Y0-BYA-560
DISCARDED

State and Local Government in America

Third Edition

State and Local Government in America

DANIEL R. GRANT

H. C. NIXON

Allyn and Bacon, Inc. Boston

Library of Congress Cataloging in Publication Data

Grant, Daniel R
State and local government in America.

Includes bibliographies.
1. Local government—United States. 2. State governments. 3. Federal government —United States. I. Nixon, Herman Clarence, 1886- joint author. II. Title.
JK2408.G68 1974 320.9'73 74-16409

Contents

1 **State and Local Government in American Society** **1**

The Importance of State and Local Government: Old and New Elements 2
The Changing Environment of State and Local Government 9
The Character of a State and Its Communities: Fifty Patterns 20

2 **The States in the Federal System** **27**

States' Rights and States' Revolt 28
Constitutional Relations of States and Nation 32
Federal–State Cooperation: The "New Federalism" 35
Efforts to Reverse the New Federalism 48
Interstate Relationships 53

3 **Cities in the Federal System** **58**

The Constitutional Status of Cities 59
Early Federal–City Relations 62
Recent Federal–City Relations 63
Emerging Problems in Federal–City Relations 71

4 **Liberty Under Law: The Police Power** **84**

State Police Power and the Federal Judiciary 86
Local Aspects of National "Quasi-Police" Powers 103

5 **State Constitutions** 107

Features and Contents of State Constitutions 113
State Constitutions Under Attack 116
Constitution Making and Remaking 119
Other Methods of Constitutional Change 136

6 **Voters and Voting** 139

Qualifications for Voting 146
The Registration of Voters 150
General Problems of Voting 151

7 **Parties, Nominations, and Elections** 155

Party Organization and Operation 160
The Nominating Process 171
Elections and Electoral Problems 178

8 **Political Interest Groups and Public Opinion** 184

The Diversity of Interest Groups 185
Sources of Interest-Group Strength 190
Comparative Patterns of Pressure Systems 193
Interest-Group Methods 198

9 **The State Legislature: General Features** 205

Composition: Who Are the Legislators? 208
Structure: The Institutional Setting 218
Powers and Functions 226

10 **State Legislation: Process and Problems** 230

Fifty Patterns of Legislative Procedure 231
Floor Formalities and Activities 233
Unofficial "Rules of the Game" 238
Committees: Active and Inactive 239
The Role of the Party 243
Pressure Groups and Lobbyists 245
The Heritage of Malapportionment and the Impact of Reapportionment 248
Efforts to Evaluate the Fifty State Legislatures 263
Direct Legislation: The Initiative and Referendum 269

11 **The Governorship** **272**

The Governor as Lawmaker 276
A Case Summary: The New York Governor's Special Session 279
Problems of Vacancy and Succession 282
Trends in the Governorship 285

12 **The Governor and Administration** **289**

The Governor as General Manager 289
The Governor's Administrative Powers 291
Practical Restraints Upon the Chief Administrator 302

13 **Problems of Organization and Personnel** **307**

Administrative Organization and Reorganization 308
The Civil Service Reform Movement 318
Current Problems 324

14 **Finance** **330**

Expenditures 331
Revenues 335
State–Local Financial Relationships 350
Financial Planning 352

15 **The Judiciary** **355**

Common Law and Equity 356
The Judicial Hierarchy 358
The Judges 361
Judges and Politics 363
Judicial Politics: The Case of Louisiana 364
The Drama of Justice 366
Problems of Modernization 370

16 **Local Government: The County** **375**

Other County Officers and Agencies 382
County Reform Efforts 384
The New England Town 389

17 **Local Government: The City** 391

City Charters 392
Forms of City Government 395
Who Runs the City? 406
Municipal Administration 410
Regional City 415

18 **Local Government: Metropolitics** 418

Problems of Governing Metropolitan Areas 425
Proposed Remedies 429
Metropolitics and the Future 452

19 **Law Enforcement: Protective and Corrective Activities** 456

Central State Forces 459
County Authorities and Activities 462
Urban Police 465
Prison Administration and Correctional Activities 469

20 **Public Policy toward Private Enterprise** 476

Regulation of Public Utilities 477
Banking, Finance, and Insurance 481
Consumer Relations 482
Trades and Professions 485
Labor Relations 487
Agriculture 488

21 **Highways, Public Improvements, and Natural Resources** 491

Highways and Rural Roads 492
Other Transportation Improvements 495
Public Buildings, Facilities, and Urban Renewal 500
Conservation and Eco-Politics 504

22 **Education, Health, and Welfare** 511

Education 512
Health Agencies and Hospitals 520
Public Welfare 525

Index 531

Preface to the First Edition

The two authors of this text have combined their differing talents and experience in an effort to provide a factual and dynamic interpretation of state and local government in our changing American society. The work is primarily concerned with setting in perspective a concept of state and local government as a growing organic process. It is based partly on our experience in teaching, research, and governmental activity, and partly on general observation and reading of new and old works. Attention is given to such masters as Alexis de Tocqueville, James Bryce, and Lincoln Steffens, as well as to the most recent empirical studies of state and local political behavior, including urban, suburban, and metropolitan politics.

We have approached the subject with a recognition that our American society is a compound community of communities of communities, with major and increasing proportions of an urban population, an industrial economy, and national problems in a complex and changing world. We have endeavored to present a general understanding and understandable portrayal of the functioning processes of these community governments below the national level, on all fronts and fields, including the political, legislative, executive, and judicial. We have given attention to our continental geographic base, cultural heritage, and institutional developments as backgrounds for our contemporary multiplicity of governmental units with their unending continuity and continuous change in a highly technological age.

We have sought to offer an accurate view of the relationships among these numerous and varied units of government, both in realistic and hopefully idealistic terms. In this aim we have also given attention to the growing role and relationships of our national government with respect to the governance of states and state subdivisions. State and local government in America today cannot be viewed correctly without an appreciative understanding of the helpful, guiding, and occasionally restraining hand of the national government. In this connection we have also manifested concern for analyzing the relationships between the governing personnel and the governed in the American complex democracy. We have noted the needful role of experts in all units and branches of government in modern America, with appreciation, however, for the proverbial proviso that the expert should be "on tap" rather than "on top."

Special acknowledgment should be made of the assistance received from several sources, first of all to the Vanderbilt University students who obediently "tried out" parts of the manuscript in state and local government classes in 1961 and 1962. Parts have also been tried out on our colleagues, and the process has doubtless tried the patience of these and others, including members of our families and of our publisher's editorial staff. Professor Vincent V. Thursby, of Florida State University, made invaluable contributions in the early stages of the manuscript. Our indebtedness is gratefully acknowledged to Professors Robert J. Harris and John C. Wahlke, of Vanderbilt University, Professor Wilder W. Crane, Jr., of the University of Wisconsin at Milwaukee, and Professor Landon G. Rockwell, of Hamilton College. Mrs. Daniel R. Grant served faithfully above and beyond the call of domestic duty as typist and proofreader. All of these, however, are clearly absolved of any form of contributory guilt.

We hold to a philosophy of the positive and constructive approach to state and local government in the various and complementary aspects. We recognize that in American civilization today the good life is sought in increasing measure through governmental action. While it is not the purpose of this book to insist on any special definition of good government, we do hold that an essential ingredient in the quest for good or effective government is popular understanding of state and local government—what it is and how it works. It is in this spirit we hopefully offer this text to teacher and student.

February 1963

Daniel R. Grant
H. C. Nixon

Preface to the Second Edition

Due to the illness and subsequent death of my esteemed co-author and friend, H. C. Nixon, the work of revising the first edition has been primarily my own responsibility. Although the changes in state and local government in the past five years and the resultant pressures for revision of the first edition have been unprecedented, I have attempted throughout to retain our original approach—a balanced treatment of the very latest research findings and the more traditional views.

This revised edition incorporates a virtual avalanche of change in state and local government: the explosion of "creative federalism" legislation from the "War on Poverty" to "Model Cities"; the creation of the cabinet-level Department of Housing and Urban Development; the legislative reapportionment revolution with its chain reaction of political and administrative effects; the agonizing social crisis in the cities; and the acceleration of efforts to reorganize and adapt governmental structure in metropolitan areas. The increased research output of political scientists and other social scientists has been a tremendous help in the revision effort. The use of graphic material has been expanded considerably.

Helpful suggestions were made by Professors I. Ridgeway Davis, of the University of Connecticut, and James Owen, of Albany (Ga.) Junior College, who reviewed the entire manuscript. I am grateful for these and other suggestions made by professors using the first edition, as well as by my long-suffering students at Vanderbilt University subjected to both the printed and spoken word. I am also indebted to Mrs. Scarlett G. Graham for research assistance in many phases of the revision. Finally, I want to acknowledge with special thanks the genuinely collaborative assistance of my wife, Betty Jo Grant, in indexing, typing, and proofreading, as well as backstopping the rest of the work of revision.

January 1968 **Daniel R. Grant**

Preface to the Third Edition

Because readers of the first and second editions of this book have been kind enough to say they appreciate its basic approach and organization, I have resisted the temptation to give the third edition a major face-lifting by reshuffling chapter organization or making similar structural changes. While incorporating the latest trends, research, and problems in state and local government, and updating statistical data, a conscious effort has been made to retain the most popular feature of the two previous editions: a balanced treatment of the older and newer approaches to the study of state and local government, with genuine respect for the values of each. I have tried to discuss traditional reform subjects without falling into advocacy and to discuss the more sophisticated empirical research efforts of political science without losing the introductory student or the non-major in political science in meaningless abstractions.

New subjects and new emphases in this edition include: perspectives on ethnic and black politics; the new politics of ecology and consumerism; increased federal involvement in local law enforcement; comparative research on state "policy outputs"; constitutional and judicial trends affecting state and local government; trends in federalism and intergovernmental relations, including revenue sharing; developments in metropolitics; and the diverse results of a growing volume of political science research at the subnational level of government.

As in the previous editions, I am indebted to many for assistance in preparing this volume, but especially to my wife, Betty Jo, who shares heavily in the "noble experiment" to test whether a political scientist turned college president can revise his textbook.

June 1974

Daniel R. Grant
President, Ouachita Baptist University

State and Local Government in America

1

State and Local Government in American Society

A political paradox pervades the study of contemporary state and local government in the United States. Any realistic analysis of what has been occurring in government in the fifty states and the thousands of communities within them during the first three-quarters of the twentieth century is sooner or later complicated by two apparently contradictory facts. First, the power picture of national–state–local relations is characterized by what is variously described as a trend toward "national domination," "centralization," the "eclipse of states' rights," the "decline of local autonomy," and the "movement of power to Washington," to name only a few of the descriptive phrases commonly used. Second, state and local governments are spending more money, employing more people, creating a greater impact, and, in short, are more important now than ever before in our history. Few would deny the first statement, but the second may come as a surprise. How valid is the assertion that the national government, especially during the past half-century, has won a long series of power struggles with the states and their subdivisions; and that this has occurred in the face of the growing and unprecedented importance of state and local governments? The answer to this question is sought in this chapter. Old and new elements are examined, and the added question of "Why?" leads us to consider the revolutionary social and economic changes in the environment of state and local government.

A political paradox

The Importance of State and Local Government: Old and New Elements

Predictions of state decline

Not many years ago some political scientists were predicting the "withering away" of our states, not in the Marxian sense, but as an historical inevitability. The states were considered to be obsolete appendages too small to handle problems of regional or national scope and too large or with unnatural jurisdiction to handle local problems. During the crisis period of the Great Depression of the thirties, one critic went so far as to say, with some logic in the light of the times:

> Is the state the appropriate instrumentality for the discharge of these sovereign functions? The answer is not a matter of conjecture or delicate appraisal. It is a matter of brutal record. The American state is finished. I do not predict that the states will go, but affirm that they have gone.[1]

The political virility of the states was underestimated, however, and new life has grown out of both new and old factors. In striking contrast to the "states are dead" theory is the surprising discovery that the nation's largest growth sector in the 1960s and 1970s is not national defense, automobile manufacturing, or even the federal government. The largest growth sector is state and local government.[2]

Any assessment of the significance of state and local government today must recognize their vastly increased services and expenditures, the close relationship of their activities to the individual citizen, and their roles as a proving ground for national leaders, as experimental laboratories, and as an essential element in federalism and in the functioning of the American political party system.

Growth of all levels of government

Much of the explanation of the paradox referred to in the preceding paragraphs is found in the tremendous growth of government at *all* levels. The growth in power and functions of the national government has added more burdens and responsibilities to the states and their subdivisions than it has taken away from them. The flow of billions of dollars from Washington to state and local agencies and from state to local units calls for more government all along the line. It calls for extensive management of growing intergovernmental relations—for more government of government itself. State and local expenditures have risen phenomenally from one billion dollars in 1902 to almost 189 billion dollars in 1972. Although

[1] Luther Gulick, "Reorganization of the State," *Civil Engineering* 3 (August 1933), pp. 420–421.

[2] *See The Financial Outlook for State and Local Government to 1980* (New York: Tax Foundation, Inc., 1973), p. 11.

the national government has spent more annually than state and local governments since about 1935, a recent upsurge in state and local spending has narrowed the gap considerably. The ratio now stands at about 60–40 for the 410-billion-dollar total for all levels of government. State expenditures increased almost sevenfold between 1950 and 1972, jumping from 12.8 billion dollars to 87.2 billion dollars, including aid to local governments. City and other local government expenditures have expanded at a similar pace. These surprising facts of fiscal life have not gone unnoticed by nationally organized taxpayer groups whose watchdog activities have been focused mainly on the national government. In recent years, a committee of the National Association of Manufacturers, reporting on the federal budget, cited the much greater acceleration of purchases of goods and services by state and local governments compared to the national government.

The steady growth of state and local government is reflected unmistakably in the increase in number of employees, both numerically and proportionately, compared with federal employment levels. While federal employment of civilians (approximately 2.8 million in 1972) has risen only slightly since 1950, state and local employment has more than doubled (4.3 million to 10.8 million) in the same period. State and local government domination of the public employment picture may be seen in Figure 1–1. The relative requirements for personnel of the various state and local functions are indicated in Table 1–1. Even if the 5.6 million public education employees shown in Table 1–1 are excluded, state and local governments employ many more persons than the federal government. Many of the newer demands made upon state and local governments are among the most expensive to meet, both in personnel costs and equipment and construction costs. Pollution abatement, slum clearance, public housing, urban renewal, mental health programs, highway construction and maintenance, and new public works have all been responsible for the growth of state and local expenditures, taxes, and employment. Public schools remain the largest single cost item for state and local government, as national defense does for the national government.

Intimate character of state and local functions

State and local government encompasses a wide range of human relationships. It provides more material for realistic fiction than does the operation of the national government, and has been treated in this century by such writers as Theodore Dreiser, Herbert Quick, and Robert Penn Warren. Within their own borders state and local units have the primary responsibility for regulating relations between the sexes, including marriage, divorce, alimony, property rights of wives and widows, and punishment for bigamy, rape, and other types of misbehavior. Most civilian murders are crimes against a state, not the United States, although national statutes may be violated simultaneously: if, for instance, murder were

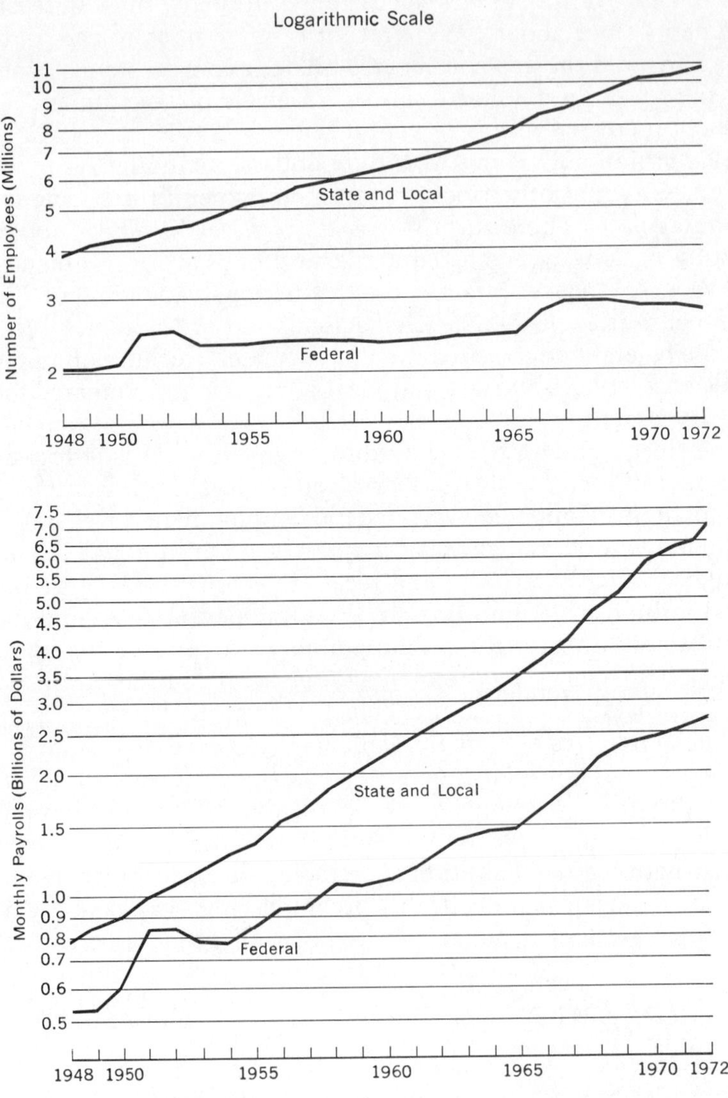

Figure 1–1. State and Local Share of Public Employment and Payrolls, 1948–72 (Logarithmic Scale). *Source:* Advisory Commission on Intergovernmental Relations, *American Federalism: Into the Third Century: Its Agenda* (Washington, D. C.: U. S. Government Printing Office, 1974), p. 4.

committed in connection with a post office or a federally insured bank were robbed. Professional groups, such as lawyers, physicians, accountants, and public school teachers, are licensed under state laws. Making and recording land titles, issuing birth certificates, licensing motor vehicles,

Table 1–1. Number of State and Local Government Employees in 1972, Classified According to Field of Employment

Field of Employment	*Number of Employees (in thousands)*	*Percent*
Education	5,626	52.0
Teachers	(2,652)	(24.5)
Highways	605	5.5
Health and hospitals	1,078	9.9
Police protection	547	5.0
Fire protection	276	2.5
Public Welfare	291	2.6
Correction	164	1.5
Natural resources	194	1.7
Financial administration	251	2.3
All other	1,776	16.4
Total	10,808	100.00

Source: U. S. Bureau of the Census, *Public Employment in 1972* (Washington, D. C.: U. S. Government Printing Office, 1973), p. 3.

requiring dog tags, rendering "shots" compulsory to prevent disease, and administering many kinds of inspection fall within state and local jurisdiction. Every vote in a national election for president must be cast in a political subdivision of a state under the supervision of local officials. States rather than the national government provide for the routine chartering of private corporations, whether corner laundries or billion-dollar giants operating in interstate commerce under national regulations.

A road to the White House

State and local politics and administration have long been a testing arena for political gladiators en route to national leadership. The state governorship has been a key spot for presidential and vice-presidential hopefuls (see Table 1–2), although the U.S. Senate seems to have supplied more aspirants in recent years. Governors have dominated major third-party tickets. Some observers go further than simply arguing that the governorship increases the political availability of a presidential candidate; they contend that gubernatorial experience in such large states as New York, California, or Ohio contributes to presidential effectiveness or even greatness.

A road to Capitol Hill

Whether such experience is accepted as the *sine qua non* for presidential greatness or not, few would deny that state and local governments make a significant contribution to the training of national leaders, legislative and judicial as well as executive. Many a legislator has reached Congress via his county courthouse or his state capital. John Jay and Justice

Table 1–2. Governors Who Became Presidential or Vice-Presidential Nominees, 1912–1972 (Governors Shown in Capital Letters; Asterisk Denotes Winner)

	Republican	*Democrat*
1912	William H. Taft	WOODROW WILSON*
	James S. Sherman	THOMAS R. MARSHALL
1916	CHARLES EVANS HUGHES	WOODROW WILSON*
	Charles W. Fairbanks	THOMAS R. MARSHALL
1920	Warren G. Harding*	JAMES M. COX
	CALVIN COOLIDGE	Franklin D. Roosevelt
1924	CALVIN COOLIDGE*	John W. Davis
	Charles G. Dawes	CHARLES W. BRYAN
1928	Herbert Hoover*	ALFRED E. SMITH
	Charles Curtis	JOSEPH T. ROBINSON
1932	Herbert Hoover	FRANKLIN D. ROOSEVELT*
	Charles Curtis	John N. Garner
1936	ALFRED M. LANDON	FRANKLIN D. ROOSEVELT*
	Frank Knox	John N. Garner
1940	Wendell L. Willkie	FRANKLIN D. ROOSEVELT*
	Charles L. McNary	Henry A. Wallace
1944	THOMAS E. DEWEY	FRANKLIN D. ROOSEVELT*
	JOHN W. BRICKER	Harry S. Truman
1948	THOMAS E. DEWEY	Harry S. Truman*
	EARL WARREN	Alben W. Barkley
1952	Dwight D. Eisenhower*	ADLAI E. STEVENSON
	Richard M. Nixon	John J. Sparkman
1956	Dwight D. Eisenhower*	ADLAI E. STEVENSON
	Richard M. Nixon	Estes Kefauver
1960	Richard M. Nixon	John F. Kennedy*
	Henry Cabot Lodge	Lyndon B. Johnson
1964	Barry Goldwater	Lyndon B. Johnson*
	William E. Miller	Hubert H. Humphrey
1968	Richard M. Nixon*	Hubert H. Humphrey
	SPIRO T. AGNEW	EDMUND S. MUSKIE
1972	Richard M. Nixon*	George McGovern
	SPIRO T. AGNEW	R. Sargeant Shriver

Major Third Party Candidates

1912	Progressive	1948	Dixiecrat
	THEODORE ROOSEVELT		J. STROM THURMOND
	HIRAM JOHNSON		FIELDING WRIGHT
1924	Progressive	1968	American Independent
	ROBERT M. LA FOLLETTE		GEORGE C. WALLACE
	Burton Wheeler		Curtis LeMay

Source: Adapted and revised from Glenn E. Brooks, *When Governors Convene* (Baltimore: The Johns Hopkins Press, 1961), p. 130.

Holmes can be cited among jurists who have served on both state and federal benches. A reverse movement of officeholders may also occur, with a national position preceding a state office. Ex-congressmen have become governors, and a few, like A. B. Cummins of Iowa and the elder Robert La Follette of Wisconsin, sandwiched tenure as governor between service in the lower and upper houses of Congress. Fiorello La Guardia and John Lindsay of New York and Maury Maverick of San Antonio became mayors after service in Congress, and Hubert Humphrey began his political career as mayor of Minneapolis. Many administrative appointees have switched service from one level of government to another. Political party officials also cross the lines of local, state, and national organizations. This easy mobility from job to job provides a by-product of mutual understanding among numerous parts of the American system.

Experimental and non-*experimental states*

One of the classic arguments for continuation of strong state and local governments has been the virtue of having fifty separate "experimental laboratories," each operating under the democratic process to test, on a small scale, various political innovations. In practice, this function has been performed only to a limited extent. The states are rigidly *non*-experimental in outlook toward certain features of governmental structure and procedure, such as separation of powers, an elective governor, and the bicameral legislature. The one exception which seems to prove the rule is Nebraska's willingness to experiment with a unicameral legislature. In matters of policy and legislation several states have shown greater willingness to break new ground, so that many programs of the national government in such fields as financial reorganization, labor regulation, and welfare legislation had the benefit of prior testing by at least a few states. Fair employment practice legislation at the national level was preceded by a variety of such programs in several states and cities. Other examples include "no-fault" insurance legislation and electoral devices such as initiative, referendum, recall, and the presidential primary.

State innovators and laggards

The recent use of states as the objects of political science studies of "comparative policy outputs" of political systems has shed additional light on the nature and extent of innovation in states. Jack L. Walker, for example, in studying why some states adopt innovative policies more readily than others, has given each state an "innovation score" based on a state's record of early or late adoption (or non-adoption) of eighty-five different programs in fields such as welfare, health, education, and conservation. Table 1–3 records New York, Massachusetts, California, and New Jersey as the leading innovators, and Mississippi, Nevada, Wyoming, and South Carolina as the foremost laggard states. Walker warns against rigid stereotyping, however, by pointing out that in spite of ranking last in the composite innovation score, Mississippi was the first state to adopt the general sales tax in 1936 and the first to authorize city and county gov-

Table 1–3. Composite Innovation Scores for the American States[a]

New York	.656	Kansas	.426
Massachusetts	.629	Nebraska	.425
California	.604	Kentucky	.419
New Jersey	.585	Vermont	.414
Michigan	.578	Iowa	.413
Connecticut	.568	Alabama	.406
Pennsylvania	.560	Florida	.397
Oregon	.544	Arkansas	.394
Colorado	.538	Idaho	.394
Wisconsin	.532	Tennessee	.389
Ohio	.528	West Virginia	.386
Minnesota	.525	Arizona	.384
Illinois	.521	Georgia	.381
Washington	.510	Montana	.378
Rhode Island	.503	Missouri	.377
Maryland	.482	Delaware	.376
New Hampshire	.482	New Mexico	.375
Indiana	.464	Oklahoma	.368
Louisiana	.459	South Dakota	.363
Maine	.455	Texas	.362
Virginia	.451	South Carolina	.347
Utah	.447	Wyoming	.346
North Dakota	.444	Nevada	.323
North Carolina	.430	Mississippi	.298

[a] Alaska and Hawaii were omitted because of inadequate data on their years of adoption of legislation.

Source: Jack L. Walker, "The Diffusion of Innovations among the American States," *American Political Science Review* 63 (September 1969), p. 883.

ernments to issue bonds for industrial plants leased to private firms.[3] The research of Walker and others into what causes some states to be more innovative than others is discussed in chapter 10.

The underlying significance of state government has been, and continues to be, its power position within the workings of the federal system. In the formal *constitutional* sense it is quite clear that the state, like the old grey mare, "ain't what she used to be," because of issues settled both recently and as early as the days of Jefferson and Lincoln. Yet in the *political* sense the states still play a prominent part in shaping the character of

[3] Jack L. Walker, "The Diffusion of Innovations among the American States," *American Political Science Review* 63 (September 1969), pp. 880–899; revised in "Innovations in State Politics," in Herbert Jacob and Kenneth N. Vines (eds.), *Politics in the American States: A Comparative Analysis*, 2nd ed. (Boston: Little, Brown and Co., 1971), pp. 354–387.

national party nominating conventions, determining the makeup of the congress, and influencing the selection of judges. Thus, the political facts of life in the United States are frequently "federal facts"—that is, related to the peculiar position of states in our elections, parties, and legislation—rather than "national facts," such as one might expect to find in England, France, and other nations without a federal form of government. While formal constitutional federalism may seem to be waning in the United States, political federalism remains virile principally because of the political virility of the fifty states. States' rights, discussed in detail in the next chapter, are probably much less dependent upon the Supreme Court for their preservation than they are upon the political power and behavior of states *as states.* In his study of *American Federalism: A View from the States,* Daniel J. Elazar supports the contention that "the states maintain their central role because of their *political* position in the overall framework of the nation's political system, a position supported by the Constitution but which transcends its formal bounds."[4]

Persistence of political federalism

The Changing Environment of State and Local Government

Governmental institutions, like people, are molded in large measure by their environment; when drastic changes occur in that environment, corresponding governmental changes may be expected sooner or later, in one form or another. The environment of state and local government has been undergoing revolutionary changes in recent years and, while no exhaustive analysis is possible here, it is possible to identify briefly some of the mainstreams of change which have involved all state and local governments. Among the more important kinds of change are the three "isms" of population movement—urbanism, suburbanism, and metropolitanism. In our increasingly mobile nation, almost 40 million people move to a new place of residence every year. These and other factors, such as economic bigness, the impact of depression and of hot and cold war, and the development of a mass culture, help to explain the character of state and local government.

The ever-growing tide of urbanism in the United States is demonstrated clearly by a few figures from past census reports on the proportion of the U. S. population living in cities of 2,500 or more:

[4] Daniel J. Elazar, *American Federalism: A View from the States,* 2nd ed. (New York: Thomas Y. Crowell Co., 1972), p. 1.

Year	Percent Urban	Year	Percent Urban
1790	5.1	1900	39.7
1820	7.2	1920	51.2
1840	10.8	1940	56.5
1860	19.8	1960	69.9
1880	28.2	1970	73.5

Urbanism and rural decline

The change from 5 percent to nearly 75 percent of our population living in cities, or from one out of twenty to almost three out of four Americans, explains many things about our government that are too often not understood. The multiplication of governmental functions, transfer of many local functions to the state or national capital, steadily rising taxes and expenditures, and the feeling that even local government has lost much of the "personal touch" that it once had—all may be attributed in large measure to the fact that we are now a heavily urbanized nation. The last census report further evidenced the urban trend, so long in the making; it showed that all but eight of the fifty states are classified as more than 50 percent urban. Of the remaining rural states, only one (Vermont) is less than 35 percent urban, and eighteen states are more than 70 percent urban. Even in Texas, four out of every five persons live in cities. California ranks highest in urbanization with 90.9 percent of its population urban, and New Jersey is a close second with 88.9 percent urban.

An urban nation

In 1960 and 1970 the rural decline in the United States was not merely *relative* (representing a decreasing proportion of an increasing total) as in previous census years; the decline was *absolute* as the rural population actually decreased in number from almost 54.5 million to just over 54 million in 1960 and to 53.9 million in 1970. The political effect of the leveling off and decline of the rural population is not so important in itself as it is in relation to the urban explosion. The problem of legislative apportionment was further aggravated and the rural "rotten boroughs" of legislative representation became even more abhorrent to the badly outvoted, swelling urban populace.

Persistence of rural power

The change to a predominantly urban nation did far more than complicate the problem of legislative representation, however. A prerequisite to understanding state and local government is appreciating the change that urbanization has wrought in the demands made upon government. Where once the rural character of the population resulted in political concern for *agriculture* and the good life on the farm, the urban chorus now cries out through pressure groups, party platforms, and elections for more and more attention to what has been called *urbiculture,* and the good life

From agriculture to "urbiculture"

in the city. The steady decline of the farm population (from 15.6 million to 9.7 million from 1960 to 1970) has resulted in an amazing drop; less than 5 percent of the nation's population are now living on farms. The focus of politics has been changing faster than we who are in the midst of it realize. Problems on the farm that were the responsibility of the individual, such as waste disposal, water supply, fire protection, transportation, recreation, and even health, have become complex and costly group responsibilities in congested cities. State legislatures, long accustomed to a relaxed condition of non-involvement in many of the more pressing problems of city government—blight, pollution of air and water, economic and racial ghettos, and snarled traffic patterns for the urban masses—were finally confronted with demands from urban majorities on a one-man–one-vote basis. The avalanche of state legislative reapportionment that followed the Supreme Court's decisions in 1962 (*Baker* v. *Carr*) and 1964 (*Reynolds* v. *Sims*) is finally taking the sting out of H. L. Menken's characterization of overrepresentation of rural interests as "barnyard government."[5]

Flight to suburbia

An added dimension to urbanism, vastly accelerated in recent years, has been the flight to suburbia by more than 75 million Americans. There are numerous reasons for this mass movement of population to fringe areas surrounding the major cities—the desire for more room, cleaner air, quiet, social status, lower taxes, and many more. It constitutes a dynamic social revolution on wheels, with its peak still unreached, which is already dealing heavy blows to our traditional patterns of state and local politics. The suburbs of our great metropolitan areas have now become the home of more people than our central cities. The central cities showed a population gain in 1960 of 6.2 million (11.6 percent) over 1950; the 1970 gain was less than 4 million (6.4 percent). Even this slight gain for the central cities is misleading because most of it resulted from the annexation of new territory. Without such annexations the 1970 increase for central cities would have been only 0.1 percent. The metropolitan suburbs by 1960 had mushroomed with an increase of 19 million, almost 46 percent over their 1950 population, with another 16 million increase (27 percent) in 1970. The total population living in central cities in 1970 was 63.8 million; the suburban total was a much larger 75.6 million. Even those core cities with larger populations find themselves frequently outvoted by their suburbs. In the early years of the growth of suburbs it was quite common to refer to the look-alike "homogenized suburbs," implying that if you've seen one, you've seen them all. The new folklore suggested a stereotype of middle-class, white, business-oriented, Republican population in all suburbs. More

[5] *See* chapter 10 for a discussion of urban and rural representation. For an inventory and appraisal of the study of urbanization in the social sciences, *see* Philip M. Hauser and Leo F. Schnore, *The Study of Urbanization* (New York: John Wiley and Sons, 1965).

recent studies, such as the excellent analysis by Frederick Wirt and others, have dissected this modern mythology of suburban sameness and found a great diversity in political, economic, and physical characteristics.[6]

Central city decline

Perhaps even more dramatic than the growth of suburbia has been the actual decline in population of many of our largest and oldest cities in the 1950s and 1960s, the first decline in history for most of them. Of the ten largest cities in 1950 all but one (Los Angeles) were reported in the 1960 census as losing population. New York City's suburbs gained by 38.9 percent but the city decreased by 1.4 percent. Chicago lost by 1.9 percent while its suburbs gained 64.9 percent. Among the heaviest losers in 1960 were Boston (13 percent); St. Louis (12.5 percent); Pittsburgh (10.7 percent); and Detroit (9.7 percent). Both Pittsburgh and Boston have suburbs which contain three times as many people as the area within their city limits. The nation's capital has not been spared; its population declined by 4.8 percent while its Virginia and Maryland suburbs gained a thumping 87 percent. The 1970 census report confirmed the trends of the previous decade, with a few modifications. The largest core cities lost population again, with the exception of Los Angeles (+ 13.6 percent), Houston (+ 31.2 percent), and New York (+ 1.5 percent). The rate of decline actually increased in Chicago, St. Louis, Pittsburgh, and Cleveland, but the decline slowed down in Boston, Detroit, Washington, Philadelphia, and San Francisco.

Political impact

These two developments—the rise of suburbia and the decline of the core city—like urbanism and rural decline, have separate but related effects on state and local politics and administration. The centrifugal suburban pull is serving as a kind of shock treatment for sleepy, rural-oriented county government in the United States. For counties that can survive the shock of sudden pressure and demand for the full gamut of urban services by thousands of demanding citizens no longer served by a core city, a new and vigorous local government may result. For others, a pathetic paralysis of ill-adapted political and administrative structures is inevitable.

The core city, too, is undergoing dramatic social and political change. The loss of its tax base, growth potential, and, perhaps most serious of all, the loss of the leadership potential of those who separate themselves politically by moving to the suburbs, all contribute to different kinds of blight in the heart of our cities.[7] In many ways the impact of suburbanism

[6] Frederick M. Wirt, Benjamin Walter, Francine F. Rabinovitz, and Debora R. Hensler, *On the City's Rim: Politics and Policy in Suburbia* (Lexington, Mass.: D. C. Heath and Co., 1972).

[7] For an early landmark study of the nature of the suburban movement and its political implications, *see* Robert Wood's *Suburbia: Its People and Their Politics* (Boston: Houghton Mifflin Co., 1959). A collection of empirical studies and essays on suburbia may be found

on state legislative apportionment may eventually overshadow the impact of urbanism. Under the reapportionment changes of the 1960s many of the large core cities gained additional representatives, but in most cases their own suburbs gained *more*. Furthermore, the effect of the 1970 census was to reduce the gains of the largest cities; and these former city seats went for the most part to the suburbs. The big city–rural rivalries of earlier days may well be replaced in many respects by legislative cleavage between core cities and suburbs.[8]

Defining "the urban crisis"

In the aftermath of the debilitating urban riots and civil disorder of the 1960s, "the urban crisis" has become a household term for social scientists, news analysts, and lay citizens alike. It has come to mean many things to many people and borders on a cliché or rhetorical formula in the language of politics, used to suit the purpose of the particular commentator of the moment. Most commonly, the term "urban crisis" is defined in the press and in political circles as a series of problems such as poor housing, crime, lack of public transportation, growth of drug use, riotous youth, and official corruption. From this viewpoint the urban crisis is the conglomerate threat and challenge posed by the physical deterioration of the city, the failure of its public services, and the decay of moral standards.[9] Some observers, particularly urban mayors and managers, have contended that this definition is too diffuse and argue that many of these problems may be traced simply to a lack of money. They therefore define the urban crisis as basically a fiscal crisis.[10] Still others have tried to go beyond mere cataloging of urban problems or statements on the revenue-raising difficulties to explain the deeper basis of the urban crisis. James Q. Wilson

---

in W. A. Dobriner (ed.), *The Suburban Community* (New York: G. P. Putnam's Sons, 1959). These studies should be read in the context of the later and more critically rigorous analysis of Wirt, et al., *On the City's Rim.*

[8] *See* William J. D. Boyd, "Suburbia Takes Over," *National Civic Review* 54 (June 1965), pp. 294–298.

[9] This classification of definitions of the urban crisis relies heavily on the excellent analysis of Peter K. Eisinger in his paper prepared for the 1973 annual meeting of the American Political Science Association (New Orleans, September 4–8), "The Urban Crisis as a Failure of Community: Some Data." For other related studies, see his article, "The Conditions of Protest in American Cities," *American Political Science Review* 67 (March 1973), pp. 11–28; and also Frances Fox Piven, "The Urban Crisis: Who Got What and Why," in Robert Paul Wolff (ed.), *1984 Revisited* (New York: Alfred Knopf, 1973), pp. 165–201; U. S. Environmental Protection Agency, *Our Urban Environment: And Our Most Endangered People* (Washington, D. C.: U. S. Government Printing Office, 1971); National Commission on Urban Problems, *Building the American City* (New York: Praeger, 1969); and Edward C. Banfield, *The Unheavenly City* (Boston: Little, Brown and Co., 1970).

[10] For related studies, *see* John V. Lindsay, *The City* (New York: Norton, 1970); Douglas M. Fox, "Federal Aid to the Cities," in Fox (ed.), *The New Urban Politics* (Pacific Palisades, Calif.: Goodyear, 1972); and Werner Z. Hirsch, Phillip E. Vincent, Henry S. Terrell, Donald C. Shoup, and Arthur Rosett, *Fiscal Pressures on the Central City: The Impact of Commuters, Nonwhites and Overlapping Governments* (New York: Praeger, 1971).

and Daniel P. Moynihan, for example, contend that the urban crisis may be best understood as a crisis of mood—a "failure of community," as illustrated by such symptoms as a pervasive unease, a sense of isolation, estrangement, and massive powerlessness.[11] Moynihan contends that the failure of community-sustaining norms and institutions was a strong causal factor in promoting legislation to combat youth crime in the 1950s and later in the legislation of the 1960s for anti-poverty and other social programs, as well as in many of the political movements for urban decentralization and community self-determination.[12] Peter Eisenger sought to test the validity of the failure-of-community thesis in a study of Milwaukee residents. He found that people neither understand nor seek control-sharing arrangements, but are worried primarily about things related to economic survival and housing; and that they view these needs from a personal rather than community perspective. Eisenger concludes that understanding the urban crisis as a failure of community, as it has been defined in the literature, is of questionable empirical validity.[13]

The difficulty faced by researchers on this subject is illustrated by an effort of the Kerner Commission to compare cities experiencing serious riots with those experiencing no riots. The data collected in 1967 became irrelevant in the spring of 1968 when three of the five cities chosen to represent non-riot cities experienced some of the most severe civil disorders of the 1960s.[14]

Metropolitanism is not a precise technical term, but a word born out of necessity to describe the advent of a new creature on the political scene—the loose-jointed, often chaotic, yet interrelated mass of people in the larger cities and their suburbs. It is the product of an accelerated urbanism and suburbanism in the frozen context of horse-and-buggy local governments. The growth of metropolitan areas in the United States has compelled the Census Bureau to devise new schemes of reporting population to make it clear that the economic and cultural city of Boston (or Chicago or San Francisco) is a great deal larger than the legal city. It began reporting "metropolitan districts" in 1920 and changed to two terms in 1950, the "urbanized area" and the "standard metropolitan area." The jargon grew further in 1960 with the SMA becoming the "Standard Metro-

[11] *See* James Q. Wilson, "The Urban Unease: Community vs. the City," *Public Interest* 12 (Summer 1968), pp. 25–39; and Daniel P. Moynihan, "Toward a National Urban Policy," in Moynihan (ed.), *Toward a National Urban Policy* (New York: Basic Books, 1970), p. 5.

[12] Daniel P. Moynihan, *Maximum Feasible Misunderstanding* (New York: Free Press, 1969), pp. 10, 14.

[13] Eisenger, "The Conditions of Protest," pp. 11–28.

[14] P. H. Rossi, R. Berk, and B. Eidson, *The Roots of Urban Discontent* (New York: John Wiley and Sons, 1974).

politan Statistical Area." In justice to the Census Bureau it must be said that the metropolis almost defies permanent definition.[15]

Metropolitan nation

The 1960 and 1970 census reports made it clear that the United States is not merely urban; it is distinctly metropolitan and becoming more so each year. The number of metropolitan areas rose from 168 to 212 between 1950 and 1960, and to 264 by 1972. Their population grew from 89 million to 143 million in the two decades. Thus, 71 percent of the people of the United States live within the orbit of large cities; about one-half of this metropolitan population live in the fifteen largest areas. As early as 1960 these metropolitan areas accounted for about three-fourths of the nation's economic activity—79 percent of all bank deposits, 78 percent of all manufacturing payrolls, and over 70 percent of all local tax revenue. In terms of geography, two-thirds of the American people live on two percent of the land. To complicate matters further, just when the "metropolitan area" began to make some headway toward acceptance in laymen's language, sociologists and political scientists began to talk about the developing "super-metropolitan area" or "megalopolis," formed when two or more metropolitan areas grow together. The most publicized of these is a 600-mile-long "Linear City" on the Eastern Seaboard, stretching from lower New Hampshire through Boston, New York, Philadelphia, Baltimore, Washington, and northern Virginia. This great metropolitan complex reaches into ten states and thirty-five major metropolitan areas, and contains more than 35 million persons. A similar linear city on the West Coast is developing from Los Angeles to San Diego, and perhaps eventually up to San Francisco. As depicted in Figure 1–2, many metropolitan areas, even the small and medium-sized ones, have spilled across state boundary lines to become interstate cities.

The megalopolis

Fragmentation of government

The impact of metropolitanism on state and local government has primarily wrought a fragmentation of local government (considered in detail in chapter 18). Robert C. Wood describes fragmentation in the extreme in *1400 Governments*, an analysis of the pattern of local government for the New York metropolitan region.[16] All metropolitan areas are

[15] The major difference between the "urbanized area" and the "standard metropolitan statistical area" is that the SMSA is based on the whole county or contiguous counties, with a few exceptions, while the urbanized area includes only those reasonably contiguous portions of counties meeting urban criteria. Both must include at least one city of 50,000 inhabitants or more. In 1971 the U.S. Office of Management and Budget issued a revised set of criteria for determining metropolitan status, permitting reasonable equivalents to the 50,000 population core city to be included. This added 21 SMSAs to the 1970 total of 243.

[16] Robert C. Wood, *1400 Governments* (Cambridge: Harvard University Press, 1961). For the most comprehensive treatment of the socioeconomic and political aspects of the metropolitan area, *see* John C. Bollens and Henry J. Schmandt, *The Metropolis: Its People, Politics, and Economic Life*, 2nd ed. (New York: Harper and Row, 1970).

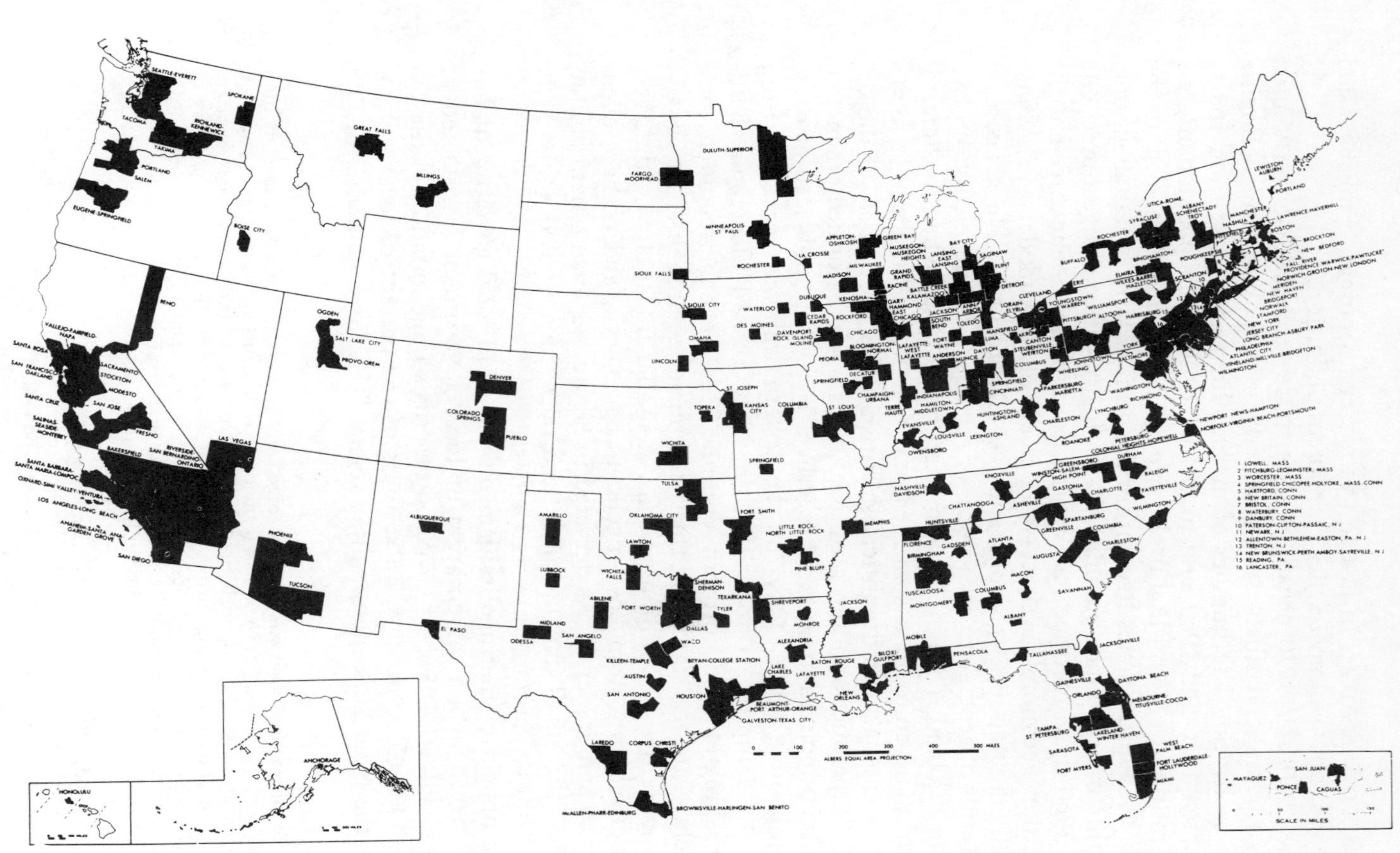

Figure 1–2. Standard Metropolitan Statistical Areas, 1972. *Source:* U. S. Department of Commerce, Social and Economic Statistics Administration, Bureau of the Census.

faced with a multiplicity of local governments, on a smaller scale than New York, to be sure, but still universally perplexing when it comes to grappling with a variety of area-wide problems. It is out of this context of inadequate local authority or competence that centralization arises, sometimes in the direction of the state capital and sometimes toward Washington. The problems of "metropolitics," metropolitan explosion, urban–suburban rivalries, and related subjects, in recent years have provided the stimulus for a whole host of "metro" studies and political consolidation movements. With such high stakes as mass transit, tax rates, crime control, public health, local self-government, control of zoning, and metropolitan planning, it is clear that the protagonists of metropolitan reform have "just begun to fight."

Population changes in the United States have not been limited to urbanism, suburbanism, and metropolitanism, although these are most common to all fifty states. The 1970 census revealed massive in-migration (net) totals for California (1.8 million) and Florida (1.3 million) during the 1960–1970 decade. Several states and communities have been affected by special types of mass movements of population with racial, economic, and political overtones. The western movement of the "Okies" and "Arkies" during the depression of the 1930s, with its accompanying welfare problems, is familiar to us all. Blacks have moved in large numbers from southern farms and towns to cities outside the South; the total out-migration of nonwhites reached an all-time high of nearly 1.5 million during the 1950s. Continued migration of blacks from the South in the period from 1960 to 1970 (1.4 million) surprised demographers who had been reporting a slowing down of the out-migration. The destination states receiving the largest numbers of blacks through migration were New York (396,000); California (272,000); Illinois (127,000); Michigan (124,000); and New Jersey (120,000). More blacks—2.2 million—live in the state of New York than in any other state, North or South, and 1.7 million live in New York City. Four states outside the South—New York, Pennsylvania, Illinois, and California—have a black population of a million or more. The 1970 census reported that every state in the union except Vermont has more than 1,000 blacks.

Racial, economic, and political migrations

Racial tension is not a monopoly of the South. Black migration to the North and West has accelerated to such an extent that a projection of trends indicates in the following tabulation a majority no longer living in the South by the mid-1970s. The percentage of blacks in the U. S. population is as shown on following page.

A swelling tide of Puerto Ricans has migrated to New York since World War II.[17] In the wake of the Cuban crisis, thousands of refugees from that

[17] For an early study of this movement *see* Oscar Handlin, *The Newcomers: Negroes*

Region	1940	1950	1960	1970
North	22%	28%	34%	39%
Northeast	11	13	16	19
North Central	11	15	18	20
South	77	68	60	53
West	1	4	6	8
Total	100	100	100	100

nearby country flooded the city of Miami and other coastal cities. A majority of Oriental groups—Japanese, Chinese, and Filipino—reside in western states, notably California and Hawaii, but totals of 10,000 or more in New York and Illinois for each of the three groups reflect sizable settlements in the New York and Chicago metropolitan areas. The American Indian population was nearly 800,000 in 1970, almost one-half of whom were living in the West. These and other groups quite naturally tend to live together as subcommunities within larger cities (or on Indian reservations), complicating the task of political, economic, and cultural assimilation. With the possible exception of Indian settlements, their more immediate impact is upon local and state governments, rather than upon the national government.

A national economy

If population movements have been the most significant influence in the environment of *local* government, economic changes have undoubtedly been most significant in the changing role of *state* government. The simple term "economic bigness" hardly does justice to the revolutionary impact which this development has had upon state government and the federal system. Nothing even approaching the full extent of the impact of the growth of modern business and labor across state boundary lines was realized until the dark hours and years following the economic crash of 1929. The impact on the states came with devastating suddenness, as described in contemporary accounts by Luther Gulick:

> Where were the states when the banks went under? Powerless Maryland, hysterical Michigan, safety-first New York! Where were the states when all the railroads were on the verge of passing into the hands of the bondholders and suspending operation? Where were the states in regulation of power and the control of utilities? Where are the states now in regulating insurance companies, with their fake balance sheets and high salaries? Where were the states in controlling blue sky securities? Where were the states in preventing destructive business competition and in protecting labor and the public? Where

---

and Puerto Ricans in a Changing Metropolis (Cambridge, Mass.: Harvard University Press, 1959).

> were the states in the development of security through social insurance? In none of these fields affecting economic life was it possible for any state to do anything decisive without driving business out of its jurisdiction into areas where there was no regulation and no control.
>
> The same kind of sectional self-interest made it impossible for any state to go forward boldly with public improvement programs to offset industrial contraction.[18]

The growth and recognition of a tremendous national, and even international, economy, rather than fifty state economies as previously assumed, is a force to which state governments are still reacting and adjusting, sometimes rapidly but more often slowly or almost imperceptibly. Greater emphasis on the "purely local," expansion of grant-in-aid programs, and the birth of "cooperative federalism," rather than "competitive federalism," are all a part of this adjustment. Through it all, the states have continued to grow vigorously.

Social changes

Some aspects of the dynamic American society have been changing so fast in recent years that sociologists have been kept working overtime on analytical studies, and political scientists have hardly begun the task of relating these studies to politics and government in a meaningful way. The new-found physical mobility of the population, for example, is producing a variety of social and political changes—some good and some bad as judged by traditional values. Physical mobility provides greater opportunity for people to move away from economic or social "dead-end streets" and provides industry with a more flexible manpower situation. Yet this same mobility has produced a rootlessness and a breakdown of "primary controls" with a resulting higher rate of crime, increasing personal insecurity, lack of community identification, low political participation, and other social problems.[19] A later stream of analysis of modern society, with Erich Fromm[20] and David Riesman[21] as chief spokesmen, emphasizes the "lonely crowd" aspects of urban living and timid conformity to the expectations of the group. The American culture is said to be a "mass culture," with entertainment, literature, music, fashions, and comic strips all mass-produced, prepackaged, and distributed by coast-to-coast communications media.[22] The implications of a mass culture upon

Effects of physical mobility

A mass society?

[18] Gulick, "Reorganization of the State," p. 421.

[19] *See,* for example, R. E. Park and E. W. Burgess, *The City* (Chicago: University of Chicago Press, 1925).

[20] Erich Fromm, *Escape from Freedom* (New York: Holt, Rinehart and Winston, 1941).

[21] David Riesman, *The Lonely Crowd* (New Haven: Yale University Press, 1950), and *Faces in the Crowd* (New Haven: Yale University Press, 1952).

[22] *See* B. Rosenberg and David M. White (eds.), *Mass Culture* (Glencoe, Ill.: The Free Press, 1957); William Kornhauser, *The Politics of Mass Society* (Glencoe, Ill.: The Free Press, 1959); and Maurice R. Stein, *The Eclipse of Community: An Interpretation of American Studies* (Princeton, N.J.: Princeton University Press, 1960).

the theoretical basis of a federal system to provide for local differences are intriguing, to say the least. It is doubtful, however, that a mass culture has developed sufficiently to undercut the strength of sectionalism and localism in politics.

The Character of a State and Its Communities: Fifty Patterns

Network of history

In spite of evidences of a mass culture, it must be recognized that each state still remains different in significant ways from all others, and that these differences are important politically. The fifty states collectively provide an exhibit of national diversity. State histories, for example, read like the stories of many different nations. Their historical origins are pictured in Figure 1–3. Thirteen former British colonies entered the Union as states ratifying the Constitution as provided by the Convention of 1787. Sixteen states are products of the eighteenth century, twenty-nine came into the Union in the nineteenth century, and three trans-Mississippi commonwealths and two non-contiguous territories acquired statehood in the twentieth century. Thirty states moved up to statehood from the status of organized territories. Vermont, Kentucky, Tennessee, and Maine were carved out of original claims or domains of other states, and West Virginia was admitted as the loyal part of Virginia during the Civil War. The republic of Texas, which had won a war of independence from Mexico, was annexed as a state by Congress in 1845. California, part of the Mexican cession of 1848, was the scene of a gold rush in '49 and became a state the following year without any preliminary territorial step. Eleven southern states were involved in a bloody war of secession, which, in its failure, stirred up a temporary constitutional question as to whether these states as state entities had been out of the Union for the war period or had merely been interfered with by disloyal elements. Oklahoma has had a unique history as a combination of two territories, both before and since gaining statehood in 1907. One of these, the Indian territory, was established in 1834 for the relocation of five Indian tribes from states east of the Mississippi. Portions of this territory were thrown open in 1889 to individual homesteaders, and thousands rushed in at the scheduled noonhour signal, finding, however, that many had evaded the guards and staked out choice claims ahead of them. These "sooners" provided a nickname for Oklahomans. The Territory of Oklahoma was created in 1890 and subsequently combined with the Indian territory to give the nation its most Indianized state, socially and politically. Louisiana is the most distinctive example of a state with a French–Spanish colonial background that continues to influence its civil institutions today.

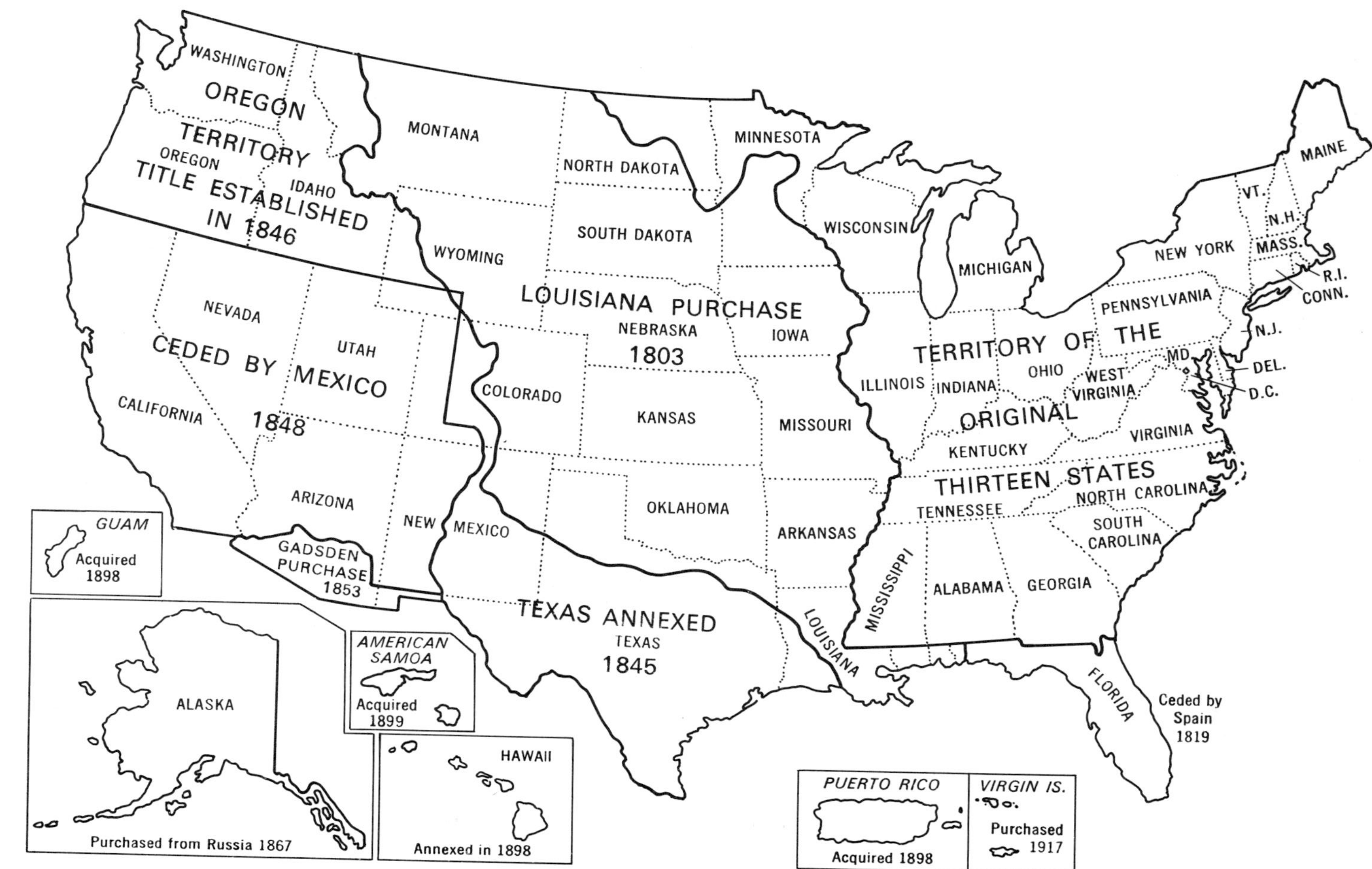

Figure 1–3. Major Acquisitions of Territory by the U. S. *Source:* U. S. Bureau of the Census, *U. S. Census of Population, 1960.*

Lands and people

The states present a mosaic of inequalities of physical geography; these inequalities are guaranteed by the Constitution, which protects all the states against compulsory division or combination. Alaska has 475 times Rhode Island's area of 1,214 square miles, and Texas is more than 200 times Rhode Island's size. California is nearly as large in area as Oregon and Washington combined, Pennsylvania could cover Delaware nineteen times, North Carolina is three-fifths larger than South Carolina, and Maine dwarfs the other New England states. Table 1–4 indicates the size and ranking of the states as to area.

Table 1–4. Area and Population of States, 1970

State	*Population*	*Rank in Population*	*% Increase in Population, 1960–1970*	*Gross Area (sq. miles)*	*Rank in Area*
United States	203,211,926		13.3	3,615,211	
Alabama	3,444,165	21	5.4	51,609	29
Alaska	300,382	50	32.8	586,400	1
Arizona	1,770,900	33	36.0	113,909	6
Arkansas	1,923,295	32	7.7	53,104	27
California	19,953,134	1	27.0	158,693	3
Colorado	2,207,259	30	25.8	104,247	8
Connecticut	3,031,709	24	19.6	5,009	48
Delaware	548,104	46	22.8	2,057	49
Florida	6,789,443	9	37.1	58,560	22
Georgia	4,589,575	15	16.4	58,876	21
Hawaii	768,561	40	21.5	6,424	47
Idaho	712,567	42	6.8	83,557	13
Illinois	11,113,976	5	10.2	56,400	24
Indiana	5,193,669	11	11.4	36,291	38
Iowa	2,824,376	25	2.4	56,290	25
Kansas	2,246,578	28	3.1	82,264	14
Kentucky	3,218,706	23	5.9	40,395	37
Louisiana	3,641,306	20	11.8	48,523	31
Maine	992,048	38	2.4	33,215	39
Maryland	3,922,399	18	26.5	10,577	42
Massachusetts	5,589,170	10	10.5	8,257	45
Michigan	8,875,083	7	13.4	58,216	23
Minnesota	3,804,971	19	11.5	84,068	12
Mississippi	2,216,912	29	1.8	47,716	32
Missouri	4,676,501	13	8.3	69,686	19
Montana	694,409	43	2.9	147,138	4
Nebraska	1,483,493	35	5.1	77,227	15
Nevada	488,738	47	71.3	110,540	7

Table 1–4. *Continued*

State	*Population*	*Rank in Population*	*% Increase in Population, 1960–1970*	*Gross Area (sq. miles)*	*Rank in Area*
New Hampshire	737,681	41	21.5	9,304	44
New Jersey	7,168,164	8	18.2	7,836	46
New Mexico	1,016,000	37	6.8	121,666	5
New York	18,236,967	2	8.7	49,576	30
North Carolina	5,082,059	12	11.5	52,712	28
North Dakota	617,761	45	−2.3	70,665	17
Ohio	10,652,017	6	9.7	41,222	35
Oklahoma	2,559,229	27	9.9	69,919	18
Oregon	2,091,385	31	18.2	96,981	10
Pennsylvania	11,793,909	3	4.2	45,333	33
Rhode Island	946,725	39	10.1	1,214	50
South Carolina	2,590,516	26	8.7	31,055	40
South Dakota	665,507	44	−2.2	77,047	16
Tennessee	3,923,687	17	10.0	42,244	34
Texas	11,196,730	4	16.9	267,339	2
Utah	1,059,273	36	18.9	84,916	11
Vermont	444,330	48	14.0	9,609	43
Virginia	4,648,494	14	17.2	40,815	36
Washington	3,409,169	22	19.5	68,192	20
West Virginia	1,744,237	34	−6.2	24,181	41
Wisconsin	4,417,731	16	11.8	56,154	26
Wyoming	332,416	49	0.7	97,914	9

Source: U. S. Bureau of the Census, *U. S. Census of Population, 1970* (Washington, D. C.: U. S. Government Printing Office).

Area is not the only geographic variation. Some states have problems of flood control; others are concerned with irrigation. There are twenty-four coastal states, a group of Great Lakes states, Mississippi River Valley states, mountain states, and so on. The large state of Texas or elongated states like Tennessee or California have enough sharp differences in their physical geography to give multiple-state characteristics to their public life.

The distribution of population among and within the states is far from even. Table 1–4 also gives significant 1970 population statistics for the states. California, at the top in 1970, has sixty-five times the population of Alaska, the least populous state. New York's 8.7 percent increase was not enough to hold on to its 1960 position of most populous state, and a 27 percent increase for California gave it first place honors in 1970. Pennsylvania holds third place. The rate of gain for several populous states is considerably above the national average (13.3 percent), while a rate much below that average applies to many rural states; three states, North Dakota, South Dakota, and West Virginia, actually lost population. Many states have densely settled metropolitan areas as well as wide-open spaces with few inhabitants. Texas has Houston and Dallas and also its sparsely populated cactus counties. A number of states have a considerable proportion of the total population concentrated in a single city or metropolitan area, such as New York, Chicago, Denver, Baltimore, Milwaukee, New Orleans, and Atlanta. A traveller would note differences in the immigrant stocks of the states as he moved from Massachusetts to Virginia, to Louisiana, to Wisconsin, and to states in the Southwest.

Economic activities

Economic activities vary among the states in spite of trends toward national standardization. The preeminent economic activity of a state is often singled out to emphasize the variety of the states—at times almost to the point of caricature. In agriculture there are wheat states, cattle states, corn and hog states, cotton states, tobacco states, and other groupings, although with considerable overlapping. West Virginia is important for coal, Louisiana for oil and natural gas, Florida for winter tourists, Maine for summer tourists, Wisconsin for dairy products, Kentucky for whiskey and horses, and so on. Illinois, thanks to Carl Sandburg's characterization of Chicago, is known as "hog butcher for the world." New York and New Jersey, between them, have the world's largest waterfront business. Pennsylvania leads in the iron and steel industry, Michigan in automobile manufacturing, California in movie productions, and Delaware in charters for corporations with operating establishments flung, empire-like, across the continent. Nevada is the state most conspicuous for legalized gambling.

Aside from differences in types of economic activity, the states show variations in the amount or extent of enterprise within their borders. Banking, for example, is less extensive in Ohio than in New York but greater in the Buckeye state than in Wyoming. Texas grows more cotton than any other cotton state, and Iowa raises more hogs than Virginia in spite of the reputation of Virginia hams.

All these lands, people, and properties make up the states as well as the nation, giving reality and vitality to laws and constitutions. The state governments, along with local units, derive powers, funds, and problems from them, as does the national government, under the federal equation. The states, through their governments, actually own fractions of these lands and properties, and they employ people in the functions of governance and service for all, with predominant emphasis on private economy, under a living constitutional system.

Tocqueville, observing and analyzing democracy in America a few years after Jefferson's death, emphasized that the United States had a central government with a network of local administration. According to him, the diversity of local units and administrative agencies constituted a significant bulwark against the tyranny of a national majority. No particular party, leader, or group could carry or control all of the numerous localities, and at no time would all these numerous localities move with unanimity toward dictatorship or destruction. In other words, the variety of political opinion and administrative practice among the communities and commonwealths would tend to safeguard the democratic nation from the evils of democracy itself.[23]

Diversity and democracy

The general pattern as observed by the astute Frenchman was to prevail for the next hundred and more years after his report on America. His analysis is essentially applicable to government in the United States today, although many successful and unsuccessful attempts have been undertaken to streamline the system from top to bottom. The nearest approaches to disruption of the pattern of diversity have occurred through solidarity of national action for survival in critical times of war and depression. But, if Tocqueville could revisit our country today, he might offer the reminder that, thanks to diversity, the United States, with all the defects of federalism and localism, has so far escaped totalitarian government of the right and of the left. He might be disturbed by the tendency toward standardization under the impact of mass communication media, and at the bizarre Watergate exposé, but he could note that we have as yet arrived at no such soulless and traditionless utopia as set forth in Aldous Huxley's *Brave New World* or George Orwell's *1984.*

The pattern today

The study of state and local government is a close-up study of balancing freedom and power, rights and responsibilities, politics and administration, in a constitutional democracy. It is a study of living institutions shot through with imperfections. Through organic growth and political folklore, these institutions are as much a part of American society as freshman and sophomore classes are a part of the traditional society of the campus. If they did not exist, they would, in some form or fashion, have to be created, despite their imperfections and despite their perennial productivity of headaches for central authorities. The significant question for investigation is not whether but how to live with them.

Living problems

[23] Alexis de Tocqueville, *Democracy in America* (New York: Alfred A. Knopf, 1945), I, especially Chapters 16–17. Tocqueville noted other American factors besides local government as safeguards against tyranny by the mass majority. Among these factors were the power and inherent conservatism of the legal profession and the restraining influence exerted by religion which was widely accepted and characterized by democratic diversity. In this connection *see* Elazar, *American Federalism*, pp. 79–116, for an interesting discussion of the relationship of the American political subcultures to the federal system. He identifies three subcultures—individualistic, moralistic, and traditionalistic, and suggests that they are strongly tied to particular states and sections of the country.

SUPPLEMENTARY READINGS

The American Assembly. *Goals for Americans: The Report of the President's Commission on National Goals.* New York: Columbia University Press, 1960. Reprinted by Prentice-Hall, New York, 1960. *See* especially Chapters 10 and 12.

Banfield, Edward C., and Wilson, James Q. *City Politics.* Cambridge, Mass.: Harvard University Press and the M.I.T. Press, 1963.

Benson, G. C. S. *The New Centralization.* New York: Holt, Rinehart & Winston, 1941.

Bollens, John C., and Schmandt, Henry J. *The Metropolis: Its People, Politics and Economic Life,* 2nd ed. New York: Harper and Row, 1970.

Brogan, D. W. *The American Character.* New York: Alfred A. Knopf, Inc., 1944.

Campbell, Alan K., ed. *The States and the Urban Crisis.* Englewood Cliffs, N. J.: Prentice-Hall, 1970.

Dye, Thomas R. *Understanding Public Policy.* Englewood Cliffs, N. J.: Prentice-Hall, 1972.

Greer, Scott. *The Emerging City: Myth and Reality.* New York: Free Press of Glencoe, Inc., 1962.

Jacob, Herbert, and Vines, Kenneth N. *Politics in the American States,* 2nd ed. Boston: Little, Brown and Company, 1971.

Key, V. O. *American State Politics.* New York: Alfred A. Knopf, 1956, Chapter 1.

Maass, Arthur, ed. *Area and Power: A Theory of Local Government.* Glencoe, Ill.: The Free Press, 1959.

Nixon, H. C. *Possum Trot.* Norman: University of Oklahoma Press, 1941.

Reagan, Michael D. *The New Federalism.* New York: Oxford University Press, 1972.

Riker, William H. *Federalism: Origin, Operation, Significance.* Boston: Little, Brown and Company, 1964.

Sanford, Terry. *Storm Over the States.* New York: McGraw-Hill Book Co., 1967.

U. S. Advisory Commission on Intergovernmental Relations. *American Federalism:* Into the Third Century: Its Agenda. Washington, D.C.: U. S. Government Printing Office, 1974.

Wirt, Frederick M.; Walter, Benjamin; Rabinovitz, Francine F.; and Hensler, Debora R. *On the City's Rim: Politics and Policy in Suburbia.* Lexington, Mass.: D. C. Heath and Co., 1972.

2

The States in the Federal System

The American form of democratic–republican government is a system of federal relationships of the states and the national government to each other and to the people under the central Constitution. The members of the epochal convention of 1787 at Philadelphia established a national government and turned a "League of States" into a "Commonwealth of commonwealths, a Republic of republics, a State . . . composed of other States. . . ."[1] They provided for a stronger central government than that of the old Confederation of 1781, which had lacked direct compulsory power over citizens. But they avoided setting up a unitary government which would have destroyed the states as political entities, leaving them merely geographical divisions of the national government, much like the territorial "departments" of France. They combined a new national government with the state governments, so that each inhabitant of a state would normally have rights, privileges, and responsibilities under two governments, without having to go through one to reach the other. This is the essence of federalism, "a device for dividing decisions and functions of government,"[2] which Americans have applied to the United States in a developmental period of more than 180 years.

Essence of American federalism

No two federal systems are completely alike. Each is *sui generis*—that is, in some measure, unique. American states differ, in function and

[1] James Bryce, *The American Commonwealth*, vol. 1, 3rd ed. (New York: The Macmillan Co., 1903), p. 15.

[2] Morton Grodzins, "The Federal System," in *Goals for Americans* (New York: The American Assembly, Columbia University Press, 1960), p. 265. *See also* his *The American System: A New View of Government in the United States*, Daniel J. Elazar, ed. (Chicago: Rand McNally and Co., 1966).

power, from the provinces of Canada, the Swiss cantons, or the so-called "republics" of Soviet Russia. If we say that federalism is a division of powers between general and regional governments which are coordinate and independent in their respective spheres, there must be some principle determining the fundamental division. Under the American Constitution, the general government is one of delegated powers; the states possess "reserved" powers. The provinces of Canada, in contrast, were to possess specifically delegated powers under the organic act, while the general or Dominion government was to have the residue. Judicial interpretation has tended to limit strictly the powers of the Dominion government, however, and to effect a practical reversal in the power relationship.[3]

Federalism not standardized

Constitutional changes and historic developments have made American federalism quite different today from what it was in the era of Hamilton, Jefferson, and Madison. Both the inner meanings and the descriptive terms or labels have shifted. Partly as recognition of the status of the states, "union" served to denote the federal system in popular usage up to the end of the Civil War. The framers of the Constitution looked forward in the preamble not to a "nation," but to "a more perfect Union." Daniel Webster, espousing a national view of the Constitution in opposition to the South Carolina doctrine of states' compact, emphasized "Liberty *and* Union, now and forever, one and inseparable!" Andrew Jackson answered the South Carolinians with the toast, "Our Union, it must be preserved!" Abraham Lincoln used political strategy and "Union" troops to save the "Union" or the "Federal Union" from disruption. In his prophetic words at Gettysburg, however, he invoked "a new birth of freedom" for "this nation, under God." Victory and consequent reunion brought forth a wider use of such terms as "nation," "national," and "nationalism" to describe America and American government. "National" was to compete with "federal" as a label for the central government and its many administrative agencies of the twentieth century.[4] "National Guard" became the proper designation of the constitutionally recognized "Militia of the several States," whether serving under orders of the president or of a governor.

A changing pattern

States' Rights and States' Revolt

Debates over states' rights in the American federal system are as old as the nation and as new as the last political campaign. Different interests and

[3] *See* K. C. Wheare, *Federal Government*, 2d ed. (New York: Oxford University Press, 1951), on the various applications of federalism.

[4] Regardless of its technical incorrectness, "federal" is accepted usage for designating the central government of the American system. The press says "federal courts," "federal administration," "federal Congress," etc., even though "federal" technically refers to the relationship between states and nation or to the form of the whole governmental system, rather than to the national government only.

sections have used the doctrine of states' rights in efforts to shape or limit national policy to their liking. Reliance on this doctrine has at different times characterized articulate minorities or groups out of power in national politics. The Jeffersonians used it in criticism of the Alien and Sedition acts of 1798, and then, once in power, incurred the states' rights wrath of New Englanders over the Louisiana Purchase and the War of 1812. South Carolina based its unsuccessful venture into nullification in the Jackson period on strong states' rights views of the Constitution.

Before the Civil War

The peak of intellectual analysis of the states' rights doctrine was reached in the speeches and writings of John C. Calhoun in behalf of his native South Carolina and South. Expanding on comments of Jefferson and refining the teachings of another Virginian, John Taylor of Caroline, he militantly argued that the Constitution was a compact made by the states in their sovereign capacity, not by the people in any national capacity. The central government, by this theory, was a non-sovereign creature or agent of the states and must not violate the compact under the penalty of justifying state nullification or even secession. The Calhoun thesis was set forth in the Constitution of the Southern Confederacy, which begins with the words, "We, the People of the Confederate States, each State acting in its sovereign and independent character, in order to form a permanent Federal Government . . . ." Southern historian Frank L. Owsley once suggested that a symbolic gravestone of the Confederacy should carry the inscription: "Died of State Rights." He referred to the irony of the South's failure to win its war for states' rights and slavery, the result in large measure of the factional divisions, obstructions, and disunity inherent in states' rights.[5]

The Civil War, often called in the South the War Between the States, marked the climax in the conflict over the meaning and application of federalism. It brought about the overthrow of the institution of slavery and added both strength and clarity to the meaning of national power, producing provisions in constitutional amendments to prevent state interference or discrimination in the sphere of human freedoms and civil or political rights. But the war and the constitutional changes left the way open for a continuing recourse to states' rights for purposes short of rebellion.

Climax and after

The Supreme Court might say in 1869 that a state could not secede,[6] but that high tribunal was destined in the next century to put the stamp of unconstitutionality upon a number of regulatory measures of Congress on the ground of encroaching on the reserved powers of the states. It was also to sustain a body of national legislation against such complaints and to find occasion to uphold and disallow sundry state enactments under test

[5] Frank Lawrence Owsley, *State Rights in the Confederacy* (Chicago: University of Chicago Press, 1925).

[6] *Texas* v. *White,* 7 Wall. 700 (1869).

by the Fourteenth Amendment. The states' rights argument, in plain terms, was to remain potent, although many of the new champions would be corporation lawyers rather than spokesmen for states or state governments. Democratic leaders made political appeals to states' rights in opposition to the New Nationalism of President Theodore Roosevelt, and Republicans resorted to a similar gospel after the New Deal era of Franklin D. Roosevelt as they worked their way back to power under Eisenhower and Nixon. There is no sign that the states will pass into eclipse for lack of argument or diversity of opinion with respect to their status.

States' rights and tidelands oil

Two of the strongest twentieth-century controversies that have involved the issue of states' rights are the contest over the control of "tidelands oil" and the integration–segregation conflict. Illustrating the stake which the great business corporations have had from time to time in fighting for states' rights, the tidelands issue found oil companies objecting strenuously to national control of the submerged offshore oil deposits. Professor Robert J. Harris has described the intermingling of economic interests and political theory in this contest as follows:

> The solicitude of the oil companies for states' rights is hardly based on convictions derived from political theory but rather on fears that Federal ownership may result in the cancellation or modification of state leases favorable to their interests, their knowledge that they can successfully cope with state oil regulatory agencies, and uncertainty concerning their ability to control a Federal agency.[7]

Contrary to most of the earlier contests, the tidelands controversy ended with a victory by the states' rights advocates. Taking their battle into the election of 1952, the oil interests secured a promise from the Republicans, who were not unmindful of important votes in Texas, Louisiana, and California, to return tideland jurisdiction from the national government to the states. The promise was fulfilled following the Republican victory in 1952.

Desegregation and "interposition"

The controversy over racial desegregation in the South brought with it a vigorous reassertion of many of the older states' rights arguments, including the less familiar doctrine of "interposition," a twin brother of the more familiar "nullification." The idea of interposition is that a state can "interpose" its authority between an unconstitutional act and the people of the state. The Supreme Court's desegregation decision in *Brown* v. *Board of Education*[8] prompted a hundred southern congressmen to draw

[7] Robert J. Harris, "States' Rights and Vested Interests," *Journal of Politics* 15 (November 1954), pp. 457–471.

[8] 347 U. S. 483 (1954).

up the "Southern Manifesto" in 1956 with a thundering attack upon the Supreme Court for its "naked judicial power," "clear abuse of judicial power," and "derogation of the authority of Congress," and with strong commendation for the doctrine of interposition and for those states "which have declared the intention to resist forced integration by any lawful means." As a political device to rally massive southern opposition to desegregation, the significance of interposition could not be ignored. As a constitutional doctrine, however, interposition was invalid from the start, and was even weaker when it was attempted against Supreme Court decisions than when attempted against acts of Congress, as it had been in all previous efforts. If there was any hope for interposition it evaporated in the Little Rock crisis of 1957 and the "Ole Miss" crisis of 1962. Governor Faubus "interposed" Arkansas National Guard units between a federal court desegregation order and Little Rock Central High School, but President Eisenhower removed the "interposers" with units of the United States Army. Subsequent interventions by national authority to insure law enforcement, as in the New Orleans school crisis in 1960 and the Montgomery "freedom-rider" tensions, made use of U. S. marshals, rather than troops, in an effort to reduce the antagonisms involved. The effort of Governor Ross Barnett to use interposition to block the admission of black student James Meredith to the University of Mississippi was countered first by U. S. marshals and finally by U. S. troops. Governor George Wallace's vow to "stand in the doorway" at the University of Alabama to resist a federal desegregation order was carried out, but it became a merely symbolic resistance since he eventually stepped aside in the face of greater federal power.

Institutional significance

In the light of current usage it is difficult to avoid the cynical impression that the states' rights argument is merely a political football in the hands of first one and then another competing team, as determined by shifting circumstances of the contest. But it should be remembered that the great debate on the issues of federalism has spanned close to two centuries. It would be difficult to cast the adherents of any given point of view exclusively in roles of agents of wisdom and goodness.

The states' rights argument during much of its long history has served, wisely and unwisely, as a conservative support for the unbroken continuity of political institutions. Whatever changes it has sought or accepted have generally been changes of restoration rather than of novel revision. It has pointedly invoked institutional history and prescriptive law rather than philosophical systems or theories of nature. It manifests more concern with rights bequeathed by the past than with responsibilities called forth by the future. The competing argument in the great debate has likewise avowed allegiance to the institutions of federalism, the law of the Constitution, and the teachings of precedent, but has advocated broader highways of interpretation for an expanding traffic of centralized government.

The never-ending debate is a functional organism of our federated democracy. It tends to shape our political institutions to an ever-growing synthesis of the ideas of such men as Hamilton and Jefferson, Webster and Calhoun, Louis D. Brandeis and Robert A. Taft, Wayne Morse and Barry Goldwater, and, perhaps, John Kenneth Galbraith and William F. Buckley, Jr. Words balance words and works balance works, again and again, while the states hold their position on a moving landscape of federated powers. In the process, our system of states succumbs neither to prophecies of doom nor to blueprints of national utopia.

Constitutional Relations of States and Nation

Reserved powers of the states

The national Constitution contains important provisions concerning state powers, guarantees, and limitations. The Tenth Amendment has figured significantly in Supreme Court cases involving the borderline between state and national powers. It is a single sentence, saying: "The powers not delegated to the United States by the Constitution, nor prohibited by it to the States, are reserved to the States respectively, or to the people." Strictly speaking, this is more of a clarification than a grant of powers. In the distribution of powers in the federal system, the national government has only such capacity for action as is delegated expressly or by implication in the Constitution, while the states have unlimited powers except for restrictions or prohibitions provided in the Constitution. The national government must look to the Constitution for powers; the states must look to that document only for limitations. The powers "reserved to the States" are too numerous and flexible to mention and are not classified in the Constitution, although the states limit their own governments through their own constitutions. The principal reserved power is the "police power," which is discussed in chapter 4, along with the major federal limitations placed upon it.

National restrictions on the states, while few, are significant, and carry the strength of the supremacy clause of the Constitution with its binding application upon state courts. Moreover, the Supreme Court of the United States has the final word in reviewing questions of federalism in cases arising under the Constitution. There can be no deadlock between state and national governments in the exercise of American sovereignty.

Guarantees to the states

The Constitution provides a few general guarantees or protections for the states. Every state is guaranteed "a republican form of government," although that phrase has never been clearly defined in official terms.

The courts have avoided interpreting the point on the ground that it is a "political" matter and is to be determined by the executive and legislative branches of government. In the Dorr rebellion in Rhode Island in the 1840s, the president gave assistance to the claimants whom he deemed the properly constituted authorities, and this action was upheld by the Supreme Court.[9] Congress may pass on the question of what constitutes republican form by denying seats to persons from states concerned, a process applied to southern states pending measures of reconstruction after the Civil War. For the number of states and the length of our constitutional history, the need or demand for invoking this guarantee has been comparatively slight. It has been held by the courts that republican form was not violated by such practices as initiative and referendum elections and the denial of suffrage to women prior to the adoption of the Nineteenth Amendment.[10]

The Constitution provides that the United States shall protect each of the states "against invasion; and on application of the legislature, or of the executive (when the legislature cannot be convened) against domestic violence." This protection has been requested a few times, but in recent years state officers and state troops (National Guardsmen) have been adequate to take care of problems disruptive of order. The national government does not have to wait for a state request to handle violence affecting United States property, business, or laws. President Cleveland ordered troops to Chicago on the occasion of a railway strike in 1894, although Governor John P. Altgeld of Illinois opposed this action. Cleveland was technically protecting the mail service.

It might be noted that Article V of the Constitution, in providing for methods of amendment, stipulates "that no State, without its consent, shall be deprived of its equal suffrage in the Senate." This stipulation was in the nature of a proviso limiting the amending power.

Eleventh Amendment

Vesting the Supreme Court with original jurisdiction in cases between states indicates respect for state dignity or sovereignty. This respect was further emphasized by the comparatively speedy proposal and ratification of the Eleventh Amendment, which became effective in 1798. This was immediately occasioned by the Court's sustaining a civil suit against the state of Georgia by a citizen of South Carolina.[11] This seemed at the time an undue restriction on state power, although there was clear language in Article III of the Constitution to support the decision. The

[9] *Luther* v. *Borden,* 7 How. 1 (1849).

[10] *Pacific States Tel. and Tel. Co.* v. *Oregon,* 223 U. S. 118 (1912); *Minor* v. *Happersett,* 21 Wall. 162 (1875).

[11] *Chisholm* v. *Georgia,* 2 Dall. 419 (1793).

Eleventh Amendment eliminated the restriction for the states by providing that the "judicial power of the United States shall not be construed to extend to any suit in law or equity, commenced or prosecuted against one of the United States by citizens of another State, or by citizens or subjects of any foreign State." The constitutional change was not necessary to protect the state against suit by its own citizens.

The Eleventh Amendment does not preclude action in lower federal courts by injured persons against state officials for violation or denial of rights provided in the Constitution. Furthermore, states and the national government may voluntarily provide for claimants of official debts or damage to come into court for settlement.

Prohibitions on the states

The national Constitution not only reserves broad powers and establishes important guarantees to the states; it also imposes certain restrictions on state practices. These restrictions are to be found in the original text and in certain amendments adopted after the Civil War. No amendment prior to that war reduced the comparative power of the states in the federal system. A large number of cases decided by the Supreme Court have hinged on these constitutional restrictions, and so have a few laws of Congress. Detailed discussion of the chief limits on state powers may be found in chapter 4.

Exclusive national powers

The states are denied certain powers which are delegated to the national government. These concern areas such as war, standing armies, foreign relations, foreign and interstate commerce, legal-tender money, patents and copyrights, tariffs, naturalization of aliens, maritime law, and the government of territories or colonies.

States and foreign relations

Although the conduct of foreign relations is delegated to the national government and denied to the states, the states do participate, in effect, in American foreign relations in a variety of indirect ways. Action of state legislatures or state officials has on many occasions complicated our relations with other nations, such as the California restriction on landholding by Japanese residents in President Wilson's administration and the removal of Italian citizens from jail in New Orleans by a lynching party in 1891. "Red light" bandit Caryl Chessman received an eleventh-hour sixty-day reprieve from the gas chamber in 1960 when the U. S. State Department relayed to Governor Pat Brown of California an Uruguayan protest against his execution. Uruguayan officials had feared hostile demonstrations at the forthcoming visit of President Eisenhower to Uruguay. Other State Department efforts to influence state and local actions have been less successful, such as the insistence of Mayor Miriani of Detroit on snubbing Soviet deputy premier Koslov when he visited that city in 1959, after two appeals from the State Department for an official welcome. Mayor Lindsay of New York touched off an international incident in 1966 by cancelling a red-carpet city greeting and dinner for King Faisal of Saudi Arabia, because of remarks considered offensive to Jews.[12]

No state shall "pass any bill of attainder, *ex post facto* law, or law impairing the obligation of contracts, or grant any title of nobility."[13] The Fourteenth Amendment specifies that citizens of the United States are citizens of the state where they reside and further states:

> No State shall make or enforce any law which shall abridge the privileges or immunities of citizens of the United States; nor shall any State deprive any person of life, liberty, or property, without due process of law; nor deny to any person within its jurisdiction the equal protection of the laws.

Part of this language is taken from the Fifth Amendment, which restricts the national government.

Important constitutional provisions equally restrict the state and national governments. Among these provisions are the amendments prohibiting slavery and suffrage discrimination.

New states on equal footing

Congress in admitting a state to the Union may enforce restrictions on the initial constitution and government as the price of admission. Once in the Union, however, a new state is on a par with the others in the constitutional system. Most advance pledges have been observed, but there are exceptions. Oklahoma disregarded a requirement not to remove the state capital from Guthrie within five years after admission.[14] Arizona, after admission, restored a constitutional provision for the recall of judges which had been deleted as a prerequisite to admission. The equality which the new state enjoys does not render it free to violate contracts or conditions relating to property which have been imposed as requirements for admission. It is a political equality.[15]

Federal–State Cooperation: The "New Federalism"

To give only the formal constitutional picture of national–state relations would be to give an incomplete one, for it is easy to conclude that Ameri-

[12] For a detailed account of the states' involvement in American foreign relations, *see* Dennis J. Palumbo's "The States and American Foreign Relations" (Unpublished Ph.D. dissertation, University of Chicago, 1960).

[13] Article I, section 10.

[14] *See Coyle* v. *Smith*, 221 U. S. 559 (1911), where the Court, sustaining the Oklahoma law which provided for the removal, established the principle that new states enter the Union on a footing of constitutional equality with the original states.

[15] *See Stearns* v. *Minnesota*, 179 U. S. 223 (1900) and *Ervien* v. *United States*, 251 U. S. 41 (1919), cases in which such nonpolitical, or business, conditions were enforced.

can government is a kind of layer cake with its functions and activities carefully parceled out either to the states or to the national government, and with the states parceling out some of their functions to local governments. According to Morton Grodzins:

Layer cake or marble cake?

> A far more accurate image is the rainbow or marble cake, characterized by an inseparable mingling of differently colored ingredients, the colors appearing in vertical and diagonal strands and unexpected whirls. As colors are mixed in the marble cake, so functions are mixed in the American federal system.[16]

Cooperative federalism

Irrespective of whether the layer-cake analogy for American government actually was at one time a true picture (Grodzins contended it *never* was), few would deny that today federal–state relationships are characterized far more by cooperation, coordination, and the sharing of power than by separation and competition. State government, national government, and local government may get together in joint action on a highway project, in fighting an epidemic, or in running down a "public enemy number one" wanted for trial in their several courts. All three may act jointly in serving farmers through a county agent, in assisting welfare clients, in providing lunches for needy school children, in utilizing hydroelectric power, and in numerous other ways. The state may receive money from the national treasury and use it for direct benefits to citizens or through the agency of local governments, according to legal provisions at Washington and the state capital. The citizen as taxpayer may know which government is taking his money, but the citizen as recipient does not always know which government or governments should be credited for the services. Taxes increasingly go to the central government, whether state or national, and expenditures flow increasingly from the center. The criteria for taxing and for spending reflect the disparate resources of the different levels of government and the need to equalize governmental services in rich and poor jurisdictions.

Two studies of the federal system, as seen by governmental officials and made by the U. S. Senate Subcommittee on Intergovernmental Relations,[17] provide additional insights for the difficult task of categorizing the

[16] Morton Grodzins, "The Federal System," from *Goals for Americans.* Copyright 1960 by *The American Assembly,* Columbia University, New York. (Reprinted by permission of Prentice-Hall, Inc., Englewood Cliffs, New Jersey), p. 265. *See also* Daniel J. Elazar, *American Federalism: A View from the States,* and Grodzins' *The American System.* The origin of the analogy apparently goes back to an earlier use by Joseph E. McLean, *Politics Is What You Make It* (Washington, D.C.: Public Affairs Committee, 1952), p. 5. Grodzins' and Elazar's view that American federalism has always been more like the marble cake is disputed by Harry N. Scheiber, "The Condition of American Federalism: An Historian's View," U. S. Senate Committee on Government Operations, Subcommittee on Intergovernmental Relations (Washington, D. C., 1966).

[17] U. S. Senate, Subcommittee on Intergovernmental Relations, Committee of Govern-

American brand of federalism as it now exists. A "composite theory of federalism," blending features of both the competitive and cooperative concepts, emerged from the various views of state and local officials surveyed in the first study. The four attitudinal positions and the percentages of the total sample holding each attitude were: Orthodox States Righters (ultraconservatives), 11 percent; Neo-Traditionalists (moderate conservatives), 43 percent; Pragmatic Cooperative Federalists (realistic liberals), 33 percent; and New Nationalists (ultraliberals), 13 percent. The composite, or hybrid, theory represents a consensus of the two middle groups—approximately three-fourths of the state and local respondents—and is said to resemble a marble-cake cut into layers.

Composite or hybrid theory of federalism

Federal aid officials—primarily middle management executives—are reported by the companion study to hold still another and rather unusual view of federalism. Some of the distinguishing characteristics of this view are said to be (1) a unifunctional and professional bias; (2) a specialized program and bureau emphasis; (3) an anti-state and locally elected-official bias; and (4) a generally unsympathetic attitude toward the power position of the states, the *general* units of local government (as opposed to special districts), and Congress' role as strengthener of the federal system. This unflattering report on federal aid officials' attitudes concluded that theirs is an atypical interpretation of our federal system, resembling none of the "cake analogies," but rather a large brick of harlequin ice cream containing 143 flavors, one for each current aid program. Deil S. Wright has added to the word pictures of federalism by speaking of "vertical functional autocracies" and "picket-fence federalism."[18]

Federalism viewed by aid officials

The interplay of federal, state, county, and city responsibility in most contemporary governmental activity may be illustrated by the following description of the work of the health officer, known as "sanitarian," in a rural county in a border state:

The case of the interrelated sanitarian

> The sanitarian is appointed by the state under merit standards established by the federal government. His base salary comes jointly from state and federal funds, the county provides him with an office and office amenities and pays a portion of his expenses, and the largest city in the county also contributes to

ment Operations, *The Federal System as Seen by State and Local Officials*, 88th Cong., 1st sess (Washington, D.C.: U. S. Government Printing Office, 1963), and *The Federal System as Seen by Federal Aid Officials*, 89th Cong., 1st sess. (Washington, D.C.: U. S. Government Printing Office, 1965). *See also* the interpretation of the first report by R. W. McCulloch, "Intergovernmental Relations as Seen by Public Officials," *Annals of the American Academy of Political and Social Science* 359 (May 1965), pp. 131–134. A more general review of intergovernmental relations is the symposium edited by Willis D. Hawley, *Where Governments Meet: Emerging Patterns of Intergovernmental Relations* (Berkeley: Institute of Governmental Studies, University of California, 1967).

[18] Deil S. Wright, "The States and Intergovernmental Relations," *Publius* 1 (1972), p. 24.

> his salary and office by virtue of his appointment as a city plumbing inspector. It is impossible from moment to moment to tell under which governmental hat the sanitarian operates. His work of inspecting the purity of food is carried out under federal standards; but he is enforcing state laws when inspecting commodities that have not been in interstate commerce; and somewhat perversely he also acts under state authority when inspecting milk coming into the county from producing areas across the state border. He is a federal officer when impounding impure drugs shipped from a neighboring state; a federal-state officer when distributing typhoid immunization serum; a state officer when enforcing standards of industrial hygiene; a state-local officer when inspecting the city's water supply; and (to complete the circle) a local officer when insisting that the city butchers adopt more hygienic methods of handling their garbage. But he cannot and does not think of himself as acting in these separate capacities. All business in the county that concerns public health and sanitation he considers his business. Paid largely from federal funds, he does not find it strange to attend meetings of the city council to give expert advice on matters ranging from rotten apples to rabies control. He is even deputized as a member of both the city and county police forces.[19]

Centralized taxing with decentralized spending

Intergovernmental relations are more prevalent in disbursing than in collecting public funds. The pattern in government as in business points toward centralization and standardization of financial management for reasons of economy, efficiency, and accountability. The closer government is to the people, the harder it finds the task of extracting revenue from the people, but the easier or less restrictive it finds the role of spending available funds. The national government surpasses most of the fifty state governments in the effectiveness and efficiency of revenue policies, including taxation and borrowing. The fifty state governments likewise surpass most of the thousands of local jurisdictions in revenue management, although many of the local jurisdictions surpass their state governments in this respect. Moreover, centralized taxes on incomes, business, and business transactions of a burdensome nature are less disruptive of the private economic system than would be equivalent exaction through a variety of taxes imposed by many local units of government. Hence, the national and state governments collect billions in revenue to be expended through decentralized local channels with accountability to central authorities. Such a pattern of government seems to fit into a pattern of human behavior. Many a respectable citizen complains bitterly because he pays heavy taxes to the national government but at the same time he praises his governor or local official for achieving progress based partly on federal funds made possible by the taxes he objects to. To spend is more politic than to tax, and intergovernmental relations seem to thrive on joint sponsorship of popular projects and services.

[19] Grodzins, "The Federal System," pp. 265–266.

The beginnings of federal aid

Much of the expansion of government has been brought about by federal aid to the states. Federal aid is not new—it is as old as the Constitution, although it has taken on new scope and variety since 1900. In planning for territories beyond the Alleghenies before Washington became president, Congress provided for land grants to support public education in the future states. This policy was followed for other territories and states carved out of the national domain. The land-grant colleges, launched under legislation enacted during the Civil War to meet vocational needs, exemplify federal and state cooperation in sponsoring higher education. The older states containing no United States lands were given titles to lands in other states which were to be sold and the proceeds used to help underwrite the costs of such colleges. Congress subsequently adopted plans for cash support for experiment stations and extension services at these colleges. The Smith–Lever Act of 1914 inaugurated further aid for agricultural education in the form of federal–state support of farm demonstration agents in the hundreds of rural counties on a fifty-fifty basis. Early federal aid for internal improvements and the later land grants for railroads in the states and territories foreshadowed the federal–state highway program of the twentieth century.

The "good roads" movement

The Federal Aid Road Act of 1916 anticipated the large-scale policy of federal aid to the states known today. The coming of the automobile stimulated an existing demand for improvement of public roads, a legitimate government enterprise. County and private maintenance could no longer meet the needs of modern America. Organizations and individuals got behind a "good roads" movement, on which many state leaders and national legislators founded political careers. To accommodate interstate and local traffic and to offset the financial inadequacies of many states, the federal government was brought into the picture. There was no hesitancy on scores of "bureaucracy," "creeping socialism," or "violation of states' rights." Government and people, as on other occasions, were meeting a condition, not following a theory. It was understood that both the state and national governments possessed the constitutional power to develop public highways. Congress has the expressed authority to "establish post offices and post roads" as well as the implied power to provide transportation facilities for defense and possibly for other purposes. The "post roads" power was not a mere pretext for granting federal aid, as the new system of rural free delivery of mail was rapidly spreading over all important roads.

Congress and the state legislatures coordinated efforts in expanding the matching pattern, which was to become a permanent practice for highway construction as well as for other purposes. Under this policy Congress grants money to the states for specified purposes, provided the states match the funds or meet a specified ratio and also comply with certain other requirements as to standards of work. Every offer is an inducement, not a club, and state acceptance is virtually the universal rule. By 1973 the national government was annually advancing close to five billion dollars to the states for the aid of primary highways, secondary or feeder roads, urban connections, and the new interstate highways. This aid has combined with state gasoline taxes in providing the chief means for establishing the most extensive highway system in the world.

Joint administration

The federal highway legislation of 1916 set up standards of cooperation for the state and national governments in the administration of joint projects, with the states exercising the initiative within defined limits and the government at Washington acting in an advisory, supervisory, and auditing capacity. The states were required to have or to establish central highway departments or agencies to execute their part of the undertakings. A national agency eventually known as the Bureau of Public Roads was set up to manage the national phases of the work. It was first in the Department of Agriculture, then moved to the Federal Works Agency, the Department of Commerce, and, finally, the Department of Transportation. Much of the local government responsibility for road construction and maintenance thus passed to the joint central management of state and national authorities.

Other uses of grants-in-aid

Highways are not the only purposes served by federal grants-in-aid. As already indicated, agriculture and education receive assistance, and the Great Depression of the 1930s brought vast sums of federal money to the states for relief and welfare activities, much of it on a non-matching basis. Local units of government also shared in various ways in federal grants in those days of need; this sharing was to continue after the back of the depression was broken. Not only city streets but also city building and sewage projects were made legitimate purposes for federal aid. The problem of planning for civilian defense in the event of atomic warfare opened up a broad new field of federal aid to the states and their urban communities.

Social security

A vast amount of federal financing in cooperation with the states is involved in the system of Social Security, which was started by congressional legislation in 1935, amended in 1939, and widely expanded after World War II. Besides receiving grants-in-aid for important welfare purposes, all the states are eligible for funds for insuring workers against unemployment. The funds are derived from taxes on payrolls of employers. The national tax for the purpose is compulsory, but a 90 percent credit or offset is allowed for state collections from the taxpayer for unemployment insurance. There is also provision for financial assistance to the state "for the proper and efficient administration of its unemployment compensation law and of its public employment offices" out of the remaining federal 10 percent. Wisconsin already had a plan of unemployment insurance, and all the other states fell in line with plans and funds after the action by Congress in 1935. Subsequent discussion will show wide variations among the states in the scope and methods of unemployment insurance. But all of them have met national standards through legislative and administrative action, including the establishment of personnel merit systems extending down to county administrative employees.

Federal aid escalation in the 1960s

A virtual tidal wave of new programs involving federal grants-in-aid was passed by Congress in the mid-1960s, bringing the total number of grant programs to more than 170. One special budget analysis reported an increase in categorical aid programs from 71 in 1950 to 530 in 1970. They are administered by some twenty-one federal departments and agencies; their annual outlay rose sharply from 7 billion dollars in 1960 to 24 billion in 1970 and an estimated 43 billion in 1973. (See Table 2–1.) A complete cataloging of these new programs would require more space than is available, although some of the details are given in subsequent chapters. Indeed, one of the current "best sellers" among government documents is the *Catalog of Federal Aids to State and Local Governments*, a large volume published annually by the Legislative Reference Service of the Library of Congress.

War on poverty

While the number and variety of newly authorized grants-in-aid in the 1960s was staggering, the bulk of them were intended as part of a two-pronged attack on poverty and urban problems. The cornerstone of the anti-poverty program was the Economic Opportunity Act of 1964. The act relied heavily on cooperative federalism to achieve such objectives as help-

Table 2–1. Federal Grants in Relation to Federal Domestic Outlays and State–Local Revenue, 1955–1973

		As percent of	
Fiscal year	*Grants (billions)*	*Federal domestic outlays*[a]	*State–local revenue*
1955	$3.3	11.9%	10.4%
1960	7.0	16.4	11.6
1964	10.1	17.9	12.4
1968	18.6	20.9	15.8
1970	24.0	21.9	15.9
1971	29.8	23.5	17.9
1972 (est.)	39.1	25.8	21.1
1973 (est.)	43.5	27.0	21.1

[a] Excludes outlays for defense, space, and international programs.

Source: Federal Budget, Fiscal Year 1973, Special Analysis P, as quoted in Tax Foundation, Inc., *The Federal Budget for Fiscal Year 1973: Future Implications* (New York, 1972), p. 8.

ing low-income families meet problems of education, vocational rehabilitation, job training and counseling, health, welfare, and employment. Parts of the poverty program, such as VISTA (Volunteers in Service to America), a kind of "domestic peace corps" helping to meet needs of impoverished groups, were operated directly by the national Office of Economic Opportunity. Most of them were grant-in-aid programs, such as "Operation Head Start," which assists local school systems in providing preschool experience for children from low-income families. The role of the states, and of the governor in particular, in the anti-poverty program very quickly became the subject of a continuing debate and congressional conflict. President Nixon's landslide re-election in 1972 was interpreted as a mandate to dismantle some of the more controversial aspects of the war on poverty, including the Office of Economic Opportunity. Some of the more popular programs were retained and transferred to traditional departments.

Attacking regional poverty

Regional aspects of poverty were given attention in the Area Redevelopment Act of 1961 and, more specifically, in the Appalachian Regional Development Act of 1965. Grants and low-interest loans were made available to eligible areas for industrial development and improvement of related public facilities. Opposition soon developed for allegedly encouraging the "pirating" of industry from one section to another. The Appalachian program was an interesting departure from past practice in two respects: it focused initially on a single hard-core poverty region, involving twelve states, and it was based on a new concept of cooperative federalism. Major decisions in initiating, supervising, and coordinating various economic redevelopment projects were delegated to the states participating in the Appalachian Regional Commission, with an unusual arrangement for decisions by a majority of the states, subject to a veto by a federal representative designated by the President. Much of the money involved was earmarked for road construction, a fact that drew criticism from some quarters. The rationale provided was the need to link previously inaccessible "pockets of poverty" to economic centers outside its environs. Following passage of the Public Works and Economic Development Act of 1965, five additional multistate regional planning commissions were established during 1966 and 1967, extending the Appalachian idea to regional poverty in the Ozarks, New England, the Atlantic Coastal Plains, the Upper Great Lakes, and the "Four Corners" of Utah, Arizona, Colorado, and New Mexico.

While the urban emphasis in federal aid programs has been growing for some time, it reached a highwater mark during 1965 when Congress sharply increased its output. In one single measure—the Housing and Urban Development Act—grants were authorized for basic water and sewer facilities, neighborhood facilities, advance acquisition of land, open space and urban beautification, code enforcement assistance, rent supplements, demolition of unsafe structures, and support for councils of elected local officials. Other legislation focusing on urban needs in the same year included the Water Quality Act, Clean Air Act Amendments, Solid Waste Disposal Act, Public Works and Economic Development Act, Law Enforcement Assistance Act, Highway Beautification Act, the extension of the Juvenile Delinquency Control Program, and the expansion of the Economic Opportunity Program.

Growing urban emphasis

Possibly the most far-reaching aspect of the federal-aid escalation of the 1960s was passage of two major programs of aid to education: the Higher Education Facilities Act of 1963 and the Elementary and Secondary Education Act of 1965. The 1963 act may prove to be as much a turning point for American colleges and universities as was the passage of the Morrill (land-grant college) Act a century earlier. Federal aid for education prior to 1963 had been approached gingerly *through* higher education for ancillary purposes such as research, educating veterans, training scientists, or training foreign language teachers. The 1963 act took a long step in the direction of aid *for* higher education by authorizing grants directly for faculty development, facilities, and student aid other than loans. Passage of the 1965 act authorizing assistance for elementary and secondary education was also precedent breaking, for it encompassed both direct aid to public schools and indirect aid to parochial schools. In this case the church–state controversy, which had blocked federal aid to schools for many years, was blunted by tying the school aid program in large measure to the war on poverty.

New landmarks in education assistance

Federal aid, particularly for welfare purposes, has not escaped challenge in the courts. Two Massachusetts suits claiming unconstitutionality of the Federal Child Hygiene Act reached the Supreme Court for decision in 1923. The Court, rejecting the argument that the law, through federal aid, was effectively inducing the states to yield a portion of their sovereign rights, dismissed the cases as not having a jurisdictional basis under the constitutional tax clauses.[20]

Federal aid before the courts

A somewhat similar case against the unemployment insurance features of the Social Security program brought forth a sweeping majority opinion by Justice Cardozo. This opinion denied the employer's claims of unconstitutionality, unfairness, and abuse of the federal tax power, holding that the congressional provisions were not coercive but were designed to facilitate voluntary joint action by the national and state governments in meeting welfare problems of vital concern to both. The Court observed that "the relief of unemployment" was a task in which "nation and state

[20] *Massachusetts* v. *Mellon* and *Frothingham* v. *Mellon*, 262 U. S. 447 (1923).

may lawfully cooperate."[21] That lawful cooperation was to expand without effective constitutional challenge.

Appraisal of federal aid

The federal aid technique enables the national government to walk the tight-rope of avoiding legal encroachment upon reserved powers of the states by entering into partnership with state governments. The United States government in this manner seeks to maintain national standards in public service by providing aid at the weakest spots. Federal aid to state education may bring funds from the wealthier sections to poorer sections for children who are likely in time to seek opportunity in the wealthier sections. The grant-in-aid policy serves partly to balance or distribute the financial burden of government in the federal system. Table 2–2 shows the

Table 2–2. Proportion of State and Local Revenue Received From Federal Aid, 1971–72

	Revenue (Per Capita)			
State	*Total*	*From Own Sources*	*From Federal Government*	*Federal Aid as Percent of Total*
U. S. Average	$798.87	$648.79	$150.08	18.8
Median State	756.41	608.04	159.90	21.1
Alabama	612.57	441.32	171.25	27.9
Alaska	1,593.72	1,057.91	535.81	33.6
Arizona	771.86	634.98	136.88	17.7
Arkansas	576.87	418.15	158.72	27.5
California	1,031.36	828.71	202.65	19.6
Colorado	830.88	655.59	175.29	21.1
Connecticut	843.48	723.18	120.30	14.3
Delaware	929.89	756.20	173.69	18.7
Florida	668.34	567.44	100.90	15.1
Georgia	685.39	530.83	154.56	22.5
Hawaii	1,034.07	798.28	235.79	22.8
Idaho	692.86	528.59	164.27	23.7
Illinois	831.84	668.45	163.39	19.6
Indiana	662.39	570.68	91.71	13.8
Iowa	727.00	623.00	104.00	14.3
Kansas	716.61	591.91	124.70	17.4
Kentucky	614.77	466.45	148.32	24.1
Louisiana	738.11	576.46	161.65	21.9
Maine	722.31	554.78	167.53	23.2
Maryland	801.13	678.03	123.10	15.4

[21] *Steward Machine Co.* v. *Davis*, 301 U. S. 548 (1937).

Table 2–2. *Continued*

State	Revenue (Per Capita) Total	From Own Sources	From Federal Government	Federal Aid as Percent of Total
Massachusetts	888.80	728.90	159.90	18.0
Michigan	859.55	716.84	142.71	16.6
Minnesota	894.19	747.15	147.04	16.4
Mississippi	647.80	470.32	177.48	27.4
Missouri	652.65	522.81	129.84	19.9
Montana	861.94	634.25	227.69	26.4
Nebraska	722.48	606.55	115.93	16.0
Nevada	988.54	816.22	172.32	17.4
New Hampshire	639.32	525.17	114.15	17.9
New Jersey	789.00	665.91	123.09	15.6
New Mexico	845.83	594.31	251.52	29.7
New York	1,119.79	937.44	182.35	16.3
North Carolina	592.07	472.21	119.86	20.2
North Dakota	783.02	609.63	173.39	22.1
Ohio	633.50	538.90	94.60	14.9
Oklahoma	683.82	515.31	168.51	24.6
Oregon	797.14	608.04	189.10	23.7
Pennsylvania	740.85	620.17	120.68	16.3
Rhode Island	756.41	598.09	158.32	20.9
South Carolina	566.21	446.24	119.97	21.2
South Dakota	785.06	615.04	170.02	21.6
Tennessee	599.00	462.67	136.33	22.7
Texas	624.71	500.98	123.73	19.8
Utah	752.79	552.78	200.01	26.6
Vermont	907.92	686.03	221.89	24.4
Virginia	647.73	525.45	122.28	18.9
Washington	876.04	714.23	161.81	18.5
West Virginia	680.88	484.20	196.68	28.9
Wisconsin	836.08	721.82	114.26	13.7
Wyoming	1,027.53	748.21	279.32	27.2
District of Columbia	1,428.67	752.20	676.47	47.3

Source: Adapted from U. S. Bureau of the Census, *Governmental Finances in 1971–72.*

difference in relative importance of federal aid among the fifty states. It tends to synchronize continent-wide spending with decentralized needs and with the centralized taxing power, borrowing power, and monetary power of the United States government.

Federal aid is sometimes criticized as a form of bribery to the states to waive their constitutional rights, as centralized extravagance in government, and as an unfair method of taking from the more provident states which have made a real tax effort and giving to the less responsible states which have been willing to impose only light taxes upon their citizens. It is further criticized as a distorting influence upon state governments to slight important needs outside the scope of federal aid in favor of too much attention to fields in which there is national help. Opposition is strongest in realms where public and private enterprise are both involved, as in housing and education. In public education additional issues arise over the separation of church and state, in connection with the question of aid to parochial schools, as well as over racial segregation.

Diverse roles for states

Friends of federal aid are sometimes among its critics, at least in terms of the failure to develop a consistent or coordinated approach from time to time, place to place, and function to function, especially with respect to the role of the states. Norman Beckman has cataloged the wide diversity of state roles in federal aid programs: a "channel" in "701" planning assistance to smaller communities; a "priority-setter" in sewage treatment and hospital construction grants; a "planner" in the federal-aid highway program; a "partner" in the River Basin Commission title of the Water Resources Planning Act; an "approving body" in the Land and Water Conservation Fund; a "legislative enabler" for most of the programs of the Department of Housing and Urban Development; and a "non-participant" in the Farmers Home Administration's grant and loan program for waterworks and sewage disposal plants.[22] William G. Colman attributes the tendency of state and local officials to criticize the administration of federal aid to the confusing proliferation of grants and the continual amending of older grants, and concludes:

> Grants-in-aid are increasing, in numbers and magnitude, at a rapid rate and we may come to a situation where grants-in-aid are an impenetrable jungle of legal, financial, and political and professional interlacings which will sorely try the minds of officials at all levels—Congressmen, Cabinet members, Governors, mayors, and county officials—in trying to maintain any kind of rational legislative and administrative direction of the areas of Government affairs in which grants play so large a part.[23]

A much more elaborate system of federal–state–local cooperation was launched by the Omnibus Crime Control and Safe Streets Act of 1968,

[22] Norman Beckman, "For a New Perspective in Federal-State Relations," in *State Government* (The Council of State Governments), 39, Autumn 1966, p. 270.

[23] Testimony of the executive director of the Advisory Commission on Intergovernmental Relations before the U. S. Senate Subcommittee on Intergovernmental Relations, Committee on Government Operations, as quoted in its report, *The Federal System as Seen by Federal Aid Officials*, p. 5.

with 1970 amendments; this act required each state to have a comprehensive criminal justice plan approved by the federal Law Enforcement Assistance Administration. This program, the first to use the controversial "block-grant" concept, places strong coordination responsibility on the states, but has a guaranteed "pass-through" of funds to local government, making certain the localities receive their share. (See chapter 19.)

In spite of the growing complexity in the pattern of federal aid and the inconsistencies in the various roles of the states, Beckman contends that the system is working reasonably well and he suggests paraphrasing Emerson: "A foolish consistency in Federal–State relations will continue to be the hobgoblin of little minds, adored by little statesmen and philosophers."[24] Whether the quest for consistency and coordination in federal aid is achieved or not, it is clear that the general trend is toward an increasing reliance upon federal grants-in-aid by the states and their local units. It remains to be seen whether the enactment of the revenue-sharing program in 1972 will cause a reduction in reliance on categorical grants-in-aid, or will merely become an additional layer on top of other federal aid programs. (See chapter 14.) The 1973 amendments to the Older Americans Act, with greatly expanded appropriations, stand as clear testimony to the continuing strength of "clientele politics" and suggest the rocky road that faces advocates of a more rational and integrated approach to the financing and administering of federal grant programs. The 1973 legislation went against the grain of the Nixon administration proposals for federal grant consolidation and a "comprehensive service approach." It isolated a particular clientele to be served (older Americans) by a separate administrative structure.[25]

Continuing strength of "clientele politics"

There are other ways, outside the scope of grants-in-aid, by which the national and state governments work together, formally and informally. Congressional legislation frequently dovetails with state laws. An example is the provision against the interstate shipment of prison-made products into states where the sale of such merchandise is illegal. In support of petroleum conservation, the Connally Act of 1935 banned interstate shipment of "hot oil" produced or supplied in violation of state law.

Other forms of cooperation

A high degree of uniformity in state inheritance levies resulted from the national policy, started in 1926, of allowing persons liable for federal inheritance taxes a credit or offset of up to 80 percent of the national obligation for payment of state inheritance taxes. This provision was unsuccessfully challenged by the government of Florida, which had been

[24] Beckman, "For a New Perspective," p. 270.

[25] For a critical review of this legislation, *see* Robert B. Hudson, "State Politics, Federalism, and Public Policies for Older Americans," a paper prepared for the annual meeting of the American Political Science Association, New Orleans, Sept. 4–8, 1973; and Robert H. Binstock, "Interest Group Liberalism and the Politics of Aging," *The Gerontologist* 12 (1972), pp. 265–280.

attracting aged rich from other states by its lack of inheritance levies. But the arrangement was satisfactory to the states having such a tax, and Florida within a few years moved into line to get funds which otherwise would fall to the United States government. Only Nevada is now without this tax. Congress took a long step toward eliminating the interstate and intercity confusion over daylight saving time by enacting the Uniform Time Act of 1966. States were permitted to exempt themselves from uniform federal provisions for daylight time only by specific legislation on a statewide basis. States were thus generally prepared for a uniform policy to attack the energy crisis of the mid-seventies. With a few exceptions the states followed federal leadership in moving holidays to Monday so that five of the nine legal public holidays provide a guaranteed three-day weekend.

Executive and administrative cooperation

Officials of federal and state governments cooperate in many kinds of activities, both informally and through legal arrangements. The Federal Bureau of Investigation gives technical instruction and assistance to state law enforcement officers and aids in tracking down particular criminals. Federal and state health authorities work together, as do their colleagues in the agricultural agencies. The Tennessee Valley Authority cooperates with state agencies and institutions in numerous activities. Important state and private libraries serve as depositories for United States government documents as a service to the public. Many other cooperative activities might be cited such as President Theodore Roosevelt's initiation of the annual state governors' conference to explore problems common to the states and the nation, at the time notably that of conservation. Experience during World War II revealed that federal–state cooperation could take place with surprising speed when the circumstances required it. Barely a week after the attack on Pearl Harbor, the Office of Price Administration asked the governors to set up cooperative machinery in the states for the rationing of scarce commodities. The result was one of our more remarkable administrative feats, a nationwide rationing program beginning with tires, automobiles, and sugar, put into action in the space of three weeks. It was a committee of federal and state officials that made plans for the nationwide 35 mph speed limit enforced during World War II by all states for the conservation of tires and gasoline.[26]

Efforts to Reverse the New Federalism

Within the past two or three decades there have been several serious and well-organized efforts not only to *halt* the trend toward increased federal

[26] For details of these and other examples of federal–state cooperation, *see* Glenn E. Brooks, *When Governors Convene* (Baltimore: The Johns Hopkins Press, 1961).

responsibilities, expenditures, and grants-in-aid, but also to *reverse* the trend by returning to the states as many functions as possible. The first and second Hoover Commissions on Executive Organization (1947–49 and 1953–55), the Kestnbaum Commission on Intergovernmental Relations (1953–55), and the Joint Federal–State Action Committee (1957–59), were all concerned in varying degrees with minimizing federal activities. The almost monotonous failure of each group to accomplish this purpose should not have been surprising to anyone who has followed the history of the development of increased federal responsibilities, and who has observed with some degree of realism the interplay of forces which produced and sustain the new "cooperative federalism." It is certainly ironic that one of the few tangible results of the Kestnbaum Commission's recommendation was legislation *increasing* federal responsibility in the field of civil defense.

Four special study commissions

Why have such efforts to reverse the centralization trends been so unsuccessful? A brief account of the work of the Joint Federal–State Action Committee should be helpful in answering this question.[27] The JFSAC came into existence as a result of an address by President Eisenhower to the Governors' Conference in 1957 calling for a committee to move from the study phase to the action phase in the matter of reallocating responsibilities and taxes in the federal system. The President suggested the following tasks for the committee:

The Joint Federal–State Action Committee

1. To designate functions which the states are ready and willing to assume and finance that are now performed or financed wholly or in part by the federal government;
2. To recommend the federal and state revenue adjustments required to enable the states to assume such functions; and
3. To identify functions and responsibilities likely to require state or federal attention in the future and to recommend the level of state effort, or federal effort, or both, that will be needed to assure effective action. In designating the functions to be reassumed by the states, the committee should also specify when those functions should be assumed—the amounts by which federal taxes should be reduced—and increases in state revenues needed to support the transferred functions.[28]

The governors responded quickly and the committee which was subsequently established seemed, on the surface at least, to have every prospect of success in its task. The President's appointees were distinguished

[27] This account relies heavily on the description by Brooks, *When Governors Convene*, pp. 100–105.

[28] *Proceedings of the Governors' Conference*, 1957, p. 99, as quoted in Brooks, *When Governors Convene*, p. 101.

and able men, including three leading members of the President's cabinet and the director of the Bureau of the Budget. Ten governors represented the Governors' Conference on the committee, and the chairmanship was shared by a governor and a national official. Morton Grodzins has summarized the initial favorable prospects of the committee as follows:

An auspicious beginning

> There existed no disagreements on party lines within the committee and, of course, no constitutional impediments to its mission. The President, his cabinet members, and all the governors (with one possible exception) on the committee completely agreed on the desirability of decentralization-via-separation-of-functions-and-taxes. They were unanimous in wanting to justify the committee's name and to produce action, not just another report.[29]

The committee worked for more than two years before abandoning its efforts. At the outset it began with caution, avoiding such tough problems as employment security, public assistance, and highway construction, and easing into the less controversial matters, such as migratory labor, flood insurance, federal lands, estate taxes, state taxation of interstate business, vocational education, and municipal waste treatment plant construction. Only in the case of the last two programs did the committee recommend transfer from federal to state hands. These two programs, which concerned vocational education and municipal waste treatment plants, accounted for about 2 percent of all federal grants to the states in 1957, or less than 80 million dollars. Effectuation of even these modest proposals bogged down in the difficulties of finding an acceptable financial arrangement for the transfer to the states. Glenn Brooks reports that the Governors' Conference "responded warily to the work of the committee." The first co-chairman of the committee, Governor Lane Dwinell of New Hampshire, made the following comment in 1958 on the difficulties of getting down to specific cases:

Resistance to change

> Nothing is easier . . . than to speculate *philosophically* on the respective roles of the various levels of government. On the other hand . . . nothing is more difficult than to attempt to spell out recommendations for the assignment or reassignment in specific areas. As is ever the case, interested groups are willing to modify or alter relationships in other fields than their own; but when it concerns a subject matter close to their own hearts, not even divine intervention is permissible without much and heavy protest.[30]

President Eisenhower included in his legislative recommendations to Congress the withdrawal of the national government from vocational

[29] Grodzins, "The Federal System," p. 268.

[30] *Proceedings of the Governors' Conference*, 1958, pp. 11–12, as quoted in Brooks, *When Governors Convene*, p. 103.

education and waste treatment programs, with corresponding credits on the federal local telephone tax. Any chances of adopting his plan were destroyed when Congress repealed the local telephone service tax in its entirety. The governors showed no enthusiasm for taking over two federal programs if that required re-enacting locally a tax just repealed nationally by Congress. Columnist Roscoe Drummond expressed the belief that the states had no desire to take back any functions. Concerning the work of JFSAC he concluded that nothing was accomplished. "No State has acted to take back a single function." Three reasons stood out, in his view, for the failure: (1) governors of the wealthy states did not fear national encroachments; (2) those governors who genuinely wanted to take over certain federal programs were unwilling to pay the political price involved in raising the necessary taxes, even if the way were paved by federal abandonment of the same taxes; and (3) some governors "would rather have the states' rights issue to talk about than to solve." The latter governors, according to Drummond, are really opposed to the performance of certain services by *any* level of government, national or state, and the claim that the service should be performed by the states rather than the national government is merely a smoke screen for their opposition to the activity itself.[31]

Reasons for failure

The constitutional amendment route to bolstering states' rights was attempted in the early 1960s by a group of state legislators and other officials proposing three amendments to the U. S. Constitution: (1) eliminating all constitutional restraints on the way the states apportion their legislatures; (2) permitting states to amend the U. S. Constitution by state legislative action alone, bypassing congressional action; and (3) creating a "court of the union" made up of the fifty state chief justices to review decisions of the U. S. Supreme Court. In the wake of rural unhappiness with the reapportionment decisions and the southern unhappiness with the desegregation decisions, the first two proposed amendments were approved by mid-1963 by about a dozen of the thirty-four states necessary to call a constitutional convention, but only five approved the third amendment. Opponents began to sound the alarm against what they called the "disunion amendments" and Chief Justice Earl Warren called for "a great national debate" before approving amendments that would radically change the character of our institutions. After 1963 support for the amendments steadily faded.

Proposed "court of the union"

The postscript to the fruitless efforts to reverse the "new federalism" may seem strange, indeed, but a new (permanent) Advisory Commission on Intergovernmental Relations (ACIR) was created by act of Congress in

[31] *New York Herald Tribune,* Aug. 5, 1959, as summarized in Brooks, *When Governors Convene,* pp. 104–105.

1959. After this enactment the JFSAC, which had no statutory basis, discontinued operations and gave its records to the new commission. Membership on the advisory commission was made so substantially different from that of the JFSAC that one former governor expressed the fear that there was an attempt to "outflank the governors" with local government officials and state legislators.[32] Only four governors were appointed to the twenty-six member commission, along with four mayors and three county officials. The insignia appearing on some of the commission's earlier reports contained the slogan: "FOR A MORE PERFECT UNION—FEDERAL, STATE, LOCAL," possibly symbolizing a new status for *local* governments in a three-way partnership. The advisory commission's functions coincide in many respects with previous commissions, but the first few years of its existence demonstrated striking differences from its predecessors: (1) the ACIR is clearly committed to cooperative federalism, accepting the idea that most problems are not given to simple analysis and solution by any one level of government; (2) it has not approached improvements in the federal system by means of debating primarily the "grand alternatives" of centralization v. decentralization, but has focused on specific current problems and practical recommendations; (3) it has shown a greater concern for the urban and metropolitan aspects of intergovernmental relations; and (4) its permanence, as opposed to "single-shot status," seems clearly to be established.[33]

Advisory Commission on Intergovernmental Relations

The number and scope of the publications of the ACIR have been of a magnitude far in excess of the general public's awareness. It has contributed close to one hundred publications, many of them formal Commission reports which set forth recommended solutions for intergovernmental tax and fiscal problems, metropolitan organization problems, and other problems related to federal, state, and local relationships.

ACIR's progressive–conservative proposals

More than a dozen reports deal with metropolitan problems, reflecting a Commission conviction that the problems of metropolitanism and governmental fragmentation constitute the greatest single domestic threat to the preservation of the federal system. A kind of progressive–conservative corollary to this theme in the ACIR reports is a new doctrine seldom

[32] Brooks, *When Governors Convene*, p. 107.

[33] For appraisals of the character and work of the ACIR, *see* Daniel J. Elazar, "The Continuing Study of Partnership—The Publications of The Advisory Commission on Intergovernmental Relations," *Public Administration Review* 26 (March 1966), pp. 56–68; Deil S. Wright, "The Advisory Commission on Intergovernmental Relations: Unique Features and Policy Orientation," *Public Administration Review* 25 (September 1965), pp. 193–202; the record of the joint hearings of the Subcommittees on Intergovernmental Relations of the House and Senate Committees on Governmental Operations, *5-Year Record of the Advisory Commission on Intergovernmental Relations and Its Future Role*, Congress of the United States, 89th Cong., 1st sess., May 25–27, 1965; and *10-Year Record of the ACIR*, 92nd Cong., 1st sess., November 1971.

preached before: that it is the duty of the national government consciously and deliberately to stimulate both preventive and corrective action at state and local levels both to strengthen the state's role and to provide rational area-wide metropolitan solutions. Thus far, the ACIR has been able to reassure those jealously guarding the states' prerogatives, while retaining the confidence of the representatives of strong urban interests. Its adopted "Agenda for the Seventies" shows no signs of decline or relaxation; it calls for action to "build stronger states, revitalize local government, restore fiscal balance, strengthen policymakers, and achieve balanced growth." The detailed recommendations in each category constitute a kind of model charter for U. S. intergovernmental relations.[34]

Interstate Relationships

State-to-state obligations of "full faith and credit"

Intergovernmental relations for the states are not all vertical (between a state and the national government); there are also horizontal relationships among states. These were given some attention by the Founding Fathers, though not very much, but in recent years the area of interstate cooperation has grown steadily. The Constitution requires that "Full faith and credit shall be given in each State to the public acts, records, and judicial proceedings of every other State." This enjoinder applies only to civil matters, for no state is expected to enforce the criminal laws of another. A deed, mortgage, contract, will, property judgment, or other civil instrument executed and recorded according to law in one state is recognized and accepted in every other state concerned. A marriage in one state is recognized in another, although the marriage laws of the two states may differ. "Full faith and credit" usually applies to divorces in the case of removal of divorcees from state to state. The United States Supreme Court has held, however, that North Carolina need not recognize a migratory divorce secured in Nevada by actual inhabitants of North Carolina, who,

[34] For a summary of ACIR recommendations to the states for restructuring and modernizing local government, *see Unshackling Local Government: A Survey of Proposals by the Advisory Commission on Intergovernmental Relations,* Rev. ed., House Committee on Government Operations, 89th Cong., 2nd sess. (Washington, D.C.: U. S. Government Printing Office, 1966). It draws heavily from three ACIR reports: *State Constitutional and Statutory Restrictions on Local Government Debt* (1961); *State Constitutional and Statutory Restrictions upon the Structural, Functional, and Personnel Powers of Local Government* (1962); and *State Constitutional and Statutory Restrictions on Local Taxing Powers* (1962), but brief descriptions are given of all reports issued by the ACIR through April 1968. Among the reports published since 1968 are *Public Opinion and Taxes* (1972); *Urban America and the Federal System* (1969); *In Search of Balance: Canada's Intergovernmental Experience* (1971); *Multistate Regionalism* (1972); and a series of volumes on *Substate Regionalism and the Federal System* (1973 and 1974).

according to proof, had never become bona fide residents of Nevada.[35] Subsequently, the Court held that where both parties participate in the proceedings and have opportunity to contest the jurisdictional issues, the decree may not be subjected to attack in the courts of another state on the ground of jurisdiction. Full faith and credit must be accorded to the decree.[36]

Another state-to-state obligation concerns the rendition of fugitives accused or convicted of crime. The Constitution states:

> A person charged in any State with treason, felony, or other crime, who shall flee from justice, and be found in another State, shall on demand of the executive authority of the State from which he fled, be delivered up, to be removed to the State having jurisdiction of the crime.

Rendition of fugitive criminals

Under this provision as supplemented by national legislation, a fugitive, to be extradited, must be officially accused of committing a crime within the borders of the state seeking his return. If a person, for example, commits murder in Louisiana and is arrested as a fugitive in California, the governor of Louisiana sends a signed requisition, with a copy of the indictment, for return of the fugitive. Normally the governor of California honors the requisition, and the prisoner is brought back by a Louisiana officer to be tried in a court of the latter state. However, there are occasional exceptions to the policy of returning fugitives, with no provision for overriding the will of a governor refusing to honor a requisition. The Supreme Court has declined to intervene. A conspicuous case some years ago was that in which the governor of New Jersey declined to honor a Georgia requisition for Robert Elliott Barnes, who told his story in *I Am A Fugitive From A Georgia Chain Gang!*[37]

Disputes and agreements between states

The framers of the Constitution authorized two important methods for deciding disputes and adjusting problems between states. Article III extends the judicial power of the United States to controversies between two or more states, with the Supreme Court having original jurisdiction in such cases. Many disputes have been settled in this manner. Article I, section 10, permits a state, with the consent of Congress, to enter into an "agreement or compact with another State." Congress and groups of states have utilized this permission, expressed or implied, for more than a hundred interstate compacts. Most of the earlier compacts were merely agreements on boundary lines, but more recent compacts have ventured into

[35] *Williams* v. *North Carolina*, 325 U. S. 226 (1945).

[36] *See Sherrer* v. *Sherrer*, 334 U. S. 343 (1948), and *Coe* v. *Coe*, 334 U. S. 378 (1948).

[37] Robert Elliott Barnes, *I Am A Fugitive From A Georgia Chain Gang!* (New York: Vanguard Press, 1932).

areas of economic and social regulation where two or more states share the same problem.

Interstate compacts

One of the better known compacts established the Port of New York Authority in 1921, with New York and New Jersey jointly tackling the construction and management of port facilities, interstate bridges, tunnels, bus and truck terminals, and airports. Several interstate compacts deal with the conservation of natural resources, such as the Columbia River salmon runs and the migratory fisheries of the Atlantic states, where action by one state would be futile. Other examples among the growing number of compacts are the Tri-State Transportation Commission Compact, ratified by New Jersey, New York, and Connecticut in 1965, creating an official planning agency for the three-state metropolitan area, and the Interstate Air Pollution Compact, ratified in 1965 by Indiana and Illinois, creating a commission to study and recommend, and to enforce if state agencies do not act.

Interstate–federal compacts

A 1971 compilation of interstate compacts by the Council of State Governments[38] revealed the steady growth to a total of 160 compacts in operation, 47 of these adopted in the 1960s. Recently, compacts have been increasingly used to secure broad intergovernmental cooperation in functional areas such as corrections, education, health, nuclear energy, planning and development, transportation, and welfare. In addition, interstate–federal compacts have been used to create a commission uniting the powers of both levels of government and creating a regulatory agency of several states. The Delaware River Basin Compact, adopted in 1961, is an example of what some at the federal level consider an improper way of organizing intergovernmental river basin management which should not be repeated. Nevertheless, similar instruments were subsequently formulated for the Susquehanna and Potomac River Basins, in spite of the doubts of some federal agencies about the wisdom of giving up their independence of action to an interstate–federal commission. This joint commission coordinates federal, state, local, and private actions affecting the resources of a river basin. One of the more ambitious efforts to utilize the interstate compact for regional planning and policy formulation is the Southern Growth Policies Board, established initially by nine states in 1971. It is open to the 17 southern states and is aimed at helping the states achieve sound and balanced growth, rather than the haphazard expansion typical of the post-World War II period.

The future growth and effectiveness of interstate compacts is by no means clear. As states move more and more into regulatory and service fields, they run into increasing difficulties of interstate negotiation and congressional approval. States have urged Congress to adopt consent-in-

[38] Council of State Governments, *Interstate Compacts, 1783–1970* (Lexington, Ky., 1971).

advance legislation in certain fields as a means of encouraging intergovernmental cooperation, but advance consent has only rarely been given. A variety of political crosscurrents, including opposition pressures from federal agencies, constitutes obstacles to many proposed interstate compacts. The "consent-of-Congress" requirement has been held by the Supreme Court to apply only if the interstate compacts tend "to increase the political power in the states, which may encroach upon or interfere with the just supremacy of the United States.[39] After efforts of the Conference of Southern Governors to obtain congressional consent to a regional education compact were rebuffed, the Conference in 1948 decided that consent was not required after all and proceeded to put the plan into operation. The plan involved joint state tax support for professional and higher education for both whites and blacks in the southern states, but because it was looked upon by many as a device to preserve segregated education, the Senate sent it back to the judiciary committee by a vote of 38 to 37. The southern argument that, since education is one of the states' reserved powers, the compact did not require congressional approval, seems to have prevailed. As a device to preserve racial segregation, however, the contracting states could hardly expect it to obtain court approval.[40]

Requirement of congressional consent

The interstate compact is by no means the only method of interstate cooperation. Through the years various interstate organizations have arisen to work in a multitude of ways for cooperation among states. The oldest is the National Conference of Commissioners on Uniform State Laws, organized in 1892. Its purpose has been to simplify transactions across state lines, and more than 170 "model laws" have been drafted and recommended to state legislatures. The major successes have tended to deal with commercial matters; all states have adopted the model laws on negotiable instruments, warehouse receipts, and stock transfer. Progress in adopting the others has been less successful; only eleven model laws were accepted by as many as forty states. Several organizations of state officials,

Other forms of cooperation

[39] *Virginia* v. *Tennessee*, 148 U. S. 503.

[40] For details of the political and constitutional issues involved in the Southern Regional Education Compact, *see* Vincent V. Thursby's *Interstate Cooperation* (Washington, D.C.: Public Affairs Press, 1953). On interstate compacts generally, *see* Weldon V. Barton, *Interstate Compacts in the Political Process* (Chapel Hill: The University of North Carolina Press, 1967); Richard H. Leach and R. S. Sugg, *The Administration of Interstate Compacts* (Baton Rouge: Louisiana State University Press, 1959); and Frederick L. Zimmermann and Mitchell Wendell, *The Interstate Compact Since 1925* (Chicago: Council of State Governments, 1951), as well as their biennial analysis of interstate compact developments, "Interstate Compacts," in *The Book of the States, 1972–73*, pp. 257–270. Professor Leach has also written an interesting case study of conflict between the Port of New York Authority and a congressional committee, "War on the Port Authority," in Rocco J. Tressolini and Richard T. Frost (eds.), *Cases in American National Government and Politics* (Englewood Cliffs, N. J.: Prentice-Hall, 1966), pp. 10–19.

including governors, attorneys general, budget officers, and chief justices, have been established on a national basis.

The Council of State Governments, established in 1925, has been called the "holding corporation" or "clearinghouse" for interstate cooperation. Serving as an overall umbrella for interstate exchange of information, conferences, and research projects, "Cosgo" acts as secretariat for several of the organizations of state officials and publishes *The Book of the States* (a biennial reference book on state government), *State Government* (a monthly journal), and special reports from time to time. It has been an active participant in the recent national studies of intergovernmental relations.

SUPPLEMENTARY READINGS

Anderson, William. *The Nation and the States: Rivals or Partners?* Minneapolis: University of Minnesota Press, 1955.

Clark, Jane. *The Rise of a New Federalism.* New York: Columbia University Press, 1938.

Cooke, Jacob E., and Cooke, Jacob E., eds. *The Federalist.* Middletown, Conn.: Wesleyan University Press, 1961. *See* Federalist papers 8, 44–46.

Elazar, Daniel J. *American Federalism: A View from the States.* 2nd ed. New York: Thomas Y. Crowell Co., 1972.

Goldwin, Robert A., ed. *A Nation of States.* Chicago: Rand McNally and Co., 1962.

Greene, Lee S.; Jewell, Malcolm E.; and Grant, Daniel R. *The States and the Metropolis.* University, Ala.: University of Alabama Press, 1968.

Leach, Richard H., and Sugg, R. S., Jr. *The Administration of Interstate Compacts.* Baton Rouge: Louisiana State University Press, 1959.

Maass, Arthur, ed. *Area and Power: A Theory of Local Government.* Glencoe, Ill.: The Free Press, 1959.

MacMahon, A. W., ed. *Federalism, Mature and Emergent.* Garden City, N. Y.: Doubleday and Co., 1955.

Mason, Alpheus Thomas. *The States Rights Debate: Anti-federalism and the Constitution.* Englewood Cliffs, N. J.: Prentice-Hall, 1964.

Reagan, Michael D. *The New Federalism.* New York: Oxford University Press, 1972.

Reeves, Mavis Mann, and Glendening, Parris N. *Controversies of State and Local Political Systems.* Boston: Allyn and Bacon, 1972.

Seidman, Harold. *Politics, Position, and Power.* New York: Oxford University Press, 1970.

Sundquist, James L., and Davis, David W. *Making Federalism Work.* Washington, D. C.: The Brookings Institution, 1969.

Thursby, Vincent V. *Interstate Cooperation: A Study of the Interstate Compact.* Washington, D. C.: Public Affairs Press, 1953.

U. S. Advisory Commission on Intergovernmental Relations. *Metropolitan America: Challenge to Federalism.* U. S. House of Representatives, Committee on Government Operations, 89th Congress, 2nd Session, August 1966. *See also* various reports by the ACIR.

U. S. Commission on Intergovernmental Relations. *A Report to the President for Transmittal to the Congress.* Washington, D. C.: U. S. Government Printing Office, 1955.

Vile, M. J. C. *The Structure of American Federalism.* New York: Oxford University Press, 1961.

White, Leonard D. *The States and the Nation.* Baton Rouge: Louisiana State University Press, 1953.

3

Cities in the Federal System

The urban view of federalism

Although it is essential to view the federal system through the eyes of the states, this view by itself is not enough. It is becoming increasingly important to look at the federal system through the eyes of cities. The former view is traditional and time-honored, whether in classroom courses in American government and history, or in U. S. Senate orations on the illustrious origins of states' rights. But the rising tide of urbanism, suburbanism, and metropolitanism in the United States has thrust a third force into the workings of federalism, and its magnitude is too great to ignore or to accommodate with a few minor adjustments in the system.

The rural and agricultural America described by Katherine Lee Bates in "America the Beautiful," with her "spacious skies," "amber waves of grain," "purple mountain majesties," and "fruited plain," is an America seen by most urbanized Americans only in their memories or on vacation trips. In the fourth stanza Miss Bates seems to have prophesied present reality with her reference to "alabaster cities" seen only in patriots' dreams. A few of the implications of the shift from a nation with only a 5 percent urban population in 1790 to a nation 73.5 percent urban in 1970 were touched upon in chapter 1. It is the purpose of this chapter to consider more fully the relationship of cities and the federal system. This involves more than the impact of cities on the federal system; it includes the oft-ignored other side of the coin—the impact of the federal system on cities and, perhaps more important, on metropolitan areas.

The Constitutional Status of Cities

It is no accident that American history is filled with accounts of political, economic, and even military activity revolving around the doctrine of states' rights, with almost no corresponding activity involving a doctrine of "cities' rights." Under the federal Constitution, cities simply have no rights as cities. The city is completely ignored by the Constitution and its language is not the place to look if one is studying the legal status of cities. So far as the federal Constitution is concerned, the only existing subnational level of government is the state. Cities, not being mentioned, are thus nonexistent in the formal sense.

Constitutional silence on cities

In sharp contrast to this rather amazing constitutional picture of urban nonexistence is the actual picture of federal awareness of cities. As early as 1960, in their study of *The Federal Government and Metropolitan Areas*,[1] Connery and Leach describe the staggering scale of some of the federal operations within the New York metropolitan area alone: fifty-two slum clearance and urban renewal projects involving federal grants of 120 million dollars; commitments for 90,000 low-rent government housing units to the extent of 30 million dollars per year for forty years; 10 million dollars to help construct ten airports between 1947 and 1957, with 6 million dollars pledged for additional work; 129 million dollars for highway and bridge construction between 1953 and 1957, not counting any funds for the new interstate expressway system; 16,000 home mortgages insured by FHA in 1955 alone, totaling 170 million dollars, with an even larger number guaranteed by the Veterans Administration in the same year; Veterans Administration hospital construction exceeding 54 million dollars during 1957, with additional grants of 10 million dollars and 3 million dollars for hospitals by the Public Health Service and Defense Department; and thirty projects for port improvement in the New York area by the Army Corps of Engineers, totaling well over 100 million dollars, and involving commitment by the Corps to maintain them at federal expense when completed. Undoubtedly a follow-up study of federal assistance to the New York metropolitan area today would make the earlier totals seem meager by comparison. In her study of urban lobbying in the federal arena, Suzanne Farkas reported that a total of more than 1.3 billion dollars of federal funds were in the expense budget of New York City for the fiscal year 1970–71.[2] This picture of federal involvement can be found, in lesser pro-

Federal operations in cities

[1] Robert H. Connery and Richard H. Leach, *The Federal Government and Metropolitan Areas* (Cambridge, Mass.: Harvard University Press, 1960), pp. 7–8.

[2] Suzanne Farkas, *Urban Lobbying: Mayors in the Federal Arena* (New York: New York University Press, 1971), p. 6.

If the President Is Interested in Summitry

Figure 3–1. Editorial cartoon by Paul Conrad. Copyright © Los Angeles Times Syndicate. Reprinted with permission.

portions, in each metropolitan area in the United States and the pressure for greater involvement continues, as illustrated in Figure 3–1.

State supremacy over cities

It is important to realize, therefore, that federal–city relations are characterized by a constitutional and political paradox. In spite of a growing network of direct and indirect communication lines between city governments and federal agencies, the city continues to be solely a creature of one of the fifty states, subject to such obligations, privileges, powers, and restrictions as the state sees fit to prescribe. The state may create or destroy cities, which are simply "municipal corporations." With respect to *all* units of local government, including cities, "the state giveth and the state taketh away." To the extent that cities exercise power to collect taxes, regulate traffic, or enact city zoning ordinances, they are actually exercising the *state's* powers, reserved under the Tenth Amendment of the federal Constitution and duly delegated to the cities by state constitutional or statutory provision. An early effort in a few state courts to establish a doctrine of the inherent right of local self-government, such as Judge Cooley's famous Michigan decision in 1871,[3] was never able to dislodge the state supremacy doctrine. (See chapter 17 for a discussion of the municipal charter and home rule.) The larger cities have increasingly complained of state restrictions and callous disregard for urban problems and needs. State officials, in turn, are equally critical and suspicious of city mismanagement and corruption. A classic example of state–city friction and resentment was the establishment of competing study commissions for New York City in the early 1970s. On Governor Nelson Rockefeller's recommendation the legislature created the "Scott Commission" to study governmental operations in New York City. It was attacked by Mayor John Lindsay and several Democratic leaders, and a counter-commission (the Vanden-Huevel Commission) was appointed to study state–city relations. Although their reports in 1972 and 1973 demonstrate expected contrasting views of city problems, state legal supremacy remains clear.[4]

Federal limitations on cities

The picture of the constitutional status of cities is not complete without a consideration of the effect on cities of federal restrictions on states. While states may be supreme over cities, the federal government is supreme over states in many areas; these federal limitations apply with equal strength to cities. There are many such limitations but four will serve to illustrate. (1) The "obligation of contracts" clause in the Constitution forbids any state to pass a law impairing the obligation of contracts; this has come to mean that a municipal corporation cannot normally withdraw from an agreement, whether that agreement is a franchise permitting a transportation company to have a thirty-year monopoly on mass transportation service, or a simple contract to borrow money. On occasion, however, the state's police power takes precedence over the obligation of contracts, as discussed in chapter 4. (2) The "tax immunity" decisions of the Supreme Court have come to mean that post offices, arsenals, navy yards, and other federal property cannot be taxed by a city except where Congress gives its consent. (3) The "equal protection of the laws" clause applies to the action of city officials and has come increasingly into the spotlight in civil rights cases where racial discrimination is charged against city schools, parks, buses, libraries, and similar services. It is this restriction which makes racial segregation of residential areas by city zoning reg-

[3] *People* v. *Hulburt*, 24 Mich. 44 (1871).

[4] For an account of contrasting views of these commissions on the "decentralization fad," *see* Frank J. Macchiarola, "Political Decentralization in New York City: A Progress Report," a paper prepared for the annual meeting of the American Political Science Association in New Orleans, Sept. 4–8, 1973.

ulations unconstitutional. (4) The "due process of law" clause becomes a federal limitation upon cities when an attempt is made to take the "life, liberty, or property" of a person (his freedom of speech, for example) in a manner the courts have come to consider arbitrary, unreasonable, or unfair.

Early Federal–City Relations

How can we explain the apparent discrepancy between the completely negative constitutional view of federal–city relations and the drastically revised picture one gets from looking at the realities of extensive present-day federal involvement in urban affairs? The explanation is found primarily in the use which the federal government has made of its own powers—especially the war powers, commerce powers, and spending powers, and the inevitable impact of such action on the growing urban sector of the nation. As a result of exercising its delegated and implied powers the federal government began to have direct and indirect contacts with cities, although prior to 1933 most of them were of a peripheral nature and more or less accidental.

Depression assistance

The turning point in federal–city relationships was probably in 1932, even before the Roosevelt administration came to power. The year is termed by Professor Roscoe Martin "a sort of geologic fault line in the development of the federal system."[5] It was in that year that Congress first mentioned the word "municipalities" in a federal statute and authorized the Reconstruction Finance Corporation to make loans to states and cities in economic distress because of the depression. Although a self-liquidation restriction stymied the early operation of much of this program, it was a forerunner for a great deal more federal acceptance of direct responsibility for problems in urban centers previously thought to be purely a local responsibility. In 1933 and the years immediately following, the New Deal poured forth an avalanche of anti-depression programs through newly created "alphabetical" agencies—FERA, CWA, WPA, PWA, NRA, and many others. Many of these agencies were authorized to deal directly with the cities as well as with states, and the city–federal contract mushroomed into use as a very common instrument in intergovernmental relations.

PWA and WPA

Between 1933 and 1939 the Public Works Administration made grants to states, cities, and other public bodies for approved public works projects, with up to 30 percent of the cost paid outright and the remaining 70 percent financed through federal loans. Cities applied for such assistance

[5] Roscoe C. Martin, *The Cities and the Federal System* (New York: Atherton Press, 1965), p. 111.

directly to the PWA, were required to observe federally prescribed standards, and were subject to PWA inspection and audit. A different agency, the Works Progress Administration, was more exclusively an emergency work relief program aimed at immediate reduction of unemployment. Local units of government made application to the WPA and agreed to provide most of the material and equipment, while the federal government furnished the labor and much of the administration for the projects. WPA was made the butt of many anti-administration jokes, including the label "we piddle around," but its efforts to cushion the effects of the depression resulted in the construction of thousands of miles of city streets and sewer lines, thousands of school buildings, as well as hundreds of hospitals and airports. The states were bypassed by most of these programs and tended to lose face in the process; however, most cities were highly satisfied with this newly acquired recognition which had previously been denied them.

War programs

Direct federal–city relationships were continued and expanded during World War II, particularly in the fields of emergency defense housing and airport construction. Even the local jails came into direct relationship with the federal government, growing out of the overcrowded conditions of federal prisons and their need to transfer some of their prisoners. Local jails were eligible for this "extra business" only if they complied with rather rigid federal standards for facilities and operation.

Recent Federal–City Relations

Urban problems as national problems

As the relationships between cities and the federal government became more complex in the years after World War II, it became clear that these could no longer be considered merely "emergency programs" with the obvious flavoring of depression or war. In an increasing number of federal aid programs there is an open avowal of federal responsibility to assist in meeting certain urban problems, such as mass transportation, urban renewal, and the preservation of open spaces. Congress has responded to the growing tendency of pressure groups and study groups interested in particular urban problems to speak of urban problems as *national* problems and to organize themselves on a *national* scale. Recent examples would include the *National* Committee on Urban Transportation, the *National* Committee on Uniform Traffic Control Devices, the *National* Outdoor Recreation Resources Review Commission, the *National* Commission on Urban Problems, and a *national* Municipal Manpower Commission, to name only a few. Even the President's Commission on *National* Goals included as part of the "goals at home" the necessity of reversing the "process

'Help!'

Figure 3–2. From *The Herblock Gallery* (Simon & Schuster, 1968).

of decay in the larger cities," and for improving living conditions both in central cities and suburbs.[6]

The urban path to Washington

City officials have long contended, and with considerable justification, that they have been forced to go to Washington as a last resort, after exhausting all efforts to secure help from the rural-dominated state government in attacking the new problems on the urban scene. The cities have become increasingly convinced that their plea for help, as portrayed in Figure 3–2, receives a more sympathetic ear in Washington than at their state capital and that their political leverage is weak at the state capital

[6] The italics in this paragraph have been inserted by the authors.

and strong in Washington. "Rural domination" through malapportioned state legislatures gave cities a made-to-order argument for bypassing the states and going directly to Congress with requests for financial assistance. It is not by chance that four of the more important national associations of local officials—the National League of Cities, the United States Conference of Mayors, the National Association of Counties, and the International Association of Chiefs of Police—have established their main offices in Washington, D. C. Nor is it surprising to hear Mayor Thomas Currigan of Denver state:

> We depend on Washington far more than on our own state government. . . . Matter of fact we even have better rapport with the federal people than the state people—and the state house is right across the street.[7]

Suzanne Farkas gives solid confirmation to the growing reliance of urban mayors on national government policies and funds for cities, and the emergence of an urban interest network at the national level.[8] She examined an extensive list of major issues on the lobbying agenda for "generalist urban lobby groups" between 1960 and 1970 and concluded that their major commitment is to housing and urban development issues.

At the beginning of 1966, the national government was administering between 75 and 100 separate programs involving financial assistance for urban development, depending on how narrowly urban development is defined. More than three-fourths of these programs were authorized during the preceding fifteen years. Many of them, as indicated in the previous chapter, were enacted during 1965, the peak year for "The Great Society" legislation in the Johnson administration. Some of the more recent areas of federal–city relationships are considered briefly in the discussion which follows.

Federal housing programs

Present federal activities in the field of housing reflect a historical background of wide diversity in origin and purpose. Beginning with the construction of some 16,000 units for shipyard workers during World War I, the federal government moved into additional housing programs in the depression of the thirties, during World War II, and in the post-war period. These programs were aimed at alleviating threats of widespread mortgage foreclosures on homes, providing more capital for private home construction by guaranteeing new mortgages, insuring small loans for home modernization and repair, providing low-rent public housing through hundreds of local housing authorities, and providing liberal housing credit for veterans under the so-called "G. I. Loan Program."

[7] Jules Loh, "Beleagured Cities Turn to Washington for Aid," an Associated Press article in the Nashville *Tennessean*, Jan. 16, 1966.

[8] Suzanne Farkas, *Urban Lobbying: Mayors in the Federal Arena*, pp. 35–68.

The changing housing philosophy

In recent years an increasing crescendo of criticism of federal housing programs has arisen, including charges that they are an "unrelated hodgepodge," have caused the rapid construction of "crackerbox suburbs," have shown little imagination in their design of low-rent public housing as barracks-like blockhouses, have been guilty of a bias against apartment houses, have not been adequately linked to other federal aid programs such as those for express highways, and have shown a concern "too little and too late" for relating housing programs and policies to overall urban planning. Some of this criticism and changing philosophy has come from the housing officials themselves, as illustrated in a 1957 speech by Housing Administrator Albert M. Cole with surprising relevance in the 1970s:

> Twenty years ago we thought in terms of individuals, of houses to shelter them, of special aids administered through special and separate governmental units. Then we recognized that this was too limited, too piecemeal. We began to think in terms of local areas and neighborhoods and we tried to bring some unity into government aids through a loose coordination in a single overall agency.
>
> In the Housing Act of 1954 we moved another long step forward. We dealt with the community as a whole and with housing in relation to other aspects of the community. In the urban renewal program, we established an approach that was based on overall planned action for the whole community and on closely integrated administration of government aids.
>
> But as we top one hill and look ahead, we find an even wider horizon ahead of us—another hill to climb if we are to continue to progress. In these few years I have discovered that even the community is not the final entity that we must consider—that it is part of a growing and expanding urban economy which moved with giant strides not only into the suburbs but into the interurban stretches that no longer define the country and the town. Today it is in these broader terms that we must think and plan—the community as part of the region, the neighborhood as part of the community, the individual home as part of the neighborhood. This is a far cry from the hope of twenty years ago that we could solve our city's problems of slums and bad housing simply by providing good homes for low-income families and tearing down the city's slums one by one, as we went along.[9]

The Housing Act of 1949 set forth a national goal of "a decent home and a suitable living environment for every American family," and provided assistance for slum clearance and urban redevelopment. The Housing Act of 1954 introduced the broader concept of "urban renewal"; it provided federal assistance to local communities not only for clearing and

[9] Address before the National Housing Conference, Washington, D. C., June 17, 1957, as quoted by Connery and Leach, *Federal Government and Metropolitan Areas,* pp. 11–12. By permission of Harvard University Press, Cambridge, Mass.

redeveloping slum areas, but also for preventing the spread of slums and urban blight through rehabilitation and conservation measures in deteriorating areas. The federal assistance included survey and planning advances, loans, and capital grants of up to two-thirds of the net project cost. Subsequent legislation liberalized the matching provisions by considering approved private renewal expenditures as part of the localities' matching obligation. Under urban redevelopment a slum area is acquired through the power of eminent domain, the slum structures are cleared, the area is planned for re-use, and the cleared area is sold to private (or public) developers who are committed to develop it in compliance with the community plan.

Slum clearance and urban renewal

Another step in the ever-broadening concept of slum clearance and urban renewal was the enactment in 1966 of a proposal by President Johnson for a "demonstration cities" program, involving far more than housing. In a special message to Congress he described it as "larger in scope, more comprehensive, more concentrated than any that has gone before," and called for the selection of sixty to seventy cities to demonstrate how the physical rehabilitation of slum areas can be combined with the social rehabilitation of the people living there. This emphasis and approach were aimed, at least in part, at meeting the charge that past programs relied predominantly on the "federal-bulldozer" approach. Shortly after passage of the legislation by Congress, the program was unofficially renamed the "model cities" program, presumably to avoid any invidious connotation of the term, "demonstration."

The "model cities" program

The Housing and Urban Development Act of 1968 launched a number of new financing programs pledging federal aid in building or rehabilitating 26 million housing units in the next decade. Private lending institutions became heavily involved, government subsidies filled the interest-rate gap, and housing "starts" reached record highs in the early 1970s. However, moderate-income families were primarily benefitted. The mysterious numerical jargon of different federal housing programs—sections 221(d)(3), 235, and 236, became the new passwords of the housing industry.[10]

Another program of federal assistance to cities which grew out of housing legislation was the program of assistance for urban planning. The Housing Act of 1954 and later amendments not only authorized grants to state planning agencies for planning assistance to cities of less than 25,000 population, but grants also have been authorized to state, metropolitan,

Urban planning assistance

[10] *See* the critical analysis of federal-housing programs by Committee for Economic Development in *Financing the Nation's Housing Needs* (New York, 1973). For a study of the planning process in the model cities program in New York City, with emphasis on the role of the planner and residents, *see* Edward M. Kaitz and Herbert Harvey Hyman, *Urban Planning for Social Welfare: A Model Cities Approach* (New York: Praeger, 1970).

or regional agencies for planning on a metropolitan basis. By 1960 close to 100 metropolitan areas, urban regions, and special areas had received federal approval for planning projects. By 1966 metropolitan planning agencies had been established in about three-fourths of the metropolitan areas in the country with the assistance of this "701" program. More than 400 projects for metropolitan regional planning, as well as 77 state-wide plans and more than 1,300 projects in small urban areas were funded on a two-thirds federal matching basis during its first eleven years of operation. Federal grants have thus encouraged community-wide planning that is not limited to the boundary lines of the patchwork quilt of local governments.

Open-space preservation and urban beautification

A program to assist state and local public bodies in open-space land preservation was created by Congress in the Housing Act of 1961. It originally provided for federal grants of up to 20 percent of the cost of acquiring land to be used as permanent open space, and up to 30 percent if it involved a substantial portion of a metropolitan area or urban region. Subsequent amendments raised the federal share to as much as 50 percent, and even to 90 percent for special projects demonstrating new and improved methods of achieving urban beautification and improvement. A logical extension of the concept was made by a 1965 amendment permitting federal grants for acquiring developed land, where open-space land is unavailable, and clearing it for use as open-space land. Approved uses of the open space are for parks and recreation, conservation of land or other natural resource, and for scenic or historic purposes. Its basic objectives are to help localities curb urban sprawl, blight, and deterioration, and to encourage a more desirable pattern of urban development than the asphalt landscape.

Recreation for the metropolis

Although the federal government has long been involved in recreation through its national parks, national forests, and reclamation projects, it has only recently begun to recognize that recreation is primarily an urban and metropolitan problem. The congestion of urban living, coupled with the steady increase in automation-produced leisure time, has meant that recreational pressure groups have become metropolitan pressure groups in large measure. In their search for recreation for the metropolis, such groups have shown no reluctance to petition Washington, rather than to limit their activity to state capitals.

Urban mass transportation

In 1961, the federal government took official notice in a specific way, for the first time, of the urban problem long considered to be the most frustrating and perhaps even the most hopeless—mass transportation. Congress responded to pleas of help for these floundering enterprises in American cities by authorizing two programs of modest assistance. One was a mass transportation demonstration program involving grants from the Housing and Home Finance Agency (now HUD) to public agencies for the demonstration of new urban transportation methods, techniques, and systems designed to carry out urban transportation plans and research. The

1961 act authorized up to two-thirds of the cost of such "pilot projects" to be paid by the federal government, but it was required that the project be applicable or relevant to the urban transportation needs of *other* areas. In the same act Congress authorized low-interest loans, when unobtainable from private sources, for the acquisition, construction, or reconstruction and improvement of mass transportation systems in urban areas. The program was expanded beyond the modest pilot-project scope by the Urban Mass Transportation Act of 1964. It authorized 375 million dollars to be spent over a three-year period on capital costs and expansion and improvement of mass transit systems, public or private, in metropolitan and urban areas. The assistance, on a federal two-thirds share basis, must be made through public bodies and its limitation to capital costs avoids federal involvement in operating problems. Commenting on the enormity of the urban mass transit problem, Michael N. Danielson points out that a three-year, 375 million dollar program—less than one-tenth the amount of federal highway expenditures—is only a "symbolic first step" in the direction of "modernizing dilapidated commuter lines, unclogging city highways, and developing balanced metropolitan transportation systems dedicated to moving people rather than motor vehicles."[11] Following 1965 legislation authorizing the Secretary of Commerce to undertake research and development on high-speed ground transportation, Congress passed the Urban Mass Transportation Assistance Act of 1970, aimed at preserving and upgrading urban public transportation at a cost of a billion dollars per year.

Urban highways

The federal aid program for urban streets and expressways involves important informal federal–city relations, but the states have insisted on keeping the formal relationships "very proper" in the constitutional sense, with the federal–state contacts being the primary ones. Cities have chafed under the arrangements, feeling that the result was the dominance of a *rural* roads program. The federal Bureau of Public Roads actually started as an agency of the rural-oriented Department of Agriculture where it remained until 1939; but a succession of moves and reorganizations since that time have given it greater urban orientation and a home in the Department of Transportation. In recent years urban political strength in Washington has been apparent in the increased share of federal highway aid earmarked for use in cities and in federal officials' encouragement of state highway officials to work more closely with cities. For example, state highway departments are required to hold public hearings on all proposed highway construction giving all affected cities an opportunity to state their views. Subsequent project requests from the state to the federal Bureau of Public Roads will be rejected unless accompanying transcripts of

[11] Michael N. Danielson, "Cities in Trouble," *National Civic Review* 54 (December 1965), p. 586.

public hearings indicate the affected cities have been consulted. Even the vast program for the Interstate Highway System is essentially an urban highway program. As originally proposed it was a highway network linking the great cities of the nation, but Congress gave it the "interstate" label in apparent deference to the sanctity of federal–state relations. Even so, as Connery and Leach suggest, "it might more correctly be called the Intercity Highway System, because people want to go in and out of cities, not in and out of states."[12] The roads carry not only long-distance traffic between 90 percent of the nation's cities, but carry a heavy load of urban and suburban commuter traffic.

Airports

In contrast to the pattern of highway assistance, federal–local relationships in airport construction have been direct, bypassing the states from the beginning. Prior to World War II a considerable amount of federal money was spent for constructing city airports, but it was a by-product of the depression public works programs rather than a result of a specific national airport program. Approximately 550 airports were constructed during World War II with emergency military considerations being dominant. The basic question of which level or levels of government should be responsible for airport planning, construction, and operation was finally determined in the Federal Airport Act of 1946, which essentially provided for a direct federal–local pattern. States can be bypassed by local governments applying for federal assistance unless specifically prohibited by state law. The federal government is responsible for preparing and revising annually a national airport plan, and any "public agency" may seek assistance for projects consistent with the federal plan.

Military installations and defense industries

One of the strongest influences which the federal government has on cities today comes not from a consciously designed urban program, but is a by-product of the federal government's most expensive activity—national defense. Citizens of Norfolk, San Diego, Corpus Christi, or Detroit do not need to be told how much military installations or defense industries can shape the physical, economic, and social development of an urban area. City chamber of commerce representatives vie with each other for each new prospective defense establishment, confident that it is synonymous with prosperity; but city planners, traffic officials, and budget directors know that there is another side to the picture. The need for large undeveloped tracts of land usually results in a location far beyond the boundaries of the city, leaving such vital matters as street design, traffic control, and land-use planning and control in the hands of ill-prepared township or county officials. By the time adequate controls have come into existence, the ribbon-like developments around the project have frequently become eyesores as well as serious problems of public health, education, law enforcement, and the like. This is a very complex and relatively

[12] Connery and Leach, *Federal Government and Metropolitan Areas*, p. 48.

unexplored problem of federal–local relations, particularly with respect to governmental obligations and opportunities for making cities livable communities.

Civil defense

The impact of civil defense policies and programs on the shape of cities is *potentially* greater even than that of military programs and installations. Any really serious effort to prepare the nation for atomic attack would involve an industrial dispersion program of such magnitude as to make contemporary suburban sprawl seem mild by comparison. It is clear that the problem of civil defense is first of all a problem of the metropolitan areas, both because of the greater vulnerability which their congestion brings, and because they contain a majority of our human and industrial resources. Yet civil defense programs thus far have been distinguished by their failure to make any appreciable impact on cities and, in the absence of greatly heightened Cold War tensions, there seems to be little prospect for such impact. A program of federal grants-in-aid to states on a 50–50 matching basis is designed to help states and local governments acquire civil defense equipment and train civil defense workers. Federal–local relationships are normally routed through the states, but can be direct under certain circumstances.

Water resources

Although the federal government has long been involved in the development and use of water resources—Congress authorized the first river improvements in 1924—it has been only recently that cities as such have fought their way into the policymaking process for water. The federal government's relation to water resources has become unbelievably complex, involving the very old programs of improving navigation in rivers and harbors, the later programs of flood control, irrigation, and power development, and the more recent activities of water pollution control, and the growing problem of water for human and industrial consumption. Irrigation policies have come increasingly under fire from cities seeking to satisfy their swelling population's seemingly unquenchable thirst. Water used for irrigation is lost for downstream urban use, and the federal government must ultimately decide whose priorities are higher. Urban involvement in stream pollution, sometimes as the offender and sometimes as the plaintiff, has also increased in recent years, especially in the wake of the surge of interest in ecology. Federal regulations and grant-in-aid programs relating to water quality and clean air are discussed in chapter 21; the city is heavily involved in both.

Emerging Problems in Federal–City Relations

The foregoing summary of federal programs affecting cities in fairly direct ways has not described in any detail the content of such programs; more detailed treatment of the specific program content may be found in later chapters. The purpose of such a brief panorama has been to focus attention on what seem to be steady and perhaps even inevitable trends toward closer federal–city ties. Out of these trends and new relationships several basic problems or questions emerge, however.

Fragmented metropolitan areas and the federal government

Most federal aid programs, whether for urban expressways, urban renewal, or civil defense, are strongly influenced at the performance level by the fragmentation of "natural metropolitan communities" into small bits and pieces of governmental units. As mentioned in chapter 1, metropolitanism in the United States, which has 264 metropolitan areas, has been inevitably accompanied by a proliferation of local governments. Varying from more than a thousand governments for New York and Chicago to smaller metropolitan areas having less than ten governments, the average is about 90 local governments per metropolitan area. In addition to 2 or 3 counties, 15 or 20 cities, and several towns or townships, the typical metropolitan area is also governed by about 50 assorted special-purpose districts or authorities for water, sewage disposal, fire protection, schools, and the like. With a few rare exceptions, federal agencies have felt compelled to deal with these separate governmental fragments rather than with the metropolitan area as a single entity, for the simple reason that virtually no metropolitan area is a single political entity. An increasing number of federal programs require all approved projects to comply with a "regional plan." But this is difficult to enforce meaningfully when so many metropolitan areas have no comprehensive regional planning or have only recently begun such planning.[13] With some exceptions, Congress has not seen fit to use the federal spending power to coerce fragmented local governments into some degree of metropolitan coordination; but by its silence, Congress has undoubtedly strengthened the independent status of the small cities and special districts which make metropolitan and regional planning and development so difficult. The result is frequently a case of federal failure to see the metropolitan forest because of focusing attention on the separate city trees.

City trees and metropolitan forests

Effects of special districts

Several of the reports of the Advisory Commission on Intergovernmental Relations have been critical of this situation, not only of the state and local governments' failure to bring order out of metropolitan chaos, but also of the national government's tendency to encourage the creation of new special districts. These units, discussed in detail in chapter 18, are attractive to federal agencies because they can be given legal autonomy from many of the state and local problems of staffing, salaries, geographic jurisdiction, borrowing authority, and "political interference." However,

[13] On this point, *see* Norman Beckman, "How Metropolitan Are Federal and State Policies?" *Public Administration Review* 26 (June 1966), pp. 96–106. He takes an optimistic view of the prospects for both federal and state officials to take an area-wide view of the metropolis.

each new special-purpose district tends to have the effect of weakening general-purpose governments and complicating the task of coordinating metropolitan area planning, decision making, and operations. The ACIR has urged a reversal of this trend by recommending:

> . . . that the Congress and appropriate Executive agencies take legislative and administrative action to remove from Federal aid programs for urban development all organizational limitations which require or promote special purpose units of local government to the disadvantage of general purpose units of local government (i.e., municipalities, towns, and counties.) Other factors being equal, general purpose units of government should be favored as Federal Aid recipients. Special purpose recipients should be required to coordinate their aided activities with general purpose governments.[14]

Uncoordinated federal programs

Strangely enough, a situation somewhat analogous to metropolitan fragmentation can be found at the federal level. The federal fragmentation is functional rather than geographic, however. There has never been a federal *urban* program presented in a package to Congress in the same way that a *farm* program is packaged for legislative purposes. Connery and Leach point out that urban programs "are created as isolated units and are administered in isolation from one another," and contend that the result is "a jungle of disconnected programs and projects, strewn among a variety of administrative agencies."[15] Their appraisal would doubtless be even more harsh if it had been made after the establishment of the antipoverty program, with its bewildering array of new and revised federal projects involving the cities.

The federal highway program is probably most often cited as an example of isolation from other programs. Urban highways are only one part of the urban transportation problem which includes traffic and parking problems, and bus, railroad, and air facilities and policies. To take it a step or two further, the whole transportation problem is only one part of the problem of land-use planning which, in turn, is only one part of overall metropolitan planning. Such coordination of the interstate highway program with public housing and urban renewal programs as has actually occurred has tended to be too limited and too late, and it has taken place in spite of the organizational isolation of the federal programs.

[14] Advisory Commission on Intergovernmental Relations, *Impact of Federal Urban Development Programs on Local Government Organization and Planning,* prepared in cooperation with the U. S. Senate Committee on Government Operations, 88th Congress, 2nd Sess. (Washington, D. C.: U. S. Government Printing Office, 1964), p. 23. *See also* ACIR reports on *The Problem of Special Districts in American Government* (1964), *Intergovernmental Responsibilities for Water Supply and Sewage Disposal in Metropolitan Areas* (1962), and *Performance of Urban Functions: Local and Areawide* (1963).

[15] Connery and Leach, *Federal Government and Metropolitan Areas,* p. 98.

Similarly, the airport planning responsibility of the federal government has not been geared to an integrated view of the various urban problems related to federal programs. Even with respect to the single function of aviation, conflicts are not uncommon between the civilian and military programs in their impact on cities. Some years ago the city of San Diego had the unusual experience of having one agency of the federal government declare its airport obsolete; the agency approved the city's proposed new site, only to have another federal agency object to the location on grounds of interference with the nearby naval air station. As the federal government moves into more and more areas—recreation, open-space preservation, water supply, water pollution control, mass transportation, and other areas closely related to the life of cities—this problem of coordination at the federal level is becoming increasingly important.

The information gap: vertical and horizontal

Some observers are beginning to warn of a serious "information gap" concerning the new tidal wave of grant-in-aid programs enacted in the mid-1960s. The gap has both vertical and horizontal dimensions. Not only do local officials increasingly need an elaborate "score card to identify the federal players," for example, the five separate federal aid programs available for sewage facilities, but officials in a specific program give only a low priority to knowledge of, and coordination with, related federal programs. The 1965 study of *The Federal System As Seen by Federal Aid Officials* concluded that the

> . . . great majority of these middle-management administrators are unsympathetic to efforts at the national or urban field levels which are geared to interrelating federal urban development programs and to injecting a broad-gauged metropolitan viewpoint into the administration of such programs. And most of this distrust is rooted in fear—fear of change, fear of delay, fear of a dilution of individual program goals, fear of meddling by inexpert generalists, fear of dual or triple supervisory procedures, and fear of a diminution of bureau or agency autonomy.[16]

In terms of its committee structure and processes, even the Congress is badly fragmented when it comes to a comprehensive approach to urban problems. Professor Fred Cleaveland cited this segmental character of urban interests in Congress and suggested that the creation of the executive Department of Housing and Urban Development in 1965 might stimulate some corresponding institutional change in the legislative branch, such as a joint committee on urban affairs, as proposed by the National League of Cities.[17]

[16] U. S. Senate Committee on Government Operations, *The Federal System*, p. 92.

[17] Frederic N. Cleaveland, "Congress and Urban Problems: Legislating for Urban Areas," *Journal of Politics* 28 (May 1966), pp. 289–307.

To understand some of the dilemmas faced by the cabinet-level Department of Housing and Urban Development in its task of coordinating federal–urban programs, it is helpful first to review its origins. For many years a variety of proposals were advanced for a new agency at the federal level devoted entirely to urban affairs. They varied from a simple interagency committee, generally recognized as a rather feeble administrative device, to a proposal for a cabinet-level Department of Urban Affairs. The latter proposal was not a new idea by any means. A Department of Municipalities was suggested as early as 1912. In more recent years it was not uncommon to have speeches in Congress on behalf of a Department of "Urbiculture" to counterbalance the rural-minded Department of Agriculture. The arguments for such a department centered around the growing need for an effective spokesman for urban interests in national policymaking at the cabinet level. It was pointed out that 80 percent of our population lived on farms or in rural areas in 1862 when the Office of Agriculture was established, but with urban population pushing toward that same percentage today, special recognition of the urban dweller's needs was now called for. It was argued that existing urban programs at the federal level, without the addition of any new ones, were already of sufficient size to warrant departmental status and that the correction of the "step-child status" of several of the urban programs was long overdue. Persuasive administrative arguments were given in favor of such a Department of Urban Affairs. These arguments centered upon the failure of fragmented federal agencies with isolated urban programs to treat "the whole city" in coordinated fashion, rather than in unrelated segments, as often happened. Another administrative argument pertained to the convenience of establishing a central contact point in Washington for all federal relationships with cities, rather than requiring city officials to go back and forth among several agencies in handling their business with Uncle Sam. Finally, it was contended that creating a single cabinet-level department would be the quickest and most effective way to accelerate much-needed research on a variety of urban problems, providing a unified information center for and about cities.

Origins of HUD

Arguments pro

The idea of such a department was not without its critics, however, and not all of them were persons unfriendly to urban interests. The principal arguments against an urban affairs department were given by Connery and Leach, in a three-pronged summary: "politically unwise, administratively unsound, and functionally unnecessary."[18] Politically, it would be difficult to avoid the "big-city" brand on the department with the word "urban" tending to alienate not only certain rural interests but also some suburban interests, which are often as opposed to the big city as

Arguments con

[18] Connery and Leach, *Federal Government and Metropolitan Areas*, p. 182.

their rural neighbors. Administratively, the feasibility of extracting the "'urban aspects" of all or parts of the federal programs and placing them in a single department was seriously questioned. It would be the only department based on a geographical concept, causing some to term it an "organizational misfit" likely to create more problems than it would solve.

The Department was finally created by the Housing and Urban Development Act of 1965, and President Johnson appointed HHFA Director Robert Weaver as its secretary and the first black cabinet member. Professor Robert Wood, a political scientist from MIT and specialist in metropolitan problems, was appointed undersecretary. The Department was directed in its enabling legislation to "assist the President in achieving maximum coordination of Federal urban programs," and the secretary was instructed to exercise leadership at the direction of the President in coordinating such programs. Presumably the President is the chief urban coordinator and the HUD secretary is to be his principal means of achieving this unity of action. Yet, of the 100 or more federal programs affecting the cities, only a comparatively small segment was placed within HUD; FHA and FNMA, public housing, urban renewal, college dormitory construction, mass transportation, basic water and sewer facilities, and metropolitan planning were the major ones. Left outside HUD were many programs equally important to urban development: education, health, welfare, anti-poverty, air and water pollution, manpower and employment, highways, economic development, and many others. Senator Edmund Muskie summarized his doubts about the prospects for coordination in a speech to the Senate:

Urban programs in and out of HUD

> HUD, in essence, is another department among formidable equals such as HEW, Agriculture, Commerce, and Labor. Its powers of coordination—yet untested—are only as effective as the degree to which these other Federal agencies will give up some of their autonomy and cooperate. If the past record of voluntary cooperation among Federal agencies is any indicator, HUD will have tough going unless a strong and positive mandate of program coordination is assured for this new department, and effective machinery for carrying out that mandate is put into operation.
>
> At this time I am not sure whether the mandate or the machinery for effective coordination is sufficiently strong to pierce the veil of traditional Federal functionalism, and to spur interagency cooperation.[19]

Continuing problem of coordination

During its first year of operation, HUD's infant bureaucracy had to jockey for jurisdictional position with the departments of HEW, Interior, and Commerce concerning such programs as pollution control, urban park land, and high-speed railways. Both HUD and the Department of Commerce felt the administrative tremors of the soon-to-be established twelfth

[19] *Congressional Record*, vol. 112, no. 52, March 25, 1966.

cabinet department—transportation. President Nixon's proposal to meet this continuing problem of coordination, in 1971 and again in 1973, was a cabinet-level Department of Community Development.

Are cities outgrowing states?

The question of whether the cities are outgrowing the states is hardly a *recently* emerging problem, for it has been asked by many students of government for many years. In the 1920s Professor Charles E. Merriam repeatedly affirmed his belief that "the nation and the cities are vigorous organs," but that states are stumbling blocks which neither govern the cities nor permit the cities to govern themselves.[20] Merriam's contention that the states are going downhill has hardly been borne out in recent history (as discussed in chapter 1), but the question continues to crop up in various contexts. The burgeoning growth of metropolitan areas across state boundary lines makes one wonder whether interstate cities, like interstate commerce, must inevitably come under federal regulation. The 1970 census revealed that more than one out of five citizens live in the thirty-two interstate metropolitan areas, comprising more than forty-six million persons. (*See* Table 3–1.) Millions more live in metropolitan areas that border but do not yet cross state lines. This makes it conceivable that the time may come within the next generation or so when more people live in interstate cities than in intrastate cities.

The interstate metropolis

State departments of community affairs

In spite of the pressures of interstate urbanism, many states have established state-level departments of community affairs (DCAs) in an effort to respond positively to the urban crisis. In setting up one of the largest and strongest DCAs, New Jersey seemed to be attempting to prove that its cities had not outgrown the state. The department provides guidance, training, and information to local communities in the field of housing; and it possesses strong regulatory powers. The New Jersey DCA exercises controls over relocation, low-income housing development, and new communities for retirees; and it provides financial assistance for relocation and urban renewal and for various other housing-related programs. One study of the DCAs, however, concludes that their overall record is unimpressive:

> . . . most DCAs remain toothless tigers with minor amounts of financial aid to bestow or regulatory power to apply. Few have grown significantly from their origins as antipoverty technical-assistance units ambivalently spawned by OEO in 1965. The legislatures that did not create cabinet-level DCAs in the heat of the urban riot era seem disinclined to do so now. Furthermore, most of the leadership that launched the DCA movement in the middle 1960s has left the state scene.[21]

[20] *See* W. Brooke Graves, *American State Government,* 3d ed. (Boston: D. C. Heath and Co., 1946), p. 943.

[21] Lawrence O. Houstoun, Jr., "Are the States Relevant?" *City* 6 (Summer 1972), p. 44.

Table 3–1. Interstate Metropolitan Areas, 1970

Metropolitan Area	*States with Part of Territory*	*Number of County Areas*	*1970 Population*
New York–Northeastern New Jersey	N.Y.–N.J.	13	16,178,700
Chicago–Northwestern Indiana	Ill.–Ind.	8	7,612,314
Philadelphia	Pa.–N.J.	8	4,817,914
Washington	D.C.–Md.–Va.	7	2,861,123
St. Louis	Mo.–Ill.	7	2,363,017
Cincinnati	Ohio–Ky.–Ind.	7	1,384,851
Kansas City	Mo.–Kans.	6	1,253,916
Portland	Ore.–Wash.	4	1,009,129
Providence–Pawtucket	R.I.–Mass.	8	918,781
Louisville	Ky.–Ind.	3	826,553
Memphis	Tenn.–Ark.	2	770,120
Toledo	Ohio–Mich.	3	692,571
Allentown–Bethlehem–Easton	Pa.–N.J.	3	543,551
Omaha	Neb.–Iowa	3	540,142
Springfield–Chicopee–Holyoke	Mass.–Conn.	4	529,922
Wilmington	Del.–N.J.–Md.	3	499,493
Davenport–Rock Island–Moline	Iowa–Ill.	3	362,638
Chattanooga	Tenn.–Ga.	2	304,927
Binghamton	N.Y.–Pa.	3	302,672
Duluth–Superior	Minn.–Wisc.	2	265,350
Huntington–Ashland	W.Va.–Ky.–Ohio	4	253,743
Augusta	Ga.–S.C.	2	253,460
Columbus	Ga.–Ala.	3	238,584
Evansville	Ind.–Ky.	3	232,775
Lawrence–Haverhill	Mass.–N.H.	2	232,415
Parkersburg–Marietta	W.Va.–Ohio	3	199,000
Wheeling	W.Va.–Ohio	3	182,712
Steubenville–Weirton	Ohio–W.Va.	3	165,627
Fort Smith	Ark.–Okla.	4	160,421
Fall River	Mass.–R.I.	2	149,976
Fargo–Moorhead	N.D.–Minn.	2	120,238
Sioux City	Iowa–Neb.	2	116,189
Texarkana	Tex.–Ark.	2	101,198
			46,245,022

Source: Adapted from U. S. Bureau of the Census, *1970 Census of Population*, Vol. I, "Characteristics of the Population," Part A, Section 1, pp. 171–190, with later additions.

Lion In The Streets

Figure 3–3. From *The Herblock Gallery* (Simon & Schuster, 1968).

Determining federal and state responsibility

Whose responsibility is it, ultimately, to govern the giant cities in such a way as to solve or alleviate the frustrations of blight, congestion, slum housing, open-space disappearance, and unplanned sprawl? Is the answer to be sought in increased federal–city relationships? Some observers, including Connery and Leach, conclude that "federal involvement in metropolitan areas is no longer a matter of conjecture," and that the federal government *inevitably* will move in the direction of further commitment.[22] Urban interest groups argue for greater federal leadership and assistance by pointing out that while slum dwellers now outnumber farm dwellers, the federal government spends far more in assistance for each farm family than for each slum family. The cartoon in Figure 3–3 is

[22] Connery and Leach, *Federal Government and Metropolitan Areas,* p. 8.

illustrative of the pressure that arises for increased national spending when slum conditions continue to exist.

The increasing difficulty of developing a "comprehensive national urban policy" that makes any significant distinction between "urban policy" and "national policy" has been well stated by Suzanne Farkas:

> The difficulties of the urban lobbyist are increased by the necessity to project the justifying and unifying idea of urban lobbying—representation of the *total* urban interest. Since almost 70 percent of the population live in urban areas, the urban interest would appear to encompass most of the interests of American society. What, then, distinguishes "urban" from "national?" If urban interests could be spelled out simply as "the interests of the vast majority of urbanites," this would not solve the problem. Most things will impinge on urban dwellers, if only negatively; even the ostensible exclusively rural interest in farm subsidy is deceptive. Since subsidies on farm products affect the prices that the urbanite has to pay for food, the urban slum dweller cannot leave farm-subsidy policy solely to a Congressional Committee on Agriculture.[23]

A warning to states

Still others, such as the Kestnbaum Commission, do not consider increased federal involvement inevitable; their message is principally one of warning to the states:

> If States do not give cities their rightful allocation of seats in the legislature, the tendency will be toward direct Federal-municipal dealings. These began in earnest in the early days of the depression. There is only one way to avoid this in the future. It is for the States to take an interest in urban problems, in metropolitan government, in city needs. If they do not do this, the cities will find a path to Washington as they did before, and this time it may be permanent. . . .[24]

In his discussion of the growing role of cities in "the expanded partnership" of federalism, Roscoe Martin devotes one chapter to "The Case of the Reluctant State," and is highly critical of the states' capacity "to react positively and effectively to the demands of a new age." He concludes:

> . . . that state constitutions are outmoded and inflexible; that the legislatures, identified as the keystone of the democratic arch, are not representative; that

[23] Suzanne Farkas, *Urban Lobbying: Mayors in the Federal Arena.* Copyright © 1971 by New York University. Reprinted by permission of New York University Press.

[24] U. S. Commission on Intergovernmental Relations, *A Report to the President for Transmittal to the Congress* (Washington, D. C.: U. S. Government Printing Office, 1955), pp. 39–40.

> resources, partly from deliberate choice, are inadequate; that the atmosphere is not congenial to the embrace of new programs; and that the state horizons are severely limited by prevailing mythology. . . .
>
> [The] vast new problems of urban America are unique in the experience of the states, which react to them in an impatient and sometimes a truculent manner. Nothing would please the states more than for the cities and their problems to dematerialize into thin air. . . .
>
> Many observers believe that the states will prove equal to the challenges of the metropolitan age. The wish doubtless is father to the thought, and the thought perhaps to the hope; but one who allows hope to sire expectation ignores a considerable body of evidence.[25]

Opposition to federal intervention

The most vigorous opponents of federal action in urban affairs have been taxpayers' groups fearful of the impact of such programs on their tax bill. Their arguments rely heavily on states' rights and on such suggestive questions as that expressed in this title from an article in a business news magazine,[26] "Should Uncle Sam Be Your Mayor?" Governor Smylie of Idaho, in dissenting from a recommendation of the Advisory Commission on Intergovernmental Relations for federal financial assistance to metropolitan area planning agencies, stated:

> I can see little justification in the assumption of a permanent financial responsibility by the National Government for a function which in a great many of our metropolitan areas is and will continue to be an intrastate affair. Our Federal system of Government under the Constitution is already characterized by a large number of grants-in-aid which began as stimulative devices but evolved quickly to the status of permanent subsidies.[27]

A multi-factoral answer

Ultimately, the determination of responsibility for containing and regulating the "urban revolution" is a *political* question whose answer will come only in part through rational arguments concerning the constitutional rights of states to be rulers of their urban households. The coercive effects of geographic, economic, and technological developments will also help to shape the answer. Probably more than any other single factor, the U. S. Supreme Court's 1962 decision in the Tennessee reapportionment case, and the quick chain reaction of the companion suits by cities in many other states, holds the key to the future in federal–state–local relationships.

[25] Martin, *Cities and the Federal System*, pp. 79–81. A more favorable view of the urban effort of the states is given in Michael C. LeMay, "The States and Urban Areas: A Comparative Assessment," *National Civic Review* 61 (December 1972), p. 542.

[26] *Nation's Business* 49 (January 1961), p. 14.

[27] U. S. Advisory Commission on Intergovernmental Relations, *Governmental Structure, Organization, and Planning in Metropolitan Areas* (Washington, D. C.: U. S. Government Printing Office, 1961), p. 44.

In reversing its long-standing policy of refusing to become involved in reapportionment disputes, the Supreme Court ruled on *Baker* v. *Carr*, but gave very few answers in the decision,[28] except to say that federal courts can entertain such cases. The months immediately following this ruling saw a veritable flood of cases brought to state and federal courts in a massive attack on the rural domination of state legislatures. In 1964 the most important of these questions was answered in the case of *Reynolds* v. *Sims*[29] when the Court declared that *both* houses of the state legislature must be apportioned on the basis of population. The actual legislative impact of the reapportionment cases is discussed in chapter 10.

The impact of the reapportionment cases

Two seemingly contradictory conclusions may be drawn concerning the broad policy significance of the reapportionment cases, one relatively disturbing to "states' righters," and the other more comforting to them. As a symbol of Supreme Court interference in the "private affairs" of the states, these conclusions will undoubtedly be placed alongside several others which are currently anathema to states' rights advocates. Yet it is entirely possible that this particular "interference" by the Supreme Court may have released the log jam which long blocked states from responding to urban pressures for assistance. It is possible that the urban path to Washington is already too well travelled for any significant turning back. If the states put their houses in order by accepting urban problems as state problems, one of the strong arguments for direct federal–city relationships will be blunted.[30]

[28] 369 U. S. 186 (1962).

[29] 377 U. S. 533 (1964).

[30] For a more detailed discussion of the metropolitan challenge to states, *see* Lee S. Greene, Malcolm E. Jewell, and Daniel R. Grant, *The States and the Metropolis* (University, Ala.: University of Alabama Press, 1968).

SUPPLEMENTARY READINGS

Advisory Commission on Intergovernmental Relations. *Governmental Structure, Organization, and Planning in Metropolitan Areas.* Washington, D. C.: U. S. Government Printing Office, 1961.

———. *Impact of Federal Urban Development Programs on Local Government Organization and Planning.* Washington, D. C.: U. S. Government Printing Office, 1964.

Baker, Gordon E. *The Reapportionment Revolution: Representation, Political Power, and the Supreme Court.* New York: Random House, 1965.

Betters, Paul V. *Recent Federal–City Relations.* Washington, D. C.: United States Conference of Mayors, 1936.

Cleaveland, Frederic N., et al. *Congress and Urban Problems: A Casebook on the Legislative Process.* Washington, D. C.: The Brookings Institution, 1969.

Commission on Intergovernmental Relations. *The Impact of Federal Grants-in-Aid on*

Structure and Functions of State and Local Governments. Washington, D. C.: U. S. Government Printing Office, 1955.

Connery, Robert H., and Leach, Richard H. *The Federal Government and Metropolitan Areas*. Cambridge, Mass.: Harvard University Press, 1960.

Danielson, Michael N. *Federal–Metropolitan Politics and the Commuter Crisis*. New York: Columbia University Press, 1965.

Farkas, Suzanne. *Urban Lobbying: Mayors in the Federal Arena*. New York: New York University Press, 1971.

Grant, Daniel R. "Federal–Municipal Relationships and Metropolitan Integration." *Public Administration Review* 14, Autumn 1954, pp. 259–268.

Harris, Fred R., and Lindsay, John V., eds. *The State of the Cities: Report of the Commission on the Cities in the "70's."* New York: Praeger, 1972.

Long, Norton E. *The Unwalled City*. New York: Basic Books, 1972.

Martin, Roscoe C. *The Cities and the Federal System*. New York: Atherton Press, 1965.

Moynihan, Daniel P., ed. *Toward a National Urban Policy*. New York: Basic Books, 1970.

National Resources Committee. *Our Cities: Their Role in the National Economy*. Washington, D. C.: U. S. Government Printing Office, 1937.

Reynolds, Harry W., Jr., ed. "Intergovernmental Relations in the United States." *The Annals of the American Academy of Political and Social Science* 359, May 1965.

U. S. Advisory Commission on Intergovernmental Relations. *State Action on Local Problems*, 1972. Washington, D.C.: U. S. Government Printing Office, 1973.

Vernon, Raymond. *Metropolis: 1985*. Cambridge, Mass.: Harvard University Press, 1960.

Willbern, York. *The Withering Away of the City*. Tuscaloosa: University of Alabama Press, 1964.

See also readings listed for chapters 2 and 18.

4

Liberty Under Law: The Police Power

Two threads

The web of government developed by our states and localities has two significant threads of thought and practice, intertwined in an ever-lengthening development. One perpetuates the idea of liberty for the individual with respect to his person, opinion, and property. It embraces substantive and procedural guarantees traceable to origins in the Magna Carta, British common law and statutes of rights, doctrines of natural rights, and American prenational experience. The other thread, also a heritage from earlier times, is the concern for community interests and the recognition of citizens' responsibility for serving or respecting essential public interests. The twin threads of the individual's right and the public's power are roughly defined by the phrase "Liberty under Law." The public power is manifest in various forms, fundamental among them the power to tax, the power of eminent domain—that is, the power to take private property for public use—and the police power. It is the reconciliation of liberty with authority in the form of the police power that is the concern of this chapter.

The American states historically have led the nation in emphasizing bills of rights and in the broad exercise of police power. They have followed, with degrees of imperfection, the teaching that there must be liberty but not the liberty to injure others. When states have been thought to be remiss in providing such protections, the national government, through constitutional change or judicial interpretation, has buttressed or modified state protections and powers against discriminatory practices. It has not reduced the length or strength of the great threads in the web of state government. The purpose or ultimate effect of the Civil War amendments, for example, was to place all persons, regardless of color, on the same basis with respect to rights and powers. In one application of those amendments the "white primary" was held unconstitutional as a denial on racial grounds of the rights to participate in the choice of elected officials.[1]

Scope of police power

Police power should not be thought of as simply the authority of a uniformed officer with a badge on his breast and a pistol on his belt, although it is basic to that authority. It is the general power, whether expressed, implied, or inherent, to establish and apply laws or regulations for the maintenance or advancement of public safety, health, welfare, and morals. Miscellaneous and unrelated examples of its use are provisions for milk inspection, prevention of fire hazards in city or forest, smoke control or abatement, fixing maximum interest rates, compulsory vaccination, compulsory school attendance, limits on child labor, enforcement of standards of weights and measures, zoning to exclude shops and factories from residential areas, prohibiting or regulating the sale of liquor, and banning the sale or display of obscene pictures and publications. The old "blue laws" providing rules for Sabbath observance and the modern speed laws providing rules of the road are also manifestations of police power. So is the Tennessee statute designed to prevent the public use of rattlesnakes in worship. Police power is just about as broad in meaning as government itself. It is not a specific derivative from a constitutional clause or provision. It is inherent in the very concept of government. Its limits are to be found primarily through the interpretation of other constitutional or governmental features to which it must be adjusted.

The application of police power varies according to change in the needs and circumstances of different regions and different eras. There may be differences in water regulations between desert areas and areas of heavy flood. Compulsory insurance of workers against occupational accident was brought on by the industrial revolution, and many types of health regulation had to await the scientific findings of Pasteur and others. The atomic future may expand the use of this power in ways not now foreseen.

State police power in the federal system

In the American federal system the police power belongs to the states with the exception of such power as may be delegated by the Constitution, expressly or by implication, to the national government or forbidden to the states. Thus it is necessary to look at police power in terms of federalism. The police role of the national government within the states is distinctly limited, but nevertheless effective and significant in modern times, as will be subsequently explained. It may duplicate, reinforce, or complement the role of the states, as in prohibiting the shipment of liquor into a state for delivery and consumption contrary to state law. But the average American has more day-to-day contact with the state police power,

[1] *Smith* v. *Allwright,* 321 U. S. 649 (1944), overruling *Grovey* v. *Townsend,* 295 U. S. 45 (1935).

and has more opportunities to obey or violate state or local laws and ordinances than to make contact with national powers.

State Police Power and the Federal Judiciary

The use of police power by one state or another has been challenged from time to time as unconstitutional in cases reaching the Supreme Court. The states can point to both victories and defeats for police power in these cases. From the record of such victories and defeats the scope of the state police power in the American constitutional system gradually unfolds.

Challenges under the "obligation of contract" clause

An important basis for challenge has been the provision in Section 10 of Article I of the Constitution that no state shall "pass any . . . law impairing the obligation of contracts." This prohibition was invoked in the famous Dartmouth College case, decided in 1819 by the United States Supreme Court in an opinion written by Chief Justice John Marshall.[2] The legislature of New Hampshire had modified the Dartmouth charter, presumably making valid use of its police power by partly shifting the institution from private to public control without the trustees' consent. Daniel Webster, a Dartmouth graduate, argued the case for his alma mater. The Marshall opinion, conforming to the Webster argument, pronounced the corporate charter a contract and held the statute of modification unconstitutional as an impairment of the contract. The state was not privileged to use its police power so as to impair the obligation of a contract.

Webster and legal colleagues, however, were rendered a different opinion in arguing the same constitutional point in the Charles River Bridge case[3] when Roger B. Taney was Chief Justice. The Massachusetts legislature, after chartering the Charles River Bridge corporation to build a bridge and operate it for tolls, chartered another company to build and operate a bridge nearby in effective competition with the earlier company. The Charles River Bridge group claimed that this unexpected competition was an impairment of business and of contract. Taney, writing the majority opinion, rejected the claim that monopolistic privileges were implied in the original charter, insisting that any doubt or ambiguity should be resolved in favor of the public or the community. He concluded that "While the rights of private property are sacredly guarded, we must not forget that the community also has rights, and that the happiness and well-being of every citizen depends on their faithful preservation." This Taney doctrine emphasized the power and the responsibility of the state both as grantor of privileges to vested interests and as continuous guardian of the public in-

2 *Dartmouth College* v. *Woodward,* 4 Wheaton 518 (1819).
3 *Charles River Bridge* v. *Warren Bridge,* 11 Peters 420 (1837).

terest involved in the grants. It foreshadowed the coming of a wider usage of police power by state and municipal governments, particularly in connection with utility franchises.

Almost a century after the Charles River Bridge decision, Chief Justice Charles Evans Hughes further strengthened the police power in an opinion upholding a Minnesota mortgage moratorium law.[4] This law had been passed for the relief of debtors during the Great Depression of the 1930s. The act, providing for the postponement of foreclosures, was challenged by creditors as impairing the obligation of contract. To the layman it would seem that this was a case in which the Supreme Court had no choice but to declare that Minnesota had used its police power improperly to change the terms of legally binding contracts, in violation of the federal Constitution. But the Court ruled to the contrary. This decision was not made by a "New Deal Court," occurring, as it did, three years before Franklin D. Roosevelt named a justice to the bench. The literal restraint of the Constitution is not to stand in the way of the state's use of police power within the scope of "reasonable means" for economic survival in a crisis. The police power of the state may not be contracted out of existence.

Factor of interstate commerce

The police power of the state is restricted in important ways by the power of Congress to "regulate commerce with foreign nations, and among the several States, and with the Indian tribes." The overlap of the state police power and the federal commerce power has provided material for discourse and decision by the Supreme Court in numerous cases since Marshall made their relationship important in *Gibbons* v. *Ogden* in 1824.[5] The broad opinion in this case interpreted "commerce" as including "navigation" and invalidated a New York state law which granted a monopolistic shipping license in New York waters to a group of steamboat operators, and which consequently penalized a rival operating between New York and New Jersey under a license from the national government. The state could not use its police power so as to interfere directly with navigation in interstate commerce as provided for by legislation of Congress.

In a case decided in 1852, the Supreme Court held that Pennsylvania might regulate pilotage in interstate commerce, since Congress had not regulated it, and the state regulation had only local and indirect effect on interstate commerce.[6] This by no means reversed the Marshall ruling of 1824. The doctrine that the states could not place an unreasonable or direct burden on interstate commerce and could not interfere with the valid use of the commerce power by Congress remained. The Supreme Court in

[4] *Home Building and Loan Association* v. *Blaisdell*, 290 U. S. 398 (1934).
[5] 9 Wheaton 1 (1824).
[6] *Cooley* v. *Board of Wardens of Port of Philadelphia*, 12 Howard 299 (1852).

1886 put the stamp of unconstitutionality upon statutory provisions of Illinois prohibiting certain specified rate practices by railroads moving interstate freight originating in that state.[7] Absence at the time of congressional legislation on the subject was held to be no justification for state action, since the shipping process involved was clearly national in scope and affected persons far beyond the bounds of Illinois. After Congress created the Interstate Commerce Commission and endowed it with authority over rate making, the Supreme Court sustained that agency's steps to bring Texas' intrastate rates into relation with interstate rates. The national action was designed to prevent freight-rate injury to Shreveport, Louisiana, near the eastern border of Texas, and overrode and curtailed the authority of the Texas railroad commission.[8]

A still different use of the national commerce power to check the police power of the state is illustrated by the 1946 decision of the Supreme Court invalidating a Virginia requirement for racial separation of bus passengers insofar as applicable to persons travelling in interstate commerce.[9] The opinion classed segregation by state action as an undue burden on national commerce. The national government's power under the commerce clause does not prevent state regulation under the police power, however. In the absence of conflicting federal legislation, Florida, for example, may enact a quarantine against the entry of citrus fruit into the state to protect her citrus orchards from the Mediterranean fruit fly. Similarly, interstate trucks may be required by a state to comply with a variety of specifications as to weight, height, width, and lighting, in the interest of highway safety. But the Court has ruled that Arizona cannot limit the length of interstate trains, and that California cannot keep indigent persons from moving into the state. Many other examples might be cited of the border problems arising between the national commerce power and state police power. That border is not definitely fixed in law or fact. It requires continuous reinterpretation and readjustment in the light of changing conditions.

Fourteenth Amendment

The Fourteenth Amendment, since its adoption in 1868, has provided the basis for hundreds of cases as well as extensive national legislation and investigation bearing on the scope of state police power. Its first section, after defining citizenship and determining that American citizens are citizens "of the State wherein they reside," imposes three overlapping restrictions on the states. The first is that no state "shall make or enforce any law which shall abridge the privileges or immunities of citizens of the United States." The second restriction is that no state shall "deprive any person

[7] *Wabash, St. L. and P. Ry. Co.* v. *Illinois*, 118 U. S. 557 (1886).

[8] *Houston, East and West Texas Ry. Co.* v. *United States*, 234 U. S. 342 (1913).

[9] *Morgan* v. *Virginia*, 328 U. S. 373 (1946).

of life, liberty, or property, without due process of law." The third is that no state shall "deny to any person within its jurisdiction the equal protection of the laws." It should be noted that the shift from the term "citizen" to "person" expanded the coverage of the restrictions for the purposes of law and jurisprudence. A corporation is a legal person for many purposes, although it is not an individual citizen, and aliens, of course, are persons but not citizens.

Use by private corporations

The Fourteenth Amendment, although an outgrowth of the Civil War and the emancipation of the slaves, was to be used far more extensively by private corporations than by blacks during the first sixty years of its existence as part of "the supreme law of the land."[10] Business interests failed conspicuously, however, in some of their early attempts to sidetrack state regulatory legislation by invoking this portion of the Constitution. In deciding the *Slaughterhouse Cases*[11] in 1873, the Supreme Court, with four dissents, upheld a Louisiana statute which provided for monopolistic private control of premises in New Orleans for slaughtering meat under public inspection and required all local butchers to use these facilities. The butchers complained that they were victims of abridgement of "privileges or immunities," of deprivation of "due process," and of denial of "the equal protection of the laws." The opinion of the Court emphasized the enduring regulatory power of the states in our federal system and stressed the close but not exclusive connection of the Fourteenth Amendment with the rights of ex-slaves.

Regulating businesses "affected with a public interest"

In the post-Civil War period, rapid expansion of railroads into the sparsely settled areas of the West led to transportation conditions which the western farmers thought intolerable. The farmers banded together in the Granger movement to secure legislative regulation of the railroads in the interest of adequate service at reasonable rates. The farmers also sought regulation of auxiliary services essential to movement of their produce to market. The states' regulatory power was soon challenged under the Fourteenth Amendment. In *Munn* v. *Illinois*,[12] the first of the Granger cases, the Supreme Court upheld an Illinois statute fixing maximum charges for storing grain in warehouses in large cities. Chief Justice Morrison R. Waite, in delivering the opinion, cited Taney and British authorities on police power and observed that the Illinois law was not violative of the "due process" clause of the Fourteenth Amendment, since it applied controls to private property "affected with a public interest." But just what is a business affected with a public interest? The Court subsequently stated that in

[10] *See* C. W. Collins, *The Fourteenth Amendment and the States* (Boston: Little, Brown and Co., 1912).

[11] 16 Wall. 36 (1873).

[12] 94 U. S. 113 (1876).

the Munn case it had conceived the term "affected with a public interest" as the equivalent of "subject to the exercise of the police power."[13] This somewhat circular definition simply means that the scope of the state police power in this field is determined by the slow process of judicial inclusion and exclusion, case by case.

Subsequent opinions of the Court were to show a cyclic trend toward viewing the Fourteenth Amendment of the Constitution as a businessmen's amendment, in a fashion highly disturbing to proponents of the police power. Broad clearance was set up in 1886 by the Supreme Court in a categorical statement that corporations were persons entitled to "equal protection of the laws."[14]

In 1905 the high tribunal set aside a New York statute fixing maximum hours for employees of bakeries, holding it an unreasonable use of police power in violation of the "due process" protection of the liberty of contract to sell and purchase labor.[15] This laid down a pattern for later decisions, provoking Justice Holmes, in dissent, to object to deciding cases on economic theory and to observe that the "Fourteenth Amendment does not enact Mr. Herbert Spencer's *Social Statics*." This dissenting opinion foreshadowed the majority slant of later years. In 1937 the Court frankly reversed itself with respect to state power to regulate labor conditions, Chief Justice Hughes noting in the opinion that "the liberty safeguarded is liberty in a social organization."[16]

Support for narrowing the Fourteenth Amendment's protection of corporations came from such justices as Louis Brandeis, Hugo Black, William Douglas, and others. The constitutional history of the shift is one which would fill many pages. Suffice it to say with the Court in the *Nebbia* case, where it sustained New York's regulation of the price of milk, that:

> So far as the requirement of due process is concerned, and in the absence of other constitutional restriction, a state is free to adopt whatever economic policy may reasonably be deemed to promote public welfare. . . .
> . . . The Constitution does not secure to anyone liberty to conduct his business in such fashion as to inflict injury upon the public at large, or upon any substantial group of the people.[17]

We had come a long way by the mid-1930s from the doctrine that the state's police power applied only to businesses rather narrowly conceived as "affected with a public interest."

[13] *Nebbia* v. *New York*, 291 U. S. 502 (1934).

[14] *Santa Clara County* v. *Southern Pacific Railroad Company*, 118 U. S. 394 (1886).

[15] *Lochner* v. *New York*, 198 U. S. 45 (1905).

[16] *West Coast Hotel Company* v. *Parrish*, 300 U. S. 379 (1937).

[17] *Nebbia* v. *New York*.

The story of the Fourteenth Amendment as a shield for human rights is too long to be given here except in summary of significant points. It has afforded the Supreme Court a new role as defender of humane democracy.[18] The use of the amendment for protection of human rights, at ebb tide around the turn of the century, registered a genuine revival between 1930 and 1960 when corporations were finding it a less useful weapon against state police power. The Fourteenth Amendment correlates with the advancement of blacks, although by no means is limited in application to racial relations. It involves the relationship of state and local police power to the freedoms of labor, speech, press, worship, and assembly, as well as to equality of opportunity in public education and recreation. It is the story of evolution in both procedural and substantive rights, with an increasing sensitivity of the Supreme Court to the rights of human beings.

Shield for human rights

The "due process" clause of the Fourteenth Amendment has served more and more in recent decades to require state courts to exercise fair and proper procedure in criminal cases. The Supreme Court, for example, in 1923 sent a case back to an Arkansas court for retrial on the ground that the jury had brought in a hasty verdict under the influence of a mob.[19] Some years later the court similarly interfered with the trial of a group of blacks at Scottsboro, Alabama, because the accused transients were shunted through proceedings to conviction without any advance provision for counsel.[20] A sequel to this case met similar treatment because blacks had been systematically and traditionally excluded from jury service in that Alabama jurisdiction.[21] Convictions in state courts have been set aside because they were based on forced confession of guilt. Such methods of securing conviction, in the words of Justice Black, constitute "a denial of due process of law as guaranteed in the Fourteenth Amendment."[22] Unnecessary brutality to prisoners under arrest or in custody has subjected state or local officers to prosecution in federal court under civil rights legislation passed by Congress in conformity with the Fourteenth Amendment.[23] The Supreme Court has not brought the states under the same procedural limitations as the national government, however. Until recently, such national requirements in the Bill of Rights as the right to jury trial, grand jury indictment, privilege against self-incrimination, and protection against

Right to a fair trial

[18] *See* Robert G. McCloskey, "The Supreme Court Finds a Role: Civil Liberties in the 1955 Term." *Virginia Law Review* 42 (October 1956), pp. 735–760.

[19] *Moore* v. *Dempsey*, 261 U. S. 86 (1923).

[20] *Powell* v. *Alabama*, 287 U. S. 45 (1932).

[21] *Norris* v. *Alabama*, 294 U. S. 587 (1935).

[22] *Chambers* v. *Florida*, 309 U. S. 227 (1940).

[23] 18 *U. S. Code Annotated* § 242; *see Screws* v. *United States*, 325 U. S. 91 (1945), and *United States* v. *Sutherland*, 37 F. Supp. 344 (1940).

double jeopardy have all been held as not binding on the states unless they so desire.[24] In 1961, the so-called federal exclusionary rule—making evidence obtained in violation of the Fourth Amendment inadmissible in court—was applied to the state judiciary as well.[25] Subsequent decisions require states to provide legal counsel for indigent defendants facing "serious" criminal charges;[26] to extend to defendants in state courts the same privilege against self-incrimination previously applicable under the Fifth Amendment to federal proceedings;[27] and to assure that protections against self-incrimination extend to questioning at the police station.[28] But in 1972 the Supreme Court refused to require uniform jury procedures for imposing the death penalty.[29]

Freedom of speech and press

The Supreme Court in the second quarter of the twentieth century strengthened the Fourteenth Amendment as a protection of our basic freedoms against unreasonable interference from state police power. The Court gradually absorbed the specific restraints imposed by the First Amendment upon the national government into the "liberty" protected under the Fourteenth Amendment against infringement by the states. In effect, under the rulings of the Court, the states must observe the restrictions of the First Amendment in respect to speech, press, assembly, and religion. Municipal regulations have been voided by the Supreme Court for interfering unduly with the liberties of religious, labor, and other groups wishing "to speak, write, print or distribute information or opinion." This was made clear by Justice Owen J. Roberts in a Court opinion in 1939 with numerous citations from other cases.[30] The 1949 decision in the *Terminiello* case sustained freedom of speech in a fashion that has been criticized as too restrictive of the use of police power for the local preservation of order in inflammatory circumstances.[31]

It has also been decided that publication of a newspaper or periodical may not be suppressed or enjoined by state action for obnoxious and derogatory remarks concerning public officers,[32] and in two related, but more recent, cases in Alabama the Supreme Court further strengthened freedom of the press. It ruled that a public official cannot recover libel damages unless he proves that the statement was made with deliberate

[24] *Walker* v. *Sauvinet,* 92 U. S. 90 (1876); *Hurtado* v. *California,* 110 U. S. 516 (1884); *Twining* v. *New Jersey,* 211 U. S. 78 (1908); *Palko* v. *Connecticut,* 302 U. S. 319 (1937).

[25] *Mapp* v. *Ohio,* 367 U. S. 643 (1961).

[26] *Gideon* v. *Wainwright,* 372 U. S. 335 (1963).

[27] *Malloy* v. *Hogan,* 378 U. S. 1 (1964).

[28] *Miranda* v. *State of Arizona,* 384 U. S. 436 (1966).

[29] *Apodaca* v. *Oregon,* 406 U. S. 404 (1972), and *Johnson* v. *Louisiana,* 406 U. S. 356 (1972).

[30] *Schneider* v. *State (Town of Irvington),* 308 U. S. 147 (1939).

[31] *Terminiello* v. *City of Chicago,* 337 U. S. 1 (1949).

[32] *Near* v. *Minnesota,* 283 U. S. 697 (1931).

malice.[33] Four Montgomery city officials and Governor John Patterson had sought damages from *The New York Times* and four black ministers for a full-page advertisement alleging racial oppression and soliciting funds for Dr. Martin Luther King. In a 1966 decision, the Court held that state laws —in this case Alabama's 1915 anti-electioneering statute—barring publication of political editorials on election day are a "flagrant" unconstitutional abridgement of freedom of the press.[34] Protection through the Fourteenth Amendment has invalidated the banning of movies under claims of their being sacrilegious or suggestive of crime and immorality,[35] and has served to limit state and local regulation of obscene literature. The *Roth* decision in 1957 required an obscenity test of whether the dominant theme of the material taken as a whole appeals to prurient interest, and whether the material has redeeming social value.[36] The 5 to 4 decision in the *Ginzburg* case in 1966 gave censors an additional legal weapon—the obvious motive of the publisher—in controlling obscenity.[37]

The trend of liberal Supreme Court decisions giving First Amendment protection to public portrayal of sexual conduct received a setback in a five-to-four decision in 1973 which held that juries and courts no longer need to find that material is "utterly" without redeeming social value before they declare it obscene. Chief Justice Burger wrote the majority opinion, holding that local community standards rather than national standards may be used to determine whether material is obscene, and that courts may determine whether the work "taken as a whole lacks serious literary, artistic, political, or scientific value to merit First Amendment protection."[38]

Censorship and loyalty oaths

State anti-subversion measures have had a checkered experience with the federal judiciary, with approval being given in the *Adler* case to the state's barring from employment in public schools persons holding subversive doctrines or membership in subversive organizations. The Court stated that the right of such persons to "assemble, speak, think and believe as they will" is not the "right to work for the State in the school system on their own terms."[39] Since 1960, however, the Supreme Court has struck

[33] *New York Times Company* v. *Sullivan*, 376 U. S. 254 (1964).

[34] *Mills* v. *State of Alabama*, 384 U. S. 214 (1966).

[35] *Joseph Burstyn, Inc.* v. *Wilson*, 343 U. S. 495 (1952). But a municipal ordinance imposing prior restraint on showing motion pictures through censorship of the films by municipal authorities does not "on its face" violate the First and Fourteenth Amendment guarantees of free speech and press: *Times Film Corp.* v. *Chicago*, 365 U. S. 43 (1961).

[36] *Roth* v. *United States*, 354 U. S. 476 (1957).

[37] *Ginzburg et al.* v. *United States*, 383 U. S. 63 (1966).

[38] *Miller* v. *California*, 93 S.Ct. 2607 U. S. (1973).

[39] *Adler et al.* v. *Board of Education of the City of New York*, 342 U. S. 485 (1952). A subsequent decision indicated, however, that a state violates due process of law when it dis-

down loyalty oaths required of public employees in six states—Arkansas, Florida, Washington, Maryland, New York, and Arizona. The Arizona law was said to be based on "guilt by association," making mere membership in an organization considered subversive the basis for discharge or suspension of salary. The 5 to 4 ruling declared the law unconstitutional as a violation of "the cherished freedom of association protected by the First Amendment."[40] But in 1972 the Supreme Court upheld a Massachusetts law requiring state employees and applicants not only to uphold the Constitution, but to oppose overthrow of federal or state governments "by force, violence, or by any illegal or unconstitutional method."[41] The vote was 4 to 3 (Nixon appointees Powell and Rehnquist were not on the court until after the case was heard).

Religious freedom

The Fourteenth Amendment has protected freedom of worship in ways other than by safeguarding religious speech from interference by local authorities. The Supreme Court has insisted rather strictly upon the separation of church and state in public education. Its insistence has extended to outlawing the release of time for religious activity or instruction on school premises even where such instruction was at the request of parents.[42] The school action was held to be contrary to the religious "establishment" clause of the First Amendment and, therefore, violative of the Fourteenth Amendment. Four years later, in the *Zorach* case, the Court reconsidered the problem of "released time" and approved the New York system of permitting students to go to religious centers not on public school property for instruction during the school day.[43] Reversing a former decision, the Court in 1943 overruled the action of a school board which expelled children of the Jehovah's Witness faith for refusing to salute the national flag in school exercises because of religious scruples.[44] But the practice of transporting school children in public buses to parochial schools has been upheld.[45] A 1972 decision affecting Amish parents and their children upheld their right to an exemption from compulsory school attendance laws on religious grounds.[46]

---

charges an employee on the sole ground that he has invoked the Fifth Amendment's safeguard against self-incrimination before a committee of the U. S. Senate. *Slochower* v. *Board of Higher Education of City of N. Y.*, 350 U. S. 551 (1956).

40 *Elfbrandt* v. *Russell et al.*, 384 U. S. 11 (1966).

41 *Cole* v. *Richardson*, 405 U. S. 676 (1972).

42 *Illinois ex rel. McCollum* v. *Board of Education*, 333 U. S. 203 (1948).

43 *Zorach* v. *Clauson*, 343 U. S. 306 (1952).

44 *West Virginia State Board of Education* v. *Barnette*, 319 U. S. 624 (1943), reversing *Minersville School District* v. *Gobitis*, 310 U. S. 586 (1940).

45 *Everson* v. *Board of Education*, 330 U. S. 1 (1947).

46 *Wisconsin* v. *Yoder*, 406 U. S. 205 (1972).

The relationship of local police power to religion and religious freedom is somewhat flexible and not easy to define at any one time. Through the years, all levels of government have offered special concessions to churches including tax exemption of church property and income, recognition of Sunday as a legal day of rest in every state, Sunday "blue laws," requirement of daily reading of the Bible in many public schools, and legal observance of such Christian holidays as Christmas and Easter. What happens when one's religious freedom conflicts with a state or local government regulation for public health or welfare? In recent years courts have supported the police power in three unusual cases: in spite of religious objections of parents who were Jehovah's Witnesses, a court ordered that an Rh baby be given a blood transfusion; a compulsory chest X-ray requirement at the University of Washington was held to apply to all students, including a Christian Scientist with religious objections; and a nine-year-old girl helping her guardian aunt to sell publications of Jehovah's Witnesses was held subject to the child labor law in Massachusetts.[47]

Borderline church–state relations

The perplexing relationship between the requirement of religious freedom and the state's police power, as manifested in Sunday laws, was considered by the Supreme Court in four cases in 1961. These cases challenged the constitutionality of laws in Pennsylvania, Massachusetts, and Maryland, on the ground that they impose a "Christian Sabbath" on non-Christians. Orthodox Jewish merchants who close their stores on Friday evening and Saturday are then prevented by law from being open on Sunday. The Court upheld the Sunday closing laws, saying that such laws are legal if designed to promote a day of rest and recreation. The Court served notice, however, that such laws would be declared unconstitutional if they are found, on their face or by examining their legislative history, to be primarily designed to promote religious observance and church attendance.[48] The Court rejected at the same time an appeal to review South Carolina's law against commercial movies on Sunday. The law, enacted long before the days of movies, prohibits commercial entertainments on Sunday and has been interpreted as including movies. The state court decision, from which the appeal was made, upheld the state's power to enact such a law and concluded that if it was "out of step with the times" as alleged, it was the job of the legislature, not the courts, to change it.

Sunday "blue laws"

[47] *See* Robert E. Cushman, *Civil Liberties in the United States* (Ithaca, N. Y.: Cornell University Press, 1956), Part III, "Freedom of Religion: Separation of Church and State." For the most complete history of church–state relations, *see* Anson Phelps Stokes, *Church and State in the United States*, 3 vols. (New York: Harper and Row, 1950).

[48] *McGowan* v. *Maryland*, 366 U. S. 420 (1961); *Two Guys* v. *McGinley*, 366 U. S. 582 (1961); *Braunfeld* v. *Brown*, 366 U. S. 599 (1961); and *Gallagher* v. *Crown Kosher Market*, 366 U. S. 617 (1961).

Legislation restricting birth control

Connecticut's eighty-six-year-old law prohibiting the sale or use of contraceptives or giving medical advice on birth control was invalidated in 1965. A test case was instituted following the closing by police of the Planned Parenthood Center of New Haven, Connecticut, and the Supreme Court ruled that it was an unconstitutional invasion of the right of marital privacy.[49]

Religious tests for officeholding

In still another 1961 decision in the church–state area of the law, the Supreme Court struck down a Maryland requirement that each state officeholder must make a sworn statement of his belief in a Supreme Being. In a unanimous opinion the court held that no religious test whatsoever may be applied by either federal or state governments to disqualify a person from holding public office, and that atheists have as much right to disbelieve as other citizens have to believe.[50] In recent cases concerning prayer and Bible reading in the public schools, the Supreme Court has continued its strong stand against the "establishment of religion."[51] A certain ambiguity in the court's rulings with respect to provision for voluntary prayer resulted in efforts to amend the constitution to permit voluntary prayer in public buildings. A decade of efforts failed to secure the change; in 1971 the "Wylie amendment" was forced out of a House committee by a discharge petition, only to fall short of the necessary two-thirds majority by 28 votes in a 240 to 162 favorable House vote. Opponents of the amendment contend that it is unnecessary since voluntary prayer has never been forbidden, and that the vague wording might undermine the guarantees already provided.

Equal opportunity in public education

The Fourteenth Amendment's provision for "equal protection of the laws" has come to mean much more than the guarantee of fundamental freedoms against the unreasonable application of state or local police power. According to the highest judicial interpretation, it also means equality of opportunity in state-supported institutions of learning. With that principle assumed, compulsory segregation of races in the public assemblages and facilities of one-third of the states was to burden the courts with a weighty problem of interpretation in terms of sociological jurisprudence. In this American dilemma, was segregation in itself a denial of equal protection to the minority race? And, if not, what was essential to equal protection within the pattern of segregation?

[49] *Griswold* v. *Connecticut,* 381 U. S. 479 (1965).

[50] *Torcaso* v. *Watkins,* 367 U. S. 339 (1961).

[51] *Engel* v. *Vitale,* 370 U. S. 421 (1962); and *Abington School District* v. *Schempp,* 374 U. S. 203 (1963). *See* Robert H. Birkby, "The Supreme Court and the Bible Belt: Tennessee Reaction to the 'Schempp' Decision," *Midwest Journal of Political Science* 10 (August 1966), pp. 304–319. *See* Chapter 22 for a more detailed discussion of these and other cases in connection with the education function of state and local government.

Doctrinal guidance for half a century was set forth in 1896 by the Supreme Court in *Plessy* v. *Ferguson*,[52] a case concerning racial separation in railway travel in Louisiana. The Court held that the state requirement of separation was not contrary to the "equal protection" clause but was a reasonable use of police power in accordance with established "usages, customs, and traditions." Separate but equal accommodations would meet the constitutional test. In support, the opinion pointed to legislation by Congress for segregation in the public schools in the District of Columbia. A vigorous dissent by Justice John M. Harlan, a Kentuckian, posed a point for the future with the observation that the "Constitution is color blind." After forty years the Supreme Court began to weigh the facts of institutional segregation, although without departing from the constitutional formula of the Plessy case. In 1938 it held that a black citizen of Missouri, with proper academic qualifications, was "entitled to be admitted to the law school of the State University in the absence of other and proper provision for his legal training within the State."[53] State provision for his training in another state fell short of "equality of legal right."

Sweatt and McLaurin cases

In 1950 the Supreme Court took further steps. It decided that the refusal to admit a black to the law school of the University of Texas was denial of equal protection, although he was offered training at a law school for blacks in the state.[54] The opinion pointed out that the latter school was not equal to that for whites in faculty, facilities, recognition, and opportunity for contacts. In the same session the Supreme Court decided that Oklahoma, after admitting a black to the graduate school of the state university, was denying him equal protection by segregating him in classrooms, library, and cafeteria.[55]

The Court next considered the constitutional validity of segregated public schools. The issue was no longer the equality of segregated facilities, upon which most of the earlier gains had been scored for blacks in cases before the Court. Instead, segregation itself was challenged in the light of its sociological and psychological implications. The Court gave consideration to a group of cases on this issue for a period of more than a year, extending into 1954. The cases came up from South Carolina, Virginia, and Kansas, along with one from the District of Columbia not involving the Fourteenth Amendment. The Department of Justice entered the contest against segregation. The battle of briefs in these cases provided the sharpest collision yet between the protagonists of integration and segregation. In

[52] 163 U. S. 537 (1896).

[53] *Missouri ex rel. Gaines* v. *Canada*, 305 U. S. 337 (1938).

[54] *Sweatt* v. *Painter*, 339 U. S. 629 (1950).

[55] *McLaurin* v. *Oklahoma State Regents for Higher Education*, 339 U. S. 637 (1950).

May 1954, Chief Justice Warren in a unanimous opinion of the Court in *Brown* v. *Board of Education*[56] observed categorically that in public education "the doctrine of 'separate but equal' has no place." "Separate educational facilities are inherently unequal." In terms of psychological jurisprudence, he wrote that the segregation of black children "may affect their hearts and minds in a way unlikely ever to be undone." Methods of implementing the reversal of policy were left to future argument and decision, and in an opinion one year later the Supreme Court cleared the way for enforcement through the federal district courts of the states concerned. Desegregation in the South and the North, like the building of Rome, was not to be achieved in a day. It soon became apparent that the court requirements for "all deliberate speed" would be met with more deliberation than speed.

Brown v. *Board of Education*

Segregation by law first disappeared in the District of Columbia, with slower and more gradual desegregation beginning in the border states of Delaware, Kentucky, Maryland, Missouri, Oklahoma, and West Virginia. Token integration took place in parts of Arkansas, North Carolina, Tennessee, Virginia, and Texas, with some sections following the moderate patterns of the border and others following the Deep South pattern of hard-core resistance. Efforts of the Deep South to maintain segregated education have been described by Professor Robert J. Harris as follows:

Efforts to maintain segregation

> Many of the states in the South, in addition to noncompliance with the Court's decision, pursued policies of aggressive defiance. Official resistance took such forms as public school closing and leasing laws, pupil placement laws, interposition resolutions, closing of schools by executive proclamation, and executive maintenance of segregated education by force in the name of law and order, as exemplified by the employment of state police by Governor Allan Shivers to maintain segregated education in Mansfield, Texas, and employment of the National Guard by Governor Orval Faubus in Little Rock to prevent nine children from entering Central High School. Semiofficial and unofficial defiance has also been common in the states of the former Confederacy. Leaders of thought and opinion in politics and journalism employed the ancient shibboleth, "a government of laws and not of men," to encourage lawlessness under labels like "massive resistance," as proposed by Senator Harry Byrd, and resistance by all legal means, as advocated by one hundred southern congressmen who signed the so-called Southern Manifesto. Most . . . did not overtly advocate violence, but their intemperate language and distortion of the law created an atmosphere conducive to disorder generally and encouraged such sporadic outbreaks of violence which resulted in mob action at Little Rock, Mansfield, and Clinton, Tennessee, and in bombings of schools,

[56] 347 U. S. 483 (1954).

synagogues, or churches in Nashville, Clinton, Atlanta, Birmingham, and Jacksonville.[57]

Cracks in the segregationist armor of the Deep South appeared in 1960 and 1961 when token integration was carried out under court orders in the New Orleans public school system and at the University of Georgia. Early in 1961 the Georgia legislature abandoned its rigid segregation laws and replaced them with four measures proposed by Governor Ernest Vandiver as the "most feasible method of holding integration to a minimum." The new methods emphasized local option referenda on closing and opening schools that had been integrated, tuition grants for pupils who prefer private schools to integrated public schools, and a constitutional declaration that no child can be forced to attend integrated schools against his will. Opposition to the bills in the legislature was light, but one spokesman for total segregation said, "The white flag will be the symbol of this legislature. Isn't it ironic in this, the centennial year of the Civil War, that Georgia surrenders again?"[58]

Token integration

Because neither the President nor Congress, as Professor Harris points out, had developed a policy or plan for meeting the constitutional crisis in race relations,

> . . . the burden of implementing the Supreme Court decision has fallen almost exclusively on the federal judiciary, and primarily on the United States district courts. Accordingly, one of the most important policies of social change in the twentieth century was committed to the tedious and fortuitous process of private litigation, with the final judgment affecting only the parties in controversy. The relative inadequacy of judicial precedents as vehicles for social change, in contrast to the efficiency of legislation and administration to effectuate change rapidly, has long been a theme of text writers in jurisprudence, who are amply corroborated by . . . the events that have occurred in the area of race relations since May, 1954.[59]

The major burden of overseeing and policing desegregation of the public schools was shifted away from the courts to the Congress and the Executive branch by passage of the Civil Rights Act of 1964. Of its ten titles, several related to ways and means of speeding up the snail-like pace of desegregation in some school districts. The U. S. Office of Education was required to report within two years on progress of school desegregation

Shift in enforcement burden

[57] Robert J. Harris, *The Quest for Equality* (Baton Rouge: Louisiana State University Press, 1960), pp. 154–155. For a more detailed account of state resistance measures, *see* "Race Relations Law Survey, May 1954–May 1957," *Race Relations Law Reporter* 2 (1957), p. 881.

[58] Associated Press report in the Nashville *Tennessean*, Jan. 25, 1961.

[59] Harris, *Quest for Equality*, p. 157.

at all levels, and to give technical and financial assistance, if requested, to school systems in the process of desegregating. The Attorney General was authorized to file suit for desegregation of schools in specified circumstances; and, in Title VI, where voluntary compliance had been sought unsuccessfully, federal agencies were authorized to cut off funds to discriminatory state and local programs. Passage of the precedent-breaking Elementary and Secondary Education Act of 1965 made Title VI a potent weapon in federal acceleration of school desegregation. Its implications for school politics and administration are discussed in chapter 22.

Racial balance, busing, and the Swann case

The common pattern of racial desegregation of schools, white flight to the suburbs, and the resulting resegregation brought the courts back into the picture on the twin issues of racial balance and busing. In the Swann case in 1971 the Supreme Court unanimously ruled that courts have the power to require busing of students when school authorities fail to meet their obligations to desegregate.[60] The decision involved four southern school situations, but dealt primarily with massive busing requirements in the Charlotte–Mecklenburg School System, the largest in North Carolina. The decision agreed that objections to busing may be valid if the time or distance of travel is so great as to risk the health of the children or significantly hamper the educational process. It also ruled that courts may alter school attendance zones, may group zones not having common boundaries, and may prohibit school boards from using future school construction or abandoning old ones to perpetuate or re-establish segregated systems. On racial balance, the Court said that every school need not reflect the racial composition of the system as a whole, but a court may use the racial ratio, in the school system as a whole, as a starting point to determine whether a violation exists.

The busing backlash

By the opening of school in the fall of 1971, federal judges had applied the principles of the Swann decision in cases involving more than 40 school districts. The political impact was immediate, and "forced busing" provided a potent campaign issue for the 1972 presidential election. (*See* Figure 4–1.) President Nixon warned federal administrative officials against proposing busing as a primary means to enforce school desegregation plans, at the same time promising that the government would continue to enforce busing ordered by the courts. Controversy over an anti-busing amendment caused a long stalemate on congressional legislation for aid to education, and caused Chief Justice Burger to issue an unusual opinion indicating misgivings about lower courts' interpretations of the Swann

[60] *North Carolina State Board of Education* v. *Swann*, 402 U. S. 43 (1971). For an account of an effort to achieve racial balance by state legislation, *see* Frank Levy, *Northern Schools and Civil Rights: The Racial Imbalance Act of Massachusetts* (Chicago: Markham Publishing Co., 1971).

Green light

Figure 4–1. Jon Kennedy in the Arkansas *Democrat.*

decision. While upholding extensive busing in Winston-Salem, he denied that a fixed racial balance is required in the schools. Supporters of busing, including the U. S. Civil Rights Commission, reminded opponents that, until legal segregation of the schools was ended, black children in Sturgis, Mississippi, were being transported by "forced busing" to an all black school 93 miles away, and suburban Atlanta blacks were being transported 75 miles to their appropriate segregated school. In 1974 the U. S. Supreme Court called a halt to required cross-district busing. In a 5-to-4 decision in the Roth case (*see* chapter 22), the court ruled that suburban school districts surrounding Detroit could not be forced into participation in metropolitan busing unless they were found guilty of helping to segregate schools in the metropolitan area. In spite of the many stops and starts in desegregation progress since 1954, a landmark statistical report in 1973 revealed the same percentage of black and white 17-year-olds in high school and an all-time high in the number of blacks in college—twice what it was five years earlier.

The logical extension of the decision in the Brown case to other areas of public activity has been taking place slowly but steadily since 1954. Federal courts have invalidated segregation by law in publicly supported parks, golf courses, swimming pools, and other recreation facilities; publicly operated eating places; public transit facilities; public libraries; and other state and local activities involving service to all citizens. The use of state and local authority to preserve segregation and to make other racial distinctions in a hundred and one ways has now been clearly established as unconstitutional. Although segregated swimming pools were ruled unconstitutional, blacks were turned down in 1971 by a 5-to-4 Supreme Court decision in efforts to force Jackson, Mississippi, to reopen pools on an integrated basis. Justice Burger reminded critics that "all that is good is not commanded by the Constitution and all that is bad is not forbidden by it."[61] Efforts to alleviate de facto segregation in housing, employment, and other areas of American life continue, but the emphasis has shifted more to economic and political pressures than to adjudication. The cartoon in Figure 4–2 illustrates one of the more common techniques of "sophisticated segregation" which has spread some of the spotlight of racial strife to cities outside the South.

With the retirement of Chief Justice Earl Warren in 1969 and his replacement by Warren E. Burger, an activist era of the Supreme Court seemed destined to an end. Burger's reputation as a "strict constructionist of the Constitution" was one of the major factors leading to his appointment by President Nixon. Only time will tell whether Burger and the subsequent Nixon appointees to the Court will reverse the role of the federal judiciary from a driving force for the rights of the individual against those of government and collective society.

The Burger Court, law, and liberty

The Burger Court started the decade of the seventies with a more sympathetic view of the policeman and the prosecutor in criminal cases. Burger himself responded publicly in 1971 to charges that law-and-order emphasis had brought instances of "police repression," stating that "nothing that I can see" would suggest that there is a danger of police oppression. He suggested rather that most Americans believe "that it is quite the reverse of that situation—that the law enforcement agencies simply are not able to cope with the problems of law enforcement."[62]

Even if the court decisions of the 1970s should bring the judicial trends of the 1950s and 1960s to an abrupt halt, there can be little doubt

[61] *Palmer* v. *Thompson* 403 U. S. 217 (1971).

[62] From *The New York Times* news service, as reported in the *Arkansas Gazette,* July 4, 1971.

'Those Alabama Stories Are Sickening. Why Can't They Be Like Us And Find Some Nice, Refined Way To Keep the Negroes Out?'

Figure 4–2. From *Straight Herblock* (Simon & Schuster, 1964).

that the state's police power was more than just temporarily sensitized to the rights of previously unprotected groups of citizens. The liberty aspect of "liberty under law" now has new meaning in state and local government as a result of its long day in court.

Local Aspects of National "Quasi-Police" Powers

The Constitution of the United States does not confer a "police power" as such upon the federal government. But several of the powers which it does confer afford Congress authority to exercise something very much akin to the power to regulate in the interest of the public safety, health, welfare, and morals—a kind of "quasi-police" power, "almost but not quite" the real thing. Congress uses its delegated powers in various ways to supplement or even supersede the local workings of state police power. This is notably true in the regulation of interstate commerce, and it is by no means limited to strategic attention to intrastate freight rates. Regulation of interstate trade in foods requires inspection, not at the state lines, but at places of processing, and this relieves the states of large regulatory burdens. The regulation of wages, hours, and bargaining conditions of labor in business affecting interstate commerce often brings federal "police power" to the local scene. The Interstate Commerce Commission in 1955 ordered an end to segregation of interstate passengers in southern stations. A decade later the Supreme Court upheld the use of the interstate commerce power by Congress to forbid racial discrimination in places of public accommodation.[63] The interstate commerce power is used to prohibit the shipment of prison products into states where the sale of such products is contrary to state law. There can be no practical differentiation at the state line for the regulation of aviation, radio, and TV, and, consequently, national supervision of these activities applies to both interstate and intrastate operations. National legislation against interstate kidnapping, "white slave" traffic, and auto theft duplicates state jurisdiction and aids the states in punishing violators. State regulation of the issuance and marketing of securities, as in the case of railroad regulation, proved inadequate and, to close the gap, the national government entered the field through the commerce power.

Policing interstate commerce

Congress finds constitutional powers for local regulation outside the commerce clause. Use of the mails for fraudulent purposes is punishable by legislation based on the postal power, regardless of whether or not it is interstate. Local narcotics peddling is violative of a federal tax law, as is "wildcat" distilling of liquor. In the exercise of its spending power, the national government stipulates the conditions of labor working for contractors with government contracts, not a small item in the nation's economy. The war or military powers are used to regulate civilian activities around centers where armed forces are located, and certain practices are prohibited in the interest of military morals and morale. The national government protects its own property wherever that property is located.

Other national uses of police power

Hunting migratory birds is regulated under legislation which implements a treaty. Regulation under legislation which implements a treaty poses an interesting problem in federalism. Congress attempted to regulate the hunting of migratory birds in 1913, but the law was declared unconstitutional in the lower federal courts.[64] Power to regulate the hunting of migratory birds was not one of the powers delegated to the national gov-

States, Congress, and the treaty power

[63] *Heart of Atlanta Motel, Inc.* v. *United States*, 379 U. S. 241 (1964).

[64] *United States* v. *Shauver*, 214 Fed. 154 (1914); *United States* v. *McCullagh*, 221 Fed. 288 (1915).

ernment. The United States subsequently entered into a treaty which provided for the protection of migratory birds by Canada and the United States. In implementation of the treaty Congress passed a new migratory bird act and, on test in the Court, the constitutionality of the act was sustained.[65] Congress is empowered by the Constitution to "make all laws which shall be necessary and proper for carrying into execution the foregoing [listed] powers, and all other powers vested by this Constitution in the government of the United States, or in any department or officer thereof." The power to make treaties is one of the other powers. The decision in *Missouri* v. *Holland* indicates that Congress may do something in implementation of a treaty which it could not do under the Constitution prior to the treaty's existence, that is, regulate the hunting of migratory birds. The implications for the federal system are far-reaching indeed, and considerable controversy has ensued as to the proper scope of the treaty-making and treaty-implementing authority. The "Bricker" amendment proposed in the United States Senate early in 1953 provided in part that a treaty provision in conflict with the Constitution "shall not be of any force or effect" and that a treaty "shall become effective as internal law in the United States only through legislation which would be valid in the absence of treaty." The amendment failed to pass in the Senate in 1954 by only one vote, but the issue has shown unusual survival power.

Centralized and decentralized processes

Americans of this century have utilized national processes increasingly for important applications of police power as well as for many important determinations of civil rights. They have come to rely increasingly upon the functioning of national and state governments, in coordination or in counterbalance, for the effective exercises of power and for the effective preservation of liberty. Thus do they recognize, in terms of a Toynbee synthesis of democracy, the twin principles of "Law and Freedom in History."

[65] *Missouri* v. *Holland*, 252 U. S. 416 (1920).

SUPPLEMENTARY READINGS

American Civil Liberties Union. Reports and pamphlets. New York: American Civil Liberties Union.

Bachrach, Peter. *Problems in Freedom.* Harrisburg, Pa.: The Stackpole Co., 1954.

Barker, L. J., and Barker, T. W., Jr. *Freedom, Courts, Politics: Studies in Civil Liberties.* Englewood Cliffs, N. J.: Prentice-Hall, 1965.

Burkey, Richard M. *Racial Discrimination and Public Policy in the United States.* Lexington, Mass.: D. C. Heath and Co., 1971.

Corwin, Edward S. *Liberty Against Government.* Baton Rouge: Louisiana State University Press, 1948.

Cushman, Robert E. *Leading Constitutional Decisions.* 12th ed. New York: Appleton-Century-Crofts, 1963.

Emerson, T. I., and Haber, David. *Political and Civil Rights in the United States.* 2 vols. 3rd ed. Boston: Little, Brown and Co., 1967.

Frankfurter, Felix. *The Public and Its Government.* New Haven: Yale University Press, 1930.

Freund, Paul A., and Ulich, Robert. *Religion and the Public Schools.* Cambridge, Mass.: Harvard University Press, 1965.

Grimes, A. P. *Equality in America: Religion, Race and the Urban Majority.* New York: Oxford University Press, 1964.

Hamilton, W. H., and Rodee, C. C. "Police Power." *Encyclopaedia of the Social Sciences.* Vol. 12. New York: The Macmillan Co., 1951. Pp. 190–193.

Harris, Robert J. *The Quest for Equality.* Baton Rouge: Louisiana State University Press, 1960.

Peltason, Jack W. *Fifty-eight Lonely Men: Southern Federal Judges and School Desegregation.* New York: Harcourt, Brace and World, 1962.

President's Committee on Civil Rights. *To Secure These Rights.* Washington, D. C.: U. S. Government Printing Office, 1947.

Roettinger, R. L. *The Supreme Court and State Police Power.* Washington, D. C.: Public Affairs Press, 1957.

Tussman, Joseph, ed. *The Supreme Court on Church and State.* New York: Oxford University Press, 1962.

Weintraub, Ruth G. *How Secure These Rights.* New York: Doubleday and Co., 1949.

White, Walter. *A Man Called White.* New York: The Viking Press, 1948.

5

State Constitutions

The United States is a land of constitutions, constitutional law, and constitutional interpretation. Americans have an abiding faith in the doctrine and workings of judicial review for defining or checking a multiplicity of statutes, and they place great reliance upon basic documents like written constitutions, fundamental charters, and organic acts for guidance in carrying on public affairs. As early as 1620 a small group of "Americans" aboard an anchored ship off Plymouth Rock signed a compact pledging:

Land of constitutions

> We . . . doe by these presents solemly and mutually in the presence of God, and one another, covenant and combine our selves togeather into a civill body politick . . . and by vertue hereof to enacte, constitute and frame such just and equall lawes, ordinances, acts, constitutions, and offices, as shall be thought most meete and convenient for the generall good of the colonie. . . .

Although it is evident from British experience that constitutions need not be written to be effective, Americans, from the Mayflower Compact to the most recent constitutional referendum, have insisted on prescribing and circumscribing the powers of government in textual terms. Popular priority for constitution writing may not quite attain that suggested by the cartoon in Figure 5–1, but every state inevitably has a formal constitution to establish what its officers and subdivisions may and may not do and to establish how the functions of government are to be performed. A constitution is necessary to chart the course of government within the broad field of powers reserved to the states by the Tenth Amendment of the federal Constitution.

"Now, you try to get a fire started while I draft a constitution."

Figure 5–1. From the *Rotarian*, June 1972. By permission of the publisher.

Constitutions as political documents

Venerated though they may be, state constitutions should be recognized at the outset as *political* documents. If politics "is the study of influence and the influential," as Harold Lasswell has said, and the "influential are those who get the most of what there is to get,"[1] it is not too difficult to identify the "influential" within a state by the privileges and protections they have secured in their state constitution. Taxpayers' groups and property interests have been able to secure strict and detailed limits on state legislatures' taxing, borrowing, and spending powers. The strength of veterans' groups and their lobbyists is revealed in constitutional guarantees of veterans' preference in public employment and even con-

[1] *Politics: Who Gets What, When, How,* quoted in *The Political Writings of Harold D. Lasswell* (Glencoe, Ill.: The Free Press, 1951), p. 295. This emphasis on constitutional politics follows closely Robert B. Dishman's *State Constitutions: The Shape of the Document* (New York: National Municipal League, 1960), pp. 7–8.

stitutional provisions for bonuses, pensions, tax exemptions, and other privileges. The influence of church groups, sometimes opposed to other church groups, may be measured in constitutional contests. A case in point is the conflict over outlawing bingo as a form of gambling, as Protestant groups have urged, or making it legal, as urged by Catholic groups. The influence of farm interests is reflected in a variety of special privileges, but the chief constitutional stronghold of farmers is the "rigged formula" for overrepresentation of rural areas in the state legislature. Roscoe Martin notes the overwhelming concern of most state constitutions for farmers with the statement that "every time one turns a page one stumbles over a milking stool or hears the distant whinny of the ploughmare—but not the cough of the tractor; that came later."[2]

Labor union influence, conversely, is reflected at a low level in most state constitutions. Only four states—New York, New Jersey, Missouri, and Hawaii—specifically guarantee the right to join unions and to bargain collectively. More states have passed so-called "right to work" amendments to their constitutions, actions usually regarded by organized labor as anti-labor victories for coalitions of business and farm groups. State constitutions reflect the political status of racial or ethnic groups, especially if the dominant group feels insecure in its position; but state influence may be counterbalanced by national influence, not only with respect to racial provisions but to all of the foregoing examples of constitutional politics.

Constitutions and party struggles

The status of the state constitution as one of the prizes in the power struggle between the two political parties is illustrated by Democratic party opposition to the proposed new Michigan constitution in 1963, and Republican support for it. The primary reason for Democratic opposition to it was its retention of the area principle for districting the state senate, which heavily favored the upstate Republicans and penalized the Detroit Democrats. This basis of representation was subsequently invalidated by the courts, resulting in a Democratic majority in both houses of the legislature after the 1964 elections. A second reason for Democratic opposition to the new constitution was its sharp reduction in the number of elective state officers, making appointive the auditor general, treasurer, highway commissioner, and superintendent of public instruction. The Democrats were embarrassed in their opposition by their previous support for making these positions appointive when they had been dominated by Republicans, and the Democrats controlled the governorship. But subsequent election of Republican governor Romney caused the proposed shorter ballot to be viewed as detrimental to the fortunes of Michigan's Democratic party.[3]

[2] Martin, *The Cities and the Federal System*, p. 49.

[3] *See* John H. Fenton, *Midwest Politics* (New York: Holt, Rinehart and Winston, 1966), p. 42; and Albert Lee Sturm, *Constitution-Making in Michigan, 1961–1962* (Ann Arbor: Institute of Public Administration, University of Michigan, 1963), pp. 190–193.

In the Illinois constitutional convention of 1970, debate was so acrimonious between Chicago Mayor Richard Daley's Democrats and the Republicans that one downstate delegate drew cheers from both groups when he proposed that Chicago somehow be "cut out" of the state.

State constitutions and "the supreme law of the land"

State constitutions are subordinate to "the supreme law of the land," as defined in Article VI of the United States Constitution. In other words, state governments are not to have powers in conflict with federal constitutional provisions, with congressional legislation that is constitutional, or with treaties properly made "under the authority of the United States." But these national restrictions, which are exceedingly important, are really few in number in comparison with the wide range of activities they leave open to the states. The United States Constitution leaves a great vacant space in the field of government, and each state undertakes to fill this space with a constitutional structure, using its own methods for establishing and changing this structure. A state's constitution is the supreme law of the state for all matters which fall outside the national jurisdiction or which are not forbidden to the states. It also may duplicate the national jurisdiction in significant areas over which states and the nation have concurrent powers, as in taxation or liquor regulation. In the end, the citizen may meet more overlappings than gaps of government in this constitutional duality.

Variety of lengths

The state constitutions offer a wide variety of subject matter and arrangement, along with an approximate similarity in the statement of fundamental rights and powers. They are longer than their forerunners of the Revolutionary period, when Virginia based its government on a constitutional document of fifteen hundred words. Professor Alfred de Grazia has graphed the trend towards longer state constitutions in American history, demonstrating a marked increase in length for the period from 1776 to 1910. The pattern is not clear for the constitutions adopted thereafter, although the longest for the entire span from 1776 to the middle of the twentieth century was adopted in 1921.[4] The constitutions vary in length from an estimated 7,600 words for Vermont, to an estimated 106,000 words for Alabama. Georgia wins a dubious honor with 500,000 words if purely local provisions are counted. Notable for length in addition to Alabama's are those of California, Oklahoma, and Texas. With more than 200,000 words, the Louisiana constitution was the longest for many years, but the 1974 constitution contains less than 35,000 words. Alaska and Hawaii each came into the Union with relatively brief constitutions of approximately 12,000 words. Constitutions which originated in the Victorian period "are much like the mansions of the time—massive, rambling

[4] Alfred de Grazia, "State Constitutions—Are They Growing Longer?" *State Government* 27 (April 1954), pp. 82–83.

and adorned with gingerbread."[5] The age of the various state constitutions is shown in Table 5–1.

The longer the constitution, the more likely it is that it contains legislative minutiae or deals with transitory matters. The long constitutions mentioned, as well as many others, are not limited in coverage to

Table 5–1. General Information on State Constitutions

State or other jurisdiction	*Number of constitutions*	*Dates of adoption*	*Effective date of present constitution*	*Estimated length (number of words)*	*Number of amendments*	
					Proposed	*Adopted*
Alabama	6	1819; 1861; 1865; 1868; 1875; 1901	1901	106,000	497	326
Alaska	1	1956	1959	12,000	12	11
Arizona	1	1911	1912	18,500	141	77
Arkansas	5	1836; 1861; 1864; 1868; 1874	1874	40,170	[a]	53
California	2	1849; 1879	1879	68,000	667	392
Colorado	1	1876	1876	40,190	147[b]	53[b]
Connecticut	4	1818(c); 1965	1965	7,959	5	4
Delaware	4	1776; 1792; 1831; 1897	1897	22,000	[a]	83
Florida	6	1839; 1861; 1865; 1868; 1885; 1968	1969	21,286	15	10
Georgia	8	1777; 1789; 1798; 1861; 1865; 1868; 1877; 1945	1945	500,000	1,016	767
Hawaii	3	1950; 1958; 1968	1968	11,904	41	38
Idaho	1	1889	1890	22,280	125	85
Illinois	4	1818; 1848; 1870; 1970	1971	17,500	0	0
Indiana	2	1816; 1851	1851	11,120	52	29
Iowa	2	1846; 1857	1857	11,200	41	36[d]
Kansas	1	1859	1861	14,500	93	65[d]
Kentucky	4	1792; 1799; 1850; 1891	1891	21,500	47	20
Louisiana	10	1812; 1845; 1852; 1861; 1864; 1868; 1879; 1898; 1913; 1921; 1974	1975	35,000	0	0
Maine	1	1820	1820	20,000	143	123[e]
Maryland	4	1776; 1851; 1864; 1867	1867	37,300	199	160
Massachusetts	1	1780	1780	36,000	115	97
Michigan	4	1835; 1850; 1908; 1963	1964	19,867	13	6
Minnesota	1	1858	1858	20,080	186	100
Mississippi	4	1817; 1832; 1869; 1890	1890	25,742	106	37

[5] Dishman, *State Constitutions*, p. 1.

Table 5–1. *Continued*

State or other jurisdiction	Number of constitutions	Dates of adoption	Effective date of present constitution	Estimated length (number of words)	Number of amendments Proposed	Adopted
Missouri	4	1820; 1865; 1875; 1945	1945	33,260	52	37
Montana	2	1889; 1972	1973	11,250	0	0
Nebraska	2	1866; 1875	1875	19,975	238	164
Nevada	1	1864	1864	17,270	117	70
New Hampshire	2	1776; 1784[f]	1784	12,200	135[f]	61[f]
New Jersey	3	1776; 1844; 1947	1947	16,030	23	17
New Mexico	1	1911	1912	26,136	185	88
New York	5	1777; 1822; 1846; 1849; 1894	1894	47,000	249	172
North Carolina	3	1776; 1868; 1970	1971	17,000	5	5
North Dakota	1	1889	1889	31,470	[a]	90
Ohio	2	1802; 1851	1851	30,000	195	110
Oklahoma	1	1907	1907	63,569	196	85
Oregon	1	1859	1859	23,000	284	143
Pennsylvania	4	1776; 1790; 1838; 1873; 1968[g]	1873; 1968	24,750	9	6
Rhode Island	1	1843[c]	1843	21,040	79	42
South Carolina	6	1776; 1778; 1790; 1865; 1868; 1895	1895	45,740	430	417
South Dakota	1	1889	1889	24,000	161	82
Tennessee	3	1796; 1835; 1870	1870	15,150	34	19
Texas	5	1845; 1861; 1866; 1869; 1876	1876	54,000	343	218
Utah	1	1896	1896	20,990	103	60
Vermont	3	1777; 1786; 1793	1793	7,600	200	44
Virginia	6	1776; 1830; 1851; 1868; 1902; 1970	1971	8,000	2	2
Washington	1	1889	1889	26,930	103	61
West Virginia	2	1863; 1872	1872	22,970	74	42
Wisconsin	1	1848	1848	17,966	127	98[d]
Wyoming	1	1889	1890	23,170	67	36
American Samoa	2	1960; 1967	1967	5,000	9	5
Puerto Rico	1	1952	1952	9,338	6	6

[a] Data not available.
[b] Information only available from 1912 to present.
[c] Colonial charters with some alterations, in Connecticut (1638, 1662) and Rhode Island (1663), served as the first constitutions for these states.
[d] Amendments nullified by Supreme Court. Iowa: three on procedural grounds; Kansas: one; Wisconsin: two.
[e] One adopted amendment will not become effective until the legislature enacts further legislation.
[f] The constitution of 1784 was extensively amended, rearranged, and clarified in 1793. Figures show proposals and adoptions since 1793.
[g] Certain sections were revised by limited convention.

Source: The Book of the States, 1974–75, p. 23.

fundamental principles but are used for purposes of authorizing or preventing all sorts of practices which in early days were unheard of or were left to the discretion of legislators. Until its 1974 revision, the Louisiana document regulated miscellaneous minor matters concerning local government and public administration, devoting 4,032 words to delineation of the powers, duties, mode of selection, and other matters pertaining to the Board of Commissioners of the Port of New Orleans, with special attention to the subject of bond issues. In addition, it named two Mississippi River bridges for the late Huey P. Long, and proclaimed his birthday a legal holiday forever. The Alabama constitution puts rigid limitations on local tax rates and, in consequence, has been amended frequently to provide needed taxing power for local jurisdictions. Distrust of legislatures is manifest in many constitutional details of prohibition and procedure. And court action or decision may be overruled by the constitutional process, as when a California amendment validated a primary election plan which the judiciary had rejected.

Concern for minutiae

The natural growth of government and the problems of government partly account for the expansion of the contents of constitutional texts. But straight-jacket provisions sometimes get into these basic documents in response to the whims or pressure of groups, organizations, and sections. Examples are Oklahoma's constitutional requirement that all public schools must teach the "elements of agriculture, horticulture, stockfeeding, and domestic science," the Florida ban on taxation of incomes, the New York requirement that the state's forest preserve be "forever kept as wild forest lands," and guarantees in many states against loss of legislative representation by rural units regardless of population status.

Features and Contents of State Constitutions

American state constitutional systems have much in common. Their fundamental documents reflect common features in essential matters despite a wide diversity of detail and language. Most constitutional texts start with a preamble, stating broad purposes and in many cases invoking divine guidance: "We the people of Alaska, grateful to God . . . ." Hawaii's constitution takes note in the preamble of its unique heritage: "We the people of the State of Hawaii, . . . mindful of our Hawaiian heritage, . . . and with an understanding heart toward all the peoples of the earth . . . ." As in the national Constitution, the preamble is the introduction to provisions of rights and powers, usually a collection of glittering generalities, rather than an actual statement of rights and powers.

Common features

More common than the preamble is a statement, bill, or declaration of rights, partly duplicating the provisions of the first ten amendments of the national Constitution. This feature of state constitutions, however, takes first place in historical importance and is incorporated in the main texts rather than attached in the form of amendments. It sometimes appears immediately after the preamble. Its provisions are designed, in part, to prevent state and local authorities from interfering with the individual freedoms of worship, speech, press, assembly, and petition; to safeguard private property rights; and to insure fair or proper trial and treatment of accused persons. Some old-fashioned bills of rights, as in the constitutions of Kentucky and Tennessee, provide superfluous sermons on popular sovereignty and natural rights, even asserting or implying a doctrine of revolt against abusive and arbitrary exercise of governmental power. There are also examples of modern additions to bills of rights, as in the Montana provision that "laws for the punishment of crime shall be founded on the principles of reformation and prevention." The essential points of the state bills of rights are embodied in vital traditions. Those vital traditions afford the best possible guarantee that the governments will abide by the constitutional rules. Furthermore, the Fourteenth Amendment of the national document requires that every state respect certain fundamental rights and freedoms regardless of its own written constitution.

Bill of rights

Every state constitution provides for a structure or framework of government. In general or specific terms, it outlines three branches of government: legislative, executive, and judicial. It sets forth powers, functions, and limitations for these branches and authorizes ways or means for putting men and money to work to carry on their functions. It provides for separation of powers combined with a system of interbranch checks. It has clauses or sections on such subjects as taxation and finance, administrative agencies and departments, suffrage and elections, county and city government, public education and state institutions, state lands and property, conservation, privileges and responsibilities of corporate enterprise, law enforcement, the state militia, etc. Provision of a process for amendment or revision is a usual constitutional feature. It is also common among many states, as already indicated, to have a body of miscellaneous provisions and amendments embedded in the constitution, thus making the fundamental document read more like a code of legislative statutes than a statement of the organic basis of law and government.

Framework of government

The *Model State Constitution* of the National Municipal League has influenced the development of state constitutional revision since the publication of the first edition of that work in 1921. The governmental structure in the sixth and latest edition (1963) is compared with that of a "typical" state constitution in Figure 5–2 .This "model" fills only a few pages and contains nine articles of subject matter; a final tenth article provides a "schedule" of transition from the old to the new constitutional order. This document reflects the work and thought of political scientists

Model State Constitution

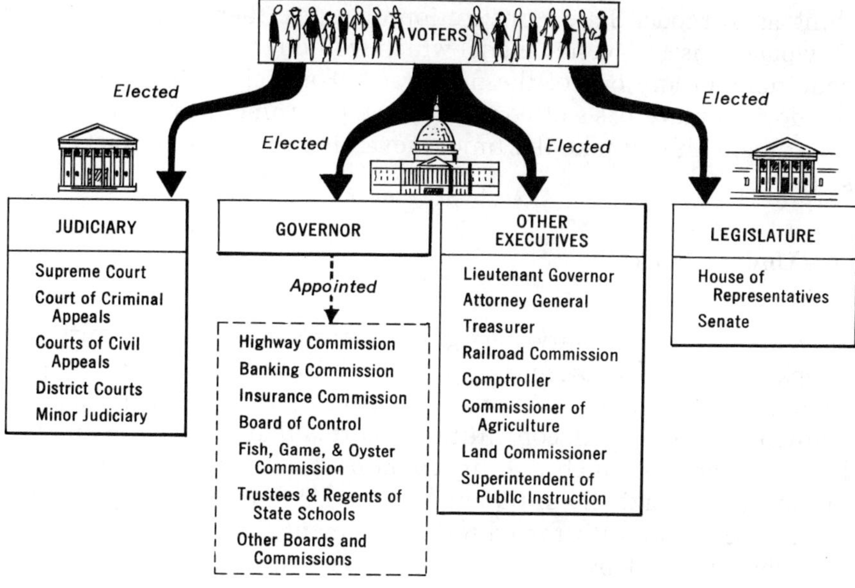

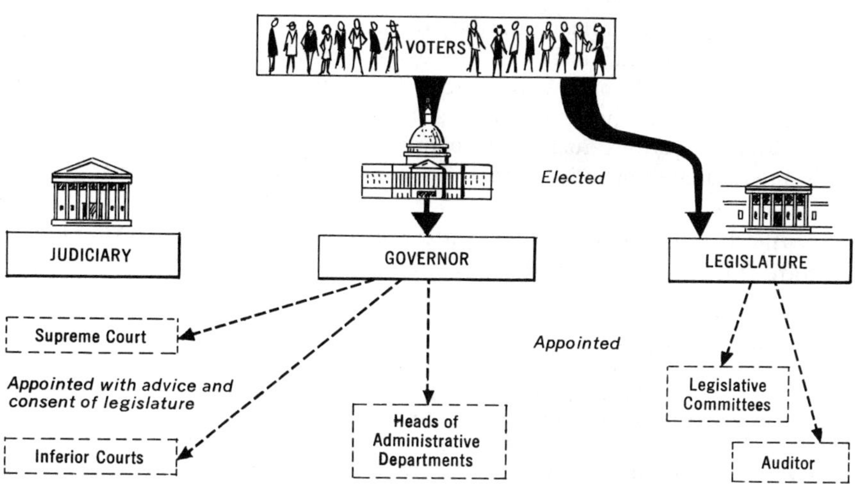

Figure 5–2. Comparison of Typical State Constitution and Model State Constitution. *Source:* Adapted from Model State Constitution, 6th ed., National Municipal League and the Texas Constitution.

and administrators as well as of lawyers and laymen. As the preface to the model constitution points out, "Strictly speaking there can be no such thing as a 'Model State Constitution,' because there is no model state." Obviously it is a suggested model which would require adaptation to fit the conditions of any one of the fifty states. For a closer acquaintance with the documentary basis of constitutional government in actual operation, the student should take the time to examine the constitution of his own state.

State Constitutions Under Attack

Widespread criticism

Students of contemporary state government approach unanimity in their attacks on the obsolescence of state constitutions and their support for thorough-going revision. After a committee of distinguished legal scholars studying the New York constitution reported that it was "literally amazed by the extent to which . . . [it] contains hollow phrases, defective provisions, and creakingly antiquated policies,"[6] *The New York Times* reinforced the report with the editorial statement that the state constitution was characterized by "haphazard arrangement, slipshod and confusing phraseology, relics of long-gone fears, verbosity, frustrated efforts to fit law to new circumstances, a testimonial to the force of inertia."[7] The late Professor Kimbrough Owen wrote of the long-winded 1921 Louisiana constitution:

> A layman who starts out to study the Louisiana Constitution . . . is confronted with a Herculean task. . . . The document will trip, entangle, infuriate and then exhaust him. The difficulties presented to the inquiring citizen include the vast detail, the dispersion of subject matter, confusing terminology, inconsistencies, errors, references to other legal documents, informal amending procedures, duplication of material, contradictions and omissions.[8]

A critique of the Florida state constitution by Professors Dauer and Havard found both its draftsmanship and its provisions for Florida govern-

[6] Inter-Law School Committee, *Report on the Problem of Simplification of the Constitution to the New York Special Legislative Committee on the Revision and Simplification of the Constitution*, Staff Report No. 1 (April 1958), p. 330, as quoted in David Fellman's "What Should a State Constitution Contain?" in W. Brooke Graves, ed., *Major Problems in State Constitutional Revision* (Chicago: Public Administration Service, 1960), p. 140.

[7] *New York Times*, June 2, 1958. © 1958 by *The New York Times Company*. Reprinted by permission.

[8] "The Need for Constitutional Revision in Louisiana," *Louisiana Law Review* 8 (November 1947), pp. 1–104, as quoted by Fellman in Graves (ed.), *Major Problems in State Constitutional Revision*, pp. 140–141.

ment to be sadly defective. The discovery of more than 200 errors of spelling and grammar by a casual count in the Florida Constitution, while of no great import in itself, was said to be indicative of many more serious deficiencies.[9] Many other individual state examples could be cited, but the final report of the (Kestnbaum) Commission on Intergovernmental Relations made a general indictment of state constitutions, concluding that ". . . many State constitutions restrict the scope, effectiveness and adaptability of State and local action. These self-imposed constitutional limitations . . . have frequently been the underlying cause of State and municipal pleas for Federal assistance."[10]

Details rather than fundamentals

Probably the most common criticism of state constitutions is failure to adhere to the axiom that constitutions should be confined to fundamentals. Defining fundamentals should involve some latitude, to be sure, but few would accept as really fundamental the South Dakota constitution's authorization for a twine and cordage plant at the state penitentiary, the South Carolina clause defining what constitutes a "durable hard surface" street in the city of Greenville, or the Texas constitutional provision for the popular election of the inspector of hides and animals. The tendency to legislate details into the constitution seems to result from an unwillingness to trust future legislatures to make even minor decisions concerning their government. A member of the Illinois Constitutional Convention of 1870 chided his colleagues on this point:

> It is assumed that when we depart from this hall all the virtue and all the wisdom of the state will have departed with us. We have assumed that we alone are honest and wise enough to determine for the people the ordinary, and in many instances even the most trivial, questions affecting the public welfare; as if the mass of people of the state of Illinois were not as competent hereafter to select others that are honest and capable as they were to select us.[11]

Effects of excessive detail

What are the effects of this common state practice of incorporating statutory details into the "fundamental law"? Professor David Fellman does not hesitate to judge the results as bad, and summarizes his arguments as follows:

> Excessive constitutional detail is bad for many reasons. It solidifies the entrenchment of vested interests. It makes temporary matters permanent. It

[9] Manning J. Dauer and William C. Havard, "The Florida Constitution of 1885—A Critique," *University of Florida Law Review* 8 (Spring 1955), p. 12.

[10] Commission on Intergovernmental Relations, *A Report to the President for Transmittal to the Congress* (Washington, D. C.: U. S. Government Printing Office, 1955), p. 37–38.

[11] Quoted by Walter F. Dodd, *State Government*, 2d ed. (New York: Appleton-Century-Crofts, 1928), p. 96.

> deprives state legislatures and local governments of desirable flexibility and diminishes their sense of responsibility. It encourages the search for methods of evading constitutional provisions and thus tends to debase our sense of constitutional morality. It makes frequent recourse to the amending processes inevitable. It hinders action in time of special stress or emergency. It stands in the way of healthy progress. It blurs the distinction between constitutional and statute law, to the detriment of both. It creates badly written instruments full of obsolete, repetitious, misleading provisions. Above all, it confuses the public, and in fact makes it certain that few will ever bother to read the state constitution. This is extremely unfortunate, since one of the main purposes of a constitution is to educate the public in first principles. How can the people be expected to respect a constitution they never read, and which may in fact be altogether unreadable. . . .[12]

The previously mentioned "forever wild" provision in New York's constitution prohibiting the removal of any trees from the state's forest preserve led to two separate constitutional crises before ski trails could be constructed in the area. Two amendments were necessary—one in 1941 permitting "not more than twenty miles of ski trails thirty to eighty-eight feet wide on the north, east and north-east slopes of Whiteface Mountain," and another in 1947 to provide for skiing on Peter Gay Mountain. Loss of flexibility to meet new problems was emphasized by Governor Driscoll in addressing the New Jersey Constitutional Convention of 1947. He warned:

> When legislation is permitted to infiltrate a constitution, it shackles the hands of the men and women elected by the people to exercise public authority. The longer a constitution, the more quickly it fails to meet the requirements of a society that is never static.[13]

Obsolescence: language and provisions

Criticisms of obsolescence extended not only to obsolete *language* (such as continued use of "doth," "hath," and "dwelleth" in the New Hampshire Constitution, and reference to citizens as "subjects"), but also to obsolete *provisions*. Archaic offices of county and township, such as justice of the peace and constable, are perpetuated in the constitutional granite of many states. Salary limits placed in many constitutions are completely obsolete today. Constitutions are cluttered with deadwood clauses related to street railway construction, dueling, Civil War disabilities, slavery, hereditary privileges, and the powers of San Francisco in connection with the 1915 World Fair, to name only a few.

As colorful as lists of outmoded constitutional clauses are, the more far-reaching criticisms of state constitutions are those which cite their

[12] Fellman, in Graves (ed.), *Major Problems in State Constitutional Revision*, p. 146.
[13] *Record of the New Jersey Constitutional Convention of 1947*, vol. I (Trenton, 1947), p. 7.

failure to deal with many contemporary problems of government. Tremendous population growth and mobility and the sudden arrival on the scene of sprawling metropolitan areas have complicated the tasks of state and local government in ways hardly imagined by the rural framers of most state constitutions. The radical nature of the change is illustrated by former governor LeRoy Collins' statement, "Florida's population in my lifetime will have shifted from eight out of ten in rural to eight out of ten in urban areas."[14] The executive article comes in for special criticism for its failure to deal with the growth of public administration and modern managerial demands on state and local chief executives. Urbanization is a development that many state constitutions simply made no provision for in the representative structure of the legislature. Constitutional provisions for local government structure and boundary lines fail to deal with the current problem of a rootless and mobile population. Who could have envisioned the need for states to go into the metropolitan water supply business? And, perhaps most serious of all, nineteenth-century constitutional articles on taxation and finance fail to deal with the demands of twentieth-century public finance. The accelerating pace and volume of change and its constitutional impact are expressed in Vermont Governor Deane C. Davis' inaugural statement: there has been "more change, more cataclysm, more invention, more progress and more deterioration than ever happened in any previous fifty years."[15]

Failure to deal with contemporary problems

Related to all of these criticisms is the charge that the amending procedure is unreasonable in many states—either much too easy or much too difficult. This is a question which can best be discussed in connection with constitution making and remaking, a subject to which we now turn.

Amendment procedures

Constitution Making and Remaking

As stated previously, our constitutions are political documents; it follows inevitably that constitution making is a highly political enterprise. The mythological image of high-principled men, an assembly of demi-gods, engaged in a selfless operation of translating abstract precepts into constitutional articles, is no more appropriate for describing a constitutional convention than it is for describing a state legislature or a city council. Constitutions help lay the ground rules for politics, and it is only natural that they should become a prize to be competed for by the various interests

The politics of constitution making

[14] *Fortune* 15 (March 1958), p. 30.

[15] Quoted from his 1971 inaugural address in Albert L. Sturm, *Trends in State Constitution-Making: 1966–1972*, p. 4. The original quotation came from *Newsweek* writer Kenneth Crawford.

making up society. The strong desire of particular groups to write into a constitution their own point of view or policy may be good or bad, depending on the student's own values. But it is important here as an essential factor in understanding constitutions. The predominant political interest of one group of constitution makers is revealed in the story told about a prominent rural member of the Tennessee Constitutional Convention of 1870. He stopped at a country store to buy cheese and crackers for the road.

> "Well, John, whar you been?"
> "Oh, I've been to Nashville—writing the new state constitution."
> "Well, what does it do?"
> "Derned if I know—but it shore gives the damn Yankees a fit."[16]

The American commonwealths virtually possess the constituent power under the federal system of independent unitary states; they are free within the framework of republican institutions to go their own way in making and modifying their constitutions. Collectively, the states exhibit evolution and diversity in the exercise of this constituent power. The state constitutions adopted during the war for independence were chiefly the work of legislatures or other revolutionary assemblies. Connecticut and Rhode Island adapted their colonial charters to constitutional purposes with few changes. Massachusetts started with a provisional arrangement, but in 1780 became the first state in the Union to establish a constitution through the combination of adoption by an elected convention and ratification by popular vote. Massachusetts' example was followed in launching the national Constitution. The method had the blessings of Jefferson and became the prevailing practice among the states. Old states have used it for acquiring new constitutions, and states in the making have used it to meet congressional requirements for admission to the Union. This method is one of the ways for revising or amending constitutions. Albert Sturm estimates that at least 224 constitutional conventions have been convened by the states from national inception through 1972.

Evolution and diversity

There are various ways of putting conventions into operation and making their work effective. A few conventions since the Civil War have been endowed with the power to promulgate constitutional provisions without popular ratification. In the present century, the 1913 and 1921 Louisiana constitutions and the 1902 Virginia constitution were not submitted to the voters.

The usual method for calling a constitutional convention is for the state legislature to provide for submitting the question to the voters in an election. Such a referendum is mandatory every ten years in Alaska, Hawaii, and Iowa, and at longer intervals in several other states. The

[16] Joe Hatcher, "Politics," in The Nashville *Tennessean,* April 23, 1962. By permission of the author.

Alaska constitution requires the secretary of state to place on the ballot the question: "Shall there be a constitutional convention?" if, during any ten-year period, there has not been a constitutional convention. In 1970 he worded the question as follows: "Shall there be a constitutional convention as required by the Constitution of the State of Alaska?" The voters approved, 39,911 to 34,472. Opponents went to court with the contention that voters were misled into believing a convention was required by the constitution; the Alaska Supreme Court agreed and invalidated the vote.[17] Another referendum was held in November 1972, and the convention call was rejected, 55,389 to 29,192. Most of the states have constitutional provisions for legislative action to secure an election on calling a convention. Such provisions are absent from a few state constitutions, but legislatures nevertheless have exercised a sort of inherent authority to provide for election of a constitutional convention and have been sustained therein by the state supreme court. Some constitutions restrict the legislatures as to when and how to call a convention election, such as requiring a two-thirds affirmative vote, passage at two successive sessions, or limiting the frequency of such action. The variety of methods in the fifty states is shown in Table 5–2.

Calling a constitutional convention

Table 5–2. Provisions Concerning Constitutional Conventions

	Procedure for calling constitutional convention			*Popular ratification of convention proposals*
State or other jurisdiction	*Vote required in legislature*[a]	*Approval by two sessions*	*Referendum vote*	
Alabama	Maj.	No	ME	ME
Alaska	Maj.[b]	No	MP	MP
Arizona	Maj.	No	MP	MP
Arkansas	Maj.[c]	No	MP	MP
California	2/3	No	MP	MP
Colorado	2/3	No	MP	ME
Connecticut	2/3[b]	No	ME	ME
Delaware	2/3	No	MP	X
Florida	[d]	. . .	MP	MP
Georgia	2/3	No	None	MP
Hawaii	Maj.[b]	No	MP	MP[e]
Idaho	2/3	No	MP	MP
Illinois	3/5[b]	No	[f]	MP
Indiana	Maj.[c]	No	MP	MP
Iowa	Maj.[b]	No	MP	MP

[17] *Boucher* v. *Bomhoff*, 495 P. 2d 77 (1972), reported in Albert Sturm, *Trends*, pp. 19–21.

Table 5–2. *Continued*

State or other jurisdiction	*Procedure for calling constitutional convention*			*Popular ratification of convention proposals*
	Vote required in legislature[a]	*Approval by two sessions*	*Referendum vote*	
Kansas	2/3	No	MP	MP
Kentucky	Maj.	Yes	MP[g]	X
Louisiana	Maj.[c]	No	MP[h]	X[h]
Maine	2/3[i]	No	None	ME
Maryland	Maj.[b]	No	ME	MP
Massachusetts	Maj.[c]	No	MP	X
Michigan	Maj.[b]	No	MP	MP
Minnesota	2/3	No	ME	[j]
Mississippi	Maj.	No	None	X
Missouri	Maj.[b]	No	MP	MP
Montana	2/3[b]	No	MP	ME
Nebraska	3/5	No	MP[k]	MP
Nevada	2/3	No	ME	X
New Hampshire	Maj.[b]	No	MP	[l]
New Jersey	Maj.[m]	No	MP	MP
New Mexico	2/3	No	MP	MP
New York	Maj.[b]	No	MP	MP
North Carolina	2/3	No	ME	ME
North Dakota	Maj.	No	MP	ME
Ohio	2/3[b]	No	MP	MP

ME—Majority voting in election.

MP—Majority voting on the proposition.

X—There appears to be no constitutional or general statutory provision for the submission of convention proposals to the electorate in these states, but in practice the legislature may provide by statute for popular ratification of convention proposals in specific instances.

Y—Popular ratification required but no provision for size of vote.

[a] The entries in this column refer to the percentage of elected members in each house required to initiate the procedure for calling a constitutional convention.

[b] The question of calling a convention must be submitted to the electorate every 10 years in Alaska, Hawaii, Iowa, New Hampshire; every 16 years in Michigan; every 20 years in Illinois, Maryland, Missouri, Montana, New York, Ohio and Oklahoma. Connecticut may submit question to the electorate after 10 years and must submit it after 20 years.

[c] In the following states, the constitution does not provide for the calling of a constitutional convention. Legislative authority to call such a convention has been established in practice in Arkansas, Indiana, Louisiana, and Texas by court decisions and precedents; in Pennsylvania by statute; in Rhode Island by advisory opinion of the court; and in Vermont by the opinion of the Attorney General. In Massachusetts the legislature exercises an unchallenged assumption of this power.

[d] The power to call a convention is reserved to petition by the people.

Table 5–2. *Continued*

State or other jurisdiction	*Procedure for calling constitutional convention*			*Popular ratification of convention proposals*
	Vote required in legislature[a]	*Approval by two sessions*	*Referendum vote*	
Oklahoma	[b]	No	MP	MP
Oregon	Maj.	No	MP	X
Pennsylvania	Maj.[c]	No	MP	MP
Rhode Island	Maj.[c]	No	MP	MP
South Carolina	2/3	No	ME	X
South Dakota	3/4	No	MP	[n]
Tennessee	Maj.[o]	No	MP	MP
Texas	Maj.[c]	No	MP	MP
Utah	2/3	No	ME	ME
Vermont	Maj.[c]	No	MP	Y
Virginia	2/3	No	MP	MP
Washington	2/3	No	ME	ME
West Virginia	Maj.	No	ME	ME
Wisconsin	Maj.	No	MP	X
Wyoming	2/3	No	ME	Y
American Samoa	[p]	. . .	. . .	ME[q]
Guam	. . .	. . .	. . .	. . .
Puerto Rico	2/3	No	MP	MP
Virgin Islands	Maj.[r]	No	MP	ME

[e] Majority must be 35 percent of total votes cast at general election; or at a special election, the majority must be 30 percent of the number of registered voters.

[f] Majority voting in election or 3/5 voting on issue.

[g] Must equal 1/4 of qualified voters at last general election.

[h] 1921 convention call was ratified by the electorate after enactment by the legislature. The document itself was not. The current convention call was by legislative act only. The act calls for ratification by the electorate.

[i] 2/3 of those voting.

[j] 3/5 voting on question.

[k] Must be 35 percent of total votes cast at election.

[l] 2/3 voting on question.

[m] The constitution does not provide for the calling of a constitutional convention. A convention was called, however, by legislation which was submitted to the people by referendum.

[n] Submitted to voters in a special election in a manner to be determined by the convention.

[o] The convention may not be held more than once in six years.

[p] Convention called by governor at 5-year intervals. Delegates elected by county councils.

[q] Approval of Secretary of the Interior required.

[r] The convention may not be held more than once in 5 years.

Source: The Book of the States, 1974–75, p. 20.

The question of calling a convention may also be put to the voters in certain states by an initiative petition. This device permits a certain number or percentage of the voters to propose an amendment or constitutional convention and requires action by the electorate to be rejected.

If, by one of these methods, a constitutional convention is called for, members of the convention are then elected, generally from legislative districts, but sometimes with the addition of a limited number from the state at large. Frequently, able men are more willing to serve in a constitutional convention than in a legislature, the rationale being that they can contribute to the formulation of the basic laws and yet not sacrifice the amount of time legislative service entails. While efforts are usually made to minimize the role of party politics in constitutional conventions, this may result not so much in nonpartisanship as in a kind of "honor system" of bipartisan equality, as in Missouri in 1943 and New Jersey in 1947. The Missouri constitution specifies that one Republican and one Democrat shall be chosen from each of the senatorial districts and fifteen at-large delegates agreed upon by the state party committees. Of the fifteen at-large delegates, seven were Democrats, seven were Republicans, and one was a self-styled "anti-New Deal Democrat" who, significantly, was selected to be president of the convention. New Jersey's efforts for party equality came through informal party agreement rather than through constitutional directive. The Michigan constitutional convention of 1961–62 was dominated by Republicans, ninety-nine delegates to forty-five, as a result of a landslide partisan victory at the polls. Only in the Detroit metropolitan area did the Democrats win, forty-one to fifteen, and elsewhere the Democrats were almost shut out, eighty-four to four.[18] The Connecticut constitutional convention of 1965, on the other hand, followed the principle of bipartisan equality, with seven members of each party elected from each of six districts, thus dividing the eighty-four delegates equally between the two parties.[19] Sturm concludes that partisan election of delegates was more common during the period from 1938 to 1968; seven of the twelve conventions called between 1966 and 1973 used the nonpartisan basis.[20]

Convention personnel

Party politics

The much debated question of whether constitutional conventions are "above politics," especially party politics, is the focus of an interesting six-state study by Swanson, Kelleher, and English.[21] Convention delegates

[18] Three vacancies occurred later and were filled by Democrats appointed by Democratic Governor Swainson. *See* Sturm, *Trends*, pp. 45–47.

[19] Karl A. Bosworth, "1965 Constitutional Convention: Its Politics and Issues," *Connecticut Government* 19 (March 1966), p. 1.

[20] Arkansas, Hawaii, Illinois, Maryland, New Mexico, North Dakota, and Tennessee. In New Jersey an equal number was elected from each of the two major parties. Law suits were required to settle the partisanship issue in Illinois (1969) and Montana (1971).

[21] Wayne R. Swanson, Sean A. Kelleher, and Arthur English, "Socialization of Constitution-Makers: Political Experience, Role Conflict, and Attitude Change," *The Journal of Politics* 34 (February 1972), pp. 183–198. The data came from a comparative study of six

Table 5–3. Delegate Attitudes Toward the Process of Constitution Making in Six States

	I. "Constitutional conventions are as political as anything else."		*II. "A constitutional convention is special and above party politics."*		*III. "Party loyalty is a strong influence in convention voting."*	
	Agree (Realist)	*Disagree (Idealist)*	*Agree (Realist)*	*Disagree (Idealist)*	*Agree (Realist)*	*Disagree (Idealist)*
New York						
Pre-convention	39%	61%	50%	50%	53%	47%
Post-convention	70	30	32	68	75	25
Illinois						
Pre-convention	45	55	46	54	41	59
Post-convention	69	31	13	87	75	25
Maryland						
Pre-convention	37	63	60	40	12	88
Post-convention	27	73	66	34	3	97
Hawaii						
Pre-convention	45	55	63	37	17	83
Post-convention	44	56	62	38	8	92
New Mexico						
Pre-convention	17	83	81	19	17	83
Post-convention	21	79	71	29	5	95
Arkansas						
Pre-convention	32	68	55	45	7	93
Post-convention	32	68	38	62	2	98

Source: Adapted from Wayne R. Swanson, Sean A. Kelleher, and Arthur English, "Socialization of Constitution-Makers: Political Experience, Role Conflict, and Attitude Change," *The Journal of Politics* 34 (February 1972), p. 189. By permission of the publisher.

were interviewed before and after the convention session to determine which of the two conflicting views they held on convention operation: (1) The "idealized" view or the "statesman" model (decision making on the basis of rational, nonpartisan, disinterested choice, viewed as quite distinct from normal state politics) and (2) The "realistic" view or the "legislative" model (conventions as mere extensions of normal legislative politics, clearly and properly responsive to interest groups, political parties, and political leaders). As reported in Table 5–3, the majority of delegates

Comparative study of delegate attitudes

state constitutional conventions (in New York, Illinois, Maryland, Arkansas, Hawaii, and New Mexico) directed by Elmer E. Cornwell, Jr., and Jay S. Goodman. For a complete study of the Maryland convention, *see* Swanson, Cornwell, and Goodman, *Politics and Constitutional Reform: The Maryland Experience, 1967–1968* (Washington, D.C.: Washington Center for Metropolitan Studies, 1970).

in the six states saw the convention in "idealistic–statesman" terms, and held to this view throughout the session. About one-third of the delegates, however, moved toward the "realist" position, especially in the New York and Illinois conventions. The authors' own views were that the New York and Illinois conventions experienced crucial partisan cleavages, but Maryland, New Mexico, Hawaii, and Arkansas appeared to avoid partisan conflicts for the most part.

Conventions are customarily unicameral and thus avoid the problems and delays of two-house deadlocks. They are also free from the check of executive vetoes. A convention may meet in a legislative chamber of the state capitol at a time when the legislature is not in session, and may split its session into two periods with a recess to provide time for study and consultation. The tradition of holding the convention in the state capital was broken by New Jersey in 1947 when the constitutional convention met on the campus of Rutgers University in New Brunswick. Delegates were said to enjoy greater insulation from the "statehouse politics" of Trenton because of their retreat behind the ivy-covered walls. Alaska followed this example and convened its constitutional delegates on the campus of the University of Alaska, five frozen miles from Fairbanks, and some 500 miles from the capital city of Juneau. The unusual protections of mid-Alaska in mid-winter could hardly be duplicated, however, in the constitutional deliberations of other American states.[22] Sturm's study of twelve conventions found all were funded by legislative appropriation, ranging from a low of $224,000 for Rhode Island to $10 million for New York. Arkansas and North Dakota were close to the median of $600,000. The average length of the twelve conventions was about seven months, excluding the Rhode Island convention which convened in 1964 and did not officially adjourn until 1969.

Physical setting

Funding

A constitutional convention is essentially similar to a regular law-making body in methods of organization and procedure, with important committees performing much of the actual work. Convention deliberations normally stimulate less parliamentary maneuvering and obstructive tactics than one sometimes observes in a legislature, although these deliberations are nonetheless subject to the pressure of groups, parties, and sectional interests from within and without. The delegates to a convention are not likely to be swamped with details and local matters, which too often plague the members of legislative assemblies.

Procedure

The work of a convention, as a rule, is cut out for it in the official call. The call may provide for consideration of only a certain number of

[22] John P. Wheeler, Jr., *The Constitutional Convention: A Manual on Its Planning, Organization and Operation* (New York: National Municipal League, 1961), and John E. Bebout and Emil J. Sady, "Staging a State Constitutional Convention," in Graves (ed.), *Major Problems in State Constitutional Revision*, pp. 67–85.

specified subjects, for unlimited power to write a new constitution, or for general power to revise or rewrite a constitution subject to specific reservations. Attempts to set limits to its activity in this manner may be ignored by the convention itself. Still, except in the case of a territory achieving statehood, every constitutional convention is primarily concerned with revision and modernization rather than with sweeping changes in the fundamentals of government. Any drastic break with constitutional traditions would only invite rejection of the proposals by the voters at the election on ratification. Conventions not infrequently receive criticism for doing too little rather than too much; i.e., for omitting meritorious proposals lacking appeal to voters.

Preconvention commissions

Constitutional conventions of modern days have come increasingly to recognize their need of research and reference staffs. It has seemed advisable in a number of cases to have a commission set up in advance of the convention to explore the whole subject of state constitutions and constitution making in order to supply the convention delegates with useful information and even recommendations for their guidance. The commission may make use of research experts in the fields of law, political science, local government, and public administration. The Alaska Statehood Committee served as the preparatory commission for that state and farmed out the research job to the Public Administration Service, a private consulting group. A New York commission in 1956 hired its own staff of researchers and consultants. The published findings of these bodies not only provide valuable service for convention members and committees but also prove beneficial in stimulating an informed public interest in constitutional problems.

Constitutional commissions

Several states have undertaken important constitutional revision by creating commissions to function in lieu of conventions, seeking thereby the advantages of the convention method without the trouble and expense of assembling such a large body. This method permits compactness and expertness of study and deliberation. It attracts less press and radio coverage while the work is in progress, although the final offerings come under public gaze when submitted for ratification. Use of the commission has come into prominence in recent years, partly because of successful experiments in Georgia and New Jersey.[23] The New Jersey legislature in 1941 created a Constitutional Revision Commission to prepare a new draft for a century-old document which had been changed by only four amendments since 1875. The resulting draft, as modified by the legislature, incurred the opposition of Mayor Frank Hague's political machine of Jersey City and failed to be ratified at the polls. But the movement for revision

[23] *See* B. M. Rich, "Convention or Commission," *National Municipal Review* 37 (March 1948), pp. 133–139.

continued, and a constitutional convention met in 1947 under the joint encouragement of Republican Governor Alfred E. Driscoll and the Democratic leader, Mayor Hague. The convention proposal was overwhelmingly approved by the voters and took effect on the first day of 1948. In 1943 the Georgia legislature created a commission, headed by Governor Ellis Arnall, to formulate a draft to replace a constitution cluttered up with more than three hundred amendments. The commission's proposal was modified by the legislature in 1945 and ratified the same year by a vote of two to one. The revision, like the work of a typical convention, fell short of the wishes of reformers, although it improved the basis of local government, abolished the poll-tax requirement for voting, and reduced the voting age to eighteen. The Georgia Supreme Court upheld the right of the people to adopt a complete revision of their constitution even though it was not submitted to them by a convention as specified in the 1877 constitution.[24]

Table 5–4. Use of Constitutional Conventions and Constitutional Commissions 1938–1972 (By Date Created)

	Constitutional Conventions			*Constitutional Commissions*		
Period	*Unlimited*	*Limited*	*Total*	*Study*	*Preparatory*	*Total*
1938–1950	5	3	8	8	0	8
1951–1955	2	3	5	3	0	3
1956–1960	1	3	4	11	2	13
1961–1965	4	1	5	17[a]	6	23
1966–1972	9	3	12	23[a]	4	27

[a] Two of these bodies had both study and preparatory responsibilities.

Source: Albert Sturm, *Trends in State Constitution-Making: 1966–1972*, p. 30.

By the 1970s the constitutional commission, in two principal forms —study and preparation commissions—had become the most significant recent development in effecting both minor and major changes in state constitutions. From 1966 to 1972, Sturm identified 38 constitutional commissions operative in 31 states; 9 commissions were created in 1969; and Illinois had 3 commissions during this period. The growing popularity of the constitutional commission (*see* Table 5–4) is probably the result of its acceptability to state legislators who prefer the greater control over commissions' recommendations than is possible or customary to hold over the constitutional convention. Florida in 1969 became the first state to provide for constitutional commissions in the constitution itself, rather than only on a statutory basis.

Growing popularity of commissions

[24] *Wheeler* v. *Board of Trustees,* 37 S. E. 2d 322 (1946).

The method of initiating proposals for constitutional change by petition is similar to the method of initiating legislation by petition, which it has paralleled as a twentieth-century development, notably in the West. Oregon adopted it in 1902, and since then it has spread to about a dozen other states. To put a proposed amendment before the electorate in this manner, a petition for such action must bear the signatures of a specified proportion or number of voters. Such a requirement might be 10 percent of the votes as in the last election for a justice of the supreme court in Oregon, a flat minimum of 20,000 signatures as in North Dakota, or 3 percent of the vote cast for governor in the preceding biennial election as in Massachusetts. (*See* Table 5–5.)

Amendments proposed by initiative petition

Most of the hundreds of amendments of state constitutions in force today originated through legislative proposal. This method has proved the most convenient and workable for making minor changes or adding one or two amendments at a time, while conventions have seemed more suitable for overhauling constitutions. Many western states have not adopted new constitutions since becoming states but have added many scores of amendments through legislative proposal as well as a few through initiative petition. (*See* Table 5–1.) All but one of the states have constitutional arrangements for legislative proposal of amendments to the voters. New Hampshire stands alone in restricting proposals to the convention process and, at the other extreme, Delaware permits passage by two successive legislatures with a two-thirds majority to put amendments into effect without further action. Among the other forty-eight states the constitutional requirements vary widely as to procedure and house majorities necessary to submit amendments to the electorate. (*See* Table 5–6.) About one-third of these states require passage of a proposal at two successive regular sessions, one state insisting upon a two-thirds majority each time. The others permit submission of proposals by action at a single session, more than half of them requiring a two-thirds or three-fifths majority of both houses. There are other restrictions, such as limiting the frequency of proposals or the number per session. Louisiana requires that proposals be introduced within the first twenty-one days of a session, except in case of an emergency and then only by a vote of two-thirds of the elected members. Custom and tradition also affect the feasibility of legislative preoccupation with constitutional change. Virginia voters adopted an extensively revised constitution in 1970, as drafted not by a convention, but by the Virginia General Assembly.

Amendments proposed by legislative action

Ratification by the electorate is normally the final step in putting constitutional amendments or revisions into effect, with most states requiring ratification of amendments proposed by legislative action or initiative petition. Many states also have constitutional provisions prescribing the popular ratification of convention offerings, and the others customarily

Ratification

Table 5–5. Constitutional Amendment Procedure: By Initiative

State or other jurisdiction	*Size of petition*	*Referendum vote*
Arizona	15% of total voters for Governor at last election	Majority vote on amendment
Arkansas	10% of voters for Governor at last election including 5% in each of 15 counties	Majority vote on amendment
California	8% of total voters for Governor at last election	Majority vote on amendment
Colorado	8% of legal voters for Secretary of State at last election	Majority vote on amendment
Florida	8% of total votes cast in 1/2 of the congressional districts and 8% of the total votes cast in the state in the last election for presidential electors	Majority vote on amendment
Illinois[a]	8% of the total votes cast for candidates for Governor at last election	Majority voting in election or 3/5 voting on the issue
Massachusetts	3% of total vote for Governor at preceding biennial state election, no more than 1/4 from any one county	30% of total voters at election and majority vote on amendment
Michigan	10% of total voters for Governor at last election	Majority vote on amendment
Missouri	8% of legal voters for Governor at last election in each of 2/3 of the congressional districts in the state[b]	Majority vote on amendment
Montana	10% of the qualified electors of the state; to include at least 10% of the qualified electors in each of 2/5 of the legislative districts	Majority vote on amendment
Nebraska	10% of total votes for Governor at last election including 5% in each of 2/5 of the counties	Majority vote on amendment[c]
Nevada	10% of total voters who voted in 75% of the counties and 10% of the voters who voted in the entire state at the last general election	Majority vote on amendment in two consecutive general elections
North Dakota	20,000 electors	Majority vote on amendment
Ohio	10% of electors which must include 5% of voters for Governor at last election in each of 1/2 of the counties	Majority vote on amendment
Oklahoma	15% of legal voters for office receiving highest number of votes in last general state election	Majority voting in election[d]
Oregon	8% of the total votes for Governor at last election	Majority vote on amendment
South Dakota	10% of total votes for Governor in last election	Majority vote on amendment
Wyoming	15% of those who voted in last general election and resident in at least 2/3 of the counties of the state	Majority of those voting in the preceding general election
Virgin Islands	Not less than 10% of qualified voters of the Territory	Majority vote on amendment at next general election

[a] People may petition to amend only the Legislative Article (Article IV).

[b] Legislature is empowered to fix a smaller percentage.

[c] Votes cast in favor of amendment must be at least 35% of total vote at election.

[d] If amendment is voted on at general election, ratification is by majority voting in election. If it is voted on at a special election, ratification is by majority vote on the amendment.

Source: The Book of the States, 1974–75, p. 22.

Table 5–6. Constitutional Amendment Procedure: By the Legislature

State or other jurisdiction	*Legislative vote required for proposal*[a]	*Approval by two sessions*	*Ratification by electorate*	*Limitations on the number of amendments submitted at one election*
Alabama	3/5	No	MA	None
Alaska	2/3	No	MA	None
Arizona	Maj.	No	MA	None
Arkansas	Maj.	No	MA	[b]
California	2/3	No	MA	None
Colorado	2/3	No	MA	None[c]
Connecticut	[d]	[d]	MA	None
Delaware	2/3	Yes	None	None
Florida	3/5	No	MA	None
Georgia	2/3	No	MA	None
Hawaii	[e]	[e]	MA	None
Idaho	2/3	No	MA	None
Illinois	3/5	No	[f]	None[c]
Indiana	Maj.	Yes	MA	None
Iowa	Maj.	Yes	MA	None
Kansas	2/3	No	MA	5
Kentucky	3/5	No	MA	2
Louisiana	2/3	No	MA[g]	None
Maine	2/3[h]	No	MA	None
Maryland	3/5	No	MA	None
Massachusetts	[i]	Yes	MA	None
Michigan	2/3	No	MA	None
Minnesota	Maj.	No	ME	None
Mississippi	2/3[h]	No	MA	None
Missouri	Maj.	No	MA	None
Montana	[j]	No	MA	None
Nebraska	3/5	No	MA[k]	None
Nevada	Maj.	Yes	MA	None
New Hampshire	3/5	No	[l]	None
New Jersey	[m]	[m]	MA	None
New Mexico	Maj.[n]	No	MA[n]	None
New York	Maj.	Yes	MA	None
North Carolina	3/5	No	MA	None
North Dakota	Maj.	No	MA	None
Ohio	3/5	No	MA	None
Oklahoma	Maj.	No	ME[o]	None
Oregon	Maj.	No	MA	None
Pennsylvania	Maj.	Yes[p]	MA	None

Table 5–6. *Continued*

State or other jurisdiction	*Legislative vote required for proposal*[a]	*Approval by two sessions*	*Ratification by electorate*	*Limitations on the number of amendments submitted at one election*
Rhode Island	Maj.	Yes	[q]	None
South Carolina	2/3	Yes[r]	MA	None
South Dakota	Maj.	No	MA	None
Tennessee	[s]	Yes	ME[t]	None
Texas	2/3	No	MA	None
Utah	2/3	No	MA	None
Vermont	[u]	Yes	MA	None
Virginia	Maj.	Yes	MA	None
Washington	2/3	No	MA	None
West Virginia	2/3	No	MA	None
Wisconsin	Maj.	Yes	MA	None
Wyoming	2/3	No	ME	None
American Samoa	3/5	No	MA[v]	None
Guam[w]	——	——	——	——
Puerto Rico	2/3[x]	No	MA	3
TTPI[y]	——	——	——	——
Virgin Islands	2/3	No	MA	None

MA—Majority vote on amendment.

ME—Majority vote in election.

[a] In all states not otherwise noted, the figure shown in this column refers to percentage of elected members in each house required for approval of proposed constitutional amendments.

[b] General Assembly limited to three; no limit on number of initiative proposals.

[c] Legislature may not propose amendments to more than six articles at the same session in Colorado; Illinois: three articles.

[d] Majority vote in each house in two sessions or 3/4 vote in each house in one session.

[e] Approval by 2/3 vote in each house in one session or by majority in two successive sessions.

[f] Majority voting in election or 3/5 voting on amendment.

[g] If five or fewer political subdivisions of the state are affected, majority in state as a whole and also in affected political subdivision(s) are required.

[h] Two-thirds of those voting on issue in each house; Mississippi: should include not less than a majority elected to each house.

[i] Majority of members elected sitting in joint session.

[j] Two-thirds of total combined membership of both houses.

[k] Votes cast in favor of amendment must be at least 35 percent of total vote at election.

[l] Two-thirds of voters on amendent.

[m] Three-fifths of all members of each house; or majority of all members of each house for two successive sessions.

(Table footnotes continued on page 133)

accept ratification of convention drafts as necessary and proper practice. South Carolina and Mississippi further require that popular ratification of legislative proposals be reinforced with subsequent passage by the legislature to make constitutional changes effective.

Ratification elections are sometimes crucial, and the constitutional work of a legislature or convention may come to nought unless a statewide campaign is launched to explain the issues to the voters. New York and other states have experienced rejection of revision proposals at the polls. The recent trend is toward the utilization of citizen organizations, leaders, and experts to secure ratification. Such groups actively supported ratification of new constitutions in Missouri in 1945, New Jersey in 1947, and Michigan in 1963. The spade work of such groups is no less significant than the spade work performed in advance of the drafting of the proposals.

The final draft of a constitutional convention is usually submitted for acceptance or rejection as a whole at the polls. Through technical requirement or convention decision, however, proposals may be passed upon separately, as is normally the case with amendments presented by the legislative or petition process. Of a group of amendments offered separately, one may pass, while another may fail. A simple majority is adequate for popular ratification or constitutional changes in most states. But there are a few exceptions, as in Minnesota, where the majority for ratification of an amendment must be a majority of those voting in the elec-

---

[n] Amendments dealing with certain sections on elective franchise and education must be proposed by 3/4 vote of the legislature and ratified by 3/4 vote of the electorate and 2/3 vote in each county.

[o] The legislature, by 2/3 vote, may require a special election on amendments. If the amendment is voted upon at a special election, ratification is by a majority vote on the amendment. The legislature may amend certain sections of the constitution relating to the Corporation Commission by simple majority vote, without popular ratification.

[p] Consecutively elected.

[q] Three-fifths of voters on amendment.

[r] Final approval in legislature by majority of quorum after popular ratification.

[s] Majority members elected, first passage; 2/3 members elected, second passage.

[t] Majority of all citizens voting for Governor.

[u] Two-thirds vote Senate, majority vote House, first passage; majority both houses, second passage. Since 1910, amendments may be submitted only at ten-year intervals.

[v] Approval by Secretary of the Interior required.

[w] The Guam legislature has no authority to amend the "Organic Act." Action to amend can be accomplished only by the U .S. Congress.

[x] If proposed amendment is approved by a 2/3 vote in the legislature, it is submitted to voters at a special referendum; if approved by a 3/4 vote in the legislature, the referendum is held at next general election.

[y] The Congress of Micronesia has no authority to amend or change an order of the Secretary of the Interior, but it may petition and request the Secretary to do so.

Source: The Book of the States, 1974–75, p. 21.

tion; in Illinois, where a proposed amendment is adopted if approved either by a majority of the electors voting in the election or by two-thirds of the electors voting on the amendment; and in Tennessee, where a legislative proposal must be ratified by a majority equal to the majority cast for governor. Such a requirement is an arithmetical handicap for the amendment, since voters are normally more attracted to names of persons of prominence on the ballot than to impersonal propositions. Under such conditions, much more than a simple majority must be cast for a constitutional proposal in order to put it over. Attesting to the effectiveness of such an arithmetical handicap, Tennesseans until 1953 were able to claim the dubious honor of having the "oldest unamended constitution in the world."[25]

Proliferation of constitutional detail through a flood of amendments goes on unabated in some states. In the half-century since the adoption of the Louisiana constitution in 1921, that state has adopted 494 amendments—over three-fourths of the 659 proposed amendments placed before the voters. In 1962 a bumper crop of 32 amendments out of 48 proposed was adopted by Louisiana voters in a single election, but the voters revolted in the general election of 1970 and rejected 53 amendments—22 general and 31 local. One of the arguments for adoption of a new Georgia constitution in 1945 was the fact that the old 1877 constitution had been amended 301 times in 68 years. Yet pressure for local-application amendments led to 655 changes in 25 years for the 1945 Georgia constitution. California's 1879 constitution has been amended 358 times.

Probably the best recent example of a state in persistent search of some way—almost *any* way—to achieve a comprehensive revision of an outmoded constitution is the long-term effort of Kentucky revisionists.[26] The need for constitutional reform was cited as early as 1924 in the report of a firm of management consultants, Griffenhagen and Associates; the constitution was labeled, in subsequent reports, as an anachronism and "a detailed 1890 plan for a static Kentucky." The rural interests of 1890 quite naturally dominated the writing of the constitution, and their values persisted long after Kentucky's urban pressures began to call for a more flexible, fundamental law. The most commonly mentioned weaknesses were constitutional salary limitations, an antiquated system of lower courts, a limit on the legislature to one sixty-day session every two years, the requirement that the governor share executive authority with several other elected officials, and the virtual absence of local home rule.

Kentucky's frustrating revision efforts

All efforts at major constitutional revision prior to 1966 came to

[25] *See* William H. Combs, "An Unamended State Constitution: The Tennessee Constitution of 1870," *American Political Science Review* 32 (June 1938), pp. 514–524.

[26] *See* David A. Booth and John E. Reeves, "Kentucky Unorthodoxy," *National Civic Review* 55 (June 1966), pp. 310–316.

grief. The constitution is quite specific concerning the revision process, discouraging some of the more ingenious expedients attempted in states with more ambiguous constitutional language. Only the two following methods are specified. (1) The general assembly may propose amendments subject to the approval of the voters at the next general election; but there is the proviso that only two may be submitted for vote in any election, no amendment may relate to more than one subject, and if defeated, it cannot be submitted again for five years. (2) A constitutional convention requires affirmative action by two successive legislative sessions and approval by majority vote at the next election for state officers. The majority is made more difficult to obtain by requiring that the vote must equal one-fourth of the votes cast in the preceding general election.

Methods of formal change

Constitutional reformers were dissatisfied with the results of the first method, and major efforts to secure a constitutional convention failed in 1931, 1947, and 1960. In 1964 a new chapter in the seemingly hopeless yet endless story of constitution revision attempts in Kentucky was initiated when, on the suggestion of Governor Edward T. Breathitt, the legislature created a fifty-member "Constitution Revision Assembly." The assembly was *not* a constitutional convention—it was an agency of the Legislative Research Commission to carry on a program of study, review, and examination of the state constitution. It was something of a cross between an elaborate commission and an unconventional convention, and the membership was very distinguished. Over a period of twenty-two months, they worked diligently and produced a proposed new constitution —not dramatic in innovation, but likely to be considered by most students of state and local government as a vast improvement over the old document.

An unconventional convention?

After considering several alternative courses of action in attempting to secure adoption of the proposed constitution, the 1966 General Assembly rejected the more legally sure but politically doubtful alternatives in favor of a bold attempt to "activate" a so-called "revolutionary section" of the Bill of Rights. The draft was submitted directly to the people in November 1966, without further procedural ado. Following successful tests in circuit court and in the Kentucky Court of Appeals, the referendum was held on schedule under a previously unused section of the Bill of Rights which bestows on the people "at all times, an inalienable and indefeasible right to alter, reform or abolish their government in such manner as they may deem proper." Some proponents of constitutional revision applauded the proposed constitution but worried about the method chosen to implement it, fearing that the procedural issue would obscure the substantive issue.

Initiation by "revolutionary" action

Although Governor Breathitt gave a strong endorsement to the proposed constitution and there seemed to be little opposition in the early months before the election, the usual pattern of opposition forces began to arise as the election neared. Strongest opposition was found among local government officials whose elective constitutional positions would have been made appointive. The most common opposition arguments concentrated fire on increased state power in general, and increased administrative power in particular. The proposed constitution was rejected by an overwhelming majority of Kentucky voters, with more than a ten to one negative vote in many counties and no lower than a two to one negative vote in any county. Thus, another chapter ended in the frustrating efforts of constitutional reformers to "move state and local government into the twentieth century." The difficulty of achieving constitutional modernization by the popular referendum route and the lack of popular appeal of many reform dogmas were again demonstrated.

Overwhelming rejection in 1966

Other Methods of Constitutional Change

Constitutions grow in ways other than through formal amendment. Every state constitution is subject, more or less, to modification and development through judicial interpretation, statutory amplification, and official custom or usage. And state constitutions, like state statutes, may become invalid through national action, as has happened with respect to questions of suffrage and issues of racial discrimination.

Change through judicial interpretation

A constitutional provision can be and sometimes is judicially interpreted to permit governmental action which, according to an earlier judicial interpretation, it prohibited; and for all practical purposes the constitution means what the judges say it means. Kentucky courts, for example, finally ruled that long-standing constitutional restrictions on salaries could be interpreted in the light of an increased cost-of-living. More often, however, the scope of a provision is extended by gradual interpretation to accord with the governmental needs of a developing community. The courts of our states and of the United States in dealing with matters fundamental to our governmental system constitute, in effect, continuing constitutional conventions.

Legislative elaboration

Insofar as a constitution deals with matters which are bound to be rendered obsolete by rapidly changing conditions, an easy mode of change becomes essential to the functioning of government. One such method is through ordinary legislation designed to supplement or even to circumvent the intent of the framers. Oregon in 1956 submitted to the voters an amendment designed to alter the constitutional prescription of a $1,500 annual salary for its chief executive. The salary appropriated for the governor for 1955 was just ten times the constitutional limit, indicating legislative recognition that the salary set by the constitution was obviously out of keeping with current economic conditions. If, on the other hand, the constitution sets up a skeletal framework, allowing legislative discretion in the prescription of details and in the adaptation to changing conditions, the role of the legislature is no less important. The 1947 constitution of New Jersey, for example, vests the judicial power in a "Supreme Court, a Superior Court, County Courts and inferior courts of limited jurisdiction." Then it provides that the "inferior courts and their jurisdiction may from time to time be established, altered or abolished by law." Perusal of the 1956 study of *State Intermediate Appellate Courts* published by the Institute of Judicial Administration demonstrates in this one area of government the degree to which legislative enactments augment constitutional provisions, even determining such fundamental matters as jurisdiction. Footnotes to the study include more references to statutes than to constitutions.

Usage also has its impact upon the constitution, modifying its provisions or determining the way in which provisions will be applied or even judicially construed. An example of commingling forces for constitutional change is afforded by *Schardein* v. *Harrison et al.*[27] In that case Kentucky's Court of Appeals, applying the principle that "legislative or executive construction of constitutional provisions adopted and acted upon with acquiescence of the people for many years is entitled to great weight with the courts," permitted an incumbent to succeed himself despite constitutional ambiguity as to whether he was eligible to do so. Party practices obviously determine the way in which the government operates in many instances without being covered wholly in constitution or law. A broad view of the constitution, which would hold that the constitution consists of everything determinative of the structure and functioning of the government, would take into account changes wrought in the fundamental law by practice. Many analysts believe modification of a constitution by means other than formal amendment is at least as important as modification by formal amendment.

Understanding state constitutions

Reading over a state constitution, then, will provide one with only a limited understanding of its meaning. As with the United States Constitution, it is necessary to have an acquaintance with a number of significant statutes, court opinions, and practices of executive officials in order to know what the constitution means today. In other words, we must look at the state government both as a whole and in terms of its operating parts to get a valid view of its constitutional features. The foundation takes on meaning according to the superstructure which it sustains, and it must not

[27] 18 S. W. (2d) 316 (1920).

be pictured in isolation or detachment. Hence, all the chapters of this text throw light on the meaning of the living state constitutions, and the student should take care to treat this chapter more as an introduction than as a full explanation of the state constitutional system.

SUPPLEMENTARY READINGS

Allen, Tip H., Jr., and Ransone, Coleman B., Jr. *Constitutional Revision in Theory and Practice.* University, Ala.: Bureau of Public Administration, University of Alabama, 1962.

"Constitutions." Continuing article in *The Book of the States.* Lexington, Ky.: Council of State Governments.

Dauer, Manning J., and Havard, William C. "The Florida Constitution of 1885: A Critique." *University of Florida Law Review* 8, Spring 1955, pp. 1–92.

Graves, W. Brooke, ed. *Major Problems in State Constitutional Revision.* Chicago: Public Administration Service, 1960.

Hobbs, Edward H., ed. *Yesterday's Constitution Today: An Analysis of the Mississippi Constitution of 1890.* University, Miss.: Bureau of Public Administration, University of Mississippi, 1960.

Keith, John P. *Methods of Constitutional Revision.* Austin: Institute of Public Affairs, University of Texas, 1949.

National Municipal League, State Constitutional Studies Project. A series of background studies published in 1960 and 1961:

Dishman, Robert B. *State Constitutions: The Shape of the Document.* Rev. ed. 1968.

Baker, Gordon E. *State Constitutions: Reapportionment.*

Rich, Bennett M. *State Constitutions: The Governor.*

Heady, Ferrel. *State Constitutions: The Structure of Administration.*

Rankin, Robert S. *State Constitutions: The Bill of Rights.*

———. Individual state convention studies beginning in 1969:

Cornwell, Elmer E., Jr., and Goodman, Jay S. *The Politics of the Rhode Island Constitutional Convention,* 1969.

Wolf, George D. *Constitutional Revision in Pennsylvania: The Dual Tactic of Amendment and Limited Convention,* 1969.

Connors, Richard J. *The Process of Constitutional Revision in New Jersey: 1940–1947,* 1970.

Meller, Norman. *With an Understanding Heart: Constitution Making in Hawaii,* 1971.

O'Rourke, V. A., and Campbell, D. W. *Constitution-Making in a Democracy.* Baltimore: Johns Hopkins Press, 1943.

Pollock, James K. *Making Michigan's New Constitution.* Ann Arbor: George Wahr Publishing Co., 1963.

Sturm, Albert L. *Trends in State Constitution-Making: 1966–1972.* Lexington, Ky.: The Council of State Governments, 1973.

———. *Thirty Years of State Constitution-Making: 1938–1968.* New York: National Municipal League, 1970.

Temporary Commission on the Revision and Simplification of the Constitution of New York State. *First Steps Toward a Modern Constitution,* New York State Legislative Document No. 58, 1959.

Uhl, Raymond, et al. *Constitutional Conventions: Organization, Powers, Functions and Procedures.* Columbia, S. C.: Bureau of Public Administration, University of South Carolina, 1960.

U. S. Advisory Commission on Intergovernmental Relations. *State Constitutional and Statutory Restrictions upon the Structural, Functional, and Personnel Powers of Local Government.* Washington, D. C.: U. S. Government Printing Office, 1962.

6

Voters and Voting

Voting is an ancient and modern process by which individuals participate in group decisions. By means of voting, officers and lawmakers are selected to govern and policies are adopted to guide officers and lawmakers in governing. Under dictatorial rule, it may be a manipulative technique of satisfying the governed by permitting them to approve what is predetermined or inevitable. In democratic government, it is a process by which a majority decides issues and bestows both power and responsibility upon the few of their own choosing. More citizens take part in voting than in any other phase or feature of democratic government. This mass participation, particularly in America, is centrally regulated by constitutional provisions, statutes, and administrative decrees. Despite centralized red tape and bureaucracy, however, actual voting is decentralized. Polling facilities, in city and country, are distributed among convenient locations in such a way that neighbors cast ballots under the supervision of neighbors.

Voting as a function of government

Until recently it was customary for political science textbooks to state that under our Constitution there is no such thing as a *national* right to vote. In a technical sense this is still true in spite of the trends toward federalization of voting qualifications. Like many other features of American government, voting qualifications are determined separately by each state, subject to an increasing number of important national checks or reservations. The Fifteenth Amendment prohibits the denial of the vote to American citizens "by the United States or by any State on account of race, color, or previous conditions of servitude." The Fourteenth Amendment has been used effectively to reinforce the Fifteenth to protect black voters as participants in primary elections. The Nineteenth Amendment

Chiefly a state constitutional responsibility

prevents suffrage discrimination "on account of sex," and the Twenty-fourth Amendment outlaws the poll tax as a voting requirement in the nomination and election of federal officials. The voting age was lowered to eighteen by the Twenty-sixth Amendment. The Voting Rights Act of 1965 places certain states under severe restrictions concerning racial discrimination in the regulation of voting. According to Article I and the Seventeenth Amendment, voters for senators and representatives in Congress shall in each state "have the qualifications requisite for electors of the most numerous branch of the State legislature." A degree of indirect control over the suffrage is conferred upon Congress by the provision that each branch shall be judge of the "elections, returns and qualifications of its own members."

Development of universal suffrage

The story of suffrage expansion among the American commonwealths parallels the growth of political democracy in the whole Western world. The age of Jackson emphasized the role of the common man and his right to vote without a property qualification. Universal white male suffrage became the vogue in most of the states in this era, although it came about in Rhode Island only after a Dorr's Rebellion jolted the conservative elements to relinquish voting restrictions handed down from colonial times. This general movement toward political democracy more than matched the enfranchisement of men of the middle classes in Great Britain by the epochal Reform Bill of 1832. American blacks and British laboring classes could lay claim to manhood suffrage by 1870; fifty years later the women of these two countries as well as of many others were voting. The right or privilege of suffrage, however, was not made absolute in any state. There were conditions to be met and obstacles to be avoided, as will appear in our subsequent look at voting management and procedure.

Nonvoting

The technical establishment of universal suffrage brought new problems to American governments and electorates. Formidable tasks arose in connection with registering voters and supervising voting, particularly in populous areas with high mobility of many classes of people. Furthermore, there is a significant lack of voting in the United States, particularly in local or minor elections and in places or regions where one party or political faction predominates. Participation in state and local elections is greater when they happen to be coupled with the election of a president. Those who vote for governor in off-year elections ordinarily number from three-fourths to four-fifths the total of those who vote for governor in presidential years. Many potential voters neglect to register or qualify, and many who qualify often fail to go to the polls on election day. Millions who might vote do not vote, even in national elections. The proportion of non-voting is particularly high in some of the southern states. The extent to which Americans fail to exercise their privilege and duty is readily apparent from a contrast between totals of potential and actual voters in a given election.

Studies of nonvoting

Much of what we know about voter participation is based on studies of national elections, and it may or may not hold true in particular state and local elections. An Indiana study re-examines four familiar propositions on voter participation and suggests the generalizations on national samples may require modification at the state and local level.[1] The four propositions tested in Indiana were that voter participation increases with: (1) the competitiveness of the electoral situation, (2) the degree of urbanism of the population, (3) the prestige of the office, and (4) the totality of the election appeal. The first two were found to be "not necessarily so" in Indiana, where during at least one ten-year period close interparty races failed to bring out more voters than less competitive races, and where voter participation was found to be greater in rural areas than in metropolitan areas. Greater voting for offices with higher prestige, such as the president or the governor, than for those with lower prestige, such as the prosecuting attorney, was found to be the practice in Indiana. The number of voters attacked by the strange disease of "voters' fatigue" somewhere between the top and bottom of the ballot was not so large as might be expected. The fourth proposition was also substantiated in Indiana—more people vote in state contests if they are held during a presidential election than if not, but, again, the difference is not so great as one might expect.

Reasons for nonvoting

No fixed set of reasons can be given for nonvoting.[2] Inertia or indifference to voting responsibility is often the case, especially with citizens who have removed to new scenes or regions and have not "learned the ropes." Some fail to vote because they consider it a futile undertaking, assuming that the "machine will win anyway." Studies indicate that persons with "efficacious attitudes" are more likely to vote than those without such attitudes. A person is said to feel efficacious if he believes he can or does have some effect on the political process, and persons of upper socioeconomic status, especially the better educated, males, white persons, and city dwellers, tend to score higher on efficacy.[3] Some avoid elections because of confusion over candidates and issues. Some citizens in one-party states fail to vote in the general election on the ground that its result is predetermined in the party primary. In Mississippi's 1959 gubernatorial

[1] James A. Robinson and William H. Standing, "Some Correlates of Voter Participation: The Case of Indiana," *Journal of Politics* 22 (February 1960), pp. 96–111.

[2] Speculation as to the reasons for our poor voting record continues nonetheless. *See*, for example, Richard M. Scammon, "Why One Third of Us Don't Vote," *New York Times Magazine*, Nov. 17, 1963.

[3] *See* Lester W. Milbrath, *Political Participation* (Chicago: Rand McNally and Co., 1965), for a discussion of these and other variables related to political participation.

election only 57,617 voters went to the polls whereas 441,047 voted in the Democratic primary election determining who was to be a Democratic candidate for governor.

Even when a close race is predicted, large numbers of potential voters will stay away from the polls if they do not feel deeply about the issues. Crowded conditions and inconvenience at the polls sometimes deter urbanites, including laborers whose working time conflicts with voting hours. This problem is partly avoided in Continental Europe by holding elections on Sunday. But the shorter working day for American employees reduces this obstacle, as does the use of voting machines and other efficient methods of handling voters at the polls.

Black voting and nonvoting

Voting by blacks in the South has risen rapidly after many years of official barriers and unofficial harassment, especially during the period between 1890 and 1920. With the invalidation of the white primary in 1944, the last "fool-proof" method of excluding blacks from an effective vote was struck down.[4] As black registration and voting increase in the South, the degree of increase and the political direction of the "black vote" differs sharply both between and within the various states. In Louisiana, for example, Fenton and Vines tested the widely held belief that black registration in the South is concentrated in urban areas and discovered that no clear correlation exists between the degree of urbanism and the extent of black registration.[5] They found that black registration, if anything, is lower in the large urban centers than in rural Louisiana and attributed this to several factors: many urban blacks are rootless and feel little identity with their community or their fellow blacks; their leadership often works at cross purposes; and interest in registration is probably higher in Louisiana rural areas where the election of a sheriff is an important event. On the positive side, Fenton and Vines investigated the religious-cultural variable and the role of local politicians and concluded that both are extremely important in Louisiana. In French–Catholic parishes the percentage of black registration is more than double the percentage in Anglo-Saxon Protestant parishes. They also conclude that where black registration is high, the sheriff has almost invariably been friendly to the idea, and their vote seems to be in his factional camp.

Black voting in Texas falls into two sharply different patterns of vot-

[4] *See* chapter 7 for a discussion of the white primary.

[5] John H. Fenton and Kenneth H. Vines, "Negro Registration in Louisiana," *American Political Science Review* 51 (September 1957), pp. 707–714. For a detailed comparative analysis of black registration in southern states, *see* Donald R. Matthews and James W. Prothro, *Negro Political Participation in the South* (New York: Harcourt, Brace, and World, 1966). *See also* Harry A. Bailey, Jr. (ed.), *Negro Politics in America* (Columbus, Ohio: Charles E. Merrill, 1967).

ing behavior, according to a study by Harry Holloway.[6] In the cities black registration is high—in Austin their percentage has been higher than for the white population—and seems to approach 50 percent generally. The city blacks "form a surprisingly effective, cohesive and stable bloc oriented toward the liberal Democratic candidate, especially if he is strongly pro civil rights. And they decidedly favor candidates of their own race or of Latin (Mexican–American) extraction."[7] A different pattern exists for the rural black, however. Holloway suggests that the rural east Texas black is still behaving under the tradition of "white paternalism" and is politically manipulated in the caste system of race relations which prevails. Registration is encouraged by white officials so long as blacks function as an adjunct to the white vote, but as rural blacks develop some independence, this encouragement would normally disappear. "Paradoxically, then, the freeing of the rural Negro may well mean some drop in Negro registration in the state's rural counties."[8] A similar pattern of rural black voting in Georgia, in alliance with white factions, is described in a study by Bernd and Holland.[9] The first black in the Georgia Senate since reconstruction days was elected in 1962 from an Atlanta district. Whether the findings of the Holloway study, as well as the Louisiana and Georgia studies, would hold true for the 1970s should be the subject for further research.

Civil Rights Acts

New federal help to blacks who had been denied the right to vote was provided in the civil rights acts of 1957, 1960, and 1964, but they involved a milder approach than the Voting Rights Act of 1965. The 1960 legislation relied primarily on court action to eliminate racial discrimination in voter registration, authorizing federal judges to appoint "referees" to determine the voting qualifications of persons local officials refuse to register. Title I of the 1964 Civil Rights Act further expanded the federal government's role, but continued the reliance on court action for effectuation. For federal elections it prohibited denial of the right to vote because of minor errors or omissions on application forms—a frequently used device by some registration officials; it ruled out oral literacy tests; and it made a sixth-grade education presumptive of literacy. The Attorney General was authorized to request three-judge federal courts to hear voting rights suits, making possible immediate appeal to the Supreme Court.

The Voting Rights Act of 1965 grew out of dissatisfaction with the rate of progress in registering blacks, as dramatized by the events in Selma, Alabama, and the march on the state capitol led by Martin Luther King.

[6] Harry Holloway, "The Negro and the Vote: The Case of Texas," *Journal of Politics* 23 (August 1961), pp. 526–556.

[7] *Ibid.*, p. 527.

[8] *Ibid.*, p. 554.

[9] Joseph L. Bernd and Lynwood M. Holland, "Recent Restrictions upon Negro Suffrage: The Case of Georgia," *Journal of Politics* 21 (August 1959), pp. 487–513.

The result was congressional passage of a bill which was a major departure from the past practice of relying predominantly on the courts, by authorizing direct action by federal executive officials without intervening court action. The 1965 Act concentrates on several hard-core states or subdivisions of states, in which fewer than one-half of the adult population were registered or voted in the 1964 presidential election, and which required a literacy, understanding, or good character test. In such areas federal examiners may suspend literacy and other tests which have been used to discriminate against blacks and proceed to register otherwise qualified voters and to protect their rights on election day. Limitations of space prevents more detailed description of the provisions of the Act, but it clearly involves federal displacement of state authority over voting in those areas where there is a long history of disfranchisement of blacks.[10]

Voting Rights Act of 1965

A survey of black registration in six southern states[11] after the first full year of the Voting Rights Act revealed dramatic increases. The Voter Education Project of the Southern Regional Council reported a total of just over 837,000 blacks registered in these states in mid-1965, or less than 30 percent of the black voting-age population. By mid-1966 the number had increased to 1,289,000, or nearly 46 percent of those eligible. During the first year, federal examiners registered voters in twenty-four counties in Mississippi, eleven counties in Alabama, five parishes in Louisiana, and two counties in South Carolina. Of the total increase of over 450,000, close to 124,000 were registered by federal examiners. By 1972 the number of new black voters registered in 11 southern states exceeded 1.5 million. Increased black registration produced increased black voting, and 1966 saw an upsurge in black candidates for office, many of whom were elected.

Increased black registration

Perhaps most symbolic of the voting breakthrough was the election of a black to the potent office of sheriff in Macon County, Alabama, a milestone in that state's history. Blacks were elected to offices in increased numbers in local governments of the South; the eleven-state total increased from less than 100 elected black officials in 1965 to close to 900 in 1972. Equally precedent-shattering was the election of black mayors in the northern cities of Cleveland, Ohio, and Gary, Indiana, in November 1967. In Cleveland, where the black population is estimated at less than 40 percent of the total population, Carl Stokes first won the Democratic nomination over incumbent Mayor Ralph Locher and then defeated Republican Seth Taft, a grandson of President William Howard Taft, by a razor-thin margin. Following these early precedents, more cities elected black mayors; the number was balanced almost equally between southern and non-

10 The Voting Rights Act of 1965 was upheld by the Supreme Court in *South Carolina* v. *Katzenbach*, 383 U. S. 301 (1966).

11 Alabama, Georgia, Louisiana, Mississippi, South Carolina, and Virginia.

southern cities. Los Angeles in 1973 became the largest city to elect a black mayor, when Thomas Bradley unseated incumbent Sam Yorty. In the same year, Atlanta voters replaced Mayor Sam Massell with thirty-five-year-old Maynard Jackson, making Atlanta the seventh major city to elect a black mayor. By 1974, the number of elected black officials in the United States had tripled over the number in office five years earlier, totalling 3,000. Michigan had the greatest number with 194, followed by Mississippi with 191 and New York with 174.

Racial gerrymandering

One of the most publicized efforts of a state to prevent blacks from voting was the action of the Alabama legislature in 1957 in rearranging the boundaries of the city of Tuskegee in such an elaborate manner as to exclude all but four or five of 400 black voters, while not excluding any white voters. In the subsequent *Gomillion* case[12] the U.S. Supreme Court unanimously reversed a lower court ruling and held the Alabama gerrymandering to be an unconstitutional "essay in geometry and geography . . . to deprive colored citizens . . ." of their right to vote in municipal elections. The decision has obvious implications for other types of gerrymandering by state legislatures, making it increasingly difficult to intervene in racial discrimination cases without also intervening in cases of urban–rural discrimination. The Tuskegee decision was thus an important forerunner of the Supreme Court's reapportionment decision in *Baker* v. *Carr* in 1962. In 1964 a black minister and a Tuskegee Institute professor were elected to the Tuskegee city council. In an interesting comparative study of the actual impact of the black vote in Durham, North Carolina, and Tuskegee, William Keech reports more positive results for "legal justice" (just administration of existing laws) than "social justice" (securing changes in unjust laws).[13]

Proposed remedies for nonvoting

Various remedies have been proposed for nonvoting, which is significantly greater in democratic countries than in modern totalitarian dictatorships. Compulsory voting, with penalties for the negligent, is one occasionally offered suggestion. Such remedies have been tried in Australia, Belgium, and a few other small countries with limited success. America is not moving in that direction. Proposals for compulsory voting have been rejected in a few western states, while the North Dakota and Massachusetts legislatures have failed to make use of specific constitutional power to penalize nonvoting. The American theory is that voting should be voluntary to be worthwhile and that it should be encouraged as both a privilege and a responsibility of citizenship. Civic preaching and energetic campaigning have in recent years succeeded in bringing close to seventy

[12] *Gomillion* v. *Lightfoot*, 364 U. S. 339 (1961).

[13] William R. Keech, *The Impact of Negro Voting: The Role of the Vote in the Quest for Equality* (Chicago: Rand McNally, 1968), pp. 106–107.

million voters to the polls in elections for president; however, the number voting fluctuated between 61 and 64 percent of the adult population in the three presidential elections of the 1960s. Voting in many local elections is still extremely scant; it is extremely rare for more than 50 percent of the voters to turn out. The problems of voting and nonvoting must not be viewed in isolation. They are to be examined as important parts of a large governmental process and in relation to a group of problems, including the qualifications of voters, ballots and ballot reforms, nominations and elections, the legal regulation of parties and pressure groups, financing politics, and campaign techniques. There is much time and activity between the individual's act of voting and the establishment in office of persons chosen by his vote to govern. It is essential to look at all aspects of the electoral process. This broad approach was taken in the *Report of the President's Commission on Registration and Voter Participation*, which made a number of suggestions in 1963 for increased voter participation.[14]

Qualifications for Voting

Universal adult suffrage has always been more a theoretical ideal than a reality in American elections. Some of the historic limitations, such as minimum age and residence requirements, underwent extensive revision in the early 1970s at the hands of Congress and the Supreme Court. Until 1970 only a few states[15] had a lower voting age than twenty-one. Congress attempted in the Voting Rights Act of 1970 to lower the minimum voting age to eighteen in all elections—federal, state, local, general, special, and primary. The Supreme Court upheld the new law only as it applied to federal elections, not for state or local elections, leaving registration and voting in a state of dual confusion.[16] A movement for a constitutional amendment, already underway, was given added impetus by this electoral crisis and the Twenty-sixth Amendment was ratified in 1971 by the required 38 states in the record time of three months and seven days. The eighteen-year-old minimum voting age for all citizens at all levels became the law of the land.

The Twenty-sixth Amendment

The rationale for the states' long-standing residence requirements for voting has come under heavy pressure from increasingly mobile Americans in recent years. The idea that new residents are unfamiliar with state and local political issues and should observe a one- or two-year waiting period became less persuasive in its application to national elections. Congress

Reduction of residence requirements

[14] *See Report of the President's Commission on Registration and Voter Participation* (Washington, D. C.: U. S. Government Printing Office, 1963).

[15] Georgia and Kentucky (18), Alaska (19), and Hawaii (20).

[16] *Oregon* v. *Mitchell*, 400 U. S. 112 (1970).

recognized this in the Voting Rights Act of 1970 by reducing to thirty days the residence requirement for voting in presidential elections, and by requiring states to make special provisions for absentee voting and for registering new residents. Although this law applied only to presidential elections, it stimulated the same kinds of pressures that resulted in a uniform age requirement. In 1969, 1970, and 1972 cases[17] the Supreme Court had already made it clear that only a "compelling state interest" justified the exclusion of the franchise of persons. The Court reaffirmed the power of the states to require their voters to be bona fide residents of the state, but denied the relevance of lengthy residence requirements as a test of bona fide residence. With the invalidation of Tennessee's one-year residency requirement in 1972 it seemed clear that a common and short residency requirement for all states and in all elections was inevitable.[18]

Voting residence for students

Passage of the Twenty-sixth amendment enfranchising the eighteen-year-olds added new fuel to a long-time controversy in college communities over the question of residency for college students. Many states specifically state that persons cannot acquire residence for voting purposes while in the state as a student. Many also provide, either by statute or administrative ruling, that students who are already residents of the state must vote at the residence of their parents. Columnist William F. Buckley, Jr., described giving students the right to vote in relatively small towns containing a large university as "playing Russian roulette." He contended that ". . . in the history of college towns, individual student bodies are transitory experiences. They should not be given the power of hit-and-run drivers."[19] As in the case of length of residence, however, the trend is clearly away from the more restrictive statutes and rulings that prevent college students from voting in college towns and cities.

Until passage of the Twenty-third Amendment in 1961, *place* of residence, rather than *length* of residence, denied the residents of Washington, D. C., all voting privileges. Ratification of the Twenty-third Amendment allows the residents of the District of Columbia to elect three electors to the electoral college, but it falls far short of granting full voting rights to D. C. residents. They still have only a nonvoting representative in Congress, and Congress still controls municipal affairs for the voteless residents of the District.

All states require citizenship as a qualification for voting. There is no

[17] *Hall* v. *Beals*, 396 U. S. 45 (1969); *Evans* v. *Corman*, 398 U. S. 419 (1970); and *Dunn* v. *Blumstein*, 92 S.Ct. 995 (1972).

[18] Robert Thornton, "Election Legistlation," *The Book of the States, 1972–73*, pp. 26–27. For an analysis of the function of the residence requirement, *see* W. Ross Yates, "The Functions of Residence Requirements for Voting," *Western Political Quarterly* 15 (September 1962), pp. 469–488.

[19] William F. Buckley, Jr., "Where's a Student's Home?" *Arkansas Democrat*, Oct. 18, 1971.

national restriction on alien suffrage, and aliens were legally permitted to vote in many states until a wave of native American sentiment called for a change in the 1850s. Several states for some years continued to allow voting by aliens who had formally declared the intention of becoming American citizens; only within recent times has Arkansas joined all other states in denying the vote to noncitizens. Moreover, citizenship in all states must be without blemish of conviction of serious crime, although a pardon may restore political privileges. The pardon is not necessary in West Virginia, where their courts have interpreted the phrase, "No person under conviction for . . . ," to mean that once the sentence is served, voting rights are restored. Certain states likewise bar recognized paupers and vagrants from voting, although there are difficulties in determining the facts in the case of persons who are not living in "poor houses" as public charges. In all states the suffrage is denied to the insane and the feeble-minded, but recent studies have raised provocative questions concerning the denial of civil rights to mental patients. In one study[20] a group of patients expressed opinions and interest in political and social issues as readily as the hospital employees did and, ironically, gave little evidence of being "more illogical, inconsistent, or unprepared to fulfill their obligations as citizens than a similar group of individuals who are not identified as emotionally unstable."

Citizenship without tarnish

The educational or literacy test was developed partly as a method of restricting certain groups or classes from voting and partly for positive reasons of securing intelligent voting. Much more education is needed in the modern day than in former times because of the multiplicity of offices, candidates, and complex issues for the voter to consider. By 1970 close to a third of the states had a literacy test, a few of them allowing an alternative in the form of property qualification or an understanding of the principles of republican government. The test prevailed most extensively in the South and East, where there is more consciousness of minority groups or the "newer immigration," but it was found in all sections of the country. Administration of the literacy test was sometimes characterized by arbitrary abuse or discrimination by local officials, who were often partisan political appointees. Included in such misuses of literacy tests have been instances of "passing" uneducated whites and "flunking" college-trained blacks in the South. The use of literacy tests for purposes of racial discrimination came under fire by Congress in the Civil Rights Act of 1964 and the Voting Rights Act of 1965. The "50 percent nonvoting" formula made their suspension automatic for Mississippi, Alabama, Louisiana, Georgia, Alaska, thirty-four counties in North Carolina, and three scat-

Educational test

[20] M. R. Hertz, et al., "A Study of Opinions of Mental Patients on Social and Political Issues," *Journal of Health and Human Behavior* 1 (Winter 1960), pp. 251–58.

tered counties outside the South. Another provision permitted persons educated in American schools in languages other than English—such as the Spanish-speaking Puerto Ricans in New York City—to qualify to vote even though unable to pass the state's English-language literacy test. In addition to these statutory measures, the Supreme Court in 1965 ruled out the use of "understanding tests" where voting registrars are given discretion to determine who has passed or failed.[21] In 1970 Congress supplemented the 1965 law by suspending *all* literacy tests until 1975; this was upheld by the Supreme Court.

Property test

Two vestiges of the property qualification for voting remain. In South Carolina it provides an alternative for persons who cannot meet the literacy test. In a few states only owners of property are allowed to vote on public bond issues or special assessments. Examples of this restriction are found in the West, although universal suffrage was in part the result of a western movement. The denial of the voting privilege to paupers in a few states is the reverse application of the respect for the role of property in government.

The poll tax

The poll tax as a requirement for voting bears a kinship to the property test. It is a per capita tax of something like a dollar or two a year, and it may be cumulative so that one who skips an annual payment has to pay for two years in order to participate in an election. It is an absolute requirement, not a substitute for a property, literacy, or other qualification. The poll tax was adopted throughout the South, during a twenty-year period ending about 1910, as one of the methods for restricting black suffrage. As a few leaders predicted and a few hoped, it proved effective as a vote-reducer for both races. More than half the original poll-tax states abolished the requirement in the first half of the twentieth century, and the resulting increase in the proportion of voting in these states provided an invidious comparison for use by anti-poll-tax forces in efforts to eliminate the restriction in the five states where the tax remained in 1962—Alabama, Arkansas, Mississippi, Texas, and Virginia.

The poll tax as a requirement for voting in federal elections was eliminated by the Twenty-fourth Amendment, passed by Congress in 1962, and ratified by the necessary thirty-eight states in 1963. Of the five states affected by the amendment, Arkansas subsequently repealed the requirement of the poll tax for voting in *all* elections, but the other four retained it as a requirement for state and local elections. Congress came close to attempting an outright ban on the poll tax in all elections when it passed the Voting Rights Act of 1965, but finally settled for a declaration calling on the attorney general to seek court elimination of the poll tax voting requirement in the remaining four states. In the case of *Harper* v.

[21] *Louisiana* v. *United States*, 380 U. S. 145 (1965).

Virginia State Board of Elections[22] in 1966 the Supreme Court did just that, filling in the state and local gap left by the Twenty-fourth Amendment.

The Registration of Voters

General purpose of registration

It is necessary under modern conditions of society to have a system of registration for the double purpose of determining who should vote and providing records of those who should vote. The system in each state is set up through constitutional and statutory provisions along with administrative machinery extending from central state and county officials to functionaries of towns, wards, districts, or precincts. The systems are designed to certify eligible voters and to keep track of such voters by location or residence. Registration managers check qualifications for suffrage and administer literacy tests in most states having such requirements. They make available for use by election officials lists of registered voters at the different polling places.

The method of compiling the lists of registered voters differs among the states and even within a given state. Most states use personal or direct registration, the prospective voter being required to appear in person before the registration board or supervisor to establish his qualifications. A few of the states and less populous jurisdictions use a non-personal or indirect system of registration, registrars being charged with compiling and maintaining the lists of qualified voters. The non-personal method of registration is an obvious convenience for the voter, but it is also an obvious opening for fraud.

Permanent and periodic registration

The states have two general kinds of voter registration. All but a few states have a system of permanent registration in some form. Most of these have this type of registration for all areas and for all elections. The remaining states have periodic registration. A few states vary the registration between areas or between types of election. The term for periodic registration varies widely from Vermont, which requires annual registration, to South Carolina, which has a ten-year registration. All but a handful of states make the voter's permanent registration subject to cancellation for failure to vote at certain specified intervals. A comprehensive survey of the registration patterns in the different states makes it abundantly clear that election administration is not the product of uniform national regulations, but remains a function of state and local governments.

A voter moving from an election unit must transfer his registration to the new area; permanent registration in certain states may be forfeited upon removal or failure to vote through two elections. It is no easy matter

[22] 383 U. S. 663 (1966).

to keep tab on voters who are registered permanently or for a long period. Whatever the form of registration, precautions must be taken to guard against abuses. Otherwise it may be possible for one to vote illegally without serious risk of detection. Registration has become costly and in many jurisdictions burdensome enough to reduce the electorate.

General Problems of Voting

Secrecy: the Australian ballot

The problems of voting have tremendously increased since the Greeks applied the process of casting ballots, or small balls, to express the public choice. The spread of suffrage to the common people brought attention to ways and means of protecting the average voter from direct or indirect coercion, whether by candidates, officials, political bosses, employers, or other persons of power. One step was to end oral, or voice, voting as well as open voting by miscellaneous paper ballots and to adopt a systematic secret ballot. The Australian ballot provided the solution, incorporating new features in the secret ballot, a device which had been known in ancient times and in some of the American colonies. Under the Australian system, each voter on election day receives only one ballot (or set of ballots), which is printed at public expense and which lists all qualified candidates or proposals to be voted for. The ballots are numbered consecutively, private or incomplete ballots are not counted, and no surplus ballots are openly available for fraudulent voting. This system was adopted by Massachusetts in 1888, and subsequently by all states, although South Carolina was the lone exception for many years. Political machines may still sometimes find ways of violating the secrecy or integrity of the ballot in order to check on blocs of controlled voters, but the Australian ballot represents a decided improvement over its predecessors.

Honest counting

Secret voting, to be effective, must be accompanied by fairly conducted elections and an open counting of the returns without manipulation. In 1946 a gun battle at Athens in east Tennessee on election night ensued when a clique of politicians took the ballots from the polling place to the jail for secret counting without the presence of rival watchers. An alert opposition of young returnees from World War II insisted that the votes "be counted as cast." Election violence has not been limited to rural mountaineers, but such measures are rare.

Voting machines

Mechanical voting machines are helpful in regularizing secret voting as well as in facilitating a speedy and accurate tabulation of the results. They remove the problems of spoiled or mutilated ballots and prevent miscellaneous petty frauds. The automatic opening and closing of a curtain for each individual voting operation in the booth make it impossible for one to "stuff the ballot box" without detection. The high initial cost of the machines restricts their use to the more populous areas, although more than half the states have legalized their use.[23] There are old-fashioned city politicians who oppose the installation of voting machines for reasons of their own. Occasional complaints indicate that mechanical voting is not completely fraudproof, and may have simply inspired more sophisticated devices for adapting manipulation to automation. Administration by honest persons is still the ultimate requirement, if corruption is to be entirely avoided. It is essential, of course, to have fair and honest assistance for persons who cannot perform the mechanical operations because of physical infirmity or incapacity.

Absentee voting

Thousands of voters in modern and mobile America are absent from their city, county, or state on election days. To meet this condition, absentee voting has been widely established. The need was first realized during the Civil War, with the taking of a few steps to accommodate the members of the armed forces in the matter of voting. The practice reached great proportions in World War II when Congress and the national government provided cooperative aid to the states in the task of returning votes from the fighting fronts. Most of the states have arrangements for absentee voting, a few providing primarily for persons absent in the armed services. As mentioned earlier in this chapter, the Voting Rights Act of 1970 requires states to make special provisions for absentee voting in presidential elections for voters who cannot vote at a new place of residence. The conditions and methods for absentee voting vary widely among the states. One practice is for an eligible absentee or prospective absentee to apply by affidavit for a ballot during a specified time prior to the election. The absentee voter then marks the ballot, signs an accompanying statement before a notary public, and mails the papers early enough to reach the proper official at his place of registration in time for the ballot to be opened and counted on election day. Mass "solicitation" of absentee ballots by ward heelers opens the door to a variety of shady or fraudulent practices and intimidation of underprivileged voters. Yet the technical safeguards against such fraud and abuse complicate the process, especially for uneducated voters, who often neglect to cast their ballot in this manner.

Many American voters feel burdened with ballot complications, and the intelligent person sometimes finds it difficult to cast an intelligent vote. There are different ways of indicating or emphasizing party nominees on general election ballots. Several states use the Indiana party-

[23] *See* Harold T. Jones, "Electronics in Voting," *National Civic Review* 53 (June 1964), p. 306–310, 337, for a discussion of the prospects for faster, less expensive, more accurate vote counting.

column type. This provides a separate column for all the candidates of one party, with the party name and symbol showing at the top. The voter may mark a designated spot at the top to vote the whole party ticket without going down the column to mark each candidate. One master lever on a voting machine casts such a vote. The party-column ballot facilitates and encourages straight party voting, sometimes blind voting. About a third of the states use the Massachusetts, or office-group, type of ballot, on which the names of all candidates for a particular office are grouped together with the party designation noted for each name. This makes no provision for straight ticket voting by one stroke, since the voter must make a separate mark for each candidate of his choice. There are modifications of these general types, and sometimes ballots, particularly in local elections, may offer the names of candidates without party classification or designation. Some states and districts confront the voter with more than one ballot at the same general election. There may be one for state officers and one or more for other officers or purposes, especially if there is occasion to vote on a bond issue or a constitutional amendment. Tennesseans go to the polls in August of an election year to mark a state ballot for primary nominations and also a ballot for the final election of county officers. More will be said in the next chapter on the subject of voting in primaries.

Ballot complications

The "short ballot" is the aim of a reform movement of fairly long standing for reducing the voter's burden in making his way through the list of candidates and offerings on election day. It is not a superficial paper reform. Supporters of the short ballot have sought to reduce the number of state and local elective offices to a few of importance and responsibility. They emphasize the point that routine and technical positions in government can be better filled by appointment, particularly with the application of merit systems for the selection of civil servants. Studies revealing the advantage to a candidate of having his name near the top of a discouragingly long ballot have given support to the movement.[24] Woodrow Wilson in 1909 became president of the National Short Ballot Organization, which exerted an influence for the next few years and later was merged with the more comprehensive National Municipal League. In consequence of the movement, the ballot has been shortened or prevented from expansion in many states and municipalities. We have always had a short ballot for national officers. But the long ballot to a large extent continues for county government and plagues the voter in other local and state elections. It contributes to non-voting and makes the outcome of elections more subject to the influence of trivial factors. The long ballot is so stabilized in

The short ballot movement

[24] *See* H. M. Bain and D. S. Hecock, *Ballot Position and Voter's Choice* (Detroit: Wayne State University Press, 1957).

legal or constitutional provisions and political traditions that shift to the short ballot is a slow and difficult process. The task of the American voter demands the use of intelligence and information, as will be more abundantly indicated in the following consideration of politics and elections.

SUPPLEMENTARY READINGS

American Council on Public Affairs. *The Poll Tax.* Washington, D. C.: American Council on Public Affairs, 1940.

Bailey, Harry A., Jr., ed. *Negro Politics in America.* Columbus, Ohio.: Charles E. Merrill Publishing Co., 1967.

Bone, Hugh, and Ranney, Austin. *Politics and Voters.* New York: McGraw-Hill Book Co., 1963.

Boskoff, Alvin, and Zeigler, Harmon. *Voting Patterns in a Local Election.* Philadelphia: J. B. Lippincott Co., 1964.

Campbell, Angus, et al. *The Voter.* New York: John Wiley and Sons, 1960.

Childs, Richard S. *Civic Victories.* New York: Harper & Row, 1952.

Council of State Governments. *The Book of the States, 1966–67.* Chicago: Council of State Governments, 1966, pp. 14–34.

Harris, J. P. *Registration of Voters in the United States.* Washington, D. C.: Brookings Institution, 1929.

Keech, William R. *The Impact of Negro Voting: The Role of the Vote in the Quest for Equality.* Chicago: Rand McNally and Co., 1968.

Lubell, Samuel. *The Future of American Politics.* New York: Harper & Row, 1952.

MacKenzie, W. J. M. *Free Elections.* New York: Holt, Rinehart and Winston, 1958.

Matthews, Donald R., and Prothro, James W. *Negroes and the New Southern Politics.* New York: Harcourt, Brace & World, 1966.

McGovney, D. O. *The American Suffrage Medley.* Chicago: University of Chicago Press, 1949.

Milbrath, Lester W. *Political Participation.* Chicago: Rand McNally and Co., 1965.

National Municipal League. *Model Voter Registration System.* 4th ed. Chicago: National Municipal League, 1954.

Ogden, Frederic D. *The Poll Tax in the South.* University, Ala.: University of Alabama Press, 1958.

Porter, Kirk. *History of Suffrage in the United States.* Chicago: University of Chicago Press, 1918.

Price, H. D. *The Negro and Southern Politics.* New York: New York University Press, 1957.

Price, Margaret. *The Negro Voter in the South.* Nashville, Tenn.: Southern Education Reporting Service, 1957.

Ranchino, Jim. *Faubus to Bumpers: Arkansas Votes, 1960–1970.* Arkadelphia, Ark.: Action Research, 1972.

Report of the President's Commission on Registration and Voter Participation. Washington, D. C.: U. S. Government Printing Office, 1963.

Scammon, Richard M., ed. *America Votes.* 6 vols. Pittsburgh: Governmental Affairs Institute, 1956–1966.

7

Parties, Nominations, and Elections

State politics, as distinguished from national politics, is probably considered by many citizens to be in a condition of declining importance against the background of depression, wartime, and space age issues of national policy. The mass media spotlight primarily on national issues involving the presidency, Congress, and federal courts. Such a view runs the risk of ignoring the role and importance of state politics in much the same way that the superficial view of an iceberg might ignore the dominant seven-eighths of the mass submerged beneath the water. Certainly, little or no support for this view may be found in the writings of political scientists in recent years, whose studies reflect a contemporary revival of interest in state and local politics. Professor V. O. Key's *Southern Politics in State and Nation* was a forerunner of many more studies focusing upon politics and party systems in the individual states.[1]

Persistent importance of state politics

[1] V. O. Key, *Southern Politics in State and Nation* (New York: Alfred A. Knopf, 1949). Professor Key's *American State Politics; An Introduction* (New York: Alfred A. Knopf, 1956), includes states outside the South. Illustrative of this revival of interest in state politics would be the following studies: James Anderson, Richard Murray, and Edward Farley, *Texas Politics: An Introduction* (New York: Harper & Row, 1971); Joseph L. Bernd, *Grass Roots Politics in Georgia* (Atlanta: Emory University Research Committee, 1960); Leon D. Epstein, *Politics in Wisconsin* (Madison: University of Wisconsin Press, 1958); John H. Fenton, *Politics in the Border States: A Study of the Patterns of Political Organization, and Political Change, Common to the Border States—Maryland, West Virginia, Kentucky and Missouri* (New Orleans: The Hauser Press, 1957); and *Midwest Politics* (New York: Holt, Rinehart and Winston, 1966); Joseph P. Harris, *California Politics* (Stanford: Stanford University Press, 1955); Herbert Jacob and Kenneth N. Vines (eds.), *Politics in the American States* (Boston: Little, Brown and Co., 1965); G. Theodore Mitau, *Politics in Minnesota* (Minneapolis: University of Minnesota Press, 1960); Dan Nimmo and William E. Oden, *The Texas Political System* (Englewood Cliffs, N. J.: Prentice-Hall, 1971); Daniel

What explains this new interest in state politics? Undoubtedly the frustration of "party reform" groups interested in changing the character of our national party system has led them to an awareness that in many respects we have *fifty* party systems in the United States, rather than a single unified national party system. This, in turn, has led to recommendations that more attention be given to studies of political parties at the state level. Much of the problem of developing "a more responsible two-party system," as recommended in 1950 by the Committee on Political Parties of the American Political Science Association, was traced back to the dominant role of the separate state party organizations. As suggested in chapter 1, American federalism may have withered considerably in the formal constitutional sense, but the strength of state parties continues to give strong life to federalism in practice.[2]

Federalism and state politics

Presidential aspirants in recent years have become painfully aware of the importance of state politics and politicians in their quest for party nomination. A Brookings study of presidential nominating politics at national party conventions reveals that the role of governors in this process has come to be more and more important in recent years. In contrast to 1848, when not a single governor was a delegate to the major party conventions, and to 1908, when not quite one-half of the Republican and Democratic governors served as delegates, more than 70 percent of the Republican and Democratic governors were convention delegates in 1956. Furthermore, of those governors attending the more recent conventions as delegates, about three out of four have been chosen delegation chairmen.[3] Senators and congressmen rarely wield as much influence as governors at the national party conventions.

M. Ogden, Jr., and Hugh A. Bone, *Washington Politics* (New York: New York University Press, 1960); Jim Ranchino, *Faubus to Bumpers: Arkansas Votes, 1960–1970* (Arkadelphia, Ark.: Action Research, 1972); Stephen B. Sarasohn and Vera H. Sarasohn, *Political Party Patterns in Michigan, Wayne State University Studies,* No. 2 (Detroit: Wayne University Press, 1957); Robert Lee Sawyer, Jr., *The Democratic State Central Committee in Michigan, 1949–1959: The Rise of the New Politics and the New Political Leadership, Michigan Governmental Studies,* No. 40 (Ann Arbor: University of Michigan Press, 1960); Allan P. Sindler, *Huey Long's Louisiana: State Politics, 1920–1952* (Baltimore: Johns Hopkins University Press, 1956); Frank J. Sorauf, *Party and Representation: Legislative Politics in Pennsylvania* (New York: Atherton Press, 1963).

[2] For a discussion of the relationship of federalism to political parties, *see* William Buchanan, "Politics and Federalism: Party or Antiparty?" *The Annals of the American Academy of Political and Social Science* 359 (May 1965), pp. 107–115.

[3] Paul T. David, Ralph M. Goldman, and Richard C. Bain, *The Politics of National Party Conventions* (Washington, D. C.: The Brookings Institution, 1960), pp. 97–98. It is doubtful that the conventions of the 1960s and 1970s have changed this picture. This study points out that a governor may control his state delegation actively even if he is not present at the convention. For example, the Arkansas delegates to the Democratic convention in 1952 are said to have waited for word from Little Rock where the governor kept in communication with the various political forces.

One other factor which seems to be stimulating a new interest in state and local politics is a growing feeling among many observers that the traditional image of "bossism," irresponsibility, corruption, and obsession with patronage is not an accurate reflection of present realities. It might be well first to examine this "traditional image" of party politics, constructing it with assistance from such spokesmen as Lord Bryce, George Washington Plunkitt, Elihu Root, and Theodore Roosevelt.[4] Lord Bryce expressed what we might call the "tweedledee–tweedledum concept" of two parties which have no real programmatic differences between them:

Traditional image of party politics: lack of program differences

> Neither party has any clear-cut principles, any distinctive tenets. Both have traditions. Both claim to have tendencies. . . . But those interests are in the main interests of getting or keeping the patronage of the government. . . . An eminent journalist remarked to me . . . that the two great parties were like two bottles. Each bore a label denoting the kind of liquor it contained, but each was empty.[5]

The traditional image of the party organization's obsession for patronage probably reached its peak in the "sillygism" of George Washington Plunkitt, a Tammany Hall leader interviewed by William L. Riordin:

Dominance of patronage

> First, this great and glorious country was built up by political parties; second, parties can't hold together if their workers don't get the offices when they win; third, if the parties go to pieces, the government they built up must go to pieces, too; fourth, then there'll be h—— to pay.
>
> Could anything be clearer than that? Say, honest now, can you answer that argument? . . . When parties can't get offices, they'll bust. They ain't far from the bustin' point right now, with all this civil service business keepin' most of the good things from them. How are you goin' to keep up patriotism if this thing goes on? You can't do it. Let me tell you that patriotism has been dyin' fast for the last twenty years. Before then when a party won, its workers got everything in sight.[6]

In his oft-quoted speech on "invisible government," Elihu Root pictured the party boss in New York as irresponsible and beyond the reach of the voters:

Irresponsibility

> The ruler of the state during the greater part of the forty years of my acquaintance with the state government has not been any man authorized by the

[4] The selection of quotations is the same as used by Sawyer, *Democratic Committee in Michigan*, pp. 76–77, in a more abbreviated form.

[5] James Bryce, *The American Commonwealth*, vol. 2, 2d ed. (New York: The Macmillan Company, 1910), pp. 21, 24, 29.

[6] William L. Riordin, *Plunkitt of Tammany Hall* (New York: Alfred A. Knopf, 1948), pp. 18–19.

constitution or the law; and, sir, there is throughout the length and breadth of this state a deep and sullen and long-continued resentment at being governed by men not of the people's choosing. The party leader is elected by no one, accountable to no one, removable by no one.[7]

Corruption

In addition to the lack of program differences, the dominance of patronage, and irresponsibility, the traditional image of American party politics places strong emphasis on corruption. Theodore Roosevelt once described the boss as

> . . . a man who does not gain power by open means, but by secret means, and usually by corrupt means. Some of the worst and most powerful bosses in our political history . . . made no appeal either to intellect or conscience. Their work was done behind closed doors, and consisted chiefly in the use of that greed which gives in order that in return it may get. A boss of this kind can pull wires in conventions, can manipulate members of the legislature, can control the giving or withholding of office, and serves as the intermediary for bringing together corrupt politics and corrupt business.[8]

A new party politics?

Does this four-fold characterization of American party politics accurately reflect the political realities of the present? One point of view holds that this traditional picture is totally inaccurate because of "a new type of party politics" developing in the United States. The idea that the decline of "bossism" has been followed by the growth of a new party politics characterized by responsibility and concern for issues is found in the recent writing of many political scientists, journalists, and at least one novelist.[9] The ingredients of this new party politics have been summarized by State Chairman Neil Staebler of the Democratic Party of Michigan:

> If I may oversimplify just a little, I'd describe the mainsprings of politics as patronage, money, program and morale. Without minimizing the importance of money and patronage, I would say that the other two, program and morale, which are closely related, are more important.
>
> They are not only more important now; they are becoming steadily more so. There may never be a time when politics can be run without money. . . . But we are in a time of change when the big variable, the big determinant of who will win, the big difference between the Parties is increasingly the difference in Party morale.
>
> This is not necessarily true in every spot. We can all name certain states where patronage is all important. . . . But these areas are shrinking. . . .

[7] Robert Bacon and James B. Scott (eds.), *Addresses on Government and Citizenship by Elihu Root* (Cambridge, Mass.: Harvard University Press, 1916), p. 201.

[8] Theodore Roosevelt, *Theodore Roosevelt: An Autobiography,* 2d ed. (New York: Charles Scribner's Sons, 1925), p. 149.

[9] *See* Edwin O'Connor, *The Last Hurrah* (New York: Bantam Books, 1956), pp. 329–331.

> When the merit system was introduced it gave our political parties a great setback. . . . But it has led to the growth of a new species of Party worker, the volunteer, who works from sheer belief in Party principles and is motivated by this thing I call morale.[10]

Issue- versus job-orientation

In his comparative study of six states in *Midwest Politics,* John Fenton classifies three state party systems as "issue-oriented or programmatic" (Michigan, Wisconsin, and Minnesota), and three others as "job-oriented or traditional" (Ohio, Indiana, Illinois). Issue-oriented parties are motivated primarily by a concern for public policy and a desire to do something about it. The job-oriented parties are concerned primarily with obtaining government jobs and privileges, even though "job-oriented politicians use the issues as means of securing the support of interest groups and through them the votes to win the jobs and contracts."[11] Fenton concludes that several factors contribute to making a party system issue-oriented: (1) strict civil service systems minimizing state and local patronage; (2) repeated defeat of one party, reducing it to an empty shell; (3) well-organized interest groups with the will and nerve to seize control of the moribund party; and (4) party division of the electorate along lines related to modern political, economic, and social problems. Of special interest is Fenton's contention that not only do the more competitive two-party states tend to spend more on welfare and education than the less competitive states, but the issue-oriented political systems spend more than the job-oriented ones.

It is still too early to know whether a totally new species of party politics in the fifty states is developing to replace the traditional system of the past century. Figure 7–1 was inspired by an especially clean state gubernatorial campaign, but the cartoonist was uncertain enough to add a question mark after the caption, "End of an Era?" A recent study of the kinds of incentives that support an urban party organization (Buffalo) concluded that they continue to be "self-oriented" rather than "other-oriented" incentives, and more tangible than intangible.[12] Probably the

[10] Speech delivered to the Women's National Democratic Club, Washington, D.C., April 18, 1955, as quoted in Robert Lee Sawyer, Jr., *The Democratic State Central Committee in Michigan, 1949–59: The Rise of New Politics and the New Political Leadership* (Michigan Governmental Studies, No. 40, The University of Michigan, Ann Arbor, 1960), p. 78.

[11] Fenton, *Midwest Politics,* p. 116.

[12] Peter R. Gluck used the concepts and constructs of "exchange theory" to study incentives for 50 Democratic and 50 Republican precinct committeemen in Buffalo. *See* "An Exchange Theory of Incentives of Urban Party Organization," a paper prepared for delivery at the American Political Science Association, New Orleans, Sept. 4–8, 1973. *See also* Sidney R. Waldman, *Foundations of Political Action: An Exchange Theory of Politics* (Boston: Little, Brown and Co., 1972); and Gordon S. Black, "A Theory of Political Ambition: Career Choices and the Role of Structural Incentives," *American Political Science Review* 66 (March 1972), pp. 144–159.

End of an era ?

Figure 7–1. Jon Kennedy in the *Arkansas Democrat.*

Mixture of old and new

most accurate picture is one which recognizes a mixture, in varying degrees, of the old and the new. Certainly old-time bossism and patronage are not what they used to be, but irresponsibility, corruption, and lack of real policy concern have a persistent quality which cannot easily be dismissed. In any case, the modern student of politics should be familiar with all elements in the mixture.

Party Organization and Operation

Operational complexity

Most votes in American elections are cast for nominees of political parties. Many of these nominees appear on ballots in the general elections as the result of being selected in party primaries. Parties and party organizations affect electoral processes for all units or levels of government, whether national, state, or local. A political party might be roughly defined as a body of citizens loosely held together by an inner group of leaders and organizers for the purpose of putting its members in office through election or appointment. The party system, in all its aspects, is rather fully treated in courses and texts on American national government.[13] But it is essential at this point to review certain significant state and local features of American politics. The features vary among regions, states, and localities. Party politics is different between the state and the city of New York, between Mississippi and Minnesota, or between seaboard regions and the hinterlands. The actual power of the major parties is highly decentralized, and sometimes a local unit defies a central committee, whether state or national. Yet the party processes all reflect the historical development of the system, and no political unit is completely free from national influences. The ever-changing picture is partly national, partly federal and, in part, locally autonomous. It is also largely illustrative of Tocqueville's observation that in democratic government "the members of political assemblies . . . think more of their constituent than of their party."[14] The analyzer of this political picture must watch his step.

Two-party system with variations

America, in the states as in the nation, has a two-party system with important exceptions and variations. State and local politics in much of the lower South and in some areas outside the South has been based primarily upon a one-party system, with a frequent two-factional cleavage within the dominant party sometimes showing factors much like those of a battle between two major parties. In recent years real two-party competition has begun to develop in one-party sections of the country, with Oregon and Vermont no longer "guaranteed" for Republicans, nor all southern states for the Democrats. New York City frequently offers the voters the opportunity to vote for one of three party tickets, somewhat in contrast to the rest of the state. Third parties have at times upset or acquired the balance of power between the Democratic and Republican parties in Minnesota and states to the westward. Local voters sometimes disregard party lines and "vote for the man," as when Little Rock elected a Republican mayor in that Democratic stronghold or when Milwaukee chose a Socialist mayor. Then there are the cases of clearly nonpartisan elections of certain officers, notably of members of school boards and less consistently of judges. The two-party system prevails in a very loose sort of manner, but it prevails. It is most conspicuous in the most highly industrialized or urbanized states.

State and local politics, more than national politics, is complicated by political machines which may function entirely within one party or

[13] For more detailed and comprehensive treatment, *see* Frank J. Sorauf, *Party Politics in America,* 2nd ed. (Boston: Little, Brown, and Co., 1972).

[14] Alexis de Tocqueville, *Democracy in America,* p. 90.

may cut across party lines. The political machine is not limited to any region of the country, and it may be found under rural as well as urban conditions. It has, however, developed its most striking features in such major cities as New York, Philadelphia, Boston, and Chicago without becoming the monopoly of one party. It cannot be precisely defined or identified, for a political outfit may be a legitimate "organization" as viewed by friends or supporters and a sinister "machine" in the eyes of critics or opponents. The essential operating "kitty" of a machine may be supplied by various methods, whether fair or foul, but the solid foundation is an enforced system of rewards and punishments. Less savory ways of machine financing include assessments on public officers and employees; kickbacks from public works contractors; bribes or blackmail from holders of business permits or franchises; contributions from property owners interested in low tax assessments or lax enforcement of building codes; protection money from gambling houses, racketeers, and other exploiters of commercialized vice; and kindred methods. Among the machines which have had leaders entangled with the law, or public investigations, in the middle third of the present century are the Long machine of Louisiana, the Pendergast machine of Kansas City, the Hague machine of Jersey City, and Tammany of New York City.[15] Still other machines have held themselves above criticism on this score for year after year. Machines of both classes are consistently interested in securing and holding political power. Although political machines have been subject to much criticism through the years from the press, political scientists and the general public in more recent years have given a more sympathetic interpretation of their role, especially in their relation to the urban poor.[16]

Political machines

It was often true that a machine was the lengthened shadow of a man, a boss, who was either the founder or an heir in the line of succession. The boss, like the baseball manager, may have been an active participant in the game which he directed with authority, or he may have functioned as an invisible director giving orders from the dugout. Again like the baseball counterpart, he may have been an ex-participant, as illustrated by Boss Ed Crump, of Memphis, a former mayor and a former member of Congress, who mastered the technique of managing mayors, legislators, and governors.[17] Huey Long at the time of his assassination in

Bosses

[15] For an absorbing history of the Kansas City political organization that gave Harry Truman his start in politics, *see* Lyle W. Dorsett, *The Pendergast Machine* (New York: Oxford University Press, 1968).

[16] *See,* for example, Charles R. Adrian and Charles Press, *Governing Urban America,* 4th ed. (New York: McGraw-Hill, 1972), pp. 92–96; Thomas R. Dye, *Politics in States and Communities,* 2nd ed. (Englewood Cliffs, N.J.: Prentice-Hall, 1973), pp. 264–266; and Robert L. Lineberry and Ira Sharkansky, *Urban Politics and Public Policy* (New York: Harper & Row, 1971), pp. 78–92.

[17] *See* William D. Miller, *Mr. Crump of Memphis* (Baton Rouge: Louisiana State University Press, 1964).

1935 was both an active member of the United States Senate and the unquestioned boss of a state machine, playing both visible and invisible roles.[18] The typical boss worked his way up through minor positions in the system to a major place of power in the great game of politics. He was often a man of limited education, but college training proved no handicap to bosses like "Abe" Ruef of San Francisco and Boies Penrose of Pennsylvania. The boss as well as his machine had great power of resilience after defeat at the polls, often surviving what seemed to be their funeral. The development of professional welfare programs made it more difficult for the boss to pose as a benevolent Santa Claus for the city's underprivileged, and the adoption of merit systems, accounting systems, and other administrative efficiencies stripped the state or city boss of much of his old-time power and color. Although bosses have declined in recent years, machines still prevail on the state and local political scene.[19]

Demagogues

Demagoguery sometimes characterizes state politics, and it is by no means divorced from bossism, although the boss was a cool calculator as to what hatreds or prejudices to use in whipping up popular passions. The demagogic play on racial and religious prejudice could not be resorted to by Long in Louisiana in the ways open to a Eugene Talmadge in Georgia or a Theodore Bilbo in Mississippi. The big city bosses have generally steered clear of this bundle of tricks, although Thompson seemed to please many of his Chicago constituents in talking about hitting the King of England on "the snoot." Demogogic oratory has served at times as a potent weapon for stirring rural and Main Street people to political action against metropolitan interests, "Wall Street," and outlanders in general. But the demagogue may work either side of the fence, pro or con, liberal or conservative, and may inflame the emotions with an appeal either to "white power" or "black power."

Reformers

Reformers and reform movements arise from time to time to challenge the power of boss or machine within or without the party structure of a city or state. Grover Cleveland launched his national career as a reform mayor of Buffalo and then as reform governor of New York. Seth Low became such a mayor of the city of New York around the turn of the century and disrupted the power of the Tammany machine for a season. John Purroy Mitchel also accomplished this feat some years later. Governor Ellis Arnall became an important one-term reformer in Georgia and

[18] *See* Robert Penn Warren, *All the King's Men* (New York: Harcourt, Brace and World, 1946).

[19] *See* Raymond Wolfinger, "Why Political Machines Have Not Withered Away and Other Revisionist Thoughts," *Journal of Politics* 34 (May 1972), pp. 365–398; and Richard T. Frost, "Stability and Change in Local Party Politics," *Public Opinion Quarterly* 25 (Summer 1961), pp. 221–235. Frost reports that the boss is passing in New Jersey, but definitely not the machine. There is a great abundance of literature on American political bosses. A classic analysis by Lincoln Steffens, his *Autobiography* (New York: Harcourt, Brace and World, 1931), is based on his muckraking writings of the muckraking era.

achieved constitutional results, only to see the Talmadge machine return to power. Reform movements tend to die out through apathy of the masses or failure in leadership, or both, unless an able and politically minded leader takes charge and builds a machine of strength from top to bottom, as did Hiram Johnson in California and the elder Robert M. LaFollette in Wisconsin. Even reformers must play practical politics or sooner or later leave the field. In fact, their category overlaps with those of bosses and demagogues, as was demonstrated by a few southern governors, including J. K. Vardaman and Theodore Bilbo in Mississippi, Huey P. Long in Louisiana, and Charles B. Aycock in North Carolina. Every one of these leaders put through progressive programs in his state, although appealing for support in part to class or racial prejudice in the process. They tempered their sense of idealism or social justice somewhat by the dictates of the possible.

Reformist "party clubs"

A new-style urban political pattern with reformist implications in respect to traditional machine politics is the "party club" phenomenon. Organized within some urban political parties, often as factions within the Democratic Party, they are usually characterized by a youthful and ideologically oriented zeal. A small group organized as the Greenwich Village Independent Democrats was able in 1961, after failures in 1957 and 1959, to depose once-powerful New York Democratic leader Carmine DeSapio in his own election district, and to defeat his come-back attempt in 1963. Similar clubs have grown up elsewhere, particularly in California, and while they have generally eschewed the use of patronage and old-style political favors, they resemble traditional machines in such matters as strong reliance on individual canvassing of voters, personal relationships, and the rewards of sociability. Fred Greenstein is unwilling to designate such reform clubs as the "wave of the future" because their effectiveness thus far has been primarily in the more prosperous sections of cities, and their emphasis on ideology seems to make them prone to internal conflicts.[20]

The committee system

The major parties work through systems of state and local committees in addition to maintaining national committees and a campaign committee for each party in each house of Congress. The national committee of a major party consists of a man and a woman from each state, with additional membership from territories. This national arrangement may aid or influence internal state politics in important respects. But a state committee system has roots and life in its own state and is not under the direct control of any national organization.[21] It is thus part of the workings of federalism in the American party system. State and local committees

[20] *See* Fred I. Greenstein, "The Changing Pattern of Urban Party Politics," *The Annals of the American Academy of Political and Social Science* 353 (May 1964), pp. 1–13. The entire issue, edited by Lee S. Greene, is devoted to "City Bosses and Political Machines."

[21] For a discussion of the relative impotence of the national party committees, *see* Cor-

are most active and effective in two-party regions. Republican committees have limited functions in parts of the South, although they render aid to national campaigns and take a hand in federal patronage when their party is in national power. They are non-existent in many southern localities. Political leaders, bosses, and machines may carry on much of their party activity through the committee channels, holding power partly through committee membership and management, or yielding power through loss of committee control. In many cases, however, the men of power may use other methods of operation, leaving routine functions to the responsibility of committees.

State committees

The state "central committee" or "executive committee" of a major party varies in composition, organization, functions, and extent of control by law. This diversity results partly from the fact that party rules and state statutes on the subject vary widely among the states. Custom and practice also affect the role and importance of the state committee. The membership ranges from about a dozen up to several hundred. The members are chosen through party primaries or through state party conventions, with a few exceptions or modifications. The Democrats of South Carolina pick the members by the county convention method. The unit of selection is frequently the county, but it may be a judicial district, state legislative district, or congressional district, sometimes with the addition of members from the state at large. The officers of the committee, such as chairman, vice-chairman, and secretary, are likely to be important cogs in the system, especially in states where the membership is exceedingly large. The committee chairman customarily is selected on the basis of being satisfactory to the party's candidate for governor. He may be chosen from outside the committee membership.

A state committee which is unwieldy because of large membership finds ways of facilitating its work by delegating much of its power to act to a small executive committee of its own creation. The important work of a large committee is also likely to be planned in advance by a caucus of leaders. An important function of the state committee is to serve as a central coordinating agency for election campaigns. Another is to secure campaign funds. Through its officers, the committee also has duties in connection with arranging and scheduling the state convention, if one is held. In primary elections, the committee has both legal and party duties to make arrangements with candidates as well as with state government officials.

The party picture in the states presents a wide miscellany of local committees. The most prevalent local committee unit for the whole country is the county, but use is also made of such units as town, city,

---

nelius P. Cotter and Bernard C. Hennessy, *Politics without Power* (New York: Atherton Press, 1964).

ward, precinct, and district, and sometimes the congressional district. As with the state committee, the powers and functions of these numerous local organizations differ widely under the conditions of two-party or one-party systems, methods of nomination by primaries or by conventions, much or little party regulation by legislation, and other factors. Their official functions are of little importance in local elections which are nonpartisan.[22] The members of a local committee may be chosen by primaries, conventions, or caucuses. These party officials are important agents for getting voters properly qualified and getting out the vote for their nominees on election day. They serve as doorbell ringers, poll watchers, and campaigners at the grassroots or neighborhood level. They cooperate with speakers and candidates as well as with voters, and they overlap with the bosses and machines of their party, if they are not part and parcel of the machines.

Local committees

It is important to keep in mind the role of the candidates themselves in carrying on the work of the parties to which they belong. They carry much of the brunt of party campaigning, and they provide the leadership for rallying the committee workers. They have much to do with mapping and executing campaign strategy from top to bottom level of the party organization. The work of candidates for important office, along with that of their campaign managers, helpers, and publicity directors, adds much to the life of the party. This work constitutes the chief method of providing or presenting issues for public consideration, even if there is a formal platform offering by the party, which is often not the case. Candidates at times attract the support of ad hoc groups to supplement the activity of the regular party functionaries. The way in which citizens are recruited to become candidates for public office and to be party activists has become the subject of increasing research by political scientists in recent years. The focus is primarily on the types of persons who are political activists and/or officeholders and the reasons they become involved. Some research has emphasized "pull factors"; i.e., political recruitment into activism is thought to come primarily from external stimuli in the environment, such as being "drafted" by political party leaders or interest groups. Other research emphasizes "push factors," or factors resulting from internal self-initiation related to personal ambition, idealism, and other self-generating reasons. The work of Milbrath, Jacob, Seligman, Prewitt, Eldersveld, and others, leads to the conclusion that political recruitment involves a combination of both.[23]

Candidates and their recruitment

[22] On this point, *see* Phillips Cutright, "Activities of Precinct Committeemen in Partisan and Non-Partisan Communities," *Western Political Quarterly* 17 (March 1964), pp. 93–108.

[23] John Rehfuss summarizes the growing body of literature on political recruitment in his paper, "Political Recruitment to Local Office in Illinois Cities," prepared for the Annual

Fischetti

"No Madam, I do not give trading stamps for a vote."

Figure 7–2. Copyright © 1972 by the *New York Herald Tribune.* By permission of John Fischetti.

The personal touch

In an age of television and other mass media of communication, and of what the sociologists call "impersonal relationships in a lonely crowd," the "personal touch" is still very much the basis for a great deal of party motivation and support. The handshaking tour of candidates has become a commonplace part of the American scene; this kind of personal attention has become essential both to secure votes and to secure the loyalty of party workers. Political strategist Jim Farley once wrote about this aspect of politics:

Meeting of the American Political Science Association, New Orleans, Sept. 4–8, 1973. *See* especially Lester Milbrath, *Political Participation* (Chicago: Rand McNally, 1965); Kenneth Prewitt, *The Recruitment of Political Leaders: A Study of Citizen Politicians* (Indianapolis: Bobbs-Merrill Co., 1970); Moshe Czudnowski, "Sociocultural Variables and Legislative Recruitment," *Comparative Politics* (July 1972), pp. 561–587; Lester Seligman, "Political Recruitment and Party Structure," *American Political Science Review* 55 (March 1961), pp. 77–86; and Herbert Jacob, "Initial Recruitment of Elected Officials in the United States—A Model," *Journal of Politics* 24 (November 1962), pp. 703–716.

> . . . I'm an old-fashioned fellow who . . . still believes that the only way to get ahead in public life is to understand people and sympathize with their viewpoint. It doesn't hurt my feelings when some sophisticated gentleman of the writing craft describes me as the kind of fellow who likes to go back to the old home town and salute the neighbors by their first names while they greet me in return with a hearty "Hello, Jim." The radio is a wonderful thing—it has been a tremendous factor in promoting the success of the Roosevelt political fortunes—but, to my way of thinking, there is no substitute for the personal touch and there never will be, unless the Lord starts to make human beings different from the way he makes them now.[24]

Degree of interparty competition

One of the most perplexing questions facing the student of politics is the nature and significance of party competition, especially since genuine interparty competition at the local level may exist in only a small fraction of elections. What explains why so many districts are always safely "in the bag" for one party, and what are the effects of this situation? So little comparative research across state lines has been done on party competition that it is difficult to generalize. Heinz Eulau concludes from data gathered in Ohio that there is a correlation between degree of urbanization and degree of party competition, suggesting that advocates of a more competitive party system can take hope in the increasing urbanization of the United States.[25] This hypothesis found no support, however, when tested by Gold and Schmidhauser in Iowa. They suggest that degree of urbanization may be more related to *intra*party competition than to *inter*party competition.[26]

The fifty states have been classified by Professor Austin Ranney according to degree of party competition in *state* offices, rather than the common use of federal offices as an index of competitiveness. The interesting results are shown in Table 7–1, based on the period from 1956 to 1970. The hazards of undertaking such a classification are made apparent by the "switch" of Arkansas and Florida in 1966 with the election of Republican governors; however, they both returned to the Democratic fold in 1970. Ranney, looking for correlates of competitiveness, finds that the

[24] James A. Farley, *Behind the Ballots; the Personal History of a Politician* (New York: Harcourt, Brace and World, 1938), pp. 192–93. For a very readable account of politics in Massachusetts, *see* Murray Levin, *The Compleat Politician: Political Strategy in Massachusetts* (Indianapolis: Bobbs-Merrill Co., 1962).

[25] Heinz Eulau, "The Ecological Basis of Party Systems: The Case of Ohio," *Midwest Journal of Political Science* 1 (August 1957), pp. 125–135.

[26] David Gold and John R. Schmidhauser, "Urbanization and Party Competition: The Case of Iowa," *Midwest Journal of Political Science* 4 (February 1960), pp. 62–75. For a discussion of the influence of electoral systems on electoral competition, *see* Charles E. Gilbert and Christopher Clague, "Electoral Competition and Electoral Systems in Large Cities," *Journal of Politics* 24 (May 1962), pp. 323–349.

Table 7–1. The Fifty States Classified According to Degree of Interparty Competition (1956–1970)

One-Party Democratic	*Modified One-Party Democratic*	*Two-Party*		*Modified One-Party Republican*
Louisiana (.9877)	North Carolina (.8332)	Hawaii (.6870)	New Jersey (.5122)	North Dakota (.3305)
Alabama (.9685)	Virginia (.8235)	Rhode Island (.6590)	Pennsylvania (.4800)	Kansas (.3297)
Mississippi (.9407)	Florida (.8052)	Massachusetts (.6430)	Colorado (.4725)	New Hampshire (.3282)
South Carolina (.9292)	Tennessee (.7942)	Alaska (.6383)	Michigan (.4622)	South Dakota (.3142)
Texas (.9132)	Maryland (.7905)	California (.6150)	Utah (.4565)	Vermont (.2822)
Georgia (.9080)	Oklahoma (.7792)	Nebraska (.6065)	Indiana (.4450)	
Arkansas (.8850)	Missouri (.7415)	Washington (.6047)	Illinois (.4235)	
	Kentucky (.7170)	Minnesota (.5910)	Wisconsin (.4102)	
	West Virginia (.7152)	Nevada (.5742)	Idaho (.4077)	
	New Mexico (.7150)	Connecticut (.5732)	Iowa (.3965)	
		Delaware (.5687)	Ohio (.3837)	
		Arizona (.5663)	New York (.3835)	
		Montana (.5480)	Maine (.3820)	
		Oregon (.5387)	Wyoming (.3537)	

Source: From Herbert Jacob and Kenneth N. Vines, *Politics in the American States: A Comparative Analysis*, second edition, p. 87. Copyright © 1971 by Little, Brown and Company (Inc.). Reprinted by permission.

Correlates of competitiveness

two-party states are substantially more urbanized than the one-party or modified one-party states. (*See* Table 7–2.) While the impact of the Civil War has apparently been to keep seven southern states as one-party Democratic states for more than a century, the converse is not true: the states that fought for the Union are predominantly two-party states, rather than one-party Republican. Ranney lends his support to Eulau and concludes that the explanation is found in the greater urbanization of the

Table 7–2. Social and Economic Characteristics of States by Degree of Competitiveness

Characteristic	*One-Party Democratic*	*Modified One-Party Democratic*	*Two-Party*	*Modified One-Party Republican*
Number of states	7	10	28	5
Percentage of population urban	53	57	68	46.5
Percentage of population living in cities of over 100,000	17	20	22	5
Percentage of blacks in population	29	14.5	4	1
Percentage of foreign stock in population	3	6	23	22
Percentage of Roman Catholics among church members	16	21	44	42
Median income	$3884	$4764	$5999	$4920
Percentage of labor force in agriculture	11	8	7	17
Percentage of labor force in manufacturing	20	19	22.5	17

Source: From "Parties in State Politics," by Austin Ranney in Herbert Jacob and Kenneth N. Vines, *Politics in the American States: A Comparative Analysis*, second edition, page 90. Copyright © 1971 by Little, Brown and Company (Inc.). Reprinted by permission.

non-southern states, and in several other factors shown in Table 7–2.[27]

Degree of competition between parties is related to the behavior of legislators, or at least to the "role orientations" of legislators, according to the findings of one study.[28] Data from California, New Jersey, and Ohio seem to support the hypothesis that legislators elected from competitive districts are more likely to be district-oriented (as opposed to state-oriented) than those elected from one-party districts. Similarly, legislators from one-party districts are more likely to be state-oriented than those elected from competitive districts. Another study assumes that party responsibility in the state is a consequence of party competition; the study tested for possible intervening factors tending to inhibit or promote party responsibility. Of various possibilities—party organization, electoral mar-

[27] For a more detailed discussion of the correlates of interparty competition at the state level of office holding, *see* Ranney's "Parties in State Politics," in Jacob and Vines, *Politics in the American States*, pp. 61–99.

[28] John C. Wahlke, Heinz Eulau, William Buchanan, and LeRoy C. Ferguson, *The Legislative System: Explorations in Legislative Behavior* (New York: John Wiley and Sons, 1962), pp. 291–293.

gin, experience and leadership, ideology, and constituency—it was concluded that only constituency was an important factor.[29]

The Nominating Process

Evolution and variety

Political evolution and variety characterize the nominating process in state and local government. John Adams, years before the rise of regular parties, described a nominating caucus in a "smoke-filled" attic in advance of the town election. That method is still used in local elections, in conjunction with other methods in the making of party nominations. The rise of regular political parties brought on the party convention for the purpose of nominating candidates and drafting party platforms. After several decades the convention seemed unsatisfactory, at least to democratic reformers, and the movement for nominating primaries got under way as an accompaniment of general adult suffrage. As a result, we find a mixture of caucus, convention, and primary, not only among the states but even in a single state, as in New York. It is true, however, that party primaries have supplanted or considerably minimized the party convention in most of the states and local units of government. It should be mentioned that there still exists a practice of individual candidacy, handed down from colonial times, by which a prospective officeholder announces for election and gets his name on the ballot independently of party machinery, primary procedure, and caucus endorsement. Practical and technical problems make this method of self-nomination generally ineffective in large electorates, but it may be successful in local elections in small constituencies where personal character and contacts outweigh party influence in the voter's mind. Champions of minor parties and of unpopular causes sometimes use this technique for purposes of propaganda without any hope of election.

The caucus

The caucus method of unofficial nomination was a natural development of the growth of towns and other large voting units. John Adams, in a classic description already referred to, said of the meeting of the Boston Caucus Club in the roomy garret of Tom Dawes, "There they smoke tobacco till you cannot see from one end of the garret to the other. There they drink flip, I suppose, and there they choose a moderator, who puts questions to the vote regularly; and selectmen, assessors, collectors, wardens, fire-wards, and representatives, are regularly chosen before they

[29] Thomas A. Flinn, "Party Responsibility in the States: Some Causal Factors," *American Political Science Review* 58 (March 1964), pp. 60–71. *See also* Sarah McCally Morehouse, "The State Political Party and the Policy-Making Process," *American Political Science Review* 67 (March 1973), pp. 55–72, for an analysis of the relation of political party strength to state policy outputs, and for argument that disagrees with those studies minimizing the role of political parties in the policymaking process.

are chosen in the town."[30] This club operated without legal restriction or regulation, and similar groups operated in this manner for decades afterwards. The congressional caucus for nominating candidates for president followed this plan of eighteenth-century Boston. Despite its early vogue in high and low places, however, the caucus as the main or sole reliance for nominating candidates for office came under popular criticism with the rise of Jeffersonian and Jacksonian politics. It was denounced as unrepresentative and corrupt, and caucus by legislators for nominating non-legislative candidates was objected to as violative of the principle of separation of powers. This method of selecting nominees for president was to end in the 1820s, but steps were taken earlier to supplant it in the states.

The convention

The delegate convention was resorted to as a more democratic and representative method than the caucus for nominating candidates. It also facilitated the offering of platform issues to the voters. Delaware adopted the convention system during the presidency of Jefferson, and many other states in the North went over to this method by 1830. The nominating convention gradually spread over the entire country, with or without legal regulation. The convention system developed on a hierarchical basis. At its apex was the state convention made up of delegates from county or town units which in turn were composed of members from still lower units, such as wards or precincts. The whole convention system operated under the general direction of central and local committees. The choice at the level of the precinct unit could be little more than the work of an old-fashioned caucus, although the meeting might be designated as a "convention" or "primary." Advantage tended to rest with the alert insiders, who might meet earlier than the designated time, might fill the meeting place or bar the door to late comers, and might find other means of exercising machine control. Then there was the possibility of manipulating the state or county convention in deciding disputes between contesting delegations in favor of the preferred clique regardless of claims or evidence. These abuses, great or small, seemed conspicuous in many sections after the Civil War. They were intensified by the increase in the power and spoils of office in government, the expansion of which was geared to an expanding economy with many conflicts of interest. Like the nominating caucus in earlier times, the delegate convention proved unsatisfactory to democratic reformers and yielded to a more direct technique for nominating candidates to office in state and local units.

The primary is a method of making nominations by direct popular action. It is a preliminary election in which groups of voters choose the

[30] Charles Francis Adams (ed.), *The Works of John Adams*, vol. 2 (Boston: Little, Brown and Co., 1850), p. 144. The citation is from a diary entry of February 1763.

candidates directly without the use of delegates or representatives in caucus or convention for such purposes. It presumably permits any voter to participate in selecting the candidates to be put on the ballot of his party in the general election. Its first use has been credited to Crawford County, Pennsylvania, where both Democrats and Republicans adopted the practice before the Civil War. The primary spread to other Pennsylvania counties and was used in several states before 1900. In the early years of the twentieth century it was supported by such leaders as Robert M. LaFollette, Theodore Roosevelt, and Charles Evans Hughes as an integral part of the democratic movement of their era. Wisconsin, under the leadership and governorship of LaFollette, in 1903 established by law the first statewide primary election system in the country. Oregon followed the Wisconsin example in 1904, and then the movement spread rapidly among the different states. In 1955 Connecticut lost its distinction of being the only state with no provision for primary elections.[31] In some states, however, the primary is optional with the party committees and, in certain states, as in New York, it is not employed in choosing candidates for state office or United States senator. In Utah the primary is used only in cities of the first and second class. The Connecticut primary is resorted to only if an unsuccessful convention candidate who polls at least 20 percent of the convention vote challenges the convention outcome. His challenge is in the form of a petition calling for a primary and signed by a certain number or percentage of party members.

Rise of the direct primary

Direct primaries, as generally understood and conducted, are usually distinctly partisan. However, nonpartisan primaries are held in a number of states for local selections and for choosing certain state officers, particularly judges. Minnesota in 1912 applied this type to the selection of members of the legislature, and Nebraska has prescribed this method for the choice of the members of the state's unicameral legislature. The nonpartisan primary is designed to make local and judicial elections and officers independent of party organizations or machines and national political influence. The candidates are listed on the primary ballot without any party designation or emblem, and a majority vote is sufficient for office without a second election. There must be a second or general election if a divided vote prevents a majority in the first contest. The primary, as thus used, is a preliminary or semi-final general election. The nonpartisan primary frequently does not preclude undue political pressure and machine influence, for candidates may be earmarked and classified by leaders and bosses without the fact being stated on the ballot. Printed slates may be unofficially distributed or published in advance of the poll-

Partisan and nonpartisan primaries

[31] *See* Duane Lockard, "Connecticut Gets a Primary," *National Municipal Review* 44 (October 1955), pp. 469–470.

ing date. It is difficult to remove national party influence from all local elections, particularly in our largest cities.

Patterns in "nonpartisan cities"

Whether partisanship has actually been removed when the nonpartisan ballot has been adopted is the subject of more than one recent study. The result seems to be a variety of patterns in which the role of the party organization varies from a position of recognized dominance to that of almost complete impotence. Professor Adrian suggests the following typology for nonpartisanship in actual practice:[32] (1) cities in which it is normally impossible for a candidate to win without the support of a major party organization (e.g., Jersey City during the time of the Hague machine, and Chicago); (2) cities where both party and nonparty groups compete with slates of candidates on a reasonably equal basis (e.g., Cincinnati, Albuquerque, and Wichita); (3) cities customarily having slates supported by nonparty groups but with little or no participation by party organization (e.g., Kansas City since the fall of Pendergast, Dallas, Fort Worth, Nashville, and many others); and (4) cities in which neither party organizations nor slates of candidates are important. The third and fourth types appear to be far more common than the first two, but the fourth, often based on what Eugene Lee has called a "politics of acquaintance,"[33] may be the most common pattern of all. Under the fourth system, individual candidates typically develop their own organization, financial support, and following on an ad hoc basis. Concerning the actual effect of nonpartisanship, two recent case studies indicate that nonpartisan municipal elections do not free the electorate from the pressure of group influence or contribute to "an integrated civic life."[34]

Legal features of primaries

Primaries, whether optional or mandatory, partisan or nonpartisan, are generally regulated by state law, if one may overlook a few southern attempts to save the "white primary" by processes of delegalization. Partisan primaries are usually held on the same day for the different parties at designated voting places. The returns may be canvassed and reported by party officials as prescribed by law. Names of candidates for nomination are placed on primary ballots by various methods, including individual declaration and filing of candidacy, petition by a specified number or percentage of qualified voters, and action through a preprimary convention.

[32] Charles R. Adrian, "A Typology for Nonpartisan Elections," *Western Political Quarterly* 12 (June 1959), pp. 449–458.

[33] Eugene C. Lee, *The Politics of Nonpartisanship: A Study of California City Elections* (Berkeley: University of California Press, 1960). *See also* James Q. Wilson, "Politics and Reform in American Cities," in Ivan Hinderaker (ed.), *American Government Annual, 1962–1963* (New York: Holt, Rinehart and Winston, 1962), pp. 37–52; and Robert H. Salisbury and Gordon Black, "Class and Party in Partisan and Nonpartisan Elections: The Case of Des Moines," *American Political Science Review* 57 (September 1963), pp. 584–592.

[34] Gerald Pomper, "Ethnic and Group Voting in Nonpartisan Municipal Elections," *Public Opinion Quarterly* 30 (Spring 1966), pp. 79–97.

The petition method is widely used, sometimes along with others. The aspirant for nomination may be required to pay a filing fee, which varies for different states and offices. This is one way of financing primaries. In the greater number of states a plurality vote is adequate for nomination, but several states, especially in the South, require a majority vote, with a second primary for a "run-off" between the two leading candidates in case no one receives a majority in the first contest. The "run-off" for state nomination in such states as Texas, Louisiana, or Alabama is often a conspicuous battle with manifestations suggestive of a two-party contest. Preferential voting, the casting of first and second choice votes, has been proposed as a means of avoiding the burden of a run-off primary. Adoptions have been few, however, and preferential voting has been used more by sports writers in selecting the top ranking football or basketball teams in the nation than by the states for party primaries.

End of county-unit system

Until 1962 the Democratic state primary in Georgia operated by law as a county-unit system somewhat as the Electoral College does in the election of the president of the United States. Eugene Talmadge in 1946 won a majority of the county units and the Democratic nomination for governor with a popular vote second from the top. The rural-cherished county-unit system was abandoned after being voided by a three-judge federal court, resulting in the first Georgia primary on a popular-vote basis since 1908. The U. S. Supreme Court upheld the decision in 1963, ruling that the county-unit system violated the equal protection clause of the Fourteenth Amendment.[35] Maryland's county-unit system, in effect since 1910, was also invalidated in 1963.

The closed primary

Partisan primaries are of two types, open and closed. In a majority of the states the closed type prevails. It is based on the theory that only Democrats should vote in Democratic primaries and only Republicans in Republican primaries. Under this method the participant, besides being a qualified voter, is supposed to meet a prescribed test of party allegiance before receiving a ballot at the polls. The test varies from a simple statement of party affiliation to proof by the voter that he has supported the party ticket and expects to support it in the approaching general election. The secret ballot makes it easy in many states for a voter to meet the test without being effectively challenged as a bona fide member of the party.

The "white primary"

Court controversies have occurred in parts of the one-party South over a special application of the closed primary. Between 1910 and 1940 movements were undertaken with success to bar black voters from participation in Democratic primaries. This, in effect, denied them a voice in the election of governmental officers, since nomination in the Demo-

[35] *Gray* v. *Sanders*, 372 U. S. 368 (1963).

cratic primary is tantamount to election in these states. Blacks began to participate rather freely after 1930 in party primaries in portions of the South, particularly in North Carolina, Virginia, and Tennessee. But a series of decisions by the United States Supreme Court was required to break up the "white primary" as contrary to the Fourteenth and Fifteenth Amendments. Southern attempts, especially in Texas, to classify the primary as a private, voluntary organization, completely nongovernmental in nature, proved of no avail in the end. The Court cut through this subterfuge in the significant case of *Smith* v. *Allwright* in 1944, the last of a series of cases from Texas on the subject.[36] Thus a disguised method of disfranchisement on racial grounds came to an end in the technical and constitutional sense. A substantial participation in primaries and other elections by southern blacks has followed the outlawing of the "white primary."

The open primary

The open primary prevails in a few states, including Minnesota, Montana, Wisconsin, Washington, and Michigan. The qualifications for voting in such a primary are the same as for voting in a general election, with no legal way of preventing a Democrat or Republican from voting to nominate a candidate for the other party. In Montana and Wisconsin the voter is supplied with ballots of all parties and instructed to select the ballot of his preference, to vote for the candidates of his choice on that ballot, and to surrender the unused ballots. Minnesota uses a consolidated primary election ballot with the candidates listed in party columns, permitting the voter to choose his column in secret with the restriction that voting for candidates in two columns voids the ballot. The state of Washington has a still more wide-open primary with no semblance of party regularity in the voting booth. This system utilizes a blanket ballot listing all candidates for nomination and permitting the voter to switch freely from party to party in marking his choices. The high man of each party for each office wins the nomination. The open primary, as well as the loosely regulated closed primary, is criticized on the ground that it permits outside voters or interests to raid a party and dictate its nominations, to the extent of forcing upon the party weak or otherwise unsatisfactory candidates. The commonly accepted notion that the open primary tends to weaken party responsibility is challenged by a study comparing the voting behavior of U. S. senators from open-primary and closed-primary states. The findings indicate that whatever the causes of

[36] 321 U. S. 649. Other Texas cases involving the issue are *Nixon* v. *Herndon*, 273 U. S. 536 (1927); *Nixon* v. *Condon*, 286 U. S. 73 (1932); *Grovey* v. *Townsend*, 295 U. S. 45 (1935). For an important collateral opinion on the primary not involving the race issue, *see United States* v. *Classic*, 313 U. S. 299 (1941).

their party irresponsibility, the type of primary does not appear to be one of them.[37]

Double filing

Double filing is a system closely related in idea and purpose to the open primary. Under this plan a candidate may seek nomination for the same office by two or more parties in the same primary election. This was allowed by California until 1959 and still is by New York. Mayor La Guardia was nominated for his first term by the New York City primaries of the Republican party and the American Labor party. Double filing was limited in New York in 1947 by the legal requirement that candidates be enrolled as members of the party in which they seek nomination unless excepted from the requirement by party authorities. Governor Warren of California was nominated for re-election in 1946 by his own Republican party and by the Democrats in the same primary. In that state a candidate listed on two primary tickets must win the nomination of the party to which he belongs in order to make any other nomination effective.

Appraisal of the primary

The primary system tends to favor the large parties. A small primary vote tends to serve as an unfavorable opinion poll. In a number of states small parties are denied the use of the system for lack of showing at the polls. Most states prescribe a minimum number or proportion of the votes cast at the last preceding general election to qualify a party to enter the primary. It is 10 percent in several states, 2 percent in a few, 25 percent of the total vote cast for presidential electors in Virginia, 20 percent of the total vote cast for presidential electors in Kentucky and Oregon, and in Florida on January 1 preceding the primary election the party must have registered to vote as members more than 5 percent of the total registered voters of the state. The Republican party is out of the primary system in some of the southern states. Weak or new parties may use other means of selecting candidates, but this is likely to call attention to their inferior status.

The open primary and the nonpartisan primary are criticized as interfering with party discipline or responsibility, and the closed primary is sometimes criticized as entrusting too much public power to party functionaries. The primary has clearly tended to make nominations more democratic than formerly, although it has not met the expectations of its early sponsors. It has increased the number, routine, and expense of elections, with greater burdens for candidates, voters, and election officials, and the result is all too often virtually noncompetitive, deserted primaries. Yet there is little prospect of departure from the use of state and local primaries

[37] Ira Ralph Telford, "Types of Primary and Party Responsibility," *American Political Science Review* 59 (March 1965), pp. 117–118.

for the nominating process. The question is more one of change or improvement than of abolition of this method of making nominations for election. The problems of the primary are a part of the general electoral problem, and all of these problems must be considered together.

Elections and Electoral Problems

Importance of managing general elections

The general election is the final action in the states and local units to determine who will hold elective office. It is the climax in the great game of politics, and it requires an extensive system of rules, umpiring, and scorekeeping. There is usually an officer, often the secretary of state or a special board, to administer the election laws at the state level. The details, however, are under the charge of local officials, such as the county clerk, city clerk, or special board. Finally there are precinct inspectors, clerks, managers, and returning officers who conduct activities at the polling places. The major parties are generally represented among those conducting elections except in areas where only one party prevails. Parties with nominees are allowed to have watchers at the polls. Precinct voting may be held in public buildings, such as school houses, city halls, fire halls, and courthouses, but frequently it is necessary to rent polling places for the day. The hours for voting are determined by law and normally extend from six or seven A.M. to six or seven P.M. After the polls close the votes must be counted, certified, and reported. Local canvassing officials receive returns from the different voting places and report the results to the proper county or state authorities. The results are then officially announced, and writs or certificates of election are issued to the winners. Several days may elapse before the final official results are announced, but usually within a few hours unofficial results are announced to the public.

Contested elections

Unsuccessful candidates frequently contest close elections. The laws for contests vary, but ordinarily the defeated candidate, or in some cases a qualified supporter, may contest an election on claims of miscount, misconduct, fraud, or corruption on the part of election officials; ineligibility of the victorious candidate; illegal votes for the winner; rejection of legal votes for the loser; and bribery or intimidation in such a manner as to prevent a fair and free election. Contests may be heard by an election board or tried by a regular court, according to the law or constitution of the state, with possible appeal to the state supreme court. Denial of national constitutional rights in local elections may lead to cases in federal courts. The exposure of unsavory facts may lead to criminal prosecution of individuals. Legislatures may investigate elections, especially of their own members, and each house of Congress, of course, has full power to investigate state and local elections involving its seats.

The different ways of designating party nominees on general election ballots militate for or against party strength. The Indiana, or party-column type, as noted in the preceding chapter, encourages straight party voting. The Massachusetts, or office-group type, encourages split-ticket voting, or at least equalizes such voting with straight-party voting. There are modifications of both of these general types. Montana has the party column without provision for voting by a single mark. Texas has a column type with the unique requirement that the voter "scratch" the ballot by drawing a line through names of the candidates he opposes, the "unscratched" getting his vote. For sixty-two years the official ballot emblem of the Democratic party of Alabama carried the motto "White Supremacy . . . for the right" accompanying a drawing of a crowing rooster. In 1966 the state committee, making a bid for black votes and re-alliance with the national party, dropped the "White Supremacy" slogan, replacing it with the word "Democrats."

Party labels on election ballots

Many methods have been advanced and tried in America and other countries to provide more adequate representation of the minority than is generally found under two-party or one-party systems. Third parties sometimes poll substantial votes only to wind up with no post-election power or voice in government. Several plans have been devised to modify the workings of the simple majority or plurality rule for the selection of officers and to provide representation in government for all elements of opinion.

Problems of minority representation

John C. Calhoun anticipated this modern problem in his proposal for a concurrent majority to protect a minority geographical section from the dominance of an arithmetical majority beyond the regional border. Calhoun thought representation should reflect both numbers and interests. Representation of numbers he deemed the absolute majority; representation of interests he deemed the concurrent majority. He maintained that the "more extensive and populous the country, the more diversified the condition and pursuits of its population, . . . the more difficult is it to equalize the action of the government—and the more easy for one portion of the community to pervert its powers to oppress, and plunder the other."[38] It is necessary to guard against both the tyranny of numerical majorities and the tyranny of organized minorities.

Two of the more common proposals for more adequate minority representation are cumulative voting and proportional representation. Cumulative voting is possible in the election of groups or delegations, when several members are to be selected to represent a county in the state legislature. It is used in this way to choose members of the lower house of the

Cumulative voting

[38] Richard K. Crallé (ed.), *The Works of John C. Calhoun*, vol. 1 (New York: Russell and Russell, 1968), pp. 15–16.

Illinois legislature. By this plan a voter may cast one vote for as many candidates as there are members to be chosen from his district or cast his total number of votes for one candidate. Thus, a minority group of citizens may concentrate votes on one candidate with the hope of electing him instead of dividing support among a number of sure losers. It is a scheme for facilitating the minority voice within the framework of majority rule. Illinois voters rejected a proposed constitutional amendment in 1970 that would have eliminated this procedure.

Proportional representation

Other schemes, more mathematically accurate, have been devised for achieving the goal of proportional representation (often called "PR"). One scheme is the List plan, which proportions legislative seats among different lists of candidates on the basis of the relative votes received. It has been used in western Europe and necessitates voting for the party as a whole, rather than for individual candidates. American experiments in proportional representation have been examples or modifications of the Hare system, advanced by Thomas Hare, an Englishman, in 1859 and praised by John Stuart Mill. By this method the voter expresses a first choice for one candidate, a second choice for another, and so on for as many positions as there are to be filled. A quota is determined by dividing the total number of valid ballots cast by the number of posts or seats to be filled, plus one, and adding one to the quotient. The quota for a district casting 240,000 ballots for five positions would be $\frac{240{,}000}{5+1} + 1$, or 40,001. Candidates receiving 40,001 or more first choices are elected, and, if necessary, their surplus votes as well as the votes of the weak candidates are distributed among the next ranking candidates to attain quotas. The actual voting procedure is simple, but the counting is a complicated process that confuses many citizens.

Proportional representation has been used in a few American cities for election to the council body, but never for higher legislative chambers as in Europe, Canadian provinces, and Australian states. "PR" is praised as a method of providing representation for minority and occupational groups and for checking local political machines. It is criticized as inimical to the two-party system and as an encouragement to "splinter" parties. It was abandoned by New York City not long after World War II. One of the arguments used against it in this instance was that Communists could use it to get an official contact with the city government. The dominant party pointed to the 1945 election of two Communists, duly labeled as such on the ballot, to the city's council under the system. The Communists polled 9 percent of the votes and received 9 percent of the council's seats.[39]

[39] *See* Richard S. Childs, *Civic Victories* (New York: Harper and Row, 1952), Chapter XXVI, and Belle Zeller and Hugh A. Bone, "The Repeal of P. R. in New York City—Ten Years in Retrospect," *American Political Science Review* 42 (December 1948), pp. 1127–1148.

States have long had laws against such practices as fraudulent voting, buying votes, intimidating voters, providing liquor at polling places, or selling liquor on election days. Modern conditions have called for legislation on other campaign practices. A number of states prohibit campaign assessments on public employees. There is also state legislation forbidding political contributions by corporations, limiting campaign funds, and requiring reports on sources and uses of funds. This legislation is reinforced in different ways by national legislation on the subject, not only with respect to presidential and congressional elections but also with application to state and local contests. The Hatch Acts, taken together, not only bar federal employees from active official politics, but likewise restrict state or local employees receiving any federal funds.[40] They also prohibit political pressure on such employees for campaign contributions. Corporations are barred from contributing to national election campaigns, and federal legislation prohibits corporations, like national banks and labor unions functioning under national protection, from using their regular funds for political purposes.

Legislation on corrupt practices

A problem related to campaign finance grows out of the prolonged lapse of time between primary and general elections and, in some states, between the initial and run-off primaries. Election dates set in an earlier era when horse-and-buggy transportation and communication methods seemed to necessitate long campaigns are certainly outmoded in the era of private planes and television. Several states have taken action in recent years to reduce the hardship of prolonged and expensive campaigning by shifting the time of the primary nearer to the November general election.

Burden of prolonged campaigns

There is a serious need for revamping and clarifying legislation on the use of money in elections, whether national, state, or local. Substantial funds are necessary in all elections outside of small towns or villages. The dramatic rise in campaign costs is illustrated in Figure 7–3. The electoral safeguards of a frontier democracy are inadequate for the elaborate and high-pressure campaigning of modern America. Extensive use of money in elections might as well be recognized and made allowable by law. It is a complex task to formulate and apply fair rules for the use of campaign funds by business, labor, agriculture, and professional interests. Low limits for campaign expenditures have led to subterfuge and indirection in the collection and disbursement of funds. It would seem that effective and systematic publicity with respect to all campaign funds is a greater civic need than further restrictions on the size of campaign chests.

Inadequacy of corrupt practice legislation

[40] *See* Herbert C. Alexander and Laura L. Denny, *Regulation of Political Finance* (Berkeley: Institute of Governmental Studies, University of California, and Citizens' Research Foundation, 1966). For a case study on state campaign finance, *see* Donald G. Balmer, *Financing State Senate Campaigns: Multnomah County, Oregon, 1964* (Princeton, N. J.: Citizens' Research Foundation, 1966).

Figure 7–3. George Fisher in the *North Little Rock Times*.

Impact of Watergate

The abuses of campaign financing at the federal level, revealed by the Watergate investigations, stimulated an outpouring of state legislation in 1973 and beyond. In addition to limits on campaign contributions and expenditures and strict disclosure requirements, emphasis is placed upon administration by an independent election commission. Common Cause commended states that passed such legislation and suggested that their actions would prompt Congress and other states to enact stronger laws controlling campaign financing.[41]

[41] For details on state limitations on campaign contributions and expenditures, *see The Book of the States 1974–75*, pp. 42–47.

SUPPLEMENTARY READINGS

Bone, Hugh, and Ranney, Austin. *Politics and Voters.* New York: McGraw Hill Book Co., 1963.

Brogan, D. W. *Politics in America.* New York: Harper & Row, 1954.

Campbell, Angus; Converse, Philip E.; Miller, Warren; and Stokes, Donald E. *Elections and the Political Order.* New York: John Wiley and Sons, 1965.

David, Paul T. *Party Strength in the United States, 1872–1970.* Charlottesville: University Press of Virginia, 1972.

Dye, Thomas R. *Politics in States and Communities.* 2nd ed. Englewood Cliffs, N. J.: Prentice-Hall, 1973.

Eldersveld, Samuel J. *Political Parties: A Behavioral Analysis.* Chicago: Rand McNally and Co., 1964.

Fenton, John H. *Midwest Politics.* New York: Holt, Rinehart and Winston, 1966.

Flynn, E. J. *You're the Boss.* New York: The Viking Press, 1947.

Greene, Lee S., ed. "City Bosses and Political Machines." *The Annals of the American Academy of Political and Social Science* 353, May 1964.

Jacob, Herbert, and Vines, Kenneth N., eds. *Politics in the American States.* 2nd ed. Boston: Little, Brown and Co., 1971.

Jennings, M. Kent, and Zeigler, L. Harmon, eds. *The Electoral Process.* Englewood Cliffs, N. J.: Prentice-Hall, 1966.

Key, V. O. *American State Politics.* New York: Alfred A. Knopf, 1956.

Lee, Eugene C. *The Politics of Nonpartisanship: A Study of California City Elections.* Berkeley: University of California Press, 1960.

Levin, Murray. *The Compleat Politician: Political Strategy in Massachusetts.* Indianapolis: Bobbs-Merrill Co., 1962.

Lockard, Duane. *New England State Politics.* Princeton: Princeton University Press, 1959.

Milbrath, Lester W. *Political Participation.* Chicago: Rand McNally and Co., 1965.

Milligan, M. M. *The Inside Story of the Pendergast Machine by the Man Who Smashed It.* New York: Charles Scribner's Sons, 1948.

Prewitt, Kenneth. *The Recruitment of Political Leaders: A Study of Citizen Politicians.* Indianapolis: Bobbs-Merrill Co., 1970.

Shannon, J. B. *Money and Politics.* New York: Random House, 1959.

Sorauf, Frank J. *Party Politics in America.* 2nd ed. Boston: Little, Brown and Co., 1972.

Sprengel, Donald P. *Comparative State Politics: A Reader.* Columbus, Ohio: Charles E. Merrill, 1971.

Steffens, Lincoln. *Autobiography.* New York: Harcourt, Brace and World, 1931.

Sundquist, James L. *Dynamics of the Party System: Alignment and Realignment of Political Parties in the United States.* Washington, D. C.: The Brookings Institution, 1973.

8

Political Interest Groups and Public Opinion

There is much more to government, particularly democratic government, than the formal processes of nominations, party campaigns, elections, legislation, executive policy, administration, and judicial decision. Social forces, for good or ill, affect all phases, branches, and levels of government. The role of public opinion and the press as an influence in American government was recognized by Thomas Jefferson, Alexis de Tocqueville, and James Bryce, not to mention latter-day observers and social scientists. James Madison spoke brilliantly and prophetically in *The Federalist,* Number 10, of "a landed interest, a manufacturing interest, a mercantile interest, a moneyed interest, with many lesser interests" and observed that the "regulation of these various and interfering interests forms the principal task of modern legislation," involving "the spirit of party and faction in the necessary and ordinary operations of government." Madison realized that factional interests are inevitable and cannot be abolished or prevented in any way short of destroying liberty itself. He advanced the opinion that relief is only to be sought by means of controlling the effects.

Non-official forces

Just how important are these organized factional interests or "pressure groups?" The naive citizen may have a totally unrealistic impression of the governmental process consisting principally of well-insulated activities of voting, law making, administration, and court interpretation, and may be strangely unaware of the continuous day-to-day struggle among groups for power and influence over governmental decision makers. At the other extreme, however, perhaps in the name of sophistication, a citizen may have arrived at a cynical view of pressure groups as all powerful and of politicians and administrators as mere pawns with no real power in their

Two extremes

own right. Truth is probably somewhere in between these extremes. A more realistic view of state and local government will strike a balance which includes an understanding of the importance of both the official institutions of government and the non-official forces such as pressure groups, or political interest groups, as political scientists increasingly call them. This chapter will use the terms "interest group" and "pressure group" interchangeably.

Certain rights of private and group pressure on government are guaranteed against national interference by the First Amendment and indirectly against state or local interference by the Fourteenth Amendment. It is possible to regulate and publicize the activities of pressure groups, but the federal government has found such tasks difficult. Lower levels of government have, on the whole, made much less headway than the central authorities. It should be noted, however, that special interest may balance special interest with incidental results of public good. But there is no standing assurance of such a beneficial balance in specific cases or conditions, as municipalities and counties particularly have discovered over the years. The pressure of special interests may be offset by the influence of an independent press and of organized groups of citizens with broad purposes transcending class interests. On whatever score, government is closely linked with organized group power and with the media of mass communication. That linkage is a vital and recognized feature of modern politics.

The Diversity of Interest Groups

Types of pressure at state and local levels

Pressures exerted by many groups affect both national and state or municipal government in such fields as labor–management relations, taxation, transportation, and conservation. Many pressures are directed primarily at the national government, as is true in matters of foreign policy and international relations. Many special and general pressures are pointed chiefly or entirely at the lower levels of government, as in problems of local health regulation, school improvement, municipal vice or graft, juvenile delinquency, fire prevention, metropolitan growth and adjustment, land-use planning and zoning, and the operation of state, city, or county business. The bulk of the pressure from civil rights groups in recent years, particularly after passage of federal civil rights legislation in 1964 and 1965, has focused upon state and local governmental authorities and quasi-public community groups. Among the organizations that keep a close watch on state and local government are branches of the League of Women Voters, associations of taxpayers, chambers of commerce, labor unions and councils, teachers' associations, manufacturers' associations, farm groups, leagues of municipalities or counties, and different types of professional groups. Railroad interests and trucking interests are on the job when their franchises, operations, properties, and taxes are involved. Newspapers and other vehicles of communication maintain news coverage of all these public activities and at the same time provide channels for shaping opinion on pending issues.[1] Government agencies and administrators also issue statements of information and interpretation concerning their activities, and these statements, whether official or unofficial, are not calculated to cultivate disfavor for the policies of the issuing authorities. Administrative bureaucracies can be among the more powerful interest groups in state and local government.

A national "citizens' interest group"

A new genre of political interest group was organized in 1970 as "Common Cause," seeking to become a national "citizens' lobby." Under the leadership of John Gardner, former U. S. Secretary of Health, Education, and Welfare, its membership reached 300,000 by 1974. Although its early efforts were aimed primarily at federal legislation, it shifted during the election year of 1972 to the state level with emphasis on model state reform laws in areas such as conflict of interest, lobbying, campaign expenditures, and government secrecy. The most difficult test of an interest group like Common Cause is proving its long-term viability. Can a large number of citizens convert simple concern for good government into a common political cause for an indefinite period of time?

"Political" groups—more or less

The common notion that America is a "nation of joiners" is supported by the findings of the five-nation study of Almond and Verba which indicated that Americans have the highest degree of organizational membership (57 percent).[2] While most organizations are involved in political activities in one way or another, though in varying degrees of intensity, Almond and Verba discovered that only 24 percent of the people interviewed actually believed their organizations were engaged in politics. The differences in members' perceptions of the political nature of their organizations are shown in Table 8–1, with the highest percentage of members perceiving political involvement in the case of farm organizations, and the lowest percentage in the case of religious organizations. While a different rank order might result if actual political behavior were ranked, rather than perceptions, it is clear that all of them have a significant degree of political involvement. Although the National Rifle Association has never registered as a lobby, claiming its functions are primarily educational, it has constituted a powerful force against federal, state, and local firearms-control legislation.

[1] *See* James E. Gregg, *Editorial Endorsement Influence in Eight California Cities: 1948–1962* (Davis: Institute of Governmental Studies, University of California, 1965).

[2] Gabriel Almond and Sidney Verba, *The Civic Culture* (Princeton: Princeton University Press, 1963), as discussed by Harmon Zeigler, "Interest Groups in the States," in the first edition of Herbert Jacob and Kenneth N. Vines (eds.), *Politics in the American States*, p. 105.

Table 8–1. Perceptions of Political Involvement

Type of Organization	*Percent of Membership Perceiving the Organization as Politically Involved*	*Total Number of Members in Sample*
Farm	71	29
Civic–Political	62	111
Professional	60	41
Business	55	40
Labor	50	136
Religious	35	180

Source: Harmon Zeigler, in Jacob and Vines, *Politics in the American States,* first edition (1965), p. 105.

The example of Michigan

The variety of groups that may be mobilized for purposes of influencing basic public policy at the state level can be illustrated by the experience of the 1961–62 Michigan constitutional convention, which required registration of convention lobbyists. Albert Sturm reports that the seventy agents representing fifty-nine organizations covered a wide area of the political, economic, and social spectra of the state.[3] Business groups were most numerous, with twenty agents from general commercial and manufacturing interests, the automotive industry, transportation and related interests, utilities, banking, and real estate. The seven agents of the Michigan State Employees Association constituted the largest number registered for any single interest group. Three persons represented the Michigan Education Association. Two agents each were sent by the Michigan Municipal League, the County Road Association of Michigan, the Michigan Committee for the Protection of Property Rights, the Michigan Association of School Boards, the Michigan Farm Bureau, and the State Bar of Michigan. Labor, religious, governmental, and social reform groups, and other miscellaneous areas completed the list of officially registered lobbyists. One of the more active of the groups was the Coordinating Committee for a Sound Constitution, organized as a "citizens' lobby" by some two hundred representatives of organizations which had originally promoted the constitutional convention. The picture of interest-group influence is only partially completed by recounting the number and types of registered lobbyists because, as Sturm points out, there were many other persons, groups, and organizations who exerted an influence on the convention without being registered. Witnesses who appeared before committees, both voluntarily and on request, represented at least 150 interest groups; mail was no small

[3] Albert Lee Sturm, *Constitution-Making in Michigan, 1961–1962* (Ann Arbor: Institute of Public Administration, University of Michigan Press, 1963), pp. 129–140.

factor, with one convention leader receiving about 320 items from approximately eighty-five organizations; state and local officers and agencies expressed their views both formally and informally; and, finally, there were "built-in lobbyists" present in the form of convention delegates who were clearly associated with particular interests such as labor, farming, state employment, and higher education. Following the completion of the convention's work and in anticipation of the 1963 referendum new alliances of interest groups pro and con were organized to influence the voters who, ultimately, decided to adopt the constitution.

Interest-group aims

Most interest groups, exclusive of holders of government jobs and in contrast to political parties, are not directly concerned with winning office for their members. Their primary purpose is to influence government policy, either to achieve something or to prevent something. The influence may be applied for the purpose of securing favorable legislation or administrative decision. It may be against a too rigid or too lenient enforcement of a law or regulation where a range of administrative discretion or decision is provided, as in cases of urban zoning, formulating traffic rules, or granting permits for selling and serving beer. It may be for or against expansion of city limits; a proposed administrative reorganization; projected changes in a state constitution; the issuance of county, municipal, or state bonds; and the election of candidates because of their views on issues affecting group interests. A pressure group may have an educational, a religious, a racial, or an economic purpose, or a combination of purposes. Such a group is by no means detached from politics except organizationally. Its aims are essentially political.

Limitations of diverse groups

The special and general pressure groups have extensive overlapping of membership and it is frequently the case that an organization or its leadership lacks the support of important blocs of members. Many a citizen belongs to many organized groups serving different and even conflicting purposes. Physicians who are members of the American Legion and also of the American Medical Association cannot support both organizations when they clash over policies relating to public health or hospital services. A citizen may not be able to go along with his taxpayers' association on a program of economy and at the same time support his civic group's plan for an expensive civic auditorium.

Contrary to popular impressions, conservationists and anti-pollution forces often find their causes in conflict rather than in harmony. Traditional conservation groups—sportsmen, fishermen, and wilderness advocates—often resist the merger of pollution and conservation programs in state government, fearing that an emphasis on pollution cleanup and public health might favor urban programs and neglect rural areas. One of the more serious obstacles to the development of a well-informed citizenry, with objective and dependable news sources, is the absence of effective competition between newspapers in many cities. Yet, even in single-ownership communities a newspaper cannot completely ignore or suppress important news and publicity on men and movements it may be fighting bitterly on its editorial page. Huey Long, when governor of Louisiana, made headlines in New Orleans papers opposing him. Much of this news was favorable to Long despite slants in writing it. The press ordinarily gives the news, even in a one-paper town, because the economics of newspaper management, if not the ethics of journalism, favors news coverage. There are likewise clear limitations on tendencies toward one-sidedness and partisanship in the uses of radio and television.

Ethnic and black politics

Political scientists have traditionally contended that ethnic identity tends to have a diminishing influence on political attitudes. The gradual absorption of immigrants into the broader society has caused their separate group identity to become less and less meaningful. Their political identification with similar educational, income, and occupational groups becomes more important than race or national origin. Black politics has been considerably slower in following this trend; it is too early to describe with any certainty the characteristics of black politics in the 1970s.[4] For an extended period following the Civil War, many blacks supported the Republican party because it was the party of Lincoln and emancipation. Since Franklin D. Roosevelt and the New Deal, blacks have voted heavily Democratic.

Black political activity rose to record heights of unity and militancy in the civil rights activism of the 1960s.

Civil rights groups in the 1970s

The contrast between civil rights politics in the 1960s and 1970s is rather sharp. Civil rights activity in the decade of the sixties was characterized by police dogs in Birmingham, marches, desegregation opponents defying court orders by standing in doorways, economic boycotts, and black voter registration drives. The relative quiet, diminution of violent confrontation, and growing diversity of opinion on racial problems have puzzled many political analysts.

Explanations of apparent slowdown

One observer of the civil rights scene suggests the following reasons for the apparent slowdown in civil rights activity in the 1970s. (1) Loss of leaders: The deaths of Martin Luther King and John and Robert Kennedy left civil rights activists without the kind of inspiring leaders necessary for a regional or nationwide movement. (2) Competing issues: The anti-war movement diverted money and public interest away from civil rights and toward the Indo-China conflict. The ecology and women's liberation movements also diverted public focus. (3) Federal co-optation: With large spending programs on poverty, education, community action,

[4] Representative of the growing body of literature on black politics is Hanes Walton's *Black Politics* (Philadelphia: J. B. Lippincott Co., 1972).

and fair employment practices, all levels of government hired many of the former activists at much higher salaries than they were previously earning. A large portion of the civil rights leadership was, in effect, absorbed into the establishment. (4) Black militancy: In the latter part of the 1960s, many of the more militant blacks began to reject the concept of "integration," saying that in reality it meant "assimilation," which they rejected. They also began to reject "white liberals" and even the less militant blacks. Busing to achieve racial balance in the schools received a mixed response from black militants. (5) Tight money for civil rights activities: For several reasons, principally economic and legal, foundations became more cautious in funding civil rights organizations, and much of the available money for civil rights activists began to dry up.[5]

Sources of Interest-Group Strength

Sources of strength: (1) Size

(2) Cohesion

(3) Geographic distribution

What determines the strength or weakness of an interest group, not only for ethnic and civil rights groups, but for all kinds of political interest groups? Perhaps the most obvious source of strength is the number of members (potential voters) which the group can claim. However, size alone is not a guarantee of strength; some groups become increasingly disunited as growth occurs. The larger labor unions seldom exhibit the same cohesion in politics that they do in collective bargaining. When large size is accompanied by unity and cohesion, however, a certain degree of strength is assured. Similarly, the geographic distribution of the members of a political interest group may contribute to its strength or weakness. It would be difficult to state a single rule on the effects of having a scattered membership. A group concentrated in one city, for example, could exert a great deal of influence over the local government of that community. But such a group might well be snubbed by a state legislature as representing only a small sectional interest. Conversely, an influential statewide organization would be hard put to influence a particular city council or mayor.

(4) Status

Related to the factors of size, unity, and geographic distribution is the less tangible but equally vital factor of prestige or status. Leaders of the medical profession, the banking association, or the bar association will usually enjoy more easy access to the decision-making circles of state and local government than will representatives of migratory farm workers, "off-brand cults," or other groups which society has generally branded as having low status. Those who are not committed to working "within the system" can hardly expect to be held in high regard by the leaders in the system. (*See* Figure 8–1.) Status is not a permanent condition, nor is it

[5] *See* Jim Leeson, "Civil Rights in South Quieter in 70's," *Race Relations Reporter* 2 (March 1, 1971), pp. 10–12.

Figure 8–1. *Dunagin's People* by Ralph Dunagin. Courtesy of Publishers-Hall Syndicate.

the same from state to state or city to city with respect to similar pressure groups. Leaders of the NAACP do not enjoy the same access to the Mississippi legislature as they do to the legislatures of Illinois, Michigan, and New York. Support of the local Chamber of Commerce may well defeat a proposal in some city councils, while it may guarantee easy passage in others. Reputations vary with circumstances, and there is always the possibility that "abuse of status" may backfire. However, a prestigious membership is generally a tremendous asset to a pressure group. Although status and wealth do not always coincide, wealth is often a contributing factor in the traditional American definition of success. Everything else being equal, it is a source of interest-group strength.

(5) Organization and leadership

Organization and leadership are other factors which can make or break the power of a pressure group. A decentralized, loosely knit organization with diversified local power centers may find it difficult to act quickly, to communicate effectively, and to speak with a single voice at the time and place needed. A centralized, tightly knit organization which concentrates authority in the top leadership can take public stands quickly and is less easily outmaneuvered by opposition groups or by state and local decision makers. The degree of centralization or decentralization in a pressure group may well be the result of the quality of leadership which the group has had over several decades; group members and public officials alike look to a strong leader as the legitimate spokesman for the interests of the group. Thus, legislators will come to know that popular, able Lobbyist X *is* the State Trucking Association, whereas less popular, less able Lobbyist Y is not really the League of Municipalities—he must check back constantly with 200 mayors, during which time the battle lines and issues may have changed drastically. The importance of this factor in interest-group strength is also illustrated by the diversity of types of leaders among black civil rights groups.[6]

(6) Program

A final characteristic of a pressure group affecting its power position in the state or community, and one which may at times be all important, is the ideological content of the group's program. It is a simple axiom that a program that fits the prevailing system of values and beliefs of the public at large will have easier sledding than one which runs counter to community values, all else being equal. Granted, a good public relations campaign may make black appear to be white on occasions, but pressure groups cannot afford to put their trust in such manipulative miracles. In spite of widespread southern acceptance of the Ku Klux Klan's doctrine of white supremacy at one time, the Klan deviated from other community values relating to violence and now has little community respect or support. The brand of "obvious special privilege" on a program will weaken the pressure group, but a clear-cut goal of "fair play," "correcting a wrong," "ending discrimination," or "supporting the weak but worthy" will solidify the support of the group membership and facilitate access to public decision makers.

(7) Political environment

Another factor is the political environment in which the pressure group must operate. This is a characteristic of the state or local community rather than of the pressure group itself, but may be an important source of strength or weakness to the group. The contribution to the strength of pressure groups of the separation of powers, a federal system, and weak political parties (by providing such a variety of access points) is discussed in detail in many textbooks on American government.[7] In addition, such factors as the attitude of legislators and councilmen toward lobbying, the relative strength or weakness of the governor or local executives, and the

[6] *See* James Q. Wilson, *Negro Politics: The Search for Leadership* (New York: The Free Press, 1965).

[7] *See*, for example, Marian D. Irish and James W. Prothro, *The Politics of American Democracy*, 3rd ed. (Englewood Cliffs, N. J.: Prentice-Hall, 1965), pp. 243–244; and Totton J. Anderson, "Pressure Groups and Intergovernmental Relations," *Annals of the American Academy of Political and Social Science* 359 (May 1965), pp. 116–126.

degree of autonomy or integration of the administrative agencies affect the strength of pressure groups and will not produce the same pattern in any two states.

Comparative Patterns of Pressure Systems

Comparative studies of interest groups at the state and local levels of government have not been undertaken in any comprehensive fashion, so it is difficult to generalize about patterns of similarity and dissimilarity from state to state. We are indebted to Harmon Zeigler for his groundbreaking efforts in this respect, and the comparative summary in the next few paragraphs closely follows his analysis.[8] Table 8–2 indicates the wide range and number of the various types of interest groups that register to lobby before selected state legislatures, with a high of 439 in Florida and a low of 41 in Kansas. Numerically, it is clear that business dominates the structure of lobbying in all seventeen states, whether 30.6 percent of the population is employed in non-industrial occupations, as in South Dakota, or only 1.8 percent as in Connecticut. In South Dakota 63 percent of the interest groups registered are either business associations or single businesses; in Connecticut it is 71 percent. Does this mean it can be concluded that business interests literally "run the legislatures" and that the relative power of each type of interest group is in direct proportion to the number of groups registered? Certainly not, for the low numerical ranking of farm groups is not a true indicator of their considerable influence. Similarly, many of the business groups registered are "single-shot" affairs involving only a few days of attendance at the legislature. Even so, it seems clear from Table 8–2 and from studies of other states that business groups are the most significant part of the pressure system. One difference between the pressure system in the nation's capital and that in the state capitals should be noted: businesses tend to work more through intermediary organizations in Washington, while they tend to work more directly through their own lobbyist at the state capital.

Comparison of interest groups

Shifting from the picture of variety within each state's pressure system, it is important to consider comparatively the relative strength of each state's pressure system taken as a whole. Zeigler suggests the provocative hypothesis that in the more urbanized, industrialized, heterogeneous states, where voluntary association membership should be the greatest, the pressure system should be the weakest in its impact on state policy. His

[8] Harmon Zeigler, in Jacob and Vines, 1st ed., *Politics in the American States*, pp. 101–147. Although the cited chapter is revised with the co-authorship of Hendrik van Dalen in the second edition (1971), pp. 122–160, there are no significant departures from Zeigler's earlier direction.

Table 8–2. Classification of Interest Groups in Selected States

State	*Business*	*Single Business Corp.*	*Labor*	*Farm*	*Profes-sional*	*Reform*	*Public Agency*	*Religious and Ethic*	*Veteran*	*Other*
California (432)[a]	28.8%	23.1%	10.7%	1.9%	4.7%	4.4%	11.2%	1.1%	0%	14.1%
Florida (439)	18.7	28.2	20.1	2.3	5.7	1.1	10.3	1.0	0	12.6
Iowa (204)	36.3	10.8	8.8	2.9	5.3	6.9	7.4	7.8	1.5	12.3
Kentucky (59)	49.2	6.8	16.8	1.7	10.2	1.7	6.8	0	0	6.8
Maine (165)	40.0	16.4	8.5	3.0	5.4	2.4	14.6	.6	.6	8.5
Michigan (322)	19.9	35.4	8.1	2.1	12.1	5.0	11.2	1.6	1.2	3.4
Montana (180)	27.2	27.2	13.9	4.4	4.4	3.0	8.9	1.0	1.7	8.3
Nebraska (150)	35.3	13.3	4.7	5.3	9.1	4.7	11.3	1.3	1.0	14.0
South Dakota (92)	41.5	21.7	5.4	5.4	8.7	4.3	5.4	0	3.3	4.3
Kansas (41)	9.5	39.4	9.5	2.8	5.2	3.8	13.7	1.9	0	14.2
New York (174)	47.1	27.0	8.1	1.0	7.5	1.0	3.5	1.0	0	3.8
Ohio (173)	35.8	23.9	15.0	1.2	12.1	1.0	4.6	1.0	1.0	4.4
Pennsylvania (243)	32.8	30.8	10.3	1.0	12.4	1.2	7.8	1.6	0	2.1
Virginia (107)	18.7	62.6	8.4	3.7	1.9	0	1.0	0	0	3.7
Connecticut (175)	44.6	26.3	4.6	1.1	6.3	1.7	6.3	1.1	1.1	6.9
Indiana (136)	38.2	11.8	10.3	1.5	7.4	9.4	3.7	2.9	0	14.8
Rhode Island (60)	33.3	21.7	16.7	1.7	8.3	0	0	1.7	5.0	11.6

[a] Numbers in parentheses indicate total number of interest groups registered with the state.

Source: Harmon Zeigler in the first edition of Jacob and Vines, *Politics in the American States* (1965), p. 110.

rationale is that more open and competitive group politics limits the chance of success of any one group, with a resulting stalemate or compromise rather than total dominance. Table 8–3 presents Zeigler's classification of strong, moderate, and weak state pressure systems in relation to three variables—party competition, cohesion of parties in legislatures, and socio-economic character of the state. The reader should consult Zeigler's own analysis of the data and the limitations he points out; but, in general, he believes his hypothesis is supported despite the notable exceptions of Michigan and California and some contradictions of the four-state study by Wahlke, Eulau, Buchanan, and Ferguson. Table 8–3 indicates that pressure groups are strongest not only when political parties and legislative cohesion are weakest, but also when states have lower urban population, lower per capita income, and a lower industrialization index.

Strength of pressure systems compared

To classify some states' pressure systems as "strong" and others as "moderate" or "weak" is not to say that there is a uniform pattern of interest-group activity for those in each category. Within the category of strong pressure systems, for example, Zeigler finds four distinct "emerging

State patterns of group activity

Table 8–3. The Strength of Pressure Groups in Varying Political and Economic Situations

	Types of pressure system[a]		
Social conditions	*Strong*[b] *(24 states)*	*Moderate*[c] *(14 states)*	*Weak*[d] *(7 states)*
Party Competition			
One-party	33.3%	0%	0%
Modified one-party	37.5	42.8	0
Two-party	29.1	57.1	100.0
Cohesion of Parties in Legislature			
Weak cohesion	75.0	14.2	0
Moderate cohesion	12.5	35.7	14.2
Strong cohesion	12.5	50.0	85.7
Socio-Economic Variables			
Urban	58.6	65.1	73.3
Per capita income	$1900	$2335	$2450
Industrialization index	88.8	92.8	94.0

[a] Alaska, Hawaii, Idaho, New Hampshire, and North Dakota are not classified or included.
[b] Alabama, Arizona, Arkansas, California, Florida, Georgia, Iowa, Kentucky, Louisiana, Maine, Michigan, Minnesota, Mississippi, Montana, Nebraska, New Mexico, North Carolina, Oklahoma, Oregon, South Carolina, Tennessee, Texas, Washington, Wisconsin.
[c] Delaware, Illinois, Kansas, Maryland, Massachusetts, Nevada, New York, Ohio, Pennsylvania, South Dakota, Utah, Vermont, Virginia, West Virginia.
[d] Colorado, Connecticut, Indiana, Missouri, New Jersey, Rhode Island, Wyoming.

Source: Harmon Zeigler and Hendrik van Dalen in Jacob and Vines, *Politics in the American States,* 2nd ed., p. 127. Copyright © 1971 by Little, Brown and Co. Reprinted by permission.

patterns of group activity"—an alliance of dominant groups, a single dominant interest, a conflict between two dominant groups, and the triumph of many interests.[9] He cites the southern states and Maine as examples of the first pattern, with a non-diversified economy, relatively non-competitive party politics, and weak legislative cohesion, all of which open the door for a strong alliance of a relatively small number of interest groups. Lockard points to the "Big Three" interests in Maine—power, timber, and manufacturing—which have clearly outdistanced any rivals in political activity and power, and concludes that their "predominant authority is seldom challenged by any really sustained effort."[10] Zeigler's contention is that such an alliance becomes increasingly difficult to maintain as urbanization and industrialization of the state increase.

Alliance of dominant groups

Similarly, the national strength of such issues as environmental pollution, women's rights, racial justice, and auto safety can interfere seriously with the "low profile" power of local and regional interests in state legislatures. Ralph Nader and the late Dr. Martin Luther King have become potent forces to consider, as have women's liberation and the energy crisis.[11]

The classic example of a single dominant interest in a state is the Anaconda Company of Montana, with rough parallels provided by oil in Texas and the DuPont interests in Delaware. In recent years the dominant role of Anaconda in Montana has been diminished both by new competitors and by self-restraint in the political arena. However, the conditions in the Montana legislature earlier in the twentieth century inspired Burton K. Wheeler to write that "the Democrats controlled the House, the Republicans controlled the Senate, and the Company controlled the leaders of both."[12] While the Anaconda Company, with its elaborate network of copper mines, mills, aluminum companies, railroads, fabricating plants, and forests, is the largest single political fact in Montana, state politics is not completely dominated by Anaconda. Zeigler concludes that Anaconda "is a major actor which can claim success in many instances, but it sometimes has been forced to accept defeat."[13]

A single dominant interest

Two dominant groups—automotive labor and automotive management—have made the politics of the state of Michigan an unusual mixture

[9] *Ibid.*, p. 117.

[10] Duane Lockard, *New England State Politics* (Princeton: Princeton University Press, 1959), p. 79.

[11] *See*, for example, Leslie L. Roos, Jr. (ed.), *The Politics of Ecosuicide* (New York: Holt, Rinehart and Winston, 1971), and J. Clarence Davies, III, *The Politics of Pollution* (New York: Pegasus Books, 1970).

[12] Burton K. Wheeler with Paul Healy, *Yankee from the West* (Garden City, N. Y.: Doubleday and Co., 1962), p. 84.

[13] Harmon Zeigler and Hendrick van Dalen, in Jacob and Vines, *Politics in the American States*, p. 131. *See also* Thomas Payne, "Under the Copper Dome: Politics in Montana," in Frank H. Jonas (ed.), *Western Politics* (Salt Lake City: University of Utah Press, 1961), pp. 197–198.

of strong, cohesive two-party politics and strong, bi-factional pressure politics. Although the Michigan economy is less dominated by the automotive industry than it once was, the union–management conflict, which established deep roots during earlier years, continues to be the focal point in Michigan power struggles. The major difference in the Michigan pattern of pressure politics is the extent to which the cleavages between the two major interest groups have become institutionalized in the structure of the two parties—the automotive unions with the Democratic party and the automotive managers with the Republican party. Thus, instead of the two-party system serving as a moderating influence in group conflict, as is the case with the national parties, the Michigan parties may well have a reinforcing effect on the positions of the two major interest groups.

Conflict between two dominant groups

The final pattern among strong pressure systems is best described as the triumph of many interests with the diverse economy, two-party politics, and weak legislative cohesion of California, for example. California's legislature is normally the scene of the freeplay of interest groups unrestricted by demands from political parties. This was not always the case in California, where the railroads—particularly the Southern Pacific—once dominated both parties and the legislature. The reformism of the early twentieth century in California weakened political parties and, ironically, opened the door for freewheeling pressure groups. William Buchanan concludes that, even when the more sensational journalistic stories are discounted, California interest groups during the "lobby era" of 1942–1953 were virtually in charge of the initiation of public policy.[14] Zeigler speculates that, with an emerging partisanship in California politics, the legislature will move away from lobby dominance. The extension of this speculation is that, as states become more urbanized, industrialized, and heterogeneous, the independent influence of interest groups will decline.

Triumph of many interests

A "systems approach" study of the Texas political system by Nimmo and Oden describes the pressure system in that state as the "prime filter through which all demands to which policy makers respond must pass."[15] They contend that the formal structure of Texas government created by the Constitution of 1876 tends to insulate decision makers from popular control. Real political power is left to a set of loose and shifting coalitions among strong interest groups that are mainly conservative and grounded in the business community: oil, natural gas, beer, railroads, insurance, trucking, consumer finance, banking, the Farm Bureau, the engineering lobby, and certain religious bodies. Nimmo and Oden conclude provocatively

Texas pressure system as a "prime filter"

[14] William Buchanan, *Legislative Partisanship: The Deviant Case of California*, University of California Publications in Political Science, vol. 13 (Berkeley and Los Angeles: University of California Press, 1963), p. 143.

[15] Dan Nimmo and William E. Oden, *The Texas Political System* (Englewood Cliffs, N. J.: Prentice-Hall, 1971), p. 105.

that the Texas pressure-group system is the least studied and least understood of all Texas political subsystems; that it is closer to an elitist reality than to a pluralistic democracy; and that the less prosperous exist more as "subjects" than "citizens."

Skills v. *acknowledgement of legitimacy*

Before turning to an examination of interest-group methods, it is important to remember that no amount of skill in lobbying can overcome certain weaknesses in a group or in its particular situation. Legislative *acknowledgement of the legitimacy of the group,* that is, whether a group represents a public that deserves to be considered seriously in formulating a particular policy, is more important than lobbying skill. Skillful lobbying can take advantage of a group's recognized legitimacy, but cannot create it.

Interest-Group Methods

Interest-group methods and party relations

The methods of pressure groups are multitudinous. Many of them work directly to influence party platforms and the selection of candidates. Under the long presidency of Samuel Gompers, the American Federation of Labor developed an effective policy of endorsing the candidacy and publicizing the records of legislators favorable to labor, regardless of party. Spokesmen of pressure groups are frequently in evidence at party conventions. In fact, an American political party comes close to being a compound of pressure-group interests, one group sometimes more powerful in one party and another in the other. The relationship is reciprocal, for a party generally welcomes the civic, financial, and electoral support of powerful pressure groups, although it may seek advantage through criticizing the opposition party for pressure group connections. The support may be open and publicized, often by crusaders against graft or corruption. It may be of an undercover nature, such as gambling interests quietly seeking easy treatment. Invisible electoral pressure may be exerted by other types of vested interest with big stakes and limited popular appeal.

Lobbying

Personal lobbying is an old and continuing method of applying the power of pressure groups. Its importance is by no means limited to the national scene. Its impact is likely to be felt wherever policymaking bodies function. Land lobbies were prominent in the early days of the Republic. Railroad lobbies became significant in the latter half of the nineteenth century. In that era the Northwestern and Burlington companies, for example, had lobby bosses for work with the Iowa legislature; the Louisville and Nashville railroad company used strong pressure on legislative bodies from Kentucky to Louisiana; and Jay Gould made trips to Albany to get what he wanted in the way of favorable railway legislation or non-action on hostile bills. Other public utilities followed the railroads in this activity. The problem of regulating lobbying had to be faced by state legislatures, although with indifferent or varying success, as will be pointed out in the subsequent treatment of legislatures.

The techniques of lobbying are pluralistic. There are professionals and amateurs at the game of making personal and personable contacts with legislators and policymakers. Bribery and entertainment of lawmakers have been exposed from time to time as reprehensible forms of pressure. Lobbyists have influenced legislation by offering legal fees, retainers, and employment to legislators, their relatives, or their firms. Official patronage has been used by lobbyists of the executive branch of government to push administration bills through a legislature. Lobbyists and their sponsors sometimes draft bills to be introduced and supported by their legislative favorites.

Much of the lobbying that goes on is legitimate and even desirable or necessary. It provides valuable information and analysis for lawmakers. Indeed, research has come to be one of the more effective lobbying devices.[16] Facts and views need to be presented from different angles and by different groups in order to provide the whole picture of a complex problem. It is seemingly fair and proper that each group have the opportunity to give its case, if only to counter the bias of other groups. Constructive lobbying has at times led to advances in legislation. It might be observed that pioneer laws for specialized care and treatment of the insane were enacted in several states partly in response to unselfish lobbying by Dorothea Dix (1802–87), a New England schoolmistress turned reformer. Lobbying has its credits as well as its debits on the civic ledger.

National lobbying less corrupt?

Although the popular conception of lobbying as synonymous with bribery has been proven wrong by a number of research efforts at the national level, Lester Milbrath reports that Washington lobbyists and congressmen believe that state lobbying is more corrupt than national lobbying.[17] Those interviewed attributed to the states "more bribery," and described state lobbying as "cruder," "more obvious," and "more freewheeling and less visible" than in Congress. The present state of research does not permit us to agree or disagree with such charges, but Harmon Zeigler has pointed to certain characteristics of state legislatures and legislators which would, theoretically at least, "contribute to more corrupt lobbying techniques."[18] Limits on the length and frequency of state legisla-

[16] *See* E. F. Cooke, "Research: An Instrument of Political Power," *Political Science Quarterly* 76 (March 1961), pp. 69–87, a case study of the Pennsylvania Economy League which "has come to wield great influence over the making of public policy instead of being only a research agency."

[17] Lester Milbrath, *The Washington Lobbyists* (Chicago: Rand McNally and Co., 1963), pp. 302–303.

[18] Zeigler and van Dalen, in Jacob and Vines, *Politics in the American States*, p. 123. *See also* Harmon Zeigler and Michael Baer, *Lobbying: Interaction and Influence in American State Legislatures* (Belmont, Calif.: Wadsworth Publishing Co., 1969).

tive sessions have made it more difficult to develop internal rules and expectations, formal and informal, such as Congress has restricting the behavior of both legislators and lobbyists. The rapid turnover among state legislators also retards the development of such internal checks, and tends to give a kind of permanent "amateur status" to state legislatures. Related to this are studies which reveal that state lobbyists are frequently no more professional than the legislators, with only a small core of regulars serving as more than occasional one-time lobbyists.[19] Nor do many ex-legislators ever become lobbyists, according to a number of studies. Finally, the compensation of state legislators is considerably less than that of the national legislators, presumably leaving them more vulnerable to offers of assistance in meeting living expenses in the state capital.

Factors in degree of corruption

Lobbying does not stop when a legislative battle is ended. Whether that battle is won or lost, the effective lobbyist will shift his focus to the administrative arena, or perhaps to the courts or the voters.[20] With the growing importance of administrators in state and local government, especially in increased discretionary powers, the lobbyist's initial legislative defeat may be turned into an administrative victory or vice versa. If an interest group feels that it is not getting a fair deal from a particular government agency, it may support legislation to take the agency "out of politics," usually by establishing an autonomous board or commission. This commonly means organizing an agency in such a way that members of the most interested pressure group will control the selection of personnel and the formulation of policy or making it more difficult for a competing pressure group to gain control. Thus, roadbuilders want an autonomous state highway commission, sportsmen want an autonomous game and fish commission, PTA leaders want an autonomous board of education, doctors want an autonomous board of health, and so on *ad infinitum.* To the extent that interest groups succeed in such efforts to maximize their access to state and local officials by pulling "pet agencies" away from the rest of the governmental structure, the result is fragmented, uncoordinated government, with all of its attendant problems. Most interest groups would agree that this "isolationist approach" would not be proper for *all* state or local departments, but would insist that "this one function (or agency) is different."

Interest groups and "administrative autonomy"

Interest groups of all types are likely to rely heavily upon the use of propaganda, combined perhaps with other methods. Pressure by this

[19] Walter DeVries, *The Michigan Lobbyist: A Study in the Bases and Perceptions of Effectiveness* (Unpublished Ph.D. dissertation, Michigan State University, 1960), p. 61.

[20] *See* Clement E. Vose, "Interest Groups, Judicial Review, and Local Government," *Western Political Quarterly* 19 (March 1966), pp. 85–100. He suggests that political scientists have neglected the important role of interest groups in agitating for judicial review of state and municipal public policy.

method is as old as the "propagation of the gospel." Samuel Adams and his colleagues made excellent use of it in stirring up support for the Revolution, and Tom Paine became an effective pamphleteering propagandist during the Revolution, winning high praise from George Washington for thus stimulating popular morale. Propaganda is used at all political levels—from centers concerned with town politics to groups cultivating opinion in the sphere of international relations. Propaganda may provide useful information on public matters and contribute to popular education. But it is not primarily designed to educate or stimulate objective thinking. Propagandists seek to utilize or manipulate words and symbols in such ways as to influence belief and action toward predetermined ends. The advertising of merchandise is in reality a special type of propaganda by business interests seeking to influence or pressure prospective customers to buy their products. However, laws and standards for maintaining truth in commercial advertising are somewhat more enforceable than safeguards against political propaganda. In appealing to human feelings and emotions, political propaganda may skirt away from the truth into realms of half-truths and untruths with a skillful avoidance of technical libel.

Propaganda

Political propaganda has been closely associated with printer's ink, but in modern days it is linked also with the media of radio and television. Candidates may use all of the arts of propaganda in their campaigns, but the customary label for this as viewed by critics is "demagogy." There were demagogues long before the invention of printing, though printing expanded the possibilities for persuasion. Printed propaganda takes various forms, including the distribution of press releases, biased editorials, editorializing in the news appearing in the regular dailies or weeklies, issuing pamphlets and circulars, publishing organizational journals or periodicals under second-class mailing privileges, displaying slogans on billboards, and purchasing political advertising in newspapers. The effectiveness of these methods is strengthened by the tendency of many people to view the printed word as truth rather than with tempered skepticism. The sharp decline in recent years in the number of cities with competing daily newspapers raises important questions about the responsibility of the press in influencing political opinions.[21]

Propagandists and demagogues make use, consciously or unconsciously, of many tricks appealing to prejudice, passion, and other non-rational traits of human nature. They frequently utter glittering generalities, such as emphasizing a stand for "good government," "honesty, decency, and morality," or for opposition to "graft and corruption." They

Propaganda tricks

[21] *See* R. B. Nixon and J. Ward, "Trends in Newspaper Ownership and Inter-Media Competition," *Journalism Quarterly* 38 (Winter 1961), pp. 3–14. This study of 1,461 American cities reveals that only 61 cities have competing daily newspapers, compared with 552 in 1920.

resort to name-calling, throwing odious terms at the opposition, and expropriating lofty terms for their side. Arkansas cities managed effectively to pin the odious label, "city-killer law," to a measure making it more difficult to annex suburbs, while Florida news media interests pinned the attractive label, "sunshine law," to a bill requiring governmental meetings to be open to the public at all times. Political propagandists publicize testimony from distinguished or popular characters, testimony favorable to their cause or unfavorable to the opposition, thus seeking to establish praise or blame by association. They know the drawing power of big names is important, as advertisers recognize in using endorsements of merchandise by stars of baseball and the movies. Political testimonials from dead statesmen (Washington, Jefferson, or Lincoln), may be more effective than those from living persons, denials or retractions being impossible, although there is always the risk of counter-quotation by the opposition. They use a mental transfer device, identifying themselves or their leaders with the people, the best people, or the "plain people." Willie Stark, in Robert Penn Warren's *All the King's Men,* illustrated this trick in telling Louisiana rural voters that he was a "hick," they were "hicks," and it takes a "hick" to help a "hick." Card-stacking arguments and charges show up frequently in political propaganda. An important example of this is the fallacious assumption that events or deeds in a sequential relationship inevitably have a cause-and-effect relationship. Another technique is asking questions that have no basis in fact or logic, thereby conveying a false implication to minds of the unsophisticated. A classic example of this is, "Have you quit beating your wife yet?" It is said that Al Smith once asked an incumbent opposition leader what he did with the millions of taxpayers' dollars which he claimed to have saved. It is not difficult to inject bias into the meaning and even into the statistical analysis of complex financial data by processes of oversimplification or of deliberate confusion.

Propaganda and democracy

The power of the masters of political propaganda to make or mold mass opinion through the expanding media of modern communication and the new political role of Madison Avenue's public relations firms has led certain informed observers to despair of democracy for our time. Walter Lippmann[22] is among those who have expressed concern on this point. But there is ground for hope for democracy through diverse propaganda, counter propaganda, and analysis of propaganda. The recognition of propaganda for what it is tends to develop an immunity or resistance to its impact in its extravagant forms. Democratic freedoms permit this development in ways not possible in totalitarian systems of government. American propaganda pressure, on the whole, is greatest in the realm of

[22] *See* Walter Lippmann, *Public Opinion* (New York: Free Press, 1965), and *The Phantom Public* (New York: Harcourt, Brace and World, 1925).

national politics and policy, although much of it also impinges on federal–state relations. At the same time, propaganda is subject to extensive check and scrutiny on the national scene, thanks largely to pressure-group competition and to an able coverage by a variety of journalists and commentators. Propaganda on this large scale is subject to what Woodrow Wilson called "pitiless publicity." It has not always been effectively checked or exposed at state and local levels, as muckrakers and reformers have discovered. But no propaganda engine has quite succeeded in shaping or controlling public opinion in all bailiwicks of a state or region or the nation.[23]

Much money is required to carry on the extensive propaganda and lobbying in America today. Millions of dollars annually are spent for the purpose of influencing opinion and action in matters of government. Additional funds flow partly, incidentally, or indirectly toward the same ends, as in various informational services and publications of private and public bodies. Some of the most effective lobbying is accomplished by public and private officials who are financed and classified for other functions. The ability to make outlays for political influence and action differs widely among pressure groups, being based largely on the expectations of returns from the funds so expended. On such a basis, it is normally easier to arrange for work and money for special economic purposes than for the general good—for groups of manufacturers, laborers, farmers, and professional men than for all consumers or all citizens, however important the interests of all consumers or all citizens. The idea that everybody's business is nobody's business often means that special interests outrank the general interest in financial support for pressure politics, at least in the day-to-day movement of public affairs between elections. Meeting this discrepancy is one of the problems of state and local government, of civic education, and of citizens.

Private or fractional government

The processes of cultivating opinion and influencing government should not be blindly praised or condemned. They are flexible, yet enduring as the weather. It is important to understand them as phases of political behavior and power. They provide channels of contact between the official government of the whole community and a network of unofficial "governments" of private groups. The network includes corporation government, labor union government, club government, lodge government, church government, student government, and a miscellany of other unofficial or private governments. These fractional units function in a pattern of social interrelationships and cannot be completely divorced from formal political government to which they are subordinate in final power. A certain amount of politics and political leadership is to be found in the private establish-

[23] We are not here concerned with the use of propaganda to solidify opinion for victory in wartime.

ments, which are conducted much like state governments, requiring internal laws, regulations, and prescribed rules of procedure. Intentionally and unintentionally, the fractional groups collectively exert a pressure of large proportion on the government of the community, whether the community be nation, state, city, county, or town. The pressure also moves in the other direction. The spheres of influence of the fractional governments are altered in response to increases in the functions of the state. Our public interests and our private interests are interlinked, for better or for worse. It is necessary and proper to study these interests in their interrelationship, not in isolation.

SUPPLEMENTARY READINGS

Bentley, Arthur F. *The Process of Government.* Chicago: University of Chicago Press, 1908.

Berelson, Bernard, and Janowitz, Morris, eds. *Reader in Public Opinion and Communication.* 2nd ed. New York: The Free Press, 1966.

Best, James J. *Public Opinion: Micro and Macro.* Homewood, Ill.: Dorsey Press, 1973.

Blaisdell, D. C. *American Democracy Under Pressure.* New York: The Ronald Press Co., 1957.

Bryce, James. *The American Commonwealth.* Vol. 2. 3rd ed. New York: The Macmillan Co., 1900. Part 4.

Frost, Richard T., ed. *Cases in State and Local Government.* Englewood Cliffs, N. J.: Prentice-Hall, 1961. *See* especially Part 2, pp. 41–75.

Hacker, Andrew. "Pressure Politics in Pennsylvania: The Truckers vs. the Railroads." In Alan F. Westin (ed.), *The Uses of Power: 7 Cases in American Politics.* New York: Harcourt, Brace and World, 1961.

Hennessy, Bernard C. *Public Opinion.* Belmont, Calif.: Wadsworth Publishing Co., 1966.

Herring, E. Pendleton. *Public Administration and the Public Interest.* New York: McGraw-Hill Book Co., 1936.

Holtzman, Abraham. *Interest Groups and Lobbying.* New York: The Macmillan Co., 1966.

Key, V. O. *Politics, Parties, and Pressure Groups.* 4th ed. New York: Thomas Y. Crowell Co., 1958.

Lane, Robert E., and Sears, David O. *Public Opinion.* Englewood Cliffs, N. J.: Prentice-Hall, 1964.

Maleck, Edward S., and Mahood, H. R., eds. *Group Politics: A New Emphasis.* New York: Charles Scribner's Sons, 1972.

Milbrath, Lester W. *Political Participation.* Chicago: Rand McNally and Co., 1965.

Salisbury, Robert H. *Interest Group Politics in America.* New York: Harper & Row, 1970.

Truman, D. B. *The Governmental Process: Political Interests and Public Opinion.* New York: Alfred A. Knopf, 1951.

"Unofficial Government: Pressure Groups and Lobbies." *Annals of the American Academy of Political and Social Science* 319 (September 1958). Entire issue.

Zeigler, L. Harmon, and Baer, Michael. *Lobbying: Interaction and Influence in American State Legislatures.* Belmont, Calif.: Wadsworth Publishing Co., 1969.

9

The State Legislature: General Features

Early importance and prestige

The state legislature, with its colonial origin, is the oldest American instrumentality for the exercise of representative self-government. The colonial assembly played an important role in the course of events leading up to the American Revolution, and British interference with local legislative processes constituted a significant basis of complaint against the colonial governors and the Crown. The first half dozen specific grievances set forth in the Declaration of Independence concerned the disallowance of colonial laws and the dissolution or disruption of legislative sessions and proceedings. America had already become a land of laws and lawyers, and the idea of legislative supremacy was prominent in the minds of the revolutionists as they undertook to transform the colonies into states. The legislatures, in fact, assumed the chief responsibility for these changes, as well as for providing for representation in the deliberative body of the general government.

It was only natural that the idea of legislative supremacy would prevail in the establishment of the Continental Congress and later of the Congress of the Confederation. The patriots entertained strong desires to have a government of laws, not of arbitrary men. It required years of experience for them to accept the Hamiltonian concept of energy in the executive branch of government. Men like James Otis, Patrick Henry, and Thomas Jefferson served in the legislative body of their state or colony in the course of their public life, seeking through representative lawmaking the safeguarding of liberty.

The members of a typical state legislature are subject to a large share of the criticism which politics and politicians in America are often subject to today. There are many possible causes of the seeming decline of this branch of government since the formative years of the republic, not all of them related to its eclipse by the rise of the nation and the national Congress. The broadside attacks of the muckrakers at the turn of the century and their influence on the public image of the legislature have doubtless lived longer than the conditions which inspired such writing. Typical of this turbulent stream of literature is E. L. Godkin's denunciation of corruption in the New York Legislature in 1898:

Later "decline" in stature

> If I said, for insurance, that the legislature at Albany was a school of vice, a fountain of political debauchery, and that few of the younger men come back from it without having learned to mock at political purity and public spirit, I should seem to be using unduly strong language, and yet I could fill nearly a volume with illustrations in support of my charges.[1]

There is a nostalgic assumption by many people that modern legislators lack the goodness and wisdom of their counterparts of older times when agrarian gentlemen gave their best to the state. This view takes inadequate account of the comparative simplicity of the legislative tasks of early years and also of the shortcomings of legislatures with respect to frauds in dealing with lands, banks, and bonds prior to the Civil War. Accompanying this view, there was the more vigorous and sophisticated complaint that our growing urban centers were underrepresented in state legislatures, requiring urban majorities to appear on bended knee before rural lawmakers or "red necks" and beg for "handouts" from the legislature. Herbert Jacob has suggested that "state legislatures may be our most extreme example of institutional lag."[2]

John Gardner, Chairman of Common Cause, a "citizen's lobby," has led one of the more massive efforts to focus national attention on the need for state legislative reform. He called the state legislatures "among the most scandalously operated instrumentalities in this country." In calling for wholesale reorganization he left little doubt about his appraisal of the status quo:

> Most of them are riddled with conflict of interest, riddled with corruption and wholly inadequate instruments of self-government. The conflict of interest in the state legislatures is the worst evil they have. There are men making laws who most of the time are in the employ of the interests they are making the laws about.[3]

[1] Quoted from the *Nation* in Ralph Volney Harlow, *The Growth of the United States*, vol. 2 (New York: Holt, Rinehart and Winston, 1943), p. 310.

[2] Herbert Jacob, "Dimensions of State Politics," in Alexander Heard (ed.), *State Legislatures in American Politics* (Englewood Cliffs, N.J.: Prentice-Hall, 1966), p. 3.

[3] Quoted by UPI in the *Arkansas Gazette*, Jan. 3, 1972.

Legislatures, as noted in a previous chapter, are guided and restricted by state constitutions more than was the case during early statehood. This trend results not only from distrust of legislators, but also from alteration of old constitutions to accord with what the people conceive to be the needs of a technological age. The increase of constitutional clauses has inevitably led to more instances of judicial review of legislation, with the consequence of subordinating the legislature to the judiciary in the public mind.

Constitutional restrictions

The executive branch as well as the judiciary shares power and functions with the legislature in ways not anticipated in the simplicity of Jeffersonian days. The modern governor has ways of leading and influencing the legislature. Moreover, a vast amount of administrative machinery, partly or largely under direction of the governor, is required in order to implement the work of the legislature, since laws are not self-executing. Administrative activity, furthermore, is constant and continuous, not intermittent like the legislative process. There is meaning in the witticism that "administration is nine-tenths of the law." Until the reapportionment revolution of the 1960s, executive–administrative leaders may have been more responsible and responsive than legislative bodies to the demands of urban citizens, who in most states had a larger voice in choosing the governor and other administrative officers than in determining the legislative majority.

Although the legislature has lost a measure of its comparative supremacy, its "decline" has been more relative and apparent than absolute. This deliberative body has expanded its functional role within the pattern of constitutional and political restrictions. Occasionally, a great deal is accomplished in a single legislative session, as is seen in James D. Barber's summation of the work of one state legislature in 1959:

A more balanced view

> How does the legislature manage to get anything done? Peopled as it is with those who come to be entertained, those who come to advertise themselves, and those who come to perform a vaguely defined civic duty, the legislature appears more like a clinic than a machine for the production of law.
>
> Yet they did produce. During . . . five months . . . members of the Assembly passed more than 1,450 measures, authorizing the spending of nearly 700 million dollars. They approved nine proposed amendments to the state constitution. They reorganized the state's entire minor court system, replacing 168 local courts with a 44-judge State Circuit Court. They abolished county government—a system in effect for nearly three centuries—and distributed its functions among various states agencies. They became the fourth state legislature to enact a Uniform Commercial Code, covering virtually all commercial transactions. They made major changes in the executive branch, creating new departments of Consumer Protection and Conservation. They

> authorized the issuance of $345 million in bonds for an immense highway program.
>
> Not all their actions were of such far-reaching significance: they also took time to define the word "stop," to specify the height of junkyard fences, and to establish the Irish Heritage Association. But both critical and enthusiastic commentators agreed that the record . . . was "remarkable" and historic."[4]

Composition: Who Are the Legislators?

What kinds of people make up the fifty state legislatures? Traditional efforts to answer this question have consisted largely of descriptions of legal qualifications and of statistical studies on such factors as the legislator's age, occupation, income, experience, and representational origin. More recent research on state legislatures has begun to suggest new ways of looking at our lawmakers. The old and new in combination go a long way toward presenting a realistic picture of the members of our state legislatures.

Four types of legislators

Four categories of legislators were discovered by Barber on the basis of their "personal needs and political adaptations" revealed in interviews with members of one state legislature. They are "Spectators," "Advertisers," "Reluctants," and "Lawmakers," whose traits may be summarized as follows:

> The passive Spectators, who enjoy watching the legislative show and want to continue on, appear to have been attracted by the prestige of legislative office, thus compensating for feelings of social inferiority. The Advertisers, active but unwilling to return, are out to become known, usually for business purposes, and show occupational insecurity and marked inner conflicts. The Reluctants are legislators under protest, performing a civic duty for their small-town neighbors, but experiencing difficulty in adapting to a strange, fast-moving situation. The Lawmakers, active and tentatively committed to extended legislative service, concentrate on the substantive issues, being freed for this by personal strength and powerful adjustive techniques.[5]

Barber's classification grew out of his effort to discover why so many state legislators do not return to the legislature for a second term, a problem discussed below. He concludes that the non-repeaters tend to be the Advertisers (one session usually meets their need for publicity) and the Reluctants (even one session seems to be too many for many of these).

[4] James David Barber, *The Lawmakers: Recruitment and Adaptation to Legislative Life* (New Haven: Yale University Press, 1965), p. 163. By permission of the publisher.

[5] *Ibid.*, in abstract of Barber's original dissertation, the basis of his book.

Barber's study is full of interesting verbatim accounts of his interviews with legislators. One obviously impressed "Spectator" gave the following account of the governor's tea for the legislators:

> We were very impressed. I mean you couldn't help but be impressed. It's a beautiful home. The Governor and his wife met us graciously and gave us the full roam of the house—"Go ahead, look at anything you want. Make yourself at home. We'll see you later on." And we wandered around. It's a beautiful home. Everything in it is beautiful. And, ah, then tea was served—so we had coffee. (laughs) So we were sitting around, or standing there, and the Governor came by and he talked to everybody, and his wife talked with everybody. So—before that, we drove up in front of the house and a state trooper, there, he opened the car door. The passengers got out. I got out. The state trooper took the car, parked it for me. And, ah . . . so we had tea, and the Governor talked with us. His wife talked with us. And when it came time to leave, we departed. And again, why—a warm handshake. None of this fishy handshake, but a warm handshake. And, ah, they thanked us for coming—whereas normally we should have thanked them for being invited. They thanked us for coming. And we got out there, the state trooper, he opened the car door. And off we go.
>
> Well, as I say, we had a wonderful afternoon there. As I say, we were only there an hour, hour-and-a-half. It was very impressive. You couldn't help but be impressed.[6]

Political socialization of legislators

Another way of looking at individual legislators focuses attention on their "political socialization"—the process by which "they selectively acquired the values, attitudes, interests or knowledge that fit them for legislative roles and make them take these roles in characteristic ways."[7] In the four-state study by Wahlke and others, legislators were asked "How did you become interested in politics? What is your earliest recollection of being interested in it?" Responses to these questions reveal a great diversity of roads leading future legislators to an interest in politics. Equally varied is the *time* of political socialization, indicating that politics may become meaningful to a person either early or late in life. However, it was found that the legislator's political interest is more likely to take place at an early age, often in childhood for many of them.

Sources of political interest for legislators

What are the major sources of political interest for legislators? The summary presented in Table 9–1 gives an indication of the origins of political interest in the states of California, New Jersey, Ohio, and Tennessee.

Already well-established as an important determinant in voting behavior, *primary group influence* was acknowledged by nearly one-half of

[6] *Ibid.*, p. 31.

[7] Wahlke, et al., *The Legislative System*, p. 70.

Table 9–1. Major Sources of Political Interest of Legislators in Four States[a]

Source of Interest	*California*	*New Jersey*	*Ohio*	*Tennessee*
Primary group influence (family or friends active or interested in politics)	34%	47%	43%	42%
Political or Civic Participation (in school, pressure groups, parties; study of politics, etc.)	70	60	49	43
Particular Events or Conditions (political campaigns; war, depression, state and local conditions/issues, etc.)	42	25	21	18
Personal Predispositions (sense of obligation, admiration for politicians, indignation, power, sociability, etc.)	52	53	52	33
Socioeconomic Beliefs (liberal, conservative, religious, etc.)	16	10	6	3

[a] Percentages total more than 100 since some respondents gave more than one answer.

Source: Adapted from John C. Wahlke, Heinz Eulau, William Buchanan, and Leroy C. Ferguson, *The Legislative System: Explorations in Legislative Behavior,* p. 86. Copyright © 1962 by John Wiley & Sons. Reprinted by permission of John Wiley & Sons, Inc.

the legislators as a major source of their political awareness. The law partner who was a city councilman, the grandmother who was a "suffragette," and similarly politically active friends or members of the family are cited by the legislators. Frequently political interest is almost a matter of family inheritance or tradition: "My first recollection of politics was when I was four years old and my father was a member of the House. . . . I played here in this room when I was a little boy."[8]

Political or civic participation was named most often as a source of political interest, indicating that interest does not necessarily precede activity. The reverse is often true, as in the case of the person recruited into politics by those who sense his potentialities. Classes in civics or politics in school cannot claim large numbers of "converts" among the legislators, but some apparently acquired a *sense* of political participation in the classroom, such as the one who reported: "The man who did the most and stimulated me the most was Dr. X, the head of the government department at the university. He was a Roosevelt New Dealer and I was a good Repub-

[8] *Ibid.*, p. 83.

lican. We had some wonderful fights. I still drop in to see him whenever I'm down that way."[9]

Particular events or conditions, such as presidential elections and national or local crises like war or depression, have made profound impressions on many of the legislators. The wartime covenant or the prison-camp resolve to return home and "do something about this mess" is familiar political history. The recollection of one legislator is less somber but equally real: "During the Bryan-McKinley campaign I hanged a picture of McKinley on my bedroom wall. My father took it off and I hanged it up again. He took it off and took me to the woodshed. I've been a Republican ever since."[10] Still others cite some local problem or issue as the source of political interest for them: "Our representative bought up land and sold it to the state government for deer, fox, and such. Mad foxes were biting families. There were rattlesnakes all over. My friends and businessmen wanted to get the land back."[11]

Personal predispositions were cited in various ways by about one-half of the legislators in response to the question of how they became interested in politics. Included were power predispositions—though few mentioned this specifically—as well as such factors as sociability, indignation, sense of obligation, and the like. It seems to be akin to Barber's "personal needs" concept discussed above. This might suggest that legislators are where they are because at least *some* men are "political animals." However, Professor Wahlke and his colleagues warn that, "If there is a personality syndrome of which one may speak as 'political man,' the data do not and cannot reveal its existence among these state legislators."[12]

Finally, *socioeconomic beliefs* have had a part in stimulating political interest but, with American politics generally considered more pragmatic than ideological, it is not surprising that all the evidence points to a relatively minor relationship between beliefs and political interest. As a whole, state legislators are only slightly more concerned about liberalism, conservatism, etc., than the people they represent.

"Role orientations" of legislators

Still another way of describing who the legislators are and what they are like is to discover the legislators' own expectations of what their conduct or behavior should be—their "role orientations." Making use of "role theory" as developed principally by social psychologists and sociologists, the collaborators in the four-state legislative research project found four "purposive-roles" among legislators responding to the question: "How would you describe the job of being legislator—what are the most important

[9] *Ibid.*, p. 86.
[10] *Ibid.*, p. 89.
[11] *Ibid.*, p. 90.
[12] *Ibid.*, p. 93.

things you should do here?"[13] The four roles which the legislator may assume as decision maker are those of *Ritualist, Tribune, Inventor,* and *Broker.*

"Ritualist"

The *Ritualist* tends to stress the mechanics of the legislator's job, so overwhelming and complex are the formal rules of parliamentary procedure. Preoccupation with legislative maneuvering, the bureaucratic and routinized maze, and mastery of the legislative work-flow chart can become, for the Ritualist, an end in itself rather than a means to an end. Some Ritualists may really be opposed to lawmaking, as in the case of one who reported, "an old gentleman once suggested to me that all we should do is pass the budget and go home. He didn't like laws. I agree with him in some respects."[14] Of course, the Ritualist's role is essential to the functioning of the legislature, but it is hard to conceive of a legislature composed exclusively of Ritualists.

"Tribune"

The *Tribune* perceives himself primarily as the advocate or defender of popular demands and needs. His roots go deep in American political history to the period when the colonial legislature was expected to fight the people's battle against the British Crown and his appointed governor. The modern Tribune is not so opposed to his government as his colonial predecessor, but he is still principally concerned with knowing the needs, hopes, feelings, and desires of the people, and being their spokesman. Some legislators take the role of Tribune even though they are not *personally* committed to popular views.

"Inventor"

The *Inventor* is probably the most frustrated legislator because, in a technological age when the center of gravity for policy formulation has moved toward the executive branch, he still perceives himself as initiator and creator of public policy. He focuses attention on what he thinks are the creative aspects of his job, and his self-image is that of the thoughtful, farsighted legislator of vision and imagination. The Inventor wants to solve the state's current problems—unemployment, mental illness, taxes, and regulation—by inventive effort, and believes the legislator "should be in front of things."

"Broker"

Finally, the *Broker* is consistent with the dominant theme in studies of the legislative process as the struggle between interest groups, constituents, and administrative forces. The Broker's job is to compromise and arbitrate, and perhaps also to "coordinate and integrate" the demands of

[13] *Ibid.*, pp. 249, 494. The discussion that follows relies heavily on Chapter 11, "The Legislator as Decision Maker: Purposive Roles." The authors' "fundamental working hypothesis" was that "a significant portion of legislators' behavior is role-behavior, that this behavior is substantially congruent with their role-concepts, and that insight into the working of legislative bodies can therefore be gained by ascertaining their role-concepts. The principal objective, therefore, was to discover the main role-orientations of legislators." [p. 29.]

[14] *Ibid.*, p. 251.

Table 9–2. Distribution of Legislators' Purposive Role Orientation[a]

Role Orientation	*New Jersey*	*Ohio*	*California*	*Tennessee*
Ritualist	70%	67%	58%	72%
Tribune	63	40	55	58
Inventor	49	33	36	30
Broker	33	48	27	15

[a] Percentages total more than 100 since respondents could hold more than one orientation.

Source: From John C. Wahlke, Heinz Eulau, William Buchanan, and Leroy C. Ferguson, *The Legislative System: Explorations in Legislative Behavior,* p. 259. Copyright © 1962 by John Wiley & Sons. Reprinted by permission of John Wiley & Sons, Inc.

conflicting interests. The more naive Broker may think only in terms of an automatic balancing operation achieved by listening to all sides. But the sophisticated Broker sees the need of a tough-minded appraisal of conflicting group interests "in terms of their moral worth, the power potential of the groups in combat, and the political consequences for his own position."[15]

Does each state have the same pattern, proportionally, of Ritualists, Tribunes, Inventors, and Brokers? Table 9–2 shows the distribution of roles and the variations between the four states. For a detailed analysis the reader should consult Wahlke's book, but the authors' summary gives an indication of the significance of each state pattern:

> In general, then, the data on purposive-role orientations seem to support the assumption that orientations are shaped by both historic conceptions of the functions of the legislature and by contemporary circumstances in the governmental power structure. In all four states, the traditional institutional requirements of the legislative office, centered in the legislative mechanisms, make the Ritualist conception an appropriate orientation in the task of lawmaking. In three states, the Tribune orientation is held widely enough to suggest that the state legislature continues to be an important link between the electorate and the government. The Inventor orientation seems to be relatively unimportant, except in New Jersey where legislature and executive were controlled by different parties and where the legislature may attempt to compete with the governor in the making of state policy. The Broker orientation, probably the most realistic but also perhaps the most difficult to take under modern conditions, was less widely accepted than one might have expected, except in Ohio where economic geography would seem to have made it more salient and central in the total legislative role.[16]

[15] *Ibid.*, p. 257.
[16] *Ibid.*, p. 260.

Still other role orientations play an important part in making the legislator the kind of actor he is in the lawmaking process. The old brain-teasing question, "What determines your vote—your conscience or your constituents?" gives rise to the threefold classification of representational roles: *Trustee, Delegate,* and *Politico.* The Trustee claims to let his conscience and judgment be his guide. The Delegate proposes to follow the instructions and wishes of his constituents or other clienteles. The Politico claims to follow first one, then the other, depending upon circumstances which may require balancing one against the other. Well over one-half of the legislators in California, New Jersey, Ohio, and Tennessee were found to be Trustees, with the Delegates being least numerous. It is probably true that under modern conditions it is more realistic to be a Trustee, and it may well be a functional necessity rather than a "pious formula."[17]

Representational roles

In terms of the kinds of bills introduced and pushed by the great majority of legislators, William J. Keefe suggests that legislators seem to be preoccupied, not with statewide matters, but rather with solving local problems, meeting local pressure, conveying advantage to parochial interests, and satisfying pet peeves.[18] The major bills serving statewide purposes are more often the work of outsiders—the governor, administrative agencies, or private interest groups—while the typical "legislator's bill" is commonly what Keefe calls a "merely" bill. Such a bill " 'merely' prohibits the possession of liquor in baseball parks, prohibits the operation of boats having a horsepower rating in excess of seven and one-half on this-or-that lake, or makes it unlawful to purchase lotteries or number tickets."[19]

Local orientation and "merely" bills

A problem that has long perplexed legislative reformers is the large percentage of one-term-only members of the legislature. Close to one-half of the approximately 7,600 members are replaced every two years, primarily a result of failure to run for re-election.[20] In his pioneer study of legislative tenure and turnover, Professor Charles S. Hyneman suggests that experience in three sessions is necessary before one can hope to be effective, and concluded:

Legislative turnover

> The real task is to find why so many legislators, senators and representatives alike, choose not to run again. Devices and arrangements which reduce the

[17] *Ibid.,* pp. 281, 286. Other roles studied include "areal roles," "pressure group roles," and "party roles." *See also* Wilder W. Crane, Jr., "Do Representatives Represent?" *Journal of Politics* 22 (May 1960), pp. 295–299; and Thomas R. Dye, "A Comparison of Constituency Influences in the Upper and Lower Chambers of a State Legislature," *Western Political Quarterly* 14 (June 1961), pp. 473–480.

[18] William J. Keefe, "The Functions and Powers of the State Legislature," in Alexander Heard, *State Legislatures,* pp. 38–39.

[19] *Ibid.,* pp. 38–39.

[20] Belle Zeller (ed.), *American State Legislatures,* Report of the Committee on American Legislatures, American Political Science Association (New York: Thomas Y. Crowell Co., 1954), pp. 61, 65.

> hazards of an election year to a minimum will still not give us a body of lawmakers rich in the experience of their trade. The state legislator must be made more happy in his career. . . . The key to rehabilitation of the legislative branch is in the nature of the legislator's job and his attitude toward it.[21]

Reasons for withdrawal

The four-state legislative study sheds some light on the problem of explaining withdrawals from the legislature, but no regular pattern for all states was discovered in the reasons given by 220 who expressed unwillingness to run again. "Economic reasons" accounted for 20 percent; "personal reasons" prevented 18 percent from running again; 13 percent considered the job "too demanding"; 12 percent thought they had "served long enough"; 12 percent mentioned "political considerations"; and 13 percent were planning to seek another office. The remainder were either bored or confessed to a feeling of inadequacy.[22] Obviously, returning to the state legislature is not high on the scale of values of these persons.

Reasons for returning

But why do the others (252) want to return? The principal reason given was "involvement" in the legislative job, accounting for 58 percent, while 33 percent gave "public service" as their reason. Other reasons, including additional ones given by the same legislator, were the status value of holding office (13 percent), political contingencies (15 percent), and a variety of "private reasons" such as service to special groups and something approximating "apathy," each of which was mentioned by less than ten percent. "Responsibility to party" was mentioned by only two percent. The findings of this study indicate that in states with a more competitive party system the legislators tend to be more committed to running for re-election (in New Jersey three-fourths of the members expected to run again), but Barber found no such relationship in his study of legislators.[23]

Socio-economic background

The picture of our state legislators would be incomplete without a brief look at their socioeconomic background. It is always possible to "prove too much" from such studies, especially if it is implied that high-status legislators always support the interests of high-status citizens, or that lawyer legislators always protect lawyer interests. Although studies reveal a rather strong correlation between class position of the population as a whole and their opinion on certain public issues, there is considerable room for doubt that a *legislator's* social background correlates in any

[21] Charles S. Hyneman, "Tenure and Turnover of Legislative Personnel," *The Annals of the American Academy of Political and Social Science* 195 (January 1938), pp. 30–31. David Ray has studied long-term trends of legislative stability in "Membership Stability in Three State Legislatures: 1893–1969," *American Political Science Review* 68 (March 1974), pp. 106–112. During a 75-year period in Connecticut, Michigan, and Wisconsin, there was a substantial decline in the number of first-term legislators and a general increase in the number of legislators seeking re-election.

[22] Wahlke, et al., *The Legislative System*, p. 127.

[23] *Ibid.*, p. 123, and Barber, *The Lawmakers*, p. 163.

simple and direct way with his voting behavior in office. If, as Peter Rossi suggests, lower status groups tend to be attracted to persons of high status who have deviated from "high-status voting behavior," then the socioeconomic background of elected representatives may actually be a poor predictor of their decisions.[24] Thus, the socioeconomic characteristics of the constituents may be more important in understanding legislative behavior than such characteristics of the legislators. Even so, the individual legislator's occupation, education, race, religion, and social status undoubtedly affect his decision making in certain respects and, viewed with care, such information can be another important tool in understanding legislators and legislatures.

Lawyers tend to dominate the occupational picture of state legislators, to the extent that their critics have been known to poke paraphrased fun at them, saying we have a "government of lawyers and not of men."

Occupation

Farmers have traditionally run a close second to lawyers but in recent years their proportion of the total membership has begun to slip. In the four-state study of 1957 legislatures cited earlier, lawyers accounted for 36 percent and farmers for only 10 percent of the members. Almost every significant occupation group was represented, though very few were engaged in occupations demanding manual skills and none were in unskilled occupations. Thus, if the unskilled labor force in these four states approximates the national proportion, 20 percent of the people are "not represented" in the state legislatures in this restricted sense of the word.[25] "Laborers" accounted for 2 percent of all legislators in the recent study which included all states.[26] Occupationally speaking, state legislators are principally "upward mobile," in that they have tended to take up more prestigious occupations than those of their fathers.

Education, sex, and race

It might come as a surprise to some, but legislators come from the best-educated sector of the population; more than three-fourths have been exposed to a college education. The striking contrast between the educational level of the state legislators and that of each state's total population is demonstrated in Table 9–3. The average starting age for state legislators is in the early forties. Women are no longer curiosities in state legislatures, although the typical picture would be one or two women in a given legislature.[27] Even prior to the 1960s, blacks were found in a few

[24] Peter Rossi, "Community Decision-Making," in Roland Young (ed.), *Approaches to the Study of Politics* (Evanston: Northwestern University Press, 1958).

[25] Wahlke, et al., *The Legislative System,* Appendix 5, pp. 489–490. *See also* two articles by David R. Derge, "The Lawyer as Decision-Maker in the American State Legislature," *Journal of Politics* 21 (August 1959), pp. 408–433; and "The Lawyer in the Indiana General Assembly," *Midwest Journal of Political Science* 6 (February 1962), pp. 19–53.

[26] Zeller, *American State Legislatures,* p. 71.

[27] *See* Emily E. Werner, "Women in the State Legislatures," *Western Political Quarterly* 21 (1968), pp. 40–50. *See also* Elizabeth G. King, "Women in Iowa Legislative Politics," a

Table 9–3. Social Background of State Legislators, Selected States

	Percent College Graduates	*Percent Professional, Managerial, or Sales*	*Percent Farmers and Farm Laborers*	*Percent Catholic*	*Percent blacks (1967)*
California					
Population	10	48	2	22	5.6
Legislators (1957)	54	86	13	17	5.8
New Jersey					
Population	8	45	1	37	7.5
Legislators (1957)	63	92	2	36	4.4
Ohio					
Population	7	40	3	18	8.1
Legislators (1957)	58	88	10	23	8.8
Tennessee					
Population	5	35	10	1	16.5
Legislators (1957)	46	84	13	2	6.0
Pennsylvania					
Population	6	39	2	27	7.5
Legislators (1958)	32	76	5	34	4.4
Georgia					
Population	6	35	8	0.9	28.5
Legislators (1961)	57	78	22	0.4	4.2
Wisconsin					
Population	7	37	11	29	1.9
Legislators (1953)	40	68	22	33	1.0

Source: Thomas R. Dye, "State Legislative Politics," in Herbert Jacob and Kenneth N. Vines, *Politics in the American States: A Comparative Analysis,* p. 178. Copyright © 1971 by Little, Brown and Company (Inc.). Reprinted by permission.

of the legislatures, in non-southern states with large urban black concentrations, and several southern cities had black city councilmen. With black voting on the rise, black state legislators have been elected increasingly in the South. In 1962 an Atlanta district elected a black to the Georgia Senate, and ten blacks were elected to the 1966 Georgia legislature—two in the senate and eight in the house. Only Michigan had more black legislators (11) than Georgia. The Mississippi House of Representatives early in 1968 seated its first black member since Reconstruction days.

---

paper prepared for the annual meeting of the American Political Science Association, New Orleans, Sept. 4–8, 1973.

One other social characteristic of legislators, their predominantly rural or small-town origin and outlook until recent years, has probably inspired more articles in the Sunday supplements of newspapers than any other facet of the legislature. Accounts of legislative battles with the more numerous "country slickers" putting to flight the "city yokels" have become commonplace. Strong overrepresentation of rural districts in state legislatures, for a variety of constitutional and political reasons, has been one of the major unsolved problems of state government. This problem, with its legislative implications, is discussed in detail in chapter 10.

Structure: The Institutional Setting

The formal institutional structure of the state legislature is important and deserves careful attention, but the student must beware of a common tendency to conclude that this structure is the major determinant of the output of the legislature, or of state government generally. Herbert Jacob suggests that the legislative structure and machinery "do not shape the outputs of a state government as significantly as does the economic base of the state (on expenditure decisions), the interest-group structure (on regulation of occupations and professions), or the political culture (on regulation of political activities)."[28] If his diagnosis is correct, it is unreasonable to expect revolutionary changes in the performance and end-products of a state legislature solely through changes in formal institutional structure. It would be equally unreasonable, however, to conclude that structural changes have no effect at all. The evidence seems to support a role of moderate importance for formal structure.

The role of formal structure

All American states, except one, have the two-house, or bicameral, type of legislature, comparable to the United States Congress. The exception is Nebraska, which followed the advice of the late Senator George W. Norris in passing a constitutional amendment in 1934 to establish a unicameral legislature of thirty to fifty members. Attempts to change to the unicameral system in a few other states have met with failure.

Bicameralism and unicameralism

Bicameralism is traditional among the states. Most of the original thirteen commonwealths came into the Union with the two-house system. Georgia and Pennsylvania, which entered with the unicameral system, soon established two-house legislatures. The state of Vermont made a similar switch after being admitted to the Union. There is little immediate prospect of unicameral expansion among the states, although the Nebraska experiment has won praise, several editions of the Model Constitution issued by the National Muncipal League offer such a plan, and

[28] Herbert Jacob, in Heard, *State Legislatures*, p. 36.

unicameralism has proved satisfactory among Canadian provinces,[29] Swiss cantons, and American cities. Despite strong arguments for the one-house type, the bicameral legislature prevails in the United States for historical and other reasons, including the seldom-penetrated wall of political self-preservation.

Arguments for the two systems

One important argument for the bicameral type of legislature is that it enables one house to check another and thus avoid mistakes. The checking process is supposedly due, at least in part, to the difference in the constituencies of the members of the two houses. The various interests of the state may thus be represented differently in the two houses, so that certain interests may be able to check bills in one house, with certain others holding the reins in the other house. This is a negative argument, sometimes countered by the observation that good bills may thus be killed along with the bad. It is also true sometimes that public opinion becomes aroused over unpopular bills after the first house passes them, bringing about defeat in the second chamber.

Advocates of the unicameral legislature point to the expense and complications of the two-house system with its too prevalent opportunities for lobbying, buck-passing, and miscellaneous scheming to thwart the public will. They emphasize that the single-chamber legislature tends to center and fix responsibility on the legislators, to bring lawmakers and executive together in policymaking, to facilitate the use of competent experts, to avoid legislative delays, and to cut down the cost of legislation. Their arguments are strong but do not prevail against traditional views and ways. Our state legislatures, with their two houses, find coordination of decision and action through different makeshift techniques, including the extra-constitutional and extramural.

Size

Every state legislature, with the exception of Nebraska's chamber of forty-nine members, consists of two houses of different size and basis for membership. The upper house, or senate, varies from twenty members in Alaska and Nevada to sixty-seven in Minnesota. The lower house varies from forty members in Alaska and Nevada to 400 in New Hampshire, with a median of 100. The total number for the ninety-nine legislative chambers runs about 7,600, with additional personnel for staff and clerical work. Most of the states, as shown in Table 9–4, have two-year terms for the lower house; about three-fourths of the states elect senators for four years. A few southern states have four-year terms for both houses. Reelection is constitutionally permissible and frequently occurs, but a high rate of turnover is a persistent feature, as discussed above.

Terms

The 7,600-plus state legislators are chosen, not so much to provide the number necessary for the work of lawmaking, but to provide what seems

[29] *See* Paul Douglas, "All Canadian Provinces Use Unicameral System," *National Civic Review* 59 (February 1970), pp. 92–93.

Table 9–4. The Legislators: Numbers and Terms

State	Senate Members	Senate Term	House Members	House Term	Total for Both Houses
Alabama	35	4	105	4	141
Alaska	20	4	40	2	60
Arizona	30	2	60	2	90
Arkansas	35	4	100	2	135
California	40	4	80	2	120
Colorado	35	4	65	2	100
Connecticut	36	2	151	2	187
Delaware	21	4	41	2	62
Florida	40	4	120	2	160
Georgia	56	2	180	2	236
Hawaii	25	4	51	2	76
Idaho	35	2	70	2	105
Illinois	59	4	177	2	236
Indiana	50	4	100	2	150
Iowa	50	4	100	2	150
Kansas	40	4	125	2	165
Kentucky	38	4	100	2	138
Louisiana	39	4	105	4	144
Maine	33	2	151	2	184
Maryland	43	4	142	4	185
Massachusetts	40	2	240	2	280
Michigan	38	4	110	2	148
Minnesota	67	4	134	2	201
Mississippi	52	4	122	4	174
Missouri	34	4	163	2	197
Montana	50	4	100	2	150
Nebraska	unicameral legislature			4-year term	49
Nevada	20	4	40	2	60
New Hampshire	24	2	400	2	424
New Jersey	40	4	80	2	120
New Mexico	42	4	70	2	112
New York	60	2	150	2	210
North Carolina	50	2	120	2	170
North Dakota	51	4	102	2	153
Ohio	33	4	99	2	132
Oklahoma	48	4	101	2	149
Oregon	30	4	60	2	90
Pennsylvania	50	4	203	2	253
Rhode Island	50	2	100	2	150
South Carolina	46	4	124	2	170
South Dakota	35	2	70	2	105
Tennessee	33	4	99	2	132

Table 9–4. *Continued*

State	*Senate* *Members*	*Term*	*House* *Members*	*Term*	*Total for Both Houses*
Texas	31	4	150	2	181
Utah	29	4	75	2	104
Vermont	30	2	150	2	180
Virginia	40	4	100	2	140
Washington	49	4	98	2	147
West Virginia	34	4	100	2	134
Wisconsin	33	4	99	2	132
Wyoming	30	4	62	2	92

Source: The Book of the States, 1974–75, pp. 66–68.

Representational districts

to be the proper representation for the multitude of political units or communities, such as towns in New Hampshire, counties in many states, or districts larger than counties in certain instances. The senatorial districts or units are frequently larger than those for the lower house; but the same basis, say a county, may be used for both houses, with more elected to the lower house than to the state senate if the constituency is populous. While much attention is given to population as a factor in apportionment, especially in the lower house, this factor is actually combined in different ways with others, such as allowing at least one seat in the lower house to every county in North Carolina or to every town in New Hampshire. While technically not ruled out by the Supreme Court's one-man–one-vote requirement, it will become increasingly difficult to maintain one seat per county or town because it will necessitate abnormally large legislatures. The one-man–one-vote principal does not require single-member districts and some use of multi-member districts is made by more than half of the states.

Technical qualifications for members are comparatively simple. As to age requirements, twenty-one is generally adequate for the lower house and in several states for the upper chamber. A few states have the requirement of twenty-five for a senator. It is quite generally stipulated that a member be an American citizen and voter. The length of residence required varies somewhat among the states, as does the residence requirement for voting. Political tests are more rigid than these official standards, however. It is difficult or impossible for a candidate to win a legislative election without an established residence in the district, town, or county of substantial duration. The importance of party or political connections should not be underestimated, for they are frequently more important than such factors as formal education.

Compensation and privileges of members

The compensation for members of the legislature varies widely among the states and continues to change from year to year. California, New York, and Illinois are at the top, providing biennial compensation of $53,490, $43,000 ,and $40,408, respectively. Massachusetts, Michigan, Pennsylvania, Hawaii, Alaska, Ohio, and Florida rank next, and were the only other states in 1973 with biennial compensation at $27,000 or higher. At the other extreme is New Hampshire, which pays its legislators $200 each for the biennium. The median biennial compensation increased from less than $4,000 to more than $14,500 from 1963 to 1973. About one-fourth of the states provide compensation only on a per diem basis for legislative service, with no pay for days or periods when the legislature is not in session. As recently as 1943 over one-half of the states paid their legislators on a per diem basis, so the trend toward the salary basis is clear. The per diem pay in 1973 was $10 or less in Alabama, Idaho, Kansas, North Dakota, and Rhode Island, but was as high as $100 per day in South Carolina. Legislators in many states have their highly unrealistic compensation supplemented by allowances for travel and other official expenses, and in some cases it is not an insignificant item.[30] The low scale of compensation is rigidly determined in certain states by constitutional provision. It is clear that many states offer miserly wages for legislative service, but it would be difficult to prove that the standards of performance are proportionately higher where the pay is higher. Many ill-paid members, however, find sundry ways of rewarding themselves indirectly, if only by putting members of the immediate family, other relatives, or friends on the patronage list, sometimes as legislative clerks with little or nothing to do.

A good scale of compensation is only one of several factors which tend to make a legislative career attractive to citizens of ability and integrity. State legislators have privileges and immunities somewhat like those of members of Congress. The state constitutions generally render lawmakers free from arrest while attending sessions and going to or from sessions, except for serious crime or breach of the peace. A member thus may not be compelled to leave or miss a session to serve as a witness or answer to a civil suit in court. A member may not be officially questioned in any other place on statements made in speech or debate in the legislature. Of course, his own house may censure him or even unseat him for cause, and a member is always *politically* answerable to critics and constituents as a public figure.

Until recently the legislatures of most states were convened and organized in regular sessions biennially, usually in January of odd years. The trend toward annual sessions has gained momentum, however, and by

[30] For a table showing "Legislative Salaries and Retirement Systems," *see The Book of the States, 1974–75*, p. 73. *See also Modernizing State Government* (New York: Committee for Economic Development, 1967), p. 81.

1974 forty-two states had annual sessions required or allowed by the constitution, compared with only four meeting annually in the early 1940s. Although some of the second year sessions are limited to fiscal and budget matters, the movement to include such restrictions seems to be declining.

Legislative sessions

More than half of the states limit sessions constitutionally to seventy-five days or less. This restriction holds down the pay of members serving on a per diem basis, and it tends to bring on a confusing rush of business during the closing days of a session, sometimes resulting in surprising or unfortunate legislation. Perusal of the legislative output from almost any of these hectic sessions will afford examples of such legislation. Florida, for example, in a legislative session some years ago enacted conflicting laws with respect to the compensation to be paid county commissioners in Okaloosa County. The attorney general ruled that Chapter 29752 should prevail since it was "the last expression of the Legislature in that its final passage was three days subsequent to said Chapter 29784." Sometimes the clock is turned back at the end of a session to provide time within the constitutional limit for disposal of the cumulative load. Another device is to meet officially for only one or two days a week toward the end of the session, thus leaving many days uncounted and free for clearing up matters through committees and informal adjustment. A method used intermittently by some states with limited success is that of the split session, with a recess of at least thirty days and no bills introduced after the recess except as approved by a three-fourths majority. California was first to adopt it in 1911, but dropped it in 1958. The inadequacy of sixty legislative days for modern needs has brought about an increased reliance upon special or extra sessions, which all states authorize by call of the governor and which may be convened in some states by concerted action of the members themselves. During the decade of 1960–70, a total of 257 special sessions were held, with the reapportionment emergencies causing many of them.

Restrictions on length

The picture of a state legislative organization is similar in broad outline to the congressional structure. There must be standing committees to deal with continuing matters of importance, including finance, taxation, education, the judiciary, and rules. Special committees are created from time to time for temporary purposes, sometimes for investigative assignments. Unnecessary committees may be created in order to spread memberships and chairmanships among the legislators for purposes of privilege and publicity. The representatives or assemblymen of the lower house choose a presiding officer, generally with the title of "speaker." A majority of the states have constitutional provisions for an elected lieutenant governor to preside over the senate with a role similar to that of the vice president at Washington. A president pro tempore is available to preside in the absence of the lieutenant governor. The senate in a few states chooses its own regular presiding officer.

Organizational outline

In two-party states the majority and minority parties have caucus machinery for organizing the houses, electing officers, and choosing floor leaders to carry on the work. Political factions take over such roles in one-party states, the division sometimes being between the supporters and the opponents of the governor's program and recommendations. The organization at times may be planned and determined by bosses and machines, as exemplified in former years by the Hague machine in New Jersey, the Platt machine in New York, the Long machine in Louisiana, and the Crump machine in Tennessee. Pressure groups may also vitally affect organizational structure of a legislature toward getting the legislation they seek.

Staff and service personnel

The make-up of a state legislature extends beyond the elected membership. There must be clerks, sergeants at arms, doorkeepers, pages, and messengers. Important committees may have expert consultants or investigators on the payroll in order to handle the work with efficiency. The last few decades have witnessed steps to establish systematic services to aid legislators in different ways. Three important types of aids are legislative reference service, bill-drafting service, and the legislative council.

The pioneer example of the first type, starting in 1901, was Wisconsin's Legislative Reference Bureau developed by Charles McCarthy to provide ready and pertinent information for the use of members of the legislature. Most of the states have followed this early example, providing in one way or another for reference service as an aid to lawmaking, and in most cases the bureaus are sections of the state library, law library, or archives. Most of the states have taken steps to provide formal assistance in the drafting of bills, which is particularly useful to farmers, businessmen, and other members not versed in law. In an increasing number of states, the legislative reference service and bill-drafting service are being made administratively responsible to the legislative branch of government, rather than to the executive, in response to legislative preference for controlling their own sources of assistance. The growth of legislative councils accounts for much of this organizational shift.

All but a handful of states, following the 1933 example of Kansas, have organized legislative councils to give continuous study to legislative problems and legislative planning.[31] The size and composition of the councils vary. The membership ranges from five in South Carolina to 253 in Pennsylvania, which is one of the states numbering all members of the legislature in the council. The median size is fifteen. In some states the governor, other administrative officers, or "citizen" or "public" representatives serve on the council along with legislators. In most of the states

[31] *See* William J. Siffin, *The Legislative Council in American States* (Bloomington: Indiana University Press, 1959).

the regular membership is restricted to members of the legislature and selected generally by the presiding officers of the legislative houses. In varying degrees, the legislative council facilitates cooperation in policy-making between the chief executive and the lawmakers. It may be divided into committees for division of labor, and it has a supporting staff of research workers and advisers. Some states, with or without a formal legislative council, rely on interim committees of the legislature to serve purposes of research and planning.

Working facilities: a comparative picture

The sharp contrasts between various states in legislative working conditions, staff assistance, and facilities is presented clearly in the following condensed picture for California, New Jersey, Ohio, and Tennessee:

> The California legislature has by far the most impressive working facilities. Each member occupies a modern two-room office suite, with a full-time secretary guarding the outer room, answering mail, keeping track of his bills and making appointments for constituents and lobbyists to see him. A Legislative Council with a staff of 26 lawyers and 22 clerks is available 13 hours a day during the week and eight hours a day on weekends to draft bills or estimate their constitutionality. There is also a Legislative Analyst, with 44 assistants, responsible to the Joint Budget committee for combing the $2 billion executive budget and recommending revisions in line with legislative policy. The University of California Bureau of Public Administration makes long-range studies of specific problems; interim committees with specialized staff work on medium-range ones. The Legislative Bill Room performs prodigious feats of overnight printing to give each member (and lobbyists subscribing) copies of (1) every bill with its latest amendments, (2) a "History" which shows the current progress of all bills, (3) yesterday's "Journal," with roll-calls, and (4) today's agenda (the "Daily File") for both houses and all committees.
>
> In New Jersey each member receives a small allowance for secretarial help which ordinarily goes to his wife or to his office secretary for keeping track of legislative affairs from his home or business office. There are no offices for members and few committee rooms in Trenton, but there are caucus rooms—the Senate's air conditioned. This lack of facilities in the Capitol must be seen in the light of the Mondays-only schedule, which makes it possible for members to do the bulk of their homework while they are in their districts. A Law Revision and Legislative Services Commission has research and bill drafting offices, there is a Counsel to the Legislature and a Reference Bureau in the State Library. Records of the session are commercially published.
>
> In Ohio the legislator's desk serves as his office for the session. Here he keeps his files, reads bills, answers mail and interviews lobbyists and constituents. He shares a secretary with a number of other members. A Legislative Reference Bureau, staffed by part-time law students at Ohio State, aids in drafting bills, maintains a file of back measures and also serves as a reference library. A bipartisan Legislative Service Commission consisting of 14 legislators and a professional staff of 12 persons investigates longer-range problems, using

the customary power of a legislative investigating committee when necessary. Some subjects are referred to it for study by the Legislature, others originate with the staff of director. Although the choice of subjects bears the stamp of majority-party policy direction, the reports themselves are comprehensive, detailed and "objective." The staff, while outside civil service, is professional and free of patronage appointees.

The Tennessee Legislature operates with a minimum of paperwork. Members work at their desks or in their hotel rooms. They have available for absolutely essential secretarial chores a small pool of stenographers on leave for the session from administrative agencies. The Legislative Reference Service has a staff for bill drafting, but some of the members who feel that omnipresent influence of the Governor here prefer to take their bills to the office of the independently chosen Attorney General. The Legislature provides each member with a subscription to the private "Legislative Service," which daily duplicates copies of general bills and, occasionally, important amendments (but not local bills or resolutions). Floor proceedings are tape recorded, but not transcribed until after the session is over.[32]

The Citizens Conference on State Legislatures, headed by former governor Anderson of Kansas, found in its researches that the appropriations to operate the United States Congress more than double the amount available for operating all fifty state legislatures combined. The implications of this comparison for the quality and quantity of staff assistance and working facilities provided for state legislators are clear.[33]

Powers and Functions

The state legislature's most important single function is that of making laws. But it has important powers and functions in other fields. Its role in planning, proposing, or perfecting constitutional revision has already been discussed in the chapter on state constitutions. It has important functions in connection with investigating matters bearing on legislation and the operation of state or local government. It has the power to investigate questions of removal of unworthy state officials through impeachment proceedings. The legislature in a few states has the responsibility of selecting particular state officials; however, this role has declined except for selection of the auditor, as will be noted later, and for rare cases of inter-

More than lawmaking

[32] John C. Wahlke, Heinz Eulau, William Buchanan, and Leroy C. Ferguson, *The Legislative System: Explorations in Legislative Behavior,* pp. 50–52. Copyright © 1962 by John Wiley & Sons. Reprinted by permission of John Wiley & Sons, Inc.

[33] Norman Beckman, "For a New Perspective in Federal-State Relations," *State Government* (The Council of State Governments) 39 (Autumn 1966).

vention in disputed or inconclusive elections. The legislative selection of United States Senators came to an end in 1913 with the adoption of the (federal) Seventeenth Amendment. It is usual, however, to require that important appointments by the governor be confirmed by the state senate, but this process is not applicable to a large list of civil service appointments made under merit systems, or to officials chosen by popular election. No state parliamentary body has any special role corresponding in importance to that of the American Senate with respect to foreign relations, although action in interstate compacts shows a resemblance to treaty making. Most state legislators, moreover, have less time for public service than members of Congress and likewise less incentive or opportunity to concern themselves with all phases of the governmental process. Making laws seems about enough for them.

Lawmaking

The state lawmaking power is a broad one, subject, of course, to a few significant checks and limitations. The legislature must conform to state and national constitutional provisions or run serious risk of having enactments set aside by state or federal courts. In all states except North Carolina the legislature must guard against a gubernatorial veto or be prepared to override such a disapproval in the statutory process.

The exercise of a positive legislative role within these limitations applies to a wide range of subjects under three general classifications. There must be a large body of statutes on crime and punishment, another set of laws concerned with civil property relations among persons, and a group of enactments on governmental functions and units. The work of passing laws on criminal, civil, and public matters is always with us, and every adjourning legislature leaves in its wake additional statutes, whether of a general or special type, on the three subjects. From time to time the session laws are brought together, edited, and annotated for publication in codified form. Even the codification process is conducted according to legislation enacted for the purpose. Our fifty state-law factories never completely catch up with their work.

Financial power

Every legislature has an important role in the field of public finance under constitutional directions and restrictions. In a strict sense this role falls primarily under the classification of lawmaking, but in essence it is much more than lawmaking. It is concerned with the problems of raising revenue and providing for expenditures, of administering finance and financing administration. The legislative power of the purse is a significant power developed through the ages. It was a check on the rule of appointed governors in the colonial era. This power today calls for fiscal understanding as well as legal learning. It requires close contact and cooperation with the executive branch of government, particularly in budgetary planning and management, as will be emphasized in more detail in the subsequent chapter on state finance.

Separate powers of the two houses

The two houses of the legislature have different non-lawmaking powers somewhat after the manner of the two houses of Congress. Each is judge of the election and qualifications of its own members, and has disciplinary power over its membership. Each has independent investigative functions, although joint committees of the two houses may be created for such purposes. Each house controls its own organizational set-up, according to constitutional provisions, and makes or modifies its rules of procedure. In impeachment proceedings, the lower house makes the charges, and the other house tries the case, sometimes removing the accused from office and barring him from holding state office in the future. Oregon, a state with provisions for the popular recall of officials, disallows legislative impeachment of state officials. Besides confirming important executive appointments, the senate in a few states exercises approval power over executive dismissals. A number of state constitutions, like the federal document, require that bills for raising revenue originate in the lower house; this stipulation tends to give that house more initiatory power in dealing with appropriations. The legislative houses function in different ways as forums and mirrors of opinion or group views. Within the scope of their rules and rulings, they are free to adopt independent or concurrent resolutions to support or oppose just about any issue or movement affecting state, nation, or world. They may seek in this manner to influence the outcome of bills pending in Congress. They may call upon Congress to provide for a convention to propose amendments to the United States Constitution, and Congress shall take such a step "on the application of the legislatures of two thirds of the several States." Such a feat has never occurred, although movements to this end have been attempted, particularly for the purpose of limiting national income taxes, and for the proposed "states' rights amendments" mentioned in Chapter 3.

Power through practice

The actual role, power, and restrictions of the state legislative bodies cannot be fully determined or understood by looking merely at the technical structure or constitutional frame of reference. Of equal or greater importance in establishing the position and revealing the picture of the legislature are the political factors, methods, traditions, and accepted practices associated with this branch and the other branches of state government. The legislature gains or loses power and importance partly by the way it works, as well as by the way the executive and judicial establishments function. It is now in order to turn to the legislature at work, which will shed light on the growing problems of organization and procedure on the American state legislative front today.

SUPPLEMENTARY READINGS

Abernathy, Byron R. *Constitutional Limitations on the Legislature.* Lawrence: Government Research Center, University of Kansas, 1959.

Barbar, James David. *The Lawmakers: Recruitment and Adaptation to Legislative Life.* New Haven, Conn.: Yale University Press, 1965.

Council of State Governments. *The Book of the States,* 1974–75. Section II, "Legislatures and Legislation." Lexington, Ky., 1974.

———. *American State Legislatures: Their Structures and Procedures.* Lexington, Ky., 1971.

Farmer, Hallie. *The Legislative Process in Alabama.* University, Ala.: Bureau of Public Administration, University of Alabama, 1949.

Guild, Frederic H. *Legislative Councils After Thirty Years.* Carbondale, Ill.: Public Affairs Research Bureau, Southern Illinois University, 1964.

Heard, Alexander, ed. *State Legislatures in American Politics.* Englewood Cliffs, N. J.: Prentice-Hall, 1966.

Janda, K., et al. *Legislative Politics in Indiana.* Bloomington, Ind.: Indiana University Bureau of Government Research, 1961.

Jewell, Malcolm E. *The State Legislature.* New York: Random House, 1962.

———. *Legislative Representation in the Contemporary South.* Durham, N. C.: Duke University Press, 1967.

Kornberg, Allan. *Legislatures in Comparative Perspective.* New York: David McKay Co., 1972.

Senning, J. P. *The One-House Legislature.* New York: McGraw-Hill Book Co., 1937.

Siffin, William J. *The Legislative Council in the American States.* Bloomington: Indiana University Press, 1959.

Sorauf, Frank J. *Party and Representation: Legislative Politics in Pennsylvania.* New York: Atherton Press, 1963.

Wahlke, John C., and Eulau, Heinz, eds. *Legislative Behavior: A Reader in Theory and Research.* Glencoe, Ill.: The Free Press, 1959.

Wahlke, John C.; Eulau, Heinz; Buchanan, William; and Ferguson, LeRoy C. *The Legislation System: Explorations in Legislative Behavior.* New York: John Wiley and Sons, 1962.

Zeller, Belle, ed. *American State Legislatures.* Report of the Committee on American Legislatures, American Political Science Association. New York: Thomas Y. Crowell Co., 1954.

See also titles listed for chapter 10.

10

State Legislation: Process and Problems

The how *is important*

The chief function of the legislature is to legislate. Even those states with constitutional provisions for direct legislation by statewide election formulate most of their statutes through enactment by lawmaking bodies. In other words, the voting citizens do not directly make the laws but choose representatives to adopt the laws. This chapter is concerned with the formal procedure, the institutional controls, the human behavior, and the political forces and techniques that constitute the state legislative process. It is concerned with the problems of that process as observed in modern times, and with the various ways and means proposed for their solution. The *how* of the legislative process is both important and at the same time highly complicated. It involves both visible and invisible features or practices. Mastery of the *know-how* of lawmaking is difficult, not only for the student or observer, but also for the legislator himself. This inquiry into the actual workings of the legislative mill at the state level must, therefore, be considered as only suggestive and not exhaustive.

Caution for "legislative sightseers"

An initial word of caution is in order for the student sightseer who makes the trip to the state capitol to view personally the legislative process. The total legislative process is never on display, not necessarily because secrecy is desired, but because it is never confined to any one place or time. To "see the legislative process" would involve being in scores of executive offices, legislators' hotel rooms, committee rooms, public hearing chambers, pressure group and newspaper offices, capitol corridors, bars, coffee-shop corners, and church vestibules, to name only a few scenes of legislative decision making. Nevertheless, if all these "feeder points" are kept in mind, a visit to the legislature can be worthwhile, for it is here that all other influences must officially crystallize into laws. It should be remembered that it is both dramatic and dull, but more often dull. The following description of one state legislature might just as easily be of yours:

> Connecticut's capitol building bears some resemblance to a rococo movie place. In the Hall of the House of Representatives, the bright blue rug, the ornate fixtures, and the elaborate stained-glass windows create a certain theatrical atmosphere. There were times during the session when the action matched the setting. One thinks of the stately drama of the inauguration, the light-hearted Saint Patrick's Day celebration, and the sentimental hatchet-burying ceremony with which the session closed. Occasionally, debate was dramatic (as in the struggle to reform the state's court system), or pathetic (as in the attempt to save a local hospital), or comic (as on questions of deer-hunting with bows and arrows and operation of barber shops on Washington's birthday). The original verse recited during the session would fill a small but entertaining volume. For the visiting legislative buff, the session had its moments.
>
> But they were few and far between. Considered as pure entertainment, the day-to-day operations of the House—the long-drawn-out committee hearings, the readings of the calendar, the perfunctory debates on minor bills and irrelevant resolutions—could not sustain for long interest of an audience of outsiders. As one who watched a considerable number of House sessions (often alone in the gallery), the writer confesses that he often found his attention wandering to the pigeons conspiring on the window-sills. Most of the time, to the mere observer, the proceedings of the House are dull.[1]

Fifty Patterns of Legislative Procedure

Like the human fingerprint, each state legislature is unique. It has formal and informal configurations of power and procedure all of its own, like other states in some respects, but totally different in others. It is only one part of the structure of power in the state's political system and is thus functionally interdependent with four other *major* political variables: the executive establishment, political parties, pressure groups, and the legislators' constituencies.[2] It is essentially this web of relationships, unique in varying degrees in each state, which explains the state's legislative decision-making process. A state legislative pattern depends upon a number of "ifs." *If* the governor dominates, the legislature may be principally a

Unique configurations of power and procedure

[1] James David Barber, *The Lawmakers: Recruitment and Adaptation to Legislative Life* (New Haven: Yale University Press, 1965), p. 23. Reprinted by permission of the publisher.

[2] This discussion is based upon the analysis in John C. Wahlke, et al., *The Legislative System: Explorations in Legislative Behavior* (New York: John Wiley and Sons, 1962), p. 245.

ratifying agency or may be preoccupied with checking executive usurpations. *If* the political parties are strong and policy-oriented, the legislature may function primarily as an arena for disciplined partisans to support the majority or minority leaderships. *If* the constituencies are effectively assertive, the legislature tends to focus on carrying out popular mandates. *If* pressure groups dominate, the legislature may function as an institution for compromising and integrating group conflicts. Of course, to these "ifs" must be added various constitutional requirements and limitations as well as a backdrop of history, customs, and traditions.

The four-state legislative study by Wahlke, Eulau, Buchanan, and Ferguson provides an excellent illustration of interstate variations in the legislative process. Notice the differences in what are judged to be the "essential elements" in each state's legislative system:

> *California:* (1) the vast number of bills; (2) the essential part played by the author; (3) the open committee hearing and the overt part taken by lobbyists in decision-making; (4) the "'automatic calendar" which gives every bill some consideration if the author asks it; (5) the importance of the floor vote; (6) the wide range within which the outcome of any given issue is unpredictable, depending as it does upon the actions of certain members who remain until the last essentially free agents; and (7) the irrelevance of political parties.
>
> *New Jersey:* (1) the small size of the legislature; (2) the strength of partisanship; (3) the dominant part played by the majority caucus *as a group;* (4) the irrelevance of committees; (5) the impersonalism achieved by rotation of members in the Assembly and officers in both chambers; and (6) the inability of the minority to make a responsible contribution to policy development.
>
> *Ohio:* (1) the complete fusion of chamber and majority party leadership, administered by presiding officers; (2) the smooth functioning of this leadership to the point where it is secure enough to treat the opposition permissively on occasion; (3) the importance of committees as the heart of the legislative process; (4) the general resemblance to congressional procedures; and (5) the formalization of structure and process required by the size of the lower house.
>
> *Tennessee:* (1) high turnover and brief sessions; (2) initiative almost entirely in the hands of the Governor, represented by his floor leaders; (3) the importance of floor action as the central point of decision; (4) the amount of time and attention devoted to local bills in a variation of the "unanimous consent" procedure; and (5) the negligible part played by political parties.[3]

Types of conflicts

State legislatures also differ in the type of conflicts that consume the members' energy and dictate their rivalries and alignments. For example, striking differences are shown in Table 10–1 between the Ohio and New Jersey legislators' concern about "labor conflicts," which are very impor-

[3] *Ibid.*, pp. 61, 62, 64, 65.

Table 10–1. Importance of Legislative Conflicts in Four States

Type of Conflict	*Percent Declared "Important"*[a]			
	California	*New Jersey*	*Ohio*	*Tennessee*
Urban–Rural	65%	53%	79%	91%
Party	26	96	49	23
Governor	18	76	36	89
Liberal–Conservative	58	22	52	29
Labor	65	18	61	54
Regional	69	18	17	13

[a] Figures are for members of lower house only, in each state.

Source: Adapted from John C. Wahlke, Heinz Eulau, William Buchanan, and Leroy C. Ferguson, *The Legislative System: Explorations in Legislative Behavior,* p. 425. Copyright © 1962 by John Wiley & Sons. Reprinted by permission of John Wiley & Sons, Inc.

tant to the former, but relatively unimportant to the latter. Party conflicts rank quite low in importance in California and Tennessee and exceptionally high in New Jersey. The urban–rural conflict is the only type rated important by over half of the legislators in all four states. Conflicts with the governor are ranked high in New Jersey and Tennessee but much lower in California and Ohio. In the description of state legislative procedure which follows, an effort is made to focus attention on both the similarities and the differences between states, insofar as they seem significant.

Floor Formalities and Activities

Talk, tactics, and legislation

It takes a vast amount of talk and manipulative tactics to translate democratic will and policy into law in representative assemblies, wherever those assemblies are located. Much of the debate and discussion is essential to free government, as emphasized by John Stuart Mill and many others.[4] Much of it is likewise unessential, if not definitely detrimental in itself, but partly unavoidable. Similarly the miscellaneous tactical maneuvers are employed constructively and otherwise, both to accomplish and to prevent the taking of steps, whether for public or private interest. Through such a combination of talk, action, and compromise, thousands of bills are adopted into statutes in the fifty states each biennium, while many more thousands of introduced bills are sidetracked during the legislative

[4] T. V. Smith, *The Legislative Way of Life* (Chicago: University of Chicago Press, 1940), deals with the relationship between talk and legislation in America.

process, never to become law. Some idea of the magnitude of the legislative load is afforded by consulting *The Book of the States'* biennial inventory of the number of legislative introductions and enactments in regular and extra sessions. Most of the legislatures introduce more than 1,000 bills in the regular session; New York leads the way with as many as 15,000 in one session. Very few states actually enact as many as a thousand bills into law in one session; only eight did in either 1971 or 1972, California's 1,821 topping all others.[5]

In this complicated process, significant technicalities and formalities are observed to systematize the lawmaking game. The average state legislature thus functions with a continuous mixture of inefficiency and discipline, with somewhat less systematic performance than is to be observed in Congress. It is more amateurish than the national legislative branch.

The quorum and majority

The question or problem of a quorum may arise in any type of deliberative body, public or private. All members cannot be present all the time, and yet regular business presumably cannot be carried on with too few present. Hence a quorum must be determined or defined in proportion to the total membership, or as a fixed number of members who must be present for official action or decision. Such a stipulation is designed to insure representative government against minority rule. The customary requirement parallels the provision in the federal Constitution that a majority of each house of Congress "shall constitute a quorum to do business; but a smaller number may adjourn from day to day, and may be authorized to compel the attendance of absent members, in such manner, and under such penalties as each House may provide." There are exceptions to the majority requirement, however, as exemplified in the Tennessee constitutional provision that two-thirds of the membership be present for a quorum. A provision like this may at times enable a stubborn minority through concerted absenteeism to block majority action. Even though a majority of the membership favor and can pass a bill; two-thirds of the members must be present under such a rule to permit action. There are stories of Tennessee legislators breaking a quorum and delaying the legislative game by crossing the nearby Kentucky border to become immune from arrest for non-criminal conduct. Normally, the lack of a quorum is corrected by calling in absentees from adjacent rooms or neighboring quarters or having them brought to the floor by sergeants-at-arms. But raising the question of a quorum, with consequent roll calls and rounding up of members, is one of the techniques for carrying on a legislative filibuster.

[5] The others were: Illinois (1,787); Connecticut (1,361); North Carolina (1,248); New York (1,214); Massachusetts (1,119); Texas (1,067); and South Carolina (1,046). *See The Book of the States, 1974–75*, pp. 84–85.

The passage of a bill, according to the state constitution, may require affirmative action by a majority of a quorum, as in Congress, or it may require a majority vote of the total membership, as in Iowa and Tennessee. Kentucky requires an affirmative vote by two-fifths of those elected and a majority of those voting. In the New Hampshire house a majority constitutes a quorum, but, if less than two-thirds of the elected members are present, two-thirds of those present must assent to render any action valid. A roughly similar rule governs action in the New Hampshire senate. Non-controversial bills and resolutions are often passed by a one-sided voice vote without a large attendance and without any check or challenge as to the matter of a quorum or a constitutional majority. This is particularly likely to occur in the case of local bills, in which only the members from the communities involved have an interest.

Introduction and readings of bills

No proposal becomes a bill for official consideration by a legislative chamber unless it is formally introduced by a member, group of members, or committee of that house, or is received with a certificate of adoption from the coordinate house of a bicameral legislature. Non-members, even high state officials, have no technical power to introduce bills, however much initiative and influence they may exercise in preparing drafts of laws and pushing them to adoption through a variety of means, including at times actual lobbying on the floor. Any member may introduce bills without limit, regardless of actual authorship, even to the extent of tossing in crackpot proposals "by request," but with no assurance that his offerings will get beyond the introductory stage. According to the practice in the state, a member introduces a bill by speaking from the floor or by filing it in the "hopper" to be announced in due course by the clerk or presiding officer, who then assigns it to an appropriate committee.

On its sojourn through one house a bill is given three readings, actual or nominal, unless it becomes stranded along the way without reaching the point of decision for adoption or defeat. A few states, Nebraska and the Dakotas included, have reduced the requirement to only two readings. Separate readings on separate days are required in all states, either by constitutional provision or by rules of procedure. Full oral readings were essential and also feasible in the days of simple government when convenient facilities for printing and distributing copies of pending bills were lacking. But such ample renderings on the floor are neither necessary nor feasible for handling the mass of complicated proposals, which the modern lawmaker must ponder and study for himself or in consultation with experts to approach an understanding of the problems involved.

The first reading, customarily by title only, occurs when the bill is introduced or is announced as having been introduced. The second reading, either in full or by title, is part of the process of considering the bill as reported by the committee to which it was assigned. This reading is usually accompanied by debate, perhaps by committee of the whole house, and this is the appropriate time for offering amendments. In many states the crucial vote on a bill is at some stage in the second reading. After passing the second reading, with or without change, the bill is ready for its third reading but must normally await its turn. At the last reading, debate is not customary but may take place with attention centered on the measure as a whole. The proposal of amendments at this stage requires unanimous consent. After passing the third reading, whether by title or in detail, the bill is engrossed and put in form for the certification signature of the presiding officer. It is now ready for consideration by the other house, or, if it has come from the other house in identical form, it is ready for its way to the governor's desk and most likely the statute books.

Orders of business and calendars

Legislative bodies conduct floor activities normally in accord with orders of business and calendars, making exceptions and digressions through unanimous consent, special orders, and the like. The daily order of business includes such items as the prayer by the chaplain, roll call, corrections of the journal, petitions and memorials, reports of committees, introduction of bills, bills on first reading, bills on second reading, bills on third reading, special business, unfinished business, and miscellaneous business.

The calendars are really lists of bills completed by committees to be taken up in sequence on designated days. Local bills, for example, may be placed on a separate calendar and be considered exclusively on specified days, as Mondays. There may be calendars for general bills, for unanimous consent items, and for other matters. Urgent or favorite bills may get top priority through unanimous consent or through special rules of a powerful rules committee, steering group, or informal majority leadership. This special treatment, in effect, reduces the priority of other bills and also reduces the likelihood of their getting attention by the deliberative body. But this discretionary treatment is part of the process of legislative politics, and it frequently is necessary for the passage of constructive legislation and avoidance of chaotic conditions near the end of a session.

Voting

Legislative houses cast votes on bills and motions in different ways. One method is by unanimous consent, with the raising of no voice of opposition and announcement by the presiding officer that the point is carried or ordered. Another is the voice vote (*viva voce*), with the chair judging whether the yeas or the nays have a majority. If there is doubt, there may be a show of hands to be counted or a division, with members passing by tellers in two groups to be counted. There are legal and constitutional ways for requiring a vote by roll call, with every member present responding to be recorded as voting for or against the motion or as being present but not voting. This is a slow process unless electric devices are used. A number of states have installed electric voting systems, with push buttons at each member's desk and with a scoreboard to flash each vote as well as to indicate the results. This method preserves a mechanical record of the voting proceedings.

Floor management: the speaker

There are ways of regulating and limiting debate in legislatures in order to get the work done. This is more noticeable and necessary for assemblies of large membership than for the small bodies. Most of the state senates and Nebraska's unicameral legislature fall in the latter classification, but the lower houses generally operate under procedural regulations that may be highly restrictive of freedom of discussion. The rank-and-file member of a lower chamber is likely to find it difficult at strategic times to get the opportunity to speak. Also he is likely to find his time limited to a few minutes when he does get the floor. Not only does the lower house make more use of rules limiting debate than the upper house, but the speaker of the house is often in a position to exercise more power and partisanship than the presiding officer of the senate.

The speaker of the lower chamber is invariably chosen from the membership. He becomes the chief spokesman for the majority party, group, or faction of the house over which he presides, keeping in intimate contact with the other leaders of the majority. That majority may be further strengthened through political line-up with executive leadership as exemplified by the governor. Under such circumstances, it is not easy to overrule the speaker. He has an effective power of recognition, with no little discretion to give the floor to friends and withhold it from enemies. He has the important power to appoint the members of standing committees and to assign bills to committees for study and report. He is in a position to make partisan interpretation and application of the rules in doubtful or borderline cases, although custom, politics, and majority opinion are checks on excessive abuse of this power. The speaker may rank next to the governor for his role in state political management.

Rule breaking and journal keeping

It might be said that all rules of legislative procedure are made to be broken. This observation applies to upper and lower houses. There are rules for breaking rules, for suspending them by unanimous consent or by a two-thirds vote. Even if rules are set forth in the state constitution, there are ways of adopting special orders that such rules have been applied when, in fact, they have not been applied. It is a type of legal fiction to record three readings for a bill when there may have been no actual readings. It is a further fiction, as is sometimes the case, to assume that the readings occurred on three separate days when the so-called readings were rushed through in one day. There are also fictions as to the presence of a quorum. It is an undisguised fiction at the end of a session to turn the official clock back and hold it short of midnight while the planet perhaps makes a complete revolution on its axis. These fictions are written up and authenticated in the journal of the house concerned as if they were not fictions. And the law is what the journal says is the law when the session ends, and the members go home; sometimes to discover in leisure what they did in haste. It is, furthermore, the practice of courts and attorneys general to accept the certified journals at face value, refusing to go behind them to check the process of a separate branch of government. Nevertheless, fiction, including the legislative variety, need not be inherently detrimental. There is hope that it may serve useful public purposes.

Unofficial "Rules of the Game"

Legislative procedure involves far more than written rules. Some unwritten rules are more important than official ones and the consequences of their violation may be a great deal more serious. The four-state legislative study provides an interesting catalog of such rules-of-the-game described by legislators themselves. The rules are grouped into six categories according to their primary function.[6]

(1) *Rules primarily intended to promote group cohesion and solidarity.* Respect for other members' "legislative rights" ranks high among these rules ("support another member's local bill if it doesn't affect you or your district"; "don't steal another member's bill"; "accept the author's amendments to a bill"). Another rule is that of impersonality ("don't deal in personalities"; "oppose the bill, not the man"; "don't criticize the moral behavior of members"). Others related to promoting group cohesion and solidarity include the rule of modesty ("don't be a prima donna"; "don't talk for the press or galleries"); the rule of respect for other members' "political rights" ("respect the incumbent status of other members"; "don't embarrass him in his district"); and the rule of institutional patriotism ("defend the legislature and its members against outsiders").

(2) *Rules that primarily promote predictability of legislative behavior.* Ranking above all other rules in frequency of mention is the rule of performance of obligations ("keep your word"; "abide by your commitments"). Related to this is the rule of advance notice of changed stand ("notify in advance if you can't keep a commitment"). Two rules concerning predictability relate to openness—openness of aims ("be frank in explaining bills"; "don't conceal real purpose of bills or amendments"); and openness in opposition ("don't conceal your opposition"; "notify in advance if you're going to oppose or introduce amendments").

[6] The discussion that follows is adapted from tables in Wahlke, et al., *The Legislative System*, pp. 146–147; pp. 160–161. The material has been greatly condensed but much of the language is theirs. The authors are indebted to Professors Wahlke, Eulau, Buchanan, and Ferguson and to John Wiley and Sons, Inc., for granting permission to use it in this form.

(3) *Rules that primarily channel and restrain conflict.* Perhaps the best example of rules to ameliorate conflict is the rule of conciliation ("be willing to compromise"; "don't be a perfectionist"; "accept half a loaf"). Closely related are the rules of seniority ("respect the seniority system"); and of apprenticeship ("respect older members"; "don't try to accomplish too much too soon"). In the states with more competitive party systems frequent mention was made of following caucus or conference decisions and observing "senatorial courtesy" in the more narrow sense of controlling appointments.

(4) *Rules that primarily expedite legislative business.* The most obvious rule to expedite legislative business, and one which ranked high in frequency of mention, is self-restraint in debate or, simply, "don't talk too much." Related to this is restraint in opposition ("don't fight unnecessarily"; "don't be opposed to everything"). Others deserving some mention include application ("don't leave after your own bill has been considered"); restraint in bill introduction ("don't introduce too many bills or amendments"); and commitment to job ("take the job seriously").

(5) *Rules that serve primarily to give tactical advantages to an individual member.* Some rules relate not so much to group purposes as to the personal self-interest of the legislator. Examples of these are courtesy, sociability, gracefulness in defeat, caution in commitments, negotiation, and self-restraint in goals.

(6) *Desirable personal qualities cited as rules.* Some legislators, when asked to name the unofficial rules-of-the-game, mentioned various personal qualities which did not fit readily into any of the above categories. Ranking first is integrity, followed by personal virtue, objectivity, ability and intelligence, and non-venality.

Possibly more significant than the rules-of-the-game are the methods legislators have of punishing those who fail to comply. Sanctions for enforcement are shown in Table 10–2, ranked in order of their frequency of mention by legislators in the four states. The arsenal of weapons is imposing, with obstruction of the non-complying legislator's own bills being most frequently mentioned. Ostracism, mistrust, loss of political perquisites and rewards, denial of special privileges, and public ridicule, are all recognized in lesser degrees of strength. Reprimand in party caucus is apparently significant only in states such as New Jersey where party discipline is high.

Committees: Active and Inactive

Legislative bodies rely heavily upon committees of different kinds and sizes for much of the actual work of investigation and lawmaking. They

Table 10–2. Sanctions for Enforcing Rules of the Game Perceived by Legislators in Four States

Sanction	*Proportion of Legislators Naming Each Sanction in* Calif.	N.J.	Ohio	Tenn.
Obstruction of His Bills: abstain or vote against him; bottle up his bills in committee; amend his bills; pass them only if of major importance to general welfare.	55%	42%	57%	72%
Ostracism: give him the "silent treatment"; subtly reject him personally.	24	14	31	29
Mistrust: cross-examine him on floor, in committee; don't put any trust in him.	34	14	25	12
Loss of Political Perquisites, Inducements, and Rewards: take away patronage, good committee assignments; report to constituents, local party organization.	15	9	19	4
Denial of Special Legislative Privileges: denial of unanimous consent; otherwise delaying bills.	9	8	4	2
Reprimand: in caucus, in private.	—	12	[a]	1
Overt Demonstrations of Displeasure: ridicule, hissing, laughter, etc.	3	1	2	3
Miscellaneous Other Sanctions	5	12	[a]	3
No Sanctions Perceived	7	14	11	10

[a] Less than 1%

Source: John C. Wahlke, Heinz Eulau, William Buchanan, and Leroy C. Ferguson, *The Legislative System: Explorations in Legislative Behavior,* p. 154. Copyright © 1962 by John Wiley & Sons. Reprinted by permission of John Wiley & Sons, Inc.

use committees to originate, revise, and report bills as well as to pigeonhole or bury numerous proposals, thus preventing them from reaching the floor for time-consuming consideration. The committee system provides a division of labor among legislators, opens official ways for engaging the services of non-member experts and advisers, and affords direct opportunity for individuals and groups to present pertinent facts and opinions on pending bills with which they are concerned. The system has superfluities but is, nevertheless, indispensable for modern democratic government.

Indispensability of committees

There are several types or classes of committees and committee functions. The most general is the *standing* committee for the consideration of all bills and matters in a particular field of interest, such as revenue, appropriations, labor, or the judiciary. There may be *special* or *select* committees to look into temporary problems, such as election frauds, civil disorders, or administrative scandals, to make reports and recommendations, and to pass out of existence when the special task is completed. There may be *interim* committees to make studies or investigations between sessions of a legislature. It becomes necessary to set up a *joint conference* committee, with members from both houses, to iron out differences when a bill passes both houses but in different form or language, and the house of first passage will not accept the changes. This is sometimes the only way of obtaining inter-house unity of action on significant measures in such fields as financial policy, administrative reorganization, or regulation of economic enterprise. Several states, for example, Maine, Massachusetts, and Connecticut, make extensive use of standing joint committees to consider bills in the first instance in order to minimize deadlocks between the two houses.

Types of committees

Many state legislatures have excessively numerous standing committees, particularly in the lower house, with Mississippi having 40. A few senates have large numbers, Texas topping the list with 46 and several others having just under 40. Counting the house, senate, and joint standing committees, the number comes to 83 for Mississippi. Several states have but little less. The smallest number is unicameral Nebraska's 13. A survey by the Council of State Governments indicated that the median number of house standing committees dropped from 39 in 1946 to 18 in 1969, while the median for the senate committees dropped from 31 to 16. According to the study made by the Committee on American Legislatures of the American Political Science Association, it would be feasible for state legislatures to limit the number of standing committees to about 12.[7]

Multiplicity and size of committees

Many of the committees have large memberships. North Carolina's 71 committees range from 8 to 63 members. At the other extreme are several states, among them Wisconsin and Massachusetts, where there are committee memberships of less than 5. Large memberships provide committee representation for various groups and regions of a state, but such memberships in combination with numerous committees inevitably en-

[7] Belle Zeller (ed.), *American State Legislatures,* Report of the Committee on American Legislatures, American Political Science Association (New York: Thomas Y. Crowell, Co., 1954), p. 100.

tail an extensive duplication of members, often making it impossible for a legislator to attend all of his committee meetings, even if he can keep up with when and where the meetings are to be held.

The committee process

The *modus operandi* of standing committees varies somewhat among legislatures and among the committees of any particular legislature. The rules committee, because of its continuous connection with house proceedings, invariably has the prerogative of meeting at any time of the day or night. Most or all other committees are generally required to avoid conflict of time with the regular floor sessions, except for urgent reasons and with special house permission. They are expected to meet evenings, mornings, or over weekends, leaving the regular afternoons clear for attendance on the floor. In considering bills, important committees hold public hearings and also meet in executive session to prepare reports on their assignments. Unimportant and "graveyard" committees sometimes rock along for months or more without meeting or report, particularly if a dominant chairman is opposed to action. It becomes common knowledge that legislatures are equipped with "hot-running" committees and "cold-running" committees, with "committee stacking" the method of determining committee temperature on specific questions.[8]

A large committee with heavy duties has certain characteristics of a legislative chamber at work, with a schedule or calendar of items for consideration and, perhaps, with a division of functions among subcommittees for investigation and report to the full committee. The chairman of such a committee often exercises significant powers to divide up the work and to guide, speed, or delay attention to measures assigned to his group. A committee hearing may take less than a day or may extend over several days or weeks, with all sides on pending proposals having their say and with members putting questions and arguments to the different advocates.

One-third of the states require every committee to report on every bill referred to it, whether the report be favorable, unfavorable, or without recommendation. This stipulation tends to prolong legislative sessions. The remedy in many states for committee neglect is to discharge a committee from handling a bill and recall the bill to be placed on the calendar of the chamber for debate and vote. The step for recall may be taken by majority action or petition. Such a move, however, is not easy and is no guarantee of final passage when the showdown comes. An unfavorable report by a committee may be counteracted by a motion to substitute the original bill or a minority report for the committee version, but this strategy is likewise no guarantee of adoption. The rank-and-file member might conclude from the fate of his bill that the Ark would not have been built if Noah had depended upon a committee and a legislature.

[8] *See* Loren P. Beth and William C. Havard, "Committee Stacking and Political Power in Florida," *Journal of Politics* 23 (February 1961), pp. 57–83.

The work of legislative committees varies widely in quality, and different opinions of the same committee work doubtless vary. One of the less favorable appraisals of committee work is found in a legislator's statement reported in Barber's legislative study:

> I've seen different members of the committee—not that I'm knocking them personally, but this is just a broad statement—they got holes in their shoes. Their heels are run down. Their ties got spots on them. And the way I visualize it, now, you see, you see them sitting there, so austere, listening to a (high official) making counter-claims about these points, and you know they probably haven't got a dime for a cup of coffee. (laughs) Yet they're to judge, or pass favorably on these matters that go into millions of dollars![9]

Quality of committee work

High quality is said to be more likely in legislatures with few and relatively small committees that can be streamlined for the exercise of both power and responsibility with less opportunity for bypassing the public interest. The streamlining of committee functions is not only meritorious in itself; it is also an index of general concern for streamlining and strengthening the legislative process. Committee work has been facilitated and improved through the rise and expansion of expert assistance. As pointed out in the preceding chapter, this assistance includes bill-drafting service, legislative reference service, and legislative councils. But the quality of work of legislative committees can rise no higher in the long run than the quality of the legislature itself.

The Role of the Party

Question of party's importance

If someone asked you which political party has the majority of members in your state legislature, you probably could answer quickly. But if you were asked *how important* party membership is in the legislative process in your state, you might have a more difficult time answering. Political scientists specializing in the legislative process find it very difficult to generalize about the legislative role of parties for all fifty states; even within individual states this can be a hazardous job. The ascribed role of party in one legislative session may come unglued one or two sessions later.

Two-party, one-party, and no-party legislatures

Statistical studies of party membership of legislators do give *some* answers. Many states, most of them in the South, are predominantly one-party states. In some respects they become *no-party* states because there is no reason for tight party discipline to protect partisan control of legislation such as might be expected in competitive two-party states. Four state legis-

[9] Barber, *The Lawmakers*, p. 40. By permission of the publisher. The last two sentences in this quotation appear in Barber's dissertation, p. 67, but not in the published version.

latures[10] consisted entirely of Democrats in 1961 and six others were more than 90 percent Democratic. By 1965 only Mississippi's legislature was entirely Democratic.[11] As mentioned in the previous chapter, legislative organization in such states tends to follow factional lines rather than party lines. Several states are considered strongly Republican, but no state legislature is wholly Republican and only one state, Vermont, was as much as 80 percent Republican in 1961. Vermont dropped to around 70 percent Republican in 1965. Two states, Minnesota and Nebraska, require non-partisan election of their legislators.

Party influence on legislative behavior

Statistics on nominal party membership, however, cannot tell who are "party men" in the legislature and who are not. Recent studies reveal wide variations in the extent of partisanship in legislatures, not only between states but also between houses and between parties within one state.[12] The device used in the four-state legislative study to tackle the question of party influence was to seek an evaluation by the legislators themselves. Their own ratings, summarized in Table 10–3, show a striking contrast between strong influence in New Jersey, moderate influence in Ohio, still less influence in California, and the least influence in Tennessee. The relatively high rating given Republican influence on legislative behavior in Tennessee reflects a feeling that the Republican minority occasionally swings the balance of power between Democratic factions on such issues as redistricting or segregation. As some Democrats expressed it: "You never thought about the Democratic Party unless the Republicans were trying something—for example, reapportionment".[13] A different pattern appears in Ohio where the minority party in a two-party competitive legislature is rated low in influence on individual members. As one House member described it:

> No one has told me to vote for or against something because I'm a Democrat. I don't know, though; it may be different with the Republicans. I think that they are closely associated with their party because they are in control. No one bothers us (i.e., the Democrats) because they know that the Democrats can't deliver.[14]

On the whole, a kind of quasi non-partisanship seems to exist for the *majority* of state legislatures for *much* of the time, certainly more so than

[10] Alabama, Louisiana, Mississippi, and South Carolina.

[11] *The Book of the States, 1966–67*, p. 45.

[12] *See*, for example, W. J. Keefe, "Comparative Study of the Role of Political Parties in State Legislatures," *Western Political Quarterly* 9 (September 1956), pp. 726–742; Warren Moscow, *Politics in the Empire State* (New York: Alfred A. Knopf, 1948); and W. Duane Lockard, "Legislative Politics in Connecticut," *American Political Science Review* 48 (March 1954), pp. 166–173.

[13] Wahlke, et al., *The Legislative System*, p. 359.

[14] *Ibid.*, p. 357.

Table 10–3. Evaluations of Party Influence on Legislative Behavior by State

Evaluation[a]	*New Jersey*	*Ohio*	*California*	*Tennessee*
Much/considerable influence				
Republicans have	37%	34%	1%	16%
Democrats have	22	1	5	3
Both parties have	33	16	—	1
Some/increasing influence				
Republicans have	—	7	5	16
Democrats have	1	6	15	4
Both parties have	—	5	34	3
Little/no influence				
Republicans have	1	2	8	2
Democrats have	—	17	—	4
Both parties have	6	12	32	51

[a] The percentages refer to the proportion of all interviewees making a specified evaluation of a particular party's influence on legislative behavior. The percentages do not refer to the proportion of legislators belonging to one party or the other, nor to the normal voting strength of each party in the legislature.

Source: John C. Wahlke, Heinz Eulau, William Buchanan, and Leroy C. Ferguson, *The Legislative System: Explorations in Legislative Behavior,* p. 355. Copyright © 1962 by John Wiley & Sons. Reprinted by permission of John Wiley & Sons, Inc.

Quasi non-partisanship of legislatures

for Congress. The frustrating efforts of Professor Wahlke and his colleagues to find a demarcation line between the "party man" and the "independent" or "maverick" in the legislature led them to the conclusion that "ambivalence and uncertainty about the meaning of 'party' is a fact of political life, felt by the legislators themselves; it is not just a reflection of the state of political research."[15] Chaffey and Jewell have focused on part of this question in a recent study of the selection and tenure of state legislative party leaders in eight states. They conclude that the more professional legislatures tend to have less turnover of party leadership, longer periods of apprenticeship for leaders, a more established pattern of succession, and fewer contests for leadership posts.[16]

Pressure Groups and Lobbyists

The popular stereotype of lobbying in the state legislature is a picture of legislative weaklings engaged in daily "surrender exercises" to merciless

[15] *Ibid.*, p. 376. For further research on this subject, *see* Alan Rosenthal, "An Analysis of Institutional Effects: Staffing Legislative Parties in Wisconsin," *Journal of Politics* 32 (August 1970), pp. 531–562.

[16] Douglas Camp Chaffey and Malcolm E. Jewell, "Selection and Tenure of State Legislative Party Leaders: A Comparative Analysis," *Journal of Politics* 34 (November 1972), pp. 1278–1286.

attacks from marauding bands of wicked lobbyists whose weapons are principally money and the power of political reprisal. That this is gross exaggeration of the contemporary state legislature should be obvious to the conscientious student of politics. What, then, is the role of pressure groups and lobbyists in the state legislative process? Much of the answer is supplied in chapter 8, but it may help to consider the question again from the legislator's point of view.

Exaggerated stereotype

The friendliness or hostility of legislators toward pressure groups, and awareness of them, were measured in the four-state legislative study, with legislators classified into three groups:

1. Facilitators: Have a friendly attitude toward group activity *and* relatively much knowledge about it.
2. Resisters: Have a hostile attitude toward group activity *and* relatively much knowledge about it.
3. Neutrals: Have no strong attitude of favor or disfavor with respect to group activity (regardless of their knowledge of it), or, have very little knowledge about it (regardless of their friendliness or hostility toward it).[17]

Facilitators, Resisters, and Neutrals

An almost equal number of Facilitators and Neutrals were found, 36.5 percent and 36.7 percent, respectively, with the remaining 26.8 percent Resisters. The realism of this classification is supported by the response of legislators to the question of why they thought the legislature might work better or worse in the absence of pressure groups. Although 63 percent of the Facilitators considered pressure groups indispensable to the legislative system, only 14 percent of the Resisters held this opinion. Resisters were the group most frequently expressing less favorable opinions, including the view that pressure-group activity "is a wholly disruptive force which ought to be eliminated."

Legislators' views of lobbyists' influence

Although legislators disagree on how influential lobbyists are, few feel that the omnipotent devil stereotype is an accurate picture of lobbyists. The four-state study found that most go no further than the legislator who said, "Lobbyists do affect the vote. Maybe they don't change your vote—lobbyists are only effective with those who are undecided—but they can sure make you bleed."[18] While most legislators were found to agree that pressure groups can, on occasion, make them "bleed," ultimate influence of the lobbyists is downgraded by such statements as:

> Legislators aren't really influenced much by lobbyists in the way people think. We go to their parties because we like free meals and parties. But no one ex-

[17] Wahlke, et al., *The Legislative System,* p. 325.
[18] *Ibid.*, p. 340.

> pects that to affect your vote. I don't know that any lobbyist ever really could buy anything.[19]

The authors of this four-state study do not reject the proposition that one of the central functions of the legislature is the "accommodation of interest group demands." Their findings add further weight to it but suggest, in addition, that in "refereeing" the group struggle, legislators may view the pressuring lobbyists with a much more impartial or "public-minded" eye than is generally believed. Concerning the quotation above alleging that free meals and parties do not really buy votes, Professor Wahlke and his colleagues concluded:

> Cynics will no doubt write off such comments as platitudinous talk for public consumption, but the impression of interviewers in all four states was that such views represent genuine convictions. Legislators themselves seem to be not only much more sophisticated in their estimates of the relative power and merits of various groups than they are generally given credit for, but also much more adept at parrying the thrusts of these groups and devising their own counterpressures against them.[20]

Regulation of lobbying

The frequent call to "do something about lobbyists" probably comes as much from disgruntled groups nursing wounds suffered from a recent legislative defeat as from any other source. Their lobbyists may have lost to other lobbyists. However, the call to regulate lobbying has received strong popular support from time to time, particularly as some example of abuse is brought to light. The problem of preventing abuses while protecting the right to be heard is not a simple one. The legislature is intended primarily to serve the public interest; yet it is composed of private persons and is steadily confronted with urgent pressure from private groups. The private pressures are concentrated, while pressure for the public interest is likely to be diffused. Moreover, private interests have the constitutional rights of speech, press, and petition, and lawmakers cannot be shut in, like a trial jury, and shielded from contact with interested parties. They certainly cannot be shielded from contact with the governor and other executive officers, who may lobby or exert other types of pressure. Pressure through propaganda and appeals to public opinion cannot be checkmated except through exposure or counter propaganda. But further measures may be offered to check personal lobbying around legislatures.

At times there have been more private lobbyists than public legislators at a state capitol, and such conditions have provoked severe criticism for their actual or alleged influence in corrupting the lawmakers. As

[19] *Ibid.*
[20] *Ibid.*

in many other ventures, individual states preceded the national government in seeking to regulate or restrict lobbying activities. Georgia, in 1877, adopted a constitutional provision declaring that "lobbying is a crime." Massachusetts and Wisconsin pioneered with legislation on the subject prior to 1900, and more than thirty other states have subsequently adopted statutes to combat the evils of the "third house." Wisconsin passed a new lobby control law in 1957, one of the strictest in existence. It prohibits the buying of meals, drinks, or anything of value for a legislator, thus attacking head-on the problem of where to draw the line between harmless courtesies and corrupting favors.

Important features of lobbying laws require the registration of paid lobbyists, the names of the sponsors, and the terms of compensation. Failure to comply with the requirements may subject the violator to fine, imprisonment, and denial of registration. The legislation has proved difficult to enforce, although it is said to have improved the practice of lobbying in a few states like Wisconsin. There are sundry and subtle ways of evading the regulations or secretly violating them. There is no legal method, for example, to prevent the election of a powerful lobbyist to the legislature, as hypothesized in Figure 10–1, where he can ply his trade with skill. Nominally unpaid lobbyists cannot be easily exposed or restricted, particularly if they are also important political bosses. There is a degree of hope for the public good in the diversity of purpose and competitive balancing of power among the special interests seeking legislative blessings through lobbying and other pressure tactics. Employers and employees may battle as lobbyists. So may railway and trucking spokesmen. Group may balance group and unintentionally promote the public interest, partly by exposing each other to the public eye. Lobbyists cannot completely disregard the effect of public opinion. (*See also* the discussion of pressure groups in chapter 8.)

The Heritage of Malapportionment and the Impact of Reapportionment

Prior to the historic reapportionment decisions of the Supreme Court in 1962 (*Baker* v. *Carr*)[21] and 1964 (*Reynolds* v. *Sims*),[22] rural domination of state legislatures was the pervasive and overriding fact of political life in state and local government. Although it is now a condition of the past, its strong influence for more than half of the twentieth century has left an indelible imprint on state legislative tradition. It is impossible to under-

[21] 369 U. S. 186.
[22] 377 U. S. 533.

BOARD MEMBERSHIPS
CORPORATION STOCK
LEGAL FEES
GIFTS
LAW-MAKER
GeoFisher
"Easy, Girls - I'm Married - Have To Watch My Conflict Of Interest, You Know. Hee Hee Hee!"

Figure 10–1. George Fisher in the *Arkansas Gazette.*

stand the legislatures of the 1970s apart from the apportionment and reapportionment struggles of the preceding half-century.

Aggravation of the rotten borough

H. L. Mencken, in one of his rare lapses into optimism, once predicted that the "rotten borough" could not last. Writing in 1928, he observed that, "The yokels hang on because old apportionments give them unfair advantages. The vote of a malarious peasant on the lower Eastern Shore counts as much as the votes of twelve Baltimoreans. But that can't last. It is not only unjust and undemocratic; it is absurd."[23] If Mencken could have seen the Maryland legislature and its apportionment at the time of the 1960 census, and that of the great majority of other states, he would have discovered that the rotten borough not only survived but,

[23] Quoted by Anthony Lewis, "On the Trail of the Fierce Gerrymander," *New York Times Magazine,* Feb. 19, 1961, p. 17.

in the face of the rising tide of urban growth, thrived in more extreme circumstances than ever. A state senator from one Eastern Shore county (Kent) in 1961 represented 15,481 Marylanders, while one from Baltimore County represented 492,428. Over three-fourths of Maryland's population in 1960 lived in the four largest counties plus Baltimore City, but they elected only one-third of the members of the upper house of the state legislature.

Maryland was merely one example of the rotten borough—a term originally applied to certain British districts prior to the parliamentary Reform Bill of 1832. Legislative malapportionment in 1961 existed in different degrees in nearly all of the fifty states. Only two states, Wisconsin and Massachusetts, had rural and urban representation approximating the democratic ideal of "one man, one vote," according to Gordon E. Baker in his study of urban–rural imbalance.[24] The 1960 census indicated that urban underrepresentation was getting worse rather than better, especially in those states deliberately basing their representation on land area or something else besides number of people. In California, the 6,038,771 people in Los Angeles County were represented by one state senator, the same representation granted to the mountain peaks of the Sierra Nevadas and the 14,294 people living in that district. New Jersey's Essex County, with its 923,545 people, had only one state senator, while Cape May County's 48,555 people were also represented by one senator.

Limits on big city representation

The fine art of gerrymander provides another method for bolstering rural legislative supremacy, with boundary lines of multi-county districts drawn to suit special needs. Muscogee County, Georgia (containing the city of Columbus) was the victim of a party tradition of "rotating" the nomination for state senator among the three counties of the district. Two rural counties (Chattahoochee and Marion) were joined to Muscogee County in Senate District 24 and each was given the privilege by the state Democratic party of nominating the senator once every three legislative sessions. With nearly 90 percent of the district's population, Muscogee County had no real senate representation in two sessions out of three, thanks to a gerrymandered district plus party rotation rules in a one-party state.

Some states were even less subtle in their method of limiting urban representation than the above examples of representing area or governmental units rather than people. A few state constitutions specifically

[24] Gordon E. Baker, *The Reapportionment Revolution: Representation, Political Power, and the Supreme Court* (New York: Random House, 1966). *See also* such studies of individual states as E. H. Hobbs, *Legislative Apportionment in Mississippi* (University Miss.: Bureau of Public Administration, University of Mississippi, 1956). For a discussion of methods of measuring malapportionment, *see* Glendon Schubert and Charles Press, "Measuring Malapportionment," *American Political Science Review* 58 (June 1964), pp. 302–327.

limited the representation of the most populous county to prevent its dominating the state legislature. For the three counties of Delaware, representation in both houses of the legislature was frozen in the constitution of 1894. New Castle County, with two-thirds of Delaware's population, was restricted to a permanent two-fifths minority status in the legislature as specified in the constitution.[25] Cook County, with over one-half of Illinois' population, was limited to twenty-four of the state's fifty-eight senators.

Balking legislatures

Probably the most frustrating cause of underrepresentation for urban people was simply the failure of the legislature to obey a constitutional requirement for reapportionment after each census. By 1961 six censuses had come and gone since legislators last reapportioned the states of Alabama and Tennessee, even though it was clearly required every ten years. Indiana and Louisiana had not reapportioned since 1921 and many others were not up-to-date with the letter of their constitutions. Far more were out of step with the *spirit* of their constitutions, having carried out "token" reapportionment without making a genuine adjustment for population changes.

Results of malapportionment

What were the results of this fairly consistent pattern of overrepresentation of the rural areas within states? The answer rural people give is obviously different from the answer of urban people. To rural people the result seemed to be the preservation of state government sympathetic to rural needs and interests, and the prevention of domination by city people who have no understanding of their problems. To urban people the argument was the converse, except that they could claim that if one group *must* be governed without sympathy or understanding, it should be the minority and not the majority which is thus overruled. While there was merit in arguments to protect minority groups from oppression, it was difficult to conceive of continued rural domination of state legislatures in a democratic nation 70 percent urban. In the final analysis, most arguments for continued overrepresentation for farmers, pastures, counties, and land area generally boiled down to a defense of rural people as "better" or "safer" citizens than city people.

City people contend, with a considerable amount of evidence, that rural legislators frequently vote against legislation desired by large cities, such as governmental reorganizations, increased taxing power, urban-type regulatory authority, daylight savings time, and welfare legislation. Some southern cities have had their "moderate" approach to racial problems wiped out by rural segregationists dominating the legislature. The greatest amount of friction may be found in the division of the state's tax dollar, particularly in such matters as rural versus urban highways. State legis-

[25] Actually amounting to 7 out of 17 senators and 15 out of 35 representatives.

latures have been very reluctant to share with the cities the revenue from motor vehicle taxes, and have tended to appropriate it for use outside cities. This has compelled cities to finance their streets and expressways from the over-burdened property tax, even though the bulk of motor vehicle use may be inside the large cities.

Several studies have suggested that the importance of urban–rural conflict in legislatures may have been exaggerated. David Derge found that conflicts between core city and suburbs, between parties, and between factions are more common in the Illinois and Missouri legislatures than urban–rural conflicts.[26] White and Thomas contend that urban–rural conflicts are more satisfactorily explained in terms of conflict among social, economic, and cultural interests which historically have been associated with urban and rural areas. They predict the future inability to describe such conflicts even superficially as urban–rural differences.[27]

Although Professor Robert Friedman finds that "urbanness and ruralness" are much less useful in explaining American politics than "more detailed interest groupings," he concludes that because legislators still *think* in terms of urban–rural conflicts, they must, by definition, be included as an important part of the political process.[28] M. C. Havens studied urban–rural cleavage in the Alabama legislature and found that urban–rural alignments do take place to a significant extent, though not on the majority of roll-call votes.[29] (*See* Table 10–1.) However, in a study of Florida, which was one of the most extreme cases of malapportionment, Havard and Beth concluded that any correspondence between legislative acts and the will of the majority of the people was largely accidental.[30]

The inadequate representation of urban people is often distasteful to the leaders of organized labor and to other groups opposed to rural guidance. The underrepresented groups often seek results through the legislative power of the governor, who most likely appreciates urban votes. For important types of legislation and investigation, urbanites may skip an unsympathetic state government entirely and look to Congress for

[26] David R. Derge, "Metropolitan and Outstate Alignments in the Illinois and Missouri Legislative Delegations," *American Political Science Review* 52 (December 1958), pp. 1051–1065.

[27] John P. White and Norman C. Thomas, "Urban and Rural Representation and State Legislative Apportionment," *Western Political Quarterly* 17 (December 1964), pp. 724–741.

[28] Robert Friedman, "The Urban-Rural Conflict Revisited," *Western Political Quarterly* 14 (June 1961), p. 495.

[29] M. C. Havens, *City Versus Farm?* (University, Ala.: Bureau of Public Administration, University of Alabama, 1957).

[30] William C. Havard and Loren P. Beth, *The Politics of Mis-Representation: Rural–Urban Conflict in the Florida Legislature* (Baton Rouge: Louisiana State University Press, 1962).

action, perhaps under the interstate commerce power. According to the President's Commission on Intergovernmental Relations, the unrepresentative character of state legislatures exerted a centralizing influence on the American federal system. Legislative neglect of the underrepresented urban communities "has led more and more people to look to Washington for more and more of the services and controls they desire."[31] The Commission notes that "The same shift of population which has resulted in State legislatures becoming less representative of urban areas has had the effect of making the United States Senate more representative of these areas, because Senators, elected at large, must depend heavily upon urban voters, even in predominantly rural States."[32]

Malapportionment and centralization

Why was it impossible, at least prior to *Baker* v. *Carr,* to reapportion state legislatures to reflect twentieth-century realities in population? The answer is found in a combination of obstacles to change: the vested interest of legislators, economic and sectional interests that cut across urban–rural cleavages, abnormal restrictions on revising old constitutions, and public apathy. The desire of legislators to preserve the status quo is well known. Professors Steiner and Gove report that legislators, even when forced to act (as in the case of Illinois in 1955), still can be expected to work on behalf of the following vested interests:

The politics of apportionment

1. Individual preservation, the desire to be in a "safe" district.
2. Mutual preservation, the willingness of members to cooperate with each other in protecting incumbents against potential challengers.
3. Political party preservation, the desire of the leaders of each political party organization to maximize its strength in the legislature.
4. Bloc preservation, the desire of members of voting blocs—whether based on geographic, economic, or ideological cohesion—to retain existing personnel and strength. Such blocs are often bipartisan, and their membership is relatively small.[33]

The politics of reapportionment is not simply a rural versus urban conflict. Urban business groups sometimes oppose reapportionment and the resulting increase in urban legislative strength because of a preference for the more conservative policies of rural legislators. As a Salt Lake City businessman, opposed to reapportionment in Utah, explained, "It's better the way it is. People from the country are less radical."[34] Even the leader

[31] Commission on Intergovernmental Relations, *A Report to the President for Transmittal to the Congress* (Washington, D. C.: U. S. Government Printing Office, 1955), p. 39.

[32] *Ibid.*, p. 40.

[33] Gilbert Y. Steiner and Samuel K. Gove, *The Legislature Redistricts Illinois* (Urbana: University of Illinois, Institute of Government and Public Affairs, 1956), p. 71.

[34] Ernest H. Linford in Robert S. Allen (ed.), *Our Sovereign State* (New York: Vanguard Press, 1949), p. 350.

of the normally urban-minded AFL–CIO in a southern border state maintained that he received more sympathetic consideration from "intelligent rural legislators" than from the "bums" elected at-large from the metropolitan counties.[35] Geographic and partisan factors may also work at cross purposes with simple urban interests. Highly urban San Francisco once helped reject a proposal which would have increased its strength in the California senate, fearing the additional consequence of multiplying the legislative strength of Los Angeles and Southern California. The urban push for reapportionment often loses steam when it is discovered that the principal benefits will go to the opposition political party, currently in a minority status. Such was the case in Tennessee where much of the gain went to solidly Republican east Tennessee.

Economic and sectional crosscurrents

A seemingly inevitable result of repeated frustration of reapportionment efforts, whether at the hands of a recalcitrant legislature or of a rigidly unchanging constitution, was creeping public apathy. Even under the most favorable conditions, representation and apportionment issues competed poorly with such hardy perennials as schools, roads, pensions, and taxes. Nevertheless, in some states—e.g., Oregon, Washington, Colorado, Minnesota, Illinois, and New York—the public interest in this issue was aroused to a considerable degree.[36] In several states political frustration led to court action, in an attempt to compel the fulfillment of a constitutional obligation. Early results of such efforts were not encouraging, with the judiciary refusing to dictate to its "sister" under the doctrine of separation of powers. The plaintiffs were given the hollow prescription that the only remedy was to elect a legislature that would perform its duty and were told it was a political question, not a judicial one.[37]

Public apathy

Courts and reapportionment

Court action concerning reapportionment finally became more bold and imaginative in the late 1950s. A federal district court in Minnesota in 1958 accepted jurisdiction in a case demanding at-large election of legislators because of failure to reapportion since 1913. With a veiled threat of subsequent action, the court postponed a decision to afford the legislature another opportunity to "heed the constitutional mandate to redistrict."[38] This unusual assertion of judicial power was followed by a

[35] Wilder Crane, "Tennessee: Inertia and the Courts," Chapter 17 in Malcolm E. Jewell (ed.), *The Politics of Reapportionment* (New York: Atherton Press, 1962), p. 317.

[36] Gordon E. Baker, *State Constitutions: Reapportionment* (New York: National Municipal League, 1960), p. 39. *See also* his study, *The Politics of Reapportionment in Washington State,* "Eagleton Case Studies in Practical Politics" series (New York: Holt, Rinehart and Winston, 1961).

[37] *Colegrove* v. *Green*, 328 U. S. 549 (1946).

[38] *Smith* v. *Holm*, 220 Minn. 486 (1945), quoted in *Magraw* v. *Donovan* (Minn. Fed. Dist., 3d Div.), Civil 2981 (July 10, 1958).

long legislative struggle and finally by passage in 1959 of the first redistricting bill in Minnesota in forty-six years. Though the bill fell far short of the prescribed population basis, it offered substantial improvement for the urban areas, and especially for the five-county Twin City metropolitan area. The Supreme Court moved to eliminate one kind of gerrymandering in 1960 when it held that the Alabama legislature could not re-draw the city limits of Tuskegee so as to exclude virtually all black residents.[39]

Baker v. Carr *and aftermath*

The Tennessee legislature met in 1961 under the threat of U. S. Supreme Court action, but failed to follow the Minnesota legislature's example. The almost immediate result was a 6-to-2 landmark decision reversing the no-jurisdiction precedent of *Colegrove* v. *Green,* but leaving to the lower federal courts the task of deciding whether actual discrimination exists in violation of the Fourteenth Amendment. The case of *Baker* v. *Carr* set forth three main propositions: (1) voters may sue for relief from any unconstitutional interference with their right to vote; (2) a complaint that discriminatory and arbitrary state apportionment violates the Fourteenth Amendment, whether well-founded or not, is a claim falling within the jurisdiction of the federal courts; and (3) merely because such a claim raises a political question is not sufficient cause for dismissing such a case.

Reaction to this decision was electric, varying from the charge by more than one southern senator that it was a "death blow" to states' rights, to the prediction that it would so reform state government that the "look-to-Washington" trend will grind to a halt. Justice Frankfurter, the only remaining member of the Court who cast one of the four majority votes in the 1946 Colegrove decision, wrote a vigorous dissent in the 1962 case, calling it "a massive repudiation of the experience of our whole past in asserting destructively novel judicial power." While arguments with counter-arguments were still ringing, however, politically starved cities lost no time in moving through the judicially opened door. Rural-minded state legislatures shook off a half-century of lethargy and began frantic explorations in special sessions to discover whether limited concessions to the cities might stave off more drastic judicial action. The unprecedented activity during the six months following *Baker* v. *Carr* included the adoption of reapportionment laws by eight legislatures in special sessions, the filing of forty-eight law suits in thirty states, the handing down of forty-one lower court decisions, and the initiation of ten constitutional amendments affecting reapportionment.

As auspicious as this beginning was, it was not until the Supreme Court decided to go all the way with "one-man–one-vote" in *Reynolds* v.

[39] *Gomillion* v. *Lightfoot,* 364 U. S. 347 (1960).

Sims (1964)[40] that the full extent of the court's requirement became clear. By a vote of 8 to 1, the Court held that both houses of the legislature must be apportioned on a population basis, rejecting the so-called "federal analogy" which defends the right of a state senate to imitate the U. S. Senate and represent geographic areas or political units rather than people. The federal analogy was held to be "inapposite and irrelevant" because the states are not little federal unions in which counties and cities have a similar legal relationship to the states as the states have to the nation. Chief Justice Warren concluded that "legislators represent people, not trees or acres" and that they "are elected by voters, not farms or cities or economic interests." Figure 10–2 indicates one cartoonist's interpretation of the Reynolds decision. The Reynolds decision touched off an opposition movement for a constitutional amendment designed to permit states to decide whether they want one house of their legislature apportioned on some basis other than population. Led by Senator Dirksen of Illinois, the proposed amendment failed to get the necessary two-thirds vote of the Senate on more than one occasion.

Population basis for both houses

The amazing reapportionment revolution started by *Baker* v. *Carr* was given additional wind currents by *Reynolds* v. *Sims,* and it took only about two years to result in substantial adherence to the equal population principle in virtually all of the fifty states. Answers have begun to emerge to questions about the mechanics of apportionment and districting, such as the mathematical extent of disparities in district population allowed; the required frequency of reapportionment; the approved population base; the issue of multi-member versus single-member districts; and the age-old problem of gerrymandering. Early in 1973 the Supreme Court pulled back from requiring absolute mathematical exactness of equality in the districts of the Virginia House of Delegates. In a 5-to-3 ruling,[41] it approved a plan with variation of 16.4 percent from the largest to the smallest district. Reapportionment every ten years was not specified as a rule by the Court, but it was endorsed as "a rational approach" to the task of adjusting to population movements and growth. The Court has permitted reasonable variations among states in determining what "population" shall be used as a base for equal representation—census figures, citizens only, or registered voters—so long as it does not appear to result in malapportionment. While the Court approved the use of a registered-voter base in Hawaii as a reasonable means of excluding tourists and military personnel from calculations, it served notice that it was not endorsing

Effect on mechanics of representation

[40] 377 U. S. 533. Five companion cases were decided at the same time, involving New York, Maryland, Virginia, and Colorado. The Reynolds case involved Alabama. For an in-depth account of the New York case, *see* Calvin B. T. Lee, *One Man, One Vote: WMCA and the Struggle for Equal Representation* (New York: Charles Scribner's Sons, 1967).

[41] *Mahan* v. *Howell,* 93 S.Ct. 979 (1973).

Sanders in The Kansas City Star

"Great Scott! We've lost our vote!"

Figure 10–2. Sanders in *The Kansas City Star.*

this method for all times or circumstances.[42] Although multi-member districts are frequently criticized as discriminatory against urban minorities of blacks and Republicans, the Court has given qualified endorsement to their use. The majority of states have one or more multi-member districts.[43]

No and yes on multi-member districts

For a brief four days in 1971 it seemed that the Supreme Court had ruled that the at-large election of state legislators from multi-member districts is an unconstitutional device, designed to avoid black or other minority representation. This was the ruling for Hinds County (Jackson),

[42] *Burns* v. *Richardson,* 384 U. S. 73 (1965).

[43] For an analysis of various criteria for reapportionment, *see* Howard D. Hamilton (ed.), *Reapportioning Legislatures: A Consideration of Criteria and Computers* (Columbus, Ohio: Charles E. Merrill, 1966). Details on reapportionment in each state are in a 400-page compendium edited by William J. D. Boyd, *Apportionment in the 1960's: State Legislatures, Congressional Districts* (New York: National Municipal League, 1967). *See also* Boyd's "Apportionment and Districting: Problems of Compliance," *National Civic Review* 60 (April 1971), pp. 199–203.

Mississippi; the court required that this most populous county in the state be divided into single-member legislative districts.[44] In the same year, however, the same court declined to rule out the multi-member district in Marion County (Indianapolis), Indiana, even though it tended to reduce the chances of minority candidates.[45] Although there seems to be no way to avoid the uncomfortable aura of inconsistency about the two decisions, the most plausible explanation is that the court gave the benefit of the doubt to Indiana but not to Mississippi, with its long history of legal segregation and disfranchisement of blacks.

Partisan gerrymandering

As the number of ways to malapportion a legislature has been steadily reduced by court action, gerrymandering remains one of the last devices for accomplishing this purpose. Although racial gerrymandering of the city of Tuskegee's boundaries was outlawed in the *Gomillion* case, the issue of partisan gerrymandering has not been dealt with by the courts. Since it is doubtful that an easily administered test for determining gerrymandered district boundaries can be developed by the courts, the odds are against judicial efforts to apply the equal protection clause in this field. It may well remain the only unpenetrated part of Justice Frankfurter's "political thicket" of legislative representation.

Assessing reapportionment effects

Alleged effects of malapportioned state legislatures have been catalogued by such critics as H. L. Mencken for many years and have been accepted somewhat "on faith" by advocates of reapportionment. When it became apparent that malapportionment was coming to an end, the predicted results were simply the opposite conditions to those catalogued ills—more financial and technical aid to cities, less arbitrary state interference with city government, greater state concern for the core-city problems of blight, congestion, and poverty, and less "red-neck" conservatism, racial bigotry, and bias against the stereotyped sinful, corrupt cities. While it is still too early to assess actual effects, it is already clear that at least one intervening variable is modifying the expected results. The suburbs, not the central cities, have made the greatest gains in legislative representation and stand to gain even more in coming years. As William J. D. Boyd has expressed it, "The United States is an urban nation but not a big-city nation. The suburbs own the future."[46] Even before the Baker decision David and Eisenberg reported that while most core cities were still somewhat underrepresented in state legislatures, their plight was not nearly so acute as that of suburban counties.[47] Thus, the earlier image of

Greater suburban than urban gains

[44] *Conner* v. *Johnson*, 402 U.S. 690 (1971).

[45] *Whitcomb* v. *Chavis*, 403 U. S. 124 (1971).

[46] William J. D. Boyd, "Suburbia Takes Over," *National Civic Review* 54 (June 1965), pp. 294–298.

[47] Paul T. David and Ralph Eisenberg, *Devaluation of the Urban and Suburban Vote* (Charlottesville, Va.: Bureau of Public Administration, University of Virginia, 1961).

the reapportioned legislature reflecting the dominance of the "urban syndrome" of Democrats, liberals, organized labor, Catholics, blacks, and other racial minorities must give way to a more complex mixture including the "suburban syndrome" of Republicans, conservatives, business interests, protestants, and whites. Both stereotypes are overdrawn; the suburban population especially is more diversified than this suggests. As Malcolm Jewell warns, "The suburb has confounded political prognosticators, and the suburban voter has been more often stereotyped than analyzed."[48]

Party changes, North and South

The impact of suburban gains on party strength in the legislature varies between regions and, in certain cases, between states in the same region. The predictions of Democratic urban gains in the North were supported by the early experience of such states as Michigan, New York, New Jersey, and Illinois, but the effect of gains in suburbia, where neither party has consistently had a stronghold, is to temper the long-run hopes of northern Democrats. One study of party changes in the Indiana legislature concluded that Republicans gained despite a reapportionment designed by Democrats, with the 1968 election giving 73 percent of the House to Republicans, although they polled only 54 percent of the vote for secretary of state.[49] In the South there are other factors involved besides reapportionment, but it has helped to provide for a growing two-party competition for the first time in several state legislatures. Intraparty splits and shifts of power can be expected particularly for the Democrats in southern states and for the Republicans in northern states. The fact that the bulk of reapportionment legislation was engineered by predominantly Democratic legislatures, while Republican strength was at a low ebb nationally, must be listed as a Democratic advantage. Growing black political strength is taking place both North and South, but constitutes a sharper break with the past in the South.

Quality impact

Some of the hopes of good government groups for an improved quality in state legislatures as a result of ending malapportionment may prove to be ill-founded, in spite of the strong "moral case" for reapportionment, according to Herbert Jacob.[50] He points out that the political skill and legislative experience of "rural stalwarts" may be replaced by the inexperience and short-term career interest of urban amateurs, who tend to stay in the legislature for shorter periods. Others point to the healthy effect of all of the publicity and citizen interest accompanying the court

[48] Malcolm E. Jewell, "The Political Setting," in Alexander Heard (ed.), *State Legislatures in American Politics*, p. 81.

[49] George C. Roberts, "A Districting Dilemma," *National Civic Review* 59 (June 1970), p. 305.

[50] Herbert Jacob, "The Consequences of Malapportionment: A Note of Caution," *Social Forces* 43 (December 1964), pp. 256–261.

action, constitutional conventions, and other events focusing attention on the legislature as people want it to be. To the extent that citizen interest and involvement have been stimulated to a higher level, this may account for more legislative change than reapportionment, *per se*, has caused.

Policy impact

One of the more difficult unanswered questions about the effect of one-man–one-vote apportionment is whether the hopes of its liberal backers for more welfare-oriented legislatures will be borne out in practice. Does reapportionment really make a difference in the "policy outputs" of a state legislature? A study by Richard I. Hofferbert challenges the common assumption that it does make a difference.[51] He was unable to find any significant relationship between the degree of numerical equality in a state's apportionment system and either (1) the state's "welfare orientation rank"—a reflection of the level of financial support for various education and welfare programs, or (2) the level of direct state aid to the two largest cities in the state.

Malapportionment and state policy outcomes

Thomas Dye has found some association between better representation for urban areas and higher public expenditures for education, but he concludes that both are more likely a product of the socioeconomic development of the state. As a result of his systematic inquiry into the forces shaping policy outcomes in the American states—education, health and welfare, highways, taxation, and the regulation of public morality—Dye reports that malapportionment appears to have little independent effect and that economic development is the key variable:

> On the whole, the policy choices of malapportioned legislatures are not noticeably different from the policy choices of well apportioned legislatures. Policy differences which do occur turned out to be a product of socioeconomic differences among the states and not a direct product of apportionment practices. Certainly malapportionment gives more weight to the political influence of rural voters. And reapportionment may noticeably affect the style and character of state politics. But there is no empirical evidence that reapportionment will bring about any substantial changes in state programs in education, welfare, highways, taxation, or the regulation of public morality.[52]

Professor Jewell has critically analyzed the methodology and implications of studies such as those by Hofferbert and Dye and points to the twin difficulties of measuring malapportionment and of trying to use

[51] Richard I. Hofferbert, "The Relation Between Public Policy and Some Structural and Environmental Variables in the American States," *American Political Science Review* 60 (March 1966), pp. 73–82.

[52] Thomas R. Dye, *Politics, Economics, and the Public: Policy Outcomes in the American States* (Chicago: Rand McNally and Co., 1966), p. 294. He reaffirms this position in Jacob and Vines, *Politics in the American States*, pp. 173–175.

interstate correlations to measure the effects of malapportionment. He asks "Why should we expect a well apportioned legislature in an overwhelmingly rural state to pass more liberal legislation or give more state aid to large cities than a poorly apportioned legislature in an overwhelmingly urban state?"[53] He cites the example of some of the poorest and most rural states in the South—Mississippi, South Carolina, and Tennessee—which were among the most malapportioned, but which would probably not have adopted more "liberal" policies even if their largest cities had been adequately represented. In spite of the scarcity of statistical support from the few early research efforts, many observers are convinced that the performance of newly reapportioned legislatures, such as those in Virginia, Michigan, and Colorado, clearly indicates a much greater willingness to grapple with urban and metropolitan problems than was true of previous legislatures, as well as a greater willingness to levy the taxes required for such programs.[54] Whether or not this is merely a high, early season batting average that will fade with the passing of time is a question that only time and more systematic research can answer. But these early observations are more relevant to Professor Jewell's assertion that "The effects of malapportionment on policy outputs can be best evaluated not by measuring differences among states with different degrees of malapportionment, but by studying the response of state legislatures as a whole to the challenges of the metropolis."[55]

Greater concern for metropolitan problems

In making a call for much more research on the hard question of what difference state legislative reapportionment really makes, Bernard C. Hennessy states the need as follows:

A call for research

> We need to study comparative policy outcomes, empirically and if possible quantitatively. We need to ask whether there is a greater sense of fairness, justice, or feeling-of-being-adequately-represented among the electorate after apportionment; and whether legislator-constituent contact, and/or other measures of this sense-of-being-represented, bears out these important attitudes related to citizen efficacy and democratic theory. We need to ask if the articulation of federal, state, and local systems is made more efficient (functional) by reapportionment: does reapportionment based on one-man-one-vote help the bright locals (city councilmen, county supervisors, village aldermen) get promoted to the state legislatures, or to Congress? Or, if promotion of talent is

[53] Malcolm E. Jewell, "Will *Baker* v. *Carr* Save the States?" (Unpublished paper delivered at the annual meeting of the Southern Political Science Association, Gatlinburg, Tennessee, Nov. 10–12 1966), p. 3.

[54] *See* Kenneth T. Palmer, "Legislatures Seen Helpful to Cities," *National Civic Review* 59 (May 1970), pp. 262–263.

[55] Malcolm E. Jewell, "Will *Baker* v. *Carr* Save the States?" p. 9. *See also* Yong Hyo Cho and H. George Frederickson, "The Effects of Reapportionment: Subtle, Selective, Limited," *National Civic Review* 63 (July 1974), pp. 357–362.

Modern carpetbaggers

Figure 10–3. Jon Kennedy in the *Arkansas Democrat.*

not deemed to be functional for democratic pluralism, do the bright locals get heard and recognized at the higher levels under reapportioned systems?[56]

To this research agenda could be added other questions, including some very broad ones which tend to defy empirical research, such as whether or not reapportionment will "save the states" from being bypassed by the new federal–urban partnership. Will the reapportioned legislature be too suburban oriented to tackle *core-city* problems—not merely urban problems generally? Perhaps core-city and suburban representatives can be expected to stick together on such matters as increasing state aid for education, expressways, and mass transit, and perhaps for home rule legislation. But we can quite likely expect rural–small town alliances with metropolitan suburbs on such subjects as core-city taxes,

Ambivalence on core-city issues

[56] Quoted from an untitled note by Bernard C. Hennessey, ed., in *National Center for Education in Politics: Bulletin* 14 (June 1966), p. 4.

welfare legislation, annexation, and metro-type governments, with a negative stance on these measures. There are very few basic issues of state and local government, and very few incumbent officials (*see* Figure 10–3) that the reapportionment revolution will leave untouched as it continues to effect change in state political structures.

Efforts to Evaluate the Fifty State Legislatures

Political scientists generally shy away from judging the "goodness" or "badness" of political institutions and processes. They have tried increasingly in recent years to restrict their role to describing and explaining political phenomena, rather than prescribing or advocating. This role is often unclear to students and other observers because political scientists as private citizens are frequently active and vocal in prescribing, judging, and advocating all kinds of political ideas and programs. The frustrations of trying to separate facts from values are well known.

As long as this warning is kept in mind, it should be useful to review a recent massive effort by the Citizens Conference on State Legislatures to develop a yardstick by which to measure the fifty state legislatures—i.e., their decision-making capabilities as determined by their structure, organization, rules, and procedures. The fourteen-month study under the direction of Larry Margolis, and financed by the Ford Foundation, was entirely normative, depending on value judgments and preferences; it made no pretense to be an exercise in social science. It assumed that a state legislature should be functional, accountable, informed, independent and representative, and thus evaluated all legislatures against the acronym "F.A.I.I.R." The related criteria and subcriteria are outlined in Table 10–4.

Information was gathered on each state and, with the criteria weighted according to relative importance, the rank order of each state on the F.A.I.I.R. criteria was determined, as shown in Table 10–5. Under this system California ranked first in functional, third in accountable, second in informed, third in independent, and second in representative, making it first in overall ranking. Alabama, on the other hand, ranked forty-eighth in functional, fiftieth in accountable, forty-ninth in informed, fiftieth in independent, and forty-first in representative, making it fiftieth in overall ranking. Figure 10–4 presents the overall rankings in a map of all fifty states.

Those who attempted this evaluation confess to several limitations. The rankings are relative to other states and not to some absolute ideal; they show one state to be "better" or "worse" than another, but not how much better or worse. The differences between the tenth and twentieth

Table 10–4. The F.A.I.R. Criteria for Evaluating State Legislatures

GENERAL STRUCTURE OF THE EVALUATIVE APPARATUS

FUNCTIONALITY	**ACCOUNTABILITY**	**INFORMATION HANDLING CAPABILITY**	**INDEPENDENCE**	**REPRESENTATIVENESS**
Criteria Subcriteria	**Criteria** Subcriteria	**Criteria** Subcriteria	**Criteria** Subcriteria	**Criteria** Subcriteria
A. Time and its Utilization 1. Restrictions on the Frequency, Length and Agendas of Sessions, and Interim Periods 2. Techniques for the Management of Time Resources 3. Uses of Presession Time **B. General Purpose Staff** 4. Personal Aides and Assistants to Leaders and Members **C. Facilities** 5. Chambers 6. Leader's Offices 7. Committee Facilities 8. Facilities for Service Agencies 9. Member's Offices	**A. Comprehensibility in Principle** 1. Districting 2. Selection of Leaders 3. General Complexity 4. Explicit Rules and Procedures 5. Anti-Limbo Provisions 6. Planning, Scheduling, Coordination and Budgeting **B. Adequacy of Information and Public Access to it (Comprehensibility in Practice)** 7. Public Access to Legislative Activities 8. Records of Voting and Deliberation 9. Character and Quality of Bill Documents 10. Conditions of Access by Press and Media	**A. Enough Time** 1. Session Time 2. Presession Activities **B. Standing Committees (as Information Processing and Applying Units)** 3. Number of Committees 4. Testimony 5. Facilities **C. Interim Activities** 6. Interim Activities 7. Structure and Staffing 8. Reporting and Records **D. Form and Character of Bills** 9. Bill Status and History 10. Bill Content and Summaries	**A. Legislative Autonomy Regarding Legislative Procedures** 1. Frequency and Duration of Sessions 2. Expenditure Control and Compensation-Reimbursement Powers 3. Reapportionment **B. Legislative Independence of Executive Branch** 4. Access to Information and Analysis 5. Veto Relationships 6. Lieutenant Governor Problem 7. Budget Powers 8. Miscellaneous **C. Capability for Effective Oversight of Executive Operations** 9. Oversight Capabilities 10. Audit Capability	**A. Identification of Members and Constituents** 1. Identification **B. Diversity** 2. Qualifications 3. Compensation 4. **Voting Requirements** **C. Member Effectiveness** 5. Size and Complexity of Legislative Body 6. Diffusion and Constraints on Leadership 7. Access to Resources 8. Treatment of Minority 9. Known Rules 10. Bill Reading

Table 10–4. *Continued*

D. Structural Characteristics Related to Manageability

10. Sizes of Houses

11. Standing Committee Structure

E. Organization and Procedures to Expedite Flow of Work

12. Origination and Sponsorship of Bills

13. Joint Committee Usage

14. Treatment of Committee Reports

15. Anti-Limbo Provisions

16. Emergency Procedures

17. Bill Carry-over

F. Provisions for Management and Coordination

18. Continuity and Powers of Leadership

19. Inter-House Coordination

G. Order and Dignity of Office

20. Order and Decorum

11. Information on Legislators' Interests

12. Information on Lobbyists

C. Internal Accountability

13. Diffusion and Constraints on Leadership

14. Treatment of Minority

11. Quantity and Distribution

12. Timeliness and Quality

E. Professional Staff Resources

13. General Research Coverage

14. Legal

F. Fiscal Review Capabilities

15. Fiscal Responsibility

16. Staff Support for Fiscal Analysis and Review

17. Fiscal Notes

D. Interest Groups

11. Lobbyists

E. Conflicts and Dilution of Interest

12. Dilution of Interest

The accompanying table shows the criteria and sub-criteria used in evaluating state legislatures' potential for meeting their responsibilities under the American system of government. The lettered headings (A, B, C, D, etc.) are the criteria, and the numbered headings are the sub-criteria. The 10 sub-criteria under Representativeness, for example, make up the three criteria of "Identification," "Diversity," and "Member Effectiveness." Information supplied by state legislators and staff members on the basis of a questionnaire was used in determining the content of the numbered sub-criteria. The sub-criteria, in turn, were used to determine a score for a state on each of the criteria. Combined and weighted scores on the criteria then yielded a state's score on a major characteristic. A final, overall ranking for a state relative to the other 49 was derived from its combined scores on all five major characteristics. The result is a clear indication of how well each legislature is equipped to be functional, accountable, informed, independent and representative.

Source: Citizens Conference on State Legislatures, *Report on an Evaluation of the 50 State Legislatures* (Kansas City, Mo., 1971), p. 29.

Table 10–5. Rank Order of State Legislatures by Overall Rank and F.A.I.I.R. Criteria

Overall Rank	*State*	*Functional*	*Accountable*	*Informed*	*Independent*	*Representative*
1	California	1	3	2	3	2
2	New York	4	13	1	8	1
3	Illinois	17	4	6	2	13
4	Florida	5	8	4	1	30
5	Wisconsin	7	21	3	4	10
6	Iowa	6	6	5	11	25
7	Hawaii	2	11	20	7	16
8	Michigan	15	22	9	12	3
9	Nebraska	35	1	16	30	18
10	Minnesota	27	7	13	23	12
11	New Mexico	3	16	28	39	4
12	Alaska	8	29	12	6	40
13	Nevada	13	10	19	14	32
14	Oklahoma	9	27	24	22	8
15	Utah	38	5	8	29	24
16	Ohio	18	24	7	40	9
17	South Dakota	23	12	15	16	37
18	Idaho	20	9	29	27	21
19	Washington	12	17	25	19	39
20	Maryland	16	31	10	15	45
21	Pennsylvania	37	23	23	5	36
22	North Dakota	22	18	17	37	31
23	Kansas	31	15	14	32	34
24	Connecticut	39	26	26	25	6
25	West Virginia	10	32	37	24	15
26	Tennessee	30	44	11	9	26
27	Oregon	28	14	35	35	19
28	Colorado	21	25	21	28	27
29	Massachusetts	32	35	22	21	23
30	Maine	29	34	32	18	22
31	Kentucky	49	2	48	44	7
32	New Jersey	14	42	18	31	35
33	Louisiana	47	39	33	13	14
34	Virginia	25	19	27	26	48
35	Missouri	36	30	40	49	5
36	Rhode Island	33	46	30	41	11
37	Vermont	19	20	34	42	47
38	Texas	45	36	43	45	17
39	New Hampshire	34	33	42	36	43
40	Indiana	44	38	41	43	20
41	Montana	26	28	31	46	49
42	Mississippi	46	43	45	20	28

Table 10–5. *Continued*

Overall Rank	*State*	*Functional*	*Accountable*	*Informed*	*Independent*	*Representative*
43	Arizona	11	47	38	17	50
44	South Carolina	50	45	39	10	46
45	Georgia	40	49	36	33	38
46	Arkansas	41	40	46	34	33
47	North Carolina	24	37	44	47	44
48	Delaware	43	48	47	38	29
49	Wyoming	42	41	50	48	42
50	Alabama	48	50	49	50	41

Source: Citizens Conference on State Legislatures, *Report on an Evaluation of the 50 State Legislatures* (Kansas City, Mo., 1971), p. 29.

ranking could be very small. Finally, the rankings fail to show progress that is taking place in a number of state legislatures. They are like a "stop-action" photograph showing where the states stand, but not where they have been or where they are going.[57] Admittedly controversial, the report is a useful tool to prospective political reformers as well as political researchers.

Legislative variables and policy outputs

The relative importance of reforming the state legislative structure and processes would seem to be downgraded considerably by some of the recent research focusing on the policy outputs of the fifty state governments. Thomas R. Dye, for example, has concluded that environmental conditions, such as state wealth, urbanization, education, and industrial development, shape both the political system and public policy of states.[58] This relegation of the state's political system, including its legislative process variables, to a somewhat incidental role is disputed by William L. Shade and Frank J. Munger. Their recent analysis of a broad spectrum of variables indicates that legislative professionalism, interparty competition, and information level all have an independent effect as strong determinants of state policies.[59] In his research on how state innovations are adopted and spread to other states, Jack L. Walker concludes that a process

[57] Citizens Conference on State Legislatures, *Report on an Evaluation of the 50 State Legislatures* (Kansas City, Mo., 1971).

[58] Thomas R. Dye, *Understanding Public Policy* (Englewood Cliffs, N. J.: Prentice-Hall, 1972), p. 262.

[59] William L. Shade and Frank J. Munger, "Consensus, Conflict and Congruence: Policy-Making in the American States," a paper prepared for delivery at the American Political Science Association, New Orleans, Sept. 4–8, 1973. Shade and Munger accept the strict environmentalist interpretation in the case of policies subject to strong influences beyond state boundaries, but reject it when policies are determined by influences internal to state systems. *See also* Ronald E. Webber and William R. Shaffer, "Public Opinion and American State Policy-Making," *Midwest Journal of Political Science* 16 (November 1972).

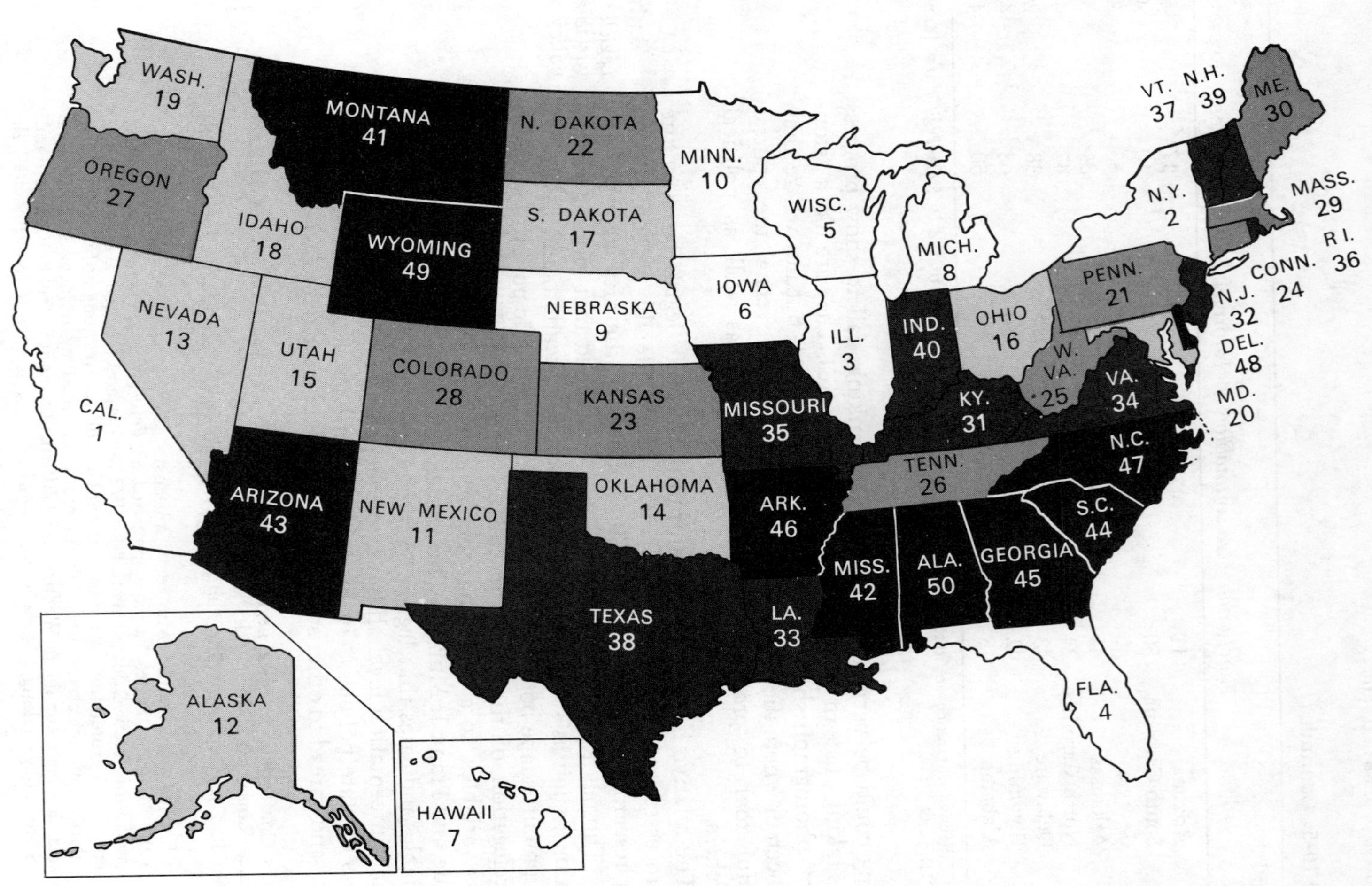

Figure 10–4. Ranking of State Legislatures in the U. S. on F.A.I.I.R. Criteria. *Source:* Citizens Conference on State Legislatures, *Report of an Evaluation of the 50 State Legislatures* (Kansas City, 1971), p. 26.

of emulation and competition, against a background of natural reluctance to take risks, has resulted in regional groupings of states with roughly similar levels of public service. As discussed in chapter 1, innovative legislation correlates strongly with the larger, wealthier, more industrial, and urbanized states.[60] State legislatures are more inclined to take "policy cues" from a state that has already adopted a new program if that state is viewed as a point of legitimate comparison. Supplementing and reinforcing this process is the system of interstate communications by which states become aware of new developments. Walker outlines a network of research centers, national associations of professional administrators, interest groups, and various kinds of voluntary associations, which connect pioneering states with more parochial ones.

When legislatures adopt innovations

Direct Legislation: The Initiative and Referendum

The legislative process is not necessarily a *representative* process, as we are constantly reminded by ballots greatly enlarged by the "initiative and referendum" in many states. Popular dissatisfaction with legislatures during the muckraking days brought about a movement around the turn of the century for direct methods in the lawmaking process, particularly in the West. With the reformist zeal of the Progressive era carrying the day, almost half of the states adopted constitutional provisions for supplementing or restricting the legislative program through the widely heralded initiative and referendum, generally coupling this weapon with a direct recall of important executive officers. As the Progressive movement slowed up, so did adoptions of "I and R," and only Alaska has adopted them since 1917.

This system of legislation by direct democracy calls for a vote by the electorate to pass on a proposed law or constitutional matter if a petition is properly presented with a sufficient number of voters' signatures, say 8 or 10 percent of the number participating in the last preceding election. An initiative petition asks for a vote on a proposed law in the face of legislative neglect or opposition. The initiative in some states is *indirect*, with the proposal going first to the legislature, rather than the electorate, unless the bill is not passed by the legislature. In the *direct* initiative the proposal goes straight to the voters, bypassing the legislature completely. A referendum petition asks for a popular vote to give the people a chance to reject or accept some legislative enactment. This is sometimes called the *protest* referendum, in contrast to the *compulsory* referendum on consti-

[60] Jack L. Walker, "The Diffusion of Innovations Among American States," *American Political Science Review* 63 (September 1969), pp. 880–899.

tutional amendments or other issues which the legislature is required to submit to the electorate, and the *voluntary* referendum which may or may not be called for by the legislature at its discretion. Examples of the latter would be a "right to work" bill or a large bond issue considered "too hot" for the legislators to handle by themselves. In such circumstances there is a fine line of distinction between a genuine desire to let the people rule and the urge to "pass the buck."[61]

The critics of direct legislation are numerous, arguing that to bypass the legislature actually weakens the legislature and confuses legislative responsibility, that such a device assumes more expertness and interest on the part of the voters than realism would support, that an already long ballot is made much longer, and that in practice "I and R" have given undue advantage not to "the people" but to well-organized and well-heeled pressure groups. Contemporary proponents, while recognizing that the high hopes of its originators have not been fulfilled, defend these direct methods as a kind of shotgun over the door available to the people in our pluralistic political structure when all else seems to fail. It seems clear, in any case, that those states using direct legislation are not inclined to abandon it. As an impact on the legislative process, it has hardly equalled the modern governorship, which is our next subject for consideration.

[61] For an interesting study of a referendum, *see* Raymond E. Wolfinger and Fred I. Greenstein, "The Repeal of Fair Housing in California: An Analysis of Referendum Voting," *American Political Science Review* 62 (September 1968), pp. 753–769. The use of the initiative by ecology groups in California in two different cases, one successful and one unsuccessful, is compared by Carl E. Lutrin and Allen K. Settle, "The Public and Ecology: The Role of Initiatives in California's Environmental Politics," a paper presented at the annual meeting of the American Political Science Association, New Orleans, Sept. 4–8, 1973.

SUPPLEMENTARY READINGS

Baker, G. E. *The Reapportionment Revolution: Representation, Political Power, and the Supreme Court*. New York: Random House, 1966.

Blair, George. *American Legislatures: Structure and Process*. New York: Harper & Row, 1967.

Breckenridge, A. C. *One House for Two*. Washington, D. C.: Public Affairs Press, 1958.

Buck, A. E. *Modernizing Our State Legislatures*. Philadelphia: American Academy of Political and Social Science, 1936.

Congressional Quarterly Service. *Representation and Apportionment*. Washington, D. C., 1966.

Francis, Wayne. *Legislative Issues in the Fifty States: A Comparative Analysis*. Chicago: Rand McNally, 1967.

Hamilton, Howard D., ed. *Legislative Apportionment*. New York: Harper & Row, 1964.

Hanson, Royce. *The Political Thicket: Reapportionment and Constitutional Democracy*. Englewood Cliffs, N. J.: Prentice-Hall, 1966.

Heard, Alexander, ed. *State Legislatures in American Politics*. Englewood Cliffs, N. J.: Prentice-Hall, 1966.

Jewell, Malcolm E., ed. *The Politics of Reapportionment.* New York: Atherton Press, 1962.

Keefe, William J., and Patterson, Samuel A. *The Legislative Process in the United States.* New York: Random House, 1966.

Kornberg, Allan. *Legislatures in Comparative Perspective.* New York: David McKay Co., 1972.

Lane, Edgar. *Lobbying and the Law.* Berkeley: University of California Press, 1964.

"Legislation." Continuing article in the annual *The Book of the States.* Chicago: Council of State Governments.

"Legislative Reapportionment." *Law and Contemporary Problems* 27, Spring 1952.

McKay, Robert B. *Reapportionment: The Law and Politics of Equal Representation.* New York: Twentieth Century Fund, 1965.

Neuberger, R. L. *Adventures in Politics: We Go to the Legislature.* New York: Oxford University Press, 1954.

Schubert, Glendon. *Reapportionment.* New York: Charles Scribner's Sons, 1965.

Walker, Harvey. *The Legislative Process.* New York: Ronald Press, 1948.

See also titles listed for the preceding chapter.

11

The Governorship

The governorship might be described in many respects as a small-scale edition of the American presidency. It has standardized features with a margin of fluctuation according to the state, the time, and the man on the job. It is a venerable American office, stemming from colonial times and characterizing the state establishments from the beginning. Restrictions on the office by the makers of the first state constitutions on the basis of bitter experience with colonial governors did not prevent social prestige and distinction from becoming attachments of the chief executive. This was true in the early national period when the governorship was held by men like Thomas Jefferson and Edmund Randolph in Virginia, John Hancock in Massachusetts, and George Clinton in New York. It became no less true in later eras when the office was to constitute a marker on the road to the White House for such leaders as Grover Cleveland, Woodrow Wilson, Theodore Roosevelt, and Franklin D. Roosevelt.[1]

General importance and prestige

Governors have been strong and weak, competent and incompetent, leaders and followers, honest and dishonest. Many have acquired permanent nicknames, such as "Soapy" Williams, "Kissin' Jim" Folsom, "Ma" Ferguson, and Huey "Kingfish" Long. There have been clowns, dictators, demagogues, and grafters; the federal prison has opened and closed the door for more than one governor in the current century. But who would contend that the majority have been any less honest and capable than the executives of American business, labor, or other institutions? Many have been strong leaders, indicated by those who became president and by

Various types of individuals

[1] *See* Table 1–2 in chapter 1.

Table 11–1. State Governors' Ages at Inauguration: 1940–1970

Ages	*1940–50*	*1950–60*	*1960–70*
30–39	10	24	24
40–49	63	68	73
50–59	57	41	44
60–69	28	17	14
70–79	2	4	—
80–89	1	—	—

Source: Samuel R. Solomon, "Governors, 1960–1970," *National Civic Review* 60 (March 1971), p. 130. Reprinted by permission.

others like Hiram Johnson of California, Frank Lowden of Illinois, Harry Byrd of Virginia, Robert La Follette of Wisconsin, Gifford Pinchot of Pennsylvania, John Connally of Texas, Alfred E. Smith, Thomas E. Dewey, and Nelson Rockefeller, the last three from the Empire State. Most of them exemplified mastery of both the political and the administrative spheres of state government, although in distinctly different ways.

Accent on youth

On the whole, the accent is increasingly on youth among the state governors; in the 1960s, the median beginning age was 46, compared with a median age of 51 during the 1940s. According to Samuel R. Solomon's study of 156 governors during the 1960s, 24 became governors in their thirties; in the 1940s, only 10 were elected at this age.[2] The largest number of governors (73) were in their forties, with 44 in their fifties, and 14 in their sixties (*see* Table 11–1). The formal education of governors has continued to rise steadily; over 95 percent have attended college. The legal profession is the dominant vocation of men who become governors, accounting for nearly 60 percent, with business in second place with 20 percent, and the once prominent farming and ranching occupations declining to only 6 percent.

Term and turnover: ex-governors

The turnover in the office of governor is rather extensive in most of the fifty states. The reasons for this are historical, constitutional, and political. The two-year term was once a contributing cause, but other limitations are involved. Table 11–2 indicates not only the near unanimity of states operating under a four-year term, but the steady trend away from shorter terms since original statehood. In 1972 Iowa, Kansas, South Dakota, and Texas were the latest to switch to the longer term. About one-fourth

[2] Samuel R. Solomon, "Governors, 1960–1970," *National Civic Review* 60 (March 1971), pp. 126–146.

Table 11–2. Changes in Length of Governors' Term, 1780–1974

Year	*Number of States*	*1-Year Term*	*2-Year Term*	*3-Year Term*	*4-Year Term*
1780	13	10	1	2	0
1820	24	10	6	4	4
1860	34	5	16	2	11
1900	45	2	21	1	21
1940	48	0	24	1	23
1974	50	0	4	0	46

Source: Abridged and updated from Table 2, "Length of Term of State Governors, 1780–1964, p. 187 from *The American Chief Executive* by Joseph E. Kallenbach (Harper & Row, 1966). Updated with information from *The Book of the States, 1974–75,* p. 147.

of the states providing for a four-year term, however, forbid a regular incumbent to succeed himself, and close to one-half limit the governor to two consecutive terms. After Governor George Wallace of Alabama made an unsuccessful attempt to secure a state constitutional amendment (later secured) permitting him to succeed himself, his wife, Mrs. Lurleen Wallace, was elected in 1966 to succeed him. She became the first woman to serve as governor of Alabama and the third in U. S. history. He was elected to a new term in 1970. Factors other than legal ones often contribute to compulsory retirement of governors after one term, even after excellent performance. Many have found the office a blind alley with respect to a political future. Only a few from a few states can entertain hopes of candidacy for president. A governor may go to the United States Senate but, if so, he is likely to hold the seat for a long time, leaving little opportunity for another governor to move in this direction. A few former state executives become state or federal judges, and a few are appointed to important administrative posts in state or nation. Some become lobbyists. Many return permanently to private life and enterprise, often in law or business.

Aspects of the governorship

The annual salary of the governor ranges upward from $10,000 in Arkansas to $85,000 in New York, not including the governor's mansion and certain expense funds. By 1975, only Arkansas and North Dakota paid their governor less than $20,000, and eight paid $50,000 or more. Besides the requirements of citizenship and residence, a minimum age of 30 is usually stipulated; however, for political reasons one almost necessarily needs the experience of more than 30 years to win a governorship. Candidates for the office are nominated by party primaries in most of the states, although a few states, including New York, still cling to use of the party convention for this purpose.

The governor's role embraces a broad range of powers and functions, although it is generally hedged with more restrictions and division of authority than the role of the president. The governor is the ceremonial and traditional head of the state, and he speaks officially for the state in important relations with other states or the national government. He is commander-in-chief of state troops when they are not in national service, and there have been constitutional provisions for him to command the "navy" of the commonwealth. Under his responsibility for law enforcement, he may order out state troops to preserve order and, under the federal Constitution, he may request and receive military aid through order of the president to check "domestic violence." He has powers of appointment and removal of officers or employees as prescribed and limited by constitutional and statutory provisions of his state. In a majority of the states the governor has broad or restricted powers of pardon, parole, and commutation of sentence. In a few states he is an important member of a board with jurisdiction in such matters. The governor has a measure of supervisory power over central administration, but this power varies widely from state to state, partly according to whether the executive branch is integrated under him or shared with a number of other elected officers. (This phase of state administration will be considered in the next chapter.) The governor has a miscellany of powers to issue proclamations, orders, rules, and regulations, to call special elections as necessary and required, and to serve as an ex officio member of sundry boards or commissions. He is in a position to exercise important powers and employ strategic methods in formulating and initiating policy, including the making and blocking of legislative policy.

General role

Some students of state politics, noting the increasing failure of governors to win the presidential or vice-presidential nomination of the major parties, suggest that the modern state governorship has increasingly become a politically vulnerable office. Not since Adlai Stevenson in 1956 has either of the two major party candidates for the presidency been a state governor; in both 1960 and 1964 not even a vice-presidential nominee was a govenor. Austin Ranney compared the "staying power" of incumbent U. S. senators with that of incumbent governors in 1966 and 1968, and found that in the elections of these two years 88 percent of the senators survived while only 67 percent of the governors survived.[3]

New political vulnerability of governors?

Governors are now faced with tremendously increased demands for more and better schools, recreation facilities, highways, and other services which, coupled with inadequate state revenue sources, keep them in

[3] Austin Ranney, "Parties in State Politics," in Herbert Jacob and Kenneth N. Vines (eds.), *Politics in the American States*, p. 116.

the constant hot water of financial crisis. In the early 1950s Karl Bosworth observed that state taxes were so much smaller than the federal income tax and local property taxes that arguments about reducing costs of administration seldom generated much heat.[4] But in more recent years, with the steady rise in state costs and in pressures for new and improved services, the governor is finding it far more difficult to satisfy the voters and to be all things to all people. Increasingly the governor's political fate is tied to "the one big tax battle" at some point during his term of office. This line of reasoning would suggest that the presidential prospects of governors may some day soon be no better than it has been all along for the battle-scarred and weary mayors of the large cities. It is much too early, however, to sound the death knell for the large states' governorship as a stepping-stone to party presidential nominations.

While governors do, on occasion, become U. S. senators, it has been especially difficult for a governor to survive the hazards of being an "instant senator." This is a situation where a governor resigns and has himself appointed to the senate to fill an unexpired term. In Kentucky, Governor A. B. ("Happy") Chandler was able to win the Senate seat by election in 1940 after having arranged for his own appointment to replace Senator Logan who died in 1939. But many others have failed in attempting the same thing; this, too, may be a part of the new political vulnerability of governors. A study by Hain and Smith reveals a recent increase in the rate of congressional candidacies for the office of governor. It concludes that this is explained in part by the increasing attractiveness of the office of governor in many states. They find that, while congressmen are running for governor more often, they are winning less often; however, this probably reflects the shift from convention nomination to direct primary nomination, and a shift toward junior congressmen running for governor rather than more seasoned veterans.[5]

The Governor as Lawmaker

The governor has distinct constitutional powers enabling him to influence the legislature, provided he has the personal capacity and political

[4] Karl Bosworth, "The Politics of Management Improvement in the States," *American Political Science Review* 47 (March 1953), pp. 84–99.

[5] Paul L. Hain and Terry B. Smith, "Congressional Challengers for the Office of Governor," a paper prepared for delivery at the Annual Meeting of the American Political Science Association, New Orleans, Sept. 4–8, 1973. They studied 78 incumbent U. S. Representatives who sought election as governor from 1901 to 1971, and found considerable support for the argument of Joseph A. Schlesinger and Gordon S. Black that differences in career risks encourage some officeholders to seek advancement while others are trapped in place. *See* Black's "A Theory of Political Ambition: Career Choices and the Role of Structural Incentives," *American Political Science Review* 66 (March 1972), pp. 144–159.

arrangement or apparatus to utilize them. The powers to call special legislative sessions, to recommend measures by speech or message, and to veto bills belong technically to the weak governor as well as to the strong one, but ability and skill are necessary to make effective use of these techniques. The convening of special sessions is normally more important for the governor than for the president, since state legislators spend much less time than congressmen in regular session. The governor in about a third of the states has the additional power of exclusively specifying legislative matters for consideration by a special session.[6]

Constitutional powers

Of the forty-nine states with provision for the governor's veto, about one-fourth allow the "pocket" veto at the end of sessions and more than four-fifths have the item veto, which came into practice after the Southern Confederacy adopted it in the Civil War. Under the *pocket veto,* a bill fails to become law unless signed by the governor before a specified time after adjournment of the legislature. The *item veto* enables the governor to prune individual parts or figures from an appropriation bill without rejecting the whole measure. Most states providing for the item veto restrict it to appropriation bills. The veto power is of particular importance to the governor as unfinished business piles up for a legislature at the end of a session with little or no time for repassage of bills rejected by the chief executive. Sometimes popular but questionable legislation is passed and sent to the governor in order to saddle him with the "rap" for disapproval. Studies and observations[7] indicate that less than 5 percent of bills passed by the legislatures are vetoed by governors and that less than 10 percent of vetoed bills are subsequently enacted. The trend in new and revised constitutions is to increase the period of time allowed for the governor to act on legislative bills.

The affirmative vote necessary to override the veto varies. Some states apply the congressional pattern of requiring a two-thirds majority of each house. Requirements in other states range through a clear majority, a three-fifths majority, a two-thirds majority of the membership of each house, a simple majority, and a three-fifths majority of those present. North Carolinians have debated for many years the pros and cons of their "holdout status" against giving the veto power to the governor. Former governors Terry Sanford and Luther Hodges support the veto power as a part of the traditional system of checks and balances, and doubt that North Carolina is the only one of the fifty states that is right in this practice. On the other hand, former governor Dan K. Moore believes the sys-

North Carolina's vetoless governor

[6] The subjects are stated in the call which, however, does not bar the legislature from undertaking impeachment proceedings under the constitution.

[7] *See* F. W. Prescott, "The Executive Veto in Southern States," *The Journal of Politics* 10 (November 1948), pp. 659–675; and F. W. Prescott, "The Executive Veto in American States," *Western Political Quarterly* 3 (March 1950), pp. 98–112.

tem has worked well over the years and that the governor has enough power. The only serious effort to give the North Carolina governor the veto failed in 1933 when a proposed constitutional amendment which passed the legislature was never submitted to the people for a vote because of an election law technicality.

Frequency of divided government

Divided government, in which the party of the governor fails to control the legislature, is surprisingly frequent in the states; only ten southern and border states avoided it from 1946 to 1970. In a study by Thomas R. Dye[8] it was discovered that at any given time almost one-third of the states were experiencing divided government, and twenty-two states were in this predicament in 1958. Dye reported that Democratic governors are more likely to face hostile legislatures than Republican governors, a confirmation of earlier studies by V. O. Key. Of the governors facing an opposition majority in at least one house between 1954 and 1962, 70 percent were Democrats and only 30 percent were Republicans. Increased Republicanism in the South has resulted in increasingly divided government. Republican governors Rockefeller (Arkansas) and Kirk (Florida) had to face Democratic legislatures in 1967, as later so did Virginia's first Republican governor (in 1969) since the 1880s, Linwood Holton. Although majority control of the legislature is important to the success of the governor's legislative program, one study makes the surprising finding that it is not true that the more seats the governor has to spare, the more successful he will be.[9] Modest majorities are apparently more susceptible to gubernatorial leadership and influence than overwhelming majorities.

Extra-constitutional ways

The governor has extra-constitutional ways of influencing lawmakers. He may strike bargains crudely or constructively by exercising or not exercising his technical legislative as well as his patronage powers. He may find other influential methods for throwing his executive weight around for legislative purposes. He may come into office with a well-formulated and much publicized program and steadfastly insist upon translating it into law and fact. He may make effective appeal to public opinion through speech and press for support of his program, particularly if the offerings meet recognized needs. He may devote the major portion of his work to the problems of legislation, which Theodore Roosevelt said he found to be necessary as governor of New York. He may step forward as the actual as well as the nominal boss of his party in his state. Woodrow

[8] Thomas R. Dye, "State Legislative Politics," in Jacob and Vines, *Politics in the American States*, p. 154; Austin Ranney has extended the analysis to 1970 in the second edition, p. 109.

[9] Sarah P. McCally, "The Governor and His Legislative Party," *American Political Science Review* 60 (December 1966), pp. 923–942. *See also* her related discussion in Sarah McCally Morehouse, "The State Political Party and the Policy-Making Process," *American Political Science Review* 67 (March 1973), pp. 55–72.

Wilson gave advance announcement of such leadership in his election campaign for governor of New Jersey and followed up this notice by attending the legislative caucus of his party contrary to expectation and without invitation. In spite of the division of authority with other elected officers, the governor may unify his party or faction more than the president, who must build his program upon the diverse interests of his continent-wide backing. Going beyond his party or political faction, a governor may shrewdly divide the power and balance the interests of pressure groups in order to attain his objectives. He may also resort to the strategy of composing or reconciling the demands of different geographic regions of the state, for his constituents are not limited to one political subdivision as are those of a member of the legislature. Governors like Huey Long in Louisiana have been known to discriminate in their legislative influence against sections or cities that furnished heavy opposition to their election. If not a political weakling or a subservient tool of invisible spoilsmen, the chief executive may speak to and for the people in advancing state policy. He may utilize his station to transmit expert knowledge on important subjects of public concern. Despite the circumscription of his power and the onerousness of his office, the governor is in a better position than any other officer in his state to speak as the chief lawmaker for all—as the tribune of the people.[10]

A Case Summary: The New York Governor's Special Session

The governor and the special session

The influence of a strong and purposeful governor over the legislative process may be seen in a case study of New York Governor Nelson Rockefeller's experience with a special session of the state legislature.[11] The two main proposals of a controversial nature on the agenda for the special session were a multi-million dollar program of state aid to help schools and colleges to build fallout shelters and a reapportionment bill for the state's congressional districts. New York's constitution permits the governor to call the legislature into special session only "on extraordinary occasions," and Warren Weaver, Jr., suggested in *The New York Times* that:

[10] *See* Coleman B. Ransone, Jr., "Political Leadership in the Governor's Office," *Journal of Politics* 26 (February 1964), pp. 197–220, for a discussion of the growing role of the southern governor in political leadership during the decade of 1950–1960. For an effort to relate variables such as the governor's influence and the state political party structure to the policymaking process, *see* Sarah McCally Morehouse, "The State Political Party and the Policy-Making Process," *American Political Science Review* 67 (March 1973), pp. 55–72.

[11] *See* the excellent summary by Warren Weaver, Jr., "The Governor's Show," *New York Times*, Nov. 13, 1961, which the authors have relied upon for these paragraphs.

> There were few compelling reasons offered this week, however, as to why the shelter program and reapportionment could not have been postponed for seven weeks, to await the convening of the regular session. There remained only the purely practical reason that it was a lot easier to pass these controversial bills intact by the convenient and somewhat ruthless mechanism of the special session.[12]

Why should it be easier to pass the governor's proposals in a special session? More than any other factors, time and publicity work against the deliberative role of the legislature during special sessions. The text of the New York shelter bill, thirty-eight legal-sized pages long, was not made public until mid-morning of the Wednesday before the opening Thursday session. Although copies were sent special delivery to the senators and assemblymen, many who had left home early for the trip to Albany saw the bill for the first time Thursday morning before the session convened at noon. A general outline of the shelter plan had been made public three weeks earlier, but the withholding of the full details on the legislation decreased the likelihood that substitutes or amendments might be drafted. While there is no constitutional obstacle in New York to prolonging a special session for a week or more to consider amendments to the governor's proposal, most legislators are anxious to return to their homes and are reluctant to go beyond a day or two for the special session. Thus, the governor called the signals with the shelter bill and the pressure of time tended to produce a "take it or leave it" situation. This was most effective in its impact on the Republican legislators, of course, for any action resulting in pushing the session over into the next week would appear to be disloyal to Governor Rockefeller.

Pressures of time and publicity

The governor's hand was also strengthened by the publicity circumstances peculiar to a special session. The public spotlight was clearly aimed at the legislature and, even more significant, such scrutiny was easily focused on the legislator's vote on a single issue. The normal committee delays and procedural red tape so common to a regular session were not available to dissipate the public awareness of what was going on. Perhaps most important of all, Governor Rockefeller was able to call the session at such a time, and define the issue in such a manner, that some lukewarm legislators felt that a vote against his shelter bill might well be considered by the public as a vote against protecting school children's lives. The bill passed intact after brief debate.

The governor enjoyed similar success with the reapportionment proposal, a much more partisan measure. The twenty-six-page bill and accompanying maps of the new districts were made public just as the special

[12] *Ibid.*

session convened on Thursday. The bill became a law on Friday, slightly more than twenty-four hours later. Amendments were even less likely than in the case of the shelter bill because the task of drawing congressional district boundary lines is a highly technical process, even under more leisurely conditions, and the Democrats had little chance to alter a measure adopted on straight party lines.

If the shelter and reapportionment bills had been submitted to a regular session of the legislature, there can be little doubt that both would have received extensive study and some revisions at the hands of both Republican and Democratic legislators. In the circumstances of a special session, however, the legislative initiative and key controls were shifted into the hands of a resourceful governor.

Special sessions in Arizona: pro and con

A study by Roy D. Morey of the Arizona governor's use of the special session supports the idea that it is a means of increasing the governor's "legislative batting average," but also indicates it is not an unmixed blessing for him.[13] Unless used with prudence and skill, it can boomerang, resulting in loss of political face and effectiveness by the governor. Morey lists the following potential pitfalls: (1) The governor's prestige is placed more squarely on the chopping block in a special session than in a regular one. (2) Calling special sessions may be pounced upon by the press and opposition groups as waste of the taxpayers' money. (3) If sessions are called too often, intense antagonisms may develop against the governor. He cannot use the special session again and again to bludgeon the legislature into submission. (4) The governor can be caught on the horns of a dilemma if the special session adjourns without meeting his demands. To call the legislators back runs the risk of compounding the antagonism, but to give up may project an unfortunate political image of gubernatorial weakness.

Batting average: special sessions v. regular sessions

Even so, Morey found that Arizona governors from 1912 through 1963 were twice as successful in special sessions as in regular sessions. The governors achieved a cumulative success of 45 percent during special sessions compared with only 23 percent during regular sessions. Each of the eleven governors studied had a better batting average during special sessions. Morey also found that the high percentage of enactments occurred when the governor kept his call to the lowest number of items; that a difference in party affiliation between the governor and legislature was not a determining factor in gubernatorial success; and that external crises, such as wars and depressions, did not insure greater executive–legislative cooperation.

[13] Roy D. Morey, "The Special Session: Asset or Liability," *Southwestern Social Science Quarterly* 46 (March 1966), pp. 437–444. *See also* his *Politics and Legislation: The Office of Governor in Arizona* (Tucson: University of Arizona Press, 1965).

Problems of Vacancy and Succession

Vacancy and succession procedures

Vacancies occur in different ways prior to the expiration of a governor's term. Sometimes the succession is associated with bitter politics and controversy. The governor may die or may become incapacitated for duty, although the latter status may be difficult to determine. He may resign or be removed through impeachment proceedings. In certain states he may be recalled by a popular vote in a special election. If the state has the office of lieutenant governor, that officer succeeds to the vacant governorship, except in cases of popular recall. In the eleven states without a lieutenant governor, the presiding officer of the senate or the speaker of the house normally becomes the chief executive for the unexpired term. As in the national government, there may be a further line of succession for possible emergency. The successor may serve as "governor" or as "acting governor" according to constitutional language and interpretation. The lieutenant governor has a regular administrative post, with commensurate salary, in Indiana, but in most states he is primarily a contingent executive, except for instances of membership on boards or councils. Presiding over the state senate, with or without committee appointment power, is his usual function. In many states he serves as acting governor during the governor's absence from the state. There have been occasions when the acting official upset the executive apple cart under such circumstances, by the dramatic pardoning of long-term prisoners or other action contrary to the wish or policy of the absent governor. Governors at times have hesitated to leave the state even for a short period, not wishing to turn the reins of government over to the personal or political opposition. The Alabama constitution protects the governor during his temporary visits beyond the border by providing that there be a twenty-day absence before the lieutenant governor exercises the higher authority.

Absence of any procedure for determining inability of the governor in Louisiana in 1959 proved to be a source of embarrassment and, doubtless, of entertainment to the people of the state and the nation. Governor Earl Long was taken, against his will he alleged, to a mental clinic in Galveston, Texas, and when released he was committed to a state mental hospital in Louisiana on court order obtained by his wife. Long was released in subsequent court action and proceeded to dismiss the state police chief, the head of the state department of hospitals, and the director of the hospital to which he had been committed. Although the attorney general gave an opinion during the month of these events that the executive power resided with the lieutenant governor, he refused to assume such powers.[14] In recent years several states have added constitutional provisions for determining the inability of the governor to perform his duties or for clarifying lines of succession.[15]

Resignation

The governor resigns sometimes for straightforward reasons and sometimes for purposes of political strategy. An example of the former was the resignation of Governor Earl Warren of California to accept appointment by President Eisenhower as Chief Justice of the Supreme Court. An example of finesse would be the resignation by a governor under an agreement or cordial understanding in advance that his successor will reciprocate by appointing him to a vacant seat in the United States Senate. The Kentucky example of A. B. ("Happy") Chandler was cited earlier in this chapter. There have been resignations under embarrassing circumstances, as when an Indiana governor a few decades ago surrendered office to serve time in the federal penitentiary at Atlanta for conviction of fraud.

Impeachment

Provisions for impeachment proceedings against the governor and other officials are found in the constitution of every state except Oregon, which relies entirely upon the recall process for removal. In most states the impeachment pattern approximates the formula provided for dealing with officers of the national government. The lower house of the legislature adopts articles of impeachment, generally on the basis of a committee investigation and report. This adopted statement then goes to the senate, which conducts a trial, hearing testimony and argument from both sides, with the lower house providing the prosecution and the defendant utilizing counsel in his own behalf. In the end the senate decides the question, usually under the requirement of a two-thirds vote for a verdict of guilty. The punishment consists of removal from office and disqualification to subsequent holding of state office. Any conviction carrying a prison sentence must be decided through a separate trial before a tribunal of the judicial branch. There have been only a few removals of governors by impeachment trials in the twentieth century, including one in New York, one in Texas, and two in Oklahoma. A few impeachments have failed to result in removal, including three in Oklahoma and one in Louisiana. In these cases the senate votes for conviction were below the required total. The successful action in Texas against Governor James Ferguson in 1917 had a bizarre sequel in the subsequent election of the ousted official's wife, Miriam ("Ma") Ferguson, to the office in a campaign which heard the slo-

[14] *See* Bennett M. Rich, *State Constitutions: The Governor* (New York: National Municipal League, 1960), p. 11.

[15] Delaware (1969), Georgia (1968), Massachusetts (1968), Missouri (1968), New Hampshire (1968), Oregon (1972), South Carolina (1972), and South Dakota (1972).

gan, "Two governors for the price of one." Mrs. Ferguson was not a career woman and was considered a proxy.[16]

The recall

Twelve states have provisions for the recall of the governor and other state officials by popular vote. The recall is a method of holding an election for the removal of an officer in response to a petition by a designated percentage of voters. Oregon, first to adopt state recall (1908), requires the signature of 25 percent of the voters for an election; Kansas requires only 10 percent; the others approach Oregon rather than Kansas. The petition contains a statement of reasons or claims justifying the recall. The election is held within a specified time, and the results of the balloting determine whether the officer relinquishes or retains office. In several states simultaneous voting provides for a contingent successor, but three states require a subsequent election in case of removal. Only one governor has been removed through a recall election; the victim was Lynn J. Frazier of North Dakota, who had stirred up opposition over agrarian reforms. Soon after his removal in 1921, he was elected to the United States Senate. The recall has been less effective at the state level than impeachment proceedings. It has found more use in local government. It is not a judicial process and imposes no punishment of disqualification.

Disputed titles to the office

The full annals of the American state governorship would cover exciting controversies over titles to office affecting a tiny few of the many hundreds of individuals who have held that public position. The Dorr rebellion in Rhode Island over outmoded suffrage restrictions brought about a clash in 1842 between two governors or would-be governors prior to collapse of the Dorr movement. Duplicating claims to the governorship in Louisiana and in South Carolina were ended in 1877 when President Hayes withdrew federal troops from those states, letting political nature take its course. When a North Dakota governor became involved in a federal trial in the 1930s, the lieutenant governor undertook to administer the office, and the state supreme court ousted the governor. Following the ensuing election, the residential qualifications of the winner were challenged shortly after he assumed office. A court decision again disqualified a governor, and again a lieutenant governor took charge, giving the state four governors in less than a year.[17]

Georgia presented a more explosive case in 1947, following the death of Eugene Talmadge, the governor-elect, on the eve of his inauguration. M. E. Thompson, the newly elected lieutenant governor, undertook to assume the governorship, and so did Talmadge's son, Herman, who had

[16] More than 3,000 pardons were granted in her two-year term, often with her husband as legal spokesman for the applicant. Pardon columns appeared in the press. The Fergusons had an agrarian reformist appeal.

[17] R. L. Miller, "The Gubernatorial Controversy in North Dakota," *American Political Science Review* 29 (June 1935), pp. 418–432.

been counted in as second in the race for the governorship as the result of precautionary write-in votes. Backed by state troops and legislative action, Herman Talmadge exercised control of the office and moved into the governor's mansion. His men made short shrift of outgoing Governor Ellis Arnall's gesture toward retaining power pending the constitutional determination and qualification of a successor, but Thompson was able to use a capitol office as president of the senate. The state government, except for routine matters, marked time for two months before the Georgia supreme court resolved the Talmadge–Thompson duel in favor of Thompson. Young Talmadge then moved out but won the next election for a return engagement. Just twenty years later Georgia found itself in the midst of another gubernatorial Donneybrook, when neither Republican Howard (Bo) Callaway (451,032) nor Democrat Lester Maddox (448,598) received a majority of the votes in the general election, thanks to nearly 60,000 write-in ballots cast for Ellis Arnall. Segregationist Maddox had been an upset winner over Arnall previously in the Democratic primary. An 1824 provision of the Georgia constitution directs the legislature to choose between the two highest if no one has a majority. In the post-election maneuvering Callaway backers argued for a runoff election between the two, Maddox supporters argued for legislative selection, the American Civil Liberties Union proposed a new election open to all candidates, and a three-judge federal court held that the legislature could not make the choice because it was malapportioned. The U. S. Supreme Court acted quickly in a 5-to-4 ruling that the legislature could act since there is no federal requirement for direct election of governors, and the legislature had previously been allowed until May 1968, to correct its malapportionment. The legislature then proceeded to elect Maddox governor.

Georgia governor disputes: 1947 and 1967

Trends in the Governorship

The multiple roles of the governor have increased in the twentieth century both through determinism and design. More people with more occupational interests inevitably call for more government at all levels, including the state level. The trend toward increased government emphasizes centralization or partial centralization of many functions, such as the administration of education, highways, and law enforcement. The governor shares much of this administration through appointive or supervisory powers.

Reasons for an increasing role

As president, Theodore Roosevelt emphasized the importance of the role of the governors individually and as a group in intergovernmental cooperation. The cooperation may be interstate or between the states and the national government in tackling common problems such as conservation. That general policy of cooperation has continued in many ways, as exemplified by the annual sessions of the Governors' Conference and by regional conferences. The intergovernmental role of the governor involves both cooperation and conflict. The new "explosion" of federal-aid programs in the 1960s increasingly involved the governor in the pressures of intergovernmental tension and conflict, often over federal guidelines for the elimination of racial discrimination, or in disagreements over anti-poverty programs. One controversy centered on whether to permit governors to veto particular anti-poverty projects. After a brief experience with permissive legislation to this effect, Congress approved a compromise limiting the scope of the veto and making it subject to overriding by the Director of the Office of Economic Opportunity. Continued tension can be expected over this irritant to the strong defenders of states' rights, as suggested in Figure 11–1.

Growing role in intergovernmental relations

State legislatures, like Congress, have discovered that all the details of modern government cannot be put down specifically in statutes and that a degree of operational choice or discretion must be left to the executive, particularly the chief executive. There developed the parallel necessity for legislative reliance upon the governor and his aides to formulate or recommend policy in the complex technical matters of modern government. Part-time legislators cannot master the intricate problems confronting the states today, and an able governor may provide answers to the problems, becoming the chief lobbyist among lobbyists.

Gains through reorganization

The governor has gained power in varying amounts through governmental reorganization in more than half of the states in the last fifty years. Three states, New York, Virginia, and Massachusetts, achieved reorganization by constitutional amendment. Many others, notably Illinois, made sweeping reorganizational changes through legislative enactment, with stimulative leadership by governors supported by effective research on the subject. Under the influence of Governor Lowden, Illinois in 1917 scrapped more than 100 agencies and offices and allocated their functions among nine departments, although not involving the constitutionally elective offices. This definitely increased the power of the governor both through appointment and through supervision. Virginia and New York went further toward a short ballot for state officers and toward establishing the governor at the top of an administrative hierarchy. The governorship has found new strength in the spread to three-fourths of the states of executive budget-making and fiscal control, particularly where reorganization has become most extensive and effective. The flexible role of the governor in this field is further considered in the subsequent chapter on finance.

The reorganization movement is continuous, and the governors are in a position to sponsor and utilize studies by professional experts on the

Figure 11–1. Justus in the *Minneapolis Star.*

subject. It cannot honestly be said that the movement resulted in radical or even major alteration of state governmental structure in the post-World War II period. But studies continue to be authorized and afford grist for the mill of political pressures for strengthening administrative structures. It is not an extravagant observation to say that reorganization and modernization of state administration have transformed and continue to transform the governor "from figurehead to leader."[18]

[18] On this point, *see* Leslie Lipson, *The American State Governor: From Figurehead to Leader* (Chicago: University of Chicago Press, 1939). At least one authority on state government has called for a moratorium on suggestions for strengthening the governorship until more evidence is available on whether this helps to solve state problems. *See* Samuel K. Gove, "Why Strong Governors?" *National Municipal Review* 53 (March 1964), pp. 131–136.

SUPPLEMENTARY READINGS

Abernathy, Byron R. *Some Persisting Questions Concerning the Constitutional State Executive.* Lawrence: University of Kansas Government Research Series No. 23, Government Research Center, 1960.

Beyle, Thad L., and Williams, J. Oliver, eds. *The American Governor in Behavioral Perspective.* New York: Harper & Row, 1972.

Brooks, Glenn E. *When Governors Convene.* Baltimore: The Johns Hopkins Press, 1961.

Cross, W. L. *Connecticut Yankee: An Autobiography.* New Haven, Conn.: Yale University Press, 1943.

Gantt, Fred, Jr. *The Chief Executive in Texas: A Study in Gubernatorial Leadership.* Austin: University of Texas Press, 1964.

Governors' Conference. *Proceedings.* Annual publication. Lexington, Ky.: Council of State Governments.

Hutchinson, W. T. *Lowden of Illinois.* Chicago: University of Chicago Press, 1957.

Kallenbach, Joseph E. *The American Chief Executive: The Presidency and the Governorship.* New York: Harper & Row, 1966.

Lipson, Leslie. *The American State Governor: From Figurehead to Leader.* Chicago: University of Chicago Press, 1939.

Macdonald, A. F. *American State Government and Administration.* 6th ed. New York: Thomas Y. Crowell Co., 1960. Chapter 7.

Morey, Roy D. *Politics and Legislation: The Office of Governor in Arizona.* Tucson: University of Arizona Press, 1965.

Perkins, J. A. "American Governors, 1930 to 1940." *National Municipal Review* 29, March 1940, pp. 178–184.

Ransone, Coleman B. *The Office of Governor in the United States.* University, Ala.: University of Alabama Press, 1956.

Schlesinger, J. A. *How They Became Governor.* East Lansing: Bureau of Social and Political Research, Michigan State University, 1957.

———. "The Governor's Place in American Politics." *Public Administration Review* 30, January–February 1970, pp. 2–9. *See also* in this same issue several articles (pp. 10–41) by other authors in a symposium on the state governorship.

Smith, Alfred E. *Up to Now: An Autobiography.* New York: Viking Press, 1929.

See also titles listed for chapter 12.

12

The Governor and Administration

Although the governor's role as political leader has been strong since the beginning of our nation, it is only in recent decades that he has gained real strength in the field of administration. The most significant twentieth-century changes in the role of the governor have taken place in his relationship to law enforcement and program execution, rather than in his position as chief legislator, chief ceremonial representative of the state, or political chief of the state's majority party or faction. As our state governments have become financial giants, governors are more and more finding it impossible to shut off from their concern the administration of the state's affairs as "mere work for the clerks." The politically minded candidate of today who campaigns successfully for the office of governor finds himself, often unhappily, transformed into a chief administrator responsible for day-to-day managerial decisions.

The governor's new role

The Governor as General Manager

Prior to 1900 most governors had little to do with administration. This resulted in part from the early preference of the people for the legislative branch, a carryover from the days when the colonial governors were so unpopular; in part from the highly decentralized character of state administration; and in part from the fact that administration did not occur on a very large scale. Governors themselves were chiefly interested in the legislature, politics, and party leadership; the usual grant of "executive power" found in the early state constitutions offered them little oppor-

Early emphasis on non-administrative functions

tunity to behave any other way. Constitutionally, the governor was made "head of state" with miscellaneous powers on ceremonial occasions as well as the pardoning power and control of the militia, but he was certainly not a "head of administration." Administration was left vaguely responsible to the state legislature, and later directly to the people, but not to the chief executive. This scanty administrative power and the lack of coordination of independent offices and agencies were observed by Tocqueville in his American travels in 1831.

Constitutional limitations

About the turn of the century, as popular demands upon government increased, it began to be recognized that there was a serious discrepancy between the constitutional or legal picture of the governor and the picture of the governor as seen by the people generally. The popular notion of the governor was that he had all the power necessary to see that the laws of the state were enforced. However, prior to the turn of the century, Woodrow Wilson described the administrative weakness of the governor:

> The governor . . . is not the 'Executive'; he is but a single piece of the executive. There are other pieces coordinated with him over which he has no direct official control, and which are of less dignity than he only because they have no power to control legislation, as he may do by the exercise of his veto, and because his position is more representative, perhaps, of the state government as a whole, of the people of the state as a unit. Indeed it may be doubted whether the governor and other principal officers of a state government can even when taken together be correctly described as 'the executive,' since the actual execution of the great majority of the laws does not rest with them but with the local officers chosen by the towns and counties and bounded to the central authorities of the state by no real bonds of responsibility whatever.[1]

Wilson's description of the constitutional position of the governor is still valid in many states, although statutory changes and other factors have tended to make the formal constitutional picture unrealistic today. Even so, the legal position of the governor in most states is much weaker than that of the president in the government of the United States, because the governor shares responsibility for the executive branch of the government with several other elected executives.

The emerging general manager

The extraordinary expansion of governmental activities and the growing importance of the administrative side of state government have made changes in the administrative role of the governor inevitable. The powerful forces of scientific management in industry and crusading reform in municipal government spilled over into both state and national levels of government with the result that on the state level, during the

[1] Woodrow Wilson, *The State: Elements of Historical and Practical Politics,* rev. ed. (Boston: D. C. Heath and Co., 1909), p. 330.

past half-century, the governor has begun to secure recognition as the "general manager" of state government. The state reorganization movement, based on the necessity for unity of command, effective coordination, internal responsibility, and administrative leadership, has undertaken to provide for the entire executive establishment in state government a general manager in the person of the governor. The governor's increasing managerial responsibilities have now been recognized in most states; the states seem slowly but surely to be granting additional administrative power to the governor for performing his new job.

The Governor's Administrative Powers

Strict construction of powers

Although most state constitutions vest the governor with "the supreme executive power," little if any definite authority is conferred on the governor by this provision because state courts have applied the rule of strict construction to the powers of the governor more often than have the federal courts in the case of the president. Only specific grants of authority are recognized. Differing court interpretations of seemingly equal grants of authority in the various states make it hazardous to generalize on the basis of constitutional and statutory provisions alone. Other variables of even greater importance, such as the effect of political strength, personal appeal, or custom upon the administrative power of a governor, make it obvious that no single pattern can be said to describe the governor's administrative power. Nevertheless, three major administrative powers are possessed by every governor in varying degrees: (1) the power of appointment and removal; (2) the power of fiscal management; and (3) the supervisory power. These are the principal means by which the governor makes his impression on the administration of state affairs.

The power of appointment

The power of appointment is one of the most important powers possessed by the governor, affecting not only his control of the administrative branch but his relations with the legislature as well. No governor can have complete confidence in subordinates whom he has not selected, nor can he properly be held responsible for the actions of such persons. Personal appointment of subordinates does not guarantee their responsibility, but it makes the probability considerably greater. Exercise of the appointing power is not as simple as it might seem. Appointments are frequently made under a great deal of pressure of many kinds. There is the practical requirement that the winning candidate for governor must choose most of the people who will help him operate the state government even before he takes the oath of office. He realizes that, although no one of his appointees can make a success of his administration, any one of the many persons appointed can seriously damage his administration by incompetence or dishonesty. There is seldom a shortage of applicants for the various positions, but salary limitations and insecurity of tenure make it exceedingly difficult to find capable people for the jobs. Few department heads can expect to serve longer than the limited tenure of the governor.

Appointing power not inherent

All states are generally agreed on a strict constructionist interpretation of their constitutions vis à vis the appointing power; i.e., it is not inherently and exclusively an executive function. The history of court interpretation of the governor's appointing power reveals the predominant opinion that such power must be expressly granted in the state constitution or by statute. In the first state governments, the power to appoint administrative officers was largely in the hands of the legislature, and early in the nineteenth century the choice of such officers was transferred to the electorate. The governor was looked upon as a political figure, in whom the power of appointment did not rest any more properly than in other divisions of the government. Since state constitutions generally have made little mention of the governor's power of appointment, recent increases in the use of this power result from legislative action proliferating new offices and boards. Furthermore, the state reorganization movement has increased the governor's power to appoint department heads in many states.

Restrictions on appointing power: senate confirmation

In spite of the increase in the governor's power of appointment in recent years, there are many restrictions upon this authority. In most states a large number of important appointments are made subject to confirmation by the senate. This restriction is defended on the ground that it requires the governor to make better appointments since they will have to run the gauntlet of legislative scrutiny. In practice, however, no such superiority has been demonstrated under this system, and there is considerable evidence that the confirmation requirement serves to destroy the personal responsibility of the governor for appointments.

Legal qualifications

Another restriction on the appointing power of the governor is the practice of writing into the law special qualifications for an appointee to a certain office. For example, the law may specify that each member of a board must represent a different geographic area of the state or that an officer must possess certain professional qualifications, such as five years of experience in banking for one to be appointed bank commissioner. Some years ago the Arkansas legislature passed a bill stipulating that the governor's appointees to the five-member hospital board had to be a doctor, a lawyer, a farmer, and two businessmen, but Governor Ben Laney vetoed it, on the ground that it would be unwise to limit membership on the board to a few professions and occupations.

Buffer boards

Another common restriction on the governor's appointing power, particularly in states that have no merit system to prevent the ravages of the spoils system, is the "buffer board" created with long and overlapping terms of office in the hope of taking an agency or institution "out of politics." The governor's influence is usually limited to the appointment of one board member each year, although a strong governor finds many devices for arranging for more than one vacancy. Buffer boards serve, where effective, to prevent clearcut change in state policy. The influence of the outgoing governor lingers after his departure, and the only consolation for the new incumbent is recognition of the fact that his influence will also grow and ultimately confront his successor with the same deterrent to change. (*See* Figure 12–1.)

Civil service

Civil service laws constitute a limitation on the governor's appointing power only to the extent that the merit system may effectively diminish pressure and influence in those areas where the governor would otherwise make or influence appointments. Here again, the strong governor is able to find and use many loopholes. It should be remembered that the

'One of us has got to go'

Figure 12–1. Jon Kennedy in the *Arkansas Democrat.*

civil service laws do not apply to the higher ranking bureau and department heads and to other exempted categories of positions.[2]

Elective administrators

One other restriction on the governor's appointing power, a serious limitation in some states, is the popular election of many other administrative officers besides the governor. At its worst this practice saddles the governor with a cabinet of department heads not of his own choosing who manifest varying degrees of hostility and aloofness from the governor's administrative leadership. Such elective administrators may even conceive of themselves as rivals to the governor and pursue alternative policies in order to impress the public with their fitness to succeed or perhaps to replace him. The long ballot, which results from the election of administrative officials, dates back to the second quarter of the nineteenth century, when the Jacksonians considered it self-evident that government could be derived from the consent of the governed only if the people elected their administrative officials as well as their legislature. It was not until many years later that the problem of fixing the responsibility for the conduct of big government began to make evident the necessity for the short ballot. Some states have been able to limit this restriction on the governor's appointing power by retaining only one or two elective officials in addition to the governor. In New Jersey the only other elective officer is the auditor, and he is elected by the legislature. The two newest states, Alaska and Hawaii, have limited the number of popularly elected administrative officials to two and three, respectively. Other states have simply bypassed the elective officers by giving important responsibility to the newer appointive officers, while at the same time whittling away the powers of the independent officers, leaving many of them mere figureheads. This is often the practical substitute for a constitutional amendment altering or abolishing an office that retains the sentimental support of the people.

The states in Table 12–1 rank highest in number of departments headed by independently elected officials, excluding governors, lieutenant governors, and auditors.

It is easy to exaggerate the modern significance of popularly elected state officials as limitations on the governor's power, especially in view of the relative unimportance today of many of these elective offices. The Jacksonian argument for electing administrators seems to have run its course in the nineteenth century; its impact remains primarily on offices

[2] For an excellent case study of the patronage decision-making problems of Governor Averell Harriman of New York, *see* Daniel P. Moynihan and James Q. Wilson, "Patronage in New York State, 1955–1959," *American Political Science Review* 58 (June 1964), pp. 286–301. It is an analysis of efforts to optimize the attainment of two potentially conflicting goals: staffing the government competently and acquiring and maintaining control over the state party.

Table 12–1.

State	Number of Elected Department Heads	State	Number of Elected Department Heads
South Carolina	10	South Dakota	7
Oklahoma	10	Texas	7
Louisiana	11	Washington	7
Mississippi	9	Alabama	6
North Dakota	9	Idaho	6
Georgia	8	Illinois	6
North Carolina	8	Kansas	6
Arizona	7	Kentucky	6
Florida	7	Nebraska	6
Nevada	7	New Mexico	6

Source: Adapated from Committee for Economic Development, *Modernizing State Gov. ernment* (New York, 1967), p. 83.

Decline of Jacksonian argument

created before such major state functions as highways, welfare, and health came into their own. The only one of the very large departments headed by an elected executive in more than one-half of the states is education. The following tabulation shows the number of states electing various administrators:[3]

Governor	50	Labor Commissioner	5
Attorney General	42	University Regents	5
Lieutenant Governor	41	Mining Commissioner	4
State Treasurer	39	Inspections	2
Secretary of State	38	Tax Commission	2
State Auditor	25	Highway Commissioner	1
Superintendent of Education	20	Board of Equalization	1
Public Utilities Commission	13	Printer	1
Board of Education	13	Railroad Commission	1
Agriculture Commission	12	Corporation Commission	1
Controller	11	Commissioner of Charities	1
Insurance Commissioner	8	Secretary of Internal Affairs	1
Land Commissioner	7	Custodian of Voting Machines	1

The power of removal

The governor's power of removal is the indispensable counterpart of the power of appointment. One without the other is of doubtful potency for purposes of administrative control, since the appointing power cannot be exercised when no vacancy exists. As a general rule, the power of removal must be specifically provided by the state constitution or statutes,

[3] Adapted from *The Book of the States, 1974–75*, pp. 148–149.

since state governors are held not to acquire a power of removal from their general executive power or their power of appointment. There is no "Myers case for states" which gives to the governor extensive removal power over administrative officials in the way in which the 1926 Supreme Court case did for the president. Two states, Missouri in 1945 and New Jersey in 1947, provided in their constitutions extensive power for the governor to remove appointive state officials, although this does not apply to boards and commissions in New Jersey.

Regulation of removals

The most common statutory and constitutional provision dealing with the governor's removal power is the requirement that removals must be "for cause only." Although this undoubtedly serves to deter a governor somewhat, since courts have generally held it to require a definite statement of charges and opportunity for a hearing, it is the governor himself who has full power to decide whether the evidence sustains the charges. In practice, the governor's removal power is frequently much stronger than the constitution, statutes, and court decisions indicate. In states where a newly elected governor is usually strong politically, there is always a large group of holdover officials who voluntarily resign when the new governor takes office. Furthermore, the governor may request an official to resign, whether he was appointed for a definite term or not and whether the governor has the removal power or not; such a request may be honored in preference to the probability of an unhappy and prolonged "cold war" existence in the state government. As a final resort, the determined governor who controls the legislature may oust the uncooperative official by the device known as the "ripper bill"—a legislative act abolishing the office or agency and creating a new one, usually with an only slightly altered name.

Removals in practice

Few governors have gone so far as Governor Eugene Talmadge of Georgia, who demonstrated how members of one of that state's most independent boards, the state highway board, might be removed. In April 1933, he tried to have certain highway department employees fired, and in order to achieve this he omitted their names from the quarterly budget which was sent to him for approval. The chairman of the board protested this act and, in June 1933, Governor Talmadge invoked martial law and removed the chairman and one member from the board, with state troops escorting the chairman from his office. The remaining member of the board was placed in charge and the governor appointed two other persons to fill the vacancies. The ousted chairman and member of the board brought suit, but they were unsuccessful. The case is obviously not typical, but it serves as a reminder that realistic appraisal of the governor's power of appointment and removal must include not only constitutional and statutory provisions, but also such factors as the governor's personality and political strength and the traditions and practices which have developed in the state.

Because available financial resources set a maximum limit on all that state government can do, the management of finance becomes an inescapable responsibility of the governor. Fiscal management, broadly conceived, consists of budget making and budget execution. The first hundred years of our nation's history in these two fields witnessed expansion of fiscal machinery without any significant modification of the ideas on which that machinery was originally based. The center of gravity for the whole system continued to be the legislature. But even within the legislature there came to be such a scattering of responsibility among various legislative committees and subcommittees that pork-barrel and other wasteful appropriations were made easy, and a general view directed toward financial planning was made impossible. Dispersion of financial responsibility in the administrative branch was even worse. The traditional fiscal officers—assessors, collectors, treasurers, comptrollers, and auditors, all jealous of their independence—usually devised their own bookkeeping methods without regard for the needs of other fiscal offices. With the creation of new, uncoordinated agencies, separately concerned with particular taxes, debt, investment and the like, it became increasingly difficult in matters of state finance, if not impossible, for the right hand to know what the left hand was doing.

Power of fiscal management: early history

Since about 1920 there has been a reversal of the trend toward financial dispersion and a steady movement in the direction of consolidation. Improvements in both legislative and executive organization and procedure have gone far toward creating an orderly and responsible financial system. Probably the most significant development of all has been the increased role of the governor in both budget making and budget execution. The "executive budget," making the governor the budget-making authority, has been adopted in forty-six states, and in three other states the governor is chairman of a budget board or committee. In Arkansas the legislative council is the authority for budget recommendations, but the governor's appointive director of finance and administration takes on active role in preparation of the budget in actual practice. Budget making involves the bringing together of estimates of total requirements of the government, comparison of estimates with past and present expenditures, calculation of probable income, preparation and submission of the budget document to the legislature, adoption of the budget, and enactment of bills designed to carry it into operation. Budget formulation is the basic instrument for statewide planning, and the manner of its use, misuse, or neglect by the governor is crucial in determining his success or failure in office. The critical importance of a favorable recommendation from the governor for agency budget success in the legislature has been documented in a study by Ira Sharkansky.[4]

Recent fiscal trends: budget making

[4] Ira Sharkansky, "Agency Requests, Gubernatorial Support and Budget Success in State Legislatures," *American Political Science Review* 62 (December 1968), pp. 1224–1231.

The theory and practice of budget execution—controlling state expenditures—have undergone changes equally as fundamental as those in budget making. Before three or four decades ago, an appropriation was considered an *order* to spend the amount appropriated to a department. However, this doctrine has gradually been replaced by the principle that an appropriation is an *authorization* effective only so far as necessary, and subject to the specific or general authorization of the governor. It is now standard practice to vest the governor with one or more control devices intended to insure proper use of funds already duly authorized by the legislature. Some of the more common devices for executive control of expenditures include the administrative pre-audit or control through accounting, the quarterly allotment system, central control of purchasing, and approval of transfers from one appropriation item to another. Different states give the governor these control devices in differing combinations and in varying degrees of strength. For example, the administrative pre-audit may be very weak, primarily checking illegality, or it may be exceptionally strong, authorizing disallowance of expenditures which seem unwise. No realistic appraisal of a governor's administrative power can be made without careful examination of his role in fiscal management.

Budget execution

A power as essential to a governor as to any business executive, but one which receives little formal recognition by state constitutions, is the supervisory power. The governor is not an operating official in the sense that he actually executes the law himself, but it is his constitutional job to "see that the laws are faithfully executed." He must oversee and direct the administrative process, fixing the major policies supplementary to legislation and directing the operations of state agencies. Many areas of authority already discussed relate to the supervisory power, such as appointments, removals, and finances, but there is more to it than this. In essence, it is the governor's power to make his wishes known and secure acquiescence in them, a power that varies according to his ability to use certain methods or devices for supervision and direction. These devices include the requirement of information, informal investigations, individual and group conferences, orders and directives, approval of administrative acts, and the use of staff agencies. While the constitutional and statutory provisions relating to the supervisory power of the governor are important, and while it cannot be denied that most states need better legal recognition of the governor's supervisory role in administration, in the final analysis no amount of enabling legislation can make an effective supervisor out of a personally weak or disinterested governor. Individual case studies of governors reveal that such factors as personality, prestige, personal interest in administration, and political power are strong determinants of the supervisory power.

The supervisory power

In this connection a word should be added concerning ministerial and discretionary powers. The governor's powers are either ministerial, in which case he has no choice in the manner of exercising them or whether to use them, or discretionary, in which case he may decide whether, when, and how to exercise such powers. The more difficult it becomes for the lawmakers to spell out in the constitution and statutes the exact circumstances when a governor should act and the specific action which he should take, the more prevalent becomes the practice of granting discretionary powers to the governor.

Ministerial and discretionary power

In a different and practical sense every governor demonstrates the discretionary nature of executive power when he crusades for vigorous law enforcement in one or two "pet fields" about which he may have campaigned for reform, while permitting administrative relaxation in certain other departments of state government. In effect, every governor has the discretionary power to pick and choose from among the state laws those which will receive special attention, with the result that a state may have few if any arrests for violation of truck weight limits under one governor and drastic enforcement of such measures under another. This is actually an extra-legal type of discretionary power, but no picture of the governor's role in administration is complete without it.

Gubernatorial control viewed by administrators

One way of looking at the administrative power of the governor is to find out how top administrators compare his control over them with legislative control, a method used in a study by Deil S. Wright.[5] As indicated in Table 12–2, state administrators were asked whether the governor or the legislature exercised greater control over their department, had the greater tendency to cut department budget requests, and gave more sympathetic support to department goals. The results indicate a lower "control rating" for the governor in the first two questions, but a higher rating with respect to sympathy for agency goals. More administrators expressed preference for control by the governor, however, than for legislative control. Wright concludes from his study that governors, far from having dictatorial or predominant control over state administrators, apparently do not function as primary power wielders over them, at least in the eyes of the administrators themselves. Wright did find, however, that stronger *formal* powers of the governor (appointing, veto, and budgetary powers, and tenure potential) correlated significantly with administrators' perceptions of stronger gubernatorial control, giving some support to the assumptions of "executive leadership" reformers.

An interesting comparative study of selected measures of the formal strength of the governors has been made by Joseph A. Schlesinger; the

[5] Deil S. Wright, "Executive Leadership in State Administration," *Midwest Journal of Political Science* 9 (February 1967), pp. 1–26.

Table 12–2. Comparison of Gubernatorial Control over Top Administrators with Legislative Control, as Viewed by the Administrators

Who Exercises Greater Control?	*Percentage*
Governor	32
Each About the Same	22
Legislature	44
Other (and No Answer)	2
	100
Who Has Greater Tendency to Reduce Budget Requests?	
Governor	25
Legislature	60
Other (and No Answer)	15
	100
Who Is More Sympathetic to Agency Goals?	
Governor	55
Each About the Same	14
Legislature	20
Other (and No Answer)	11
	100
Which Type of Control Do You Prefer?	
Governor	42
Independent Commission	28
Legislature	24
Other (and No Answer)	5
	100[a]

[a] Percentages do not add to 100 because of rounding.

Source: Adapted from Deil S. Wright, "Executive Leadership in State Administration," *Midwest Journal of Political Science* 11 (February 1967), p. 4. Reprinted by permission of Wayne State University Press.

results are shown in Table 12–3. While recognizing that many aspects of gubernatorial power are virtually impossible to measure, such as status and personal leadership qualities, Schlesinger has measured the governor's tenure potential and his appointive, budgetary, and veto powers. With a maximum total rating of 20, the fifty state governors ranged all the way from a low of 7 for Texas to a high of 20 for New York, Illinois, and Hawaii. Although the larger states tend to rate higher in the formal strength of their governors, Schlesinger warns that governors in smaller, less complex states may be *relatively* stronger.

Table 12–3. A Combined Index of the Formal Powers of the Governors

	Tenure potential	*Appointive powers*	*Budget powers*	*Veto powers*	*Total index*
New York	5	5	5	5	20
Illinois	5	5	5	5	20
Hawaii	5	5	5	5	20
California	5	4	5	5	19
Michigan	5	4	5	5	19
Minnesota	5	4	5	5	19
New Jersey	4	5	5	5	19
Pennsylvania	4	5	5	5	19
Maryland	4	5	5	5	19
Utah	5	3	5	5	18
Washington	5	3	5	5	18
Ohio	4	4	5	5	18
Massachusetts	5	5	5	3	18
Wyoming	5	2	5	5	17
Missouri	4	3	5	5	17
Alaska	4	3	5	5	17
Tennessee	3	5	5	5	17
Idaho	5	4	5	3	17
North Dakota	5	1	5	5	16
Kentucky	3	4	5	4	16
Virginia	3	5	5	3	16
Montana	5	3	5	3	16
Nebraska	4	3	4	5	16
Connecticut	5	4	4	3	16
Delaware	4	1	5	5	15
Oklahoma	4	1	5	5	15
Alabama	3	3	5	4	15
Wisconsin	5	2	5	3	15
Colorado	5	1	4	5	15
Louisiana	4	2	4	5	15
Georgia	3	1	5	5	14
Oregon	4	2	5	3	14
Nevada	5	2	5	2	14
Arizona	2	1	5	5	13
South Dakota	1	4	5	3	13
Maine	4	2	5	2	13
Vermont	2	4	5	2	13
Kansas	2	2	4	5	13
Arkansas	2	4	3	4	13
Iowa	2	3	5	2	12
New Hampshire	2	2	5	2	11
Rhode Island	2	3	4	2	11
New Mexico	1	1	5	3	10

Table 12–3. *Continued*

	Tenure potential	*Appointive powers*	*Budget powers*	*Veto powers*	*Total index*
North Carolina	3	2	4	1	10
Mississippi	3	1	1	5	10
Indiana	3	5	1	1	10
Florida	3	2	1	3	9
South Carolina	3	1	1	3	8
West Virginia	3	3	1	1	8
Texas	2	1	1	3	7

Source: Joseph A. Schlesinger, "The Politics of the Executive," in Herbert Jacob and Kenneth N. Vines (eds.), *Politics in the American States: A Comparative Analysis,* 2nd ed., p. 232.

Practical Restraints upon the Chief Administrator

Importance of other factors

The discretionary power in the office of governor, and varying views of his control of departments, calls to our attention an additional dimension of the governor's role in administration. Simply to describe the administrative powers of the governor is not enough. Even when his extra-legal powers are considered, one still does not have a realistic view of the actual governor, only of the potential governor. Whether the powers are utilized, how they are utilized, and the practical obstacles to their utilization are equally important parts of the picture of the governorship. The performance of the governor depends upon such additional factors as demands on the governor's time, his ability, personality, background, training, and interest in politics as compared with administration.

Demands on governor's time

No single fact is more apparent from an intensive study of the work of the governor than the insistent demands made upon his time by non-administrative activities. A study of the persons and groups that called on the governor of Arkansas during four reasonably typical days produced the classification of purposes of calls shown in Table 12–4.[6]

Administrative duties overshadowed

Over 60 percent of the conferences that occupied this governor's time concerned such matters as requests for jobs and special favors or consisted of social calls and visits by representatives of civic, youth, and church organizations. The requests for jobs presumably would be fewer in a state with a merit system but, if the total for these non-administrative matters amounted to no more than one-half of the calls, it would still constitute a very important drain on the time of one charged with responsibility for directing the administrative process of state government. It

[6] Daniel R. Grant, "The Role of the Governor of Arkansas in Administration" (Unpublished Ph.D. dissertation, Northwestern University, 1948), pp. 30–39.

Table 12–4. Classification of Purpose of Visits to the Arkansas Governor's Office

Purpose of Call	*Percent of Total Number of Calls*
Requests for jobs	23
Requests for special favors	13
Requests from civic, church, and school organizations	12
Problems of administrative officials	10
Criticisms of governmental policy or actions	7
Social calls	6
Reporting confidential information	5
Requests for clemency	4
Requests for extradition	2
Miscellaneous and unknown purposes	18
	100

Source: Adapted from Daniel R. Grant, "The Role of the Governor of Arkansas in Administration" (Unpublished Ph.D. dissertation).

should be noted that conferences with administrative officials accounted for only 10 percent of the callers received by the governor, ranking fourth in the list of groups seeing the governor.

Gubernatorial conferences classified

In his comprehensive study of the Texas governorship, Fred Gantt, Jr., classifies the personal conferences with the governor—those in which constituents were unwilling to settle for letters, phone calls, or being received by a lesser official—into a dozen or so types.[7]

1. Protests about action, or lack of action, on the part of a state agency.
2. Requests for the governor to write a letter to a national organization (e.g., to help a city bid for a national convention).
3. Requests for clemency.
4. Conferences on prospective appointments to public office.
5. Conferences on speaking engagements.
6. Conferences on proposed legislation.
7. Conferences with department heads.
8. Departmental requests for deficiency appropriations.
9. Requests to intervene in labor disputes.
10. Swearing-in ceremonies for important public officials.
11. Ceremonial presentations.
12. Ceremonial signing of bills, proclamations, etc.
13. Receiving important visitors from other places.

[7] Fred Gantt, Jr., *The Chief Executive in Texas: A Study in Gubernatorial Leadership* (Austin: University of Texas Press, 1964), pp. 88–89.

Another "time and motion" study of a governor in action was made by the New Hampshire "Little Hoover Commission" covering a three-week period of Governor Sherman Adams' activities. The demands of interviews, meetings, writing and making speeches, correspondence, phone calls, and travel required work weeks of 68, 67, and 56 hours. Although department heads and officers in New Hampshire seemed to fare better than those in Arkansas in obtaining time with the governor, such interviews still accounted for less than 7 percent of his work week. Coleman B. Ransone, Jr., who includes this and other analyses in his book on the governorship, concludes that by far the most time-consuming function of the governor is his many-sided job of public relations, with the result that either his roles as policymaker and general manager are crowded out or he carries an almost impossible burden of work.[8]

Predominance of public relations

Simply from the standpoint of time demands, the answering of mail and phone calls is extremely burdensome on the governor, though probably less of an emotional drain than personal conferences. Governor Al Smith of New York once observed that his energy was so consumed by trivial clerical and routine details that he had little time left for the more important functions of office. Gantt reports that when Texas Governor W. Lee ("Pappy") O'Daniel was regularly imploring the citizens to "write a letter telling me your views," the volume of mail became so great that his staff ran six weeks behind in replying. One such reply was as follows:

Pressure of the routine and trivial

> I trust you will pardon delay in answering your letter of January 25 addressed to Governor O'Daniel. . . . I am sure you will understand when I tell you that this office has been receiving from two to three thousand letters daily since the inauguration, and the Governor's correspondence necessarily has been neglected.[9]

O'Daniel's volume of mail was apparently a record for Texas governors, with Governor Allan Shivers reporting about 1,000 letters and about 200 telegrams a day; most other governors reported considerably less. Gantt's study of Governor Beauford Jester's correspondence for an entire month revealed a daily average of fifty-five incoming and ninety-eight outgoing pieces of mail. On one occasion Governor Shivers reported receiving 543 applications for tickets to the Texas–S.M.U. football game, along with 202 requests for help in securing hotel reservations for the game.

In addition to the diversion of competing demands, a governor's lack of interest in his role as general manager may result in a virtually headless administrative establishment, even though the legal framework provides

[8] Coleman B. Ransome, Jr., *The Office of Governor in the United States* (University, Ala.: University of Alabama Press, 1956), pp. 152–154.

[9] Quoted in Gantt, *Chief Executive in Texas*, p. 80.

for a strong chief administrator. Many governors have had exclusively legislative or judicial experience; it is safe to say that their primary concern is with legislation and traditional politics, rather than with what they consider to be the less political area of administration. Such political activities can be particularly time-consuming for a governor who combines his normal political role with aspirations for further office-holding or who conceives his governorship as a stepping-stone to another office.

Preoccupation with politics

The activities of New York's Governor Harriman for three months following adjournment of the state legislature in 1955 indicate the time and interest which a governor may give to politics and public relations. He made at least forty-nine public appearances outside of Albany in ninety-one days, including a trip to Florida, four trips to Washington, D. C., three to Buffalo, two to Syracuse and Suffolk, and at least one each to Nassau and Westchester counties and the cities of Massena, Ogdensburg, Lake Placid, Bear Mountain, and Olean, as well as frequent shuttling between Albany and New York City. He met with Adlai E. Stevenson at least four times, conferred with the visiting prime ministers of Thailand and Italy and the foreign minister of France, addressed nine political fund-raising dinners, and spoke at three college commencements. Travelling by trains, automobiles, commercial airlines, National Guard planes, the Conservation Department's fish-stocking plane, and by helicopter, he still was surpassed in his travels by New York governors Al Smith, Franklin D. Roosevelt, and Thomas E. Dewey, when they were campaigning for the presidency.[10]

Many other factors may operate to make the actual role of the governor different from the potential role pictured by his legal powers and responsibilities. None is more important, however, than the personal qualities of the man himself. Ability or lack of ability, forcefulness or weakness, and ambition for higher office or the absence of such ambition, all are important determinants in the governor's performance. In addition, the customs and expectations of the people help condition the governorship, as well as such circumstances as depression, prosperity, war, and peace.

Personal qualities

All of these are factors complicating, if not frustrating, the role of the governor in administration. Demands on the governor's time, preeminent concern for political matters and public relations, and the lack of previous experience in public administration make some analysts doubt whether the elective governor can perform effectively as the general manager of state administration. The most frequent proposals for improvement are to increase the governor's professional staff assistance to make his time count for more in the administrative field, or to create the office of assis-

Proposals for improvement

[10] Leo Eagan, "Harriman Gets Around," *New York Times*, July 5, 1955.

tant governor. This official would be, in effect, a highly paid director of administration responsible to the governor. Occasionally a "state manager plan" is proposed along the lines of the council–manager plan for cities, but the motion has had few seconds. Coleman B. Ransone may well be right in concluding that the most fruitful approach probably combines the elimination of certain of the lesser functions of the governor, reduction in the time spent on other functions, and provision for more adequate professional staff assistance in carrying out his many responsibilities, particularly with respect to administration.

SUPPLEMENTARY READINGS

Alexander, Margaret C. *Development of the Power of the Executive in New York.* Northhampton, Mass.: Smith College Studies in History, 1917.

Fairlie, J. A. "The Executive Power in the State Constitution." *The Annals of the American Academy of Political and Social Science* 171, September 1935, pp. 59–73.

Faust, M. L. *Manual on the Executive Article.* Columbia, Mo.: Missouri Constitutional Convention of 1943, 1943.

Goodsell, Charles T. *Administration of a Revolution: Executive Reform in Puerto Rico under Governor Tugwell, 1941–1946.* Cambridge, Mass.: Harvard University Press, 1965.

Graves, W. B. *American State Government.* 4th ed. Boston: D. C. Heath and Co., 1953.

Highsaw, Robert B. "The Southern Governor—Challenge to the Strong Executive Theme?" *Public Administration Review* 19, Winter 1959, pp. 7–11.

Kammerer, G. M. "The Governor as Chief Administrator in Kentucky." *Journal of Politics* 16, May 1954, pp. 236–256.

Mitau, G. Theodore. "The Governor and the Strike." In Richard T. Frost, ed., *Cases in State and Local Government.* Englewood Cliffs, N. J.: Prentice-Hall, 1961.

New York State Constitutional Convention Committee. *Problems Relating to Executive Administration and Powers.* Albany, 1938.

Ransone, Coleman B. *The Office of Governor in the South.* University, Ala.: Bureau of Public Administration, University of Alabama Press, 1951.

Rohr, C. J. *The Governor of Maryland: A Constitutional Study.* Baltimore: Johns Hopkins Press, 1932.

Ruskowski, C. W. *The Constitutional Governor.* Boston: Bruce Humphries, 1943.

Scace, H. E. *The Organization of the Executive Office of the Governor.* New York: Institute of Public Administration, 1950.

See also readings listed for chapter 11.

13

Problems of Organization and Personnel

The three major elements of administration that concern state and local executives are organization, personnel, and finance. Each of these affects the others to such an extent that it is difficult and somewhat misleading to discuss them separately, but each has had its own peculiar historical development, constituting an essential part of the understanding of state and local government. This chapter deals with organization and personnel, and the next chapter is devoted to finance.

The "big three" of adminis-tration

Some people are afflicted with the habit of assessing the relative importance of organization and personnel as they relate to public administration; and organization usually comes out a poor second in such comparisons. Effective administration undoubtedly depends in large measure upon the skill, integrity, and energy of the individual persons who make up the public service; however, it is not fair to try to calculate this value in contrast to that of the structure within which the personnel operate. It is like comparing the relative merits of the contributions of oil and water in the operation of a steam engine—each is essential in its own way. In spite of the importance of personnel, it would certainly be naive to conclude that forms of government have little effect on administrative efficiency. Not only does the form of organization help or hinder able administrators, but certain forms of organization tend to attract capable personnel while other forms tend to discourage their entry into the public service.

Organization v. personnel

Administrative Organization and Reorganization

Multiplication of activities and agencies

One of the outstanding developments in the history of state government is the multiplication of state functions and activities and the accompanying growth in number and scope of administrative agencies. Because of this expansion, problems have arisen which were never dreamed of by those who were originally responsible for the administrative systems in our states. As early as 1900 many states possessed no less than 100 officers, boards, and commissions, most of them independent and uncoordinated. Some states had as many as 200 such agencies, and one study of California revealed a total of 360 administrative boards, commissions, and agencies, ranging from the Board of Guide Dogs for the Blind to the Yacht and Ship Brokers Commission. This expansion of governmental machinery was carried out in an unplanned, haphazard fashion, the spoils motive frequently dominating. After their creation, these officers, boards, and commissions tended to magnify the importance of their activities with requests for increased staffs and higher appropriations and to seek to preserve their independent status.

Dispersed administrative structure

Initial efforts to reform state administrative organization got underway a decade or so after the turn of the century, with most of the concentration upon a set of defects found in varying degrees in the administrative set-up of all of the states. The problem primarily singled out for attack has been the dispersal of the administrative structure. Instead of all activities or services of the same functional character being combined, such as public welfare or public works, each activity or service was separate and distinct, with little or no relation to other like activities or services. Typical was the administration of activities related to agriculture in Virginia in 1910, which was carried on by five independent agencies instead of a unified department. The legislative practice of creating new departments for new activities, with no reference to their proper relationship to others, inevitably resulted in a planless structure of numerous uncoordinated agencies.

Boards and buck-passing

Another practice that has been strongly criticized is the extensive use of boards and commissions for "purely administrative" or ministerial activities. The plural-headed agency is said to be characterized by slow action, lack of initiative, and lack of professional competence. Furthermore, the use of boards and commissions either constitutes a limitation upon the governor's power of direction or provides a perfect "cover-up" for passing the buck through the scattering of responsibility.

The long ballot, resulting from the large number of elective state administrative officials, has been criticized as much for its effects upon the administrative structure of the state as it has for its contribution to non-voting or uninformed voting. Some elective officials are specifically provided for in the state constitution, particularly such older offices as secretary of state, attorney general, treasurer, auditor, and superintendent of public instruction. The duties of the secretary of state are mainly ministerial in character, though quite numerous, and consist of a miscellany of functions varying from affixing the great seal on official state documents to certifying election results. The attorney general has the twofold task of acting as legal counsel to state officials, including the governor, and representing the state in civil suits and occasionally in criminal cases. Both the treasurer and auditor head clerical and accounting offices whose work is largely routine in nature, and only in the case of the auditor does logic indicate independent status. The superintendent of public instruction is less commonly elected, but this method of selection still remains in about a third of the states.

The long ballot

The constitutionally elective officers, along with those made elective by legislative act, have become in many cases administrative "touch me nots" in terms of their relations with the governor. This confronts the governor with subordinates who are not actually subordinate, making it totally unrealistic to speak of a governor's cabinet in the sense of the president's cabinet. The existence of such elective offices renders administrative coordination difficult and creates areas of unaccountability within the executive branch of state government. The same result is achieved frequently by the practice of fixing terms of state officers so that they do not coincide with the governor's term of office. Mistakenly considered to be a means of "keeping politics out" of particular agencies, this practice more often has the effect of prolonging the politics of a defeated regime for several years.

Administrative "touch me nots"

Other problems on which the state reorganization movement focused attention have been defects in the organization for financial administration and, to a lesser extent, for personnel administration. The basic organizational weakness in the fields of finance and personnel is little different from that in other fields, but the impact of multiplication and dispersion of independent officers and agencies in these fields is undoubtedly greater. The dollars-and-cents cost of a dispersed state fiscal organization became more and more obvious, and state surveys did not fail to point out this cost.

Poor fiscal organization

Beginnings of reorganization

The movement for state administrative reorganization is usually said to have received its start about 1909 or 1910. The People's Power League of Oregon published a plan for reorganization of the state government in 1909 and again in 1911. The plan provided for concentration of executive power in the hands of the governor, subject only to the check of an independent auditor; it also provided for closer relations between the governor and legislature. In 1910, Governor Charles Evans Hughes of New York stated in his annual message to the legislature:

> It would be an improvement, I believe, in state administration if the executive responsibility were centered in the governor who should appoint a cabinet of administrative heads accountable to him and charged with the duties now imposed upon elected state officers.

The proposal for reform of the national administration made by President Taft's Economy and Efficiency Commission in 1912 caused the state reorganization movement to gain momentum. Although Congress took no action on this report, several state legislatures were influenced by it to such an extent that they immediately established efficiency and economy commissions to study their state administrative organization and methods. By 1935 more than thirty states had made investigations and recommendations.

Federal stimulus

The first comprehensive reorganization plan was adopted by Illinois in 1917. Under the leadership of Governor Frank O. Lowden, the legislature abolished more than 100 separate offices, boards, and commissions, consolidating their activities in nine functionally organized departments. A similar effort in New York had failed at the polls two years prior to the Illinois reorganization. Massachusetts in 1918 and 1919 was next to reorganize, followed by eight additional states within four years. In 1923 reorganization plans were adopted in Tennessee, Maryland, Pennsylvania, and Vermont. By 1938, twenty-six states had more or less remodeled their administrative structures, three of them by means of constitutional revisions and the others by statutory changes.

The example of Illinois

New impetus was given to the reorganization movement by the 1937 report of President Roosevelt's Committee on Administrative Management which gave its blessing to the principles upon which state reorganization had proceeded. Reorganization continued throughout World War II and after, although somewhat less sweeping than in the early period of the movement and consisting in some cases of "re-reorganizations" in states which had been overhauled previously. Taking their cue from the 1947 Commission on Organization of the Executive Branch of the Government of the United States (Hoover Commission), many states authorized administrative surveys of various types in 1949 and subsequent years. The peak year for these surveys was reached by 1952 when a total of thirty-three states had set up "little Hoover" commissions.[1]

"Little Hoover" commissions

[1] For an example of comprehensive reorganization proposals submitted by governors Rockefeller of New York, Hatfield of Oregon, and Brown of California, *see* James R. Bell and Earl L. Darrah, *State Executive Reorganization* (Berkeley: Institute for Governmental

The "little Hoover" commissions did not succeed completely—not one resulted in an overall reorganization—but the trend toward positive action in state administrative reorganization accelerated sharply in the late sixties and early seventies. Of the thirty-seven "substantial reorganizations" by states since the first by Illinois in 1917, one-third of them took place between 1965 and 1972. Out of more than thirty reorganization studies in recent years, the following states adopted substantial—more than just partial—reorganizations, as determined in a Council of State Governments survey by George A. Bell.[2]

New surge in the sixties and seventies

1967	Wisconsin
1968	Colorado and Florida
1969	Massachusetts
1969–70	Delaware and Maryland
1971	Arkansas, Maine, Montana, and North Carolina
1972–73	Georgia, Kentucky, South Dakota, and Virginia

Maryland consolidated 246 agencies into eleven cabinet-level departments, and Arkansas combined 60 into 13. Several other states had significant partial reorganizations, including California, which established four "super agencies" in 1968. Governors in many states now have authority to reorganize the executive branch by executive order, subject to legislative veto.[3]

The reasons for the new surge of executive streamlining activity vary, of course, but Bell asserts that the most important single factor is the openness to change accompanying the one-man–one-vote legislative reapportionments. Federal agencies have also provided encouragement with technical and financial assistance. Through the years, however, increasing pressures to find ways of fixing responsibility in the midst of greater size and complexity of government have continued to be the basic reason for reorganization.

Reapportionment begets reorganization

This movement has been based upon principles or standards which are considered worthy aims with respect to the organization and integration of state administration. It is contended that these standards are no longer theoretical, but are based upon experience and supported either partially or entirely by actual practice in a number of states. Although no

Standards of reorganization

Studies, University of California, 1961). *See also* Lynn W. Eley, *The Executive Reorganization Plan: A Survey of State Experience* (Berkeley: Institute of Governmental Studies, University of California, 1967).

[2] George A. Bell, "State Administrative Organization Activities, 1970–1971," *The Book of the States, 1973–74,* pp. 137–146.

[3] Several states have granted the governor this authority by constitutional provision in recent years: Illinois (1970), Kansas (1972), Maryland (1970), Massachusetts (1966), North Carolina (1970), and South Dakota (1972).

exact classification of these basic standards of reorganization has ever been agreed upon, probably the five most commonly accepted standards are the following: (1) functional departmentalization of administrative agencies; (2) concentration of administrative authority and responsibility in the governor; (3) the undesirability of having boards for the purely administrative work; (4) establishment of staff and auxiliary agencies responsible to the governor; and (5) provision for an independent audit.

Functional departmentalization

According to the principle of functional departmentalization, state agencies performing similar or closely related activities should be organized and operated within the same department. Such consolidation would eliminate overlappings and effect savings by reducing the number of employees needed. Moreover, reduction of the hundred-odd virtually independent agencies into a dozen orderly departments would remove one of the greatest obstacles to central administration of all agencies by the governor.

Concentrated authority and responsibility

Probably the basic standard of the reorganization movement, and the one upon which most of the others rest, is the concentration of authority and responsibility in the governor. It is considered not only unwise administrative practice but also unjust to impose a duty upon the governor or any other official without giving him authority commensurate with that responsibility. It is contended that the proper way to hold the administration accountable to the people is to center authority and responsibility at a single point, so that both deeds and misdeeds may be credited to the proper place. This principle requires elimination of most elective administrators, extension of the governor's appointing power to include all department heads, provision for a governor's cabinet, and establishment of a four-year term of office for the governor and other state officials. In a related trend of the 1960s and 1970s, approximately one-third of the states now require joint election of the governor and lieutenant governor as a team, like the president and vice-president. Consistency would also require the elimination of restrictions that prohibit a governor from running for re-election, since the governor is otherwise insulated from this important democratic device for reward or punishment.

Undesirability of boards

Boards or commissions are deemed undesirable for "purely administrative" activities because they are generally found to be inefficient. The single-headed agency is preferred for greater initiative, professional competence, quicker action, and clear location of responsibility. It is conceded, however, that boards or commissions may be attached advantageously to departments that are required to perform duties of a policy-determining, quasi-legislative, or quasi-judicial character.

In keeping with the expanded administrative role given to the governor, it is recommended that the various staff and auxiliary services of administration be coordinated and made responsible to the governor. According to this principle, the well-equipped governor will have adequate assistance in personal office staff, a planning agency, and central offices for the budget, accounting, purchasing, and personnel administration. During the 1960s a trend developed in the direction of uniting many of these functions in a single state department of administration and finance.[4]

Coordinated staff services

Most of the state reorganization survey groups have recommended a complete separation of the functions of financial control and accounting from those of independent auditing and review. This recommendation is based on the assumption that the control and accounting functions are executive in character and should be performed by an officer directly responsible to the governor, while the functions of post-audit and review belong to the legislature.

Independent audit

One suggestion for accomplishing administrative reorganization is to grant power to the governor, similar to that possessed by the president, to initiate reorganization proposals subject to subsequent disapproval by the legislature during a specified period of time. A few states have adopted such authorizations by statute in recent years, and Alaska became the first of several states to incorporate such a plan in their constitutions. Such provisions make it clear that the legislature retains authority over the powers and functions of departments, however.

Executive initiative in reorganization

Efforts for administrative reform at the state level have been matched by similar movements aimed at county and city governments, with some significant differences. The assumptions of the reorganization movement at the local level have been virtually the same as at the state level, and include many of the same arguments for integration of the administrative structure, as well as similar forces contributing to separatism and dispersion. Reorganization of city government has often revolved around the proposal for a complete change in form of government, such as the commission plan or the council–manager plan. This is partly true in the case of county reorganization, which has recently focused on the adoption of a county–manager system or the provision for a "chief administrative officer." County reorganization has proceeded at a snail's pace, easily the slowest of all levels of government, occurring primarily in the highly urbanized counties. Problems of administrative organization uniquely related to cities and counties are discussed subsequently in chapters 16, 17, and 18.

Parallel movements in cities and counties

The reorganization movement has not been without its critics. Although most political scientists have been in general agreement with the

[4] For a brief account of this development *see* Joe E. Nusbaum, "State Departments of Administration: Their Role and Trends of Development," *State Government* 35 (Spring 1962), pp. 124–129.

standards of reorganization and the movement as a whole, there has been criticism of both the practice and the theory of the reorganization movement. One frequent criticism, which occasionally finds much popular support, is the contention that reorganization would concentrate too much power in the hands of the governor. Abolition of the constitutionally elective officers is condemned as undemocratic, and the proposal to make the governor responsible for every administrative agency is said to stake too much on the ability of one man.

Criticisms of reorganization

Many have criticized the efforts to abolish boards and commissions. It is said that the best work often comes from private individuals who feel an urge to serve and that many boards of private individuals have been characterized by this spirit of voluntary service. Other arguments put forth in defense of boards and commissions are: a board will keep politics out of a department; where its members' terms overlap it guarantees continuity; group decision is frequently indispensable; and a board meets the need for group and sectional representation. This preference for the independent commission was expressed by 28 percent of the top administrators in the study by Deil Wright, discussed in the preceding chapter.[5] Control by the governor was preferred by 42 percent and legislative control was preferred by 24 percent. When Wright analyzed these preferences in terms of the existing method of appointment, it seemed clear that those under independent commissions generally preferred to remain that way, while those already appointed by the governor preferred to retain that structure.

Boards defended as valuable

The contention is made that the spoils system is nourished rather than eliminated by reorganization. According to this argument the governor's control of the spoils system is consolidated by his increased appointing power over higher administrative officers. Not only is the control of spoils, formerly scattered among independent agency heads, transferred to the hands of the governor, but he is in a better position to bypass civil service restrictions simply because of the added influence which his new powers under reorganization have given him.

Spoils system strengthened

The charge has been made that many reorganizations have been only "paper reorganizations" characterized by reshuffling of bureaus rather than genuine consolidation. As a result, there has been no reduction in agencies, personnel, or expenditures. Examples are cited of groups of miscellaneous state agencies that have been thrown together loosely into a new department, solely for the sake of paper symmetry. In New Jersey the courts have even recognized the nature of paper reorganization by declaring that even though the New Jersey Turnpike Authority is placed by law in the State Highway Department, it actually is "in but not of" the Highway Department.[6]

Reshuffling of bureaus

[5] Deil S. Wright, "Executive Leadership in State Administration," pp. 1–26.
[6] Bennett M. Rich, *The Government and Administration of New Jersey* (New York: Thomas Y. Crowell Co., 1957), p. 256.

The criticism has been made by others, particularly by line officials, that the staff agencies are too strict. It has been said that the reorganizers have instituted excessive financial control, especially through budget bureaus, and that the finance officers have been given too preeminent a position.

Control agencies too strict

Another criticism, less frequently voiced but in many ways more serious, concerns the wisdom of compelling the governor to perform the functions of chief administrator or general manager of the executive branch when his chief interest, his capabilities, and even the major demands of his constituents all direct him toward political, legislative, and ceremonial leadership. The tendency of non-administrative functions to monopolize the governor's time and interest casts some doubt upon the assumptions of a movement that undertakes to make the politician a general manager. These critics would say that "you can lead a political horse to administrative water but you can't make him drink."

Governor uninterested in administration

Finally, there is a very large group, particularly among political scientists, which makes the single criticism that the reorganization movement has not gone far enough in its changes. In effect, it does not attack the principles upon which the reorganization movement is based, but it contends that there has been an inadequate application of these principles. This group points out that no state has adopted all the component parts of the reorganization program in their entirety. They would be the first to admit further than many reorganizations have resulted merely in a shuffling of bureaus on paper, rather than in genuine integration of administrative agencies. The cartoon in Figure 13–1 was inspired by the constitutional independence of the Arkansas Highway Commission, which caused it to be left out of the 1971 administrative reorganization.

Partial reorganizations

These criticisms of administrative reorganization, coupled with the opposition of those having vested interest in the status quo, have made progress rather slow. Probably no force has been stronger in defeating reorganization proposals or in effecting compromises than the constitutionally independent officers and the personnel of independent boards and commissions. The attitude of the forces opposed to administrative reorganization is exemplified by the following historical account of the 1931 defeat of a reorganization plan in Arkansas. The description was written by the secretary of the Arkansas History Commission.

Opposition from affected agencies

> Slick brain trusters of the National Institute, Inc. [*sic*] plainly had the governor sold wholeheartedly on this plan of theirs which looked, on paper, like the setup of an ideal plan of government. . . .
>
> Governor Parnell's faith in this new streamlined system as a cure-all of much that is complained of as ill in government is not to be questioned. Deceived by his own naive enthusiasm, he thought he might induce the Legislature to submit the plan to a referendum vote of the people as proposals for amending the

Figure 13–1. George Fisher in the *North Little Rock Times.*

> constitution. However, the Legislature was cold to the scheme as a contrivance calculated to put it in the power of the governor to make himself a dictator. Once that impression got around, the majority would have no part of that which the New York doctors of political science had prescribed.[7]

Defense of status quo by clientele groups

The one-sided nature of the state historian's account of the fate of reorganization in Arkansas can be explained in large measure, perhaps, by the fact that the proposed functional departmentalization would have swallowed up the state history commission, eliminating its status as an independent agency. While each state has had its own peculiar circumstances leading to the defeat of reorganization proposals, this distrust of "slick brain trusters" and fear of dictatorship undoubtedly are shared by a large segment of the legislators and voters. Farmers have long resisted any

[7] D. T. Herndon, *Annals of Arkansas* (Little Rock: Arkansas History Commission, 1947), p. 272.

suggestion that the state's agricultural extension service should be subject to general control by the governor and legislature, and have sought to exercise their own close control through the private state Farm Bureau. The Parent–Teachers Association reacts vigorously against bringing the education department under too great purview of the governor. And organized sportsmen are always ready for an explosive counterattack against any effort to "coordinate" the fish and game commission with other conservation and natural resource agencies.[8]

Accomplishments of reorganization

In spite of criticism and opposition, few people in states that have experienced major reorganization now desire to return to the conditions existing before reorganization. The accomplishments of the state reorganization movement cannot be evaluated fully until more adequate, comprehensive analyses have been made of the results of reorganization, but there is agreement on at least a few of its accomplishments. It is generally agreed that responsibility can be more easily located in the reorganized administrative system, and many would cite this as the principal benefit attributable to reorganization. In terms of economies, it is difficult to show actual dollars-and-cents savings through reorganization; but there can be little doubt that reorganization has resulted in more and better service per tax dollar. One of the inevitable results of increased public confidence in government in a reorganized state is the demand for new services or for expansion of existing services, making tax reductions impossible. Finally, the administrative work of the reorganized state is undoubtedly better planned than that of the unreorganized state. The credit for this rests with the governor's new-found executive leadership. The governor finds it less difficult to take an all-embracing view because of the more simplified structure of government and the assistance of new staff agencies. Information is more easily obtained, and long-range planning becomes attainable.

For any who might suspect that structural reorganization makes no real difference in the informal power relationships, Deil Wright's study of top administrators in state government provides a partial answer. He found that the administrators' *perceptions* of gubernatorial control—as compared with legislative control—generally support the hypothesis that more formal power correlates with more actual control. As indicated in Table 13–1, the governor was named most often as primary power wielder in those states where the formal powers are "strong" or "moderate"; the legislature was named most often in those states where the governor's formal powers are "weak" or "very weak." It would seem that reorganization *does* make a difference. Wright also warns against concluding that governors actually have "monopoly powers" in reorganized states.

[8] For a case study of such an effort, *see* Thomas H. Eliot, "Reorganizing the Massachusetts Department of Conservation," in Edwin A. Bock (ed.), *State and Local Government: A Casebook* (University, Ala.: University of Alabama Press, 1963), pp. 315–334.

Table 13–1. Relationship of the Governor's Formal Power to Top Administrators' Perception of the Governor's Actual Power

Who Has Greater Control over Agency Affairs?	*States in Which Formal Powers of the Governor Are:*			
Percent Naming	*Strong*	*Moderate*	*Weak*	*Very Weak*
Governor	37	41	25	21
Each About the Same	28	21	23	16
Legislature	35	38	52	63
Total	100	100	100	100

Source: Adapted from Deil S. Wright, "Executive Leadership in State Administration," *Midwest Journal of Political Science* 11 (February 1967), p. 12. Reprinted by permission of Wayne State University Press. The table makes use of an index of formal powers of the governors developed by Joseph A. Schlesinger, "The Politics of the Executive," in Jacob and Vines (eds.), *Politics in the American States: A Comparative Analysis*, p. 229.

The Civil Service Reform Movement

Importance of personnel

Structural reform in state and local government was actually preceded by civil service reform, although the two movements have proceeded at about the same pace since 1900. There can be no doubt at all that the finest organization conceivable is doomed to failure if it is manned by untrained, unscrupulous, and undependable employees. There should be no doubt that such an organization will also fail under the ever-increasing demands of modern society if it is manned by mediocre and half-trained employees, however honest they may be. Although some still have the notion that the public service can get along all right with well-meaning "second raters," experience has increasingly demonstrated that the public service in the mid-twentieth century demands the best personnel that can be found.

Origins of spoils system

A history of personnel management in state and local government has been until recent years primarily a history of the "spoils" system. Although Andrew Jackson is sometimes blamed for introducing the spoils system into American politics, many made use of the system before he did. Even colonial America operated under a spoils system of a sort. Colonial governors tended to treat public office as a special preserve of a privileged class, the British aristocracy. This became the source of friction between the colonial legislature and the royal governor concerning his appointing power. After the Revolution, the short terms and rotation of office prevalent in state governments made possible a new kind of spoils system long before Andrew Jackson was elected president. The statement of Senator Marcy of New York in 1832 that "to the victor belong the spoils" signaled not the beginning of the spoils system, but merely its spread from state and local government to the national level. Aaron Burr, the first "boss" of Tammany Hall, had applied it most skillfully in New York City after defeating Alexander Hamilton in 1800. Thus, while spoils activity was relatively insignificant at the national level from 1800 until 1829, it flourished vigorously at state and local levels. From 1829 to 1883 the doctrine of party monopoly went virtually unchallenged at all levels of government.

Evils of spoils system

The spoils system at its worst has had a disastrous effect on the efficiency of state administration. At best it has been a crude and frustrating mechanism for selecting and supervising public administrative personnel. With party activity the chief criterion for selecting employees, state and local employment became a temporary and uncertain occupation which the most capable persons had no desire to enter. The spoils system had a demoralizing effect on administration, with the quality of personnel caught in a downward spiral of short tenure of office, high labor turnover, and a general public inclination to think of public employees as incompetent and lazy. Low prestige contributed to still greater labor turnover which, in turn, contributed to still lower prestige.

The spoils system has been both a blessing and a curse to the governor and to the mayor. As a means of strengthening party or faction, of insuring the loyalty of the public service, and of giving the chief executive strong bargaining power with his legislative body, the spoils system was defended for years as essential to democratic leadership.[9] As the tasks of public administration became increasingly technical in character, however, the effects of the spoils system not only became more damaging to the administrative process, but they became an increasingly serious burden upon the governor in his new role as chief administrator of a multimillion-dollar public business. Governors began to find it intolerable to spend the greater part of each working day speaking to the many friends of the previous campaign who had "clients" in need of a job. This was all the more serious because the greatest pressure always came during the first few months of the governor's term of office, when most of his time was needed for consideration of the important initial decisions of his administration. A comparison of governors' inaugural addresses with their farewell addresses reveals an interesting contrast in their recommendations concerning patronage. The silence of the incoming governor is followed by statesmanlike pronouncements from the outgoing governor on behalf of a strengthened civil service.

Dissatisfaction with the spoils system grew during the post-Civil War period, but did not find tangible expression until 1880 when the New York Civil Service Reform Association was organized. It later became known as

[9] For an excellent analysis of post-reform problems of a governor in making patronage decisions, *see* Daniel P. Moynihan and James Q. Wilson, "Patronage in New York State, 1955–1959," pp. 286–301.

the National Civil Service Reform League and is now the National Civil Service League. Civil service reform was given a dramatic push in 1881 by the assassination of President Garfield by a disappointed office seeker. This incident mobilized strong support for a federal law, passed in 1883, which required examinations to test the abilities of job applicants. Later in 1883 the state of New York established a civil service commission with authority to administer competitive tests for state employment, and Massachusetts followed in 1884. Although for more than twenty years these two states were the only ones to adopt the merit principle, by 1900 there were eighty-five civil service commissions in the cities of the nation.

Beginnings of reform

Early in the present century (1905) Wisconsin and Illinois began a new era of civil service reform by setting up civil service commissions. Colorado and New Jersey followed in 1907 and 1908, and by 1920 Connecticut, California, Ohio, Kansas, and Maryland had fallen into line. Another lapse in activity followed, and it was not until 1937 that new converts to the merit system began to appear. In that year five states adopted the merit principle for state employment, and subsequent adoptions brought the total number of states to about two-thirds of the fifty. In addition to these states, which have what the Public Personnel Association terms "general coverage," the remainder of the fifty have complied with a 1939 federal requirement by enacting civil service laws applying to state workers associated with certain federal grant-in-aid programs.

Extension of civil service

Some of the states considered to have general coverage have experienced difficulty in continuing to manifest genuine conversion to the merit principle. Many have accepted the merit principle in name only and have devised numerous ingenious means of continuing patronage appointments. Temporary and interim appointments, tampering with examination scores, coercion to secure waivers from the top candidates, and exemption of particular classes of appointments are just a few of the possible methods of defeating the intent of a civil service law. Other states have repealed their civil service laws after only a brief trial period. In spite of occasional defections from the ranks, the general trend has been clearly in the direction of tightening up and extending the scope of state civil service laws. A new federal push for stronger state personnel systems came with the passage in 1970 of the Intergovernmental Personnel Act. It provides for grants to the states for improvement of personnel administration, for public service fellowships, and for interchange of personnel among various levels of government. New federal aid restrictions have extended prohibitions against discrimination on the basis of age, sex, and physical disability, in addition to race, religion, and political party. Counties still lag far behind cities and states in adopting civil service systems, except for the larger, more urban counties.

Circumvention of civil service

The original emphasis of the civil service reform movement was largely negative—that is, its design was to "keep the rascals out" by means of a watchdog-type enforcement of competitive entrance examinations. Other aspects of personnel management were neglected or omitted from the functions of the civil service commission. However, the merit system has come to mean far more than keeping the spoilsmen out of office. The modern personnel department is engaged in a wide variety of activities aimed at recruiting, selecting, supervising, and promoting the best qualified persons for the public service. Its many responsibilities include recruitment, examination, certification, position classification, pay policy, in-service and other training programs, performance evaluation records, discipline and removals, safety and welfare programs, and many other related activities.[10]

Essentials of personnel management

Recruitment, examination, and certification are the first functions of personnel management in the chronology of a person's entry into the public service. Recruitment, still a neglected phase of personnel management in many states, includes all activities aimed at attracting candidates for public employment. Too often recruitment amounts to little more than posting an unattractive mimeographed announcement of examinations on the same bulletin board that contains reward notices for fugitive criminals. In recent years the more progressive cities and states have adopted "positive recruitment" programs, utilizing a variety of modern methods to actively seek the best qualified persons for state employment.

Recruitment, examination, and certification

The civil service examination program, the oldest and at one time almost the exclusive personnel function, continues to be of vital importance to the merit system. Examinations for applicants may be oral, written, or physical performance tests, or they may test achievement, aptitude, or physical fitness. Tests may be based on a competitive or pass scale and administered to individuals or groups. In the assembled, or group, examination the candidates are brought together in one or more examining rooms to answer specific questions in writing. The unassembled, or individual, examination involves more personal and individual evaluation of education, experience, and qualifications, and is used for positions where the number of applicants is small and the opening is in the higher grades of the civil service. Examinations are essential aids in judging an applicant's probable future success or failure in the public service.

Following an examination, the civil service commission does not make appointments. Instead, most states provide for certification by the commission to the appointing authority of the three highest on the eligi-

[10] For a comprehensive study of the manpower problems of the second largest governmental unit in the United States—New York City—which is not a newcomer to civil service, *see* David T. Stanley et al., *Professional Personnel for the City of New York* (Washington, D. C.: The Brookings Institution, 1963).

ble list, from which he makes his selection. This "rule of three" is defended as allowing discretion for the appointing officer, at the same time providing a deterrent against partisan appointments.

Position classification

In many ways position classification is more appropriately the first function of personnel management, insofar as providing the foundation on which most other personnel activities must rest. Although considered highly technical and mysterious by some employees, it simply consists of grouping positions with similar duties into classes which permit uniform treatment. Without a position-classification plan, employees performing essentially the same duties in several different departments of state government may be on different salary scales, depending on the department's political power, prestige, and similar factors. A position-classification plan not only makes possible equal pay for equal work, but has many other uses. It provides the information necessary for intelligent recruitment and examination. Increasing information on the qualifications necessary for the higher positions in the state public service facilitates transfers and promotions within the service. Mobility of personnel is seriously limited without a classification plan. On the basis of the classification plan, in-service training programs are inaugurated, designed both to improve employees' performance and to prepare them for higher positions. Probably the fundamental rule in position classification is the fact that it is the *position* which is classified—not the person who fills the position. Thus the determining factors are the duties actually required by the job, and not the exceptional talents of the person who happens to be filling the position when it is classified.

Discipline and dismissals

Discipline in the public service varies from comparatively mild measures, such as warning or reprimand, to more stringent forms, such as suspension or dismissal. Between these extremes are such alternatives as loss of seniority, demerits from efficiency ratings, loss of privileges, and demotion in rank. The desire to protect employees from unwarranted dismissal—particularly political removal—has led in many jurisdictions to the enactment of elaborate appeal procedures which make the civil service commission a quasi-judicial agency. Some kind of hearing is guaranteed to employees dismissed in such cases, and it often takes on the appearance of a formal trial, complete with legal counsel, testimony, cross-examination, and jury decision (by the commission) of guilty or not guilty. Such an appeal procedure is defended as essential to protect the innocent from the onslaught of the spoils system, especially during the formative years of a civil service system. These protective measures have been criticized, however, both for being ineffectual when a strong mayor or governor seriously wants to fire an employee and for imposing too much "red tape" upon administrators genuinely interested in removing unsatisfactory employees. The natural inclination of an administrator is to retain an incompetent employee indefinitely rather than to risk open combat in a public hearing in which all the dirty linen of the department might be washed. In spite of this unfortunate result, there seems to be no way to move from the spoils system toward the merit system in city or state government without reasonable safeguards against arbitrary dismissals.

Collective bargaining, public unions, and strikes

The whole subject of collective bargaining, at the top of any list of personnel management concerns in private business, has only recently come to be recognized as a major concern in the public sector as well. Surprisingly, membership in unions and employee associations in state and local government is already proportionately greater than in private industry. Even with public school teachers excluded, more than one-third of state and local employees are organized, compared with less than 30 percent in the private sector.[11] States have begun increasingly to pass laws that provide for collective bargaining rights or procedures approximating collective bargaining for public employees. By 1972, close to twenty states had granted state employees the right to negotiate collectively, or to "meet and confer." Three states, Pennsylvania, Vermont, and Hawaii, have granted state employees a qualified right to strike. Although the number of strikes by public employees in 1970 was five times greater than in 1960, the laws on public employee strikes do not reflect the change.

The American Assembly report in 1971 cautiously recommended a limited right to strike for public unions. It then gave the following summary analysis of the significance of collective bargaining for public employees:

> The extension of collective bargaining in the public sector is clearly modifying the civil service system. The Assembly believes that while the trend is both inevitable and desirable, the principle of merit as it relates to the recruitment and hiring of public employees should not be eliminated. . . .
>
> The history of labor-management relations in the private sector in America is loaded with pain and controversy as the price of progress and the recognition of union rights.
>
> Public unions and collective bargaining are here to stay.
>
> The price of progress need not be so dear in the public sector if all concerned recognize and respond to the urgent need for new attitudes, new legislation and new ways of working together.[12]

[11] *LMRS Newsletter* 2 (July 1971), p. 1.

[12] *Collective Bargaining in American Government,* Report of the Fortieth American Assembly, Oct. 28–31, 1971 (Harriman, N. Y.: Arden House), p. 8. For detailed studies, *see* the Brookings Institution Series, *Studies of Unionism in Government,* including Harry H. Wellington and Ralph K. Winter, *The Unions and the Cities* (1971), and David T. Stanley with the assistance of Carole L. Cooper, *Managing Local Government under Union Pressure* (1972).

Retirement

The importance of a service-wide retirement program for public employees is perhaps best indicated by reference to the state of affairs existing prior to adoption of a pension system. In the absence of adequate retirement benefits for public employees, the tendency has been to keep employees on the payroll long after their usefulness has come to an end. This understandable reluctance to dismiss persons with long years of faithful service not only clogged up the payrolls with the over-aged and incapacitated, but also clogged up promotional ladders, put off salary increases, and discouraged the entry of young men and women into state and local employment. A two-fold motivation—a combination of humanitarianism and administrative self-interest—prompted development of an adequate program of compulsory retirement and pensions.

Few states or major cities have not adopted a comprehensive pension system for their employees, although some of the systems adopted depend upon the financially unsound "cash disbursement" plan which makes no attempt to establish adequate, actuarially determined reserves. The "actuarial reserve" plan takes the guesswork out of the annual requirements of the pension fund and does not leave this to the vicissitudes of legislative economy drives. Although the old age insurance plan enacted by Congress in 1935 specifically excluded employees of state and local governments, subsequent legislation permits these groups to participate in the federal social security system. It is common practice to balance the membership of management and employees on the pension board that is charged with responsibility for administering the retirement fund.

Current Problems

Reorganization, civil service, and the governor

The movements in state and local government for administrative reorganization and for civil service reform seem to contradict each other in one respect. On the surface it seems that the "reorganizers" favor strengthening the administrative position of the governor or mayor by giving him more appointing power, while the civil service reformers favor weakening him by divesting him of great portions of his appointing power. To complete the picture, it should be noted that most textbooks in the field of state and local government appear to give strong support to *both* movements.

Different types of appointments

There is at least a partial explanation for this seeming contradiction of recommending more and less appointing power for the chief executive at the same time. The explanation lies in the types of appointments that are referred to in each case. The state reorganization movement is primarily concerned with giving the governor the power to appoint the heads of the important departments and bureaus of the executive branch, in order that he may fulfill the constitutional mandate to see that the laws of the state are faithfully executed. The civil service reform movement, on the other hand, is primarily concerned with insuring non-political appointments of clerks, technicians, and professional employees at a level lower than department or bureau head. Furthermore, civil service reform has been more concerned with the method of appointment than the source of the appointing power, although the latter is naturally involved.

Just what should be the organizational relationship of the whole function of personnel administration to the governor? This question poses one of the most perplexing problems facing those interested in improving state government. In one corner stand those who favor a strong and independent civil service commission, isolated from the office of governor in order to prevent his meddling in appointments and removals simply to pay his political debts. This independent status for the civil service commission is usually achieved by providing that the members of the commission shall have longer terms of office than the governor and that their terms shall not expire at the same time. Insulation from the governor's influence is further provided in some states by requiring that the governor fill vacancies on the commission only with nominees submitted by independent groups, such as specified university presidents. Advocates of the strong and independent civil service commission regard it as an essential part of our system of checks and balances, designed to prevent the governor and his department heads from abusing their power.

The strong and independent commission

In the opposite corner stand those who favor an integrated personnel department as one of the principal staff arms of the governor. Proponents of the integrated department point out that the governor's new role as administrative chief of the state, added to his older roles as political and ceremonial chief, makes it essential for him to have authority over personnel management. It is argued that to deprive the chief executive of authority over personnel management is to send the soldier to battle with one arm tied behind his back. One of the strongest arguments advanced for the integrated personnel department is that it is essential before the states can begin to move away from the negative, keep-the-rascals-out philosophy of personnel management to the more positive philosophy of a merit system. It is said that as long as the personnel program is not the program of the governor and the department heads, the independent civil service commission will never obtain more than begrudging and half-hearted compliance from line officials who must, in the final analysis, carry out the program.

The integrated personnel department

What is the answer to the dilemma? The doctrines of modern "positive personnel management" seem to dictate that the chief executive should have authority over the personnel department, but practical experience with the spoils system seems to dictate that the governor needs an independent check in this area. In actual practice, most states seem to be moving toward a compromise between these two extremes.

Compromise in practice

While most states cling to the idea of a commission rather than a single head for the personnel agency, there is growing recognition that most of the work in personnel management is detailed administration, rather than rule making and adjudication. Increasing authority is being placed in the office of director of personnel, the civil service commission retained primarily as a rule-making and disciplinary body. Such an arrangement permits a close relationship between the governor and the personnel director, while guarding the independent status of the commission. But the answer does not lie in a single organizational pattern. Each state will require a tailor-made plan, with due consideration to whether the office of governor in that state has outgrown the necessity for an independent watchdog to keep the spoilsmen out. Some states obviously have not outgrown this necessity. Advocates of the council–manager plan can claim with some justification that their system of government for cities is more conducive to the merit system than one under a popularly elected executive.

Gubernatorial accountability

One other problem should be mentioned as having been aggravated by the administrative reorganization movement, but it is actually as old as government itself. This is the problem of how the governor, who has come to be a powerful figure in even the most unreorganized states, can be controlled by the people in a way that avoids hamstringing a "good governor" while keeping a "bad governor" checkmated and harmless. The administrative reorganization movement has made it clear that an impotent governor cannot adequately perform the task assigned to him in modern state government and has recommended greatly increased administrative powers. Probably the most serious omission of the reorganization movement, some would contend, has been an equal concern for a strengthened system of holding the governor and administration accountable to the people. This is probably an unfair criticism, however, for many of those who advocate reorganization of the executive are also proponents of modernizing the legislature. Reorganization of the legislature along lines laid down by modern principles would sharpen this time-honored instrument for control of the executive and render it abler to ensure accord between the action of the executive and the popular will. In any case, the new growth of administrative power certainly merits thoughtful consideration of new and sensible methods of control over this power.

A close examination of the methods available to the people for controlling their state governor will reveal that in many states the system of continuing accountability of the governor—either to the legislature, the courts, or, more directly, to the people—is seriously ineffective. A case study made by one of the authors indicates that controls existing in Arkansas are not adequate for holding the governor accountable for his conduct of administration in that state.

Inadequate methods of control

> The legislative controls are subject to the limitations of a sixty-day biennial session and are often made ineffective because of the submissiveness of the legislature to the governor. There is no independent audit of expenditures subject to the legislature. The court will not compel the governor to perform either his discretionary or mandatory duties, and its chief restraint upon the governor lies in declaring acts to be unconstitutional. The biennial election of the governor has proved to be a slender reed on which to rely for obtaining responsible administration, and there is no provision for the recall. Finally, pressure groups, including political factions, wield a substantial amount of influence upon the governor, but there is no assurance that such groups represent the people as a whole.[13]

National power over state governors, applied only timidly if at all during most of American history, has flexed its muscles more definitely in segregation matters in recent years. In an unprecedented case, Governor Ross Barnett of Mississippi was enjoined by federal court against interfering with the admission of a black, James Meredith, to the University of Mississippi in the fall of 1962. A case against Barnett for criminal contempt undoubtedly helped restrain the resistance by others such as Governor George Wallace, whose "stand in the doorway" at the University of Alabama was a much milder action than Barnett's. The Supreme Court in 1964, by a 5-to-4 vote, sustained a qualified power to try and punish a governor for contempt, without a jury trial,[14] and remanded the case for further proceedings. In a 4-to-3 decision in 1965, the Court of Appeals held that the lapse of time and changed circumstances and conditions justified dismissing the criminal contempt charges against Barnett.[15] It seems clear, however, that the incidents have resulted in a broader judicial interpretation of national power over governors.

The ombudsman

It was the quest for a system of strong but responsible state administration that undoubtedly led to the suggestion of a state manager plan many years ago by Harvey Walker[16] and the proposal by William Y. Elliott and others for a responsible executive on the model of English

[13] Daniel R. Grant, "The Role of the Governor of Arkansas in Administration," p. 334.

[14] *United States* v. *Barnett*, 376 U. S. 681 (1964).

[15] *United States* v. *Barnett*, 346 F. (2nd.) 99 (1965).

[16] Harvey Walker, "Theory and Practice in State Administrative Organization," *National Municipal Review* 19 (April 1930), pp. 249–254.

cabinet government.[17] Both proposals probably deviate too far from American governmental tradition to offer much hope for realization in the foreseeable future.

The device of an "ombudsman," a watchdog or grievance commissioner to investigate citizens' complaints of administrative abuse, has been discussed with increased frequency by political scientists and citizens' groups. Originating in Sweden in 1809, the ombudsman idea was first adopted on the state level in the United States by Hawaii in 1969, followed by Nebraska, Iowa, and Oregon. Although many legislators consider the ombudsman to be a competitor and are reluctant to support the idea, it has received much popular support and seems likely to spread among the states. A similar movement has begun at the local level, and a variety of complaint-handling offices have been set up for cities.[18]

Toward a stronger state legislature

The most feasible approach to a solution at present probably lies in strengthening the state legislature so that it can adequately fulfill its function of controlling the purse strings and supervising the administration. This does not mean reliance upon the legislature as the only form of control over the governor. It simply means that the legislature seems best suited to become the bulwark of an effective system of control. Responsible administration cannot be realized without a legislature capable of efficiently handling the task of appropriating funds for administration, of controlling expenditures by means of a regular audit as well as investigations, and of being general guardian of the administrative interests of the people.

[17] William Y. Elliott, *The Need for Constitutional Reform* (New York: McGraw-Hill Book Co., Inc., 1935).

[18] *See* Stanley V. Anderson, *Ombudsman Papers: American Experience and Proposals* (Berkeley: Institute of Governmental Studies, University of California, 1969), and Bernard Frank, "The Ombudsman Concept Is Expanding in the U. S.," *National Civic Review* 61 (May 1972), pp. 232–235.

SUPPLEMENTARY READINGS

Bollens, J. C. *Administrative Reorganization in the States since 1939.* Berkeley: Bureau of Public Administration, University of California, 1947.

Bosworth, K. A. "The Politics of Management Improvement in the States." *American Political Science Review* 47, March 1953, pp. 84–99.

Buck, A. E. *The Reorganization of State Governments in the United States.* New York: Columbia University Press, 1938.

Carpenter, W. S. *The Unfinished Business of Civil Service Reform.* Princeton, N.J.: Princeton University Press, 1952.

Civil Service Assembly of the United States and Canada. *Readings in Public Personnel Administration.* Chicago: Civil Service Assembly of the United States and Canada, 1942.

See also other reports by this organization, now known as the Public Personnel Association.

Council of State Governments. *Reorganizing State Government.* Chicago: Council of State Governments, 1950.

Fish, C. R. *The Civil Service and the Patronage.* Cambridge, Mass.: Harvard University Press, 1920.

Heady, Ferrel. *State Constitutions: The Structure of Administration.* New York: National Municipal League, 1961.

Hyneman, C. S. "Administrative Reorganization: An Adventure into Science and Theology." *Journal of Politics* 1, February 1939, pp. 62–75.

Municipal Manpower Commission. *Governmental Manpower for Tomorrow's Cities.* New York: McGraw-Hill Book Co., 1962.

Nigro, Felix A. *Modern Public Administration.* New York: Harper & Row, 1965.

Peabody, Robert L. *Organizational Authority.* New York: Atherton Press, 1964.

Sharkansky, Ira. *Public Administration: Policy-Making in Government Agencies.* Chicago: Markham Publishing Co., 1970.

Stahl, O. Glenn. *Public Personnel Administration.* 5th ed. New York: Harper & Row, 1962.

Wilbern, York. "Administrative Organization." In James W. Fesler, ed., *The 50 States and Their Local Governments.* New York: Alfred A. Knopf, 1967.

Zagoria, Sam, ed. *Public Works and Public Unions.* Englewood Cliffs, N. J.: Prentice-Hall, 1972. Background papers for the Fortieth American Assembly.

14

Finance

It is not wise to learn public finance from the typical "economy candidate" who runs for the office of governor for the first time. His glib promises of greatly increased governmental services without corresponding increases in state taxes simply brand him as one of two things—a demagogue or an ignoramus. Many a victorious gubernatorial candidate in recent history has faced the prospect of unanticipated (and unpromised) new taxes or an unbalanced budget immediately upon taking office. He can usually be depended upon to speak differently about financing state government in the next election, having learned about state finance by the rigorous, school-of-hard-knocks method.

Financial demagogy

Public finance, with its concern for expenditures and revenues, is a two-edged sword that cuts across every major program and problem of state and local government. It is difficult to think of any administrative or political act which does not have financial implications. Whether it is the employment of a new engineer in the state highway department or a newspaper editorial urging replacement of a dilapidated and unsafe wing of a local hospital, money is involved.

Importance of finance

How much money do state and local governments spend and for what is it spent? What is the comparative cost of different government programs? Who decides where the money goes? Where does the money come from, and what are the major problems in extracting it from citizens? What is happening in state–local financial relationships? The answers to these and other questions are essential to an understanding of the role of finance in state and local government.

Expenditures

All levels of government—federal, state, and local—spent almost 400 billion dollars in 1972; of this amount, about 155 billion dollars, almost 40 percent of the total, were spent by state and local governments. Based on "direct expenditures" for their "own purposes," state and local governments actually spent 47 percent of the total. Except for national defense spending, which accounted for a lion's share—79 billion dollars—the federal government actually spent about the same as the total for state and local governments. State governments, which spent less than 500 million dollars in 1915, increased their expenditures five-fold to 2.5 billion dollars in 1930, and by 1952 the 1930 amount had increased five-fold to more than 13 billion dollars. In 1972 their expenditures amounted to 72.5 billion dollars. In addition, the amount distributed by state governments to local governments each year (36.8 billion dollars in 1972) has been increasing even more rapidly than the state governments' own direct expenditures.

Increased expenditures

While there can be no doubt about the great increase in state expenditures, it is incorrect to assume a 7,000 percent increase in the past half-century is proof of waste and extravagance. Increase in population and decrease in the purchasing power of the dollar must be credited, at least partially, for causing increased expenditures. Inflation makes it especially hazardous to compare annual statistics on public expenditures. When "constant dollars" are used, rather than "current dollars," the percentage increase in state expenditures during the past decade is reduced sharply. Much of the increase, however, must be attributed to expansion of state functions through steadily broadening old services, provision of new services, and state assumption of services provided previously by local governments. Those concerned about the increase may be reassured by the knowledge that the ratio of state and local expenditures to gross national product was not much higher in 1971 than in 1931. As shown in Table 14–1, even the combined percentage for federal, state, and local expenditures is well below the 1944 record, although it has been inching back up since 1946.

Causes of increase

For what is the money spent? At the state level the three major functions of education, highways, and public welfare account for close to three-fourths of annual expenditures. The predominance of the cost of education over all other functions of government was, until recent years, primarily observed at the local government level. With the state governments becoming increasingly involved in financing education, highways have dropped to second place. The fiscal importance of the three leading functions, with health and hospitals added in, is shown in Figure 14–1.

Objects of expenditure

Table 14–1. Federal, State, and Local Expenditures as a Percentage of Gross National Product, 1931–1971

Year	*Total*	*Federal*	*State and Local*
1931	16.4%	5.5%	10.8%
1936	19.5	10.5	9.0
1941	23.1	16.5	6.7
1944	49.0	45.4	3.6
1946	21.8	17.1	4.7
1951	24.0	17.6	6.4
1956	24.8	17.2	7.7
1961	28.6	19.6	9.0
1966	28.3	19.0	9.3
1971	32.2	21.0	11.2

Source: Adapted from Tax Foundation, Inc., *Facts and Figures on Government Finance* (New York, 1973), p. 33, and U. S. Department of Commerce, Bureau of Economic Analysis.

State and local governments spend more for education (64.9 billion dollars in 1972) than for highways, public welfare, and health and hospitals combined. Functions next in financial importance to all of the aforementioned are police protection, sanitation and sewerage, natural resources, housing and urban renewal, fire protection, and parks and recreation, each accounting for from one to three percent of state and local expenditures.

Variation among states

Total figures for expenditures of the fifty states may imply a uniform expenditure pattern in each state; actually, there is a considerable amount of variation from state to state. The variation is especially apparent in any state-by-state comparison that excludes local government expenditures, because state-aid programs to local governments differ greatly among the states. Even so, it is a rare thing if expenditures of a state government for education, highways, and public welfare do not account for between one-half and two-thirds of the state's total budget.

Character of expenditures

The question of where the money goes is not answered simply by an indication of the cost of particular governmental programs. Government expenditures may be classified according to current operations, capital outlays, and other objects. Considered in this light, state and local expenditures for 1972 are presented in Table 14–2.

One of the newest and most significant areas of political science research has focused on comparative state politics, emphasizing varying

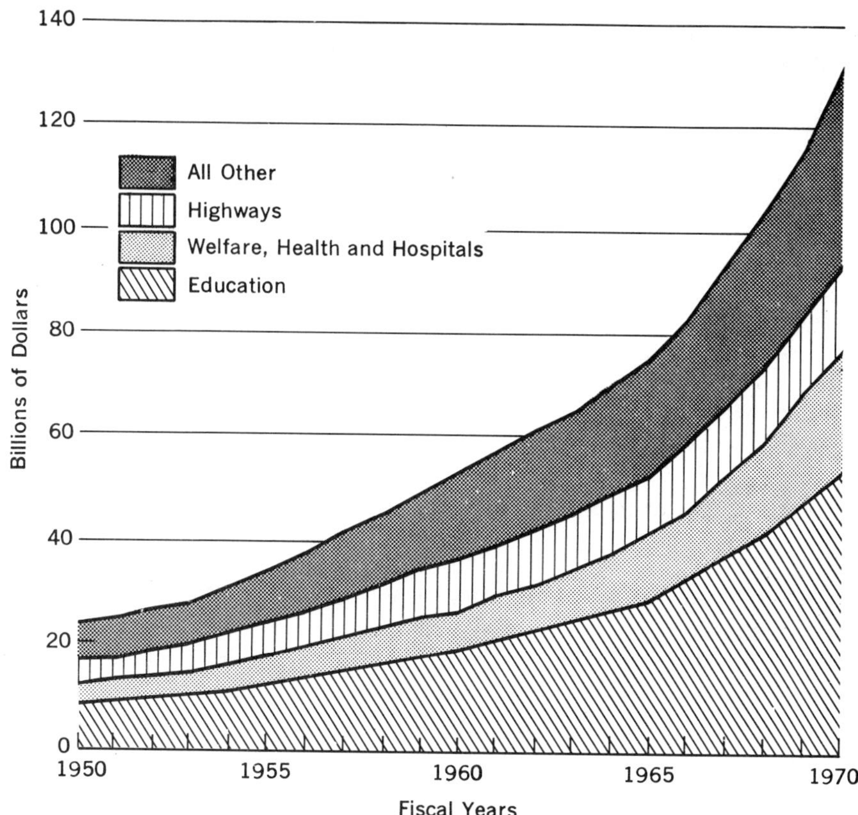

Figure 14–1. State and Local General Expenditure for Selected Functions, 1950–1970. *Source:* Advisory Commission on Intergovernmental Relations, *State–Local Finances: Significant Features and Suggested Legislation* (Washington, D. C., 1972), p. 121.

"state policy outputs" and the search for factors that show the strongest correlation with state policy variations. This kind of research is a response to criticism of preoccupation with the "inputs" of the political system—public opinion, voting, pressure groups, party politics, etc., and neglect of the task of explaining specific results of the political process. Among other measures of policy outputs used in this research is the level of state expenditures for various functions. The early results by Dye, Hofferbert, and others seemed to show that the socioeconomic characteristics of states—personal wealth, urbanization, industrialization, and education—were far more influential than political traits such as voter turnout, interparty competition, and the quality of legislative apportionment.[1] This

[1] For an excellent brief review of this literature, *see* Ira Sharkansky, *Regionalism in American Politics* (Indianapolis: The Bobbs-Merrill Co., 1970), pp. 180–181.

Table 14–2. State and Local Expenditures by Character, 1972
(In millions of dollars)

Item	State and Local	State	Local
Total expenditure	188,825	109,243	116,913
Intergovernmental expenditure	———	36,759	571
Direct expenditure	188,825	72,483	116,342
Current operation	125,630	39,790	85,840
Capital outlay	34,237	15,283	18,953
Assistance and subsidies	11,527	6,337	5,190
Interest on debt	6,893	2,135	4,758
Insurance benefits and repayments	10,538	8,938	1,600

Source: U. S. Bureau of the Census, *Governmental Finances in 1971–72* (Washington, D. C.: U. S. Government Printing Office, 1973), pp. 5, 18.

appeared to be upsetting to political scientists, especially to those who have long contended that political variables—features of the political system—have a great deal to do with the nature of policies that states enact and administer. The controversy that has ensued over the relative importance of political versus socioeconomic variables is enriching the literature of comparative state politics. Sharkansky, employing a larger concept of state politics, has discovered that certain political variables are more significant than some socioeconomic variables in their correlation to policy measures. In particular, the character of previous state expenditure decisions and the proportion of spending responsibilities assigned to state (as opposed to local) governments are found to be highly influential determinants of current state expenditures.[2] Sharkansky and Hofferbert have shown that a "turnout-competition" has a great deal to do with a policy output called "welfare-education," independent of the effects of socioeconomic factors, thus contradicting earlier studies.[3] It is important to exercise caution in interpreting the findings of this rapidly expanding literature on comparative state politics.

Political variables in state expenditures

What part of state and local expenditures goes for salaries and wages of government employees? The total payroll in 1972 was 78.7 billion

[2] Ira Sharkansky, *Spending in the American States* (Chicago: Rand-McNally, 1968); *see also* his "Economic and Political Correlates of State Government Expenditures: General Tendencies and Deviant Cases," *Midwest Journal of Political Science* 11 (May 1967), pp. 173–192.

[3] Ira Sharkansky and Richard I. Hofferbert, "Dimensions of State Politics and Policy," *American Political Science Review* 63 (September 1969), pp. 867–879.

dollars, more than 40 percent of total expenditures. Payrolls for public school teachers and other employees in the field of education accounted for more than 58 percent of all state and local expenditures for personal services. This is simply another indication of the dominant position of public schools in the requirements and problems of public finance. The gubernatorial candidate who promises to improve the financial status of school teachers is biting off a very sizable hunk of the total budget for state and local government. By the same token, the candidate who criticizes the "wasteful expenditure of vast sums of the taxpayers' hard-earned money" is very likely to be revealing his ignorance concerning the objects of state and local expenditures.

State and local payrolls

Revenues

Most of the money required to finance the ever-growing activities of state and local governments comes, of course, from taxation—federal as well as state and local. Taxes are compulsory contributions exacted by governments for public purposes. State and local taxes include levies on property, general sales and gross receipts, motor fuels, income, motor vehicles, alcoholic beverages, tobacco, corporation franchises, and estates and inheritances. A big revenue producer, sometimes omitted from lists of tax sources because of its special purpose, is the payroll assessment for the state unemployment insurance. When the three levels of government are considered separately, state government leans heavily upon three big tax sources—general sales, income, and motor fuel taxes—which account for more than 67 percent of state tax collections. (*See* Figure 14–2.) Both the federal and local governments rely on one big revenue producer: more than 83 percent of federal tax collections come from the income tax (individual and corporation), and 84 percent of local tax collections are derived from the property tax.

Governmental revenue from all sources in 1972, federal, state, and local governments, totaled 381.8 billion dollars. About 59 percent of this revenue was collected by the federal government; the state and local levels divided the remaining 41 percent on an almost equal basis. Actually, close to one-third of the grand total of governmental revenues came from nontax sources, with about 262.5 billion dollars being the total revenue from taxes at all levels of government. When taxes only are considered, federal collections accounted for 57 percent of the total for all levels of government, with the state and local levels collecting the remaining 43 percent in a five-to-four ratio. The tax totals for the three levels of government in 1972 were 153.7, 59.9, and 48.9 billion dollars, respectively; these figures exclude the payroll taxes for old-age and unemployment insurance.

Revenue totals

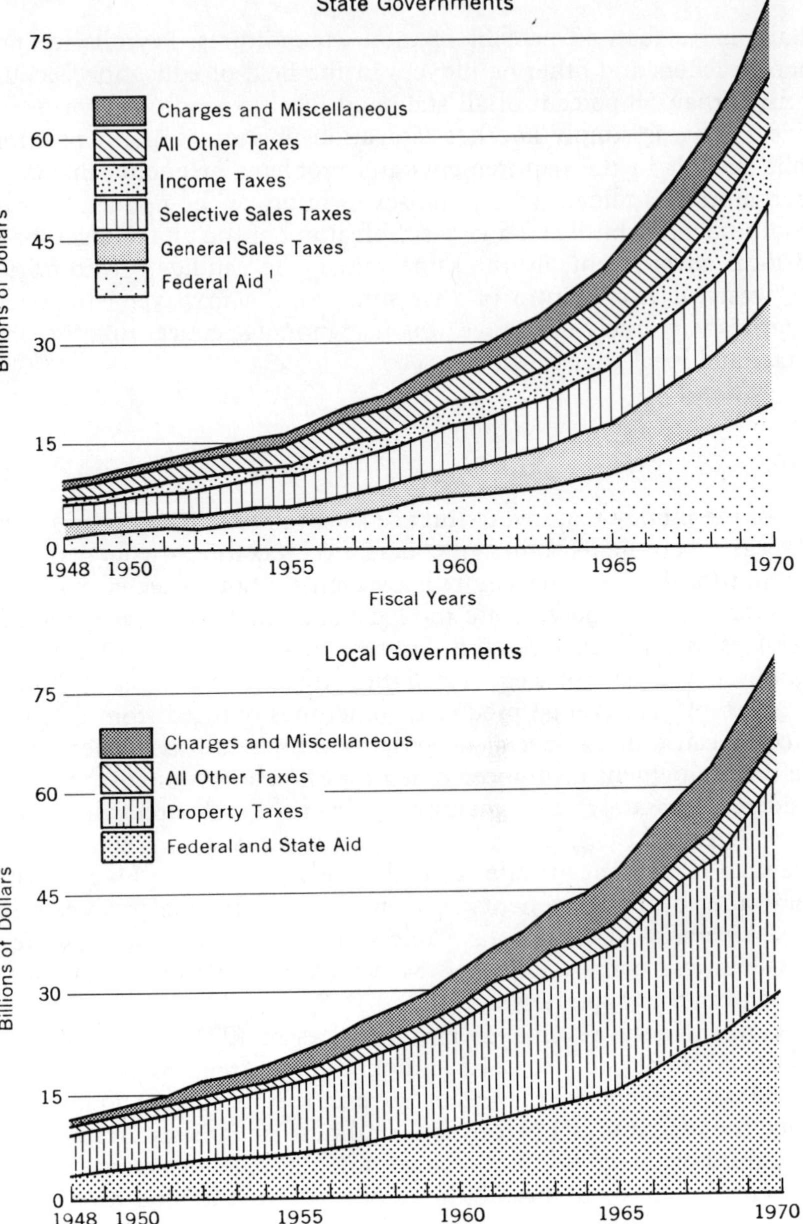

Includes minor amounts of local transfers.

Figure 14–2. Major Sources of State and Local General Revenue, 1948–1972. *Source:* Advisory Commission on Intergovernmental Relations, *State–Local Finances: Significant Features and Suggested Legislation* (Washington, D. C., 1972), p. 25.

These are the totals, but what are the trends? It should be apparent that the overall trend has been upward. Probably the most significant trends over the past fifty years are the changes in relative position of the three levels of government in their percentage of total tax collections. Beginning with 23 percent in 1916, the federal government rose to a peak of 65 percent in 1920, dropped back to 22 percent by 1932, rose to an even higher peak of 82 percent in 1945, by 1955 had dropped to 71 percent, and continued its decrease to 57 percent of all governments' tax revenues in 1972.

Trends in tax totals: absolute and relative

The percentages for local governments have followed the federal pattern in roughly inverse proportion, beginning with a very high 65 percent of the total in 1916, dropping to 28 percent in 1920, rising steadily to a peak of 56 percent in 1932, falling to the all-time low of 9 percent in 1945, and rising with some fluctuation to 15 percent in 1955 and 19 percent in 1972.

State governments' proportion of the total tax collections, however, has changed the least of the three levels of government, beginning with 12 percent in 1916 and, after less drastic fluctuations, rising only to 14 percent in 1955, 18 percent in 1966, and 23 percent in 1972. The states' proportion dropped to 7 percent in 1918 and reached a peak of 25 percent in 1940.

The trend in dollar totals from taxes during the past half-century is very clearly upward, whether the different levels of government are considered separately or together. Total local government tax collections have risen from 2 billion dollars in 1916 to 48.9 billion dollars in 1972. For state government the increase during this period was from a much smaller beginning of 0.4 billion dollars to 59.9 billion dollars. The federal government, also collecting less than local governments in 1916, rose from 0.7 billion to 153.7 billion dollars in 1972. Total tax collections for all levels of government thus increased from 3.1 to 262.5 billion dollars in fifty-six years.

Dollar increases at all levels

Before separately considering some of the more important taxes at the state and local level, it is important to note some of the constitutional restrictions—both federal and state—which limit the taxing power of state legislatures. The federal Constitution prohibits states, without the consent of Congress, from levying tonnage duties or placing duties on imports or exports. By implication, it prohibits a state from using its taxing power to evade constitutional restrictions. Thus, a state may not use its taxing power to impair the obligation of a contract or to violate the equal protection of law and due process clauses of the Fourteenth Amendment.

Federal restrictions on state taxation

Many state constitutions restrict the taxing power far more than the federal Constitution does. Some place a maximum limit on the rate of taxation, especially property taxation. Many have tax uniformity clauses which, if strictly interpreted, mean more than merely fair play and equity in taxation throughout the state, requiring that all property, personal or real, income-producing or satisfaction-producing, be taxed at a uniform rate. Such restrictive clauses may prevent a classified property tax, or progressive income and inheritance tax rates. Other state constitutions specifically prohibit certain taxes, such as an income or sales tax. In addition, most state constitutions stipulate the conditions under which the state or local governments may borrow money.

Restrictions in state constitutions

As recently as the period immediately preceding World War I, the general property tax was the principal source of revenue for state as well as local governments, accounting for more than one-half of all state revenue and virtually all local revenue. Now the general property tax has dropped almost completely out of the picture as a source of revenue for state governments, producing only 2 percent of total state tax collections in 1972, and many states have abandoned it altogether. On the other hand, the property tax remains the major source for local governments, accounting for 84 percent of local tax revenues in 1972. This persistence of the property tax as the dominant revenue source for local government—it produced 89 percent in 1902—is all the more remarkable in the face of its many criticisms.[4] The virtual disappearance of the property tax at the level of state government is attributable in part to the serious problems involved in the administration of this tax and its deviation from generally accepted principles of sound taxation.

General property tax

The property tax applies not only to *real* property, such as land, buildings, and other improvements, but also to *personal* property. Personal property consists of both *tangible* property, which includes things of intrinsic value such as jewelry, clothing, or automobiles, and *intangible* property, which includes evidences of wealth such as mortgages, stocks, bonds, and currency. In actual practice, most personal property escapes taxation. Most locally elected assessors find it expedient to permit self-assessment in the case of personal property, placing a premium on the dishonesty or temporary loss of memory of the taxpayer. Even property that does end up on tax rolls, real property for the most part, is notoriously under-assessed and unequally assessed, varying from as low as 10 percent of its fair and reasonable market value to as much as 60 or 75 percent—though not often the latter. Many other criticisms have been made of the property tax; however, at the root of most of these criticisms is the outmoded structure of the vast majority of county governments in the United

Criticisms of the property tax

[4] Frederick C. Mosher and Orville F. Poland, *The Costs of American Governments: Facts, Trends, Myths* (New York: Dodd, Mead and Co., 1964), p. 70. The book includes an excellent analysis of the relationship of taxes, expenditures, and debt to levels of government, time periods, and GNP.

States which retain a firm grip on the age-old ways of assessing and collecting the property tax.

Possibilities for reform

What can be done about the sad state of affairs into which the property tax has fallen? Many states have simply abolished it as a source of revenue at the state level, leaving it exclusively for the local governments. For a time, this took away some of the incentive for one county to assess its property at a much lower percentage of true value than another. However, the steady increase in state aid to local governments, with larger grants to the poorer counties, has made it important to avoid rewarding a county that feigns poverty simply by reducing its property assessments. Thus the problem of equalizing assessments remains. Some measures that could be adopted to improve the administration of the property tax include the improvement of recruitment and training of personnel, development of procedures which can be applied to achieve uniform results, and supervision of local assessments by the state revenue department or board of equalization. The property tax is a stable and productive source of revenue, and such improvements in its administration could go far to reduce its defects.[5] In his landmark study of the economic effects of the property tax,[6] Dick Netzer finds the property tax defective on a number of counts, but by no means worthless. Netzer does not agree that there are no realistic alternatives to this venerable tax. Rather, he suggests that both efficiency and equity could be achieved in a radical reform involving a package of the "site value" tax (related to land rents); "land value increment tax" (based on capital gains from sale or transfer of land); "user-charge-type property taxes" (financing sewerage, fire protection, etc., through service charges); and a housing tax (such as a 5 percent tax on housing costs).[7] The essential message of his study is that other choices are available and that continuation of the property tax is neither the best nor the worst of all choices.

In the early 1970s it appeared that the judicial branch of government would move into the area of property tax reform in the same massive way

[5] For a study of what the states have not done, and can do, to rehabilitate the local property tax, *see* Advisory Commission on Intergovernmental Relations, *The Role of States in Strengthening the Property Tax*, vol. 1 (Washington, D. C., 1963). *See also* the earlier study by ACIR, *Measuring the Fiscal Capacity and Effort of State and Local Areas* (Washington, D. C., 1971), for an effort to avoid some of the common pitfalls in comparing both the performance and potential performance of local governments in raising revenue. Another ACIR study focuses specifically on public school finance and analyzes in detail the current problems of the property tax: *State–Local Revenue Systems and Educational Finance: A Report Presented to the President's Commission on School Finance* (Washington, D. C., 1971).

[6] Dick Netzer, *Economics of the Property Tax* (Washington, D. C.: The Brookings Institution, 1966).

[7] *Ibid.*, p. 220.

it had over desegregation and reapportionment issues. The California supreme court took the lead in 1971 by ruling that the public school financial system was unconstitutional because of its heavy reliance on the local property tax.[8] The wide disparity in the amount of taxable property in poor and wealthy school districts, and the resulting practical limit on achieving equality of education, caused the court to find a violation of the Fourteenth Amendment equal protection clause. Within the next two years suits were filed in the majority of states. Court decisions in several states, including Texas, Michigan, and Minnesota, had already ruled against use of the local property tax to finance public education. The Texas decision was appealed and some 30 state attorneys general joined in arguing before the U. S. Supreme Court that reversal was necessary to avoid "a generation of litigation" aimed not only at school finance but at other services such as police protection and health care. In March 1973, the conservative turn of the Supreme Court became still more evident as it reversed the Texas decision by a vote of 5 to 4, ruling the Fourteenth Amendment is not violated. Justice Powell, writing for the majority, noted that the court was not endorsing the status quo, but stated "the ultimate solution must come from the lawmakers and from the democratic pressures of those who elect them."[9] Even after the Texas (Rodriguez) decision, the New Jersey Supreme Court ruled that the state's use of local property taxes to finance schools violated New Jersey's constitution. It seemed possible that cartoons such as the one in Figure 14–3 could be a little premature.

The property tax and equal protection

The general sales tax has developed rapidly as a source of revenue, and it is now one of the two principal revenue producers (29.4 percent) at the state level. It yielded more than 19.7 billion dollars in 1973 for the forty-five states levying some form of general sales or gross receipts tax. It is a tax at uniform rates upon the sale of a wide variety of commodities. It may include personal services and may extend to transactions by wholesalers as well as retailers. Strong opposition to the general sales tax has come from those who point out that it is regressive, and in effect, imposes a relatively heavier burden upon the poor than upon the rich.

The general sales tax

Nevertheless, one state after another, in time of financial crisis, has looked in desperation to the example of West Virginia which in 1921 became the first to adopt the general sales tax as a major revenue source. The number of holdouts declined steadily in the 1960s, with a dozen new states climbing on the sales tax bandwagon. Among the last to adopt were Idaho and New York in 1965, Massachusetts, New Jersey, and Virginia in 1966, Minnesota and Nebraska in 1967, and Vermont in 1969. Montana

[8] *Serrano* v. *Priest* (1971), 5 Cal. 3d 584, 487 P. 2d 1241.

[9] *San Antonio Ind. School Dist.* v. *Rodriguez* 93 S.Ct. 1278 (1973).

Surgery isn't necessary

Figure 14–3. Jon Kennedy in the *Arkansas Democrat.*

voters rejected the sales tax in 1971. Retail sales tax rates have been raised frequently through the years, especially in the sixties and early seventies, to meet growing pressures of inflation and expanded state programs. By 1974 only one state (Oklahoma) retained the rate of 2 percent; several states were at the 5 percent level, Pennsylvania was at 6 percent, and Connecticut had the highest rate with 6.5 percent. Food is exempt from the sales tax in many states. In addition to its use by the states, the sales tax is used by a steadily increasing number of cities—more than one-half of all cities over 300,000 in population. The city levy usually rides "piggyback" on the state's levy. Although largely a post-World War II phenomenon, the local sales tax was levied by 1970 in 3,500 local governments in 23 states.[10]

Preceding the general sales tax in historical origin are the sales taxes

[10] For a comprehensive analysis of the general sales tax in 1970, *see* Tax Foundation, Inc., *State and Local Sales Taxes* (New York, 1970).

on specific articles, such as gasoline, liquor, and tobacco. The gasoline tax has been adopted by every state and, until recently, it was a close second to the general sales tax in percentage of total tax collections. The state income tax is now in second place as a revenue source for all states, considered together. All states have taxes on alcoholic beverages and tobacco products (North Carolina in 1969 was the last to tax cigarettes). The tobacco tax accounted for 4 percent of 1973 state tax collections; taxes on alcoholic beverages brought in less than 3 percent. The tax on cigarettes has been increased more frequently in recent years than any other tax; undoubtedly, this trend is influenced by reports on the relationship of cigarettes to health hazards.

Sales taxes on specific articles

Close to four-fifths of the states now have an income tax, most of them enacted during the past two or three decades. Although Virginia had an income tax as early as 1843, it was not until Wisconsin adopted it in 1911 that it became apparent that it could be made administratively workable at the state level. It was the search for new revenue sources during the early depression years of the 1930s which led many other states to accept it. Although most of the states make it applicable both to corporations and individuals, a few limit it to one or the other. This tax conforms to the principle of taxation in proportion to one's ability to pay, even though the rates which the states levy are much less progressive than those of the federal government. Until 1973, the state income tax ranked a close second in importance as a revenue producer for the states, but moved into first place when the state income tax represented 31 percent of total tax collection, a significant increase from 15.7 percent in 1955. An increasing number of cities have begun to make use of an income or payroll tax, often using it as a device to tax suburbanities who work inside the central city but reside outside.

Income tax

Inheritance or estate taxes, although providing only about 2 percent of total state tax collections, are levied by every state except Nevada. The latter state has not yet yielded to the "incentive plan" provided by the federal government in 1924 which in effect penalizes any state not taxing inheritances. Congress amended the federal inheritance tax in 1924 to permit deductions to be made from the federal tax, up to 80 percent, if the state collects such a tax. Florida had no inheritance or estate tax for many years, much to the unhappiness of neighboring states that were losing wealthy retired residents to Florida. But in 1930 it finally levied an estate tax to claim the revenue which would otherwise go to the federal government.

Inheritance taxes

There is no "business tax" as such, but a variety of taxes are levied on business concerns in addition to those on property and income. Special taxes are levied on incorporation or entry into the state based upon a variety of measures. The franchise tax is collected in every state, but in revenue it cannot compare in importance with the various consumer taxes.

Unincorporated businesses are also taxed in special ways; the most common mode of taxation is the license to do business, whether for the barber, physician, peddler, newsstand, or drugstore. In addition to business taxes there are motor vehicles taxes, primarily in the form of licenses, and such levies as poll taxes and severance taxes on the extraction of natural resources.

Public lotteries

The pressing need for additional revenue and arguments over how to control illegal gambling have caused a flurry of state legislative interest in public lotteries in recent years. Eight states established public lotteries between 1964 and 1973. New Hampshire was first in 1964, followed by New York (1967), New Jersey (1970), Massachusetts and Connecticut (1971), and Michigan, Maryland, and Pennsylvania (1972). Several other states have approved referenda or constitutional amendments to clear legal hurdles for lotteries. With one or two exceptions, however, the state-run lottery has not proved to be the tax bonanza many predicted, and seems to have had little deterrent effect on the illegal numbers racket. The spectacle of several states in the New York metropolitan area competing through public billboard advertising for the gambler's dollar ("If at first you don't succeed, buy, buy again—New York State Lottery") is a new departure in state government, to say the least.

Nontax sources: federal grants-in-aid

Federal grants-in-aid constitute important nontax revenue for state and local governments, totaling over 38 billion dollars in 1972. The fiscal importance of these federal grants is indicated by the fact that it would have required an overall increase of 29 percent in state and local taxes in 1972 to replace this money if the grants had been eliminated. In many of the states the increase in state taxes required to replace federal grants would be above 50 percent. As shown in Figure 14–4, the proportion of state and local revenue coming from federal aid increased sharply between 1961 and 1972. In contrast to this, the total of federal grants to state and local governments is not a massive portion of the federal government's total financial picture. The 38 billion dollars that the federal government granted in 1972 amounted to 16.7 percent of its tax revenue, or 9.3 percent of its total revenue.

Nature and scope of grants

Although grants-in-aid are found in a wide variety of forms, the common characteristic of all forms is the central government's provision for aid for a particular service, without supplanting the responsibilities and powers of the recipient units of government which actually perform the service. Grants are usually made in the form of money, although the early land grants were an exception, as are some present grants of agricultural commodities. Most grants-in-aid are continuing arrangements, but there have been a few single-action grants.

Although the federal grant program viewed as a whole may seem to be a hodgepodge, it is the natural outgrowth of varied objectives and piecemeal development. The federal government has used the grant pri-

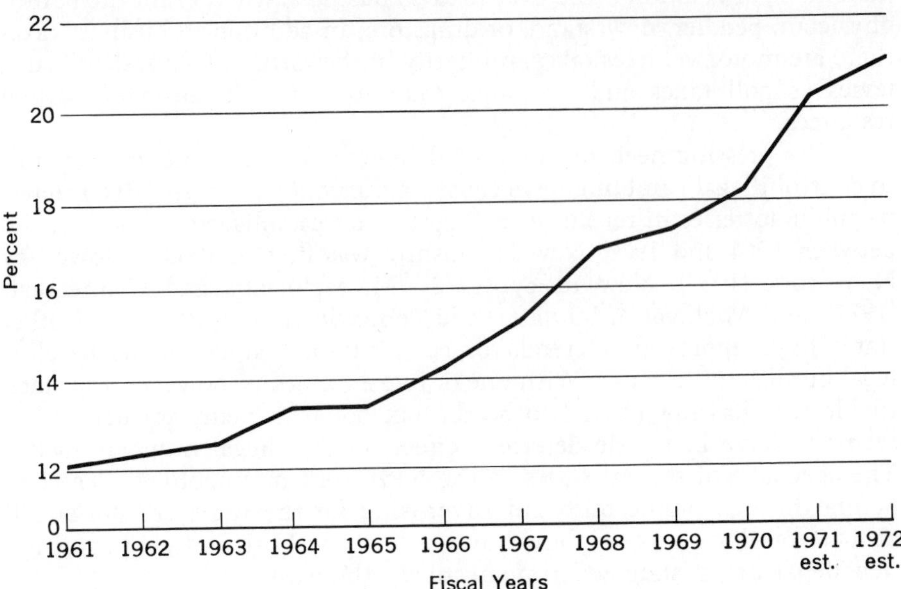

Figure 14–4. Federal Aid as a Percentage of State and Local Revenue, 1961–1972. *Source:* Advisory Commission on Intergovernmental Relations, *State–Local Finances: Significant Features and Suggested Legislation* (Washington, D. C., 1972), p. 65.

marily to achieve some national objective, such as to get the farmer out of the mud or to prevent cancer, rather than merely to help state and local governments finance existing programs. Most grants have been for services rather than for regulatory activities. The great majority of all federal grants is for a relatively small number of programs, such as public assistance, highway construction, employment security, educational assistance, and hospital construction. The largest public works program in our nation's history, the 41,000-mile interstate highway system, is being financed and administered through the federal grant-in-aid approach.

In spite of intermittent criticism and praise of the grant-in-aid system down through the years, there can be little doubt that the system has won a permanent place in the operation of our federal system. It is significant that the (Kestnbaum) Commission on Intergovernmental Relations, in spite of ominous sounds and a "show me" attitude during the early stages of its investigations, recommended no drastic changes in the grant-in-aid system when it reported to the president in 1955. With the growing proliferation of federal grants in the 1960s, described previously in chapters 2 and 3, there has been increasing pressure for broader "block grants" and for some kind of no-strings-attached tax-sharing plan. The Advisory Commission on Intergovernmental Relations endorsed a grant-consolidation plan which would permit the president to consolidate federal grant programs, subject to veto within ninety days by either house of Congress. With or without consolidation and revenue sharing, discussed in more detail later in this chapter, there is little indication that the significance of federal grants-in-aid to our state and local governments is likely to wane.

Modifications of grant system proposed

Not all governmental expenditures are made from current revenues, as desirable as this may seem to be. It is often better practice to borrow for large or unusual undertakings that cannot be budgeted on an annual basis, such as school or bridge construction. Even construction projects may be financed from current taxes in many cases, if adequate attention is given to the necessity for long-range planning and capital budgeting. The unfortunate cases of borrowing, the ones that hurt a state's credit rating, are those to finance deficits in current operations resulting from lack of proper budgeting. Borrowing may be the result either of statesmanlike action to finance an exceptionally large project without causing a greatly fluctuating tax rate, or of unstatesmanlike action to avoid increasing taxes during an election year to finance increased costs in current operations.

Public borrowing

During the first few decades of the nation's history, the states imposed no constitutional limits upon the debt which the legislature might incur. Legislative abuses of this financial liberty brought the states in some cases to the brink of disaster and led the people to adopt constitutional clauses restricting the borrowing power. The numerous defaults of the 1840s, for example, constituted sufficient evidence to the people of legislative ineptitude. Within a fifteen-year period 19 states incorporated restricted borrowing clauses in their constitutions.[11]

In spite of state constitutional limitations on borrowing and on total debt, state and local indebtedness has been increasing fairly steadily. Indebtedness of all local governments is now more than two times as great as that of state governments, although the ratio was more than seven-to-one in 1929. Local indebtedness increased from 11.6 billion dollars in 1929 to 118.5 billion dollars in 1972. State indebtedness was 1.6 billion dollars in 1929 and has risen more rapidly, percentage-wise, to a total of 51.6 billion dollars in 1972. As shown in Table 14–3, the combined state and local indebtedness has risen steadily in this century; however, its relation to the national debt has fluctuated. Its percentage of total public indebtedness has consistently increased since 1952, a fact that is

[11] For an interesting account of public credit on the state level, *see* B. U. Ratchford, *American State Debts* (Durham, N. C.: Duke University Press, 1941).

Table 14–3. Gross Debt of Federal, State and Local Governments, 1902–1972 (in billions)

Year	*Total*	*Federal*	*State*	*Local*	*State–Local Percentage of Total*
1902	$3.3	$1.2	$.2	$1.9	64.1%
1913	5.6	1.2	.4	4.0	78.8
1922	33.1	23.0	1.1	9.0	30.5
1932	38.7	19.5	2.8	16.4	49.6
1942	91.8	72.4	3.3	16.1	21.0
1952	289.2	259.1	6.9	23.2	10.4
1962	379.0	298.2	22.0	58.8	21.7
1972	597.4	427.3	51.6	118.5	28.4

Source: Tax Foundation, Inc., *Facts and Figures on Government Finance* (New York, 1973), p. 22.

often overlooked by alarmists concerned with the size of the national debt. As a percent of state and local tax revenues, or of personal income, the total state and local indebtedness has shown only modest increases or decreases through the years.

Forms of borrowing

Public borrowing is usually accomplished through bond issues, which may be for terms of from ten to forty years or longer. Longer terms are discouraged because the interest to be paid over such periods becomes excessively burdensome, and because it is considered unwise to extend the term of the bond beyond the anticipated life of the improvement which the bond issue is to underwrite. Many cities today are paying interest and principal on bonds for streets long since worn out and repaved.

The two principal forms of bonds are sinking-fund and serial bonds. In the first type, a sinking fund is established with annual payments adequate for payment of the debt on the date the bonds mature. The plan is not infallible, however, as it is not unusual for states to delay their contributions to the fund so that unsound debt management results. In the serial bond issue a certain number of bonds mature each year and are paid off until all of the bonds are retired. No sinking fund is required, and it becomes more accurately a self-enforcing system for regular retirement of the bonded debt. The use of serial bonds is generally replacing sinking-fund bonds.

General obligation bonds v. revenue bonds

The bonds that governments issue may also be distinguished as general obligation bonds and revenue bonds. General obligation bonds are supported by the taxing power of the government concerned, thus constituting a lien on the property of the taxpayers. Revenue bonds are retired only from the revenues of a particular governmental enterprise, such as a city water department, power distribution department, or a state toll highway. General obligation bonds tend to secure a lower interest rate, thus costing the taxpayer less, but in recent years their use has been hampered by legal debt limits. Since the debt limits do not apply to revenue bonds, issuance of the latter has become a common method of circumventing such restrictions.

Other nontax revenues

Other nontax revenues for state and local governments include income derived from sale of portions of the public domain and from operation of various public enterprises. Sale or lease of mineral rights, rental of camp sites, and sale of timber from public land produce this kind of revenue. The principal state-operated enterprises providing revenue are alcoholic beverage stores, toll bridges, and port facilities. A little more than one-third of the states have entered the wholesale and retail liquor business. At the local level the municipally operated water systems, power distribution systems, and bus or trolley systems are among the most common public service enterprises.

Principles of "sound taxation"

Regardless of the level of government, the more generally accepted principles of sound taxation are the following: (1) the tax should have a reasonable relationship to one's ability to pay; (2) it should be a reasonably convenient tax to pay; (3) it should be characterized by certainty, that is, it should be generally clear to the taxpayer how much he must pay and the basis on which it is figured; and (4) it should be an economical tax to collect, requiring minimum administrative costs. Many of the problems of our tax systems stem from failure to measure up to these standards suggested by Adam Smith in the eighteenth century. By these standards it must be recognized that the general sales tax and the property tax, the principal sources for state and local governments, respectively, can hardly qualify as "sound taxation." By the same token, the income tax, which plays a lesser role than the former two on the state and local levels, nearly qualifies in all respects. The regressive character of state and local taxation—tending to place a relatively heavier burden on lower income persons than on higher income persons—especially in comparison with the federal tax structure, has been revealed by more than one study.[12]

Overlapping taxation

The quest for an improved tax structure for state and local government reveals many serious revenue problems. One of the most perplexing is the growth of double and overlapping taxation between the different levels of government. There was a time when revenue sources were rather clearly segregated for the federal, state, and local levels, so that each level of government tended to avoid disturbing the others. During the depression scramble for new revenues, however, the states invaded the federal

[12] *See,* for example, Tax Foundation, Inc., *Tax Burdens and Benefits of Government Expenditures by Income Class, 1961 and 1965* (New York, 1967), p. 18.

government's field of income taxation, and the federal government invaded the states' field of gasoline taxation, followed by many more duplications. It is extremely doubtful that it will ever be possible to segregate tax sources according to governmental level again. The two principal alternatives most commonly proposed have been a system of federally collected, state-shared taxes, or a system whereby each level would continue to collect its own taxes but make some reciprocal arrangement for distributing the revenue. The latter plan would not eliminate the cost of duplicating collection facilities, but it would avoid the dispute over possible surrender of the states' taxing power to the federal government.

Federal tax-sharing: the "Heller Plan"

One of the best known of the various federal–state revenue sharing proposals in the 1960s was the "Heller Plan," named for the former chairman of the Council of Economic Advisers under presidents Kennedy and Johnson. Professor Heller recommended federal distribution to the states each year of 1 to 2 percent of the amounts reported as net taxable income by all individuals; each state's share would be determined on the basis of its population. In 1966 two percentage points would have amounted to 5.6 billion dollars for the states, with only minimal federal strings attached to its use.[13] The per capita basis for sharing would have some equalizing effect by transferring some funds from high-income to low-income areas, and it would be over and above existing and future conditional grants.

Related tax-sharing proposals

The Heller Plan and a host of other proposals for revenue sharing in recent years have stimulated a great deal of discussion and inquiry about such issues as the growing power of the national government, the competence, capacity, and effort of state governments, the need for income equalization between states, and the relationship of cities and counties to any revenue-sharing plan. Congressman Henry Reuss, for example, proposed that 5 billion dollars per year be shared with the states, but only after each state has a plan for modernization of its government acceptable to one of four "regional coordinating committees." Congressman Melvin Laird introduced revenue-sharing bills regularly between 1958 and 1968, including one calling for a no-strings-attached distribution to the states of 5 percent of the federal personal income tax. The bills carried an equalization feature that reserved a portion of the federal tax donation exclusively for the lower one-third of the states ranked in per capita income. The Advisory Commission on Intergovernmental Relations endorsed a "tax-credit plan" with some of the same effects, but with an additional goal of inducing states to levy and use more effectively the income tax. The effect of a 40 percent federal tax credit for state income taxes, for ex-

[13] Walter W. Heller, *New Dimensions of Political Economy* (Cambridge, Mass.: Harvard University Press, 1966), pp. 145–147.

ample, would be to subtract the amount of state income tax a person pays from his net tax obligation to the federal government, up to a maximum of 40 percent of that obligation.

In his 1971 State of the Union message, President Nixon recommended a general revenue-sharing plan with emphasis on decentralizing the government of the United States and restoring decision-making power to the lower levels of government. He proposed distribution to the states of a portion of federal income tax revenues—estimated at $5 billion the first year and more in the future. Each state's share would be based on its population, with a small bonus for states with high taxes relative to average income. The states would have to distribute about half of their federal allocation to their local governments, based on tax collections by each city, county, and town. Critics of the Nixon proposal, especially Chairman Wilbur Mills of the powerful House Ways and Means Committee, described it variously as a political play, "representation without taxation," and a Trojan horse that would ultimately bring irresponsibility and increased federal control to state and local government. Others argued that revenue-sharing windfalls would grant an undesirable reprieve to archaic, outmoded features of state and local governmental structures that should be held under pressure for reorganization, improvement, and possible consolidation.

Debate over revenue sharing

Congressman Mills' opposition to revenue sharing helped to block its passage in 1971, but Mills broke his own log-jam by offering a counterplan late in 1971. Mills' proposal, adopted with some modification late in 1972 as the Intergovernmental Fiscal Coordination Act, called for a $5.3 billion-a-year aid program for states and localities and retained some congressional control. It received early support from state and local officials as standing the best chance of passage and was eventually endorsed by President Nixon. The Mills formula provided a larger share to local governments, earmarked for broadly designated fields, in order to meet high priority demands made upon them. Some weighting of allocations according to the proportion of low income residents was also provided for. Payments to states included an inducement to appropriate use of the state income tax to meet revenue needs. Ironically, with the inauguration of general revenue-sharing payments in 1973, President Nixon's new budget proposals for cutbacks in *categorical* grants-in-aid caused many governors and mayors to charge that a "cruel hoax" had been perpetrated, sharing with one federal hand and stealing with the other. The reaction was just another indication that grants-in-aid will not die easily, even with the addition of revenue sharing.

Adoption of revenue sharing in 1972

A cruel hoax?

Although a 1973 survey of U. S. public opinion revealed solid support for the new revenue-sharing form of federal aid (56% in favor, 18% opposed, and 26% no opinion), the same survey showed continued preference for federal "strings" over local discretion. The question and the national response were: "When the federal government gives funds to state and local governments, do you feel the money is used more efficiently when it is given out for specific purposes or when it is given out for the state and local governments to use as they think best?[14]

Continued preference for strings

For specific purposes	48%
As they think best	30%
No opinion	22%

The American public seems to want both kinds of federal aid.

Other revenue problems: earmarking

Many state and local governments are plagued with the problem of the earmarking of revenue sources for specific objects. Nothing can be more frustrating to effective budgeting efforts than a conglomeration of taxes which are required by law to be spent for specific purposes. The practice of earmarking has a very natural origin in the desire of a pressure group interested in a single function of government to secure with certainty more money for that particular function, for example, to designate that all revenue from the gasoline tax be spent for highway purposes. It is also the only way, on occasions, to make a tax increase palatable to the public. Earmarked taxes in the long run make it exceedingly difficult to adapt the revenue program to changing needs. Although states earmark taxes for everything from Confederate pensions (Louisiana and Texas) to sick fishermen (Alaska), the bulk of earmarked revenue goes to education, highways, and welfare.[15]

Tax exemptions

Another problem facing every governmental jurisdiction is the extensive concession of tax exemptions, not only for educational, religious, and charitable institutions, but for other governments, homesteads, and veterans. Although such exemptions make the taxes higher for other people, they are defended as essential for the encouragement of worthy causes and seem to be well established. Some modification in practice has been obtained by means of voluntary "payments in lieu of taxes" by some governmental jurisdictions.

State–Local Financial Relationships

The picture of state and local finance is not complete without a few comments on trends in the financial relationships between state and local

[14] U. S. Advisory Commission on Intergovernmental Relations survey data reported in *County News* 5 (Oct. 5, 1973), p. 3.

[15] Tax Foundation, Inc., *Earmarked State Taxes* (New York, 1965). This study summarizes the major criticisms of earmarking, as well as the arguments for it, on pp. 24–28. *See also* James M. Buchanan, "The Economics of Earmarked Taxes," *Journal of Political Economy* 71 (October 1963), pp. 457–469.

levels of government. During the past few decades, state supervision and control over local finances has been steadily expanded until it covers in varying degrees nearly all phases of financial administration. This may include supervision of tax assessment and collection, limitations on the kinds and rates of taxes, control over budgets and expenditures, limitations on the procedure and maximum total of debt incurrence, supervision of accounts, conduct of audits, and financial assistance in the form of shared taxes or grants-in-aid.

Scope of state supervision of local finances

Of all of these areas of state–local fiscal relationships, undoubtedly the one of greatest change is that of shared taxes and grants-in-aid. Especially since the end of World War II, local governments have been caught in the squeeze between increased costs for public education and other functions and the exhaustion of local taxing and borrowing powers. State legislatures have responded increasingly to pressure from local governments by voting new grants-in-aid and providing for state-administered, locally shared taxes. As already discussed, a distinction is usually made between grants-in-aid and shared taxes, but this distinction often becomes blurred. As a general rule, shared taxes have few if any "strings" attached; they retain their identity by originating from a specific tax. Grants-in-aid are made for a particular activity, without regard for the origin of the funds, and frequently impose a matching requirement.

Shared taxes and grants-in-aid

In all, the local governments received 36.8 billion dollars from the states in 1972, almost one-third of the total revenue of the local governments in that year. Education has been the most important single object of state aid to local governments; its purpose is to improve teachers' salaries, to construct buildings, and to improve educational standards in general. Close to two-thirds of total state aid to local governments has gone for education in recent years.

There can be no doubt that the substantial state assistance in recent years has resulted from such factors as the fiscal inadequacy of local units of government and the increasing demand for higher minimum standards of service within the various states. However, one question that has not been adequately answered as yet concerns the effect of this increased aid upon the degree of honest effort by local units to raise funds locally. Is the increased aid causing some cities and counties simply to reduce the financial effort they were formerly making? Some states have already found this to be true and have taken the next logical step of tying state assistance to a formula which measures local effort. This, of course, requires accurate state information on actual local assessment levels. Further centralization of state–local financial relationships is thus made inevitable. (Efforts of the Advisory Commission on Intergovernmental Relations to study this problem were cited earlier in this chapter.)

Implications of increasing state assistance

Related to this problem, but more fundamental in its implications, is the question of whether state aid is not actually serving to perpetuate marginal and submarginal units of government in serious need of consolidation or elimination.[16]

Financial Planning

Something must be said about the crucial role of financial planning or budgeting in state and local government to supplement the earlier treatment of legislative and gubernatorial roles in finance. A budget is simply a financial plan, and the budgetary process is simply the planning process in public finance. It is the process whereby resources are apportioned among competing demands. If there is any single document that tells what a government plans to do, it is the budget. It is the major device through which responsible leaders in government plan and ultimately decide what facilities and services should be provided and when.

The budget: a financial plan

The budget is a twentieth-century phenomenon in America. New York City is credited with pioneering public budgeting in this country in 1907, followed by many of the states and larger governments after 1910. The federal government followed suit in 1921 by abandoning the old legislative budget system and providing for an executive budget procedure. The executive budget, which places responsibility for the preparation and recommendation of the budget upon the chief executive, was discussed in chapter 12 as a part of the governor's role in financial management.[17] Progress in adoption of the executive budget at the city level actually preceded that at the state level; however, county governments lag sadly behind, and budgeting in any real sense of the word simply does not exist, except in a few reorganized urban counties.

Growth of the executive budget

The form of the appropriation act of state legislatures is closely tied in with the problem of financial planning. Two alternative types have been the segregated or itemized appropriation act and the lump sum or unrestricted appropriation act. The itemized appropriation act, often required by the state constitution, is criticized for not permitting administrators the discretion and flexibility of action essential to execute public policy with

Itemized v. *lump sum appropriations*

[16] For detailed analysis of state–local financial relationships, *see* the various studies by the U. S. Advisory Commission on Intergovernmental Relations, including: *Local Nonproperty Taxes and the Coordinating Role of the State* (September 1961); *State Constitutional and Statutory Restrictions on Local Government Debt* (September 1961); *State Constitutional and Statutory Restrictions on Local Taxing Powers* (October 1962); *Investment of Idle Cash Balances by State and Local Governments* (January 1961, with supplement, January 1965); *State Technical Assistance to Local Debt Management* (January 1965; and *Measuring the Fiscal Capacity and Effort of State and Local Areas* (March 1971, with supplement, January 1972).

[17] *See* Council of State Governments, *Budgeting by the States* (Chicago, 1967), for a detailed study of budgeting in all fifty states.

reasonable dispatch and efficiency. The lump sum appropriation is far more desirable in the hands of a wise administrator, but is subject to abuse in the hands of a less dependable administrator.

The allotment plan

A third proposal, known as the allotment plan, is gaining increasing support in many governmental jurisdictions. This system makes use of the lump sum type of appropriation, but combines it with quarterly or monthly allotments made only upon approval of an itemized quarterly or monthly work program. Again, the emphasis of this development in fiscal practice is upon improved financial planning with responsibility placed upon the chief executive of the state or local government.

Performance budgeting

The PPB movement

The two most recent attempts to improve public budgeting were the emphasis on the adoption of "performance budgeting" in the 1950s and the planning–programming–budgeting (PPB) movement of the late 1960s. Performance budgeting was a reaction against the more narrow preoccupation with control over spending. It focused attention on the use of the budget to achieve efficient management of the activities and services performed by public agencies. The more recent PPB movement gained national prominence through its use by the Defense Department as an aid in evaluating expensive weapon systems. The PPB idea spread quickly to state and local governments, offering hope of applying modern economic and systems analysis to the policymakers' task of relating current program choices to future policy objectives.

Incremental innovation

A Brookings Institution study of the implementation of these budget innovations in the states, conducted by Allen Schick, reveals a great deal more PPB rhetoric by state budget officers than actual employment of PPB at the center of their decision-making apparatus.[18] Although Schick found at least half of the states claimed to be considering or adopting the new system, it seemed unlikely that the PPB techniques would become more than an additional layer of bureaucratic routine, even in the "five most innovative states—California, New York, Wisconsin, Hawaii, and Pennsylvania." Shick blamed the disappointing results on lack of political support from governors and legislators; a damaging gap between performance and the inflated promises initially surrounding PPB; and a lack of flexibility in adapting the precepts of PPB to changing conditions. The new approach, however, seemed to threaten the long-established practices of state budget officers and the prerogatives of legislators.

A half-century of budget reform has gone through three phases of emphasis: effective *control* of dollars, performance-oriented *management,* and more rational program *planning.* The real challenge in public finance, and more particularly in financial management, is to attain a reasonable

[18] Allen Schick, *Budget Innovation in the States* (Washington, D. C.: Brookings Institution, 1971).

Three-fold goal in public finance

and workable synthesis of these three related goals, which often pull our governments in opposite directions. The basic problem is how to effect peace between the economy drive, the service drive, and the rational-decision drive. In more simplified form, it is the ancient conflict between democracy and efficiency; it undoubtedly holds the key for those citizens interested in preserving and strengthening the sub-national levels of government.

SUPPLEMENTARY READINGS

Blakey, R. G., and Blakey, Gladys M. C. *Sales Taxes and Other Excises.* Chicago: Public Administration Service, 1945.

Break, George F. *Intergovernmental Fiscal Relations in the United States.* Washington, D. C.: Brookings Institution, 1967.

Buck, A. E. *The Budget in Governments of Today.* New York: The Macmillan Co., 1935.

Burkhead, Jesse. *Government Budgeting.* New York: John Wiley and Sons, 1956.

Commission on Intergovernmental Relations. *A Report to the President for Transmittal to the Congress.* Washington, D. C.: U. S. Government Printing Office, 1955.

Council of State Governments. *Federal Grants-in-Aid.* Chicago: Council of State Governments, 1949.

Dye, Thomas R. *Politics, Economics and the Public.* Chicago: Rand McNally and Co., 1966.

Ecker-Racz, Laszlo L. *The Politics and Economics of State–Local Finance.* Englewood Cliffs, N. J.: Prentice-Hall, 1970.

Hirsch, Werner Z. *The Economics of State and Local Government.* New York: McGraw-Hill Book Co., 1970.

Kilpatrick, Wylie. *State Supervision of Local Finance.* Chicago: Public Administration Service, 1941.

Maxwell, James A. *Tax Credits and Intergovernmental Fiscal Relations.* Washington, D. C.: Brookings Institution, 1962.

———. *Financing State and Local Governments.* Washington, D. C.: Brookings Institution, 1969.

Mosher, Frederick C. and Poland, Orville F. *The Costs of American Government: Facts, Trends, Myths.* New York: Dodd, Mead and Co., 1964.

Municipal Finance Officers' Association of the United States and Canada. *Financial Planning for Governments.* Chicago: Municipal Finance Officers' Association of the United States and Canada, 1949.

Netzer, Dick. *Economics of the Property Tax.* Washington, D. C.: Brookings Institution, 1966.

U. S. Advisory Commission on Intergovernmental Relations. *Tax Overlapping in the United States.* Washington, D. C.: U. S. Government Printing Office, 1961.

———. *Measures of State and Local Fiscal Capacity and Tax Effort.* Washington, D. C.: U. S. Government Printing Office, 1962.

———. *Federal–State Coordination of Personal Income Taxes.* Washington, D. C.: U. S. Government Printing Office, 1965.

———. *State–Local Revenue Systems and Educational Finance, A Report Submitted to the President's Commission on School Finance.* Washington, D. C.: U. S. Government Printing Office, 1971.

Wright, Deil S. *Federal Grants-in-Aid: Perspectives and Alternatives.* Washington, D. C.: American Enterprise Institute for Public Policy Research, 1968.

15

The Judiciary

Courts constitute one of the three basic divisions of state government, as of the United States national government. The state judiciary may restrain or support the role of governor or legislature, approving or disapproving policies through the exercise of the power of judicial review. More state laws have been set aside by state courts as contrary to state constitutions than have been invalidated by the United States Supreme Court under terms of the federal Constitution. Moreover, state judges are bound by the "supreme law of the land" clause of the federal document, regardless of state laws and constitutions, and they occasionally rely upon this provision for invalidating state action.

Significance of state courts

Along with the role of constitutional interpretation, state courts, centrally and locally, provide a wide spectrum of governmental contact for citizens. They exercise an important function in the affairs of men, often having the final word in regulating or umpiring the relations of man to man and of man to the state. Collectively, they try many more cases than do the federal courts, and within any one state the state courts try more cases than do the federal courts within that state. About 3,000,000 cases a year are handled in state and local courts, compared with about 140,000 in federal courts. They handle more human drama, whether the issue be property or crime.

Reasons for broad jurisdiction

The broad jurisdiction of state courts in subject matter stems from constitutional and historical factors. In the American system of federalism, as defined by the Tenth Amendment, these courts are not restricted to delegated or enumerated powers, as is the federal judiciary. They have wide functions and responsibilities in the field of police power, described in chapter 4. To a greater degree than the federal courts, state courts have served as vehicles for transplanting and perpetuating the principles and practices of British jurisprudence in America, exemplified by the use of common law and equity and by the institutionalized justice of the peace. It is significant that the American Revolution wrought no fundamental change in our judicial institutions and ways of justice. The state courts became direct heirs of the colonial courts and grand-heirs of the British judiciary.

Common Law and Equity

The rise of common law

The origin and development of our state systems of courts and jurisprudence cannot be understood without taking into account the growth, application, and meaning of the English common law, which has spread to the United States, Canada, and other countries. That body of law has vitally affected the legal commandments of all of our states except Louisiana, which was influenced by the Napoleonic Code and its antecedents. Even in Louisiana there has occurred a partial fusion of English and French doctrines, particularly in criminal law. It is difficult to convey in a few words the concept of common law as expounded by such men of legal learning as Coke and Blackstone in England and Kent, Story, and Holmes in America. Elements of the common law came into vogue as early as the thirteenth century through the formulation by judges of rules based on recognized customs common to the British realm. These rules served for trying cases that involved points and issues not covered by the prevailing statutes. The decisions and their commentaries constituted efforts to apply established principles and common sense to civil and criminal matters. The system grew with time as judges relied upon former court opinions, thus adding precedent to precedent. This body of judge-made law had reached a high stage of crystallization when it became doctrinal baggage for export to America. But it had attained a wide scope, more suited to the functions of the state judiciaries than to the prescribed jurisdictions of our federal courts.

Common law and statutes

It should be noted that statutes, as they come into existence, take precedence over the common law in case of conflict or discrepancy. That has been true in both England and America. Statutory law may duplicate, amplify, modify, or displace common law. This statutory encroachment varies among the states according to the completeness or comprehensiveness of statutes and codes, but common law seems never to perish. A change in common-law doctrine by state legislation is exemplified in the industrial era by the legislative requirement for compulsory compensation to workers for accidents incurred on the job. The statutes relieve the employee of much of the burden of proving damage and take from the employer much of the immunity handed down through the common law of a simpler society. Modern state constitutions also contain many provisions that deviate from the precepts of common law. The common law, however, has strongly influenced the applied meaning of state statutes and constitutions as interpreted by the courts, both state and federal. State laws and court opinions have been upheld by the Supreme Court of the nation on the basis of their accordance to the common law, and thus not violative of the federal Constitution. This point was set forth both before and after the adoption of the Fourteenth Amendment.[1]

Both state and federal courts try cases in equity, although state suits of this type are far more numerous. Equity applies to civil matters, not directly to criminal cases. It, too, originated in England, and arose through the crystallization of the common law by the judges. The rigidities of common law became inadequate for settling unprecedented disputes and for dispensing preventive or corrective justice not measurable in legal or monetary terms. For more flexible remedies Englishmen turned to their king, who found it convenient to leave such matters to the royal chancellor ,who thus became known as "the keeper of the king's conscience." The practice expanded into a separate system of jurisprudence and came under the administration of a chancery court. The development of this type of justice brought forth a body of chancery rules, based partly on the principles of Roman law and Canon law. The system eventually facilitated the just settlement of complicated cases without the use of juries. Equity expanded by the time of Shakespeare to the importance of the common-law jurisprudence, and it accompanied the latter system to the New World, where both were to become essential features of the American pattern of justice.

Equity proceedings in England and America today are circumscribed and regulated by statutory provisions, but nevertheless they serve modern needs flexibly. Equity hearings and decrees frequently offer the best or only means of satisfying the miscellaneous interests of a group of adult and minor heirs to an estate not covered by a will. Equity writs of injunction serve definite purposes of preventing property damage by one person to another. In past years such writs have been applied rather extensively to labor disputes, but this use has become somewhat limited by legislation, especially by laws permitting collective bargaining and peaceful picketing. It should also be remembered that equity decisions may be appealed from the trial court of a state to higher courts for proper reasons and even to the United States Supreme Court, should a national constitutional right be

[1] Supreme Court opinions on this point are cited in chapter 4 in the discussion of police power.

involved. Equity suits in federal courts between citizens of different states may also be appealed on constitutional grounds. It might be said that the equity process is, in a sense, extra-legal, but, in its flexibility, it may not become illegal or unconstitutional. Only a few states, Arkansas, Delaware, Mississippi, and Tennessee, have separate chancery courts and chancellors. The others have law and equity jurisdictions in the same courts, as is true of the federal judiciary. Thus, equity has been considerably reduced as a separate procedure in America, although certain of its features remain significant. It is an integral part of the system of justice.

The Judicial Hierarchy

One process, central and local

The state judiciary roughly duplicates the federal judiciary in hierarchical features of centralization and decentralization. No sharp example of autonomy is to be found at any point from bottom to top, although there are wide variations of actual merit and method among the states and among the courts. The trial judge with the smallest territorial basis of selection and jurisdiction is always an arm of the law and the state. In that capacity he is subject to higher authority in his dispensation of justice. He represents part of a larger system in its central and local applications. The prosecuting "party" of a murderer in any original trial court, for example, is not the "county" or the "city" but the "state." The highest points of constitutional interpretation may be raised and applied or rejected in the trial court, with or without the possibility of appeal.

Lowest of the classes of state courts

The state judicial systems embrace three or four classes of courts, as shown in Figure 15–1, with additional types for special purposes in the larger states and in important urban centers. At the bottom are minor courts presided over by justices of the peace, other local magistrates, or police judges, frequently without the qualification of formal legal training. These courts function without juries and dispose of no major matters, either civil or criminal, although they may conduct preliminary hearings to determine whether an accused person shall be held in jail or placed under bond for a jury trial for homicide.

The justice of the peace ("J.P.") once performed useful functions in rural neighborhoods and villages prior to the existence of speedy transportation and communication. But this part-time officer has been subjected to criticism in recent years, sometimes for operating "marriage mills" at convenient points or near a state line and sometimes for improvising a fee racket. There have been complaints of cooperation between justices of the peace and rural constables in "speed traps" for collecting advance fees and fines from passing motorists who could not tarry for court proceedings in a country home, store, or shop.[2] Since the party initiating a suit

[2] For an account of one "speedy" trial in which a homemade grocery table served as a

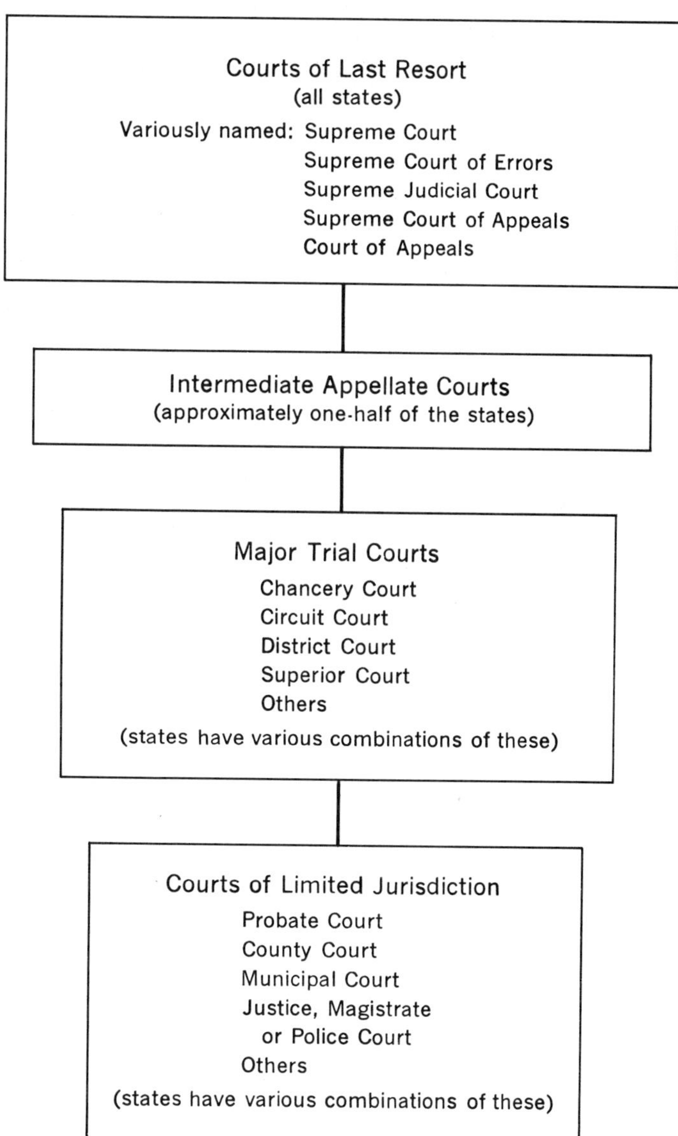

Figure 15–1. The State and Local Judicial Hierarchy.

before a justice of the peace often wins the case, it has been cynically observed that "J.P." signifies "judgment for the plaintiff." The makeshift

judge's bench, *see* James P. Economos, "Justice, Safety, and Traffic Courts," *State Government* 25 (January 1952), pp. 9–11; 20–21.

minor courts, rural and urban, have bred distrust in many instances for reasons of inadequacy, subservience to the fee system, and connection with unsavory politics.[3] The dissatisfaction has led to their being supplanted or supplemented in a number of states and cities with more systematic courts and professional judges who exercise somewhat greater authority and serve larger territorial jurisdictions. These improved tribunals have such designations as municipal courts, general sessions courts, and courts of common pleas.

Regular trial courts

Between the courts of minor jurisdiction and the appellate courts are the regular trial courts, or tribunals of "first instance," in which most American suits of importance begin and end. Cases are sometimes shunted to these courts from the minor courts, and a number of cases are appealed for one reason or another to higher courts, but the work of these state courts stands as the main component of our administration of justice. Officially, these courts are classified as "circuit," "district," or by other designations. Juries are used in these courts, and each trial is presided over by a single judge. The geographical jurisdiction is customarily limited to a county or city, although in rural regions of limited needs a judge may "ride circuit," holding sessions in county after county in rotation. Lawyers may also "ride circuit" along with the judge, as did Abraham Lincoln. There is often a separation of functions in populous centers between criminal and civil courts, regardless of whether equity is in a different jurisdiction. Where there is too much work for one judge, a court may have two or more divisions, with a trial judge for each. The judges are almost invariably qualified lawyers, both because of technical necessity and because bar associations insist upon professional training for the bench.

Higher courts

Every state has a highest court of appeals, generally called the supreme court, although other titles are used in New York, Massachusetts, and a few other states. This court consists of from three to nine judges, the number most often being five or seven. Most of its work is devoted to cases coming up from lower state courts, although it has original jurisdiction in special types of cases in a few states. It sits without a jury. In many states it has the responsibility of formulating rules of procedure for the whole judicial system of the state within the framework of constitutional and statutory provisions. In a few states the supreme court may be required to render advisory opinions on vital matters, such as the constitutionality of pending legislation, if requested by the governor or the legislature. There is no appeal from this state court, except to the United States Supreme Court on federal constitutional grounds. To relieve the highest court of excessive burdens, many of the more populous states maintain other

[3] In Leon County, Florida, for example, candidates for justice of the peace have won regularly on the platform promise that they will do nothing in the office.

courts of appeal, which constitute a class or grade above the trial courts and have the final word of review in many cases or types of cases. Close to one-half of the states have established such intermediate appellate courts.[4] Large questions of state constitutionality, however, can hardly be put at rest until the supreme court renders an opinion. The high state courts may be called upon to test the constitutionality of statutes, and the legality as well as the constitutionality of administrative performance.

Special courts

Special courts of different kinds are to be found on the fringe of the hierarchical system, notably in highly urbanized regions. These courts may handle such matters as domestic relations, juvenile delinquency, probation of wills, small claims, and the like. Much of their work is of an informal nature and partly free from battles by attorneys, although through proper channels it may be reviewed for possible reversal by higher courts.

It is also true that in modern state government, as in the national government, there are administrative bodies with power to conduct hearings and render decisions which are binding in the regulation of civil affairs, unless invalidated upon review by a judicial court. Administrative tribunals and administrative law are essential to all levels of government. This type of adjudication may be applicable to such problems as tax disputes, intrastate or local utility rates, urban zoning, licensing and location of liquor stores, enforcement of health and sanitary measures, abatement of pollution evils, and removal of fire hazards. The first "housing court" in the nation was established by the Massachusetts legislature in 1971, its jurisdiction limited to housing issues for the city of Boston. County governing bodies are officially labeled as "courts" in a few states, including Missouri and Tennessee, although most of their functions are not judicial or even quasi-judicial in nature.

The Judges

Method of selection

About one-half of the states choose judges by popular election, in striking contrast to the method used for the federal bench. Many bar associations oppose selection by popular vote as an interference with the independence and continuity of the judiciary. But lawyers individually and collectively often exercise a strong influence for the election of qualified judges. Many groups, including workers, farmers, and crusaders for direct democracy, insist upon making the choice by popular vote as the best means of checking the influence of special interests. A few states have election of judges

[4] For a good description of this level of state courts, *see* Daryl R. Fair, "State Intermediate Appellate Courts: An Introduction," *Western Political Quarterly* 24 (September 1971), pp. 415–424.

by the legislature, and others have appointment by the governor with confirmation by legislature, senate, a council, or a commission. California adopted a constitutional amendment in 1934 to combine the methods of appointment and election for putting judges on the supreme and appellate courts. Under this plan a vacancy is filled for an initial term through appointment by the governor with the joint approval of the chief justice, another judge, and the state attorney general. Successive terms are won by election, with no opposing candidates on the ballot, but with voters having opportunity to approve or disapprove. In a way, the judge runs on his record and, if he is rejected, gubernatorial appointment of another judge is in order. The Missouri constitution, adopted in 1945, contains provisions approximating the California plan but requiring the governor, in making an appointment, to select from a list of three submitted by a commission consisting chiefly of judges and lawyers of the state or district.[5] With strong support from the American Bar Association and related professional groups, ten states adopted the Missouri pattern, or a similar plan, during the 1960s.

Qualifications, tenure, and compensation

The state constitutions and statutes give rather limited attention to judicial qualifications aside from matters of age, citizenship, and residence. There are general or indefinite requirements that judges have legal knowledge or experience, but these standards are more contingent upon popular and professional opinion than upon technical stipulations. In many ways and in many states it is essential that a prospective judge have political insights and connections to win a place on the bench. The political factor does not in itself exclude professional competence.

The length of terms for which judges are chosen varies among the states and also sometimes among classes of courts. For the highest court the term is only two years in Vermont, six years in one-third of the states, and seven years or more in the others. The term runs until the incumbent is seventy years old in New Hampshire, for life in Massachusetts, and for the "term of good behavior" in Rhode Island. It is customary in many high and low jurisdictions to re-elect short-term judges who have given satisfaction and retained the confidence of the legal profession.

The salaries of judges are fixed sometimes by constitutional provisions, but more frequently by statutory enactment. The scale in most states ranges rather generally below the compensation given the federal judiciary. The annual compensation for members of the highest court

[5] For individual state provisions, *see* "Final Selection of Judges," *The Book of the States, 1974–75*, pp. 120–133 (Table 6). For a discussion of the Missouri Plan as a "different kind of politics" for judicial selection, and as opposed to a plan for taking judicial selection "out of politics," *see* Richard A. Watson and Rondal G. Downing, *The Politics of Bench and Bar: Judicial Selection under the Missouri Nonpartisan Court Plan* (New York: John Wiley and Sons, 1969).

ranges from $22,500 in Montana to $50,000 in Pennsylvania. Many states pay the chief justice more than the associate justices, with $500 and $1,000 the most usual additional compensations. Salaries received by intermediate appellate judges range from $22,360 in Oklahoma to a maximum of $48,000 in Pennsylvania. Justices of the peace and certain other minor court magistrates rely, of course, upon fees for compensation.

Removal of judges

Judges, like other officials, may be removed in one way or another for sufficient cause or demand, although this is not a common occurrence due to the slow and cumbersome method of impeachment. Eight states provide for the recall of judges by popular election. Some states provide for removal of a judge by the governor at the request of the legislature, and in others a joint resolution by the two houses of the legislature is effective for removal. Judges, moreover, are not technically immune from prosecution for crime. Removal has in rare cases been accomplished indirectly by legislative manipulation of a judge's jurisdiction.

Judges and Politics

Courts in political process

Are judges just as much "in politics" as mayors, councilmen, or governors? To say that we have "a government of laws and not of men" often leaves the impression that courts and judges perform a cut-and-dried operation of applying unambiguous and impartial law to human situations in a way that places it outside the boundaries of the political arena. An increasing number of political scientists are moving in the direction of correcting this highly unrealistic picture of the judicial process by studying the courts as a part of the political process. This does not mean that there are no distinguishing features of the judicial process and judicial institutions, but it does mean that judicial decisions involving money, office, votes, services, life, and liberty determine in part who gets what, when, and how, in our society. The courts are thus unavoidably enmeshed in politics.

Judges as political umpires

Professors Sayre and Kaufman, for example, in their excellent book *Governing New York City,*[6] describe the governmental process in New York City as a "contest for prizes," and point to the judges as important participants in the contest. Their role is usually, though not always, that of umpire rather than of player, but the outcome of a contest is in large measure dependent on what the umpires do. Sayre and Kaufman point

[6] Wallace S. Sayre and Herbert Kaufman, *Governing New York City* (New York: Russell Sage Foundation, 1960). The authors have relied heavily on their discussion found on pp. 528–531 and 536–538. *See also* W. J. Keefe, "Judges and Politics," *University of Pittsburgh Law Review* 20 (March 1959), pp. 621–631. For an interesting attempt to compare and contrast the behavior of state and federal judges, *see* Edward N. Beiser, "A Comparative Analysis of State and Federal Judicial Behavior: The Reapportionment Cases," *American Political Science Review* 62 (September 1968), pp. 788–795.

out that in settling disputes judges do much more than affect the immediate litigants—they are determining the "rules of the game" for all kinds of present and future power struggles by overturning state legislation, local legislation (much more frequently), or administrative rules, regulations, and specific actions. They settle election contests with far-reaching effects and decide whether to invalidate inequalities in legislative representation. The rewards in the power struggle to influence the decisions of government—the "contest for prizes"—are distributed in a manner strongly affected by what judges say the rules of the game are.

Judges in and from New York City, 315 of them, are involved in the political struggle in another way, according to Sayre and Kaufman. They are the formal appointing officers for the nonjudicial staffs of the courts, involving several thousand employees. Many of these are subject to civil service and other legal and practical restrictions, but the judges still run a sizable job-dispensing operation and many of the jobs are considered to be highly desirable.

Political distinctiveness of judges

Even though judges are in many respects like all other participants in the contest for the stakes of politics, Sayre and Kaufman warn against the possibility of overstating the case and of overlooking some important differences. For example, the Anglo-Saxon tradition of juridical independence is reflected in many devices which reduce considerably the accountability of the courts to elected legislatures and executives and grant some degree of immunity to pressure and retaliation. Furthermore, the avenues of access to, and bargaining with, judges by various political groups are restricted by such factors as the formalized procedure of adjudication, the strong weight given to legal precedent, and the ethical norms of the profession. But, on the whole, Sayre and Kaufman are more fearful that the student of politics will fail to recognize judges as participants in the contest for the rewards of politics than that he will fail to recognize certain differences between judges and the various other participants.

Judicial Politics: The Case of Louisiana

The importance of viewing the behavior of judges in the broad political context is illustrated by the study of the political involvement of judges in Louisiana by Herbert Jacob and Kenneth N. Vines.[7] In studying the

[7] Herbert Jacob and Kenneth Vines, *Studies in Judicial Politics* (New Orleans: Tulane Studies in Political Science, vol. VIII, 1963). The authors are indebted to Professors Jacob and Vines for permission to make liberal use of their material for purpose of this summary. Two selections by Vines, "The Selection of Judges in Louisiana," and "Political Functions of a State Supreme Court," and one by Jacob, "Politics and Criminal Prosecution in New Orleans," have been used in these paragraphs.

selection of judges in Louisiana, Vines discovered that over 80 percent of the judges had held political office (usually elective) before coming to the court. Although the state constitution requires that judges be "learned in the law" and that they have experience in legal practice in the state, only a minority of them had actually pursued a substantial career in private law practice. Instead, Louisiana judges came to the bench after political careers as state legislators, as state law enforcement officials, or as parish and municipal officials. Vines concludes that these judges bring their political values and viewpoints of state politics to their performance on the courts.

Although a tradition of re-election and long tenure in most cases has given Louisiana judges relative freedom from the cares and costs of campaigning, there is still the practical possibility that a judge will have to face opposition if he does not give continuous and careful attention to state politics. Professor Vines discovered that the Louisiana Supreme Court, during twelve selected years, had abundant opportunities to "take sides" in intraparty and factional disputes in that one-party state, with a total of 204 cases involving such matters as elections, the appointment and removal of governmental officials, and disputes among governmental agencies. In deciding these cases, the court made important determinations affecting the allocation of power and personnel in state politics. When Huey Long successfully dominated the state from 1928 to 1935, the State Supreme Court helped him at critical points by deciding in favor of Long-backed candidates in election contests and by backing Long in disputes with state officials.

Two cases will help to illustrate the relation of the Louisiana Supreme Court to the creation and domination of the Long faction. The first was decided following the death of one of the anti-Long justices; the court helped maintain a voting majority of four justices favorable to the Long faction. Governor Huey Long is reported to have promised John B. Fournet a place on the Supreme Court as a reward for having helped quash the removal proceedings against Long when Fournet was Speaker of the Louisiana House of Representatives. The death of an incumbent judge, Winston Overton, just two days before his bid for re-election in the Democratic primary in 1934, provided the opportunity, but not without some unusual assistance from the Court. The only opponent to Overton was Thomas Porter, an anti-Long candidate, and a Louisiana statute clearly prohibited the entry of any new candidate within three days of the election. The election was held as scheduled and Porter received well over a majority of all votes cast. Instead of declaring Porter the party nominee, however, the party committee called for a second primary one month later. Fournet qualified for this primary and defeated Porter by a slight majority. The State Supreme Court became involved when Porter sought an injunction against Fournet's entry into the race. With three judges dissenting, the Court refused to grant the injunction, claiming that the Court had no jurisdiction and that the party committee's decision had to be followed.

Some four years earlier, the Louisiana Supreme Court helped Long keep control of the state after he moved from the governor's office to the United States Senate in 1930. Following Long's election to the Senate, Lieutenant Governor Cyr took the oath of office for governor as provided in the state constitution. Long did not accept this, however, and had Alvin King, president *pro tempore* of the Senate, take the oath for governor. Cyr filed suit for intrusion into office and received a favorable decision in district court; but the state supreme court overruled and held that the courts were without jurisdiction in the dispute. Judges were thus the instruments for Long to continue his domination of the office of Governor.

A different facet of Louisiana judicial politics, the politics of criminal prosecution in New Orleans, was examined by Professor Jacob. A study of political influences bearing upon judicial discretion in the disposition of criminal cases revealed different patterns of leniency, depending on which political faction was in power. Jacob discovered that a district attorney backed by the traditional political machines of New Orleans, the "Old Reglars," was tougher and less lenient in his handling of cases than a district attorney supported by a middle-class reform movement. Also studied was the impact of increased racial tensions on the prosecution of blacks in New Orleans between 1954 and 1960. Based on dismissal of cases because of non-prosecution or dismissal of the affidavit, Jacob discovered not only that blacks were treated more harshly than whites in the criminal courts, but that the harshness of the treatment (compared with the treatment of white defendants) increased as racial tensions grew between 1954 and 1960. Thus, whether one looks at intraparty factional politics or at racial politics, one can expect to find extensive judicial involvement in many states.

The Drama of Justice

Participants and roles

Judges are officially the central figures in courts and court proceedings, but the drama of justice requires a cast of many other characters for formal performance in all hearings above the level of minor tribunals. It might be said that in trial courts the participants ordinarily appear in person, but in an appeal the higher courts rely primarily upon transcription, examining the script, as it were, and hearing arguments over its correctness in applying legal or constitutional standards to the factual story. The initial suit opens with one party pitted against another, that is, plaintiff versus defendant, or "state" versus defendant. Normally each party has a lawyer or a team of lawyers, the prosecuting counsel in criminal cases being known by some such title as "district attorney," "state's attorney," "solicitor," "attorney general," or "assistant officer." Each party is entitled to have witnesses, whether experts or laymen with direct knowledge. Affiliated with the courts are enforcement or administrative officers to serve papers, announce court, maintain order in court, guard prisoners, bring in witnesses, and wait upon juries. In important trials, exclusive of equity cases, there are trial juries, unless the right of jury hearing is mutually waived. There are clerks and stenographers to handle records, documents, and correspondence.

The trial jury

The right of trial by jury has been handed down for centuries. It is designed to ensure amateur and indigenous qualities in the performance of justice and prevent external or tyrannical professionalism. The trial jury, known as petty or petit jury, usually consists of twelve persons drawn from the jurisdiction of the court. The Supreme Court in 1970 ruled that a jury of less than 12 members meets the constitution's guarantee of a trial by jury. A few states actually use the smaller jury, and federal civil trials now use smaller juries. Potential jurors are selected somewhat by lot from a large list of eligible voters, freeholders, or taxpayers, with some gaining automatic excuse or discretionary excuse from the judge for occupational or urgent personal reasons. Further screening is undertaken for a particular trial, eliminating those with formed opinion or known prejudice in the case as well as those with interest in the outcome through kinship or other close affiliation with a party to the suit. The problem of selecting juries in civil rights cases is illustrated in Figure 15–2. Finally, each side is allowed a limited number of peremptory challenges for disqualification. This prerogative is often exercised to the full extent by the counsel on each side in important criminal trials. Days may be required for the process of selecting and qualifying a jury for a highly publicized criminal trial.

The trial jury exercises the important role of passing upon the truthfulness and weight of evidence for the determination of the verdict, with guidance from the judge as to the meaning of the law and the significance of the evidence in so far as the jury finds it to be true. The jury, not the judge, establishes guilt or innocence and in civil cases grants or denies the claims of the plaintiff.

Traditionally the jury verdict must be unanimous, but unanimity has been removed in several states for civil cases and in a few for criminal cases. In a five-to-four decision in 1972 the Supreme Court held that unanimous jury verdicts are not required for state criminal convictions.[8] The two states involved in this decision were Louisiana, permitting 9-to-3 votes, and Oregon, permitting 10-to-2 votes for conviction. The opinion

[8] *Johnson* v. *Louisiana*, 406 U. S. 356 (1972), and *Apodaca* v. *Oregon*, 406 U. S. 404 (1972).

'A Guy's Entitled to a Jury of His Peers, Ain't He?'
©1965 HERBLOCK
THE WASHINGTON POST

Figure 15–2. From *The Herblock Gallery* (Simon & Schuster, 1968).

of dissenting justices pointed to the incongruity of the continued requirement of unanimous verdicts in federal courts to protect property rights, while permitting state courts to deprive a person of his liberty with only a majority verdict.

A few states require a unanimous verdict only for sentence of death or life imprisonment. If a jury fails to reach a required unanimous verdict, the result is a mistrial, with choice to the prosecution of retrying or dropping the case.

The grand jury

The grand jury is also a feature of our system of justice inherited by way of the English common law. Its work actually precedes that of the trial jury in criminal procedure. It is selected in a manner much like the method used in choosing members for the trial jury, but without challenges as to qualification by opposing attorneys. It varies in size up to twenty-three members. It is an investigative body, not a trial board, and much of its work is performed in secret. It looks into specific and general matters of crime and misconduct within the jurisdiction of the court it serves. Since its members are normally laymen, it is largely dependent upon the prosecuting attorney for advice and guidance in considering cases for possible indictment or "true bills." Unanimous agreement is not required to bring a true bill, an indictment calling for trial on a specific charge. It may report a "no true bill" for a person held for grand-jury investigation if the facts clearly point to such a conclusion.

The Fifth Amendment of the national Constitution provides that no person, except in the armed forces, "shall be held to answer for a capital, or otherwise infamous crime, unless on a presentment or indictment of a Grand Jury." The Supreme Court of the United States has never held this provision to be a requirement that the states restrict themselves to indictment by grand jury, however, and many states provide constitutionally for trial of criminal cases on an affidavit or information by the proper prosecuting attorney in the jurisdiction of the trial court. Thus the grand jury is only an alternative method of bringing an accused to trial in a number of states, especially for cases not involving felony. The grand jury works somewhat less expeditiously than an expert prosecuting staff reviewing and investigating the accused. Whatever the method of presentment, the accused still has the protection of a jury trial and a defense lawyer when he appears in the "court of first instance." The grand jury may still perform useful functions in checking the work of local government officials, whether for indictment, general criticism, or exoneration. In special or unusual crime waves, special grand juries may be called into session for speedy action, and such bodies sometimes take effective initiative in civic house cleaning, working secretly to provide a grist of indictments for the mills of the trial courts.

Hearings of appeal

The appellate process is by nature a technical game, and its roster of participants consists primarily of judges and lawyers. A losing or disappointed party to a civil suit or a party convicted in a criminal case may wish to appeal to a higher court. The "state" or prosecution has no appeal from a verdict of acquittal, although a chronic criminal may be held for a subsequent trial for another alleged violation. The seeker of appeal may not get it, and, if he gets it, he may still lose his case. His counsel prepares motions and papers for appeal and argues the case in the higher court, if the latter allows the hearing for legal or constitutional reasons. The appellate court always functions with a plurality of judges, and one of them writes the opinion of the court in each case. There may be dissenting opinions. The court may uphold or reverse the ruling of the lower court and put an end to the case unless there can be appeal to a still higher tribunal. It may find errors in the lower ruling and send the case back for a retrial by the first court. Its disposition of the case accords with its interpretation of points involved in the record, the law, and the constitution. There have been exceptional instances of cases reaching appellate courts two or three times, with trial and retrial in the court of original jurisdiction. Much of this type of procedure, however, has been eliminated in civil cases by the systematic administrative handling of many damage matters, as in the automatic compensation for injury to industrial or corporate employees. Civil cases are sometimes settled "out of court" by mutual agreement between the parties, thus terminating the litigation. But the "law's delay" still characterizes our state justice in more ways than one, as will be subsequently noted.

Problems of Modernization

Dilemma of old and new

The judiciary constantly faces problems of adjusting old principles to new conditions, of maintaining old wine in new containers in a new age. Such problems confront the courts more than other branches of government, and they confront the state courts more sharply than they confront the federal judiciary, which has concern with a smaller variety of cases and powers. The problems of adjustment are also more difficult for the state systems, because the state courts function generally within a much greater circumscription of constitutional and statutory regulations than do the federal courts. These legal regulations may tell the state judge not only what to do but how. The state trial judge normally exercises somewhat less mastery in directing and expediting proceedings in his court than a comparable member of the federal bench. He plays a much less forthright role than a regular trial judge in England, where court procedure has been simplified and technical manipulations have been reduced. The American state courts offer more opportunities than others for field days for lawyers, with comparative costs of litigation running high, particularly in long-drawn-out civil cases. Yet lawyers have voiced much of the criticism of outmoded features of these courts.

Reform movements

Movements for statutory or constitutional reform or improvement of the judicial systems of the several states have been in evidence throughout most of the present century. The early call for overhauling organization and procedure was highlighted by Roscoe Pound, a Nebraska lawyer and law professor, who was to continue and expand his influence for improvement after becoming dean of the Harvard Law School. Criticisms and proposals for change have come from the American Bar Association, the American Judicature Society, the publications of the American Academy of Political and Social Science, and other sources. Social workers and social reformers have exerted pressure for certain types of judicial specialization, notably in the realm of juvenile delinquency, in which Judge Ben Lindsey became a constructive influence and authority through more than a quarter-century of service as juvenile court judge in Denver.[9]

General dissatisfaction over enlarged and crowded dockets has lent emphasis to the demands for injecting leavening elements of expertness, unity, and system into the state judicial processes, especially in populous urban regions. More than one-half of the states, with Ohio and Massachusetts as pioneers, have set up judicial councils, somewhat analogous to legislative councils, to make studies and recommendations with a view to improving or streamlining court organization and procedure. These bodies usually consist of judges and lawyers and function mainly for the purposes of research and advice, thus offering hope on a limited or gradual scale.

New Jersey court reforms

New Jersey has been a leader in seeking to coordinate and modernize the units of its judiciary through constitutional provisions adopted in 1947. As a result of these changes that state has a regular administrative director of courts, and his annual reports provide information on the status and dockets of the courts from local to supreme. The constitutional changes have tended to speed the work of the higher courts, although backlogs of cases still confront lower courts, particularly with respect to civil cases. That the effort is worthwhile is indicated by Chief Justice Vanderbilt's statement that "in our Supreme Court we have reduced the time between argument and decision from an average of 105 days under the old system to 31 days under the new, and in our intermediate court of appeals from 113 days to 23 days."[10] At the end of the third year under the new constitution, the number of cases on the calendar of New Jersey's courts was the smallest in twenty years despite increases in the number of cases initiated.

The results achieved in New Jersey are attributed by Chief Justice Vanderbilt to several factors. Popular sentiment demands high performance of the courts, and judges and lawyers strive to realize the popular expectation. Introduction of a simple system of courts is almost equally

[9] *See* R. G. Caldwell, "The Juvenile Court: Its Development and Some Major Problems," *Journal of Criminal Law, Criminology and Police Science* 51 (January–February 1961), pp. 493–511.

[10] Arthur T. Vanderbilt, "Clearing Congested Calendars," *NACCA Law Journal* 14 (November 1954), p. 335.

fundamental. Assignment of judges to the kind of judicial work in which they excel, whether it be appellate, criminal, civil, equity, probate, or matrimonial judicial work, maximizes the performance of the court system. Assignment or administrative transfer of judges to jurisdictions where there is work to be done permits concentration upon congested dockets and ensures that one judge does not sit idle while another has too much to do. The requirement of reports on work accomplished and distribution of summary reports to all the judges helps to realize a fair division of work among the judges. Standardization of rules through promulgation by the highest court of rules applicable to the entire judicial hierarchy reduces confusion and abuse of procedural technicalities. The use of pretrial conferences serves to reduce the element of surprise in trials and also to produce voluntary settlements by agreement of the parties. Finally, limiting recourse to a referee reduces the time required to secure a judgment.[11] New Jersey's achievement warrants careful study. Alaska and New York have adopted speedy trial rules setting four- and six-month deadlines, respectively, for bringing a defendant to trial after he is charged.

Auxiliary features

The states are finding various ways of reducing or avoiding the prolonged handling of controversies by the regular courts. A number of states have provided for the issuance of declaratory judgments by the courts for the benefit of potential litigants. In this way, litigants may have points of law determined in advance on the basis of facts presented and come to common understanding without further suit. Small claims courts reduce the cost and trouble of litigation for miscellaneous small matters, at the same time reducing the dockets for the regular courts. Consumer spokesmen in recent years have charged that small claims courts have become "streamlined mass collection agencies" for landlords, and contend that most of the time consumers in court are defendants rather than plaintiffs. Legal aid clinics in large urban centers facilitate the adjustment of claims and cases for citizens of limited means, sometimes using voluntary legwork by law school students. Improvement, clarification, and acceptance of performance by regulatory bodies may prevent many court cases from arising, both civil and criminal.[12] The office of Court Administrator has become an increasingly common state approach to relieving judges of many of the problems of judicial administration; 40 of the states had this office in 1972.

State and local judicial reform received an impetus from Chief Justice Warren E. Burger in the early 1970s, as he championed the cause of

[11] Arthur T. Vanderbilt, *The Challenge of Law Reform* (Princeton: Princeton University Press, 1955), pp. 85–93.

[12] *See* A. Leo Levin and Edward A. Wooley, *Dispatch and Delay* (Philadelphia: Institute of Legal Research, University of Pennsylvania Law School, 1961); S. H. Hofstadter, "Traffic Jam in the Courts," *New York Times Magazine*, Feb. 21, 1954, p. 14; and E. S. Greenbaum, "A Plea for Court Reform Now," *New York Times Magazine*, Feb. 27, 1955, p. 12.

court modernization. Although Burger's public speaking focused on many of the same court reforms proposed for several decades, he seemed to win support from state and local judges for a unified national effort in a way not previously possible. Early in 1970 Burger and several judicial organizations helped to establish the Institute for Court Management to train court administrators for positions in federal, state, and metropolitan courts. With Ford Foundation assistance, the institute began providing a six-month training course for mid-career officials to improve and modernize the administration of justice. At the urging of Burger, the American Bar Association, the Conference of Chief Justices, and other judicial organizations, a second agency, the National Center for State Courts, was established in 1971. It was an outgrowth of a meeting of 500 judges, court administrators, lawyers, and private citizens. The new center is designed as a service agency for state courts and is to serve as a national clearinghouse for new and existing research and training programs for court modernization.

Burger: new promoter of court reform

The corrective processes, to which the courts contribute, are not necessarily ended when judges, juries, and appellate bodies dispose of cases. Performance in compliance with a court decision may be a long or difficult role for parties concerned, whether in civil or criminal matters. A long term in prison may be the inevitable consequence of arrest and conviction for serious crime. In such a situation, the executive arm of government, which brought the accused to trial in the first place, undertakes to administer the punishment to the guilty according to law and court decree. Thus, both court and administration are concerned with the old and new problem suggested by the slogan, "Let the punishment fit the crime." It is not easy to solve this problem for the quarter of a million inmates of the state and federal prisons of America. Penal reform is as difficult a problem as state court reform. Prison riots on a large scale have occurred in the 1960s and 1970s in such different and far-flung states as Massachusetts, Michigan, Texas, and Washington. Preventing violations of law, apprehending violators, and managing convicted violators are large orders in our government and society. These subjects are discussed in chapter 19, after some of the unique aspects of the units of local government are considered.

Corrective processes

SUPPLEMENTARY READINGS

American Assembly. *The Courts, the Public and the Law Explosion.* Englewood Cliffs, N. J.: Prentice-Hall, 1965.

American Bar Association Journal.

American Judicature Society Journal.

Beaney, W. M. *The Right to Counsel in American Courts.* Ann Arbor: University of Michigan Press, 1955.

Cardozo, Benjamin N. *The Nature of the Judicial Process.* New Haven, Conn.: Yale University Press, 1921.

Frank, Jerome. *Courts on Trial.* Princeton: Princeton University Press, 1949.

Glick, Henry Robert. *Supreme Courts in State Politics: An Investigation of the Judicial Role.* New York: Basic Books, 1971.

Grossman, Joel B. *Lawyers and Judges.* New York: John Wiley and Sons, 1965.

Haynes, Evan. *The Selection and Tenure of Judges.* Newark, N. J.: National Conference of Judicial Councils, 1944.

Jacob, Herbert. *Justice in America.* 2nd ed. Boston: Little, Brown and Co., 1972.

Kaplan, Benjamin, and Hall, Livingston, eds. "Judicial Administration and the Common Man." *The Annals of the American Academy of Political and Social Science* 237 May 1953.

Mayers, Lewis. *The American Legal System.* New York: Harper & Row, 1955.

Murphy, Walter F., and Pritchett, C. Herman. *Courts, Judges, and Politics.* 2nd ed. New York: Random House, 1974.

Murphy, Walter F., and Tanenhaus, Joseph. *The Study of Public Law.* New York: Random House, 1972.

Pound, Roscoe. *Organization of the Courts.* Boston: Little, Brown and Co., 1940.

Radin, Max. *The Law and You.* New York: Mentor Books, 1948.

Vanderbilt, Arthur T. *The Challenge of Law Reform.* Princeton: Princeton University Press, 1955.

———. *Minimum Standards of Judicial Administration.* New York: New York University Law Center for the National Conference of Judicial Councils, 1949.

U. S. Advisory Commission on Intergovernmental Relations. *State–Local Relations in the Criminal Justice System.* Washington, D. C., 1971.

Watson, Richard A., and Downing, Rondal. *The Politics of Bench and Bar: Judicial Selection under the Missouri Nonpartisan Court Plan.* New York: John Wiley and Sons, 1969.

16

Local Government: The County

Local government has come into view frequently in the preceding chapters because that government is constitutionally and functionally interwoven with state government in important ways, including its role as a channel to federal agencies and federal funds. No unit of government is an island; intergovernmental relationships become more extensive and intensive in modern times with modern needs. Although attention is centered somewhat briefly upon some of the more specific and unique features of local government, the student should guard against any isolationist concept of the local unit or process.

Local government not isolated

The county, with its political subdivisions, is geographically the most universal jurisdiction of local government in America; and, with the New England town, it exemplifies a heritage and a continuity from British and colonial self-government. All states but three are composed of counties, the exceptions being Connecticut, Rhode Island, and Alaska.[1] Another exception is found in Louisiana, where counties are called parishes, although the difference is more in name than in actual character. The inhabitants of most cities are also inhabitants of counties and subject in various respects to county authority.

Importance of the county

[1] Counties in Connecticut, already in a state of "withering away," were abolished in 1960. Both Connecticut and Rhode Island are divided geographically into counties, but they do not have county government. "Boroughs" are authorized by Alaska's constitution, and nine have been organized in that state. The use of the word "borough" is an effort to avoid the implication that it is primarily created for state purposes, rather than for local purposes, and to avoid "importing" to Alaska the judicial decisions relating to counties in other states.

Although common to virtually all the states, the county is by no means a standardized unit of government. It has consistently and historically been more important in institutional life in the South than in New England, partly for reasons of geography and different types of colonial civic development. The states of other regions have tended to fluctuate somewhat in the development of county government between the southern emphasis and the New England de-emphasis. The population of counties varies from the 164 souls in Loving County, Texas, to the more than seven million in Los Angeles County, California. Arlington County, Virginia, covers only 24 square miles, while San Bernardino County, California, encompasses 20,131 square miles. The average area of a state's counties varies from 332 square miles in Kentucky to 8,113 square miles in Arizona, as shown in Table 16–1.

In the absence of urbanization, the county most likely becomes an important core of grassroots government and community. The county as a political entity and going concern registered a definite imprint in the

Table 16–1. Number of Counties and Average Land Area per County, by State, Ranked According to Size[a]

State	*Number of Counties*	*Area in Square Miles*
Kentucky	120	332
New Jersey	21	358
Georgia	159	367
Indiana	92	393
Virginia	98	407
Maryland	23	423
West Virginia	55	438
Tennessee	95	440
Ohio	88	466
North Carolina	100	491
Illinois	102	548
Iowa	99	566
Mississippi	82	576
Missouri	114	606
Massachusetts	12	656
South Carolina	46	658
Delaware	3	659
Vermont	14	663
Pennsylvania	66	682
Michigan	83	687

Table 16–1. *Continued*

State	*Number of Counties*	*Area in Square Miles*
Arkansas	75	700
Louisiana	62	728
Wisconsin	72	760
Alabama	67	762
Kansas	105	781
Florida	67	810
Nebraska	93	824
New York	57	841
Oklahoma	77	895
New Hampshire	10	901
Minnesota	87	920
Texas	254	1,035
South Dakota	64	1,193
North Dakota	53	1,311
Colorado	62	1,676
Washington	39	1,710
Idaho	44	1,880
Maine	16	1,938
Hawaii	3	2,138
Montana	56	2,602
Oregon	36	2,674
California	57	2,747
Utah	29	2,839
New Mexico	32	3,797
Wyoming	23	4,235
Nevada	17	6,458
Arizona	14	8,113
United States	3,043[b]	1,166

[a] Dry land and land temporarily or partially covered by water, such as marshland, swamps, and river flood plains; streams, sloughs, estuaries, and canals less than one-eighth of a statute mile in width; and lakes, reservoirs, and ponds less than 40 acres in area.

[b] The 1962 total of 3,043 had increased to 3,044 in 1972 because of Alaska's creation of 9 boroughs and the 8 city–county mergers in various states, counted by the Census Bureau as municipalities.

Source: U. S. Bureau of the Census, *Governmental Organization*, 1962 Census of Governments, vol. I, with revisions from the 1972 Census of Governments.

wide hinterlands, as those regions provided territory after territory and then state after state in the dozen decades following the adoption of the Constitution. In the hinterlands, the county, with subdistricts and townships, served as a base for bringing people and government together in such essential matters as maintaining law and order, providing schools and roads, holding elections, and legalizing land deals, mortgages, wills, and marriages. The competition between communities hoping to be designated the county seat was sometimes fierce; such stakes as the county fair, increased retail trade, and greater social and political prestige usually went to the winner. The county constitutes the locale of identification for many Americans of rural residence or background, illustrated by the memoirs of former President Truman and others. The counties themselves bear many beautiful Indian names as well as names of early national leaders, notably of Washington, Jackson, and Jefferson. A vast amount of American human history is associated with counties and is recorded in county annals.

Multiplicity of counties

The 3,044 counties in the United States, an average of 65 per state, are difficult to defend in terms of administrative or economic needs, especially those that are small in area or population or both. In days of transportation by horse and buggy over dirt roads, it was a civic convenience to establish a county small enough in area so that the courthouse would be not much more than a dozen miles from the homes of any of the citizens of the county. The farmer was thus able to do the morning milking, hitch up the buggy, drive to the county seat, transact business, and return to his home in time for the evening milking. The creation of new counties in formative eras was also sometimes stimulated by the expectation of increased opportunities for public office, improvement contracts, and official printing. Historical evidence points to such perquisites as having motivated the establishment of counties in different states of the South and Middle West. These considerations and other factors, constitutional, political, and traditional, offer almost insurmountable obstacles to the consolidation of counties, even in Texas where there are 254 or in Georgia where there are 159. Except in rare cases, the arguments of administrative efficiency and economy are of no avail for the reduction of the number of small counties throughout the land.

Rural heritage

The counties bear testimony that Americans have been largely a people of rural birth or heritage, despite the present high proportion of urban population. Although many counties are sufficiently populated to be classed as urban or semi-urban, a majority of them are primarily rural or small town in composition and retain patterns of government created by an agrarian society. Counties provide civic links between rural citizens and the outside world. County government continues to reflect strong belief in the idea of political performance by laymen or amateurs rather than by experts or professionals, unless politicians be classed as professionals. Much of it is more personalized than systematized. Ministering to the public needs of a rural county differs from the governmental administration of a big city about as much as the management of an old-fashioned country store differs from the operation of a modern department store in a metropolitan center. Rural county officials, like rural merchants, are doubtless convinced that they need not conform completely in organization or administration to the city model in order best to serve their purposes.

Growth of county government

Doubtless this rural tradition has contributed to a public image of county government as static or in decline, but this image is not supported by a close examination of growth statistics in comparison with the other levels of government. The number of county government employees increased 188 percent between 1951 and 1973, compared with federal and municipal increases of only 35 and 84 percent, respectively. The rate of increase of state employees during the same period was 170 percent, almost the same as for county governments. Thus, the effect of population increases and shifts, and the greater demand for services, appears to have had a greater *relative* impact on counties and states than on the federal government or city governments.

Schizophrenia in the urban county

Many rural-oriented county governments in recent years have been confronted with the perplexing fact that most of their citizens are city residents rather than "country folks." Some 300 urban counties now govern more than two-thirds of our nation's population. The movement from rural to urban areas in the United States between 1950 and 1960 caused more than 1,500 counties to lose population, while close to the same number were increasing in population and becoming more urban. The 1970 census showed no major change in population decline for 45 percent of the counties; 1,369 counties lost population in the 1960s. Urban and suburban demands for municipal services have caused many governments to develop a kind of split personality with a variety of symptoms of rural–urban cleavage. Undoubtedly in response to the new pressures for urban services, more than 530 counties levied a local sales tax, according to a 1972 survey. Rural residents quite naturally resist new taxes for sewerage, fire protection, or airports they feel will never benefit them, and tend to vote against governmental reform to make it impossible to administer such programs. The rural heritage and outlook of the county is not easily or quickly cast off, with a resultant schizophrenic urban county today behaving much as "new wine in old wineskins."[2]

[2] *See* Rodney L. Kendig, "A New Era Emerging for County Government," *National Civic Review* 60 (January 1971), pp. 12–16; and William N. Cassella, Jr., "County Government in Transition," *Public Administration Review* 16 (Summer 1956), pp. 223–231. For five case studies of county government in differing contexts, *see* Herbert Sydney Duncombe, *County Government in America* (Washington, D. C.: National Association of Counties,

Counties, unlike cities, are not incorporated and, unlike states, have no reserved powers. Except for some recent innovations cited later, there is no chief executive corresponding to a mayor, city manager, or governor. Almost universally the main governing authority of a county is a body of elected members with the official title of "board," "court," "commission," or other title. Although some thirty-four different titles are used throughout the United States to identify county governing boards, the most commonly used title is "board of commissioners," with "board of supervisors" running second, as indicated in the following tabulation.

The county governing board

Title of county governing board	*Number of Counties*
Board of commissioners	1,281
Board of supervisors	676
Commissioners court	254
County court	197
Boards of commissioners of roads and revenue	125
Fiscal court	120
Quarterly court	90
Quorum court	75
Police jury	60
Others (Board of chosen freeholders, Levy court, etc.)	171
Total	3,049

Source: Bureau of the Census, *Governing Board of County Governments: 1965* (Washington, D. C.: U. S. Government Printing Office, 1965), p. 3.

Main features and officers of county government

The size of the governing boards is three or five members in the case of more than two-thirds of the counties, but it extends upward to thirty or more in many counties. In two extreme cases there is a 100-member board in Wayne County, Michigan, in which Detroit is located, and a 196-member governing body for Pulaski County, Arkansas (Little Rock). The members hold such titles as "commissioner," "supervisor," or "magistrate," and, in Louisiana parishes, "police juror." The presiding officer has no regular vote or veto, and his status as chairman is decided sometimes by the members and sometimes by the voters. He has a measure of admin-

1966), pp. 155–230. It is a comparison of two rural counties (Petroleum County, Montana, and Latah County, Idaho), and three metropolitan counties (Montgomery County, Maryland; Davidson County, Tennessee; and Milwaukee County, Wisconsin). *See also* Charles E. Gilbert's study of three large suburban counties in the Philadelphia area, *Governing the Suburbs* (Bloomington: Indiana University Press, 1967).

istrative authority in applying the decisions and orders of the body. The chairman in a few states has the title of "judge of the county court," as did Harry Truman when he headed the governing board of Jackson County, Missouri.

Types of governing boards

County boards differ not only in title and size, but also in the type of membership. Any such classification of 3,049 governing bodies runs the risk of being arbitrary, but it is possible to suggest the following types, based on the official character of membership:[3] (1) Boards of commissioners or supervisors, whose primary function and accountability are as members of the county board, that is, this is their main job with the county (2,084 counties). (2) Boards of township supervisors, who have dual functions and accountability as township officials and also county governing-board members (299 counties). Some of these supervisors represent municipal governments as well. (3) Judges and justices of the peace boards, whose members serve both as board members and as judicial officials (299 counties). (4) Judge and commissioner boards, with a mixed membership consisting of a presiding officer serving both as a board member and judicial officer, and others who function only as board members (322 counties). (5) Other county governing bodies including such unusual types as the single-member "ordinary" in Georgia, and eight of the boroughs in Alaska where city officials serve with elected members of the board (forty-five counties). In 1968 the Supreme Court extended the one-man–one-vote principle to representation on county governing bodies, as well as to other units of local government.[4] In a case involving the 70,000 residents of Midland, Texas, constituting almost 95 percent of the county population, the court found discrimination because three of the five county commissioners were chosen from districts with only several hundred in population. The Midland decision brought the chain reaction started by the Baker case in 1962 to a logical conclusion, although the impetus for change in county government has just begun.[5]

The county board is both a policymaking and an administrative agency. It normally has responsibilities for the construction and maintenance of county buildings and roads, the management of miscellaneous equipment and property, and the letting of contracts on behalf of the county. It has important financial powers and duties, subject to constitu-

[3] Bureau of the Census, *Governing Boards of County Governments: 1965*, p. 2.

[4] *Avery* v. *Midland County*, 390 U. S. 474 (1968).

[5] *See* Daniel R. Grant and Robert E. McArthur, " 'One-Man–One-Vote' and County Government: Rural, Urban, and Metropolitan Implications," *George Washington Law Review* 36 (May 1968); the entire issue is devoted to the subject of reapportionment and local government. For a description of an interesting 1869 Virginia statute (dormant until 1965), providing for citizen initiation of county reapportionment through judicial action, *see* Philip L. Martin, "County Reapportionment in Virginia," *Virginia Law Review* 55 (1969), pp. 1167–1181.

tional and statutory provisions. It often has actual or adjustment powers with respect to tax rates and assessments. It may have regulatory jurisdiction over various matters. The place of the county in wide functional processes is touched upon in other chapters and in discussion of highways, education, agriculture, courts, and law enforcement, as well as more general subjects.

Other County Officers and Agencies

Turning from the county board to the other county officers, those who are generally elected include the sheriff, tax collector, tax assessor, treasurer, county attorney, coroner, and school board. A number of states provide for the election of a county school superintendent; however, many require that this officer be appointed by the county school board. The county must have a clerk or officer to keep official records as well as to record deeds, mortgages, marriage certificates, wills submitted for probate, and other legal instruments. This officer may also have charge of issuing licenses such as those for marriage, conducting particular businesses, owning automobiles, and other matters, unless provision is made for special agencies to handle them. He sometimes serves as secretary of the governing body, which may appoint him if he is not an elective official.

Miscellaneous officers and agencies

It would be impossible to list all types and titles of officers or agencies in the thousands of American counties. No county or state contains all varieties. Counties have created or expanded agencies to distribute funds under state and federal programs, as, for example, in the field of welfare. Many populous counties have separate officials or establishments for specialized functions, which may lie within the province of the central governing body in the smaller counties. Examples are election commissions, planning commissions or offices, budget and accounting authorities, and boards for reviewing tax assessments. There may be a health board or health officer, according to the size of the county. It may also be necessary to have a county engineer for duties in connection with roads and public buildings. The engineer or a county surveyor may be called upon to establish land lines for real estate owners. Many of the miscellaneous functions of government in small counties are performed by part-time officers, whether elected or appointed. This is particularly true of the coroner or medical officer; the prosecuting attorney in a rural county may carry on a private law practice along with his official duties.

The foregoing description of a widely dispersed, plural executive form of government would apply generally to 90 percent, or more, of the counties in the United States. Figure 16–1 illustrates this dispersion of power and responsibility among a variety of elective and appointive officials and

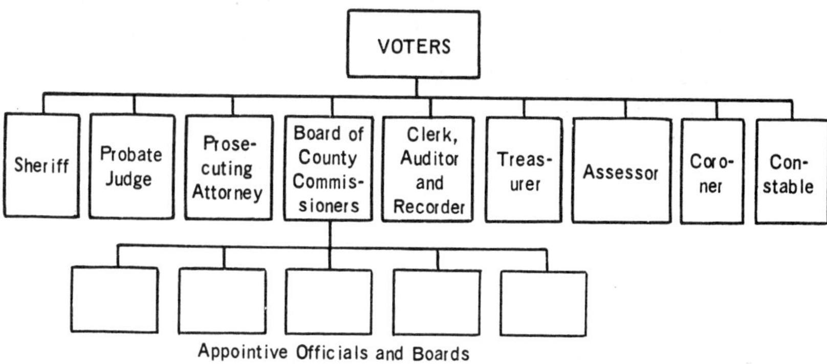

Figure 16–1. The Plural Executive Form of Government in a Typical Idaho County.

boards in a typical Idaho county. The remaining counties have some form of single executive or administrator with varying degrees of supervisory control of county administration.

Political subdivisions

The counties contain many thousand political subdivisions, such as districts, precincts, and townships. The township, as developed in a number of states from New York to the Dakotas, reflects a mixture of the New England town and the southern county. As a civic unit it must not be confused with the "township," which is a land measurement and identification term handed down from the federal public land office. However, the civic and the land units may sometimes coincide.

These subunits of different labels serve as geographical centers or areas for schools, elections, road work, tax administration, jurisdiction of justices of the peace, and the like. A great proportion are rural. The tendency is for these units to become more and more mere outlets for the administration or distribution of county government. In the past many have had internal civic activity, but they have all but lost community identity through consolidation of schools, discontinuance of magistrates' courts, and the transference of district controls to the central government of the county. With speedier transportation and communication than in early days, rural people easily turn to officials at the county courthouse for matters of local government instead of using or supporting neighborhood functionaries for such purposes. The federal government has incidentally conformed to the changing pattern by discontinuing most rural post offices and providing mail service through rural free delivery.

In the general centralization process, functions pass, in part, from state to nation, from county to state, and from community to county, with nothing left for the last outlying civic unit to absorb or centralize. With this loss of neighborhood identity, the county has a greater role than ever in serving rural constituents, developing wider community interests, and facilitating citizens' participation in government.[6]

County Reform Efforts

Criticism of county government

For decades the county has been criticized as the scene of the most backward and inefficient administration of government. It is criticized for having an unsystematized jungle of offices without a definite executive authority, for having too many elective offices, and for being at the mercy of "courthouse rings" in the distribution of patronage and contracts. In many counties fees instead of salaries still constitute coveted features of important offices, sometimes providing the object of bitter contests between rival groups. Conditions, on the whole, are not so unsavory as they have been. But, aside from questions of abuse or graft, county government is too often in serious need of constructive reform to improve or increase its role in public service, to secure a higher degree of administrative efficiency, and to avoid waste of the taxpayers' money. With a few exceptions, modernization or reorganization of county government has trailed that of city, state, and national units.

The county consolidation movement

The proposal for improving county government through consolidation of the smaller counties reached the stage of serious discussion about 1930 when it was given attention by a few state leaders, including Governor Al Smith of New York. A few state constitutions permit consolidation. But results have been rather meager. Tennessee eliminated a small county, merging it with Hamilton County, which contains the city of Chattanooga. Georgia reduced the number of its counties from 161 to 159, one of the mergers being in the Atlanta metropolitan area. Consolidation of particular functions or departments of two or more county governments has occurred in a few instances through legislative or contractual arrangements. Several counties in New Jersey, for example, have a joint sewage disposal system. Minnesota permits consolidation of health departments of counties as well as of cities and counties. During World War II southern counties sometimes pooled activities or services under the impact of national defense establishments. But the general status and identity of the numerous counties are little disturbed.

The overlappings between county government and city government in the same geographical areas raise many problems and stimulate many

[6] The problem of rural community decline is discussed by H. C. Nixon, *Possum Trot* (Norman: University of Oklahoma Press, 1941). Several states have abolished township governments or reduced them in number.

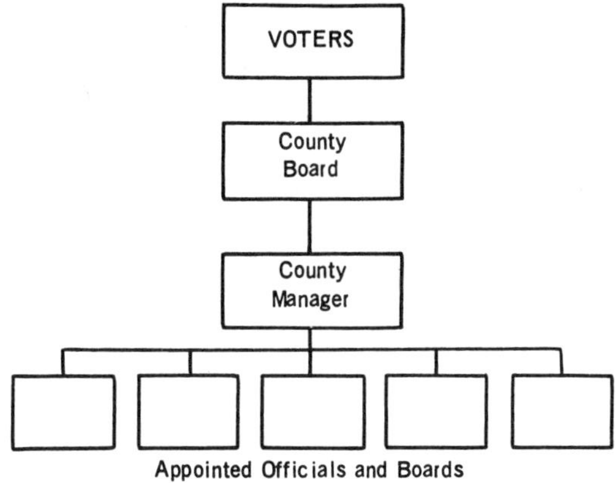

Figure 16–2. The County Manager Plan.

City–county relations

proposals in the fields of law enforcement, education, taxation, public utilities, and other matters. In New Orleans there is one administration for the city and the coterminous parish of Orleans. In particular cases in a few states, cities have been detached from counties for governmental purposes. Consolidation of functions and offices occurs more frequently, however, than the complete merging or the complete separation of city and county units. Rural and suburban citizens, along with their political spokesmen, hesitate to surrender their county prerogatives to city regimes, thereby limiting the streamlining of city–county government. Local political machines not infrequently play significant roles in the harmonious and discordant relations between city and county governments. City–county relationships and the several more contemporary cases of metropolitan city–county consolidation are discussed in greater detail in relation to metropolitan problems in chapter 18.

Improvement in administration

Counties normally have not been governed under charters or by chief executives, as have cities. But proposals to put county administration under stronger executive control have met with a measure of success, especially in highly urbanized counties. Figures 16–2 and 16–3 illustrate the two principal means of accomplishing this goal: the county manager plan and the elected county executive plan. In some counties the cumbersome governing board has been replaced with a small commission of members elected at large instead of by geographical divisions. Virginia authorizes the popular election of a chief executive, and a few counties of that state have made use of this provision. Some states, Virginia among them, permit counties to have managers chosen by the governing boards.[7]

[7] *See* G. W. Spicer, *Fifteen Years of County Manager Government in Virginia* (Charlottesville: University of Virginia, 1951).

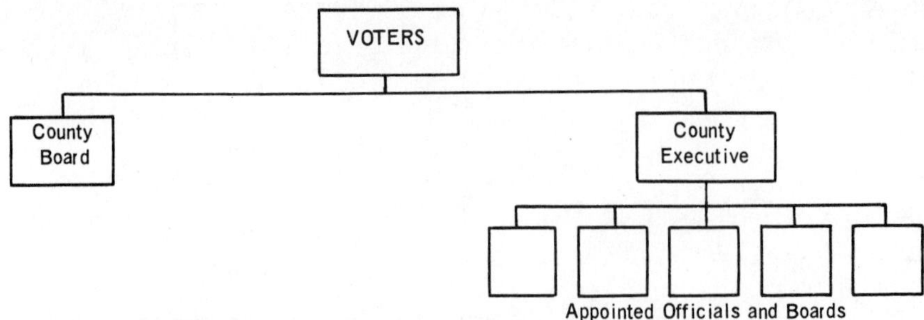

Figure 16–3. The Elected County Executive Plan.

Trend toward county administrators

The National Association of Counties established the "New County USA Center" early in 1970 to serve as a clearinghouse for information on county modernization and improvement. Its very title dramatizes the effort to break away from much of the old structure and image of county government. An increasing number of urban counties in the country have adopted the manager or chief executive type of government, and some use a modified or limited example of the plan, as illustrated by the role of a "chief administrative officer" in the counties of Los Angeles and San Diego in California. Whereas a manager possesses direct, individual authority over all administrative affairs, the CAO is the agent of the governing board, appointed by it and, performing in the name of the board, the administrative duties assigned to him by the board. The CAO generally has more restricted powers reflecting the board's unwillingness to relinquish control over such matters as the appointment of personnel, but in practice given jurisdictions may blur theoretical differences between his position and that of a manager.[8] In 1974 more than 325 counties had an appointive administrator or manager, in most cases the result of a reorganization in the 1960s. In addition, 49 counties had an elected executive. Counties that had county managers included such extreme variations in population and character as metropolitan Dade County, Florida, with more than one million persons, and rural Petroleum County, Montana, with a population of only 894. McMinn County in eastern Tennessee came under a special manager plan through special state legislation as a consequence of a serious incident at Athens, the county seat. On the night of the local election in 1946, an armed posse of aroused citizens intervened to secure a fair count of the ballots and to dislodge what they considered to be an entrenched political machine. Seventeen California counties of

[8] *See* J. C. Bollens, *Appointed Executive Local Government: The California Experience* (Los Angeles: Haynes Foundation, 1952), Chapters 1 and 5, for a consideration of the theoretical and practical differences between these two offices in the light of California experience.

over 100,000 population have chief administrative officers, and approximately one-half of all U. S. counties of more than 250,000 population have some form of appointive or elective executive.[9]

Constitutional barriers in many states make county–manager rule impossible or difficult. Urban counties here and there have reorganized their government on an executive basis through the process of special legislation; others, by law, regulation, or practice, have turned the headship of the governing board into an approximate executive office. There has been less demand in counties than in cities for statewide provisions for local home rule to permit administrative reorganization. In recent years, however, the evidence of increased pressure for home rule charters has come to be more general, with support from the National Association of Counties, metropolitan area study commissions, and other groups. Although only about 60 (less than 2 percent) of the nation's counties have home rule charters, this includes seven counties above the 800,000 population mark.[10]

County home rule

Overall merit systems exist in only a small percentage of the nation's counties. What little progress there has been in this respect is to be found in the populous or urban counties or in administrative operations subject to state and federal standards. A few states have provisions for state assistance or supervision in administering local merit systems on a county optional basis. Among these states are New York, New Jersey, and California. An example of the merit system under special or local legislation is to be found in Jefferson County, Alabama, which contains the city of Birmingham. In many rural or isolated counties it would be impossible, even with full legal or constitutional power, to inaugurate a real merit or personnel policy without reliance upon imported experts and applicants. But rural folkways may permit the development of a rule-of-thumb competence that smacks neither of expertness nor of pure spoils.

Merit systems

The funds flowing annually through the government of a large county today are well above the amount required in a year by the United States government when George Washington was president. The counties that have improved their personnel and executive systems have also generally modernized their financial management, giving attention to

County finance

[9] For a more detailed discussion of county reform, *see* "Improving County Government," *Public Management* 53 (April 1971); the entire issue of this professional journal for city and county managers is devoted to this subject; *see also* Rodney L. Kendig, "Trends in County Government," *The Municipal Yearbook, 1974* (Washington, D. C.: International City Management Association, 1974), pp. 43–46; and National Association of Counties and National Association of County Administrators, *National Survey of the Appointed Administrator in County Government* (Washington, D. C.: National Association of Counties, 1973).

[10] The seven are Los Angeles, San Diego, and Alameda counties in California, Dade County in Florida, and Erie, Nassau and Westchester counties in New York.

such features as budgeting, accounting, and central purchasing, as well as to more efficient methods of taxation. The California county of Los Angeles, with a larger annual budget than that of the city of Los Angeles, is one of those that might be cited for more effective financial organization. Many counties, however, remain behind the times in financial structure, except for accountability and regulations enforced in connection with the use of funds from the state or federal government.

Much of the revenue for county expenditures consists of allocations from federal grants or from state taxes, notably from state sales taxes, for the support of public schools, and other purposes.[11] The trends toward centralizing the financing of phases or projects of local government are examined elsewhere in chapters on state and local finance and functions. In this centralized process, a poor county with a relatively large population may receive more funds from the state treasury than its taxpayers pay into that treasury, while the citizens of a wealthy county pay state taxes in excess of the receipts from that state government by their county government for public purposes. This public equalization is somewhat similar to the policy of the national government in much of its aid to the states.

In addition to actual money, counties get other types of aid and technical assistance from their state governments. State planning agencies often provide useful information and technical advice to counties and cities. So do state offices concerned with schools, libraries, welfare, highways, parks, conservation, and other activities. Such assistance sometimes comes from the national government also, as exemplified in agricultural service, school lunch programs, welfare, and FBI cooperation. The Tennessee Valley Authority is a regional agency of the national government that has pioneered in different ways in cooperating with counties and other units and institutions to extend technical service and assistance.

Retaining the old along with the new

Counties are subject in many ways to the impact of the changing states and the changing cities. County government, like the area in which it operates, is less isolated and less autonomous than once was the case. Although it retains a heritage of self-rule from other centuries, in much of its contact with the governed in our time it functions partly as a sort of middle agent for dispensing public services, as prescribed and provided by larger centers of authority. It is other directed as well as inner directed, passive as well as active, with respect to its role and destiny. Its defenders would contend that, in the interest of balanced governance and local initiative, those larger centers should guard against neutralizing all the

[11] *The American County*, journal of the National Association of Counties, has published from time to time a revised "Federal-Aid Guide" describing the various programs of federal aid for which counties are eligible. The publication has proved to be a very popular document among county officials.

power and responsibility for decision at the county level in sacrifice to the gods of efficiency. By so doing, it may be possible to preserve a flexible union of tradition and progress at this grassroots scene of government.

The New England Town

As indicated earlier, the importance of the county as a unit of local government varies between geographical regions. New England is one region in particular where another governmental unit is closer to the people and more prominent in the public mind than the county. This unit is the New England town, long cited by philosophers as the ideal form of direct democracy, as distinguished from representative democracy. The term "town," as used in this part of the United States, refers not only to an urban area but also to the surrounding rural area. Its origins go deep into the colonial heritage of New England. The early settlement pattern of small villages surrounded by farms, coupled with common problems of severe winters and potential Indian attack, resulted in the creation of "natural" governmental areas with boundary lines generally dictated by those of the economic, social, and "military" community. This is considerably different from township boundary lines which have so often followed the arbitrary square pattern of the surveyor's lines.

A vestige of direct democracy

Although not created as municipal corporations, the New England towns have been given municipal-type functions from time to time by state legislatures, as well as certain judicial functions. The "trademark" of the New England town is the "town meeting" of all qualified voters, an institution which levies taxes, makes appropriations, determines basic policy, and elects officers. The annual town meeting is traditionally held in March, with such additional meetings as may be necessary. Besides electing the board of selectmen and the town clerk, it directly elects many other officers, though not so many as in the days when fence viewers, surveyors of hemp, surveyors of boards and shingles, sealers of leather, cutlers of staves, hogreeves, and scavengers were elected.

Town meeting government

The town meeting has lost much of its virility and feasibility in many areas because of urbanization, apathy, and the unwieldy size of such a meeting if all qualified voters should actually attend. Several variations in this form of government have been adopted in different areas, such as a *representative* town meeting based on a limited number of voting delegates, with continued right of all citizens to attend and participate in debates. An increasing number of towns have adopted a modification of the council–manager plan by providing for a town manager, chosen by and responsible to the board of selectmen. The pressure

Modern variations of town government

on the towns to provide new services and perform new functions has resulted in not infrequent legislative action to sew new patches and appendages to this old institution that is seeking to adjust to an era of rapid change.

SUPPLEMENTARY READINGS

Alaska Legislative Council and the Local Affairs Agency. *Final Report on Borough Government.* Juneau, Alaska: Local Affairs Agency, 1961.

The American County (formerly *The County Officer*). Washington, D. C.: National Association of Counties. Monthly publication.

Bebout, John E. *Model County Charter.* New York: National Municipal League, 1956.

Blair, George S. *American Local Government.* New York: Harper & Row, 1964.

Bollens, J. C. *Appointed Executive Local Government: The California Experience.* Los Angeles: Haynes Foundation, 1952.

Bollens, J. C., with John R. Bayes and Kathryn L. Utter. *American County Government: With an Annotated Bibliography.* Beverly Hills, Calif.: Sage Publications, 1969.

Bromage, A. W. *American County Government.* New York: Sears Publishing Co., 1933.

Commission on Intergovernmental Relations. *An Advisory Committee Report on Local Government.* Washington, D. C.: U. S. Government Printing Office, 1955.

Duncombe, Herbert Sydney. *County Government in America.* Washington, D. C.: National Association of Counties, 1966.

Gilbert, Charles E. *Governing the Suburbs.* Bloomington: Indiana University Press, 1967.

Gittell, Marilyn. "The Metropolitan County in New York State." *The County Officer* 27, February 1962, pp. 60–61; 99–101.

Lancaster, L. W. *Government in Rural America.* 2d ed. New York: D. Van Nostrand Co., 1952.

Martin, Roscoe C. *Metropolis in Transition.* Washington, D. C.: U. S. Housing and Home Finance Agency, 1963.

Murphy, Thomas P. *Metropolitics and the Urban County.* Washington, D. C.: National Association of Counties, 1970.

National Civic Review. New York: National Municipal League. Monthly, except August.

Snider, C. F. *Local Government in Rural America.* New York: Appleton-Century-Crofts, 1957.

Spicer, G. W. *Fifteen Years of County Manager Government in Virginia.* Charlottesville: University of Virginia, 1951.

U. S. Bureau of the Census. *Governing Boards of County Governments: 1965.* Washington, D. C.: U. S. Government Printing Office, 1965.

Wager, Paul, ed. *County Government Across the Nation.* Chapel Hill: University of North Carolina Press, 1950.

17

Local Government: The City

The American city is a modern example and adaptation of an old pattern. There were organized centers of people, wealth, and culture in ancient Egypt, Phoenicia, Greece, and Italy, where the Romans effectively applied the institutional concept of the corporate municipality. Cities and city-states of later ages provided checks or fortresses against feudalism and servile society. Transoceanic transportation and commerce stimulated a new urbanism and a new capitalism in the Western world after the discovery of a great frontier by Christopher Columbus. Dominant cities like London and Paris became capitals of great national states which supplanted the political power of a feudal network of landed lords and vassals. The city, in western Europe and eventually in America, came to be associated with sophistication and progress, even with the hope of democracy.

An ancient pattern

Yet agrarian gentlemen were often inclined to pass unfavorable judgment upon the man-made concentrations of trade, industry, and society. Thomas Jefferson recognized differences between rural and urban ways of life, considering the former as the more natural and the more conducive to happiness and hoping that his countrymen would never "get piled upon one another in large cities, as in Europe." This Jeffersonian viewpoint was prophetic of later cleavage and friction between "city slickers" and rural "hicks" and of subsequent difficulties in maintaining mutually satisfactory relations between urban and rural constituents. The city–county cleavage continues even in the face of the increasing synthesis of rural and urban living under modern conditions, including common facilities of transportation and communication.

City government in America is an intensive and really expansive pattern, but primarily it supplements rather than supplants other patterns. It lacks the feature of sovereignty of state or nation. It lacks the national, state, and county characteristics of geographical coverage, being applicable only to spots on the continental landscape.

A supplementary pattern

The municipal corporation is called into being when a community desires certain services or controls not normally provided by the county or other units of local government. It has been subjected wisely and unwisely to external centralized controls, sometimes at the dictate of rural political pressure.[1] It has been frequently subjected to stresses by the rapidity of urban or metropolitan growth, by the mobile influx of masses of nonvoters or passive voters, and by the resulting creation of problems faster than they could be solved.

City government, under these conditions, has evolved its own politics and political machines, types which were to be limited and modified by civic reforms, constitutional change, and reorganizational legislation, but nevertheless were to remain as unofficial essentials of the general pattern. American municipal government has registered vast improvements in both ethical and administrative standards since James Bryce wrote of its conspicuous shortcomings or since Lincoln Steffens and other muckrakers wrote of its corruption. City political machines have undergone processes of refinement rather than of death. This point has already been discussed in chapter 7 in connection with the old and new images of party politics, the decline of the old style city boss, and the prospects for rebuilding modified political machines.

City Charters

General features

American cities are incorporated under charters, or organic documents, which provide for boundaries, governmental powers and functions, methods of finance, election and appointment of officers and employees, and miscellaneous matters. Certain of these provisions in reality authorize a city to exercise governmental functions in the name of the state; others confer proprietary power. A city in its proprietary capacity, as operator of waterworks and other utilities, bears points of resemblance to a private company. In connection with such proprietary functions, a city is not immune to suit by private persons for claims or damage.

Municipal charters largely consist of laws which have been adopted by legislatures under constitutional authority, or of local provisions adopted under legislative and constitutional authority. Different portions

[1] *See* the discussion on this point in chapter 3.

of a charter may represent adoptions at different times and in different ways. The portions may or may not be assembled in one book, but they are often voluminous, New York City's running to several hundred pages. City charter powers, furthermore, must be interpreted and applied in the larger contexts of state and national powers. They are not to contravene the constitutional rights of persons, for example, or to offer unreasonable obstruction to the national regulation of interstate commerce.

Types or classes of charters

Charters are sometimes classified according to the methods by which they are formulated and put into effect. These methods of adoption may be indicated by designating charters as special act, general act, home rule, classified, and optional. Different methods or combinations of them may be used in the same state and cumulatively for the same city. There is, furthermore, no necessary difference between one method and another as to the actual form of municipal government resulting from the process. A mayor–council government, for example, might function under a charter adopted or modified by any method or any combination of methods.

Special-act charters

The special-act charter is of long standing and is still widely used. It involves a piece of legislation naming a specific city and prescribing its charter. It is not subject to any compulsory consideration of general standards of uniformity for municipal government in the state. Within constitutional limits and political sanctions, this charter process permits the widest variations among the cities of a state. It has been criticized by municipal reform groups for more than a century as being too much at the mercy of vindictive political machines controlling the legislature, as often leading to extensive logrolling manipulations among the legislative delegations from the important cities of a state, and as consuming a large amount of the official time of lawmaking bodies without attracting the serious attention of legislators or citizens in general. Cities resented and sought to resist what they considered to be unwarranted interference by the state legislature in the purely local affairs of individual cities.

General-act charters

The general-act charter grew out of this dissatisfaction with special-act charters, with some states (Ohio and Indiana as early as 1851) outlawing special legislation by constitutional amendment. Under this technique general municipal legislation became a sort of standard charter for all the cities of a state, at least for the regular functions of local government. As a scheme for correcting the abuses and haphazard nature of special-act charters, it proved objectionably rigid and failed to allow for local differences in needs and desires of cities. In practice the general laws were frequently supplemented by exceptions or modifications through special legislation. The mixture of general and special features offered one way of avoiding too little and too much uniformity between cities.

Other ways to achieve a blend of order and flexibility were sought in plans for classified and optional charters, especially where constitutional provisions severely restricted special legislation. In order to get around constitutional requirements for charters by general legislation, many states provided for charter differences on the basis of the population of the city. The classified system provides for a series of general charters, with each class applicable to all cities within a prescribed population range. If a leading city is in a distinct census class by itself, it may have the equivalent of a special charter without the name or constitutional obstacle. In some cases the courts have been so generous in approving single-city population classes that the practice of passing special-act charters has in effect been smuggled back into the state legislature.

Classified and optional charters

The optional charter system is somewhat like the numbered combination of offerings on a restaurant menu. The state, perhaps through constitutional provisions, offers a number of standard-form charters, allowing a municipality its choice from the published menu. The alternatives usually include the mayor–council, commission, and council–manager forms of government, plus certain variations of these forms. New Jersey in its Optional Municipal Charter Law of 1950 established an interesting procedure for municipalities considering adoption of optional plans. The law provided for election of a charter commission, the function of which is to study the form of government of the municipality, to compare it with other forms available under New Jersey law, and to recommend and explain to the community the option most suitable to its needs. The optional process is actually an exercise of limited municipal home rule. As in other processes, special legislation may be permissible and necessary or desirable to amplify or supplement optional charters, notably for large centers in highly urbanized states.

Home rule, as the term indicates, is designed to confer powers of initiative upon the local political unit with respect to the establishment or modification of the framework of local government. This incidentally reduces the burden of the state legislature in the sphere of local legislation. Home rule may result from constitutional power or legislative enactment or both, and it may apply to city charters as well as to particular changes in municipal–county or county government, including the consolidation or joint operation of political subdivisions. Legislative home rule is a less secure grant of power to municipalities than constitutional home rule, since any subsequent legislature could retract the grant if it so desired.[2]

Home rule

More than half of the states have general, limited or conditional provisions for city home rule, and some two-thirds of the cities over 200,000 in population have home rule. The movement has been rather

[2] For a good survey of the status of municipal home rule, *see* Kenneth E. Vanlandingham, "Municipal Home Rule in the United States," *William and Mary Law Review* 10 (Winter 1968), pp. 269–314.

intermittent since Missouri adopted a constitutional measure for such government in 1875. Home rule movements were most active at about the turn of the century and prior to World War I. Thereafter interest declined until the period following World War II when it registered a strong upsurge. Several states, among them Georgia, Louisiana, Maryland, Rhode Island, and Tennessee, adopted constitutional amendments in the 1950s to permit or increase home rule in their cities. Cities with home-rule charters are found chiefly in the West, the Middle West, and the state of New York; New England and much of the South rely on the older legislative methods of managing city charters.

Scope and limitations of home rule

Some states have constitutional provisions making all cities eligible for home-rule charters. Others have arrangements for applying the system to cities of specified population range, as over 3,500, over 10,000, or over 50,000. Some states require gubernatorial or legislative approval to make the adoption of home rule effective for a municipality. Michigan authorizes a governor's veto of home-rule adoptions. Sometimes home-rule constitutional provisions are not self-executing without legislative action, which may not be forthcoming. This was discovered by Philadelphia which had to wait twenty-seven years for legislation implementing the "permissive" amendment.

The expansion of home rule is partly checked for political considerations, sometimes by party interests and pressure groups with more power in the legislature than in the city. An agrarian legislature may hesitate to reduce its power over a large city of a different political complexion. Urban legislators are often sent to the state capital from counties rather than from cities. They may relish the continuous exercise of local power through special legislation, preferring not to grant home rule. Many cities may not feel "threatened" by the state legislature, particularly when the controlling local faction is a part of the controlling group at the state level.

Moreover, home rule, when granted, is never absolute and never establishes a "free city." It may stimulate local democracy, but it provides no necessary reduction of state administrative centralization, which may render any city financially dependent regardless of its type of charter. Other aspects and difficulties of home rule for cities and other units will be indicated in the next chapter, dealing with metropolitan problems.

Forms of City Government

Every American city charter, however adopted, provides for one of three general forms of municipal government, although for each form there are adaptations or variations. The three, in chronological order of origin, are the mayor–council, commission, and council–manager forms. The first is

Table 17–1. Form of Government in Cities, by Population Groups

		Form of Government							
	Number of	*Mayor–Council*		*Council–Manager*		*Commission*		*Town Meeting*	
Population Group	*Cities*	*No.*	*%*	*No.*	*%*	*No.*	*%*	*No.*	*%*
Over 1,000,000	6	6	100%	—		—		—	
500,000–1,000,000	20	15	75%	5	25%	—		—	
250,000–500,000	30	13	43%	14	47%	3	10%	—	
100,000–250,000	98	38	39%	51	52%	9	9%	—	
50,000–100,000	255	94	37%	142	56%	14	6%	5	2%
25,000–50,000	518	169	33%	291	56%	39	8%	19	4%
10,000–25,000	1,345	586	44%	597	44%	57	4%	105	8%
5,000–10,000	1,545	889	58%	511	33%	46	3%	99	16%
2,500–5,000	2,090	1,470	70%	431	21%	55	3%	135	7%
Total, all cities	5,907	3,280	56%	2,041	35%	223	4%	363	5%

Source: "The Structure of Local Government in the United States," *The Municipal Yearbook, 1973* (Washington, D. C.: International City Management Association, 1973), p. 4.

the most widely used. It constitutes the only form in vogue for American cities with a population of a million or more, and it easily dominates the choice of small cities and towns that must rely largely upon part-time officials rather than full-time administrators. The other forms have been accepted for hundreds of large or middle-sized cities below the million population limit. Since World War I, commission government, as strictly understood, has ceased to make gains and has even declined slightly, while the manager form has become widely attractive to cities of the middle bracket. The council–manager type rapidly supplanted or supplemented mayor–council government in the second quarter of the twentieth century, becoming the form most widely used by cities between 25,000 and 500,000 in population. The number of adoptions of the council–manager plan stood at about 500 in 1940, had doubled to approximately 1,000 by 1950, and had more than doubled again by 1974, reaching more than 2,600. The trend has tended to match the growth or advancement of expert management in business and industry.

Rise of three forms

City government by mayor and council is the nearest approach to the separation of powers or functions between legislature and executive in the old-fashioned way. It stems by title at least from cities of Britain or Europe, being an adaptation of the form which the colonists knew in their native land. It is defended as suitable to American urban politics, whether for good or ill. It might be described as the "most politicalized" type of urban government and, largely because of that characteristic, is not easily changed or replaced.

Mayor–council government

Many cities that retain this form, however, have found ways of modifying and modernizing it. The bicameral council that once was in fashion has become virtually extinct; Waterville, Maine, abandoned it in 1967 and Everett, Massachusetts, is the only reported survivor of council bicameralism. There are nine councilmen for Pittsburgh and Detroit, where they are chosen at large. Chicago holds to an old-style membership of fifty, elected by wards. Well over one-half of the cities with a population over 5,000 now have councils elected at large; and the percentage is much greater for the smaller cities. This poses a problem of minority and area representation and, to some extent, the citizen's feeling of loss of direct contact with "his" councilman. Proportional representation for council membership has been urged for some years by reformers for effective representation of minority groups and as a check to boss rule, but it has made little headway except in a small way with a few cities having council–manager government.

Only in the largest cities are councilmen found who are devoting full time to the city's business, and even then many divide their time between being a councilman and a businessman. A likely hypothesis concerning the kind of person attracted to the council is that the less time required for the councilman's job, the more likely it is that the community's most respected civic leaders will be found on the council. Generally speaking, smaller cities will have councils more nearly composed of leading citizens than will larger cities, but advocates of the council–manager plan contend that relief of councilmen from routine and time-consuming administrative detail is equally important in attracting community leadership to the council.[3]

It is customary for textbooks in local government to classify the various mayor–council systems in the United States as either the weak-mayor type or the strong-mayor type, some adding a third category called the hybrid type. To accept these categories uncritically is to run the risk of over-simplifying forms of city government and of neglecting the importance of the informal, "real power" picture of a city's government. Nevertheless, the classification is useful in differentiating the extremes of the power continuum for the mayor if these limitations are kept in mind.

The weak mayor

The weak-mayor plan inherits the spirit of Jacksonian democracy which calls for the splintering of government into many small parts, none of which can do a great deal of good or evil. Strong reliance is placed upon the council, not only for making policy, but for handling many administrative matters. The mayor is little more than a figurehead, competing as he does with other elected city officials and a variety of independent boards, commissions, committees, and officials who look primarily to the council for administrative direction and control. Although the mayor usually is weak in policymaking, the greater weakness is in administrative power, for he is denied the important managerial tools of organization, finance, and personnel. Unless a mayor is able to change drastically the formal structure of power by such means as a strong political position or a forceful personality, the incumbent under the weak-mayor plan is doomed by and large to the role of ceremonial head of the city. Figure 17–1 depicts the weak-mayor type of mayor–council government.

The strong mayor

The development of the strong-mayor form of government has never been conceived of as a new creation in governmental forms, since it differs primarily in degree from the weak-mayor type. Its development has had both formal and informal contributions. Like other public executives, many a technically weak mayor has discovered informal political ways of making himself strong, partly through civic necessity and partly through a natural cultivation of power. If not strong in his own political right, such a mayor may derive seeming power from a dominant political machine.

[3] For an analytical view of a city council in action, *see* J. Leiper Freeman, "A Case Study of the Legislative Process in Municipal Government," in John C. Wahlke and Heinz Eulau (eds.), *Legislative Behavior: A Reader in Theory and Research* (Glencoe, Ill.: The Free Press, 1959), pp. 228–237.

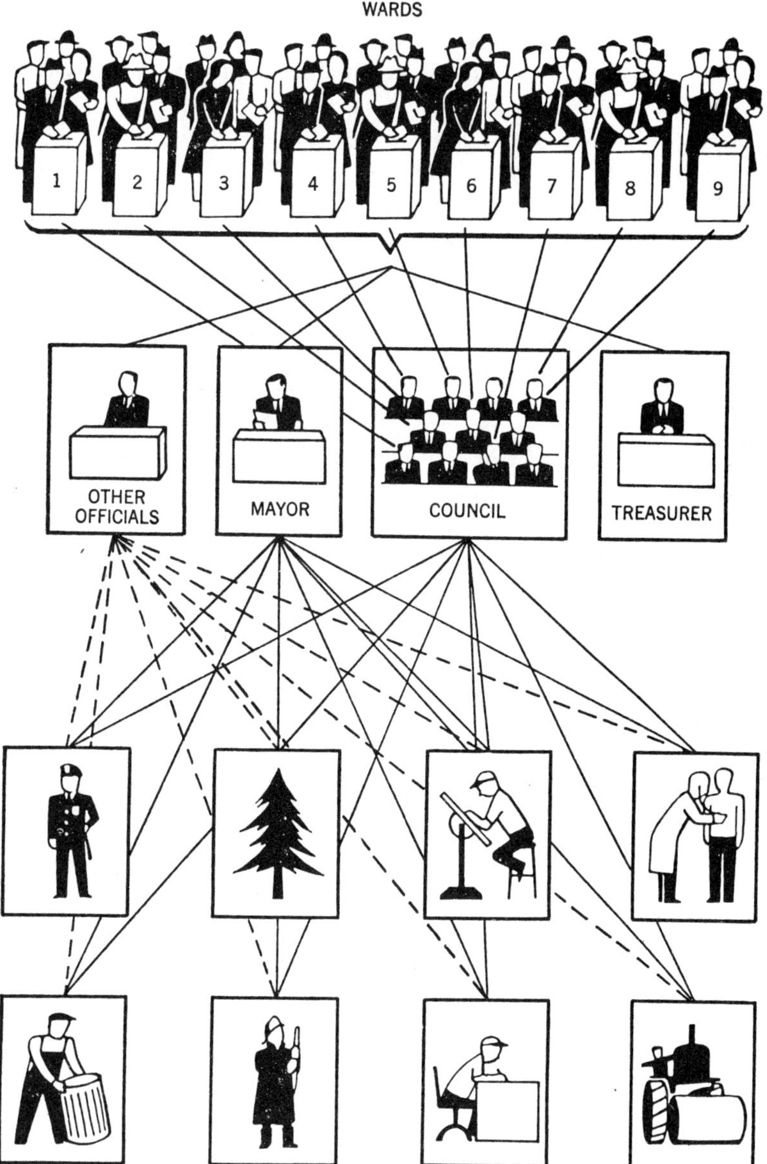

Figure 17–1. Mayor–Council Form of City Government. *Source:* National Municipal League. Reproduced by permission of the National Municipal League.

Chicago's mayors often provide effective executive government, for example, through inherent political leadership or machine support while dealing with a council that is not only legally powerful but also large. In many cities, administrative reorganization has strengthened the hand of the mayor as a genuine executive clothed with power as well as responsibility for the conduct of city affairs. An increasing number of weak-mayor cities have evolved into strong-mayor systems resembling a model of the national government that has the administrative departments clearly under the control of the president. Council surveillance over administrative details is diminished as the mayor is equipped with authority and staff assistance for administrative supervision. This includes extensive powers of appointment and removal, budget preparation and execution, day-to-day supervision, and the veto power. More recently some of the largest cities have added by charter amendment or ordinance a new feature to the strong-mayor form. They have created the position of "chief administrative officer," a kind of deputy mayor in charge of many of the more technical aspects of modern administration. The power of the "CAO" varies a great deal from city to city, but the idea is to meet the criticism that few mayors can succeed both as political leader and expert administrator, and also possibly to meet the popular challenge of the council–manager plan.

The common mixture

Most mayor–council cities fall somewhere in between the weak-mayor and strong-mayor plans, so that the most prevalent form might well be called the hybrid type. Neither the Jacksonian tradition of extreme dispersion nor the modern model of administrative integration can be said to dominate, although some elements of each can be found in most mayor–council cities today. Most cities have moved in the direction of central budgeting, purchasing, and personnel controls, but still remain a patchwork structure of independent boards and commissions not responsible to the mayor.

Commission form

The commission form of city government was designed to avoid the defects of unwieldy councils and the divided responsibility of hide-and-seek politics often involved in the old form of mayor–council government. (*See* Figure 17–2.) It got off to a dramatic start at Galveston in 1901, although approaches toward it had previously been made by other cities. A tidal wave engulfed that Texas city in 1900, entailing loss of life for thousands and property damage of many millions of dollars. Taxes could not be paid, and city services were disrupted. A huge task of reconstruction and reorganization had to be faced, and inefficient or corrupt government-as-usual was out of the question. A group of businessmen moved into the domain of public affairs, and part of their work consisted of getting a new charter from the state legislature to facilitate their emergency undertaking. Commission government was the result, and the new form, al-

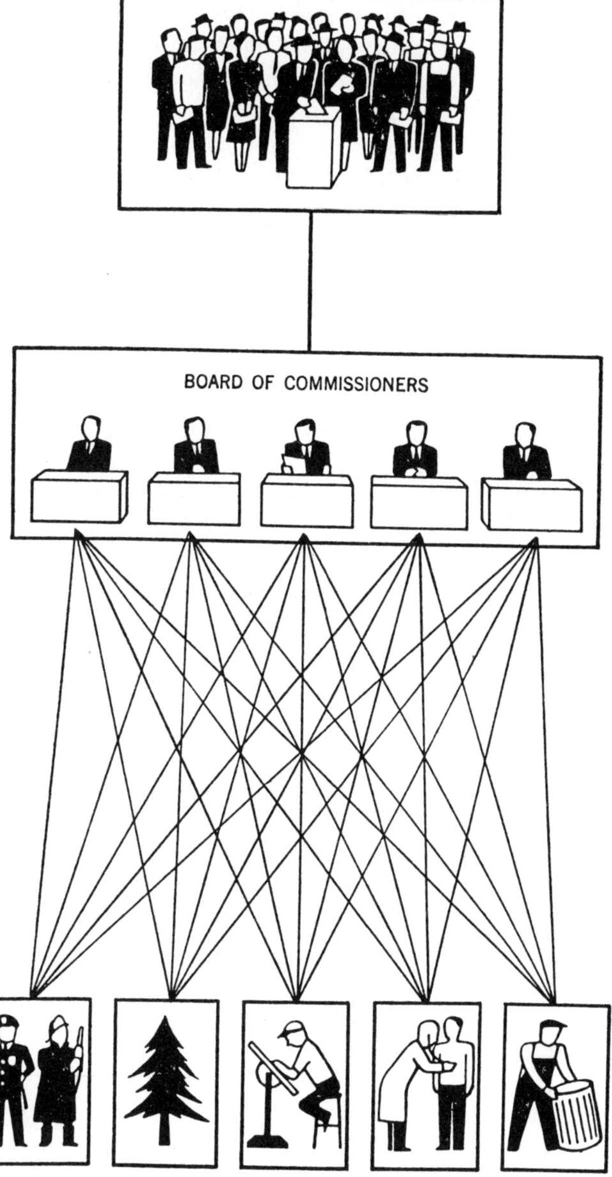

Figure 17–2. Commission Form of City Government. *Source:* National Municipal League. Reproduced by permission of the National Municipal League.

though established for temporary purposes, became permanent and provided an example for other cities, including many of smaller size as well as larger ones like Birmingham and Des Moines.

The city commission consists of three to seven members, most frequently five, who are elected at large, one of them serving as chairman and nominally the mayor. The commission as a deliberative body formulates policy much in the manner of a council; each member is administratively responsible for the management of a specific department, such as finance, public works, or public safety. Thus the same men make policy and execute it. As long as all are in agreement, government may run smoothly, but deadlocks can be unfortunate and disrupt leadership. Moreover, commissioners may tend to trade votes for the advantage of the departments over which they preside, and, where this is done, the result may be extravagant budgeting or imbalance in overall program. It is sometimes observed that the membership of a city commission, which has both legislative and executive functions, is too small for the former and too large for the latter. These shortcomings became more noticeable as a newer form of municipal government began to attract attention. Reformers and reorganization experts turned from commission to city manager as a more efficient way of meeting the growing demands made upon the American city. Galveston, birthplace of the commission plan, abandoned it in 1960 in favor of the council–manager plan.

Council–manager form

Something akin to council–manager government was established in Staunton, Virginia, in 1908, but the plan was grafted upon the mayor–council form and retained a bicameral council. Sumter, South Carolina, adopted a clear-cut council–manager form in 1912; authorities are divided on whether Staunton or Sumter should be counted the first council–manager city. But the spread of the council–manager form dates from 1914, when Dayton, Ohio, became the first large city to come under this form of municipal rule. Dayton, like Galveston earlier, had to meet sudden problems caused by a devastating flood. Civic leaders of the Chamber of Commerce, however, were already working on plans for municipal reorganization to remedy conditions of graft and inefficiency. The flood emergency intensified their effort and gave it national attention. The new charter and the new experiment lent popular impetus to the city–manager movement.

This system of municipal government recognizes the separate but coordinate functions of politics and administration. It provides for the adoption of policy, approval of financial plans, and enactment of ordinances by a council normally consisting of five to nine members elected at large on a nonpartisan ballot. The council chooses the manager, who may or may not be a resident of the city at the time of his appointment. The manager is responsible to the council, which controls his tenure and which, in turn, is responsible to the voters for the proper government of the city. All or most of the branches and agencies of the city administration, except the board or department of education, operate under the general direction of the manager, who has power to hire and fire personnel within the scope and limits of a merit system. The council's role in administration is limited to selecting and dismissing the city manager; it is prohibited from exercising direct authority over city employees. A mayor is usually selected by the council to serve only as a ceremonial officer. Figure 17–3 depicts the organization of the council–manager type of city government.

Unique features

Many claims have been made to support adoption of the council–manager plan; so many in fact, that over-enthusiastic proponents sometimes run the risk of serious disillusionment by the citizenry when *all* problems of a community are not actually solved. However, within the realm of reasonable expectation, two features of this form of government stand out above all others. One is its employment of a professionally trained, career-oriented administrator to the position of top management in municipal government, in contrast to non-professionalism in the other forms. The other outstanding feature is an institutional guarantee against stalemate between the executive and legislative branches of government, since the manager serves only at the pleasure of the council. Many other features usually associated with the manager plan, and hotly debated in campaigns for adoption, are not the exclusive property of the manager plan, and it is not unusual to find them incorporated in mayor–council charters. To mention a few: the short ballot, administrative integration, nonpartisan elections, a small council elected at large, and a council freed from petty administrative routine and detail—these are not at all incompatible with the mayor–council plan.

Regional distribution of manager adoptions

When the geographic distribution of council–manager cities is examined, a significant difference between regions appears. The use of the manager form ranges from a high 80 percent among western cities to a low of 22 percent in the Northeast. The other regions fall in between these two extremes, with the South (52 percent) being closer to the West, and the Midwest (32 percent) being closer to the Northeast. Crain and Rosenthal have analyzed the regional differences in terms of the difference in the age of western and northeastern cities, the greater enthusiasm with which the West greeted Progressivism, and the higher economic level of its population.[4]

Probably the most controversial part of the manager plan, both for governmental theory and practical politics, is the role of the manager in

[4] Robert L. Crain and Donald B. Rosenthal, "Structure and Values in Local Political Systems: The Case of Fluoridation Decisions," *The Journal of Politics* 28 (February 1966), pp. 169–195.

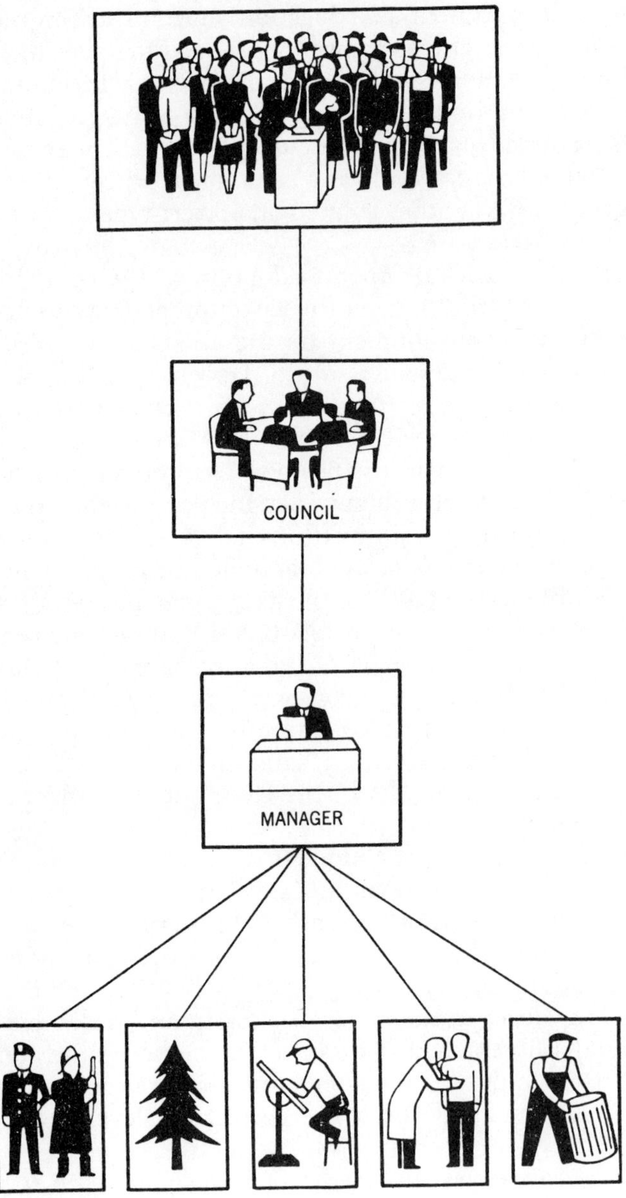

Figure 17–3. Council–Manager Form of City Government. *Source:* National Municipal League. Reproduced by permission of the National Municipal League.

policy leadership. Statements made about the theory of the council–manager plan in the early years of the movement, some by implication and others explicitly, called for a manager whose role was strictly policy execution, not policy formulation. This raised a serious question concerning the source of policy leadership, no longer provided by an elective mayor, and many argued that councils could not be expected to lead themselves and that a political vacuum existed under the manager plan. This whole controversy has been modified, though not ended, by more systematic research which examines the council–manager plan in practice as well as on paper. A study by Professor Charles Adrian of policy leadership in three middle-sized council–manager cities in Michigan revealed that the manager and administrative departments are the principal sources of policy innovation and leadership—even though the manager avoids a *public posture* of policy leadership.[5] Adrian reports other significant findings: (1) The councilman designated as mayor is not likely to become a general policy leader for the council. (2) Individual councilmen generally act as policy leaders for specific issues, and in those cases they more often act in *opposition* to particular proposals. They do not tend to be advocates or innovators.

Whence comes political leadership?

The policy role of the manager in practice is confirmed by Kammerer and DeGrove in their study of tenure problems of Florida city managers. They conclude that the manager is a political figure of considerable importance:

The manager as policy leader

> Nine out of ten of our case study cities show that citizens, civic leaders, and councilmen identify managers, both incumbents and their predecessors, with certain policy stands on many of the questions just listed. Some managers, for example, were identified as major "builders" of significant public improvements in the sense that these works stood more or less as their programs. Others were cited as the promoters and defenders of strict zoning programs to preserve a certain type and style of life. Yet others were thought of as stimulators of industrialization efforts. Some were vetoers of public construction or spending programs and defenders of the status quo.[6]

One study highlights the conflict in role expectations of managers and councilmen by contrasting their views of the city manager as policy administrator; policy innovator; political leader; policy neutralist; polit-

Manager–councilmen role conflicts

[5] Charles R. Adrian, "Leadership and Decision-Making in Manager Cities: A Study of Three Communities," *Public Administration Review* 18 (Summer 1958), pp. 208–213. *See also* Robert Paul Boynton and Deil S. Wright, "Mayor–Manager Relationships in Large Council–Manager Cities: A Reinterpretation," *Public Administration Review* 31 (January–February 1971), pp. 28–35. The issue contains a symposium on "The American City Manager."

[6] Gladys M. Kammerer and John M. DeGrove, *Florida City Managers: Profile and Tenure* (Gainesville: Public Administration Clearing Service, University of Florida, 1961), p. 29. *See also* Clarence Ridley, *The Role of the City Manager in Policy Formation* (Chicago: International City Managers' Association, 1958).

ical recruiter; and budget consultant.[7] A three-fold typology of managers was found in terms of their relation to policy initiation and advocacy in different community settings: the *administrative manager,* found primarily in homogeneous communities where he has little worry about the politics of conflict; the *factional agent,* found in communities with diverse interests, one of which is usually dominant; and the *tightrope artist,* found in cities with a multiplicity of interests, none strong enough to dominate, and requiring a manager able to maintain a delicate balance between warring factions.[8]

Any evaluation of the council–manager plan must recognize this ambivalent position of the manager with respect to political leadership. Some argue that he cannot be a strong leader, and for this reason oppose the manager plan, particularly for the largest cities, where policy matters loom so large. Others criticize the manager plan as primarily "businessmen's government," which is not responsive enough to the "labor viewpoint." Minority groups and areas at times complain that their interests are overlooked by a small council elected at large and a manager responsible to such a council. On the other hand, proponents of the plan can and do marshall an imposing array of arguments, usually centering on the idea that the proof is in the pudding—that in fact the manager plan *has* provided progressive leadership for cities and continues to meet with widespread public acceptance. Relatively few municipalities have taken steps to abandon it after trying it. City management as a career continues to grow, with an increasing number entering the field by way of graduate training and internship experience in municipal administration.[9]

Who Runs the City?

The discussion thus far in this chapter has dealt primarily with the legal roots of the municipal corporation and the more visible aspects of govern-

[7] Ronald O. Loveridge, "The City Manager in Legislative Politics," *Polity* 1 (Winter 1968), pp. 214–236.

[8] Summarized by C. Peter Magrath, Elmer E. Cornwell, Jr., and Jay S. Goodman, *The American Democracy,* 2nd ed. (New York: The Macmillan Co., 1973), p. 511.

[9] For a sympathetic account of the history of the council–manager movement by one who helped shape the movement, *see* Richard S. Childs, *The First 50 Years of the Council-Manager Form* (New York: National Municipal League, 1965). For a critique of the political thought of Childs, *see* John Porter East, *Council–Manager Government: The Political Thought of its Founder, Richard S. Childs* (Chapel Hill: University of North Carolina Press, 1965). For two articles dealing with the debate over the record of city managers in coping with social problems, *see* Delbert A. Taebel, "Managers and Riots," *National Civic Review* 57 (December 1968), pp. 554–555; and Keith F. Mulrooney, "Prologue: Can City Managers Deal Effectively with Major Social Programs?" *Public Administration Review* 31 (January–February 1971), pp. 6–13. Taebel's analysis, with supporting tables, disagrees sharply with the Kerner Commission's judgment, rather hastily concluded, that manager cities suffered more from racial outbursts.

mental structure commonly called the "form of government." It is quite possible to be a master of these subjects and still be unable to answer even in general terms the question, "Who *really* runs your city?" Do the duly elected officials really run your city? The bankers? The clergy? The newspapers? Is it the politicians or a single boss *behind* the formal officeholders? Is it a small group of wealthy oldtimers who own half of the property and have been "calling the tune" on major community decisions as long as one can remember? Or is your city government of, by, and for all the people, as democratic theory would seem to suggest? The question has obvious ambiguities and is fraught with problems of definition and assumptions, but it is still sufficiently important for an increasing number of sociologists and political scientists to have begun to focus their research interests on community power structure and decision making. Space limitations prevent a full review of all of the many community power studies completed in the last two or three decades, but it will be helpful to examine briefly a few of these studies.

A decision-making elite

Two separate studies have been made of the power structure of "Regional City" (Atlanta), a southern city of about a half-million people. The first study, by Floyd Hunter, found a single pyramidal power structure with some thirty key decision makers running the community. These men, the top business leaders in the city, stayed in communication with each other in a variety of ways, were said to make the important decisions for the community, and then pass the word down to a few hundred persons making up the next lower level in the pyramid.[10] The inner circle of decision makers did not include blacks or labor leaders, although they were acknowledged to be growing in importance. The power of this "elite" was greatest at the city level of government and diminished progressively at higher levels. Many political scientists reacted violently to many aspects of Hunter's study, including the conspiracy theory which seems to be implied, his failure to consider many subtle limitations on the power of the elite, and a methodology which seemed to guarantee that decision makers would be found, whether they actually existed or not.[11]

Atlanta revisited

A second study of Atlanta, by M. Kent Jennings, followed the Hunter study in point of time, but deviated from it significantly in the kind of power structure found.[12] Jennings studied three kinds of participants in community decision making: "prescribed influentials," or those with for-

[10] Floyd Hunter, *Community Power Structure: A Study of Decision-makers* (Chapel Hill: University of North Carolina Press, 1953).

[11] *See,* for example, Herbert Kaufman and Victor Jones, "The Mystery of Power," *Public Administration Review* 14 (Summer 1954), pp. 205–212. Hunter's book is in the same vein as C. Wright Mills, *The Power Elite* (New York: Oxford University Press, 1956), although Mills denies that his is a conspiracy theory.

[12] M. Kent Jennings, *Community Influentials: The Elites of Atlanta* (New York: Free Press of Glencoe, 1964).

mally defined political roles; "attributed influentials," or those who are perceived to be influential; and "economic dominants," or those occupying major economic posts. He concluded that the economic dominants were least involved in community decision making and exercised relatively little political power. Concerning the various decision-making roles (initiation, priority-fixing, promotion, legitimation, and implementation), the formal political leaders of Atlanta made a much stronger showing of power and influence than Hunter's previous study indicated. Jennings concludes that the power structure is not monolithic, but that it lies midway between a monolithic and an amorphous typology.[13]

Multi-centered power structure

Studies of other cities have revealed a "polynucleated" or multicentered power structure rather than a pyramidal form. Robert A. Dahl's rigorous study of "who governs" New Haven, Connecticut, provides a rich body of new insights into urban community decision making.[14] He found many centers of power in New Haven, rather than a single pyramidal elite, and each group's power depended on their supply of such political resources as time, interest, ability, experience, friends, money, etc. A combination of resources used to achieve power in one situation will not necessarily assure power in a different situation. Dahl, while denying the concept of the single elite, suggests that the mayor's office comes the closest to being a single focal point for most community decision making.

A contest for prizes

Similarly, the study of New York City by Sayre and Kaufman found no single pyramid of decision makers, but rather a system of separate and numerous islands of power.[15] They describe the political process in New York as a contest for prizes with the contestants being party leaders, officials, bureaucrats, the electorate, and a whole host of nongovernmental groups. They suggest that this "multi-centered" system of government is more favorable to the status quo than to innovations, but that over the past sixty years it has been surprisingly creative and adaptive. One of the most sophisticated conceptual and theoretical contributions to the growing list of studies of community power structure is a comparative study of four

[13] For a discussion of types of community power structure *see* Peter H. Rossi, "Power and Community Structure," *Midwest Journal of Political Science* 4 (November 1960), pp. 390–401. He suggests four types of local political structures: pyramidal (highly centralized), caucus rule (the "cozy few"), polylith (separate power structures), and amorphous.

[14] Robert A. Dahl, *Who Governs?* (New Haven: Yale University Press, 1961). The changing social and political characteristics of New Haven's mayors, as classified by Dahl in different periods of recruitment, are contrasted with Chicago patterns by Donald S. Bradley and Mayer N. Zald in "From Commercial Elite to Political Administrator: The Recruitment of Mayors of Chicago," *American Journal of Sociology* 71 (September 1965), pp. 153–167.

[15] Wallace S. Sayre and Herbert Kaufman, *Governing New York City* (New York: Russell Sage Foundation, 1960).

American communities by Agger, Goldrich, and Swanson.[16] They find several kinds of power structures and regimes defined by such facts of political life as distributions of power, illegitimate sanctions, and leadership ideologies. They conclude that American communities are, in many ways, microcosms of our national political system and, taken together, constitute a significant portion of that larger system. Two other political scientists, Bachrach and Baratz, disagreed with the "reputational" methodology of Floyd Hunter in his original study of Atlanta, but came to somewhat the same conclusion after an extensive study of power and poverty in Baltimore.

Community power and non-decision politics

They also concluded that the "mobilization of bias" in a city is to keep certain groups deprived and to protect other groups who are benefitted by the status quo. The primary method is "non-decision," by which the key questions of politics—the classic "who gets what, when, and how?"—are kept out of visible political conflict. Bachrach and Baratz contend that non-decisions in Baltimore kept black interests from coming to the forefront of the public decision-making arena for many years. However, federal aid, black protest, and changing white attitudes gradually brought black issues into the visible mainstream of local politics.[17]

The new convergence of power

A "new convergence" of power in contemporary urban politics is described by Robert H. Salisbury.[18] This structure is headed and sometimes led by the mayor, and includes two principal active groupings that provide the initiative for major community programs—locally oriented economic interests and the professional workers in technical city-related programs. Salisbury contends that whatever groups of voters constitute the mayor's successful base of support, although they are an indispensible third element of power, are severely limited in their power to direct specific policy choices. The irony behind this convergence of power elements in the modern city, according to Salisbury, is the apparent lack of resources available to this remarkable coalition of interests for solving the major urban problems now dominating the civic agenda.

There still is no easy answer to the question of who runs the city, but it is becoming increasingly clear that the single pyramidal conception is not a complete picture, at best, and is totally erroneous in many situations. Many economically powerful corporation executives refuse to "take sides" in many community issues for fear of hurting the company. Still

[16] Robert E. Agger, Daniel Goldrich, and Bert E. Swanson, *The Rulers and the Ruled: Political Power and Impotence in American Communities* (New York: John Wiley and Sons, 1964).

[17] Peter Bachrach and Morton S. Baratz, *Power and Poverty: Theory and Practice* (New York: Oxford University Press, 1970).

[18] Robert H. Salisbury, "Urban Politics: The New Convergence of Power," *Journal of Politics* 26 (November 1964), pp. 775–797.

other citizens may be highly influential but in practice take an interest in only one or two kinds of community decisions. Others appear to have unlimited power, but in reality have learned to recognize those times when it is safer not to try to cross certain lines. It does seem true, however, that the formal officials of city government are increasingly exercising power in their own right, rather than constituting mere "fronts" for invisible elite citizens hovering in the background. This should offer hope for the democratic ideal of popular control of the decision-making process in cities.[19]

Municipal Administration

Range and growth

The increase in scope and cost of municipal administration is the source of political and budgetary headaches in many of our cities, large and small. It accounts for much of the interest in the city–manager type of government, with its emphasis on efficiency and economy. The increase results from the expansion of old functions and the rise of new functions for city governments. Law enforcement is an old function, but it becomes a greater task with the creation of more laws and ordinances to enforce and the need to devise more ways for violating or evading them, often for profit. Mass transit and traffic regulation are old functions with new problems, including the seemingly unsolvable problem of adequate public and private parking. Firefighting and prevention are old functions with new and expensive methods. Old and new steps are involved in dealing with juvenile delinquency, providing recreation facilities, regulating health and sanitary conditions, maintaining water supply, administering building and rental regulations, handling welfare cases, and carrying on other important activities. Many of the larger cities also maintain airports beyond their corporate boundaries.

[19] For more detailed discussion of community power structure, *see* Peter H. Rossi, "Power and Community Structure," pp. 390–401; Oliver P. Williams, "A Typology for Comparative Local Government," *Midwest Journal of Political Science* 5 (May 1961), pp. 150–164; Charles R. Adrian (ed.), *Social Science and Community Action* (East Lansing: Michigan State University Continuing Education Service, 1961); E. W. Noland, "The Roles of Top Business Executives in Urban Development," *Research Previews* 8 (February 1961), pp. 1–8; Robert V. Presthus, *Men At the Top, A Study in Community Power* (Ithaca, N. Y.: Cornell University Press, 1964); Nelson W. Polsby, *Community Power and Political Theory* (New Haven: Yale University Press, 1963); Jack L. Walker, "A Critique of the Elitist Theory of Democracy," *American Political Science Review* 60 (June 1966), pp. 296–305; and Robert L. Crain and Donald B. Rosenthal, "Structure and Values in Local Political Systems," pp. 169–195. For an excellent summary of the essence of American city politics, categorized as "broker leadership," and a comparison with Metro Toronto's "executive-centered decision-making," *see* Harold Kaplan, "Politics and Policy-Making in Metropolitan Toronto," *Canadian Journal of Economics and Political Science* 31 (November 1965), pp. 538–551.

The wide functions of government and service bring the city into various financial and operational contacts with other units and agencies of governance, whether county, regional, state, or national. Our expanding cities are continually in need of more funds and are increasingly looking to the state and federal governments for funds. These central governments have something to say about requests for them to furnish aid to cities for public works, sewage systems, street improvements, and the like.

Administrative organization

Every city of substantial size, whatever its type of government, has an organization of agencies or departments, more or less responsible to a central authority of mayor, manager, commission, or council. The heads of the different departments as well as the members of boards and agencies may be elected by the voters or by the council, or they may be appointed by the chief executive, according to state laws, city charter, and size of the city. Each department is organized from its head to its lowest rung of common labor and manned by personnel selected by political criteria or merit tests. While organization is complex for the larger cities, it is rather simple for villages and small cities and may consist of only two key administrative officers, sometimes known as "Mr. Inside" and "Mr. Outside." The "inside" man may be the director of finance, or simply the city clerk, but he will be responsible for much of the housekeeping work related to finance, personnel, purchasing, and the routine details of administration. The "outside" man is usually named director of public works and will handle such matters as street maintenance, parks, water supply, sewers, and planning.

A large city is likely to have a personnel office or board to recruit, examine, and certify applicants for appointment by the employing officers and also to perform duties with respect to position classification, promotion, salary scales, tenure, and other employee relations. Such a city must likewise have administrative officers to conduct financial affairs, including budgeting, purchasing, accounting, auditing, and general treasury management. It must have officials and facilities for handling tax matters, such as assessment and collection of property levies, issuing licenses of various kinds and receiving payments for them, and sometimes gathering in city sales and income taxes. The management of financial and personnel matters vitally affects the scope and effectiveness of all the agencies of a city administration, for no unit of government can function without men and money.

It is further recognized in city government, as in other government, that effective operation, or line work, requires general staff work at the center. The central staff organization of an increasing number of large and medium-sized cities includes a full-time officer or agency for research, study, and advice in the wide field of city planning. The recommendations of the planning authority, insofar as they are adopted, affect both the work of the operating agencies and the trend of city development. As in other levels of government, the planning establishment is likely to be closely linked to the chief executive authority. State planning assistance may be available to urban communities, especially the smaller ones. The growing number of state-level departments of community development is discussed in chapter 3.

Land-use planning and zoning

Closely related to planning is the work or process of zoning through laws or ordinances with administration by boards or officers. Zoning is really enforced planning to designate or preserve areas for residential, commercial, industrial, or other purposes, with modifications and combinations of these classifications. It affects both public and private enterprise, and zoning authorities are often subjected to strong conflicting pressures. Once a city takes the step of seeking to regulate land use and passes a comprehensive zoning ordinance, it then is faced with the never-ending task of "holding the line" against creeping blight by "spot zoning" amendments and the granting of variances and exceptions. Decisions or recommendations of planning agencies are sometimes reversed by higher authority, such as a city council. It is common for the tradition of "councilmanic courtesy" to exist in city councils, giving the individual councilman virtually complete control over zone changes in his own district.

Dilemmas in planning theory and practice

The wide gap between city planners' aspirations and actual accomplishments is the subject of an important and disturbing analysis of the city planning process by Alan Altshuler.[20] In the light of political and administrative realities he examines the widely accepted premise that comprehensive, rational land-use planning will make cities better places in which to live, and concludes that the gap between theory and practice may be unbridgeable. Altshuler argues that as the city planner makes accommodations to avoid political opposition and controversy, he undermines his claim to professional status, and to a "rational" and "comprehensive" approach to achieving city goals. The response to Altshuler's indictment has been more intensive soul searching among those interested in city planning; the result will undoubtedly be more planning rather than less.

New-town planning

Frustration with the problems of remedial planning for old and congested cities and dissatisfaction with homogenized suburban sprawl have led some urban planners to turn to the concept of new-town planning, developed by an English urban planner in the early 1900s. Ebenezer Howard called for cities built from scratch and combining the best of two worlds—

[20] Alan A. Altshuler, *The City Planning Process: A Political Analysis* (Ithaca, N. Y.: Cornell University Press, 1965). *See also* Francene Rabinovitz, *City Politics and Planning* (New York: Atherton Press, 1969), for an assessment of the politics of planning in six New Jersey cities. *See also* John Friedman, "The Future of Comprehensive Urban Planning: A Critique," *Public Administration Review* 31 (May–June 1971), pp. 315–325.

the full variety of urban life and the beauty and serenity of the country.[21] The new-town concept in the United States was still in the embryo stage in the early 1970s, despite the two prominent experiments of Columbia, Maryland, and Reston, Virginia, and despite the inauguration in 1969 of federal assistance through the New Communities Program by the department of Housing and Urban Development. Furthermore, new-town planning in the United States is largely in private hands, while elsewhere in the world it has been primarily a governmental venture.

Reston and Columbia

Both Columbia and Reston were designed to be more than sprawling suburban bedroom communities for commuters. They were to be towns where some 100,000 people of all ages and income levels lived and worked and played, with easy access to stores, theaters, parks, churches, and places of employment. Rigid controls were adopted by the developers to prevent such things as neon signs, television antennas, permanent clothes lines, and visible trash cans. James Rouse, the builder of Columbia, planned not to make a profit for at least 10 years; he considers large amounts of "patient" money as one of the prerequisites for planning and building a new town. One of the more unusual new towns planned in the mid-1970s was "Soul City" in Warren County, North Carolina. Floyd McKissick, once head of the Congress of Racial Equality, switched his party affiliation from Democrat to Republican and supported Nixon's re-election bid in 1972. Following the Republican victory, he received a tentative guarantee of $14 million in Soul City bonds from HUD. Although planned to be open to all races, McKissick's dream is to create an urban center of 50,000 specifically directed toward developing new economic opportunities for blacks.

The new towns have their critics, as might be expected. The high cost of homes has made them predominately upper middle-class communities, although some housing for families on welfare has been provided. Early studies revealed that some of the higher income blacks who moved to Columbia worry about having turned their backs on the ghetto. Retired persons enjoyed the easy access to community facilities, but complained of the high cost of living, while teenagers expressed dissatisfaction with their relative isolation and inaccessibility to other teenagers. New-town planning is complicated by the unwillingness to trust a municipal or county government in the early stages, and by a strong reliance on private "community associations" with membership dues in lieu of town taxes.[22]

[21] Howard's *Garden Cities of Tomorrow* (Cambridge, Mass.: MIT Press, 1965) is generally accepted as the classic work on new-town planning.

[22] For a discussion of the problems of new-town governance by private homeowners' or community associations, *see* Royce Hanson, "The Current Governance of New Towns," in *New Towns: Laboratories for Democracy,* the report of The Twentieth Century Fund Task Force on the Governance of New Towns (New York: The Twentieth Century Fund, 1971).

New towns are undoubtedly the wave of the future in America, but they still had a long way to go in the early 1970s.

Public safety and fire protection

The city as a concentrated center of society requires concentrated attention to the problems of public safety. (Urban police protection is covered in chapter 19 on law enforcement.) Fire protection is more completely a local responsibility than the maintenance of law and order. Fire and police services are sometimes combined in one department, particularly in the smaller cities. But fighting fire is different from fighting crime, even though a large fire creates problems for the police. Firemen, like policemen, perform miscellaneous services besides their primary task; they may answer calls for trapped persons or animals, flooded homes, storm damage, and the like. Normally there is no attempt to corrupt fire departments and to limit their effectiveness comparable to the kinds of pressure often brought to bear upon police departments; hence, American urban fire service is generally efficient, employing competent men as well as modern mechanized equipment. However, fire losses in American municipalities far exceed the losses in European cities, largely because of differences in the construction of buildings and in methods or habits of fire protection. Many American cities have antiquated building codes, sometimes with inadequate inspection and enforcement to avoid fire hazards. Political "pull" at times relaxes the administration of regulations. Preventing fire, like preventing crime, is a large problem for urban America.

Public works and utilities

City governments are concerned with the construction, maintenance, and use or operation of various types of public works and enterprise. It is often the rule for original construction to be done by private contractors, with maintenance or operation becoming the responsibility of city authorities. Privately owned water systems were once rather common among American cities, but municipal ownership prevails widely today. Many cities in the Tennessee Valley have municipal authorities that operate under state and federal laws in purchasing electricity from TVA and distributing it to consumers. Similar municipal electric service is to be found in other river regions with public power projects. Most of our cities, however, depend upon private enterprise to provide the utilities of heat, light, power, transportation, and communication. The private companies provide and sell the services under state or local franchises and regulations, which are supposed to safeguard the public interest and also permit a fair return for the utility operations. Private enterprise in housing has been supplemented by public provision of accommodations for low-income families in crowded cities, often on lands cleared of unsightly slums. Hundreds of municipal housing authorities and projects have been launched since 1937 under state and federal legislation and local sponsorship.

Cities have been centers of art and learning since the ancient days of Athens and Alexandria. As indicated in other portions of this text, American cities generally have their own school systems within a state framework of financial support and standards. The city school board is locally elected or appointed, and the board generally chooses the superintendent. The school administration thus has a degree of technical separation from the routine politics and activities of municipal government. But through the purse and public interest the school system is linked to the fortunes of the whole urban community. It is by no means free from the influence of pressure groups, whether of teachers, parents, or local political powers. Much of the pressure is for achieving educational goals, with no little emphasis on professional standards and improvement of facilities. Sometimes, however, there are bitter battles over school issues, with victory not always on the side of progress. The politics of public education is discussed in more detail in chapter 22.

Education

Aside from public school systems, more than a dozen cities support or partly support municipal colleges or universities, notably New York, Cincinnati, Toledo, Louisville, and Omaha. Nearly every important city has a public library, customarily administered by a trained librarian responsible to a lay board. The library of a large city has a large staff and branches requiring additional personnel. The New York Public Library is one of the largest in the world, ranking next to the Library of Congress in size in the United States.

Regional City

The life, work, and culture of Americans are geared to a multiplicity of cities more than to the fifty states. For us, "civilization," as Lewis Mumford has observed, "is citification." Every important city in the United States is the hub of a regional society, a regional economy, and a regional mixture of government. Politically the large city is the central member of a community of communities, in which no member is sole master of its civic destiny, but each has autonomous ways of speeding up or retarding the order and progress of the urban whole. In the regional orbit no man, no family lives alone or in a single community, but each lives in a combination of concentric and overlapping communities. In this complex of civic units, a strong sense of community laissez faire and self-containment often prevails over and above any general concept of regional good. Intercommunity adjustment may be further hindered or complicated by the inertia or opposition of dominant private interests, although they are sometimes subject to extra-regional and national control.[23] Metropolitan communities have many aspects that conform to the needs and makings of city-states, if there were any constitutional practicability for such a step. Clearly, the regionalizing of urban life has outstripped the regionalizing of governmental institutions. We have metropolitan communities without metropolitan government.

The prospect before us

Reasons of ethics, esthetics, and maximum utility suggest the setting of limits to the laissez faire of urban communities, just as limits have been set to the laissez faire of urban individuals. Limits and standards for the purposes of regional synthesis and coordination may be applicable to landscape and skyscape, to highways and alleyways, to the construction and services of home, shop, and office. The circumscriptions at the same time should allow leeway for local community diversity, incentive, and responsibility. It might be observed that no greater problem of government this side of the Iron Curtain confronts the American people than the balanced task of functionalizing and systematizing our metropolitan regions for decent and democratic living. The next chapter explores this unfinished business.

[23] This theme is discussed, with no tendency toward understatement, in Robert S. Allen (ed.), *Our Fair City* (New York: The Vanguard Press, 1947). The nationally controlled city of Washington, D. C., is uniquely omitted from coverage by Allen's muckraking symposium.

SUPPLEMENTARY READINGS

Adrian, C. R. *Governing Urban America*. Revised ed. New York: McGraw-Hill Book Co., 1961.

Banfield, Edward C. *The Unheavenly City: The Nature and Future of Our Urban Crisis*. Boston: Little, Brown and Co., 1970.

———. *The Unheavenly City Revisited*. Boston: Little, Brown and Co., 1974.

Banfield, Edward C., and Wilson, James Q. *City Politics*. Cambridge, Mass.: Harvard University Press, 1963.

Banovetz, James M., ed. *Managing the Modern City*. Washington, D. C.: International City Management Association, 1971.

Childs, Richard S. *Civic Victories*. New York: Harper & Row, 1952.

Daland, Robert T., ed. *Comparative Urban Research: The Administration and Politics of Cities*. Beverly Hills, Calif.: Sage Publications, 1969.

Greer, Scott. *The Emerging City: Myth or Reality*. New York: The Free Press of Glencoe, 1962.

Hays, Forbes B. *Community Leadership: The Regional Plan Association of New York*. New York: Columbia University Press, 1965.

Kammerer, Gladys; Farris, Charles D.; DeGrove, John M.; and Clubok, Alfred B. *The Urban Political Community: Profiles in Town Politics*. Boston: Houghton Mifflin Co., 1963.

Lineberry, Robert L., and Sharkansky, Ira. *Urban Politics and Public Policy*. New York: Harper & Row, 1971.

Long, Norton. *The Unwalled City: Reconstituting the Urban Community*. New York: Basic Books, 1972.

Mills, Warner E., Jr., and Davis, Harry R. *Small City Government: Seven Cases in Decision Making.* New York: Random House, 1962.

Mumford, Lewis. *The Culture of Cities.* New York: Harcourt, Brace and World, 1938.

Municipal Manpower Commission. *Governmental Manpower for Tomorrow's Cities.* New York: McGraw-Hill Book Co., 1963.

Municipal Year Book. Chicago: International City Management Association. Annual publication.

National Civic Review. New York: National Municipal League. Monthly, except August.

National Commission on Urban Problems. *Building the American City: Report of the National Commission on Urban Problems.* New York: Praeger, 1969.

Peterson, E. R., ed. *Cities Are Abnormal.* Norman: University of Oklahoma Press, 1946.

Schultze, William A. *Urban and Community Politics.* North Scituate, Mass.: Duxbury Press, 1974.

Shaw, Frederick. *The History of the New York City Legislature.* New York: Columbia University Press, 1954.

Stone, Harold A.; Price, Don K.; and Stone, Kathryn H. *City Manager Government in the United States.* Chicago: Public Administration Service, 1940.

Tunnard, Christopher, and Reed, H. H. *American Skyline.* Boston: Houghton Mifflin Co., 1955.

Weaver, Robert C. *Dilemmas of Urban America.* Cambridge, Mass.: Harvard University Press, 1965.

18

Local Government: Metropolitics

Trends in metropolitics

When Charles E. Merriam made his frequently quoted statement that "the adequate organization of modern metropolitan areas is one of the great unsolved problems of modern politics,"[1] he might well have added that things would get worse before they would get better. In reporting the publication of Robert C. Wood's book *1400 Governments,* which gave a bleak picture of local government in the New York metropolitan region, *The New York Times* headlined its story as follows: "EXPERT PREDICTS REGIONAL CHAOS WITHIN 25 YEARS; More Urban Sprawl, Noise, Traffic, Air Pollution and Blight Foreseen; AREA DISUNITY BLAMED; Study Discounts Possibility of Accord Among 1,467 Local Governments."[2] While the New York region provides the outstanding example of the impact of the modern population explosion on traditional local governmental structure, it is by no means alone in its situation. The 1950 census report revealed that for the first time more than one-half of the people of the United States lived within the large urban centers designated "standard metropolitan areas"; and by 1970 the metropolitan majority had risen to 71 percent. (*See* Figure 18–1.) The government of these metropolitan areas is frequently described in such terms as "scrambled eggs," "hopeless chaos," and "political disintegration," because each metropolis is governed by a strange proliferation of counties, cities, townships, and special districts.

[1] In Merriam's preface to Victor Jones, *Metropolitan Government* (Chicago: University of Chicago Press, 1942), p. ix.

[2] *New York Times,* July 17, 1961. Wood's volume, published by the Harvard University Press, is one of nine resulting from the New York Metropolitan Regional Study.

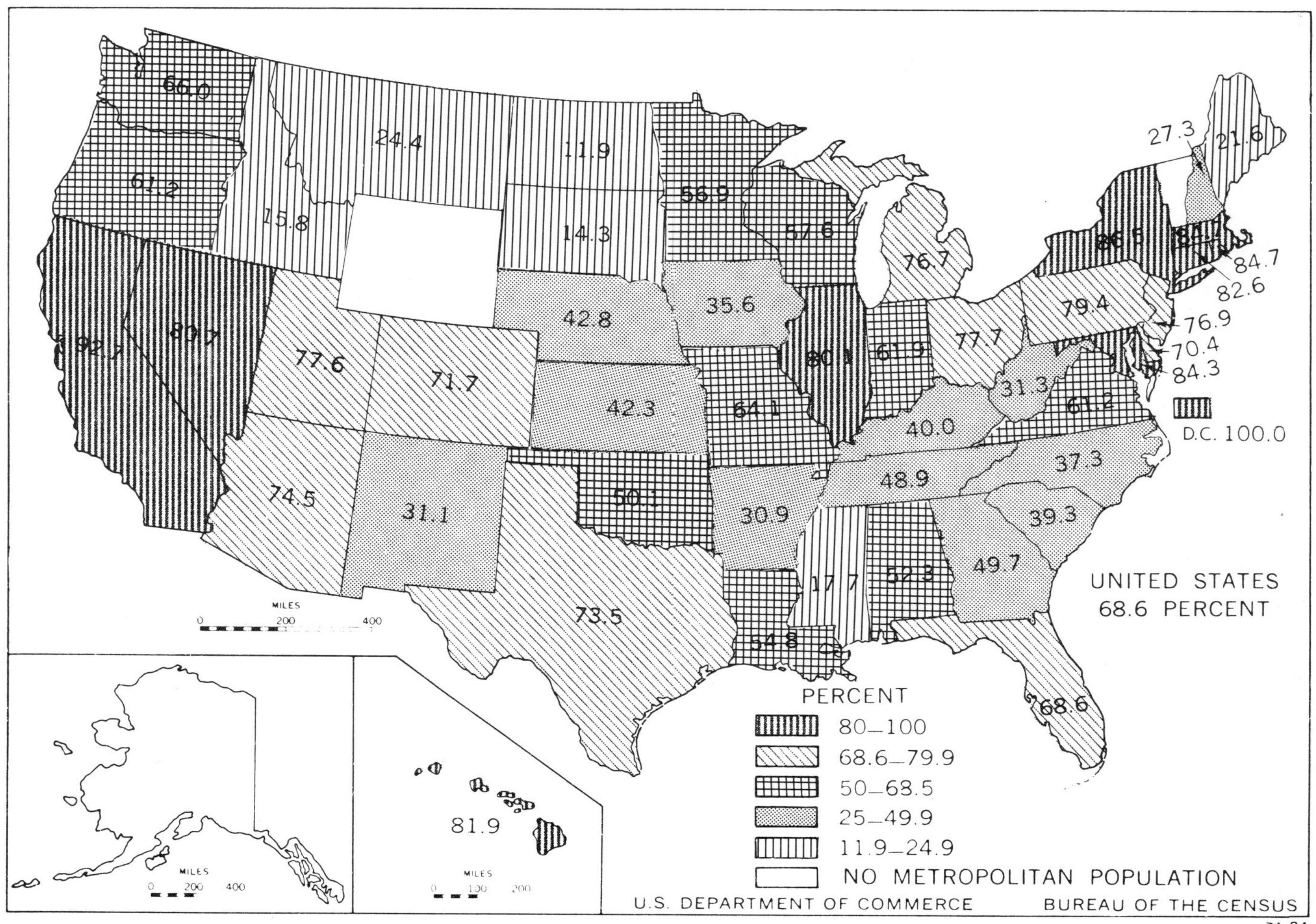

Figure 18–1. Percent of Population in Standard Metropolitan Statistical Areas by States, 1970. *Source:* Bureau of the Census, *General Population Characteristics: United States Summary* (Washington, D. C.: U. S. Department of Commerce, 1972), p. 34.

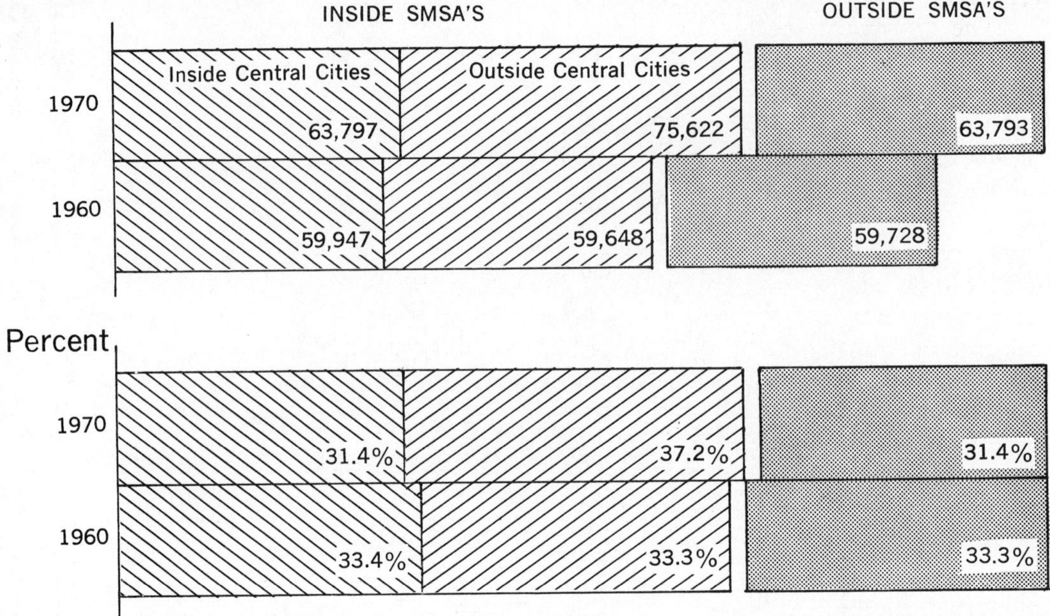

Figure 18–2. Population Inside and Outside SMSA's, 1970 and 1960. *Source:* Bureau of the Census, *General Population Characteristics: United States Summary* (Washington, D. C.: U. S. Department of Commerce, 1972), p. 34.

The outward push of the population from the central core city has been so strong that more than one-half (54.2 percent) of all metropolitan area population is now located *outside* the corporate boundaries of the central cities. (*See* Figure 18–2.) More than three times as many Bostonians live outside Boston's city limits as live inside (2,112,629 to 641,071). "Legal" Pittsburgh citizens are outnumbered by suburbanites by the same numbers as "legal" Bostonians, 1,881,128 to 520,117. Although St. Louis can rightfully claim more than 2,360,000 as the population of its metropolitan area, the incorporated city of St. Louis contains only 622,236. In even more striking contrast, the San Francisco–Oakland area numbers more than 3,100,000 in population, but San Francisco proper can claim only 715,674 as residents.

More and more the metropolis is being divided into one complex set of governments for the place of work of its citizens and another complex set of governments for their place of residence, with intricate overlapping and intertwining of the two. Because the government of metropolitan areas constitutes a special problem distinct from city government as such, this chapter gives separate treatment to developments and trends in a field that might well be called "metropolitics."

Metropolitan growth

The growth of metropolitan areas was reported in the censuses of 1920, 1930, and 1940 under the designation of "metropolitan districts," revealing a steady increase in the number of such districts, with 96 in 1930 and 140 in 1940. The aggregate population of these districts in 1940 was about 63,000,000 or 47.8 percent of the national population. The number of metropolitan areas had risen to 168 by 1950, to 212 by 1960, and to 264 by 1972; they contained more than 143 million persons, or 71 percent of the national population. The terminology used for reporting metropolitan area population has changed from time to time, but a metropolitan area usually includes a core city of 50,000 or more, plus the surrounding county (or counties) that are designated as reasonably urbanized, contiguous, and interdependent with the core city.[3]

During the period from 1930 to 1940 the central cities as a whole increased in population only 4.7 percent, while the suburbs increased 14.4 percent. Several of the central cities actually declined in population, including Philadelphia, Cleveland, St. Louis, and Boston. Between 1940 and 1950 the suburban areas continued to outgain the central core cities, 35.6 percent to 13.9 percent, although the central cities showed a more respectable rate of increase than in the previous decade.

Metropolitan growth was even more striking during the decade of the 1950s, in contrast to the slowdown in the rest of the country. The 1950–1960 increase in metropolitan population was 23.6 million, in contrast to a 4.4 million increase in the rest of the United States—or a rate of 26.4 percent and 7.1 percent, respectively. In spite of the general slowdown in population increase between 1960 and 1970, metropolitan growth exceeded non-metropolitan growth 19.8 million to 4.1 million, or a rate of 16.6 percent to 6.8 percent. Within the metropolitan areas between 1950 and 1960, the suburban fringe grew by 48.5 percent, while the core cities grew at a rate of only 10.8 percent. Between 1960 and 1970 the suburban fringe continued to outgrow the core cities, 26.8 percent to 6.4 percent. Nine of the ten largest cities in the United States lost population, accord-

[3] The Bureau of the Census replaced the "metropolitan district" with the "standard metropolitan area" in 1950, using entire counties containing a central city with at least 50,000 population, or groups of contiguous counties (or towns, in New England), as the basic unit. In addition, the "urbanized area" was utilized in its reporting first in 1950, excluding certain noncontiguous outlying areas and not relying on the county as the basic unit. In 1960 the name of the "SMA" was changed to the "standard metropolitan statistical area" and slight modifications in definition were made. Still another category, the "standard consolidated area," was devised to fit the situations of New York and Chicago, where several contiguous SMSA's appear to have increasingly strong interrelationships. In 1971 the U. S. Office of Management and Budget issued still another revision, permitting reasonable equivalents to the 50,000 population core city to be included. This added 21 SMSA's to the 1970 total of 243.

ing to the 1960 census, Los Angeles being the one exception. Houston gained population, and was a newcomer in the top ten in 1960. Seven of the top ten lost population between 1960 and 1970; Los Angeles, Houston, and New York gained.

Urban push

What are the reasons for this tremendous movement to the fringe of every large city and the accompanying stagnation or slowdown in growth of the central city? The answer is threefold, involving first of all a vigorous outward push caused by the central city itself. Such conditions in the heart of the city as smoke, dirt, noise, and congestion join to induce the inhabitants to seek a more pleasant place of residence. The in-migration of minority groups to the core city has disturbed middle-class dwellers and contributed to the "white flight" out of the city. The relentless encroachment of business and industrial establishments on residential areas, the development of slums and blighted areas, and the steady increase in property taxes also contribute to the outward push.

Suburban pull

A second factor explaining the suburban movement is the pull or magnetism of the many desirable features of the suburbs, particularly when compared with life in the central city. Clean air, more room, and quiet are important attractions, as well as the expectation of lower taxes and better government, though the latter are often deluding motivating forces. The cumulative effect of this pull of the periphery becomes clear when middle- and upper-income families feel compelled to move to the suburbs in order "to keep up with the Joneses," when retail and service establishments begin moving out to follow their customers, and when industries move to the suburbs in search of a more stable labor supply. The role of the suburbs as less vulnerable sites for defense industries is of great potential importance.

In addition to the push of the central city and the pull of the outlying suburbs, there are other factors which, while not actually causing the suburban movement, have played an important role in facilitating it. The development of modern transportation and communication methods for example, made the exodus possible. The automobile, the various rapid transit systems, and the wide expressways have transformed previously stationary city-dwellers into a highly mobile metropolitan population.

Number of local governments

One of the few things that seem forever stationary in this day of metropolitan population movements is the political boundary line. No metropolis (or state) has seen fit to create a single unit of government capable of governing an entire urban community. Rather than 264 units of local government for that number of metropolitan areas, there was a total of 22,185 separate units of government in existence within 264 standard metropolitan areas in 1972. The American metropolis may not be the *best* governed area imaginable, but it may well be the most governed, from a numerical standpoint. The distribution of governmental

Table 18–1. Number of Local Governments in Metropolitan Areas, 1957–1972

	1972	*1967*	*1962*	*1957*
Counties	444	404	310	266
Municipalities	5,467	4,977	4,142	3,422
Townships	3,462	3,255	2,575	2,317
School Districts	4,758	5,018	6,004	6,473
Other Special Districts	8,054	7,049	5,411	3,180
Total	22,185	20,703	18,442	15,658

Source: U. S. Bureau of the Census, *Census of Governments: 1972,* vol. 1, *Governmental Organization* (Washington, D. C.: U. S. Government Printing Office, 1973).

units in the metropolitan areas for 1972 and a comparison with previous years[4] are shown in Table 18–1.

Table 18–2 indicates the local governments in the twenty metropol-

Table 18–2. The Twenty Metropolitan Areas with the Largest Number of Units of Local Government in 1972

Metropolitan Area	*Number of Local Governments*
Chicago	1,172
Philadelphia	852
Pittsburgh	698
New York	538
St. Louis	483
Houston	304
San Francisco–Oakland	302
Portland	298
Indianapolis	296
Denver	272
Seattle–Everett	269
Cincinnati	260
Kansas City	256
Detroit	241
Peoria	236
Omaha	234
San Bernadino–Riverside–Ontario	233
Los Angeles–Long Beach	232
Minneapolis–St. Paul	218
Albany–Schenectady–Troy	216

Source: U. S. Bureau of the Census, *Census of Governments, 1972,* vol. 1, *Governmental Organization* (Washington, D.C.: U.S. Government Printing Office, 1973).

[4] The comparison should be interpreted with caution, however, because the figures for 1957 are for only 174 metropolitan areas, compared with 212 SMSA's existing in 1962, 227 in 1967, and 264 in 1972.

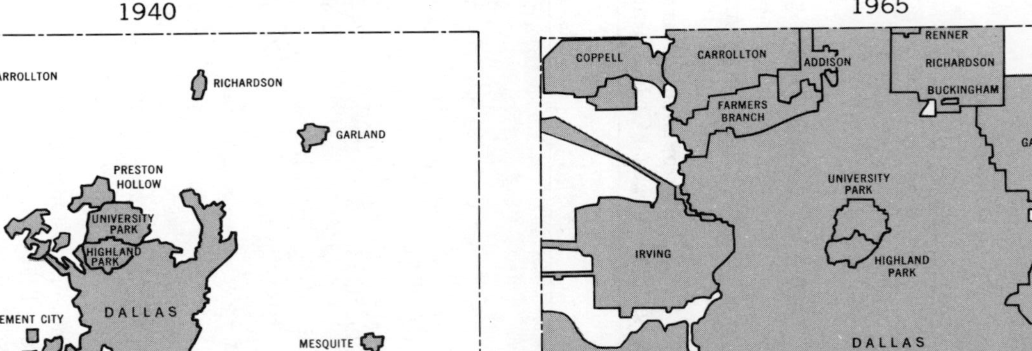

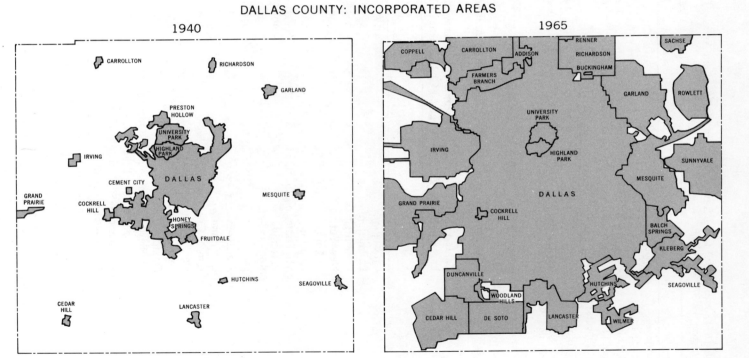

Figure 18–3. Growth of Incorporated Municipalities in Dallas County, 1940–1965. *Source:* Dallas County Planning Advisory Committee, *Report on a Cooperative Approach For Thoroughfare Development in Dallas County, Texas* (Dallas, 1967).

itan areas with the greatest number of units. If the New York area is reported separately from the governmental units in northeastern New Jersey, as is the case in Table 18–2, the Chicago area has the largest number of units, with 1,172. In thirteen metropolitan areas the number of separate units of government totals 250 or more, and in seventeen other areas the total is at least 200. In short, the statistical picture is one of extreme fragmentation of local government for all but a handful of metropolitan areas, with an average of approximately ninety governments per area. The trend is in the direction of even greater complexity and multiplication of units of government, particularly in the case of special districts and suburban cities. The high "birth rate" for new suburban cities and the development of an "iron ring" of suburbs around Dallas is shown in Figure 18–3.[5] The single exception to the multiplication trend is the number of school districts, which has dropped steadily in recent years through vigorous state action promoting school consolidations.

Problems of Governing Metropolitan Areas

Governmental effects

What have been the effects of the suburban movement upon government of the metropolitan area? What happens when cities spread out like volcanic lava, consuming the countryside and rendering their boundary lines unrealistic? Political problems of the first magnitude have resulted. Any attempt to summarize the problems of government which have arisen with the development of the metropolitan area runs the risk of oversimplification. However, a comparative study of 112 metropolitan surveys conducted between 1923 and 1957 reveals a striking similarity in the governmental consequences which seem to occur almost universally in the wake of the metropolitan explosion.[6] Summarized below are some of the more common, and more serious, problems of metropolitan government in the United States.

Financial inequalities

One of the most serious and visible results of the uncontrolled suburban movement is the financial disadvantage suffered by the central city. While more and more of the wealth of the city is moved outside the city limits and out of reach of the city tax collector, the cost of government for the central city has shown no tendency either to decrease or remain stationary. Complicating this trend are the suburbanites who escape city

[5] For an analysis of the different factors that maximize the chances that a suburban community will incorporate as a separate municipality, *see* Donald P. Hayes, "Metropolitan Decentralization Through Incorporation," *Western Political Quarterly* 18 (March 1965), pp. 198–206.

[6] *See* Daniel R. Grant, "General Metropolitan Surveys: A Summary," in *Metropolitan Surveys: A Digest* (New York: Government Affairs Foundation, 1958), pp. 1–24.

taxes and continue to aggravate the city's traffic and parking problems, use the city's streets and parks, and frequently receive many other city services without charge. All of this places an inequitable burden upon one group of metropolitan taxpayers. Bond issues for various public works, voted and paid for by the central city dwellers, are more often than not equally beneficial to suburban residents who enjoy all privileges except the dubious one of sharing the costs. The blighted sections of metropolitan areas, while paying few taxes, provide costly problems of public health, crime control, fire protection, slum clearance, and the like. These areas are almost without exception located exclusively within the central city and never in the wealthier suburbs most able to finance such services.

An additional thorn in the flesh of the central city is the fact that it suffers a serious loss of revenue from state taxes shared with cities on the basis of population, because a large portion of its "daytime" population cannot be counted. For purposes of figuring the city's share of such taxes, where a man sleeps is more important than where he works. City–suburban fiscal inequities are stressed in the 1968 report of the ACIR, based on its study of "fiscal federalism." It was discovered that the central cities' local tax burden is 50 percent greater than that of the suburbs, even though central city expenditures for education are less than in the suburbs, both on per-capita and per-pupil bases.

Unequal urban services

A second governmental problem common to most metropolitan areas is the existence of unequal services in different sections of the same metropolitan area. For cities in the early stages of metropolitanism it is the suburbanite who suffers most in this respect. Although he finds more room, fresh air, and quiet, he also frequently finds the multiple menace of inadequate sewage disposal, fire protection, police protection, and water supply, to name only a few. Prior to its 1963 metropolitan reorganization, suburban Nashville provided good examples—more than 150,000 of them—of metropolitan residents who received almost no municipal services, even having competitive, private-enterprise fire and police departments which served only paid-up subscribers.

In older metropolitan areas where suburban communities have been separately incorporated for many years, the overall result is much the same. Some of the suburban communities may well pride themselves on having the finest and most efficient city government of the whole area. This fine record is frequently possible, however, only because low-value property has been excluded from the boundaries of such cities, resulting in unwanted and underprivileged pockets of the metropolitan community being left to their own inadequate resources. In varying degrees and in different forms, metropolitan dispersion has consistently resulted in an unhealthy difference in the quality of governmental services within a given metropolitan area.

From an administrative standpoint the illogical split-up of clearly metropolitan-wide functions of government constitutes a third serious problem. This fractionalization of administration is perhaps the most universal characteristic of metropolitanism, as indicated by the 22,185 separate units of government "required" to govern 264 metropolitan areas in the United States in 1972. A typical metropolitan area has 90 units of government, most likely including: 2 counties, 13 townships, 21 municipalities, 18 school districts, 31 special districts, 4 federally supported planning districts, and 1 regional council. It requires no Solomon to point out that disease, crime, and fire are no respecters of political boundary lines. Yet what metropolitan area has had the minimum wisdom or vision to create a government with the metropolitan-wide authority necessary to cope with metropolitan-wide problems? A few cities have made progress in this direction, but the progress has been painfully limited. Metropolitan area water supply, police and fire protection, street and park "systems" "just growed," like the immortal Topsy. The result has been the haphazard creation of scores of police departments or water supply systems in a single urban area when one would be not only sufficient but also far more economical and effective. In the absence of a single, integrated, metropolitan government with authority to guide the progress of the whole urban region, unified policy formulation and execution is an impossibility.

Fractionalization of administration

In addition to the problem posed by dividing municipal administration into many illogical parts, there are troublesome and costly duplications inherent in the overlapping layers of local government. Even if large-scale annexation were to bring the metropolitan area within the boundaries of a single municipal corporation, there would still be one or more county governments and many special district governments overlapping the city and duplicating many of its activities. Very few standard metropolitan areas have tackled this problem by means of city–county consolidation or separation, so that most core cities in these areas are plagued with at least two tax assessors, tax collectors, law enforcement agencies, jails, health departments, and other agencies which operate in both city and county. This arrangement is bad at best, but is at its worst when the city and county are controlled by opposing political factions.

Many layers of government

A final problem that arises from the dispersed condition of metropolitan government, and that is probably the most serious in the long run, is the inevitable weakening of citizen control over local government in the area. Which official or unit of government is to receive the credit or blame for overall metropolitan goods or ills? Will the bewildered citizen blame the county, the central city, the suburban cities, or the many special districts for sluggish commuter traffic? Who gets the blame for an ineffective attack on an epidemic, for "gangland" type crimes in various parts

Weakening of democratic control

of the area, or for the low water pressure in the network of seventy-three different water supply systems? It should be fairly clear that citizens governed by such a maze of government as exists in metropolitan areas find it well nigh impossible to place the credit or blame for the respective deeds or misdeeds of their many governments. Democratic control by the people of the area as a whole has been dispersed and dissipated.

Metropolitan problems: real or imaginary?

A strong group of dissenting voices, disagreeing with the diagnoses of metropolitan ills, has arisen in recent years to question even the existence of metropolitan problems as such. Vincent Ostrom and others question the assumption "that the multiplicity of political units in a metropolitan area is essentially a pathological phenomenon."[7] Meyerson and Banfield disagree sharply with the view that the American city is in a state of crisis, and contend that, contrary to the common view of blight, congestion, and ineffective government, the American metropolis is one of the great achievements of all time.[8] James M. Banovetz expresses strong doubt that the core city subsidizes the suburbs because of fragmentation, and even doubts that serious problems of subsidies exist.[9] One of the most extreme attacks on metropolitan reform advocates has been made by Charles Adrian, who accuses them of "almost total lack of concern with the political process and the probable ignorance . . . of the fact that a democratic public is a 'satisficing' public and not one concerned with optimum economy."[10] Adrian accuses the metropolitan survey authors of making the false assumptions that "efficiency and economy are the highest political values held by the American homeowner," that "the core city of a metropolitan area must 'expand or die'," and that "a metropolitan area is a monolithic interest—a single community."[11]

It is too early to appraise fully the impact of this growing skepticism concerning the reality of metropolitan problems, but contrary evidence is offered by the outpouring of literature on such subjects as air pollution, water shortage, stream pollution, traffic and parking congestion, mass transit dilemmas, and the host of problems related to racial and economic ghettos. It is scarcely conceivable that one could read the six or eight most recent major books and reports on urban transportation without conclud-

[7] Vincent Ostrom, Charles Tiebout, and Robert Warren, "The Organization of Metropolitan Areas: A Theoretical Inquiry," *American Political Science Review* 55 (December 1961), p. 831.

[8] Martin Meyerson and Edward C. Banfield, *Boston: The Job Ahead* (Cambridge, Mass.: Harvard University Press, 1966), p. 2.

[9] "Metropolitan Subsidies—an Appraisal," *Public Administration Review* 25 (December 1965), pp. 297–301.

[10] Charles R. Adrian, "Metropology: Folklore and Field Research," *Public Administration Review* 21 (Summer 1961), pp. 148–149.

[11] *Ibid.*, pp. 149, 150, and 152.

ing that this is a "real" metropolitan problem clearly related to governmental fragmentation.[12] Similarly, the recent floodtide of anguished appraisals of neighborhood racial segregation patterns, in relation to the political segregation of "white power" suburban units of government from "black power" core-city units, would seem to illustrate the reality of metropolitan problems. What then explains the growing skepticism cited in the preceding paragraph? It may well be that these skeptics' real unhappiness is with the "proposed remedies," and that their tendency to downgrade the problems is a result of overreacting against what they consider to be unrealistic "dogmas of metropolitan reform," so commonly rejected by the voters.

Persistence of distress signals

Proposed Remedies

It may be said concerning remedies proposed for the various problems of governing metropolitan areas that "many are called but few are chosen." Political scientists have in recent years proposed many solutions to these problems; the more important of these proposals are summarized below, including the experience and prospects for each.

Alternative proposals

Annexation of the surrounding urbanized territory to the central city is the most commonly proposed, and perhaps the most obvious, remedy for the problem of suburbanitis. It was the method used by the nation's great cities to achieve their present size. The case for annexation is strong, both from the viewpoint of the suburbs and the central city: expensive public works, improvements, and services could be provided at lower cost than by the suburb alone; property values would rise; fire insurance rates would be lower; voting privileges in central city elections could be secured; the city's census standing would be higher; the base for financing municipal government would be broadened; and the city would bring about a suburban development consistent with its own development. For both city and suburban residents advantages result from functioning as one community, such as the capacity to make a unified attack on the metropolitan problems of disease, crime, slums and juvenile delinquency, as well as the efficiency and economy of larger scale operations. Typically strong editorial support for annexation from local newspapers is shown in Figure 18–4.

Annexation

In spite of the compelling logic of the arguments, it has been virtually impossible for the larger cities to keep pace by means of annexation with

[12] *See* the discussion on this subject in chapter 21. *See also* Advisory Commission on Intergovernmental Relations, *Metropolitan America: Challenge to Federalism* (U. S. House of Representatives, Committee on Government Operations, 89th Cong., 2nd Sess., August 1966).

The Walls Must Go

Figure 18–4. George Fisher in the *Arkansas Gazette.*

population growth on the margin of the city. Opposition to annexation is almost always strong in the suburbs, based upon several arguments: taxes would be increased; the government of the central city is corrupt or incompetent; new services would be long delayed in arriving, if they arrive at all; and annexation is a nefarious scheme of the power-grabbing politicians and tax collectors in the city hall.

Obstacles to annexation

If the suburb to be annexed is already incorporated, the opposition may be exceedingly strong because of greater community spirit and unwillingness to lose its name, identity, and independence. Once a city is surrounded by separately incorporated satellite cities, the chances of annexation are slim. Boston, for example, has never been able to annex Brookline, Newton, and Milton. The suburban cities of Pasadena and Long Beach and even wholly surrounded Beverly Hills have been successful down through the years in resisting all efforts to be incorporated into the city of Los Angeles. More recent developments in metropolitan areas are equally discouraging to proponents of annexation except in cases where the metropolitan core cities are surrounded for the most part by unincorporated territory. Minneapolis became completely encircled by incorporated cities between 1940 and 1950, and 10 new municipalities came into existence in the Chicago metropolitan area during the same period. Pittsburgh is surrounded by 190 municipalities, and Detroit by 87.

Liberalized annexation procedures

As long as each individual suburb remains the master of its fate concerning annexation, requiring a majority vote before coming under the jurisdiction of the central city, annexation must be considered a thing of the past for the older metropolitan areas. The procedure in some states, however, makes it a great deal easier to accomplish annexation. Virginia statutes provide for a special annexation court which judges the merits of each attempt, rather than allowing the voters of the city or suburbs to make the decision; annexation has been a regularly recurring process in that state. In recent years Virginia counties have increasingly resisted such annexations because of complications related to city–county separation, a matter discussed later in this chapter. Several Texas cities have been able to take advantage of home-rule charters permitting them to annex by vote of the city council without a vote of the residents of either the city or the fringe area. Since World War II some of the largest annexations in the United States have taken place in Houston, Dallas, Fort Worth, and San Antonio. The Tennessee General Assembly in 1955 adopted a new annexation procedure which borrowed from both Texas and Virginia. Pushed through the legislature by the cities, the new procedure authorized annexation by a vote of the city council, subject to possible appeal to court for approval or disapproval according to standards of community welfare and progress.

Vigorous annexation by some cities

Annexation has been used much more vigorously during the past two decades than is commonly realized, and it must not be counted out for at least some of the cities of the future. Table 18–3, showing annexations since 1948 by cities with 5,000 population or more, certainly indicates strong life remaining in the old device.

The size of the area annexed reached a peak of 1,083 square miles in 1960—in an obvious effort to prepare for the census takers—and no subsequent year has equaled that record. The *number* of annexations has continued at a high level, however, averaging more than 700 annexations per year in the 1960s. Annexations of spectacular size have taken place in some states, Oklahoma and Texas in particular; Oklahoma City has annexed approximately 553 square miles since 1959. It now has the second largest area of any city in the United States with a total land area of 641.1 square

Table 18–3.

	Area (Sq. miles) (Average per year)	Number of Cities (Average per year)
1948–51	191.4	320.0
1952–55	307.9	443.0
1956–59	537.1	524.7
1960–63	824.6	716.0
1964–66	546.6	739.7
1970–71	653.1	1,105.5

Source: Adapted from John C. Bollens, "Metropolitan and Fringe Area Developments in 1966," in *The Municipal Yearbook, 1967* (Chicago: International City Managers Association, 1967), p. 72; and U. S. Bureau of the Census, *1972 Boundary and Annexation Survey* (Washington, D. C.: U. S. Government Printing Office, 1973), pp. 1–3.

miles for its 1970 population of 366,000. City–county consolidation made Jacksonville (Florida) the largest with 766 square miles. The Los Angeles city area of 463.6 square miles was once the largest. Since 1950 Houston has expanded from 160 to 439.6 square miles, and Phoenix grew from 17.1 to 245.7 square miles. Tulsa added 116.8 square miles in a single annexation in 1966. Sierra Vista, Arizona, a city of only 6,689 population, annexed 114.7 square miles in 1971. Some states have strengthened use of annexation by establishing local boundary review boards and no-incorporation zones around municipalities.

Variables explaining successful annexation

A study by Thomas Dye[13] of factors associated with successful annexation in urban areas indicates that "social class distance" between the city and its surrounding suburbs is one of the more important variables. Thus central cities with larger proportions of middle-class residents were more successful in annexing the middle-class suburbs than were the central cities with smaller proportions of middle-class residents. Manager governments were significantly more successful in annexation than non-manager governments, perhaps harmonizing better with a suburban preference for "antiseptic, non-partisan, professionalized municipal government." The age of the settlement proved to be an important variable, with older urbanized areas having greater immobility of boundaries than younger ones. Surprisingly, the ease or difficulty of the legal procedure for annexation does not in itself provide an explanation for differences in success and failure in annexation. Similarly, the size of the urbanized area was not an important variable.

[13] Thomas R. Dye, "'Urban Political Integration: Conditions Associated with Annexation in American Cities," *Midwest Journal of Political Science* 8 (November 1964), pp. 430–446. For a critical analysis of the Virginia procedure for readjusting municipal boundaries, *see* Chester Bain, *Annexation in Virginia: The Use of the Judicial Process for Readjusting City–County Boundaries* (Charlottesville: University of Virginia Press, 1966).

In spite of successful annexations in many metropolitan areas, the fact remains that the central core cities of most of the older and larger metropolitan areas are finding it necessary to look to devices other than annexation to secure metropolitan political integration. If separate suburban incorporation could be avoided, annexation might play a surprisingly important role in the structuring of the future government for the new and presently emerging metropolis. After the straitjacket of incorporated satellite cities has been wrapped around the core cities, however, they are forced to turn from annexation to a variety of alternative proposals.

Limited metropolitan role of annexation

In the absence of annexation of the suburbs, a municipality is sometimes granted the right to exercise certain powers outside the city limits. Such extra-territorial powers have been sustained by the courts on the ground that they are essential to effective use of the intraterritorial powers granted to the city. The device takes such forms as the inspection of all sources of milk supply for a central city, even though the milkshed may extend many miles in all directions outside the boundaries of the city; the control of land platting outside the boundaries of the city; the control of contagious diseases for a certain number of miles beyond the corporate limits; the regulation of undesirable trades and the suppression of houses of prostitution within a certain distance of the city.

Extra-territorial powers

As a permanent device for furnishing integrated government to the whole metropolitan community, extra-territorial power has important limitations. The problem of financing such activities in an equitable manner is perplexing. Furthermore, the exercise of governmental power over persons having no control over the government is not conducive to cooperation over the long run.

Intergovernmental cooperation

Probably the most widely used means of coordination in metropolitan areas is that of intergovernmental arrangements for municipal activities. The prevalence of contractual and informal agreements probably can be attributed to the fact that such arrangements seldom require fundamental change in the structure of government of the area and are least disturbing to political alignments. Local governments in California have made wide use of intergovernmental agreements, especially for county provision of service to cities. Los Angeles County, for example, has close to 1,500 contracts calling for a wide range of services to more than seventy-five municipalities in the county. One aspect of this procedure is the "Lakewood Plan," named for that city of 80,000 which in 1954 was the first to contract for a whole package of services rather than contracting on a piecemeal basis. The Lakewood Plan, or the "contract cities plan" as other cities prefer to call it, has been adopted by practically all of the thirty-one cities incorporated in Los Angeles County since 1954.

The Lakewood Plan

The package of services is not the same for each city, with some tendency for older cities to begin to perform certain services for themselves.

Bollens and Schmandt point to two major limitations on the use of inter-local agreements for governing the metropolis.[14] In the first place, even in Los Angeles County where the greatest number of contracts are in effect, the great majority are concerned with the relatively non-controversial service functions, and have not resulted in an area-wide approach to the more conflict-laden functions involving regulation and control. Perhaps the severest limitation on such agreements lies in their financial nature, providing no means of serving areas with inadequate tax resources or of subsidizing the have-not areas of the metropolis.[15]

Metropolitan councils of governments

The newest form of cooperation in the metropolis is the voluntary association of local governments, usually a council of elected officials, designed to facilitate discussion and study of common problems. Some of the earliest ones organized were the Supervisors Inter-County Committee (Detroit, 1954), the Metropolitan Regional Council (New York, 1956), and the Metropolitan Washington (D. C.) Council of Governments (1957). The Association of Bay Area Governments (shortened to an unromantic ABAG) was organized in the San Francisco area in 1961 and moved vigorously into the field of regional planning. The council of governments (COG) was given a boost by the U. S. Housing and Urban Development Act of 1965 which authorized financial assistance for planning. From a modest beginning of only 12 in 1965, the number of councils of governments rose steadily to an estimated total of 350 in 1972, although there is some uncertainty over the numbers because of varying definitions. Devising a pronounceable name has continued to challenge the COG founding fathers, as in the case of the 1973 establishment of the San Bernardino Associated Governments (SAN BAG). The various steps between initiation and implementation of COG plans are shown in Figure 18–5. The COG is praised as the wave of the future by its advocates, but is viewed by its opponents as a toothless tiger or, even worse, a protector of the inadequate status quo. It has been said that a COG can be anything from an Elk's lodge to a metropolitan government. Despite the inherent weakness of voluntarism and the malapportioned structure of COG favoring the small suburban governments, they seem destined to become a common institutional addition to the metropolitan scene.

[14] John C. Bollens and Henry J. Schmandt, *The Metropolis: Its People, Politics, and Economic Life* (New York: Harper & Row, 1965), pp. 396–399.

[15] On this point, *see* Cleveland Metropolitan Services Commission, *Prologue to Progress* (Cleveland, 1959), pp. 40–41. For an analysis of the newest cooperative device, the metropolitan council of governments, *see* Metropolitan Councils of Government (Washington, D. C.: U. S. Advisory Commission on Intergovernmental Relations, 1966).

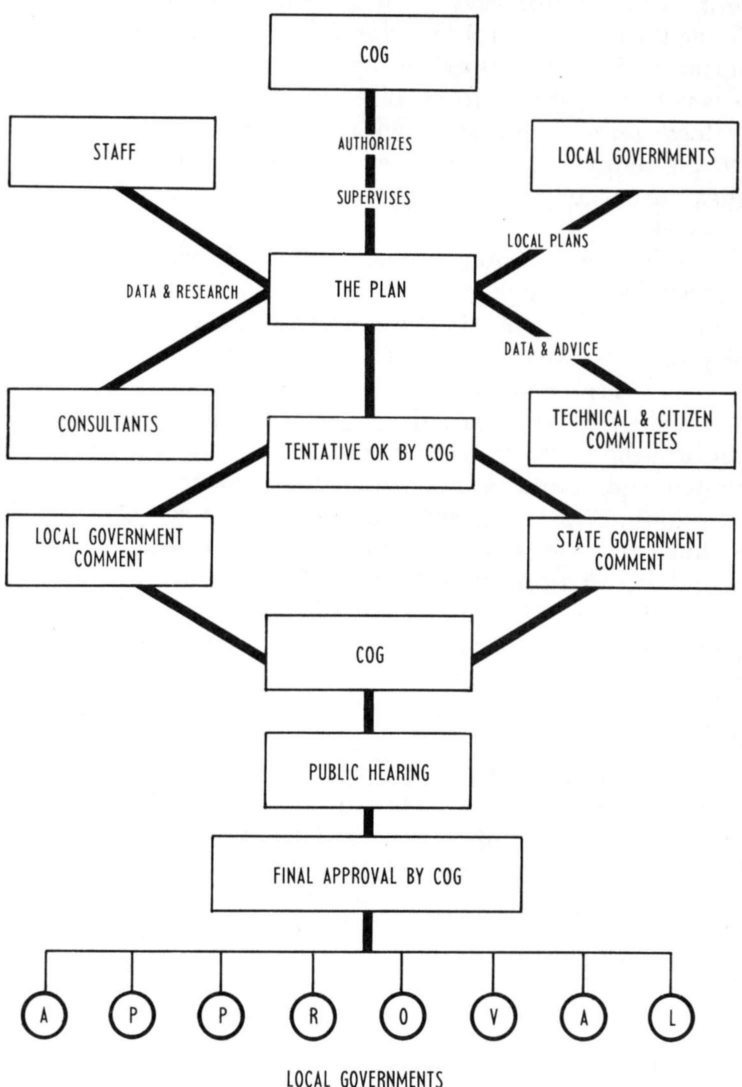

Figure 18–5. Formal Decision-Making Process in Metropolitan Councils of Governments. *Source: Metropolitan Texas: A Workable Approach to Its Problems* (Texas Research League, 1967), p. 52.

The Minnesota legislature appears to be evolving a unique hybrid between the weak COG and the all-powerful regional government in the form of the Metropolitan Council of the Twin Cities Area (Minneapolis–St. Paul). Created in 1967, the Council has been delegated increasing authority over matters of metropolitan significance. In 1974, for example, it was given authorization to review and suspend, for one year, projects of local units inconsistent with the Council's development guide. The 1973 recommendations growing out of the ACIR study of substate regionalism seem to point toward the Twin Cities "new breed of council" approach.

The federated metropolis

Where annexation has been found politically unfeasible or otherwise undesirable, some have proposed a type of metropolitan government which might be termed federal, in that there would be a formal division of powers between a central government and the constituent municipalities. Based upon a rough analogy to the relationship between the national government and the states, the larger unit of government would perform those functions that transcend municipal boundaries, while the component municipalities would continue to perform the purely local functions. The "federated metropolis" would cover the entire metropolitan area. In cases where the area coincides generally with the boundaries of a county, some plans provide for the county to become the central federated government. The federated government would be responsible for such activities as the operation of the water supply system, planning and zoning on a regional basis, tax assessment and collection, sewage disposal, traffic control of arterial streets, and other functions beyond the capacity of any one municipality. Functions retained by the existing municipalities might include fire protection, police protection, garbage disposal, and similar activities more local in character, although the difficulty of defining "purely local" is quite obvious. In a day when it has become increasingly unrealistic to attempt a division between national and state functions, and between state and local functions, any further subdivision of local functions into those which are "area-wide" and those which are purely local would seem to be moving against the stream of governmental history.

Examples of municipal federalism

For many years the city of London, having a two-tiered government consisting of a county council and several metropolitan boroughs, was the only metropolitan government which might properly be characterized as municipal federalism. But until 1964 this characterization was applicable only to the part of the city within London County, rather than to the whole of Greater London. In 1965 Parliament abolished eighty-seven of Greater London's local governments and established an enlarged two-tier form of government for thirty-two boroughs covering 630 square miles, with each borough having populations ranging from 170,000 to 340,000.[16] In 1953 the city of Toronto became the second metropolis to make use of the federal principle by uniting with its several suburbs in a federated city. Winnipeg followed suit a few years later. New York City once approached the federal form, on paper at least, but the status of its boroughs is not so independent as might be required to conform to the federal pattern. It is even less an example of federalism under its latest charter. A federated plan of urban government was proposed as early as 1896 for Boston but without success, and a federated city–county government for Alameda County in California in 1922 was defeated by popular vote. A Pittsburgh plan in 1929 came closer to succeeding than any other, but failed because it got the necessary two-thirds majority in only fifty-eight of the sixty-two local units required.

The Toronto experience

In spite of these and other failures to secure adoption, the idea of metropolitan federation is still very much alive, primarily because of the highly publicized Toronto experience and the Miami "Metro" experience, which is federal in certain respects. The "Municipality of Metropolitan Toronto" was created by the provincial parliament in 1953 and given jurisdiction over several area-wide functions, both in the city of Toronto and in its twelve suburban "satellite" cities. The federation was actually a compromise between complete amalgamation (annexation), proposed by the city of Toronto, and complete independence as defended vehemently by the suburban cities. The result was to leave the thirteen cities in charge of such activities as police, fire, health, library, and welfare services, while creating a new metropolitan level of government to handle water supply, sewage disposal, housing, education, arterial highways, metropolitan parks, and overall planning. In 1957 the thirteen local police forces were taken over by the metropolitan government, causing some critics to say that metropolitan federation is merely "disguised annexation." Metropolitan Toronto has been widely publicized for an outstanding record of accomplishment in such activities as highways, rapid transit, water supply and sewerage, and regional planning. Although the Toronto plan has given new hope to metropolitan areas in the United States, it has not been without its own problems. Representation on the twenty-five-member metropolitan council was ex officio and indirect, and equal representation for each suburb was far from equitable. Two separate studies of Toronto's metro experience by American political scientists, John Grumm[17] and

[16] For a comprehensive study of the adoption of the new Greater London plan of metropolitan government, *see* Frank Smallwood, *Greater London: The Politics of Metropolitan Reform* (Indianapolis: Bobbs-Merrill Co., 1965).

[17] John Grumm, *Metropolitan Area Government: The Toronto Experience*, Governmental Research Series No. 19 (Lawrence: University of Kansas Publications, 1959).

Frank Smallwood,[18] led to the conclusion that Toronto's remarkable record of achievement in the high-visibility public works functions was tempered somewhat by a tendency to shy away from the social service and welfare-oriented functions.

Changes in Toronto Metro

Following a comprehensive study of these and other problems by a Royal Commission on Metropolitan Toronto, additional centralization of certain functions was recommended in 1965, as well as the merger of the thirteen cities into only four. The provincial government accepted only part of the recommendations, retaining six cities (the core city plus five boroughs), and providing that welfare administration and much of school operating costs should become responsibilities of the Metro government. These changes became effective in 1967. Toronto proponents of total consolidation argue that this is another transitional step toward inevitable (and desirable) consolidation. Defenders of the federation principle contend that the merger to six cities has strengthened the federation because they are now of sufficient size, strength, and resources to become permanent, viable political units. Undoubtedly, Toronto will continue to be a most interesting testing ground for bold innovation in the field of metropolitics.

Partial federation in Dade County

The voters of Miami and Dade County in 1957 narrowly adopted (44,404 to 42,619) a two-tiered form of metropolitan government which incorporates, to a limited degree, the principle of federation. The heart of the Dade County "Metro" plan is the retention of the existing municipalities (Miami plus twenty-seven suburban cities) for the performance of "purely local" activities, with the allocation of authority to Dade County for those governmental activities which are "essentially metropolitan" in nature. During its first five years of existence, while receiving nationwide acclaim as a civic pacemaker, it was repeatedly fighting off the attacks of anti-Metro forces in the form of a multitude of lawsuits and three county-wide referendums which would have gutted the new structure. The tenure of the first two county managers was short; the first was dismissed in 1961 and the second in 1964. In addition to political battles it has had financial ones, stemming from the fact that it has many of the obligations of a city, but only the taxing power of a county. In technical terms, Dade County's Metro is more nearly a "municipalized county" than it is a federation of municipalities, since the cities as such are not represented on the board of commissioners. But whatever the classification, this "great bold venture in modern government," as second Metro Man-

[18] Frank Smallwood, *Metro Toronto: A Decade Later* (Toronto: Bureau of Municipal Research, 1963). For a more recent evaluation of the Toronto Metro experience, *see* Albert Rose, "Two Decades of Metropolitan Government in Toronto," in *A Look to the North: Canadian Regional Experience,* Guthrie Birkhead, ed. (Washington, D. C.: U. S. Government Printing Office, 1974).

ager McNayr once called it, has offered a strong ray of hope to many other American metropolises.[19]

Even before the adoption of the Miami proposal, in certain other counties in the United States political pressure from unserved suburban groups opposed to annexation and from reform groups discouraged in their annexation efforts has resulted in some cases in what might be called a "municipalized county." In spite of the county's legal position as an administrative district of the state, created to perform state functions, many states have begun to grant counties authority to provide services traditionally considered municipal in type.[20] Probably the best known example of a county performing a multiplicity of municipal functions is Los Angeles County, as mentioned previously; it has more functions than the city of Los Angeles and a budget exceeding that of the city. Among its many urban functions are street improvements, street lighting, sanitation, fire protection, police protection, library service, public parks, and regional planning. Montgomery County, Maryland, with a council–manager form of government, is serving as the *de facto* municipal government for most of the one-half million residents of the rapidly growing northwest sector of the metropolitan area of Washington, D. C.

The municipalized county

Expansion of county functions evokes much less opposition than annexation or city–county consolidation. This fact doubtless explains the rapid advances in many states in the direction of transforming the urban county into a unit of metropolitan government. Norman Beckman predicts that the county will "ride the wave of the future with regard to metropolitan governmental organization and political power."[21] His reason for stating this is that:

> County government has a priceless asset which many municipalities do not have—what students of government would term 'adequate areal jurisdiction' —but what can better be described by the word 'space.'
>
> . . . In addition to 'space' the county has high political feasibility (it exists, therefore it is feasible). It is directly accountable to an electorate that, under recent court decisions, will be reasonably representative. Finally, it has a

[19] An increasing number of studies of the Miami experience are being published. *See*, for example, Edward Sofen, *The Miami Metropolitan Experiment*, Metropolitan Action Studies No. 2 (Bloomington: Indiana University Press, 1963); Reinhold P. Wolf, *Miami Metro: The Road to Urban Unity* (Coral Gables: Bureau of Business and Economic Research, University of Miami, 1960); and Gustave Serino, *Miami's Metropolitan Experiment* (Gainesville: Public Administration Clearing Service, University of Florida, 1958).

[20] *See* Mark B. Feldman and Everett L. Jassy, "The Urban County: A Study of New Approaches to Local Government in Metropolitan Areas," *Harvard Law Review* (January 1960), pp. 526–582.

[21] Norman Beckman, "Taking Account of Urban Counties," *American County Government* 30 (October 1965), p. 68.

broad tax base and well established working relations with the state and federal governments on the one hand and the cities on the other.[22]

Problem of county organization

The one serious weakness of the movement to expand the county's functions is the fact that the county, as it is commonly organized, is still suited to the rural conditions of the horse-and-buggy era rather than to the task of administering municipal functions. Its limited powers, numerous elective officials who serve almost as separate units of government, and its cumbersome and impotent governing body are scarcely designed to facilitate effective and efficient performance of the heavy responsibilities of metropolitan government.[23] Many students of government feel, however, that it might be made suitable for local government in urban regions by drastic structural changes, such as the provision for a single county executive and the establishment of a county legislative body which is both representative and responsible.

Special metropolitan districts

One of the more popular piecemeal approaches to the problems of metropolitan government is the creation of special districts or authorities, distinct from other units of government, which have boundary lines drawn to coincide with the boundaries of the problem or problems to be solved. Special metropolitan districts are popular for a number of reasons. Experience with this device has demonstrated the ease with which seemingly insurmountable political boundary lines may be crossed. For example, the territorial jurisdiction of the Golden Gate Bridge and Highway District includes all of five San Francisco Bay area counties, all of another county, and part of a seventh. Districts meet relatively little resistance from politicians because they eliminate no jobs and usually do not disturb the organization's grip on the city government. So far as the suburban politicians are concerned, such ad hoc authorities are exceedingly popular because they lessen the pressure for annexation to the core city.

Special districts are frequently created for financial reasons, such as equalizing the tax burden over an area wider than that of existing units, or enabling a unit of government to evade established tax or debt limits. In the latter case, existing units of government in a metropolitan area may already be up to their tax and debt limits, so that the only local means of providing additional revenue to finance a desired service is to establish a new unit of government.

Among the better known special metropolitan authorities are the Chicago Sanitary District, organized in 1889, and the Massachusetts Metropolitan District Commission, dating back to 1889 for sewers, 1893 for

[22] *Ibid.* For a comprehensive treatment of the urban county, *see* Herbert Sydney Duncombe, *County Government in America* (Washington, D. C.: National Association of Counties, 1966).

[23] *See* chapter 16 for a discussion of problems of county structure.

parks, and 1895 for a water system. The growth of metropolitan areas across state boundary lines has led to the creation by means of interstate compacts of such districts as the Port of New York Authority and the more recent Bi-State Development Agency for the St. Louis area. The Port of New York Authority performs in a district of about 1,500 square miles with close to fifteen million residents.[24] Also in the New York area is the Metropolitan Commuter Transportation Authority, which began its existence in 1965 and purchased the Long Island Railroad, the most heavily traveled commuter line in the U. S.

Examples of metropolitan districts

There seems to be a growing willingness on the part of state legislatures to give special districts the power to exercise a number of functions, thus permitting multi-purpose special districts and making the title "ad hoc district" a misnomer. Some of its proponents hope that it might gradually evolve into a general area-wide government by adding functions as the failure of the smaller units of government becomes apparent. One such district was set up in 1958, the Municipality of Metropolitan Seattle, under a state law permitting cities and towns of Washington to act jointly in solving common problems. The only functions thus far are sewage disposal and water pollution, but the fourteen component municipalities may give it such additional functions as transportation, water, parks, garbage disposal, and planning. A proposal to add transportation to the Seattle authority was rejected in a 1962 referendum. A multi-purpose district was proposed for the St. Louis metropolitan area in 1959 but was defeated by popular vote.

If the value of the special district is measured in terms of the limited objective of executing a specific project, special metropolitan districts have on the whole been effective in doing the job assigned. From the broader standpoint of integrating metropolitan government, however, special districts not only weaken the bargaining power of those trying to sell annexation to the suburbs, but also add to the confusion of the independent "thousand islands" of government making up the metropolis. Such districts confuse the voters with additional layers of government and make it more difficult for the citizenry to hold government accountable. (*See* Figure 18–6.) In addition, special districts do not improve the census rating of the central city—a matter of no small importance as it relates both to promotion by the chamber of commerce and to receipts from state-collected locally shared taxes based upon population. In sharp criticism of the widespread use of special districts Roscoe Martin lists

Districts as a mixed blessing

[24] For a discussion of the shortcomings of even the highly praised Port of New York Authority, when measured on other than "its own terms," *see* Edward T. Chase, "The Trouble with the New York Port Authority," in Edward C. Banfield (ed.), *Urban Government: A Reader in Administration and Politics* (New York: Free Press of Glencoe, Inc., 1961), pp. 75–82.

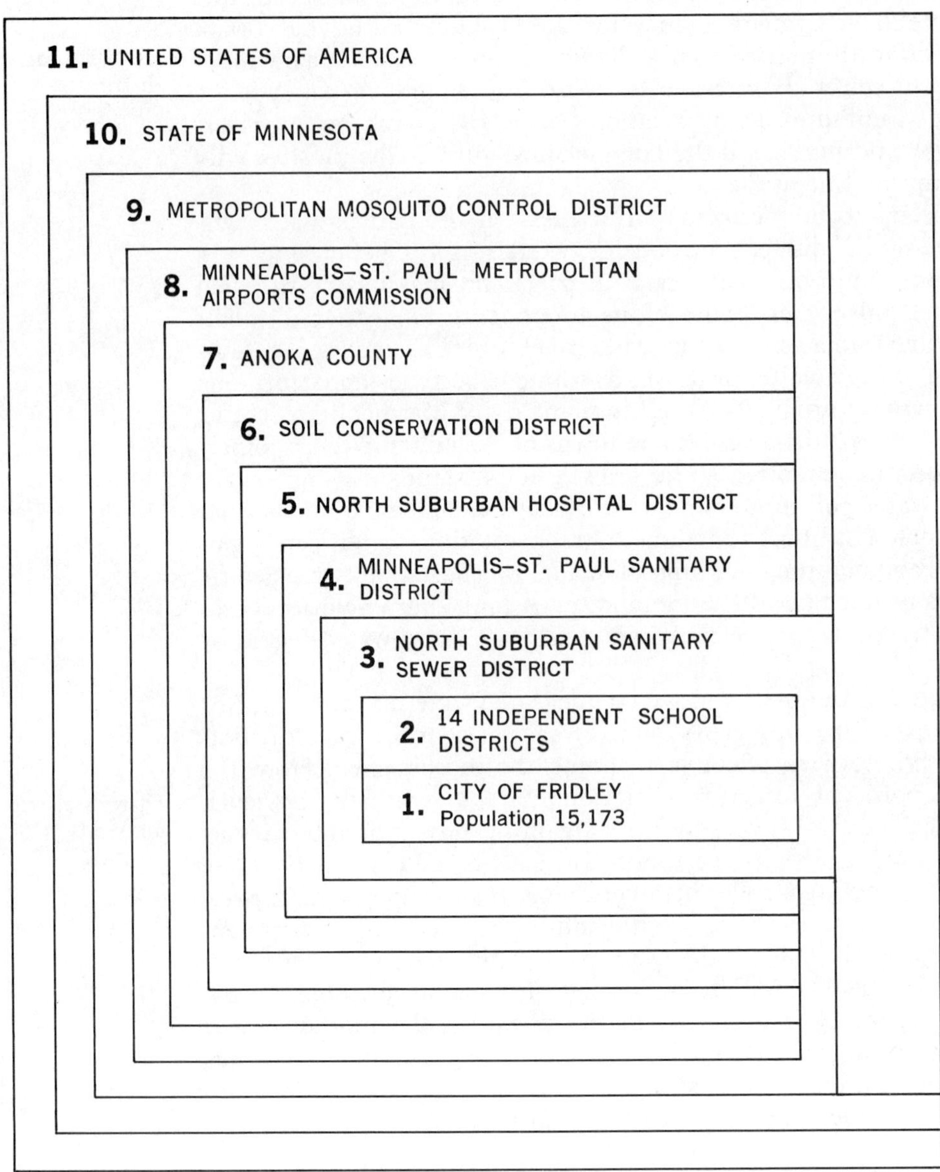

Figure 18–6. Layers of Government in Fridley, Minnesota (Minneapolis–St. Paul Area). *Source:* Committee for Economic Development, *Modernizing Local Government* (New York, 1966), p. 12.

several ill effects: it separates the program from the mainstream of city affairs; it purports to "remove the program from politics," but in practice it tends to replace the general politics of the city with a more narrow, less visible, less public, politics of a special clientele; and, finally, it "tends to atomize local government," making comprehensive planning of local programs a virtual impossibility.[25]

In spite of these long-run deficiencies, special districts continue to be very popular with metropolitan decision makers, though little known and little understood by the metropolitan public at large.[26]

City–county separation

A few cities in the United States have resorted to city–county separation in an effort to eliminate one of the layers of government under which the city resident must live and pay taxes. This involves removal of the city's territory from the jurisdiction of the county, consolidating city and county functions within the city limits and restricting the county government to the residue of the former county. The four outstanding examples are Baltimore, separated from its county in 1851, San Francisco in 1856, St. Louis in 1875, and Denver in 1903. Judicial interpretations of the state constitutions resulted in varying degrees of consolidation of city and county functions in each case. In addition to these four cases, Virginia has a unique general scheme of city–county separation for all first-class cities. When a city attains a population of 10,000 it automatically becomes for governmental purposes almost entirely separate from the county in which it is located. Second-class cities (over 5,000 population) are only partially separated governmentally from their counties, and this on a voluntary basis, continuing to make use on a pro rata basis of certain county officers and services.

City–county separation is always strongly resisted by the rural portions of the county that are to become the "rump" county. The impoverished remains of the county may find it necessary to unite with surrounding counties in the face of operating a suburban and rural government without sufficient tax resources. On the other hand, city–county separation usually seriously complicates the future expansion of the city, because enlargement of the city–county's boundaries is much more difficult than extension of the single city's corporate limits. Even though large annexations are carried out, however, it is never very long before the city has grown beyond its legal boundaries. Both San Francisco and St. Louis

[25] Roscoe C. Martin, *The Cities and the Federal System* (New York: Atherton Press, 1965), pp. 178–179.

[26] *See* Robert G. Smith, *Public Authorities in Urban Areas* (Washington, D. C.: National Association of Counties, 1969). For an earlier analysis of the nature of special districts, *see* John C. Bollens, *Special District Governments in the United States* (Berkeley: University of California Press, 1957), and *The Problem of Special Districts in American Government* (Washington, D. C.: U. S. Advisory Commission on Intergovernmental Relations, 1964).

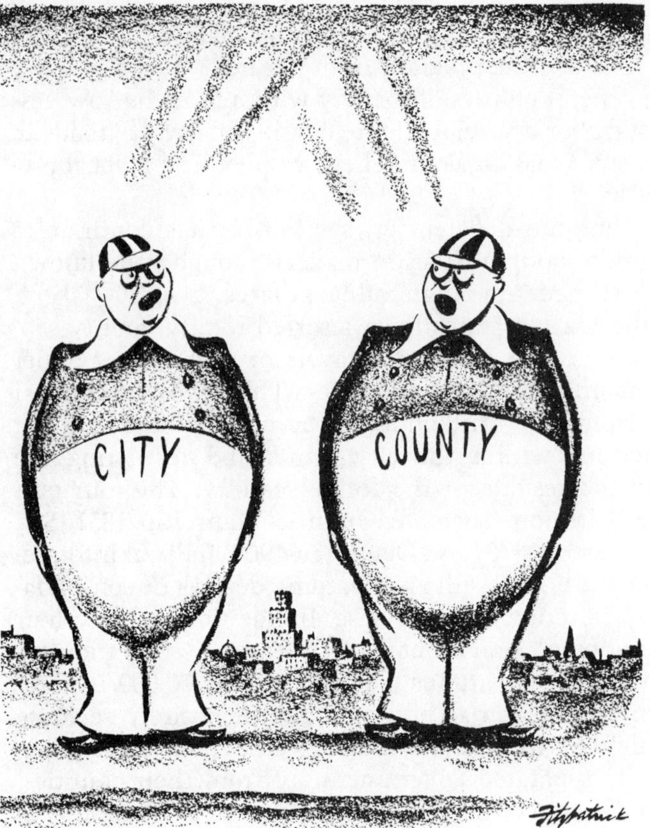

"MEET ME AT ST. LOOIE, LOOIE, —

Figure 18–7. *Source: St. Louis Post-Dispatch,* December 12, 1956. Reproduced by permission of the *St. Louis Post-Dispatch.*

have been anxious for many years to reacquire territory discarded earlier but have been unable to do so. Figure 18–7 depicts this plight. Only in Virginia has city–county separation been coupled with a practical plan for extending the city limits as the population spreads outside the city; but in recent years such expansions have met with increasing resistance even in Virginia.

City–county consolidation

City–county consolidation constitutes a slightly different method of accomplishing substantially the same result as city–county separation. Under city–county consolidation the city limits are extended to coincide with the county boundaries and the two governments are consolidated, leaving no troublesome remnant county. The effects of the two methods are identical, so far as the territory under the new consolidated city–county is concerned; it eliminates duplicate sets of officers for city and county functions and overlapping jurisdiction between city and county. More than twenty cities have adopted some form of city–county government, as shown in Table 18–4, in addition to the cities mentioned previously as having achieved a similar result by means of city–county separation. Since 1952, several mergers have taken place in the Tidewater area of Virginia; the majority of these cases involve county motivation to avoid annexation or the separation of a host of small municipal corporations, and have the effect of blocking core-city expansion.[27]

Table 18–4. Adoption of City–County Consolidations[a] by Legislative Action and by Referendum

By Legislative Action	
New Orleans–Orleans County, Louisiana	1805
Boston–Suffolk County, Massachusetts	1821
Philadelphia–Philadelphia County, Pennsylvania	1854
New York–New York County, New York	1874
New York and Brooklyn–Queens and Richmond Counties, New York	1898
Honolulu–Honolulu County, Hawaii	1907
Indianapolis–Marion County, Indiana	1969
By Referendum	
Baton Rouge–East Baton Rouge Parish, Louisiana	1947
Hampton–Elizabeth City County, Virginia	1952
Nashville–Davidson County, Tennessee (defeated in 1958)	1962
Virginia Beach–Princess Anne County, Virginia	1962
South Norfolk–Norfolk County, Virginia	1962
Jacksonville–Duval County, Florida (defeated in 1935)	1967
Juneau–Greater Juneau Borough, Alaska	1969
Carson City–Ormsby County, Nevada	1969
Columbus–Muscogee County, Georgia (defeated in 1962)	1970
Sitka–Greater Sitka Borough, Alaska	1971
Suffolk–Nansemond County, Virginia	1972
Lexington–Fayette County, Kentucky	1972
Savannah–Chatham County, Georgia	1973

[a] In addition to these listed, Baltimore, San Francisco, St. Louis, Denver, and many Virginia cities have achieved some of the same results as consolidation by means of city–county separation.

Source: Adapted from *The American County* 37 (February 1972), pp. 14–15, with additions from *County News*, periodical published by the National Association of Counties.

[27] For a discussion of the Virginia merger experience, *see* David G. Temple, "Merger in

Pros and cons of city–county consolidation

The advantages of consolidating county and city governments in metropolitan areas are fairly obvious, including such things as the taxpayers' benefit from eliminating one layer of government, the voters' benefit from the shorter ballot and more simplified structure of local government, and administrative improvements resulting from metropolitan-wide jurisdiction. This last benefit, governmental integration of the whole metropolitan area, cannot be claimed in all cases of city–county consolidation. The largest metropolitan areas in the United States spill over into more than one county as well as into neighboring states, so that consolidation with a single county would not encompass the whole urban area. Another difficulty of the consolidated city–county is the fact that future annexation to keep pace with the suburban movement necessitates detaching territory from adjacent counties, which would generally require jumping constitutional hurdles and working political miracles.

Political scientists on several occasions have pronounced city–county consolidation to be a thing of the past, only to see it resurrected as a serious proposal in some major city. The mergers of Baton Rouge[28] and East Baton Rouge Parish in Louisiana in 1947, Nashville and Davidson County in 1962, and Jacksonville and Duval County in 1967 were each declared by skeptics to be rare accidents of metropolitan reform, and not really a serious option for most cities. Yet such major consolidations as Indianapolis–Marion County, Columbus–Muscogee County (Georgia), Lexington–Fayette County (Kentucky), and Savanna–Chatham County, all occurring since the 1967 Jacksonville merger, make it clear that it is still a viable issue in metropolitan areas in the United States. The National Association of Counties (NACO) New County U.S.A. Center reported in 1972 that at least 36 areas were seriously studying city–county consolidation. The number of adoptions and continuing study activity should not obscure the fact that the odds are still about 3 to 1 against securing adoption, as indicated by a comparison of Tables 18–4 and 18–5.

City–county consolidation in Nashville

Voters of Nashville and Davidson County adopted a charter in June 1962, consolidating the city and county governments into a single metropolitan government. Four years earlier a similar proposal had been rejected by the suburban and rural voters of the county. However, an ambitious annexation drive by the city of Nashville in 1960 caused many suburbanites to look at city–county consolidation in a more favorable

---

Virginia Local Government: Issues and Implications," *University of Virginia News Letter* 40 (Oct. 15, 1963), pp. 5–8. The mergers involved the City of Hampton, the County of Elizabeth City, and the Town of Phoebus (1952); the Cities of Warwick and Newport News (1958); Norfolk County and the City of South Norfolk (1963); and Princess Ann County and the City of Virginia Beach (1963).

[28] For an appraisal of the Baton Rouge merger, *see* William C. Havard, Jr., and Floyd L. Corty, *Rural-Urban Consolidation: The Merger of Governments in the Baton Rouge Area* (Baton Rouge: Louisiana State University Press, 1964).

Table 18–5. Rejection of City–County Consolidation by the Voters, 1921–1973

City and County	*Date Rejected*
Oakland–Alameda County, California	1921
Butte–Silver Bow County, Montana	1924
St. Louis–St. Louis County, Missouri	1926, 1962
Portland–Multnomah County, Oregon	1927
Pittsburgh–Allegheny County, Pennsylvania	1932
Several municipalities–Ravalli County, Montana	1933, 1960
Macon–Bibb County, Georgia	1933, 1960, 1972
Miami–Dade County, Florida	1948, 1953
Newport News–Harwick County–Elizabeth City County, Virginia	1950
Albuquerque–Bernalillo County, New Mexico	1959
Knoxville–Knox County, Tennessee	1959
Durham–Durham County, North Carolina	1961
Richmond–Henrico County, Virginia	1961
Memphis–Shelby County, Tennessee	1962, 1971
Chattanooga–Hamilton County, Tennessee	1964, 1970
Tampa–Hillsborough County, Florida	1967, 1970, 1973
Athens–Clarke County, Georgia	1969
Winchester–Frederick County, Virginia	1970
Charlottesville–Albemarle County, Virginia	1970
Pensacola–Escambia County, Florida	1970
Anchorage–Greater Anchorage Borough, Alaska	1970, 1971
Bristol–Washington County, Virginia	1971
Charlotte–Mecklenburg County, North Carolina	1971
Tallahassee–Leon County, Florida	1971
Ft. Pierce–St. Lucie County, Florida	1972
Columbia–Richland County, South Carolina	1973

Source: Adapted from *The American County* 37 (February 1972), pp. 14–15, with additions from *County News*, periodical published by the National Association of Counties.

light and the tide turned in favor of "Metro." The unique feature of the Nashville plan is an expandable "urban services district," beginning initially with the core city's boundaries, but expanding with the urban growth and the extension of the full complement of urban services, and with a tax rate corresponding to the higher level of services. All persons are in the "general services district" and receive and pay for all area-wide services of the metropolitan government. All duplicate city and county departments, boards, executives, and legislative bodies are merged into single, metropolitan counterparts. Architects of the plan contend that it has the benefits of unified government for the entire metropolitan area

AN OPEN LETTER

TO ALL DUVAL COUNTIANS:

For a number of years many citizens throughout the county have become increasingly concerned about the inability of our outdated local government to deal with community problems effectively. The people have expressed dissatisfaction with:

- Sharply rising taxes;
- glaring examples of duplication and inefficiency in their government;
- one of the nation's highest crime rates;
- severe water and air pollution problems;
- disaccredited schools;
- the revelation of extensive graft and corruption within local government;
- disenfranchisement of the better part of our Greater Jacksonville population in the selection of leadership for the City of Jacksonville.

A host of other governmental problems—of far greater intensity in our community than elsewhere in the nation—clearly point to a need for reorganizing and rebuilding our local government.

Now, through the combined efforts of our citizenry and official action by Duval senators and representatives elected to the Florida Legislature, a plan for restructuring, reforming and revitalizing our local government has been brought to fulfillment. On August 8th, every registered voter in the county will have an opportunity to vote on the consolidation charter.

The proposed consolidated government's charter is reproduced here as a public service so that every voter will be fully informed for this extremely important August 8th referendum.

Citizens for Better Government is a grouping of concerned citizens from all walks of life in our county. Our only interest is the betterment of our community. Our ranks are open to everyone, and we urge you to join us.

The backbone of democracy is citizen involvement: Our most precious right is our right to vote. Help us if you can to work toward a Better Duval County. But whatever you do, vote your convictions on August 8th.

CITIZENS FOR BETTER GOVERNMENT
32 WEST DUVAL STREET

Vote YES for CONSOLIDATION

Consolidation: Need Has Been Building 80 Years

- **1887** Florida Constitution passed, outlining structure of present county governments. Duval population outside city: 9,589; Jacksonville population: 17,201.
- **1888** Jacksonville depopulated by yellow fever epidemic, partly through failure of community to adopt recommended sanitary safeguards.
- **1901** Jacksonville destroyed by fire; lack of adequate fire protection.
- **1917** Present Jacksonville city charter passed. Duval county population outside city: 19,000; Jacksonville population: 88,000.
- **1932** Last significant annexation to Jacksonville (City of South Jacksonville). Duval population outside city: 27,000; Jacksonville population: 135,000.
- **1955** Survey reveals more than $100 million needed to install adequate sewers, treatment plant in Jacksonville-Duval metropolitan area.
- **1960** County population outside Jacksonville exceeds city's for first time: 254,000. City population drops 3,000 from 1950 census, five years later drops below 200,000 for first time in 15 years.
- **1963-64** Two annexation attempts fail in referendums; city continues to decline.
- **1964** Community leaders demand consolidation.
- **1965** City-county schools disaccredited.
- **1965** Duval Legislative Delegation creates Duval County Local Government Study Commission under an act of the Florida Legislature. City and county contribute $20,000 each, citizens raise another $20,000 for exhaustive study of local government by 50-member Study Commission.
- **1966** Grand Jury charged to investigate corruption and graft in local government.
- **1966** Ad valorem tax assessments and general taxes reach all-time high.
- **1966-67** 10 city and county officials indicted by Grand Jury.
- **1967** Study Commission submits "Blueprint for Improvement" to the community and the Duval Legislative Delegation. Charter follows. Blueprint and charter outline plan for restructuring and consolidating local governments.
- **1967** Legislative delegation conducts public hearings to sound out citizens on charter.
- **1967** Duval Countians complain of poor service and high and inequitable utility rates in county; air-water pollution levels reach highest concentrations.
- **1967** Legislative delegation, acting on Study Commission proposals and citizen recommendations, amends consolidation charter and adopts it as state law subject to voter referendum.
- **Aug. 8, 1967** You decide. County referendum. Every registered citizen can vote.

Figure 18–8. Campaign Material for Consolidation of Jacksonville and Duval Counties, Florida. *Source:* The Florida *Times-Union* and Jacksonville *Journal,* July 2, 1967.

(533 square miles), without the inflexibilities of previous city–county mergers with respect to the problem of governing the developing suburban fringe and the more stable rural areas. If the early favorable appraisals of the first few years of Nashville Metro are dependable barometers, the Nashville plan can be expected to provide hope for many of the medium-sized and smaller metropolitan areas located entirely within single counties.[29]

Voters in the city of Jacksonville, Florida, and Duval County adopted a consolidation plan in 1967 that was patterned in many ways after the Nashville plan. After a series of financial and political crises (*see* Figure 18–8) in city and county government, a study commission recommended to the community and the Duval Legislative Delegation a "Blueprint for Improvement." The delegation adopted a city–county consolidation charter, subject to voter approval by a single majority vote. The proponents, in addition to having the normal "good-government" allies, were joined by a significant number of labor and black leaders, and the charter was adopted by a decisive two-to-one majority. Tampa and Hillsborough County, with no immediate crisis dramatizing the case for metropolitan reform, had rejected overwhelmingly a similar consolidation proposal earlier in 1967. Lexington (Kentucky) and Fayette County voters approved a consolidation by better than a two-to-one margin (36,493 to 16,060) late in 1972, effective 1974. Many similarities to the Nashville and Jacksonville pattern can be seen; both consolidation plans paid careful attention to the political consequences of the charter, and both ran a politically sophisticated campaign for adoption.

The first city–county consolidation in a northern metropolitan area in this century was approved by the Indiana General Assembly in 1969 for Indianapolis and Marion County. More intriguing than the name chosen for the consolidated government (UNIGOV) was its establishment by the state legislature *without a referendum.* Although this was a sharp departure from traditional state ground rules for consolidation (*see* Table 18–6), concessions to political expediency were made by continuing the

[29] For an analysis of the sources of support for, and opposition to, the Nashville Metro proposal, *see* Brett W. Hawkins, *Nashville Metro: The Politics of City-County Consolidation* (Nashville: Vanderbilt University Press, 1966). For a study concentrating primarily on the earlier, unsuccessful referendum in 1958, *see* David A. Booth, *Metropolitics: The Nashville Consolidation* (East Lansing: Institute for Community Development and Services, Michigan State University, 1963). For a preliminary appraisal of the post-adoption experience with metro, *see* Daniel R. Grant, "A Comparison of Predictions and Experience with Nashville 'Metro'," *Urban Affairs Quarterly* 1 (September 1965), pp. 34–54. For other studies relevant to the Nashville consolidation, *see* Roscoe C. Martin, *Metropolis in Transition* (Washington, D. C.: U. S. Housing and Home Finance Agency, 1963), Chapter IX; Herbert Sydney Duncombe, *County Government,* Chapter 10; and Daniel R. Grant, "Metropolitics and Professional Political Leadership: The Case of Nashville," *Annals of the American Academy of Political and Social Science* 353 (May 1964), pp. 72–83.

Table 18–6. Comparison of Six City–County Consolidations

	Baton Rouge–East Baton Rouge Parish Louisiana Population–267,600	*Nashville–Davidson County Tennessee Population–410,000*	*Jacksonville–Duval County Florida Population–507,200*	*Indianapolis–Marion County Indiana Population–742,000*	*Juneau–Greater Juneau Borough Alaska Population–13,895*	*Columbus–Muscogee County Georgia Population–164,235*
Date of Vote on Successful Consolidation Proposal—Votes Cast FOR and AGAINST	8/12/47 7012 for 6705 against	6/28/62 City—21,064 for 15,599 against County—15,914 for 12,514 against	8/7/67 54,493 for 29,768 against	no referendum—passed by state legislature	2/17/70 2059 for 1748 against	5/27/70 12,500 for 2,989 against
Effective Date of Consolidation	1/1/49	4/1/63	10/1/68	1/1/70	7/1/70	1/1/71
Popular Referendum Required for Consolidation Charter Passage	yes	yes	yes	no	yes	yes
State Legislation Required for Approving Establishment of Consolidated Government	no	no	no	yes	no	yes
City Area Prior to Consolidation (square miles)	5	72.5	39	84	2.34	69.5
Area of Consolidated Government (square miles)	30	533	841	402	3,108	147.8

Table 18–6. *Continued*

	Baton Rouge–East Baton Rouge Parish Louisiana Population–267,600	*Nashville–Davidson County Tennessee Population–410,000*	*Jacksonville–Duval County Florida Population–507,200*	*Indianapolis–Marion County Indiana Population–742,000*	*Juneau–Greater Juneau Borough Alaska Population–13,895*	*Columbus–Muscogee County Georgia Population–164,235*
City Population Prior to Consolidation	40,000	255,000	198,200	525,000	7,313	152,218
Population of Consolidated Government	267,600	410,000	507,200	742,000	13,895	164,235
Form—Executive	Mayor–President Council	Mayor–Council	Mayor–Council	Mayor–Council	Mayor–Council	Mayor–Council
Popularly Elected	yes	yes	yes	yes	yes	yes
Term of Office (yrs.)	4	4	4	4	4	4
Legislative Size of Consolidated Legislative Body	11[a]	41	19	29	9	10
Number Elected by District		35	14	25	0	4
Number Elected at Large	7 within city 4 in wards outside	Mayor + 5 Councilmen	5	4	9	6
Population per District		14,000	15,000	32,000	n.a.	50,000

[a] There are two separate legislative councils: One for the city: 7; one for the parish: 11 (includes 7 from city council).

Source: Adapted from *The American County* 37 (February 1972), p. 12.

separate existence of incorporated satellite cities, townships, and most county offices. Professor George L. Willis points out several factors that made UNIGOV possible: (1) strong Republican party control of the appropriate state and local governmental offices necessary to push the legislation through; (2) the convergence of partisan self-interest, traditional political attitudes and practices in Indiana, and general support of business, civic, and governmental reform groups; (3) vigorous and effective political leadership of Mayor Richard Lugar; (4) mass media support; and (5) shrewd political concessions in structuring the new government—a large 29-member council, preservation of special-service and taxing districts, and of suburban city and most county officers.[30] UNIGOV moved from transitional to permanent status on Jan. 1, 1972, with an overwhelming Republican majority of officers. Five black council members were elected, very close to what the county population ratio would call for, but doubtless a smaller percentage than would be expected if Indianapolis had not consolidated with the county.

UNIGOV for Indianapolis

Obstacles to city–county consolidation have caused many cities to resort to a more gradual approach which takes the form of consolidating single functions common to both city and county governments, without a complete political and territorial merger. Functional consolidation involves the performance by one unit of local government of an activity such as public health or sewage disposal, previously performed by two or more overlapping units, with no change in the general structural relations of these units. It may be brought about either by state action, permissive or mandatory, that reallocates the functions of local government, or by some form of contractual arrangement between the local governmental jurisdictions. One of the better-known examples of functional consolidation is the extensive plan for redistribution of functions between Atlanta and Fulton County which was approved in 1950. Although this device cannot be expected to solve the overall metropolitan problem, it can provide a means of handling certain parts of the total problem without increasing the complexity of local government in the area. Functional consolidation is sometimes called the "Fabian" approach to eventual city–county consolidation, rather than the frontal attack. But it is also possible for a piecemeal solution to one or two of the more pressing problems to slow down or delay indefinitely city–county consolidation.

Functional consolidation

Metropolitics and the Future

It is easy for advocates of integrated metropolitan government to become discouraged after running the gamut of the various proposed remedies for

[30] *County News*, June 16, 1972, p. 14.

the ills of "metropolitanism." It seems that those "solutions" which are adequate are politically infeasible, and those which are politically feasible are inadequate.[31] As early as 1950 one veteran student of the metropolis pointed out, "So far we have accomplished little more than a world's record for words used in proportion to cures effected."[32] The backward look certainly does not offer much encouragement for advocates of some kind of area-wide approach to governing the metropolis.

Frustration for reformers

Several developments in the United States, however, would seem to hold the key to the future of metropolitan government. One of these is the growing interest of the national government in the problem of governmental coordination within metropolitan areas. The U. S. Advisory Commission on Intergovernmental Relations has shown much greater concern for metropolitan areas and their governmental structures than any previous federal study group.[33] The creation of a cabinet-level department of Housing and Urban Development has already focused increased attention on obstacles to coordination in the metropolis. New federal programs requiring review and even clearance by regional planning agencies seem destined to become the rule rather than the exception. The increasingly interstate character of metropolitan areas that spill over state boundary lines presents a prima facie case for intervention by the federal government in some form.

Growing federal role

As indicated in other discussions in this book, the major unknown quantity in metropolitan development is the role of state governments. Will the reapportionment of state legislatures on a one-man–one-vote basis finally bring the states into serious concern and involvement with the issues of metropolitics? Will the increased suburban representation in state legislatures merely solidify the autonomous position of satellite cities in metropolitan areas? Or have the states been negligent so long that the mainstream of intergovernmental relations has already passed them by in favor of the national government? Some state governments have recently supported comprehensive studies of metropolitan area government, digging into questions of governmental structure which previously had been left almost exclusively to locally based study commissions.[34]

How strong a role for the states?

[31] For some reflective thinking on the relationship of American ideology to the difficulty of securing adoption of proposed metropolitan "solutions," *see* Luther H. Gulick, *The Metropolitan Problem and American Ideas* (New York: Alfred A. Knopf, 1962).

[32] T. H. Reed, "Hope for 'Suburbanitis'," *National Municipal Review* 39 (December 1950), p. 542.

[33] *See*, for example, their study of *Metropolitan Social and Economic Disparities: Implications for Intergovernmental Relations in Central Cities and Suburbs* (Washington, D. C.: U. S. Advisory Commission on Intergovernmental Relations, 1965) and *Factors Affecting Voter Reactions to Governmental Reorganization in Metropolitan Areas* (1962).

[34] *See*, for example, *Metropolitan Texas: A Workable Approach to Its Problems* (Austin: Texas Research League, 1967); *Metropolitan Virginia 1967: an Assessment* (Richmond: Virginia Metropolitan Areas Study Commission, 1967); and *The State's Biggest Busi-*

One other dimension in the future of the metropolis relates to the question of how much longer the "metropolitan community" will remain a meaningful concept. In *The Withering Away of the City*, York Willbern points out that the metropolitan city of the future will not resemble a fried egg, with a distinguishable center and outer edge, but will come to resemble "a thin layer of scrambled eggs over much of the platter."[35] If we are primarily developing the Gottman-style megalopolis[36] in several regions of the United States (encompassing several metropolitan areas merged into each other), it is exceedingly difficult to think in terms of the old, clearly defined, self-governing community. Willbern's prediction might be described as "the intergovernmental megalopolity," consisting of a network of special districts, some single-purpose and some multipurpose, several counties with increasing but segmental responsibilities, an assorted spectrum of public and private utility-type enterprises, and an elaborate variety of cooperative arrangements with higher governmental levels.

Fried eggs or scrambled eggs?

At the present time it is not clear whether American cities are headed in the direction of rational area-wide local governments for metropolitan communities, or toward the development of many headless and formless "intergovernmental megalopolities." However, there seem to be much stronger tendencies toward the latter. Connery and Leach have suggested that southern metropolitan areas have the best opportunity of any in the nation to move in the former direction "because so many of them are new and the layers of government do not lie so heavily upon them."[37] In any case, we can be sure that the field of metropolitics will constitute one of the liveliest intergovernmental battlegrounds for many years to come.

Communities or "intergovernmental megalopolities"

---

ness: Local and Regional Problems (New Haven: The Connecticut Commission to Study the Feasibility of Metropolitan Government, 1967). For a summary of the state's role in local government reorganization, *see* Daniel R. Grant, "Urban Needs and State Response: Local Government Reorganization," in Alan K. Campbell (ed.), *The States and the Urban Crisis* (Englewood Cliffs, N. J.: Prentice-Hall, 1970), pp. 59–84.

[35] York Willbern, *The Withering Away of the City* (University, Ala.: University of Alabama Press, 1964), p. 33. For a speculative discussion of black politics in the future metropolis, *see* the two-article series by Frances Fox Piven and Richard A. Cloward, "Black Control of Cities," *The New Republic* (Sept. 30, 1967), pp. 19–21, and (Oct. 7, 1967), pp. 15–19.

[36] *See* Jean Gottman, *Megalopolis* (New York: Twentieth Century Fund, 1961).

[37] Robert H. Connery and Richard H. Leach, "Southern Metropolis: Challenge to Government," *The Journal of Politics* 26 (February 1964), pp. 60–81.

SUPPLEMENTARY READINGS

Bollens, John C., and Schmandt, Henry J. *The Metropolis: Its People, Politics, and Economic Life.* 2nd ed. New York: Harper & Row, 1970.

Campbell, Alan K., ed. *The States and the Urban Crisis.* Englewood Cliffs, N. J.: Prentice-Hall, 1970.

Campbell, Alan K., and Sacks, Seymour. *Metro-*

politan America: Fiscal Patterns and Governmental Systems. New York: The Free Press, 1967.

Connery, Robert H., and Leach, Richard H. *The Federal Government and Metropolitan Areas.* Cambridge, Mass.: Harvard University Press, 1960.

Council of State Governments, John C. Bollens, Director of Study. *The States and the Metropolitan Problem.* Chicago: Council of State Governments, 1956.

Danielson, Michael N., ed. *Metropolitan Politics.* Boston: Little, Brown and Co., 1966.

Dye, Thomas R., and Hawkins, Brett W., eds. *Politics in the Metropolis: A Reader in Conflict and Cooperation.* Columbus, Ohio.: Charles E. Merrill Publishing Co., 1967.

Fiser, Webb S. *Mastery of the Metropolis.* Englewood Cliffs, N. J.: Prentice-Hall, 1962.

Goodall, Leonard E. *The American Metropolis.* Columbus, Ohio: Charles E. Merrill Publishing Co., 1968.

Government Affairs Foundation, Inc. *Metropolitan Surveys: A Digest.* Chicago: Public Administration Service, 1958.

Greer, Scott. *Metropolitics: A Study of Political Culture.* New York: John Wiley and Sons, 1963.

Gulick, Luther H. *The Metropolitan Problem and American Ideas.* New York: Alfred A. Knopf, 1962.

Hadden, Jeffrey; Masotti, Louis H.; and Larson, Calvin J. *Metropolis in Crisis.* Itasca, Ill.: F. E. Peacock Publishers, 1967.

Havard, William C., and Corty, Floyd L. *Rural–Urban Consolidation: The Merger of Governments in the Baton Rouge Area.* Baton Rouge: Louisiana State University Press, 1964.

Jones, Victor. *Metropolitan Government.* Chicago: University of Chicago Press, 1942.

Long, Norton. *The Unwalled City: Reconstituting the Urban Community.* New York: Basic Books, 1972.

Martin, Roscoe C. *Metropolis in Transition.* Washington, D. C.: U. S. Housing and Home Finance Agency, 1963.

Rush, J. A. *The City–County Consolidated.* Published by the author, Los Angeles, 1941.

Schmandt, Henry J., and Standing, William J. *The Milwaukee Metropolitan Study Commission.* Bloomington: Indiana University Press, 1965. This is one of a series of "Metropolitan Action Studies." Others include Miami, Sacramento, and Syracuse.

Studenski, Paul. *The Government of Metropolitan Areas in the United States.* New York: National Municipal League, 1930.

Sweeney, Stephen B., and Blair, George S., eds. *Metropolitan Analysis: Important Elements of Study and Action.* Philadelphia: University of Pennsylvania Press, 1958.

U. S. Advisory Commission on Intergovernmental Relations, *Governmental Structure, Organization, and Planning in Metropolitan Areas.* Washington, D. C.: U. S. Government Printing Office, 1961. *See also* other similar studies by ACIR.

U. S. National Resources Committee, Research Committee on Urbanism. *Our Cities: Their Role in the National Economy.* Washington, D. C.: U. S. Government Printing Office, 1937.

Willbern, York. *The Withering Away of the City.* University, Ala.: University of Alabama Press, 1964.

Wirt, Frederick M.; Walter, Benjamin; Rabinovitz, Francine R.; and Hensler, Debora R. *On the City's Rim: Politics and Policy in Suburbia.* Lexington, Mass.: D. C. Heath and Co., 1972.

Wood, Robert C., with Vladimir V. Almendinger. *1400 Governments.* Cambridge, Mass.: Harvard University Press, 1961.

Woodbury, Coleman, ed. *The Future of Cities and Urban Redevelopment.* Chicago: University of Chicago Press, 1953.

Yates, Douglas. *Neighborhood Democracy: The Politics and Impacts of Decentralization.* Lexington, Mass.: D. C. Heath and Co., 1973.

19

Law Enforcement: Protective and Corrective Activities

Importance to government

Government, whatever its form, is not government unless it maintains law and order. Liberty, as was emphasized in the fourth chapter, is always liberty under law. Thomas Jefferson, maximizing individual freedom and minimizing public control, left it clear that government should prevent citizens from injuring each other. Law enforcement is one of the oldest functions of government. Yet the FBI's Uniform Crime Reports show more than a doubling of crime from 1960 to 1970 in the seven categories of serious crime reported. Some might suspect this is merely a reflection of population growth, but the four serious crimes of violence (murder, forcible rape, robbery, and aggravated assault) increased twelve times faster than the population growth from 1960 to 1970, and the three serious property crimes (burglary, larceny over $50, and auto theft) increased fourteen times faster than the population. (*See* Table 19–1.) In addition to this, opinion research indicates that crimes actually committed exceed those officially reported by as much as 50 percent for robberies, 100 percent for aggravated assaults, and nearly 300 percent for forcible rapes and burglaries.[1] Even for those crimes officially reported, there is the problem

[1] Committee for Economic Development, *Reducing Crime and Assuring Justice* (New York, 1972), p. 79. In 1974, findings of the Law Enforcement Assistance Administration, based on interviews with some 22,000 persons in New York, Chicago, Detroit, Philadelphia, and Los Angeles, indicated a total of 3.1 million crimes committed, as opposed to the 1.2 million reported by police departments. If this survey is correct, crime is from two to three times as high as officially reported.

Table 19–1. Criminal Offenses Known to Police, 1960–1970

	1960	*1970*	*Increase*	*Estimated Arrests 1970*
Criminal homicide	9,000	15,812	+ 75.7%	15,230
Forcible rape	16,860	37,273	+121.1%	19,050
Robbery	107,390	348,380	+224.4%	98,210
Aggravated assault	152,000	329,937	+117.1%	155,060
4 Crimes of Violence	285,250	731,402	+156.5%	**287,550**
Burglary	897,400	2,169,322	+141.7%	358,100
Larceny over $50	506,200	1,746,107	+244.9%	748,200
Auto theft	325,700	921,366	+182.9%	153,300
3 Crimes against Property	1,729,300	4,836,795	+179.6%	**1,259,600**
U.S. population increase, 1960–1970			+ 13.3%	
Other Offenses against Property				
Vandalism				141,900
Fraud				104,600
Buying, receiving, possessing stolen property				74,000
Forgery and counterfeiting				55,500
Arson				11,900
Embezzlement				10,000
Other Offenses				
Drunkenness				1,825,500
Disorderly conduct				710,000
Driving under the influence of alcohol				555,700
Other assaults, not aggravated				348,900
Narcotic drug laws				415,600
Liquor laws				309,000
Vagrancy				113,400
Carrying or possessing weapons, etc.				120,400
Gambling				91,700
Offenses against family and children				78,500
Sex offenses (except forcible rape and prostitution)				59,700
Prostitution and commercialized vice				51,700
All other offenses (except traffic)				1,492,590
GRAND TOTAL, ALL ARRESTS (except traffic)				**8,117,740**

Source: Adapted from Committee for Economic Development, *Reducing Crime and Assuring Justice* (New York, 1972), p. 80, and FBI's *Uniform Crime Reports.*

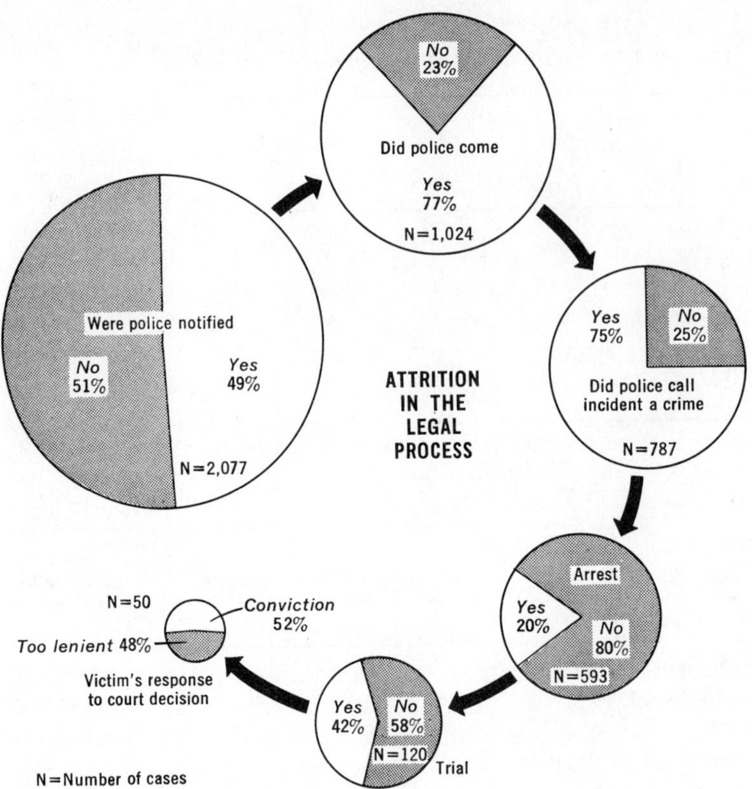

Figure 19–1. Attrition in Law Enforcement. *Source:* Published by permission of Transaction, Inc., from *Transaction,* vol. 4, no. 7. Copyright © 1967 by Transaction, Inc.

of attrition between complaint and conviction (shown in Figure 19–1) that continues to trouble society.

Theories about increased crime

The spectacular increase in crime in America is one of the social mysteries that frustrates both the expert and the layman. Reasons and theories are legion. Some sociologists stress overcrowding as the cause, citing people packed into offices, factories, homes, and mass transit devices, all of which tend to breed hostile and aggressive feelings. Another theory emphasizes the mass media's role in whetting appetites for all the material luxuries of the rich, now constantly displayed in every home by television. Still another widely held theory is that a decline in moral standards has been brought about by permissive philosophies in home and school, and by urban relaxation of the former small-town peer group pressures which enforced moral standards.

What to do about crime is in even greater dispute. The popular reaction to crime is an almost instinctive emphasis on mobilizing a counterforce—more police with more and bigger weapons, and less concern for legal protections for the suspects; there have even been civilian vigilante movements, often aimed at those different in race or culture. The recommendations of academicians, however, stress preventive and rehabilitative measures, improvements in the penal system, speedier judicial procedures, and a variety of reforms designed to coordinate and improve the whole system of criminal justice.[2] It is within this context that we shall consider the role of state and local government in law enforcement.

Law enforcement is exemplified in the nearly universal American office of county sheriff, a functionary handed down from the shirereeve of Saxon England as local keeper of the peace and enforcer of the law of the land. All units and most agencies of government are concerned directly or indirectly with the methods and effectiveness of law enforcement, of compelling obedience to legitimate authority, and preventing disturbance of the public peace or safety. The realm of law enforcement is an important area of intergovernmental relations, involving cooperation and even competition or friction. The significant state units normally involved are the state government, the counties, and the cities or towns.

All officers are state officers

All officers of the "law" in a state, except those commissioned by the national government, are state officers, whatever their local functions, duties, and powers may be. County sheriffs and deputies, city policemen and detectives, and rural constables have the direct responsibility of enforcing state laws and apprehending violators of state laws within the territorial jurisdictions of their political subdivisions. Their own election or appointment is prescribed broadly or specifically by state statutes or constitutional provisions. Federal courts and federal legislation hold them responsible as agents of the state for respecting rights of persons guaranteed by the Fourteenth Amendment. The governor in many states has important powers of supervision, removal, and replacement over designated local officers in order to prevent neglect or laxity in matters of enforcement.

Central State Forces

Every state has central agencies to facilitate or ensure the preservation of law and order in the commonwealth. The oldest of the state forces or potential forces is the "Militia," as designated by the federal Constitution,

[2] For analysis and recommendations on the police, the courts, and corrections, *see* the reports of such major study commissions as the National Commission on Law Observance and Enforcement (Wickersham Commission), 1931; the President's Commission on Law Enforcement and Administration of Justice (Katzenbach Commission), 1967; the National Advisory Commission on Civil Disorders (Kerner Commission), 1968; and the National Commission on the Causes and Prevention of Violence (Eisenhower Commission), 1969. *See also* the study of the Advisory Commission on Intergovernmental Relations, *State–Local Relations in the Criminal Justice System* (Washington, D. C., 1971).

or "National Guard," as covered by later legislation by Congress. The states are forbidden to keep troops in time of peace except by the consent of Congress, and thus the national legislature has in various ways provided for the establishment and training of the state troops, as well as for calling them into federal service with federal compensation when necessary.

The National Guard

Members of the National Guard pursue their regular civilian occupations in normal times, but are subject to call by state or national authorities. They may be ordered by the governor or his adjutant general to join their units in active duty to quell riots, to police communities visited by disaster, or to take over the whole law enforcement function in instances of complete breakdown of local administration. The Alabama state troops temporarily assumed complete administration of local government, for example, in Phenix City in the mid-1950s when the governor moved to put that gambler-ridden community under martial law.[3] The use of the National Guard by governors to police strikes has at times provoked controversy on the political front, with charges of strike breaking coming from organized labor. New Orleans authorities and citizens once complained that Governor Huey Long sent troops to patrol an open square in front of their city hall with little justification aside from factional politics. From the urban uprisings in Detroit and Newark in 1967 to the Kent State University tragedy in 1970, National Guard units were heavily involved in civil disturbances with strong social, economic, and political overtones previously seldom encountered. Although its performance has been criticized by many as provocative, amateurish, and bungling, National Guard defenders point out that from 1967 to 1970 the Guard coped with 221 disorders, including the nationwide riots of April 1968, following the assassination of Dr. Martin Luther King, and did not cause a single civilian fatality.[4] When members of the National Guard are largely or completely engaged in federal service, as in wartime, their intrastate role may be taken over by improvised home guards or state guards.

The rise of state police systems

With the rise of state police systems, state governments in modern times have been able to limit their use of the National Guard to more massive disturbances. Centralized state police systems have developed throughout the country in one form or another since the organization of the Texas Rangers in 1835 to patrol frontier regions harassed by lawless elements. Massachusetts provided for state constables in 1865, and Pennsylvania created a regular state police system in 1905. Several factors account for

[3] It might be noted that martial law is not statutory or codified law or formal military government. It is a process of superseding municipal or political authority with military rule, applicable to civilians of the area or community, under circumstances of gross peril to life, law, and order.

[4] *See* Col. George E. Moranda, "The National Guard," *The Book of the States, 1972–73*, pp. 439–442.

the growth and professional role of state agencies of public safety. Their routine performance stirs less curiosity or complaint than the sudden summoning of state troops. The universality of motor transportation on networks of superhighways requires enforcement of traffic regulations beyond the concern or capacity of local officers. State forces are likely to be best equipped to cope with inter-city or inter-county operations of major criminals, not only to apprehend them, but also to procure or test clues and evidence through scientific methods. These central agencies may provide expert aid and service to local officers, and, if they are called upon by the latter, no issue of local pride or prerogative is likely to arise. They may strengthen the hand of the law consistently in sparsely populated regions and, at times, in areas or centers of commercialized crime where local authorities may be subject to the subsidy of influential bosses of vice.

The state picture

Every state has a general police force or highway patrol or both. Three-fourths of the states have central police systems with full authority of law enforcement, and the others have state highway patrols which are concerned primarily or entirely with traffic violations, sometimes as units of the highway departments. State employees employed in police protection range in number from slightly more than 100 in North Dakota to more than 7,000 in California. There is no great degree of uniformity among the systems, but an increasing number of states select the personnel of police or patrol on a merit basis and also provide for training of the members. Racial discrimination until recently lent credence to the charge that state police forces were the nation's most segregated profession. A 1970 survey by the Race Relations Information Center found only five states with as many as 10 black troopers and 10 states with none at all.[5] In the entire nation, no more than one out of every 100 uniformed state troopers was black. Early in 1972, under federal court order, Alabama hired its first three black troopers and placed the names of more than 100 others on the eligible list.

The selection of the top officials usually is by gubernatorial appointment or at least with heavy gubernatorial influence and involvement. In a few states, the head or superintendent of the force is chosen by a board that may exercise substantial control over the activities of the agency. States with large or effective systems assign the men, on a more or less flexible basis, to routes or geographical sections for adequate territorial coverage. Some states also have a functional division, as between highway patrol service and other enforcement duties. The personnel is also likely to be organized in a military or semi-military manner, with companies,

[5] John Egerton, "States Have 250 Black Troopers," *Race Relations Reporter* (Dec. 9, 1970), p. 4.

rank, and uniforms. The Safe Streets Act has assigned states a central role in criminal justice planning at the regional and state level.

The states also have a miscellany of specialized officers or agencies for direct or indirect aid to security and law enforcement. These include such functionaries as civil-defense directors, fire marshals, game and fish wardens, liquor control officers, and different types of inspectors, who may be responsible to central regulatory agencies. There are state medical examiners to determine the cause of death in questionable or concealed circumstances. There are central offices or bureaus, with professional staffs, to make investigations with laboratory methods, including chemical and ballistic testing, and to establish evidence of crime and identification of criminals. This service is of invaluable aid to prosecuting authorities throughout the state. Such testing sometimes establishes the innocence of suspects, since the methods are free from the bias or error of eyewitnesses.

County Authorities and Activities

The sheriff

The American sheriff historically embodies the combination of a medieval factotum with a kingpin of the wild western frontier. The role of this officer has declined less in this country than in England, but our county sheriff has yielded importance to the state police and the city police, in many ways and in many regions, particularly as a keeper of the peace. He and his deputies are important enforcement and arresting officers in rural counties and in unincorporated fringes of many urban counties. The sheriff, with his subordinates, has two other regular responsibilities. He functions as an executive agent of state judicial courts in his jurisdiction, serving papers, subpoenas, processes, property attachments, and the like, in both criminal and civil matters. He guards prisoners in court and jail, administers or supervises jail quarters, provides food for prisoners, and arranges for escorting convicted persons to the penitentiary to serve sentence. He may, as in several states, have duties in connection with collecting delinquent taxes or disposing of property for nonpayment of taxes. "Sheriff's sale" has a folk meaning. Prior to the adoption of modern scientific methods of executing the death sentence and of the policy of administering this punishment in the central penitentiary in most of the states, many a sheriff, including Grover Cleveland when he was such an officer, had to fill the role of hangman, with the county jail or jail yard as the scene. Because of the availability of other enforcement forces, the sheriff today seldom exercises his traditional power to commandeer a *posse* of laymen to deal with excessive or riotous disorder.

The sheriff normally gets his position through political activity. He is chosen by the electorate in every state except Rhode Island, where selection is by the legislature. The term is likely to be for two or for four years; many states forbid a sheriff to succeed himself. This restriction does not prevent a man from winning the office for alternate terms. There have been cases of two men teaming up to hold the restrictive office between themselves, with the "out" serving as the chief deputy for the "in" for a number of terms.

The sheriff's office: fees and politics

The attractiveness of the office is enhanced in many states and counties by the retention of the antiquated fee system, fees sometimes amounting to a fortune during one term in a large county. There may be a fee for every court order, process, or warrant served by the sheriff or a deputy for whatever purpose, with additional compensation for capturing or handling prisoners. Sheriffs have been known to make handsome profits in the business of lodging and feeding prisoners, sometimes supplementing the gains by providing outside luxuries for prisoners having ample funds. The office thus tends often to become a desirable entrepreneurial undertaking, and some have been known to reap further gain by peddling lucrative protection to criminal interests. The incumbent is often enmeshed in the unavoidable business aspects of the office, whether for selfish or for unselfish motives, and thus tends to function merely as an amateur in the sphere of law enforcement. In addition to his regular staff, he may commission deputies on a nominal or honorary basis for political purposes or for authorizing privately employed guards to act in an enforcement capacity for their employers.

More than in other fields of government is vigilance on the part of citizens essential for public effectiveness in the sheriff's office. Systematic or improvised merit systems for the selection of deputies offer one answer to the problem of county law enforcement under politically chosen officials. There have also been suggestions that the sheriff be restricted to the function of process-server as officer of the court and that his enforcement or public safety role be transferred to more expert agencies.

The constable

The constable is a sort of sheriff with duties inside the county. This officer is appointed in a few states but elected in most instances by the voters of a town, township, or precinct. He generally has duties or responsibilities within his electoral subdivision. As keeper of the peace, however, he has county-wide authority in some states and may act independently of other enforcement officers. Constables have actually undertaken raids on illegal establishments overlooked by urban police and sheriff. The constable consistently acts as executive officer and process-server for minor courts or justices of the peace. This role has often become his sole or primary concern. Like the sheriff, he finds compensation through fees. Like the justice of the peace, he is only a part-time public functionary, and, like the J. P., he is tending to disappear from the civic landscape.

The coroner is also a local lay official, although he is somewhat more outmoded than the sheriff or constable. He is a popularly elected county officer in most states, and it is his function to investigate the cause of death occurring in the absence of witnesses and under circumstances indicating the possible use of unlawful means. He may have the power of assembling a jury, usually of six laymen, to conduct an inquest and render an official report on the testimony and findings. A few states, with Massachusetts as pioneer, have replaced the coroner with a local medical examiner, and the practice of choosing physicians for the office or adding medical men to the coroner's staff has been adopted as an improvement. Much of the work formerly performed by the local coroner is now handled by central state agencies or bureaus of analysis, investigation, and identification, as indicated earlier in this chapter.

The coroner

The public prosecutor

The local prosecutor is an established and essential factor in state law enforcement and criminal justice, and circumstances often combine to make him a wielder of great power. His title varies among the states. He may be designated as prosecuting attorney, solicitor, attorney general, state's attorney, district attorney, and the like. He usually serves a single county, but several small rural counties sometimes may have a circuit-riding prosecutor. He is selected by popular election in about nine-tenths of the states, most commonly for a four-year term, although there are terms of two years and of six years. He derives power from constitution, law, and custom, and is a dominant force in criminal proceedings and trial court action from first clue to conviction or acquittal. If strong and able, a lawyer in this position may inject a civic spirit of energy and action into a complacent police department, sheriff's staff, grand jury, and all investigators concerned with checking and detecting crime. Populous counties or districts may have special investigators as well as assistant attorneys attached to the chief prosecutor's office. There have been examples of softness of prosecution toward commercialized crime, but sometimes a prosecuting attorney coordinates his own militant activity with an aroused public opinion in launching an attack upon vice or racketeering. Important public careers have been started or accelerated from the office of local prosecutor, as exemplified by the elder Robert M. La Follette, Hugo Black, and Thomas E. Dewey. The office of the public prosecutor is not on the decline.

The elusive goal of "objective justice"

Public prosecution theoretically is supposed to serve at all times the ends of objective justice, not partisan injustice; however, a criminal case in court tends to become a game which the prosecuting attorney seeks to win on his own terms, leaving the defense to look out for itself or take the consequences. Wealthy or professional criminals are able to meet the prosecution with equal or superior legal talent, while many other defendants may be handicapped in this respect. The politics of harsh and lenient handling of criminal cases is discussed in chapter 15. The constitutional requirement that defense counsel be furnished in jury trials, at public expense if necessary, is often inadequate for the poor, since lawyers appointed by the court for this purpose are often unequal to the opposition in ability or experience and may at best put up a lame or nominal defense. To meet this dilemma, a number of individual counties or jurisdictions in different parts of the country have set up the office of public defender, putting this regular official on a par with the prosecuting attorney before the court. He has equal accessibility to public facilities for procuring or testing evidence. Connecticut and Rhode Island were the first states to require the system on a statewide basis, and their system became the pattern for close to a dozen states by 1970. Sometimes outside aid comes from such organizations as the American Civil Liberties Union, particularly in what seem to be conspicuous or flagrant cases of discrimination. Voluntary assistance may come from local sources, including legal-aid clinics. The number of defense counsel organizations increased sharply between 1964 and 1970 from 136 to 330, the influence of the anti-poverty war an important factor. The trial courts in approximately one-third of the states, however, continue to trust the assignment of counsel for the poor to the judge.

Public defender

Urban Police

Urban police departments constitute the most important instruments of law enforcement and public safety in the United States today. City policemen outnumber all other state and local enforcement officers combined. One policeman or marshal may suffice for a small town, but New York City requires a force of close to 30,000, and many other cities use thousands. The urban police force has a large role for several reasons. The American population has become far more urban or metropolitan than rural, and cities provide the scene of a large amount of modern crime. Moreover, urban protective vigilance must function around the clock, for the city never sleeps, part of its population being always on the move for good or for ill. Aside from directly combating crime and criminals, the city police must give constant attention to a moderate regimentation of the whole process of life, work, and play within its jurisdiction in order to prevent utter confusion. Multitudes of individuals leaving an auditorium or stadium, for example, require traffic direction, even if all the individuals should have the most saintly intentions. If fire damage leaves collapsible walls or buildings endangering life, the police must get on the job to protect the innocent and unsuspecting from self-jeopardy. Police specialists conduct searches and inquiries for missing persons, including minors and adults, whether crime is involved or not. The processes of urban civilization in the

General importance

technological age make it necessary for the police to provide guidance and assistance for the obedient as well as force and compulsion for the disobedient.

Coping with social revolution

Police responsibilities have increased in recent years because of two developments beyond the customary bounds of criminological research. One is the social alienation and rejection of "establishment" values by many of the nation's more educated youth, manifested by increased vandalism and drug abuse. The other is the growth of militancy among minority groups, resulting in serious alienation and confrontation between such groups and the police. (*See* Figure 19–2.)

From spoils to science

American urban police administration has gone through a process of incomplete evolution from spoils practices to a merit-based professionalism with a wide application of scientific techniques. This evolution has come about chiefly in the twentieth century, although progress occurred earlier in the wake of the reorganization of the London police in 1829 through reform action by Sir Robert Peel. The London "Peelers" or "Bobbies" wore copper buttons on their uniforms, from which the word "cop" was derived as a designation for an American policeman. In spite of improvement, however, many American city police departments still have far to go, and evidence of favoritism and corruption continues to appear in different parts of the country from time to time. There are a few state-

Figure 19–2. Editorial cartoon by Pat Oliphant. Copyright © *The Denver Post.* Reprinted by permission of the Los Angeles Times Syndicate.

controlled police departments, but most police forces are under local control. Hence their scientific or meritorious features tend to fluctuate with the ups and downs of local self-government. In comparison with Western Europe or Great Britain, American urban police systems have suffered because they do not attract the most competent career men. Ambitious young Americans too often have sought other outlets for their talents. Thought continues to be given by reform elements to the means whereby urban police service can be rendered an attractive career to the able, however, and some of the nation's more important cities are managing to recruit more able people for police work. The Supreme Court's more recent restrictions on police-station interrogation of suspects place an even greater premium on the recruitment and training of competent police personnel.

Departmental organization

The organization of police departments inevitably varies for different cities, particularly for cities of different size. The typical operating head, or chief of police, serves by local appointment in most cities, but is chosen by state authorities for those few departments that are under state control. The municipal superior to whom the chief is responsible varies according to city charters and forms of government. This authority may be the mayor, city manager, police commissioner, or a local board. There are variations within the variations. A commissioner, for example, may be an appointee or may be an elected member of a city commission, and he may have jurisdiction over both police and fire departments. Police boards, where used, are not uniform and are not uniformly effective. Theodore Roosevelt did a clean-up job as chairman of such a board in New York City in the 1890s.

Modern police departments are organized and operated through functional divisions in order to make use of specialized training and experience for efficient service. Traffic regulation as an expanding function calls for the concentrated attention of one branch or bureau of the force. Another task is performed by regular police patrols, who move on foot or by motor to protect life and property and arrest lawbreakers. For every large or important city there is a separate unit or division of detectives working quietly and in plain clothes to track down crime and criminals. Every such city must also have a headquarters staff that includes officers or employees for general records service, internal housekeeping, and other routine activity. A large department has a certain amount of police personnel administration. Policewomen are needed for special work among women criminals and prisoners. A city may have squads for special or temporary assignment, such as checking and investigating juvenile delinquency or raiding vice dens. A development of recent years is the auxiliary police for civil defense, which cooperates with other authorities in this functional area. The smaller cities, of course, cannot have the protection of police organization and mechanization on an elaborate scale except through central state or metropolitan arrangements.

Increasing federal involvement

The federal government has become increasingly involved in recent years in efforts to improve the standards and performance of police personnel at the state and local levels. The Federal Bureau of Investigation has for many years conducted training courses for selected state and local officers. Its National Crime Information Center (NCIC), with highly sophisticated computer storage and retrieval of criminal information, provides a high-speed law enforcement communication and data-exchange network for the United States and Canada, handling close to 1,000 inquiries daily. The number of different federal agencies involved in law enforcement and the massive task of federal, state, county, and city coordination of law enforcement are illustrated in Table 19–2.

The LEAA and early criticisms

In response to the findings and recommendations of President Johnson's Commission on Law Enforcement and the Administration of Justice, a vast new federal role was initiated by the Omnibus Crime Control and Safe Streets Act of 1968 (with 1970 amendments). This landmark legislation established the Law Enforcement and Assistance Administration (LEAA) in the Department of Justice to dispense federal grants-in-aid for the improvement of state and local law enforcement. It called for annual grants increasing to $1.75 billion by 1973. Not only is it a massive intergovernmental effort to solve a major domestic problem, the control of crime, but it also attempts to use the controversial state block-grant method to achieve cooperation among highly competitive agencies, professions, and levels of government. Local governments and urban interests lobbied strongly against the new stronger role for state government, arguing that states are inexperienced in problems of law enforcement; are encumbered by inefficient organization and rural-oriented officials; have not distributed sufficient funds to the high-crime areas; and have been responsible for two centuries of chaotic court systems, criminal codes, and penal and correctional institutions. The federal and local levels have not been spared in the early criticism of the program. The LEAA's three-member bipartisan "troika" set up for administration was plagued with friction. This led to an amendment aimed at providing more administrative unity. Early criticism of excessive local expenditures for new police "hardware" and anti-riot equipment of all kinds led to 1970 amendments requiring that close to 60 percent of the block grants to the states must be used for corrections, the entire system of courts, jails, prisons, probation and bail.

Criminal justice as a system

Probably the most far-reaching aspect of the Omnibus Crime Control and Safe Streets Act is the "systems approach" which calls for the treatment of law enforcement as "*all* activities pertaining to crime prevention or reduction and enforcement of the criminal law." Despite its inexperience and past mistakes, the states still emerged as the logical middle unit of government with adequate jurisdiction and authority, short of setting up the feared national police force. The states were considered the logical existing structure to pull the various divergent elements together into a criminal justice system. The act requires each state to establish a state criminal justice planning agency, and to submit annually a comprehensive criminal justice plan outlining its proposals for improvements. The original legislation required a 60-40 matching sum by the ultimate recipient of the grant, but the state or local obligation was reduced by Congress in 1970 to a 75-25 formula. In addition, states were required by the 1970 amendments (over their vigorous objection) to "buy-in" to the local program by paying 25 percent of the local government's matching requirement on any project. The Crime Control Act of 1973 extended the program initiated by the 1968 act, and it retained the block-grant format and the pivotal role of the states.

Prison Administration and Correctional Activities

Theories and purposes

The fifty states, with their local units, have a wide variety of prisons and correctional systems, based upon several old or new theories of crime and punishment in relationship to the nature of man. These theories are not mutually exclusive but overlap slightly with varied emphasis when applied to the multitudinous jurisdictions. Four of them should be noted: (1) There is the old, old theory that revenge should be visited by society upon the guilty person, holding him solely and individually responsible for his error and compelling him to pay his "debt" to society on the basis of an eye for an eye, a tooth for a tooth, a life for a life. (2) Closely related to the revenge theory is the general demand that punishment be sure, adequately severe, and sufficiently conspicuous to deter others from crime regardless of inclination. This idea calls for a calculated matching of crime and punishment, with large penalties to check large crimes and small penalties to check smaller violations. (3) There is the strong insistence that criminals be segregated behind walls in order to protect society from further violations by them until they learn their lesson. (4) There is a complex theory, with a modern socio-scientific bias, that assumes that society owes a debt of rehabilitation to lawbreakers, who are socially maladjusted, partly or entirely, and victims of circumstances beyond their control. These circumstances may be physical, physiological, mental, economic, or social, and ultimately deny to the individual the role of free agent. The theory of reform or rehabilitation has been particularly applied in recent times to juvenile offenders, but it is also taken seriously by many authorities and institutional officers in the treatment of adults.[6]

[6] For a comprehensive collection of old and new essays on this subject, *see* Stanley E. Grupp (ed.), *Theories of Punishment* (Bloomington: Indiana University Press, 1972).

Table 19–2. Criminal Justice Structure in the United States

	National Government	*State Governments (50)*	*County Governments (3,050)*	*Municipal (18,000) and other Governments*
I. POLICE FORCES	FBI (17,300 people) Bureau of Narcotics (2,000 people) Border Patrol (1,500) IRS-Tax Fraud, etc. (2,900) IRS-Alcohol, etc. (2,000) Treasury-Secret Service (2,500) Customs (1,400) Park Police (1,200) Sky Marshals (2,000) TOTALS. These and other units, full-time equivalent 1969: 35,500 persons	State police and highway patrols 1969 employment, full-time equivalent: 53,500 persons	Elective sheriffs and a few separate police depts.	About 35,000 separate police forces
			Total 1969 employment, full-time equivalent: 377,200 persons Of these, 15–20% are county employees, 80–85% work for municipal, township, or other governmental levels.	
			In 1967, there were 58,400 full-time and 8,400 part-time county employees	In 1967, there were 154,400 full-time and 41,600 part-time municipal employees, plus 5,900 full-time and 16,500 part-time township employees, in addition to 3,500 full-time and 9,000 part-time special district employees
II. PROSECUTION	93 District Attorneys' offices 1969 full-time equivalent employment: 5,800 plus 1,800 in indigent defense	50 Attorneys General 1969 full-time equivalent employment: 6,400	Some 3,000 Elective Prosecuting Attorneys (District Attorneys, State's Attorneys, etc.)	Usually depend, in serious offenses, on county prosecution
			1969 full-time employment equivalent: 21,800 plus 2,100 engaged in indigent defense	

Table 19–2. *Continued*

	National Government	*State Governments (50)*	*County Governments (3,050)*	*Municipal (18,000) and other Governments*
III. COURTS	U.S. Supreme Court 10 Circuit Courts of Appeals 93 District Courts Special Tax, Customs, Claims Courts 1969 full-time equivalent employment: 5,800	50 State Supreme Courts Intermediate Courts of Appeals Circuit and other Courts of Original Jurisdiction 1969 full-time equivalent employment: 15,600	Uncounted numbers of lower courts, mainly with original jurisdiction, including county courts, magistrates' courts, justices of the peace, together with special courts on traffic, domestic relations, juvenile offenders, etc. 1969 full-time equivalent employment: 63,700	
IV. CORRECTIONS	1969 full-time equivalent employment: 5,400	1969 full-time equivalent employment: 84,600	1969 full-time equivalent employment: 48,500	
			1967 employment: 32,400 full-time and 2,700 part-time	1967 municipal employment: 11,000 full-time and 200 part-time
	Prison population, Dec. 31, 1967: 19,500	Prison population, Dec. 31, 1967: 175,300	Prison population, March 15, 1970, held in some 4,000 local jails: 160,900, of whom 75,000 were awaiting trial	

Source: Committee for Economic Development, *Reducing Crime and Assuring Justice* (New York, 1972), pp. 81–83.

The prisons having the least concern with problems of human restoration are normally the city and county jails, which serve primarily for the retention of accused persons pending trial and sentence or other disposition of their cases. Such retention is not technical punishment, however unpleasant it may be, and is not to be associated with "hard labor." In many instances, however, short terms of punishment are served in such jails, sometimes by persons who serve time for lack of funds to pay fines. Because most juvenile court jurisdictions lack detention facilities other than city jails or police lockups, more than 100,000 children are held each year in these adult jails.

Local jails

There has been improvement in the living conditions and treatment of inmates in these local jails in the twentieth century. Many county jails are used jointly by the federal government for housing prisoners on a contract basis; the federal government requires that certain standards be maintained and checked by inspection. Modern health regulations apply to jails and are sometimes enforced. For a few weeks in 1955 the city of Nashville, Tennessee, was without a municipal prison because of a condemnation decision by the local health department and had to rely entirely upon county law enforcement proceedings for purposes of public safety. Many a small city or county has antiquated jail facilities, and inmates in such places have an abundance of monotonous boredom.

Many cities and counties maintain work crews of prisoners whose terms of punishment are too short for transportation to state prisons. Much of this work is on streets or roads under the eyes of armed guards and in the view of all who pass by. The prisoners may return to jail for lodging, or may in some jurisdictions be quartered in camps or workhouses, although the name of chain gang hardly applies as in former days. Many states in the nineteenth century, especially in the South, allowed "convict-lease" systems for county prisoners to work in private industries, such as mining and lumbering. This policy has been reversed by legislative compulsion as a result of pressure by social reformers and organized labor. Normally, local prison labor must be for public, not private, use.

Local prison labor

The central state penitentiaries are often superior to local jails and workhouses in scientific management and treatment of prisoners, although many state systems are inferior to federal institutions in this respect. All have difficulty in providing useful and constructive employment for those who are serving sentence. Under various state and federal statutes prison labor must not be used for the direct production of merchandise for the channels of commerce. It is often utilized for turning out items for state purposes, such as equipment and supplies for government offices or for state institutions. Penitentiary farms may provide food for the prisoners, who cultivate the crops and attend the livestock. This activity competes only indirectly with free labor, and it serves to keep the prisoners from

State penitentiaries

idleness. Prisoners also have limited opportunities for vocational training, reading, recreation, and entertainment. Inmates may issue an institutional publication somewhat on the model of a school newspaper. The best or largest of the penitentiaries are likely to have competent counselors, including chaplains, medical officers, and psychiatrists, as well as trained wardens. Serious cases of mental illness may be transferred to a special division of the state hospital for the insane.

Yet it must be said that penal institutions have only a limited success in curing criminals of criminal tendencies, of checking the "rule" of once a convict, always a convict. More than 60 percent of the nation's federal and state convicts commit crimes after prison release, and 85 percent of all crimes in the United States are committed by "repeaters." This cycle of crime has led some to describe jails as "factories of crime" and prisons as "colleges for advanced criminal education." A psychiatric expert, with clinical experience at New York's Sing Sing Prison, has urged that prisons as presently constituted be abolished, since they destroy more disturbed personalities than they reclaim. He points to the prison riots over the country as indicative of improper and unscientific treatment of the inmates. According to his view, society is more concerned with keeping persons in prison than in keeping them out. Real treatment centers for the antisocial may be around the corner, but not an immediate corner. Most states lack adequate staffs and personnel for such expert assistance.[7] All too often it is only a prison uprising such as the Attica tragedy that triggers serious prison study and reform.[8] Most recommendations for reform urge refocusing corrections on rehabilitation by more effective community-based treatment, expanded education and vocational training, and increased programs and facilities for work release. (*See* Figure 19–3.)

Juvenile delinquents

The emphasis on the philosophy of correction rather than punishment has gained wider acceptance for the institutional treatment of juvenile offenders than of adult lawbreakers. For more than a century, leaders and organizations have urged sympathetic attention to delinquent children, matching the movement for more humane care of the mentally ill. State reformatories for boys and girls often function under the name of "training school," "trade school," or "industrial school," and seek to measure up to the name. Their task is not easy, for many of the juvenile delinquents have mental limitations or emotional problems which cannot be overcome through institutional care. Furthermore, these institutions are not uniformly modern in methods and types of administrators. They some-

[7] *See* Donald H. Goff, "Correctional Programs," *The Book of the States, 1972–73*, pp. 432–438, for a brief discussion of recent correctional developments.

[8] One such study is Floyd E. Ohlin (ed.), *Prisoners in America* (Englewood Cliffs, N. J.: The American Assembly and Prentice-Hall, 1973). In 1971 a five-day convict revolt at Attica (New York) was finally quelled at a cost of 43 lives.

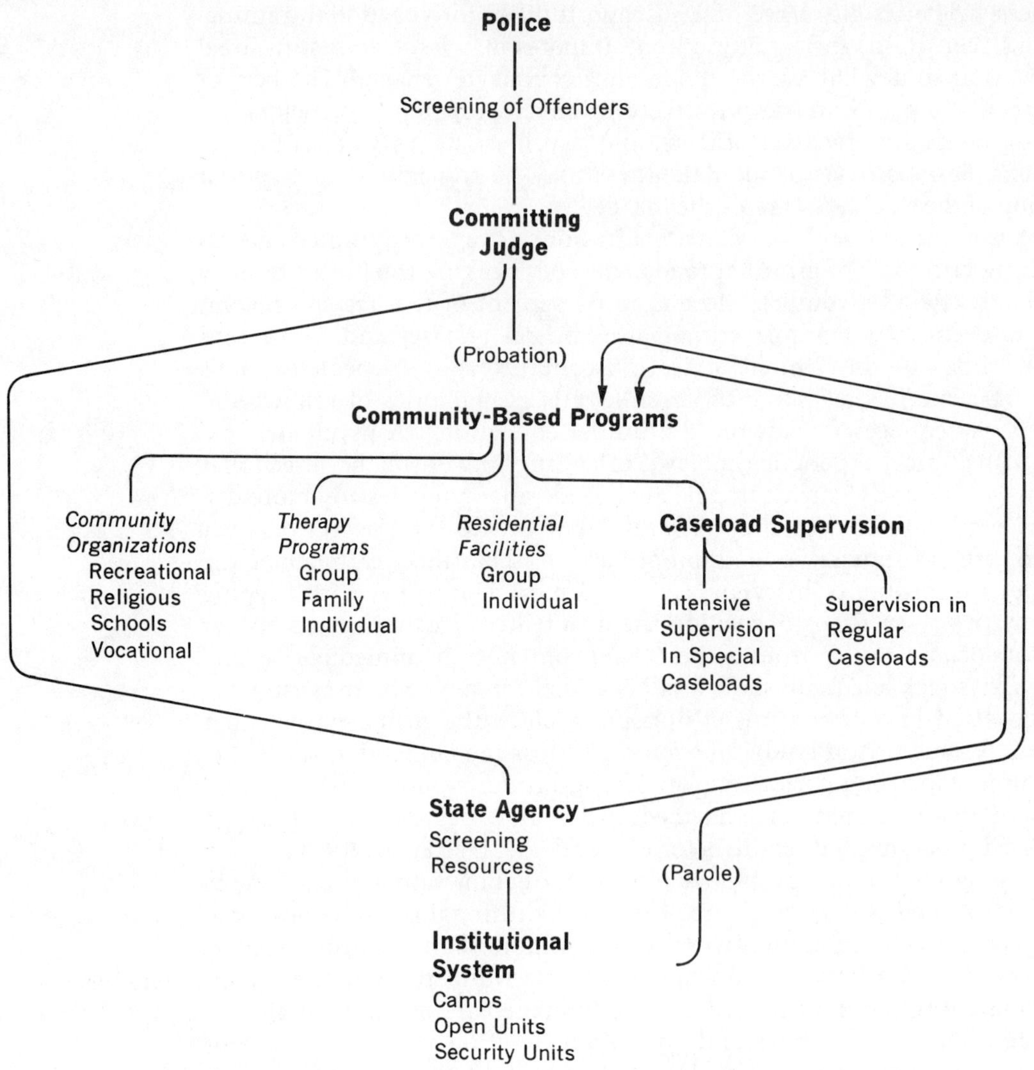

Figure 19–3. Elements of a Modern Correctional System. *Source:* U. S. President's Commission on Law Enforcement and Administration of Justice, *The Challenge of Crime in a Free Society* (Washington, D. C.: U. S. Government Printing Office, 1967), p. 182.

times have juvenile escapes. Private and public agencies give no little attention to methods of readjustment of problem children before the stage is reached for assignment to the reformatory. Through the development and training of social workers, many city school systems have visiting teachers to deal personally and individually with pupils who are falling down in work, attendance, or behavior. These professional workers have ways of getting to the root of the trouble, whether poverty, loneliness, broken home, or other difficulties, and of providing help before it is too late. Probation officers attached to local juvenile courts may also provide constructive assistance. Different service groups and clubs aid in the work of reducing or preventing juvenile delinquency.

SUPPLEMENTARY READINGS

American Prison Association. *Manual of Correctional Standards.* New York: American Prison Association, 1954.

Caldwell, Robert G. *Criminology.* 2nd ed. New York: Ronald Press Co., 1965.

Casper, Jonathan D. *American Criminal Justice: The Defendant's Perspective.* Englewood Cliffs, N. J.: Prentice-Hall, 1972.

Committee for Economic Development. *Reducing Crime and Assuring Justice.* New York, 1972.

Federal Bureau of Investigation. *Uniform Crime Reports.* Washington, D. C.: United States Government Printing Office. Semiannual publication.

Grupp, Stanley E., ed. *Theories of Punishment.* Bloomington: Indiana University Press, 1972.

International City Managers' Association. *Municipal Police Administration.* 5th ed. Chicago, 1961.

Jacob, Herbert. *Urban Justice.* Englewood Cliffs, N. J.: Prentice-Hall, 1973.

Kefauver, Estes. *Crime in America.* Garden City, N. Y.: Doubleday and Co., 1951.

Leonard, V. A. *Police Organization and Management.* 2nd ed. Brooklyn: Foundation Press, 1964.

MacIver, Robert M. *The Prevention and Control of Delinquency: A Strategic Approach.* New York: Atherton Press, 1966.

National Advisory Commission on Criminal Justice Standards and Goals. *National Conference on Criminal Justice.* Washington, D. C.: U. S. Government Printing Office, 1973.

Northwestern University School of Law. *The Journal of Criminal Law, Criminology and Police Science.*

Ohlin, Lloyd E., ed. *Prisoners in America.* Englewood Cliffs, N. J.: The American Assembly and Prentice-Hall, 1973.

President's Commission on Law Enforcement and Administration of Justice. *The Challenge of Crime in a Free Society.* Washington, D. C.: U. S. Government Printing Office, 1967.

Radzinowicz, Leon, and Wolfgang, Marvin E., eds. *Crime and Justice.* 3 vols. New York: John Wiley and Sons, 1971.

Skolnick, Jerome. *Justice Without Trial: Law Enforcement in a Democratic Society.* New York: John Wiley and Sons, 1966.

Smith, Bruce. *Police Systems in the United States.* 2nd rev. ed. New York: Harper & Row, 1960.

U. S. Advisory Commission on Intergovernmental Relations. *State–Local Relations in the Criminal Justice System.* Washington, D. C., 1971.

Wilson, O. W. *Police Administration.* 2nd ed. New York: McGraw-Hill Book Co., 1962.

20

Public Policy toward Private Enterprise

Scope and significance

Government is inevitably linked in one way or another with the economic and occupational life of its constituents. State and local units provide no exceptions to this rule. They have always manifested concern, wisely or unwisely, with problems of regulation, protection, and promotion of different types of private and professional enterprise within their borders. For these purposes they have increasingly made use of their public police power. The general constitutional aspects of this usage were explored in the fourth chapter; it seems appropriate here to take a closer look at the political, economic, and administrative ramifications of these problems and policies.

It has already been noted that in many ways state regulation led the way for national regulation of corporate business, notably of railroads. Stiff treatment and regulation of railroads have characterized a number of important governorships, including those of William Larrabee of Iowa, in the 1880s, and of B. B. Comer of Alabama, Robert La Follette of Wisconsin, and Hiram Johnson of California, in the early years of the twentieth century. Woodrow Wilson's gubernatorial term in New Jersey was characterized by the adoption of measures that lifted from that state the label "mother of trusts." Economic reform or regulation movements have occurred in local governments at times. An example is the establishment of the three-cent fare on city streetcars in Cleveland through the leadership of Mayor Tom L. Johnson, who was elected four times in the first decade of this century. It should not be forgotten that economic interests of diverse complexion rather constantly battle for the control of governmental policy at the state and local level, whether for protective labor legislation in New

York, for lenient requirements as to corporate charters in Delaware, or for concessions to new industries in Mississippi.

A varied role

The role of state and local government toward private operators and practitioners takes many forms within the American federal system. In its totality this role embraces taxation, regulation, granting corporate charters or franchises, contractual relations for public works, issuance of licenses or permits for the conduct of business and professions, inspectional procedures, offering aid or advice for the attraction of new enterprise, and various specialized or ad hoc arrangements. The role shows variations, as between an oil state like Texas and a mining state like West Virginia, or between the older textile regions of New England and newer textile regions of the Southeast, particularly in the matter of retaining or attracting manufacturing establishments. The regulation of professional boxing or of the heating of multiple-apartment buildings in New York City is a different problem from what it is in Mississippi. The state government may have more responsibility with respect to horseracing in Kentucky than in the Dakotas. One may find differences in the economic policy of state and local governments between urbanized areas and rural regions, between coastal centers and hinterlands, and between desert counties and rain belts. There is wide variety as well as similarity in the regulatory action of the numerous jurisdictions. As suggested in chapter 8, the similarities and differences between states and localities in their roles of economic regulation are determined in large measure by factors of political influence among economic groups and the question of who is able to get what, when, and how.

Regulation of Public Utilities

Certain businesses, primarily in the fields of transportation, communication, and power, have come to enjoy special privileges granted by governments; but with these privileges have come various public regulations relating to rates charged and the quality and quantity of service provided. The definition of a public utility has never been very precise, but a modern list of businesses that have come to be known as public utilities would certainly include telephone, telegraph, and power transmission companies; water, gas, and electric service companies; and such transportation facilities as the railroads, airlines, and commercial truck and bus lines; and might possibly be extended to include public markets, toll bridges and roads, airports, port facilities, and the like.

Early state and local experience with the public utility was related for the most part to transportation. Governments, ancient and modern, have manifested an interest in the routes and facilities of transportation, an interest often transcending concern merely for systems of highways. The Erie Canal represents early state development of water transportation; airports in many cases reflect modern joint action by states, municipalities, and even the federal government in providing essential conditions for the speediest form of transportation.

Historical background

Private transportation services have long been recognized in the common law as "affected with a public interest," as pointed out by the Supreme Court in *Munn* v. *Illinois*,[1] thereby developing a pattern of local, state, and federal regulation. The states pioneered in sponsoring the development of railroads through provisions for franchises, legal arrangements for securing rights of way, and sometimes direct aid, frequently with further support by municipalities. There were examples of land-grant aid by the federal government through the states as intermediaries. But the railroads of the nation got a serious taste of state regulation as a result of the Granger movement, which swept the country in the 1870s, creating a significant impact in the grain states. Strong laws were passed, sometimes rigidly fixing freight rates; the state railroad commissions were created to administer these laws. Legislation and administration went through a process of moderation with the waning of the Granger reform. Farmers and shippers realized that they needed federal regulation of rates on interstate transportation. In 1887 the Interstate Commerce Commission was provided for by Congress. But the state railroad commissions remained in existence and took on new life in the next century, although overshadowed in the transportation picture by the ICC.

Commission expansion

It became necessary to regulate other forms of moving freight and passengers besides rail, and thus the railroad commissions were generally changed in name and broadened in scope. They have frequently been named "public service commission" and are likely to have intrastate regulatory jurisdiction, not only over railways, but also over chartered bus lines, motor-freight companies, electric power, telephone services, and similar enterprises. State regulation of intrastate commerce may be prevented from jeopardizing interstate commerce or the federal regulation of such commerce. The ICC may intervene to prevent unjust discrimination against interstate commerce by intrastate rates.[2] The rapid development of cable television systems (CATV), initially as a means of serving isolated areas but more recently as multiple-channel systems providing better service and more choices in urban areas, has led an increasing number of states to move to statewide regulation of CATV. In 1974 CATV was still

[1] 94 U. S. 113 (1876). *See* chapter 4. On the subject of Granger legislation in the states, *see* S. J. Buck, *The Granger Movement* (Cambridge, Mass.: Harvard University Press, 1913).

[2] An important opinion affirming this point was delivered in the Shreveport rate case in 1914, *Houston, East and West Texas Railway Co.* v. *United States; Texas and Pacific Railway Co.* v. *United States*, 234, U. S. 342.

subject to only local regulation in the great majority of states, although industry leaders predicted 5,000 systems serving 30 million homes by 1980. The state public service commissions are organized into the National Association of Utility Commissions (NARUC), and such current issues as cable television regulation are watched carefully by NARUC, which keeps state and local interests in mind.[3]

Problems of rate regulation

Effective regulation of public utilities is not child's play, nor can it be done by well-meaning amateurs. The total investment in such utilities amounts to many billions of dollars, and the political power which can be brought to bear on a governor, a legislative body, or upon public opinion in a given policy controversy is an awesome sight on occasion. The regulation of rates charged by the utilities is undoubtedly the most difficult of the jobs faced by the regulatory commission. The courts have long held that rates fixed by the commission must permit the utility to make a "fair rate of return" on a "fair value of the utility." Determining "fairness" in the first of these two respects is not a serious problem, usually; the courts accept from 5 to 8 percent as reasonable. It is the second criterion, determining the "fair value of the utility," which has come to be the universal headache for state regulatory commissions.

Competing theories of valuation

Why is it so difficult to determine the reasonable value of a public utility? A brief examination of the possible methods which might be used will give some insight into the frustrations of conscientious commissioners. (1) Why not apply the ordinary test of market value—what it could be sold for? It is obvious that this test is impractical because giant utilities simply are not sold from day to day, or year to year, like automobiles or houses. (2) Then why not use the market value of the utility stocks and bonds? It is true that a few shares may change hands from time to time, but their fluctuations in price make it impossible to use them as an accurate measure of the entire property's value. (3) Would it not be possible to examine the profits of the enterprise and determine a fair value in much the same way as is done for competitive businesses, that is, by "capitalization of earnings"? The problem here soon becomes apparent: the utility's profits are determined in the first place by an earlier rate-making decision of the commission, and capitalizing earnings would catch both the commission and the utility in a trap of circular reasoning, always justifying the status quo. (4) Another possibility is to determine value on the basis of original cost of constructing or acquiring the property, less depreciation. Yet either inflation or deflation has the effect of making original cost a poor measure of *present* value of a public utility, and owners complain bitterly about this method in time of inflation. (5) Then why not

[3] *See* Paul Rodgers, "Developments in Public Utility Regulation," *The Book of the States, 1974–75*, pp. 523–531.

use the principle of "reproduction cost," whereby actual money invested is not the determinant, but rather the cost of recreating the public utility plant and equipment at present prices? The practical effect of fixing rates by this method is to give the owners a handsome reward if prices are higher than when the property was acquired, and to hand them a severe loss if prices have dropped since acquisition of the property. (6) The "prudent investment theory" is still another method, and a modification of the original cost doctrine. Valuation for rate-making purposes begins with original cost, but subtracts costs which would not have been made by a prudent businessman. This method obviously complicates the regulatory commission's job even further, but the philosophy is clear: a regulated monopoly should not be allowed to include foolish or extravagant expenditures in its "fair value," the basis for figuring rates charged the consuming public.

Court shift toward pragmatism

The foregoing list of possible methods of rate making is by no means exhaustive and is not given in an effort to qualify the reader as a specialist in utility rates. It should merely give some indication of the magnitude, complexity, and controversial character of this small segment of state and local regulation of business. In the case of *Smyth* v. *Ames,*[4] before the turn of the century, the Supreme Court held in effect that a formula must be used in utility valuation, making use of a variety of factors rather than relying on any one theory of valuation. Many years later in the *Hope Natural Gas* case, the Supreme Court relaxed the rigidity of this formula requirement to the extent of saying that "It is not the theory but the impact of the rate order that counts. If the total effect of the rate order cannot be said to be unjust and unreasonable, judicial inquiry is at an end."[5] This really offers the regulatory commission no guiding rule for rate-making valuations, but it does permit them a greater degree of pragmatic flexibility.

Local transportation utilities

Many municipalities exercise regulatory functions with respect to local transportation utilities. The Port of New York Authority is a bi-state metropolitan agency which operates or regulates important types of transportation facilities in several ports and municipalities. Several different kinds of metropolitan area transit authorities have sprung up in recent years, such as the San Francisco Bay Area Rapid Transit District, the Chicago Transit Authority, and the National Capital Transportation Agency. The latter agency looks toward an eventual interstate compact among Maryland, Virginia, and the District of Columbia to solve the mass transportation problems of the Washington, D. C., area.

Transportation service may be subject to other regulations outside the jurisdiction of the expert commissions. Buses, for example, are required

[4] 169 U. S. 466 (1898).

[5] *Federal Power Commission* v. *Hope Natural Gas Co.,* 320 U. S. 591 (1944).

to obey traffic regulations, and carriers of passengers must obey liquor and sanitation laws in their restaurant service. States, in an increasing number, are requiring that individual automobile owners carry liability insurance for the benefit of accident victims. In the sphere of transportation, corporations and individuals are amenable to a plurality of laws and authorities.

Banking, Finance, and Insurance

Scope of state regulations

The states undertake in varying ways and degrees to regulate private enterprise in the fields of banking, finance, and insurance. Despite the trend in recent decades toward "national" banks and "federal" loan associations, many banks, trust companies, investment houses, and lending firms continue to operate under state charter or license. Qualified state banks have become members of the Federal Reserve System and have acquired a protective status in connection with the Federal Deposit Insurance Corporation.

Financiers must comply with the requirements of the Securities and Exchange Commission for reporting and registering security issues. Intentional swindlers may receive federal punishment for fraudulent use of the mails.

The Supreme Court in 1944 reversed a long-standing position and held that insurance is commerce and is subject to federal laws and regulations if carried on across state lines.[6] Congress has used this new power with discretion, however, partly by enacting legislation to be effective in instances of state neglect of insurance regulation. In consequence, state insurance regulation has tended to expand rather than to decline, with more provision for the protection of policyholders through reserves, factual information, licensed agents, and examination of the business by official commissions or other authorities.

Financial protection for the little man

State governments and local authorities apply means and measures for the financial protection of the little man or the uninformed, although the protection is not always adequate or effective. Starting in Kansas in 1911, numerous "blue sky" laws have been passed to prohibit fraud and deception in the selling of securities. Ceilings on interest rates and other restrictions have been aimed at abuses by "personal" finance operators and loan sharks. Regulations for the prevention or exposure of bogus charities in urban communities have come into vogue.

Non-governmental activities have supplemented the efforts of public regulation in reducing these miscellaneous abuses. Legal-aid clinics have been helpful to low-income groups needing protection against the un-

[6] *United States* v. *South-Eastern Underwriters Association et al.*, 322 U. S. 533 (1944).

scrupulous. Education, publicity, and civic activities of business offer checks to frauds and flimflams. But larceny by trick, like larceny by shoplifting, continues to strike, much of it without detection.

The little man shares, of course, in the protection of enforced standards of banking and insurance. His pocketbook is safeguarded through elimination or clarification of fine-print clauses in sickness and accident policies. Improvements in this picture among all the states have been brought about by replacing the common-law doctrine and lawsuits for accident damage with automatic compensation to industrial workers. Many of these protections are applied by automatic and administrative processes, as far as they go. Others depend upon the deterrent effect of apprehending and punishing individual culprits. This action in itself means nothing in the way of financial reimbursement to the victims of fraud.

Consumer Relations

Although the name of Ralph Nader, "Naderism," and "consumerism" have become household words only recently on the American scene, the police power has been exercised for almost two centuries by states and localities to regulate industrial, mercantile, and service establishments to safeguard consumer and community interests. The regulation may have bearing on physical safety, health, pecuniary matters, moral habits, or general welfare and convenience, as well as the stability of the economic process that provides the goods and services. In the category of health and safety, shops and hotels must comply with measures to avoid fire hazards and elevator accidents; dining rooms and restaurants may be subject to test and inspection for sanitary standards of premises, equipment, and food, as well as the freedom from disease of employees; owners of apartment houses may have to meet specified requirements for the comfort of tenants; theaters and movie houses operate under precautionary regulations as to fire, overcrowding, and other hazards; drug stores have officially licensed pharmacists to fill prescriptions; dairies and milk distributors comply with standards of purity and cleanliness; and various other matters may be regulated. These procedures imply no exemption from compliance with federal food and drug regulations, although the latter may obviate the necessity for local inspection, as in the case of meat packing for both interstate and intrastate commerce.

Range of regulation: health and safety

Public surveillance provides certain economic protections for customers and clients. Grocers have been called to task for adjusting scales to short-weight outgoing merchandise. Old laws of cotton states penalized ginners and farmers for "platting" high-grade fiber around poor cotton or extraneous matter in bales. State authority to regulate warehouse rates was established in the era of the Granger movement. Farmers often are exempt from state or municipal sales taxes and license fees in marketing produce from their farms. Certain states have sought to stabilize the prices of national brands and products by preventing price-cutting of such items. Consequent court battles brought about fair-price legislation by Congress in 1952 empowering manufacturers and retailers to set prices on trademarked articles to be binding where state laws concur. This was in response to demands of conforming dealers rather than consumer pressure.

Economic practices

In the wake of the various anti-poverty programs of the 1960s, a sweeping new look at consumer protection devices at all levels of government was taken under the stinging criticisms of consumer advocate Ralph Nader and his "raiders." By the early 1970s, many states and cities had created consumer protection boards or departments and many near-sacred protections for business interests had been challenged, replaced, or at least questioned. For example, several states enacted laws that seemed to invalidate the obligation of contracts by allowing consumers a three-day "cooling-off period" during which they may cancel contracts made with door-to-door salesmen. Also outlawed in several states was the "holder-in-due-course" doctrine, long a trap for unwary installment-plan buyers who found themselves dealing with a credit bureau that has no responsibility for replacing or repairing faulty merchandise. In Massachusetts, where the state outlawed turning back the mileage reading on used cars, the Consumer Protection Division conducts "odometer raids" on used-car lots, checking vehicles on the lot and then checking with the prior owner to see if the odometer has been turned back. The trend is toward passage of comprehensive state consumer protection legislation administered by a division of the state attorney general's office, empowered to prosecute violators. One complaint has been that a haphazard proliferation of consumer protection programs has created confusion. A California study revealed 61 agencies dealing independently with different aspects of the issue.

Nader's "raiders" and their impact

One rather specialized outgrowth of the renewed interest in the welfare of the consumer has been the movement for "no-fault" automobile insurance. Growing discontent by accident victims with litigation red-tape and uncertainy in receiving compensation for medical costs and lost wages led to the proposal for legislation establishing the no-fault principle. Instead of the tort liability system, more preoccupied with fixing blame than with compensating for injuries and involving expensive lawyers' fees, "no-fault" requires the injured driver's own insurance company to compensate him; in return for this assurance, the driver's right to sue the driver of the other vehicle is restricted. Advocates contend that the

Movement for "no-fault" automobile insurance

reduction of automobile insurance rates should be the effect, rather than the chief reason for adopting no-fault insurance. Quick compensation for the injured should be the major goal. Massachusetts was the first to adopt such a law in 1970. Florida, Connecticut, New Jersey, and Michigan were among the earliest states to adopt what advocates call "authentic" or strong no-fault insurance laws, as opposed to "cosmetic" legislation which does little to reduce insurance rates and restrict damage suits.

Government policy is pressured in contrary ways by big dealers and small ones, by chain systems and independents. The pressure may prompt taxation for purposes of policy, as in using license requirements to keep tabs or limits on miscellaneous peddlers. Or demands may be made to increase the business tax per unit on extensive systems of chain stores, far above the levy upon operators of single establishments. The balancing of group pressures over revenue and regulation often determines the intrastate taxation of liquor stores and sales, with the competing interests involving consumers and non-consumers as well as dealers and producers.

Moral factors

The accessibility of goods and services to consumers is regulated in many ways under moral and social influences, with stimulus from religious teachings. This is notably true of business in alcoholic beverages, with variations, not only between states, but between communities or counties on a local-option basis. In centers where sales are permitted, moral customs account for significant restrictions with respect to minors, closing hours, Sunday business, distance of taverns and saloons from schools or churches, sale of mixed drinks versus "package stores" only, and other observances. There are local restrictions on other types of Sunday sales and services, with variations across the nation, as in curfews for baseball. Not a few blue laws remain on the books without enforcement or observance.[7] Police censorship of newsstands and bookshops for indecent material is authorized and is attempted here and there, occasionally with court contests over the differentiation between legitimate matter and obscenity. A few localities have undertaken to apply this censorship to movies. The Supreme Court trend of the fifties and sixties to restrict local discretion in obscenity regulation came to a halt with a 1973 decision by the Burger Court placing greater emphasis on local community standards in the 50 states.[8] The operation of mechanical games of chance provides problems of definition and restriction for states and municipalities, with the federal government entering the field through the tax and interstate

[7] *See* chapter 4 for a discussion of recent Supreme Court decisions relating to "Sunday closing" laws. Many are considered too difficult to enforce or unconstitutional as violations of the principle of separation of church and state. Sunday closing laws have been upheld when designed to promote a day of rest, rather than religious observance as such.

[8] *Miller* v. *California* 93 S.Ct. 2607 (1973). *See* chapter 4 for a discussion of constitutional limitations of such regulation.

commerce powers. Further examples might be cited to show that the rights of entrepreneurs and patrons are not absolute.

Trades and Professions

The states have an old but expanding function in licensing members of certain trades and professions and safeguarding the public against unlicensed practitioners. The licensing system also affords protection against unfair competition to the qualified licensees, whose influence is a factor in making and maintaining the legal requirements. It is beneficial to both clients and practitioners to keep quacks out of the way. The system incidentally facilitates merit practices in the different units of government, which must employ persons of various qualifications. Furthermore, it facilitates the acquisition and publication of accurate information on American life by government agencies, including the Census Bureau, thanks to reports from registered members of licensed groups. It has stimulated training and education in significant ways, for license standards and professional school standards have moved upward together. Public licensing provides a certain amount of underpinning for group ethics, since a license may be revoked for unprofessional practice, not necessarily or technically connected with common crime. Aside from regulatory and protective aspects, the license policy tends to provide a stamp of recognition and professionalism for the initiated.

Importance of the license system

The states have developed a wide license coverage of occupations and professions, particularly in urban and industrial regions. For example, not many years ago the New York *Legislative Manual* listed thirteen state boards of examiners, exclusive of incidental functions by subdivisions of major administrative departments, such as education, labor, and agriculture. These central boards deal with the following professions and occupational groups: law, medicine, dentistry, pharmacy, veterinary medicine, nursing, accountancy, optometry, ophthalmic dispensing, architecture, engineering and land surveying, certified shorthand reporting, and podiatry. To the occupational picture should be added sundry local permits to one-man taxi operators, plumbers, and the like. And state law provides for the recording and recognition of marriage ceremonies performed by ministers, priests, and rabbis ordained or licensed by religious authority.

Wide license coverage

Lawyers, along with doctors, make up the most consistently and continuously significant group of licensed professionals. It might be said, with a little waiving of exactness, that the state's commission lawyers govern the states. Law being the essence of government, its craftsmen compose the judicial branch, predominate in the legislative branch, and

The legal profession

hold strategic places in the executive branch. These learned craftsmen are also the architects of effective structures of private corporate government, although not seeking to change or challenge the common-law doctrine which bans corporate membership in learned professions. The law is primarily a masculine calling, with women constituting only about 10,000 members of the American bar, which numbers close to 350,000. Preparation for admission to the bar, under action or direction of the highest court of the state, can no longer be accomplished by perusing Blackstone or "reading law" as an apprentice. A combination of three successful years in an accredited law school and pre-law courses in college is coming to be the accepted approach to the examination for admission. As a result of stiff admission requirements, more than two-thirds of the lawyers of the country have attended law school, and most of them hold law degrees. Bar associations have constituted a factor in strengthening the prescribed standards, and about twenty states require that a practicing attorney be a member of at least one association.

Doctors have less occupational contact with government than lawyers. But the medical profession approximates that of law in antiquity of origin, growth, number of members, association influence, linkage with public interest, and improvement of standards of training and admission. It is a learned profession with a creed of service ethics derived from Hippocrates, the Greek "father of medicine." Yet the practice of medicine in America today is of the scale and nature of a public utility, although conducted largely as private enterprise.

Medicine

As in law, license requirements have been raised, partly through the impact of organizational pressure and solidarity. Modern medicine differs from modern law, however, in requiring longer and more expensive training for admission to practice, whatever the state and its license procedure. More human beings require individual medical service than require legal service, with consequent strain on training facilities rather than on the licensing process.

One effect of the comparative shortage of doctors and private cost of medical care for families who are neither blessed with wealth nor burdened with poverty has been the creation of a many-sided controversy over public medical policy. The question has involved the federal government, state governments, medical organizations from their national to local units, and other public or semi-public groups. It has brought about legislative gains and defeats as well as litigation and a multiplicity of proposals or movements to improve policy in ways short of "socialized medicine." Even with the passage of "Medicare" for the aged, the overall dispute is still unsettled. The issues affect not only doctors and their clients but also hospitals, medical schools, nurses, medical social service groups, and different interests concerned with providing financially for medical and hospital care through private, group, and public insurance or other cooperative arrangements.

Reciprocity and public relations

The regulation of trades and professions is administered in a large and flexible context of intergovernmental comity, mutual obligations, and public relations. Although there is diversity of standards among the fifty states and the District of Columbia, a high degree of comparability and license acceptance across state lines prevails. An architect, physician, or attorney, after proper examination and certification in one state, does not, as a rule, have to go through the whole testing process upon change of residence to another state. Flexibility also applies to transitory activities by outsiders, as when a state or federal court in the South or West admits a New York lawyer to professional participation in a case. Dr. Paul White, the Boston specialist, did not have to get a Colorado or federal license when he flew to Denver to examine President Eisenhower's heart on federal premises. Professional men qualify for expert testimony before trial or investigative bodies, whether licensed by one state or another.

The context of relationships embraces certain rights of privacy for consultants and clients. Lawyers are immune from compulsory revelation of conversations with persons whom they represent in court. Inviolability also attaches to the privacy of the doctor–patient relationship, although silence is not compulsory and factual physical data may not be privileged. Professional advisers are not immune from prosecution for knowingly committing, causing, or compounding crime in their relations with clients. Court records indicate that, for gross and reckless negligence in preparing a financial statement, a certified public accountant may be held liable to damaged outsiders as well as to his client.

Labor Relations

Common features

The states and many local jurisdictions have vital concern with labor relations and conditions in private business and industry, both because of and in spite of the important role of the national government in these matters. All the states have central administrative machinery, generally under a departmental head or commissioner, to carry on this work. All have legislation prohibiting or restricting and regulating child labor. All have provisions for employer liability or insurance for workers' compensation for accident. Local jurisdictions may enforce these measures by such means as requiring contractors to show certificate of adequate insurance coverage before issuing permits for private projects. All the states have systems of unemployment insurance in coordination and compliance with the federal Social Security provisions for financing these programs.

There are significant differences, in addition to similarities, among the states' labor policies and practices; the differences are partly reflective of regional backgrounds and outlooks. The states vary widely in licensing or not licensing members of more than fifty skilled trades and occupations outside the learned professions. They show diversity in treatment of unions. New York has a Labor Relations Board, with supporting legislation, to guarantee employees' organizational rights, to encourage collective bargaining, and to conduct elections among workers to determine the bargaining union. Less than one-third of the states have labor relations acts of general coverage. On another side of the picture, "right to work laws" prohibit or restrict the "closed shop" and "union shop" in more than one-third of the states, chiefly in the South and inland West. They usually provide that obtaining and retaining employment may not be made to depend on either membership or non-membership in a union.

Diverse features

An increasing number of states, now more than two-fifths, have commissions with mandatory power to prevent discrimination in employment on account of race, creed, or national origin, among these being most of the New England and Middle Atlantic states and the west coast states of California, Oregon, and Washington. A smaller number of states have passed laws prohibiting employment discrimination against older workers, variously defined as including persons over 40 or 45. New York and New Jersey, with the consent of Congress, established a Waterfront Commission in 1953 to replace the "shape-up" system in the port of New York by regularized and supervised hiring of longshoremen. In the decade following the passage of the Civil Rights Act of 1964 the states began slowly and then moved rapidly to yield to Title VII, which prohibits employment discrimination on the basis of sex. The argument on whether state laws establishing separate, restrictive employment standards for women are "discriminatory" or "protective" was decided in most states by repeal, invalidation, or major modification. By 1971 all states had established commissions on the status of women.[9]

Despite the multimillion membership of the unions, the states have less even standards for labor relations than for the learned professions. Union pressure, however, moves for uniform standards through national action. Labor enterprise, in the larger view, is enmeshed with interstate commerce, and the federal government is not allowed to ignore this point. Labor economics, like medical economics, is an unfinished story.

Agriculture

Farming, as an ancient and widespread occupation, is seldom outside the watchful concern of government, whether the concern be motivated by

[9] *See* Beatrice Rosenberg and Ethel Mendelsohn, "The Legal Status of Women," *The Book of the States, 1974–75*, pp. 402–410.

farm statesmanship or the farm vote. Farm problems are problems of nation, state, and locality. Farm pressure in politics continues to be important, with the decline in occupational numbers being offset by growth or strengthening organizational activity. For traditional reasons, farmers meet less avowed opposition in politics than do other groups; they are seldom denounced, even when their demands are denied or sidetracked. All states and most counties have agencies for safeguarding and serving the interests of agriculture, and this work has been expanded in many ways through federal aid and cooperation. It was not by chance that agriculture was included in the first systematic provision for federal aid to the states for applied higher education in the Morrill Land Grant Act of 1862, or that farmers in 1889 became the first occupational group to have functional representation in the president's cabinet. The governmental and organizational hookup for handling farm problems extends from Washington to the grassroots.

Farming and government

Every state has a central agency for agriculture, exclusively or in combination with related functions. The agency is likely to be a department, board, or commission, headed by a director, commissioner, or secretary. The establishment is prescribed in the constitution of several states, sometimes with requirement for popular election of the chief officer. It exercises the roles of promotion, dissemination of information, and regulation, as in enforcing measures for analysis of fertilizer, inspecting certain products or processes, and checking the spread of pests or disease among plants and animals. It maintains cooperative connections as one of four teams concerned with agriculture, the three others in the cooperative system being the federal Department of Agriculture; the agricultural college or division of the state's land-grant college; and the farm agents of the counties of the state having agricultural interests.

Agencies and functions

The governmental programs for agriculture reach the farmers chiefly through these big-four powers operating separately or in conjunction. Among the programs are agricultural experimentation and demonstration, extension service, and crop controls and supports. In many activities nonagricultural agencies are involved, including those connected with labor, health, and conservation, not to mention education.

The scope of cooperative governmental functions in agricultural relations extends to many specialized and collateral activities, partly outside the scheme of immediate production or processing of commodities for market. Many states of broad acres have public sponsorship and regulation of agricultural aviation for applying insecticides and fertilizers, making surveys of soils or crops, spotting or checking forest fires, and other purposes. State and federal forest services dispense scientific information on the care and cultivation of farm woods. Soil-conservation districts are organized on a local basis under state laws with the use of federal funds and technical assistance in developing interest and understanding of con-

Collateral activities

servation problems through meetings, informational literature, and demonstration farms. The TVA has developed fertilizer products and practices in cooperation with agricultural groups, agencies, and institutions of the Tennessee Valley.

The work of public agencies on the agricultural front extends to various phases of rural life, including home and garden, pasture and fish pond, and clubs for boys and girls. This diverse and dynamic front is not free from differences over purpose and policy among agricultural agencies and among agricultural organizations like the Farmers' Union and the American Farm Bureau Federation. Farm groups differ over relations with other interest groups in the realm of business and labor. The sharp issues of farm politics seem to be perennial.

SUPPLEMENTARY READINGS

Becker, Joseph M. *Shared Government in Employment Security: A Study of Advisory Councils.* New York: Columbia University Press, 1959.

Commission on Intergovernmental Relations. *A Study Committee Report on Federal Aid to Agriculture.* Washington, D. C.: U. S. Government Printing Office, 1955.

Commission on Intergovernmental Relations. *A Study Committee Report on Unemployment Compensation and Employment Service.* Washington, D. C.: U. S. Government Printing Office, 1955.

Crain, Robert L.; Katz, Elihu; and Rosenthal, Donald B. *The Politics of Community Conflict: The Flouridation Decision.* Indianapolis: The Bobbs-Merrill Co., 1968.

"Developments in Public Utility Regulation." Continuing article in the annual *The Book of the States.* Chicago: Council of State Governments.

Fainsod, Merle; Gordon, Lincoln; and Palamountain, Joseph C., Jr. *Government and the American Economy.* Rev. ed. New York: W. W. Norton and Co., 1959.

Fesler, J. W. *The Independence of State Regulatory Agencies.* Chicago: Public Administration Service, 1942.

Hanley, Dexter L. "Federal–State Jurisdiction in Labor's No-Man's Land: 1960." *Georgetown Law Journal* 48, Summer 1960, pp. 709–735.

Hardin, C. M. *Freedom in Agricultural Education.* Chicago: University of Chicago Press, 1955.

Jackson, Charles O. *Food and Drug Legislation in the New Deal.* Princeton, N. J.: Princeton University Press, 1970.

Killingsworth, C. C. *State Labor Relations Acts.* Chicago: University of Chicago Press, 1948.

"Labor and Industrial Relations." Continuing article in the annual *The Book of the States.* Chicago: Council of State Governments.

McCune, Wesley. *The Farm Bloc.* Garden City, N. Y.: Doubleday and Co., 1943.

Means, J. H. *Doctors, People, and Government* Boston: Little, Brown and Co., 1953.

Millis, H. A., and Montgomery, R. E. *Organized Labor.* vol. 3 of *The Economics of Labor.* New York: McGraw-Hill Book Co., 1945.

Reeves, Mavis Mann, and Glendening, Parris N. *Controversies of State and Local Political Systems.* Boston: Allyn and Bacon, 1972.

Report of the Commission on Obscenity and Pornography. Washington, D. C.: U. S. Government Printing Office, 1970.

21

Highways, Public Improvements, and Natural Resources

Much of the energy of state and local government is devoted to the acquisition, development, and preservation of routes and points of transportation; premises and facilities for the functions of education, recreation, and other public purposes; and such assets of nature as timber, water, wildlife, scenic beauty, and other resources. The role of government in this physical realm has come down from ancient times, but modern technology has provided both the means and the need for its extensive expansion.

Scope and complexity

Groups and interests, however, are far from being in accord as to just how any step of change or expansion should be taken. The location or relocation of a road or school can become a stirring issue with strong political, economic, and social overtones. Many a building program has been a source of spoils, whether in a metropolis or a sparsely settled county. Commercial exploiters and conservationists may differ sharply over public policies with respect to natural resources. Interests are frequently arrayed against interests over ways and means for financing these public undertakings. Issues of centralization versus decentralization of development or control frequently come to the front. Construction programs engage the attention of public officials from president to village alderman. Whatever the controversy, politicians like to impress constituents by visible accomplishments in stone or concrete; it is this type of governmental activity that provides some of the best examples of politics at work in an intergovernmental setting.

Highways and Rural Roads

A miscellany

The American network of through highways, city streets, and rural roads constitutes a veritable miscellany. It exhibits a combination of the medieval and the modern in physical structure as well as in methods of administration. Our thoroughfares vary widely in age, composition, width, and degree of curvature, not to mention such factors as strength of bridges, load capacity, and state of repair. The financial picture is variegated, involving local, state, or federal support or combinations of these sources, with a modern resurrection of toll systems for great turnpikes. There were examples during the depression of the 1930s of complete financing or construction of roads by the federal government, sometimes in connection with special projects. More than three-fourths of the rural mileage, which is in excess of three million, is under local control, as are most urban streets. There are examples of interurban or interstate control of highway segments, in metropolitan areas or across river boundaries. The federal government controls a rather extensive mileage on its own lands in the different states, including more than 19,000 miles in California.

State systems with federal aid

The coming of the automobile stimulated the movement for state systems of highways with the support of federal aid. Associations were formed for this purpose prior to World War I, and men were elected to Congress as advocates of "good roads." The Federal Aid Road Act of 1916 launched a program of cooperative federalism for the financial sponsorship of a continental system of major highways. The program was to undergo subsequent expansion, regardless of the political complexions of government in states or nation. To share in federal funds on a matching basis, the states had to establish central highway departments and adopt prescribed standards of performance. All states within a few years took steps toward compliance. Cooperation extended even to the uniform numbering of interstate routes, such as "U. S. 90" or "U. S. 41." Federal legislation in 1941 provided for coordinating trunk routes with connections through or around municipal areas, thus making it possible to have "townless highways" and "highwayless towns," as Lewis Mumford would say.[1] Congress in 1944 legislated against the technicality that a street is not a road (something rural state legislatures had resisted doing), and provided aid to urban centers for their portions of through highways, basing the allocations on state populations. The states accepted or facilitated this new chapter in federal–state relations.

[1] For ideas of functional relationships between highway planning and community planning, *see* Lewis Mumford, *Technics and Civilization* (New York: Harcourt, Brace and World, 1934), p. 237.

Federal aid for all highway purposes from 1921 through 1953, including emergency spending during depression years, amounted to almost 12 billion dollars. These older programs and expenditure totals now seem pale when compared with the new program for 42,500 miles of interstate expressways in progress. Initiated by the Federal-Aid Highway Act of 1956 and originally scheduled to be completed by 1972, but later extended to 1979, the system is expected to carry 21 percent of all highway traffic, although it will comprise only slightly more than 1 percent of all street and road mileage in the nation. The federal government's share of the cost of the interstate system is 90 percent, far more generous than the traditional 50–50 basis for sharing with the states. The states determine how much, if any, of their 10 percent must be borne by local governments. By 1973 more than 34,000 miles or 81 percent were already completed and in use, with an additional 4,000 miles under construction. Total cost was originally estimated to be 41 billion dollars, or an average of 1 million dollars per mile; the federal government's portion was to be about 37 billion dollars. By 1973 more than $50 billion had already been spent.

The interstate expressway system

Actual cost per mile may rise far above the average as the expressways cut their way through congested metropolitan areas. Rising costs, the difficulties of building the urban links, and conflicts over environmental impact have caused an upward revision in predicted total cost and have caused officials to be increasingly cautious in predicting the final completion date. Until 1973 the multibillion-dollar Highway Trust Fund, made up of gasoline and other road-user taxes, had been restricted to highway-related projects. The Federal Highway Act of 1973 opened the fund up to expenditures on mass transit, with $200 million authorized to be spent on the acquisition of buses in 1975, and as much as $800 million for rail transit systems in 1976.

While one is cruising smoothly down one of these four-lane expressways, it may be easy to forget that this enormous public works project is simply another highly tangible result of the political process, with all its pressures and influences, stops and starts, plans and counterplans. Decisions must be made concerning such politically volatile questions as location, how many "spokes" the major cities will have, type of construction, number and location of access points, method of financing, whether to reimburse utility companies for the cost of relocating their facilities, and whether to prohibit billboard advertising along the highways. To take billboard controls as an example, Congress authorized a bonus of one-half of one percent of the federal share to any state that will prohibit billboards for a distance of 660 feet on either side of the right-of-way. With only garden clubs and similar groups available to do battle with the billboard industry, securing passage in Congress was not easy. Only sixteen states had adopted the ban by 1962. Receiving strong support from Mrs.

Highways and the political process

Lyndon Johnson, the highway beautification campaign was further supported by the passage of the Highway Beautification Act of 1965. States were given until 1968, later extended to 1972, to ban billboards along interstate and primary highways except for commercial and industrial zones. The penalty specified for failure to comply is loss of 10 percent of federal highway funds. The act also requires the removal or screening of adjacent junkyards, with compensation provided mostly by federal funds. Pressures on Congress to authorize various kinds of billboards visible from the interstate highways continues, as does business ingenuity to find ways of communicating their commercial messages to the masses traveling the interstates.

The other federal-aid highways, known as "the ABC system," consist of (*a*) the states' "primary highway system"; (*b*) city streets that are serving as federal-aid highways; and (*c*) the states' secondary road system, consisting of feeder roads, rural free delivery mail routes, public school bus routes, and similar roads. The 800,000 miles of roads and streets in the ABC system account for 24 percent of the total miles in the nation, but carry approximately one-half of all traffic. In spite of the current emphasis on the interstate expressways, these older programs continue to have strong political support at the local level, and there seems to be little likelihood of diminished federal support. The latest addition to the various federally aided road systems is the Appalachian development highway system, involving more than 3,000 miles of new highways and local access roads to economically depressed areas. While the purposes are geared to opening up these areas for development of their economic resources, the administrative arrangements for constructing and maintaining these "anti-poverty highways" are generally the same as for other federally aided roads.

States were given a strong push in the direction of highway safety programs by federal legislation passed in 1966. States were allowed until the end of 1968 to adopt an approved program, and late in 1966 the new National Highway Safety Agency submitted to the states a list of nine proposals for safety codes. They ranged from periodic eye examinations for all drivers and mandatory helmets for motorcyclists to examination of fatally injured drivers and pedestrians for alcohol in their blood. While local state variations are permitted, a state judged to be making a poor safety effort can lose its eligibility for federal-aid safety funds and 10 percent of its federal-aid highway funds.

Local administration

Highway administration shows various stages and types of modernization in the numerous local units of government among the fifty states. More than one-half of the states divide road authority between state and county, a few divide it between state and town or township, and several have a mixture of the three units of authority. North Carolina in 1931 became the first state to apply state management and maintenance to all roads outside cities. Delaware, Virginia, and West Virginia have also adopted state control of rural roads. However, local autonomy may be restricted in other states in definite ways, either by legislation or by regulation. Central aid may be accompanied by requirements for approval by state authority or the federal Bureau of Roads. Many large cities and wealthy counties utilize effective methods and mechanization for street or road maintenance, even if political factors sometimes affect the letting of contracts for new construction. Old-fashioned kickbacks are limited or prevented by modern legislation, including the Hatch Act that covers federal aid. Spoils politics may enter into the county or city purchase of expensive equipment, as has at times occurred in state highway practices. But, spoils or no spoils, motorized civilization must be served, and so engineers are found along with politicians in highway agencies up and down the line. It is also true that community side-roads and farm-to-market routes require more local understanding than normally can be achieved at highly centralized headquarters. Little roads, like little schools, are still with us along with the big ones, though increasingly dwarfed.[2]

Other Transportation Improvements

Highways are not the only transportation concern of states and localities. There was great public interest in the development of waterways prior to the railroad era, exemplified by the completion of the Erie Canal between Buffalo and Albany in 1825.

Waterways and railways

Later in the nineteenth century, states and municipalities became active in underwriting or subsidizing railway development, sometimes even acquiring rail lines. There are still examples of public ownership of rail properties. The state of Georgia, for example, owns a line runing to Chattanooga from the heart of that state. The line is now under lease to an operating railway. Soon after the Civil War the city of Cincinnati built a rail connection to Chattanooga for the purpose of tapping the southern market. It eventually leased the road to the Southern Railway system. Other instances might be cited for the past century, including urban and interurban streetcar lines. New York City has a municipal transit system which includes over 200 miles of subway, along with a much greater bus-route mileage.

Boat, rail, and motor lines meet at the waterfront, and state port or dock facilities are to be found in such places as New York City, Mobile, and New Orleans. There are municipal terminals to serve transportation

[2] For a more detailed discussion of the politics of highway administration, *see* Robert S. Friedman, "State Politics and Highways," in Jacob and Vines, *Politics in the American States*, pp. 477–519.

on ocean fronts, inland waters, and rail sites. In 1954 New Orleans brought scattered railroads together by opening a municipal Union Passenger Terminal as a multi-million-dollar improvement project. Passenger travel by rail, which almost became extinct in the two decades following World War II, received great impetus with federal subsidization of a nationally integrated "Amtrak" system in the 1970s. Especially during the oil embargo by Arab nations, the energy crisis provided additional support for the revival of passenger rail service.

Airports

Airports vitally affect the public interest, since they require land tracts equal to plantations, and must be operated as union stations for multiple-line service, it being neither feasible nor possible for every single airline to have separate ground accommodations. Commercial aviation, furthermore, reached a stage of public encouragement and subsidy a century later than did railways and waterways. Defense and commercial air transport seem important to the nation and to the national government. The number of take-offs and landings at airports in the United States increased from five million in 1936 to sixty-five million in 1956, and was approximately double that total in the mid-1970s.

Urban and rural interest in aviation

For reasons of location and nature of service, airports are of most immediate concern to municipalities and urbanized counties; commercial airlines cannot conveniently make "whistle stops." This urban bias of aviation, when confronted by the rural bias of state legislatures, has meant that city airports have received even less sympathetic attention from state governments than city streets. The national government has turned a more sympathetic ear to urban airport promoters. Congress in 1940 appropriated funds for distribution to local governments for the development of strategic public airports deemed essential to national defense. Six years later Congress adopted broader provisions for aiding local units of government in the development of airports, authorizing the national government to deal directly with such units if not in conflict with state legislation. Many states promptly adopted cooperative legislation, some requiring that grants-in-aid and airport plans pass through state supervisory and coordinative authority. Federal, state, and local governments are working in a certain degree of unison for the making of greater and better airports. The increased use of aircraft by farmers and ranchers and the growing need for small rural landing fields may serve to stimulate greater state interest in both rural and urban airport needs. Agricultural aviation is a rapidly expanding industry involving thousands of aircraft specially designed for seeding or treating large land areas. Twenty airplanes, used in wiping out screw worm flies in Florida in 1959, covered 7,848,000 square miles, more than double the area of the United States.

Nothing illustrates the growing complexity of governmental involvement in the field of transportation quite so clearly as the mounting crisis over mass transit in metropolitan areas. It is said that it took man ten minutes to reach the center of a city in the eighteenth century, thirty minutes in the nineteenth century, and one hour today. Even after allowing for some exaggeration, such an assertion poses serious questions concerning definitions of progress and the good life. Popular magazines and professional surveys have so dramatized the problems of (and debated solutions for) urban traffic jams, inadequate parking space, deteriorating public transportation and commuter difficulties that there seems at times to be a paralysis of analysis. One of the major issues revolves around the relative merits of the private automobile and rapid mass transit, as shown in Table 21–1. The pattern of urban transportation is a complex product of technological, economic, social, and political factors, and the political ones are fast moving to the fore. Should the mayor support more freeways or mass transit? Should "public policy" be designed to change the apparent "consumer preference" for the private automobile? Will recent federal legislation for aid to urban mass transportation cause local governments to give greater emphasis to rapid mass transit? What will be the contribution of

Private autos v. mass transit

Table 21–1. Capabilities of Urban Transportation Modes

Item of Comparison	*Automotive Transportation*	*Rail-Rapid Transit*	*Bus-Rapid Transit*
1. For moving workers to and from CBD[a]	Requires expensive parking or long walk at CBD	Excellent for workers living near lines	Excellent for workers living near lines
2. For workers needing to travel for business	Essential	Not satisfactory for most such travel	Not satisfactory for most travel
3. For movement of goods	Essential	Not satisfactory for most goods	Not satisfactory for most goods
4. For recreational travel	Essential for travel outside city	Not satisfactory in most cases	Not satisfactory in most cases
5. Coverage of area	Complete, with freeways and arterials	Inferior in low-density areas. Needs feeders	Good in medium-density areas—provides own feeders
6. Capacity per track or lane	3,000 passengers per hour	To 40,000 passengers per hour	To 30,000 passengers per hour, unless limited by bus stop capacity

Table 21–1. *Continued*

Item of Comparison	*Automotive Transportation*	*Rail-Rapid Transit*	*Bus-Rapid Transit*
7. Travel time, door-to-door, non-CBD trips	Best for most non-CBD trips	Poor for most trips; requires transfers	Poor except for trips along lines
8. Travel time, door-to-door, for CBD trips	Good to poor, dependent on congestion, distance to parking	Good, for those trips from zones near transit stations only	Good for trips from zones near stops; fewer transfers
9. Vehicle comfort	Excellent—private cars; driver cannot relax	Superior, with passengers able to read newspapers unless crowded	Poorer, with less smooth operation
10. Cost per passenger mile for an 8-mile trip			
a. To CBD	6–10¢	3¢ or more	3¢ or more
b. To non-CBD place	2–6¢	3¢ or more	3¢ or more
11. Effect on CBD development	Requires parking, and would be impractical as only mode in large cities	Permits more compact CBD development by not requiring parking. Has high-capacity central area distribution system	Requires much more space than rail-rapid transit for central area loading

[a] Central business district.

Source: Donald S. Berry, George W. Blomme, Paul W. Shuldiner, and John Hugh Jones, *The Technology of Urban Transportation.* Table 29 (Evanston, Ill.: Northwestern University Press, 1963), p. 115, as adapted by Committee for Economic Development, *Developing Metropolitan Transportation Policies: A Guide for Local Leadership* (New York, 1965), p. 31.

the new cabinet-level Department of Transportation? Perhaps the most important question for local government is whether there will ever be some form of metropolitan-wide unit of government with the capacity to plan and implement a balanced system of population mobility.[3]

[3] Some of the more recent studies of the problems of urban transportation are: U. S. Department of Housing and Urban Development, *Tomorrow's Transportation: New*

Figure 21–1. From *The Herblock Gallery* (Simon & Schuster, 1968).

Systems for the Urban Future (Washington, D. C., 1968); Washington Metropolitan Area Transit Authority, *Metro* (Washington, D. C., 1969); Committee for Economic Development, *Developing Metropolitan Transportation Policies: A Guide for Local Leadership* (New York, 1965); Michael N. Danielson, *Federal–Metropolitan Politics and the Commuter Crisis* (New York: Columbia University Press, 1965); Lyle C. Fitch et al., *Urban Transportation and Public Policy* (San Francisco: Chandler Publishing Co., 1964); J. R. Meyer, J. F. Kain, and Martin Wohl, *The Urban Transportation Problem* (Cambridge, Mass.: Harvard University Press, 1965); Wilford Owen, *The Metropolitan Transportation Problem* (Washington, D. C.: Brookings Institution, 1966); George M. Smerk, *Urban Transportation: The Federal Role* (Bloomington: Indiana University Press, 1965); and Herman Mertins, Jr. (ed.), "Symposium on the Impacts of Transportation Policy Making," *Public Administration Review* 33 (May–June 1973), pp. 205–252.

Public Buildings, Facilities, and Urban Renewal

General view

Government must build. It must provide housing for the direct activities of government in capitol, courthouse, city hall, and administrative office. It must have buildings for schools, hospitals, and other institutional activities. It must have works and plants for such urban services as water supply, sewage disposal, and any other utilities not provided through private enterprise. Public parks are as much a part of urban living as are private groceries, and they require indoor as well as outdoor structures. The construction, maintenance, and administration of these various physical establishments and facilities require a constant flow of funds and the constant attention of boards or commissions and administrative directors. Much of the work in small counties may be under the direction of the regular governing body, perhaps with technical assistance from central agencies. Larger areas, including important cities, require the service of a full-time engineer or expert staff. The large city, like the state, may have a commissioner, director, or superintendent of public works. State and local planning agencies play important parts in various phases of development or redevelopment. Policymaking in these affairs by legislatures and city councils should not be overlooked.

Special features

Special types of public works in different centers and regions are influenced by geography and cultural factors. Water systems supplied by lowland rivers are not the same as those connected with mountain springs. New Orleans, with streets below the level of the Mississippi, has elaborate drainage machinery of a kind not known in a city like Denver. Reclaiming or retaining land at the water's edge for public use may be important for particular coastal or lakeside centers, not for inland plans. Boston and New York are out of the ordinary in having airports on land dredged out of the sea. Climate, geography, and social trends account for distinctive municipal developments in such centers as Miami and Los Angeles. Some local governments give more attention than others to functions of municipal ownership and operation of central stadiums and auditoriums. Cleveland's Cain Park Theatre is one of the few municipally owned and operated dramatic projects in the country. It is customary for cities served by TVA electric power to own and operate the local distribution systems. Some municipalities in other parts of the country operate gas or electric plants, occasionally under joint arrangements. Many are served by private corporations. As a result of racial segregation, the South has had problems of duplicating physical facilities for education, recreation, and other public purposes. Shifting toward integration, in turn, entails interim problems of readjusting physical arrangements.

Housing and slum clearance

Both the nation and its cities became interested in the twin problems of low-rent housing and slum clearance before President Hoover left the White House; President Roosevelt declared that one-third of the Americans were "ill housed" as well as "ill fed" and "ill clothed." The depression of the Hoover–Roosevelt period brought constructive action, but only with restriction and opposition, lest public housing constitute a socialistic interference with traditional free enterprise.

Among federal steps in the 1930s for improving housing conditions, two measures should be noted which directly call for initiative by state or local governments. Congress in 1932 authorized aid through the Reconstruction Finance Corporation for self-liquidating projects to house low-income families and for slum clearance under state or municipal auspices. But this program did not get under way effectively until 1937. Federal legislation of that year provided for federal loans and subsidies to local authorities for housing projects for low-income families and for grants for clearing slums and blighted areas. Many states and cities joined the program, and hundreds of millions in funds had been channeled into the work by the beginning of World War II.

Housing since World War II

The problems of housing increased after World War II, both for individuals and for communities. The needs were too great to be met entirely by private arrangements. One answer was the sponsorship by the federal government of credit for home ownership by veterans and others. Another consisted of the expansion of public housing projects correlatively with slum clearance or urban renewal.

Legislation was adopted by Congress in 1949 providing for a six-year housing program, a five-year slum-clearance program, and further support for rural housing. The act pointed to the goal of 810,000 urban dwelling units. It marked a change in the concept and practice of federal–municipal housing relationships, with the states playing a helpful or permissive role. Most of the states supported the program, providing for the establishment of local housing authorities. A few of them extended further state aid for the purpose. Within a few years about a thousand localities had public housing projects through federal aid, embracing a total of nearly half a million dwelling units, primarily for rental to low-income families. In the three decades following the passage of the 1937 law, the number of housing authorities rose to 1,750 but the number of dwelling units in operation did not pass the one million total until 1972.

The shift to urban renewal

Although Congress continued to use the label "Federal Housing Act," important changes have taken place in the character and scope of this legislation since the original program for low-rent housing in 1937 and the broader slum clearance and urban redevelopment assistance in the 1949 law. Subsequent housing acts have moved away from a narrow public housing emphasis toward greater emphasis on comprehensive urban renewal efforts, with a more flexible array of tools for combatting urban blight than merely to replace slums with institutional-type housing. The Housing Acts of 1954 and 1956 took note of the fact that new slums were developing at a faster rate than old ones were being cleared, and sought to encourage better planning, greater participation by private business in renewal projects, and rehabilitation and conservation of marginal property. The Housing Act of 1959 added still another dimension in local planning for urban renewal by authorizing grants for preparing a "community renewal program." The program is *city-wide* in scope, with emphasis on total community needs for urban renewal on a long-range basis.

The attack on urban blight was broadened still further by the Federal Housing Act of 1961, with two new programs of special significance for the future: (1) federal grants to help local governments to acquire land to be used for permanent "open space," and (2) loans and grants for urban mass transportation planning and for "demonstration projects" which might help solve mass transit problems. The urban planning assistance provided originally in the 1954 law, known as the "Section 701 program," was given a shot in the arm by the 1961 act, which increased the authorization for these grants from 20 million dollars to 75 million dollars, and changed the 50-50 matching basis to two-thirds federal, one-third local. The changing housing philosophy was finally reflected in the title of the legislation with the passage of the Housing and Urban Development Act of 1965. The act not only extended the urban renewal program for another four years, but also authorized an additional 60,000 units of low-rent public housing per year and provided for new and expanded programs for urban improvements. It included a new and controversial program of federal rent supplements for low-income individuals or families unable to obtain adequate housing for 25 percent of their income or less. The passage of a separate act in 1965 creating the cabinet-level Department of Housing and Urban Development made 1965 a landmark legislative year rivalling 1949 in significance. The passage late in 1966 of the Demonstration Cities and Metropolitan Development Act, discussed in chapter 3, is still another step in the direction of the "whole-city" approach to federal aid.

Broadening the attack on urban blight

Growing realization that the existing financing structure was failing to supply the volume of housing that seemed to be needed for the late 1960s and the 1970s led Congress to incorporate a variety of new approaches in the Housing and Urban Development Act of 1968. For the first time it set explicit housing goals for the nation, pledging federal aid in building or rehabilitating 26 million housing units by 1979, 6 million of these specifically for low-income families. It launched a number of new financing programs to achieve this goal: a new mortgage insurance program subsidizing the purchase of homes built by profit builders (the Section 235 program); a new subsidy for tenants in private housing built by nonprofit, limited dividend, or cooperative sponsors (the Section 236 program); and a relatively small rent supplement program designed to fill the gap between market rent and the maximum low-income families can pay. Five years after passage of the 1968 legislation, a study by the Committee for Economic Development concluded that, although the performance of the private housing market had exceeded the established targets, the "tools designed to produce housing outside the normal reach of the private housing market have proved especially disappointing."[4] HUD Secretary George Romney was especially critical in 1972 of the failure of urban renewal housing programs whose efforts were directed at unrealistic locations in the metropolitan inner cities. Rapid deterioration has continued and the government has increasingly come into ownership or control of faltering or abandoned inner-city housing.

In 1974 Congress passed the first major housing measure since 1968. In addition to continuing home ownership and rent subsidy programs, it combined seven existing programs into a new program of community development block grants. Communities are eligible on the basis of population, overcrowding, and poverty.

Rebuilding cities at a snail's pace

The legislative picture of steadily broadening assistance for rebuilding cities since the 1930s should not be permitted to obscure the fact that actual urban renewal accomplishments have been painfully modest, both in number of cities affected and scope of projects. Numerous obstacles contribute to the snail's pace: many persons in areas to be renewed oppose being relocated; prolonged court contests by property owners are common; racial issues flare up with an occasional charge that "urban renewal projects" have really become "black removal projects"; the government housing aspect of the program is often fought by private real estate interests; the red tape of intergovernmental approval, supervision, and paper work is a constant source of delay; and state governments have generally failed to assume active leadership in stimulating this work, with inaction by a few states constituting an effective roadblock against urban renewal.[5]

It has become abundantly clear that there is more to the administration of public housing and urban renewal than merely solving problems of finance, engineering, and maintenance, difficult as these may be. Administrators and lawmakers have to face or dodge problems of community relations and inter-ethnic adjustment for a diversity of clients or prospective clients. This set of dilemmas in public housing is set forth acutely on the

[4] Committee for Economic Development, *Financing the Nation's Housing Needs* (New York, 1973).

[5] In this connection, *see* the collection of readings on "Urban Redevelopment: Renew? Restore? Resettle?" in Mavis Mann Reeves and Parris N. Glendening, *Controversies of State and Local Political Systems* (Boston: Allyn and Bacon, 1972), pp. 351–408, including very harsh criticism of urban renewal by Martin Anderson.

basis of experience by Charles Abrams in *Forbidden Neighbors: A Study of Prejudice in Housing.*[6] Factors of this nature may also complicate decisions on the location of housing projects as well as plans for the disposition of blighted areas. The frustrations expressed by George Romney as cabinet member seeking to move HUD to take more affirmative action in the racial aspects of urban development indicate the massive nature of the problem. Nevertheless, urban renewal has taken root as both a basic and urgent function of government and has become a major concern of all levels of government in coming years. Abrams' *The City Is the Frontier*, written ten years after his earlier book, concedes many of the weaknesses of urban renewal programs, but presents a balanced case for its continuation with modifications.

Conservation and Eco-Politics

A many-sided task

Although "ecology" is a term that burst on the American scene as a new discovery for many in the 1960s, its concepts have deep roots in the conservation movement of an earlier era. The conservation of nature and nature's products is a many-sided task of national, state, and local units of government. It includes action through public regulation, education, or propaganda, and outright government ownership of natural resources. It is by no means limited to farm and countryside. The city of New York has some two million trees on public premises. Communion with the visible forms of nature seems essential to wholesome urban living. The industrial pollution of streams poses a threat to the economy as well as to the blessings of nature for urban communities, and at the same time it makes life unpleasant for rural areas.[7] Dwindling water supplies in and around the swelling metropolitan areas have caused cities to search many miles from home in their quest for additional sources. The abuse or misuse of soil, subsoil wealth, and growing timber has resulted in "ghost towns" and "tobacco road" regions. But proposals to check or correct destructive practices may bring conflict between special interests and the general interest, between the short view and the long view.

[6] Charles Abrams, *Forbidden Neighbors: A Study of Prejudice in Housing* (New York: Harper & Row, 1955). *See also* his *The City Is the Frontier* (1965), by the same publisher. A more controversial, and distinctly negative, appraisal of urban renewal is found in Martin Anderson's *The Federal Bulldozer: A Critical Analysis of Urban Renewal, 1949–1962* (Cambridge, Mass.: Harvard University Press, 1964).

[7] *See* chapter 18, "Who Killed the French Broad?" in Wilma Dykeman, *The French Broad* (New York: Holt, Rinehart and Winston, 1955), and David A. Booth and Paul Hebert, "Environmental Protection: The Conservation Approach," *State Government* (Summer 1971), pp. 178–184.

The concern for conservation became something of a national crusade with the disappearance of the American frontier and the rise of Theodore Roosevelt to popular leadership and to the presidency. In 1908 he called the state governors into national conference on the theme of conservation. His work was followed in the next two decades by federal legislation for national–state cooperation in checking forest fires and carrying on reforestation. A later Roosevelt brought conservation nearer home to millions in the process of expending unprecedented funds for rural relief and rehabilitation. On this front the New Deal created or expanded land improvement practices for individual farmers, soil conservation districts and associations, reforestation belts, and flood control projects, notably exemplified by the multi-purpose TVA. It brought the federal government and the farmers into closer contact with county agents, land-grant colleges, and state departments of conservation. The new patterns of relationships were to continue after the end of the depression that brought them forth. The system of federal aid or technical assistance was to remain, as were the problems of conservation, whether in regions of flood or dust bowl, whether in Democratic or Republican administrations.

The national movement

Every state serves the cause of conservation through an administrative establishment with branches or through a plurality of agencies. Fish and game regulations, for example, are administered by a separate agency in some states and by a division of the department of conservation in others. So are state parks. These departments and divisions have functions that are regulatory, educational, and promotional with respect to the resources of land, water, forests, farm woods, and wildlife. They may provide services in connection with preventing forest fires, distributing seedlings, stocking fish ponds, improving streams, and the like. They inevitably have cooperative or pressure contacts with clubs or associations of sportsmen, tourist-trade promoters, lumbermen, utility operators, and spokesmen of other interests, special or general. This variety of group interests sometimes renders difficult the balancing of policy between conservation and "development."

State agencies and activities

State conservation agencies may have working relations with other central or local authorities, including those concerned with agriculture, health, public works, planning, and law enforcement. They naturally have cooperative relations with federal agencies under the stimulus of federal aid and technical assistance, although state and national officers do not always see eye to eye on methods and measures of conservation.

One way for a government to conserve natural resources is to own and manage them. That has been distinctly recognized by the national government and even by a few local governments. Most of the states own wide tracts of land, partly as the result of federal aid or allocation in many instances. All but a few states have forest preserves, with an acreage

State ownership and management

usually ranging between a few thousand and a few hundred thousand. States topping a million acres in public forests are Idaho, Michigan, Minnesota, New York, and Pennsylvania. Public park lands are significant for many states, notably for California which has more than half a million acres. It is hardly necessary to observe that trees growing in the wide spaces of state parks may constitute timber resources just as accurately as if they were classified as forests. The states utilize their broad acres for scientific forestry, recreational resources, hunting preserves, wildlife sanctuaries, and other purposes. Some of the lands contain mineral deposits and oil reserves often for less conscious conservation.

Petroleum and natural gas

World wars, world trends, and American politics have intensified the problems of conserving and controlling the petroleum and gas resources of the nation. The states have a large scope of discretion in determining what shall or shall not be done in this crucial industry, both on private and state lands. As with other industrial resources, most of the oil states have come lately to tasks of conservation, although this reserve is not limitless and not to be replenished. Under the spur of conservationist demands and an element of supporting opinion inside the industry, the states began to act, following the early lead of Pennsylvania and New York. Most of the states concerned have become parties to an interstate compact to prevent waste and to regulate petroleum production by applying quota systems in accord with demands for the output. Congress has restricted non-quota shipments in interstate commerce. The "energy crisis" of the 1970s has provided conflicting short-run pressures, some to relax and some to tighten the restrictions on petroleum and natural gas production. However, the long-run pressure for increased conservation is unmistakable.

The states of Texas, Louisiana, and California have acquired strategic positions with respect to offshore petroleum resources under the Submerged Land Act of 1953. This measure disclaimed certain national rights or titles as set forth by the Supreme Court and undertook to "return" to the states the tidelands within their historic boundaries. Its passage fulfilled a political campaign promise of 1952, but many observers considered it a setback to national conservation. It has brought forward new points or old points of states' rights and states' responsibilities.[8]

Conservation of recreational resources

A more recent trend in conservation emphasis has been a growing anxiety over fast-vanishing open space and the lost opportunities for outdoor recreational facilities as the metropolitan mowing-machines consume the countrysides for suburban housing, shopping centers, and industrial development. The crowded metropolis is being forced to face, with an ironic twist, the problem of open space in the "Space Age." President

[8] For further discussion of this issue, in relation to states' rights, *see* chapter 2.

Kennedy took the cue in 1962 from a three-year study by the Outdoor Recreation Resources Review Commission and recommended to Congress a vast federal–state–local land-purchase program for park, recreation, and wildlife uses. The ORRRC found that the increase in use of available federal and state recreation areas by the American people had far outstripped the population growth and predicted that the pressures of urban living would continue to increase the demand for outdoor recreation. Many of its recommendations were incorporated into President Johnson's Great Society program; the Land and Water Conservation Fund Act of 1964 is one of the results. Not only is the acquisition and development of land by state and local governments for outdoor recreation encouraged, but each state is required to have a federally approved comprehensive statewide outdoor recreation plan before it may receive grants. Each state now has a liaison officer to work with the Bureau of Outdoor Recreation of the Department of Interior on this and related programs. There can be little doubt that our nation's population expansion, coupled with increases in worker productivity and leisure time, will provide increased political pressure for conservation, and perhaps reclamation, of recreational resources.

The politics of pollution: water and air

As indicated in chapter 3, the national government has become more and more involved in the problems of water and air pollution in recent years. For many years municipal and industrial wastes have been poured into the nation's streams and the atmosphere with only occasional words of reprimand from government officials and from a generally apathetic public. The myth of unlimited quantities of air and water, the strong traditions of industrial laissez faire and states' rights, and the hard financial facts of the high cost of adequate anti-pollution measures all combined to make the politics of pollution mainly talk rather than action. The unwillingness of cities and states to risk driving offending industries to less restrictive states finally led the national government to pass such measures as the Water Quality Act of 1965, the Clean Rivers Act of 1966, and the Clean Air Act of 1964. The federal Environmental Protection Agency was created in 1970 to coordinate the many diverse elements in the growing war on pollution. Federal aid to states and localities for combatting pollution is combined with a "we-will-act-if-you-don't" provision requiring water quality standards for interstate streams.

The ultimate political issue in the fight against pollution is the determination of who will pay for it. Only one part of the job is the separation of storm sewers from sanitary sewers in some 2,000 U. S. cities having a combined system for sewage and storm waters—a task estimated to cost at least 30 billion dollars. Secretary of the Interior Stewart Udall estimated that it would require 150 billion dollars and fifteen years to clean up the country's streams. Any estimate of the cost of controlling air pollution would undoubtedly be equally staggering. It cannot be predicted whether

Figure 21–2. Knox in *The Nashville Banner.*

Awaiting disaster politics?

or not the expenditure will have to await some national disaster to dramatize the need—perhaps a tragic poisonous smog in one of the major metropolitan areas of the type that killed twenty and sickened thousands in Donora, Pennsylvania, in 1948. It does seem likely that it will come in the increasingly common form of federal–state–local "partnership" programs, with all levels participating, but with the senior partner paying the major share.[9]

Water-shortage politics was for many years predominantly a concern of the arid western states and of very little concern to most of the rest of

[9] For an analysis of the politics of making governmental pollution policy and "the interests and ideas competing for domination over pollution control," *see* J. Clarence Davies III, *Politics of Pollution* (New York: Pegasus, 1970).

the nation, apathy being especially prevalent in the northeastern states. As the cities of southern California struggled with their water supply problem, other parts of the nation seemed content to leave it in the hands of state and local governments.[10] A radical shift in national opinion occurred in the middle 1960s as drought and water shortages moved to previously untouched areas. The water supply crisis in New York City, flanked by a large river and the Atlantic Ocean, dramatized the rapid changes in national opinion on water resource policy and politics.[11] Indicative of the shift is the passage by Congress of the Water Resources Planning Act of 1965 to stimulate increased federal–state–local planning and cooperation for water and related land resource conservation and development. The 1960s also saw stepped-up federal programs on desalinization of sea water, retardation of evaporation and leakage in lakes and reservoirs, transfer of water between major river basins, and, as discussed above, refinement of waste water so that it can be reused.

Water politics from West to East

Planning, as a recognized function of government, has received far more acceptance at the city level than at the state level of government. City planning and zoning involve a great deal of control over the use which private property owners may make of their land and the structures on it. Interestingly, some of the strongest supporters of this function of urban government are business and real estate groups. State planning, which has never involved much concern for "state zoning" or regulation of private property rights, has never received corresponding support or recognition as a function of state government. For a short period during the 1930s, state planning organizations were created under the stimulus of federal grants-in-aid through the National Resources Planning Board. Much of their initial work involved coordinating emergency public works projects aimed at the unemployment problem, but some progress was made toward state land-use plans, until the priorities of World War II intervened. During the post-war years state planning agencies in most states were lost in the shuffle of reorganizations which tended to downgrade any idea of comprehensive statewide planning. Many of them were given new names and made primarily responsible for attracting tourists and new industries to the state, and approving local requests for federal aid. Only about one out of four of the states has what professional planners would recognize as viable state planning agencies. The state of Hawaii,

State planning

[10] The unusual efforts of the state of California in water development are described in Reginald C. Price, "Decisions in the State's Development of California's Water during the 1960's," *Public Administration Review* 25 (December 1965), pp. 290–296. For a good summary of state developments in this field, *see Environmental Quality and State Government* (Lexington, Ky.: The Council of State Governments, 1971).

[11] *See,* for example, the series of articles, "The Crisis in Water: Its Sources, Pollution and Depletion," in *Saturday Review* 48 (Oct. 23, 1965), pp. 23–45; 75–80.

however, gives cabinet status to its Department of Planning and Research and has developed a comprehensive state plan for 1960–80, which planners hope will serve as a prototype for other states.[12]

[12] *See* H. Milton Patton, "State Planning," *The Book of the States, 1974–75*, pp. 439–442.

SUPPLEMENTARY READINGS

Abrams, Charles. *Forbidden Neighbors: A Study of Prejudice in Housing.* New York: Harper & Row, 1955.

———. *The City Is the Frontier.* New York: Harper & Row, 1965.

Anderson, Martin. *The Federal Bulldozer.* New York: McGraw-Hill Book Co., 1967.

Automotive Safety Foundation. *Urban Transit Development in Twenty Major Cities.* Washington, D. C., 1968.

Banfield, Edward C., and Grodzins, Morton. *Government and Housing in Metropolitan Areas.* New York: McGraw-Hill Book Co., 1958.

Danielson, Michael N. *Federal–Metropolitan Politics and the Commuter Crisis.* New York: Columbia University Press, 1965.

Davies, J. Clarence, III. *Neighborhood Groups and Urban Renewal.* New York: Columbia University Press, 1965.

Fitch, Lyle C. *Urban Transportation and Public Policy.* San Francisco: Chandler Publishing Co., 1964.

Freedman, Leonard. *Public Housing: The Politics of Poverty.* New York: Holt, Rinehart and Winston, 1969.

Greer, Scott. *Urban Renewal and American Cities.* Indianapolis: Bobbs-Merrill Co., 1965.

Lilienthal, David. *TVA: Democracy on the March.* New York: Harper & Row, 1944.

Maass, Arthur. *Muddy Waters.* Cambridge, Mass.: Harvard University Press, 1951.

McElrath, Dennis C.; Grant, Daniel R,; and Wengert, Norman. *Political Dynamics of Environmental Control.* Bloomington: Institute of Public Administration, Indiana University, 1967.

Mertins, Herman, Jr. *National Transportation Policy in Transition.* Lexington, Mass.: D. C. Heath and Co., 1972.

Meyer, John R.; Kain, J. F.; and Wohl, Martin. *The Urban Transportation Problem.* Cambridge, Mass.: Harvard University Press, 1965.

Moses, Robert, *Working for the People.* New York: Harper & Row, 1956.

Owen, Wilford. *The Metropolitan Transportation Problem.* Washington, D. C.: Brookings Institution, 1966.

Pinchot, Gifford. *Breaking New Ground.* New York: Harcourt, Brace and World, 1947.

Roos, Leslie L., Jr., ed. *The Politics of Ecosuicide.* New York: Holt, Rinehart and Winston, 1971.

U. S. Commission on Organization of the Executive Branch of the Government, 1953–1955. *Report on Water Resources and Power.* 3 vols. Washington, D. C.: U. S. Government Printing Office, 1955.

Wengert, Norman. *Natural Resources and the Political Struggle.* Garden City, N. Y.: Doubleday and Co., 1955.

Wilson, James Q. *Urban Renewal, The Record and the Controversy.* Cambridge, Mass.: Harvard University Press, 1966.

22

Education, Health, and Welfare

General importance

Americans, in their capacity to govern, channel billions of dollars annually into cultivating sound minds in sound bodies and reducing the toll of disease and poverty. In addition to direct expenditures, they extend various tax concessions and public privileges to privately endowed or supported institutions, organizations, and foundations that serve the interests of education, research, health, and charity on a nonprofit basis. All levels of government are involved in one way or another in this great social process, which, with the passage of time and simple ways, has outgrown the governing power and autonomy of the local communities.

Cooperative aid from centralized sources has become the established and inevitable pattern for advancing this set of social services. This trend, in its national aspects, has been pointed up by messages to Congress in recent years by presidents from both political parties, calling for aid to states, localities, and institutions for meeting "human needs" in such fields as school construction, public housing, medical research, hospitalization, child welfare service, and problems of retarded children. The trend at the same time has been emphasized by calls within the states for centralized aid to cities and counties for similar purposes, such as one governor's request for three million dollars to aid cities in maintaining day care centers for childern of working mothers, or another governor's recommendations to move his state up from the bottom of the list of fifty states in preventive and curative programs for mental health.

The states, counties, cities, and towns collectively require more funds and employ more men and women for these basic human services than for all their governmental activities in maintaining law and order and regulating private enterprise. They thus accentuate positive service, in comparison with negative restriction, in the affairs of men, although the accent may be inadequate for increasing needs.

Education

Scope, horizontal and vertical

More than one-fourth of the nation's population is enrolled in schools or colleges (over sixty million in 1973). An increasingly dominant majority of these are enrolled in state or public systems and institutions, rather than in private schools and colleges. This conglomerate process of public education involves much more than an array of teachers and pupils. It functions under central and local boards, either elected or appointed. It requires a host of administrators, including superintendents, principals, presidents, deans, and supporting staffs of secretaries, divisional managers, and specialists. Decisions concerning education are now inextricably related to the declining birth rate, the flow of migration, urban and suburban blight and sprawl, unemployment trends, "cold war" problems of defense and prestige, tax structure, technological development, race relations, and a host of other things. There are complaints of too much administrative overhead in American education, but reducing it is not easy. The public system of one of the major states might be described, in terms borrowed from interpreters of giant business, as a vertical and horizontal combination. With the first decline in public school enrollment since 1943, the quantitative problem of education began to take the back seat to various qualitative problems.

State roles

State governments, through legislative and executive functions, have the key roles in public education, despite the importance of local initiative and the variation in school merit among the localities. The states have been the essential middlemen between federal aid and the schools ever since the adoption (prior to the Constitution) of the policy of donating a section per township of western lands to the new states for educational purposes. Most states made the shift in the nineteenth century from free schools for "poor" children to free schools for all, with provisions for centralized, statewide standards for examining and certifying teachers. The states enacted compulsory school attendance laws, with Massachusetts taking the lead in 1852 and Mississippi making it universal in 1918. The states took steps to terminate many isolated one-room schools through consolidation with larger districts and provided bus transportation to and from the consolidated schools in rural regions. They have set up administrative procedures for the selection and adoption of textbooks, frequently providing them for children without cost. As indicated in chapter 14 on finance, the states appropriate or earmark central funds for distribution to local school jurisdictions. By the decade of the seventies, these supplementary funds amounted to several billion dollars annually for all the states.[1] There are tangible reasons for referring to public schools as state systems.

Higher education

Most tax-supported institutions of higher education are creations and wards of the states; and the few municipal colleges or universities are not immune from measures of state regulation and support. The state university or university system is a different entity for different states. It may embrace several campuses in different centers under one president, as in California or North Carolina; it may include the land-grant college of agriculture and mechanical arts as part of the central establishment, as in Illinois or Wisconsin; or it may separate the university in control and management from the land-grant college and other colleges of the state, as in Alabama or Texas. Some of the land-grant institutions have become universities in scope and name. Many states have separately controlled junior colleges and teachers colleges, and a separate structure still exists in many southern states for those colleges and universities established originally for blacks only. In recent years increasing state attention has been given to the establishment of "community colleges," usually defined as junior colleges offering a comprehensive program of adult education.

Many states are without any overall system or coordination for their several institutions of higher learning. But New York has a Board of Regents which exercises extensive policymaking and regulatory power over the state's entire educational system, including public schools, high schools, and higher institutions. These regents are elected by the legislature in joint session, one each year. Many states provide for the selection of university regents or trustees by gubernatorial appointment with senate confirmation under a staggered system, in an effort to prevent excessive control by any particular political administration. Undue political interference with the academic appointments or tenure of a university may bring unfavorable censure or non-recognition by associations of institutions and professional groups, and embitter alumni, as a few governors have discovered. Federal aid to state institutions also carries certain safeguards against political manipulation of academic affairs.

The local hookup

The public schools below the college level are generally more dependent upon local financing than upon state and federal aid. They are points of direct contact with units of the Parent–Teacher Association and other pressure groups supporting school improvement and expansion. They are sometimes centers of controversy over means and policy, as over the beginnings of the school lunch program which initially supplied food from surplus products by the United States Department of Agriculture. In many centers they participate in undertakings to reduce juvenile delinquency, sometimes with the direct cooperation of visiting teachers and

[1] *See* chapter 14 for this aspect and others of financing education.

other social workers. They serve in different ways as units for applying public health protections, including inoculation programs. In many rural areas the public school provides the only facility for civic forums, farm meetings, and other community activities.

School district consolidation

One of the most dramatic reorganization movements in state and local government of this century has been the increasingly successful drive to reduce, by merger, the fantastic number of school districts in the United States. Although the total number of districts was cut sharply from more than 127,000 in 1932 to about 67,000 in 1952 and still further to 15,600 in 1973, most school authorities still consider this to be far too many for best educational and economical results.[2] The consolidations have come only after grueling political fights. Opponents object to the impact of the larger consolidated schools on grassroots control of school policy, the loss of a rural community center, the "homogenizing" effects of an urbanized school on rural students, and the prospects of large bond issues for the new consolidated schools. The public, however, has generally supported the views of the proponents of consolidation, who argue that the nineteenth-century districts were geared to the transportation of that period and to the idea that few pupils would go further than the eighth grade, and that consolidated schools provide greater educational opportunity for all. The one-room school house (one-teacher elementary school), once almost a biographical prerequisite to elective office in some states, has been reduced to less than 20,000 in number, in contrast to 143,000 such schools in 1932.

Metropolitan school organization

School district organization involves not only urban–rural relationships; it has recently become a difficult intra-metropolitan problem involving urban–suburban relationships. Wealthy suburbs with a low population density may fare ten times as well, educationally, as poorer suburbs with high population density. Some suburban school districts may have "windfall tax support" from a large industrial plant, while another suburb may be blessed only with thousands of young working families with school-age children. At the same time, large "core-city" school systems are often arbitrarily separated from suburban schools, taxable wealth, and, perhaps most important, from its civic leadership, with a resultant fragmentation in educational planning and administration for the total community. This problem is closely related to the discussion of "metropolitics" in chapter 18.

The problem of racial segregation in public schools was discussed as a constitutional issue in chapter 2, but it should be included in any listing of the contemporary educational problems of state and local government.

[2] The 1972 Census of Governments makes a distinction between the 15,781 "'independent school districts" and an additional 1,457 "other public school systems" which are not actually independent units of government, but rather are dependent agencies of some other government.

Since the desegregation decision of the Supreme Court in 1954,[3] reversing the long-standing "separate but equal" doctrine, school districts in southern states have moved from crisis to crisis in a slow but steady process of compliance with the law of the land. Integration statistics can be deceiving in some respects, but the trend toward compliance is unmistakable. Of the 6,229 school districts in seventeen southern and border states, 645 had desegregated by 1957 and 976 by early 1963. By 1972, according to an HEW survey, 36.8 percent, or 2.4 million, black children were enrolled in predominantly white schools, compared with 33.1 percent in 1970 and 23.4 percent in 1968. Meanwhile, black enrollment in all-black schools in 1972 dropped to 10.9 percent, or 721,757, compared with 14 percent in 1970 and 39.7 percent in 1968. Over 300 state laws have been passed on the subject of desegregation, some to facilitate it, some to limit it to "token integration," and some to oppose it with "massive resistance." Many opposition statutes have been invalidated by the courts and others remain to be tested. When South Carolina's Clemson College admitted black student Harvey Gantt early in 1963, no southern state remained that had not experienced some degree of school desegregation.

Racial desegregation

When desegregation is measured in terms of number and percent of blacks attending school with whites, two facts become clear. First, the early years of desegregation were characterized by painfully slow compliance with the Supreme Court's decision, with less than one percent of southern black students attending school with whites as late as 1963. But equally clear is a sharp increase in these figures with the passage of the Civil Rights Act of 1964, involving the U. S. Attorney General more actively in desegregation suits, and the Elementary and Secondary Education Act of 1965, which brought the power of the federal purse to bear on lagging school districts. Perhaps the language of the Supreme Court in the Prince Edward County Case in 1964 was prophetic when they stated "There has been entirely too much deliberation and not enough speed in enforcing the constitutional rights which we held . . . had been denied . . . Negro children."[4] (*See* Figure 22–1). The federal aid "guidelines" of the U. S. Office of Education were undoubtedly responsible for the sharpest increase in desegregation which occurred in the year 1966–67 when 16.8 percent of blacks were in southern public schools with whites.

Impact of the federal purse

Segregation is not entirely a southern problem, particularly since black population outside the South is very nearly equal that inside the South. Surprisingly to some, perhaps, was the HEW report that 11 southern

[3] *Brown* v. *Topeka Board of Education*, 347 U. S. 483 (1954).

[4] *Griffin* v. *School Board of Prince Edward County*, 377 U. S. 218 (1964). For a comprehensive analysis of the impact of the Civil Rights Act of 1964 on education in the South, *see* Gary Orfield, *The Reconstruction of Southern Education* (New York: John Wiley and Sons, 1969).

Figure 22–1. From *The Herblock Gallery* (Simon & Schuster, 1968).

states had less black enrollment in all-black schools (9.2 percent) than the northern states (10 percent) or the border states (22.9 percent). Many of these school systems have a kind of de facto segregation paralleling segregated residential areas. New York City and many others now engage in "busing" pupils to schools outside their residential areas, both as a means to promote integration and to relieve crowded schools. New Rochelle, New York, and Highland Park, Michigan, were ordered by the courts to integrate schools, and many others, North and South, have been ordered to bus students in order to eliminate the discrimination resulting from segregated residential patterns. A federal district court ordered Richmond, Virginia, schools to merge with two suburban districts in order to end de facto segregation, but the decision was reversed on appeal all the way to

De facto segregation

the Supreme Court. Although the Supreme Court was expected to affirm a lower court-ordered plan for cross-district busing to achieve racial balance in Detroit and its suburbs (Roth case, 1974), the Court (in a 5-to-4 decision) overturned the lower court's ruling. The opinion, written by Chief Justice Warren Burger, had the effect of blocking metropolitan-wide busing (across district boundary lines) in other cities where it had been ordered or proposed.

Religion and public schools

Religion must take its place by race as one of the most difficult of public school problems currently troubling governmental decision makers. It is sometimes a delicate matter to provide moral or spiritual instruction without running into complaints and court cases based on the constitutional principle of separation of church and state. The issue is not simply whether individuals or groups can engage in prayer in the public schools, or even whether government officials can prescribe a particular prayer to be used in the public schools. In 1962 the Supreme Court answered the latter question in the negative in the case of *Engel* v. *Vitale*,[5] and in 1963 also held invalid in the Schempp Case[6] state and local rules requiring the reading of Bible verses and the recitation of the Lord's Prayer at the start of each day in the public schools. Equally difficult and far-reaching is the question of tax support for parochial schools, either for specific programs such as pupil transportation, free textbooks, and free lunches, or for broad assistance for teachers' salaries or for school construction or maintenance. A proposal interpreted as opening the door for tax support for parochial schools in New York was a major factor in the defeat of a proposed new state constitution in 1967. In 1973 the Supreme Court invalidated New York and Pennsylvania tuition reimbursement plans and a New York tax deduction program for their nonpublic schools, saying they effectively furthered religion in violation of the Constitution. In coming years the judicial and political issues of separation of church and state will undoubtedly be closely interwoven as they relate to the public school system.

Forces opposing federal aid

For many years the role of the federal government in public education has been a major unresolved question. The educational and ideological case for federal aid has been a persuasive one, based on the sharp differences between states in their financial resources and educational opportunity. The strongest opposition to such federal aid has come from the following groups: (1) conservative taxpayers' organizations fearing a mass transfer of the school finance burden to the federal income tax; (2) some Catholic groups who oppose federal aid that does not include aid to parochial schools; (3) some Protestant and other groups who oppose fed-

[5] 370 U. S. 421 (1962).

[6] *Abington School District* v. *Schempp*, 374 U. S. 203 (1963).

eral aid to religious schools as incompatible with church–state separation; (4) states' rights groups fearing that federal aid will lead to undesirable federal controls, a fear related particularly, but not exclusively, to segregationists' opposition to an additional federal wedge for racial integration; and (5) leaders from the wealthier states who oppose all strongly equalizing formulas as constituting too much of a "hand-out" to the poorer states. Until the passage of landmark legislation in 1963 and 1965, these political forces had consistently turned back all efforts to pass general federal aid bills in the field of education.

Turning the federal aid corner

Congress turned the corner in its efforts to provide federal aid to education when it passed the Higher Education Facilities Act of 1963 and the Elementary and Secondary Education Act of 1965. Each was the first of its kind in history and clearly represented a political accomplishment of monumental proportions. The 1963 act was less precedent-breaking in some ways, but provided assistance to higher education more openly and directly than ever before. The drafters of the 1965 act carefully walked a tight rope to avoid the church–state controversy over aid to religious and other non-public schools by basing the aid on the number of children from low-income families in the district. The emphasis was thus on aid to children, not to schools. The act included authorization for grants for purchase of textbooks and other library materials which could be loaned to private schools; grants for supplementary community-wide educational centers for services individual schools cannot provide; and grants to strengthen state departments of education. In securing passage of the 1965 act, the problem of dealing with racially segregated schools did not loom so large as previously because the passage of the 1964 Civil Rights Act had relieved the pressure considerably.[7] There should be no minimizing of the importance of the corner which has been turned, but it should be noted that the early financial impact of the 1963 and 1965 acts was less than might have been expected, due in large measure to the budget pressures growing out of the Viet Nam War and the relative slowdown in "Great Society" programs.

Following close on the heels of the legislation for federal aid to education was an unusual proposal for interstate cooperation in the field of education. Bearing some of the earmarks of a defensive action on the part of the states, a "Compact for Education" was proposed late in 1965 at a conference of several hundred political, professional, and lay leaders in education, including nineteen governors and fifty state legislators. They took

[7] For a discussion of the history of federal aid to education since 1787, and the pros and cons, *see* Alice M. Rivlin, *The Role of the Federal Government in Financing Higher Education* (Washington, D. C.: Brookings Institution, 1961), and Congressional Quarterly Service, *Federal Role in Education* (Washington, D. C., 1965).

their cue from James B. Conant, whose book, *Shaping Educational Policy*,[8] promoted the idea of an interstate compact to create a partnership between the states' educational and political leadership to facilitate the exchange of ideas, debate of goals, and stimulation of state action in education. The basic purpose is to achieve a "nationwide"—but not national—policy on education. Whatever ultimate importance the Compact for Education may have, the speed with which thirty-eight states joined the compact in just over nine months clearly demonstrates the desire of state officials to retain state initiative in the field of education. Forty-one states were members by 1972; staff headquarters were located in Denver. The compact provides for an "Educational Commission of the States," consisting of seven representatives from each member state, including the governor, two state legislators, and four appointed by the governor to represent professional and lay interests in education. The future of the Compact for Education remains much in doubt, with the pressures for "immediate" action on complex educational problems tending to leave an unwieldy commission of 350 members sidetracked as a spectator.

Proposed "nationwide" (not national) educational policy

"Politics" is commonly looked upon as the enemy of "good public schools," and a commonly proposed solution to school problems is to "take the schools out of politics." The professional educator and PTA groups are often heard advocating the elective school board and the trained superintendent as means of keeping schools out of politics. Realism suggests that this is an impossibility. A writer has described the character of elective school board politics in West Virginia in 1960:

Schools and politics

> Posts on local school boards are bitterly contested, from one end of the state to the other. "Hell," one local politician answered me, "curriculum? They don't give a damn about curriculum, half of them don't know what the word 'curriculum' means. School board means jobs—it means teachers' jobs, janitors' jobs, bus-driver jobs. They'll pass the curriculum in five minutes and spend two hours arguing about who's gonna be bus driver on Peapot Route Number One. Bus driver means a hundred and sixty dollars a month for a part-time job."[9]

The professional superintendent of schools is not really "out of politics," either. Like the professional city manager, he is inevitably a policy leader rather than a purely managerial follower, and this must be included

[8] James B. Conant, *Shaping Educational Policy* (Cambridge, Mass.: Harvard University Press, 1964). For the most comprehensive analysis of higher education policy in the United States, *see* the series of reports by the Carnegie Commission on Higher Education issued from 1968 to 1974. A list appears in Appendix G of *Priorities for Action: Final Report of the Carnegie Commission on Higher Education* (New York: McGraw-Hill Book Co., 1973), pp. 217–243; 21 supplemental publications were prepared in 1974.

[9] Theodore H. White, *The Making of the President, 1960* (New York: Atheneum Publishers, 1961), p. 99. Reprinted by permission of the publishers.

in any definition of politics. One retired school superintendent explained his decision to run for the legislature in terms of his previous relation to politics:

> After I retired from the school business, I missed the public life and the chance to meet people and appear before the public that I had had as a superintendent. I did not think of politics before this, except that as a superintendent you're always in the political business. There's a lot of politics—you have to keep everyone happy. Politics is always entering. For instance, you have to control the board.[10]

The politics of public education is still an area largely untouched by the research of social scientists, but it is clear that much of the folklore about taking schools out of politics needs careful scrutiny. There is good reason to believe that the character of a school system may inevitably be a reflection of the total political system of the community and state. If this is true, school reformers would be wise to direct their efforts at shaping or controlling the total system, rather than at futile efforts to withdraw schools from the system of community and state politics.[11]

School administration

Aside from social issues and policies, special and routine problems of administration arise, such as mapping or rearranging school districts, adjusting or streamlining city and county activities, or improving methods of purchasing supplies. The organization of administrative housekeeping is as much a need and a problem in public education as in other phases of state and local government.

Health Agencies and Hospitals

The specific role of state and local governments in promoting the health of the American people, as distinguished from *private* responsibility for

[10] John C. Wahlke, et al., *The Legislative System: Explorations in Legislative Behavior,* p. 87.

[11] For other examples of the politics of education, *see* Nicholas A. Masters, Robert H. Salisbury, and Thomas H. Eliot, *State Politics and the Public Schools* (New York: Alfred A. Knopf, 1964). *See also* the series of twelve paperbacks on *The Economics and Politics of Public Education,* published in 1962 and 1963 by Syracuse University Press; *see also* Vincent Ostrom, "The Politics of Education in a Democracy," in Joseph R. Fiszman, *The American Political Arena: Selected Reading* (Boston: Little, Brown and Co., 1962); Marilyn Gittell, "Professionalism and Public Participation in Educational Policy-Making: New York City, A Case Study," *Public Administration Review* 27 (September 1967), pp. 237–251; Mario Fantini, Marilyn Gittell, and Richard Magat, *Community Control and the Urban School* (New York: Praeger, 1970); Luvern L. Cunningham, *Governing Schools: New Approaches to Old Issues* (Columbus, Ohio: Charles E. Merrill Publishing Co., 1971); and Leigh Stelzer, "Schoolmen, Receptivity, and Community Conflict," a paper prepared for the annual meeting of the American Political Science Association, New Orleans, Sept. 4–8, 1973.

health, is not easy to define. Perhaps we can agree that if a do-it-yourself enthusiast hammers his thumb instead of the nail, his health is a private responsibility in this case. Similarly, we all agree that if the same man comes down with a highly communicable disease, state and local governments have a responsibility to prevent its spread to others in the community. But it is not enough to define public health solely in terms of prevention and private health solely in terms of curative measures. Private medical care is greatly concerned with the prevention of disease, and public health departments have well-established programs to treat tuberculosis patients, the mentally ill, and the indigent sick, as well as various patients in experimental and pilot projects. Neither is the public health program concerned only with the indigent citizen, for many of its programs are directed at persons of all economic levels. In a like manner, the division between federal, state, and local governmental responsibilities in the field of health has become blurred. Hardly a session of Congress goes by without the assumption of some additional responsibility for health care or payment.

What is public health?

The distinction between the public and private sectors of medical care is essentially a political matter, determined pragmatically by an accumulation of decisions by boards of health, legislative bodies, and occasionally by popular votes, to give governmental agencies some degree of responsibility for health problems which the private sector seems ill-equipped or unwilling to handle. Thus, through the years the accepted functions of state and local health departments have come to include communicable disease control, mental health, sanitary engineering, maternal and child health services, dental health, public health nursing, industrial hygiene, radiological health, air pollution control, emergency health services, and such auxiliary functions as public health laboratories and vital statistics.

A pragmatic distinction

Public health administration has less personnel and less historical background than the educational systems of state and local government. But this type of public activity has acquired modern significance with the development of preventive medicine, vaccines, control of communicable disease, compulsory sanitation, and appreciation of popular scientific information on health problems. States, cities, and counties maintain health agencies or officers to perform regulatory and service functions, partly in cooperation with other authorities, including the United States Public Health Service. The work is not uniformly concentrated. Milk inspection, for example, may be directed by agricultural agencies, as in a few states, instead of being directed by health officers. The city of New York has a separate scientific Department of Air Pollution Control; state conservation agencies may be charged with limiting stream pollution.

Rise of public health work

Most of the states have central health boards or commissions, with memberships of three or more, for rather infrequent meetings, somewhat like a college or corporation board. The chief administrative officer of the health agency is likely to be called "commissioner," "director," "superintendent," or "officer." His department generally serves as a clearinghouse of technical assistance, information, advice, and regulatory instruction for local health boards or officers. It may perform or direct inspectional activities, dispense vaccines, and conduct laboratory tests to advance health service or control. The board or department in some states has broad powers to issue rules or orders for compliance by citizens, institutions, and even municipalities. There are other miscellaneous functions, with variations among the states.

State agencies and functions

Public health service or power reaches citizens primarily through local agencies, which may share in federal grants-in-aid as well as receive state assistance. Full-time staffs are found in most counties, sometimes with a local physician on part-time duty as director. Most important cities have agencies separate from the county, although a single or consolidated health unit for city and county characterizes a considerable number of centers, including such metropolitan communities as Baltimore, Denver, Louisville, Memphis, Nashville, New Orleans, St. Louis, and San Francisco.

Local administration

In addition to numerous services, the local health departments exercise powers of government with respect to matters of quarantine, compulsory vaccination, inspection of products and premises, elimination of unsanitary conditions, and closure or condemnation of establishments for non-compliance. If necessary, their legitimate orders are enforced through court action. By order of the health board the city of Nashville, as noted earlier, had to vacate its police jail for a period in 1955 and depend upon county imprisonment and prosecution. The social action programs of health authorities beget opposition and criticism as well as civic support.

Hospital statistics

Statistics on the number of hospitals operated by state and local governments (over 2,250) are rather formidable, although demands are heard in many quarters for expansion and improvement. The total includes more than 575 for states, and approximately 1,680 for cities, counties, or city–county combinations. These add up to a total smaller than that for all other types of hospitals in the country, including church, private, and federal, but they represent a far greater number of beds—not far from a million. The state hospitals have an average capacity of more than 1,000 beds, a capacity that partly offsets the complete absence of public or private hospital facilities in hundreds of counties, not to mention inadequate facilities in many others. It is well to guard against relying too rigidly upon statistics, however, for private hospitals may serve public purposes under contractual arrangements with counties or cities for the care of indigent patients, and government hospitals may provide service for paying patients. Private hospitals are subject in many ways to state or local regulation.

Hospital control and administration

Public hospitals frequently have their own boards of control and administrative officers. It is a prevailing state pattern to coordinate the central hospital facilities administratively and physically with the state university medical school for practical and scientific reasons. The states also provide general and special hospital services in central or district institutions for the mentally ill, who have received increasing attention in contemporary times with the development of applied psychology and psychiatry. Special work in the field of mental illness and its cure is also found in the larger regular hospitals and medical schools. Local public hospitals vary widely in management, size, and efficiency, with many inadequacies and difficulties of distance for inhabitants of rural areas. Local hospitals, like local schools, may make gains through state and federal aid.

Foundations and associations

The public health interests are served in effective ways through nongovernmental groups and movements, as notably exemplified in the popular fights against cancer, heart disease, and respiratory diseases. The successful battles of earlier eras, such as the fight against infantile paralysis and tuberculosis, are taken for granted and often unrecognized by many of today's generation. These activities tend to supplement and support the work of public health agencies and institutions, sometimes to blaze new trails in the field of preventive measures. An example of pioneering was the Rockefeller Foundation's successful sponsorship in the early years of this century of a scientific program for removing the hookworm handicap from poor people in the rural South. Movements of enlightenment with respect to mental disorders and venereal diseases have had substantial effects and have also stimulated legislative action, including federal aid.

Federal aid: health and hospitals

Federal grants-in-aid to states and localities have exerted strong influence both on hospital construction and public health services. The Hospital Survey and Construction (Hill–Burton) Act of 1946 stimulated construction of new hospitals or additions for existing buildings; the annual appropriation began with an initial 75 million dollars and tripled within a twenty-year period. During more than twenty-five years of operation, the Hill-Burton program made grants for over 11,000 projects and nearly one-half million beds in hospitals and nursing homes. The federal share was $3.9 billion, matched by $9.8 billion from state, local, and private sources.

While urban and specialized hospitals have received assistance, the major emphasis has been upon rural and general hospitals. With the passage of Medicare for the aged, the need for additional hospital beds continues to increase. Under 1965 legislation fifty-six Regional Medical Programs, covering the entire nation, have been organized with federal funds supporting broad-based local initiative. Through such projects as coronary care training units, the regional programs are not only improving the quality and availability of diagnosis, treatment, and care of patients, but they are helping to develop new cooperative relationships within the health care system.[12]

The major areas of federal aid for specific public health programs are cancer control, heart-disease control, mental health, and venereal-disease control. Increasing criticism has been made of the "fragmentary and spasmodic" character of distribution of federal funds for public health, said to reward those states and agencies that have mastered the latter-day skill known as "grantsmanship"—a euphemistic term for begging, or putting up the best story. In recent years a debate has developed over the idea of a general "block grant" in the field of health which would permit the states increased flexibility in their support for various programs. Although this proposal has received general support from governors and other state officials, it is opposed by professional organizations interested in particular health problems (cancer, heart disease, etc.). Such groups are fearful that their particular program might be neglected. Federal officials have tended to side with the specialized grants as a means of obtaining the maximum stimulation of state and local health activity.

Block grants: pro and con

The long-standing national debate over national health insurance, labeled "socialized medicine" by its opponents, came to at least a partial climax in 1965 with the passage by Congress of the twin programs commonly called "Medicare" and "Medicaid." Medicare is the better known of the programs and, effective July 1, 1966, made some nineteen million people, sixty-five years of age and older, eligible for two types of financial assistance in paying for the costs of health care. One is a general hospital-services payment program financed under Social Security, and the other is a voluntary medical services program financed by payments from those electing to use it. Medicaid is more directly related to state governments. It considerably expanded the old Kerr–Mills program of matching federal–state grants for medical care for the needy aged. The new legislation was basically a welfare program for the medically indigent of all ages, as defined by individual states within certain federal limits. Medicaid is administered in the states by public welfare departments rather than public health departments, with one or two exceptions.[13]

Medicare and Medicaid

[12] *See* "State Health Programs," *The Book of the States, 1974–75,* pp. 368–379. *See also* John H. Knowles (ed.), *Hospitals, Doctors, and the Public Interest* (Cambridge, Mass.: Harvard University Press, 1965).

[13] For several articles on local health and welfare services in relation to more recent federal legislation, *see* the symposium in *The American County* 38 (October 1973), on "Should Counties Control Health Care Services?"

Public Welfare

To promote the public, social, or general welfare is one of the great purposes of modern democratic government. In broad constitutional coverage, it would include public education and public health, which, however, have their own functional classifications in the state and local systems. Hence welfare in more particular terms today connotes community or governmental action to relieve and prevent poverty, suffering, and human insecurity. Its modern meaning carries a more constructive psychological assumption and a stronger sense of social responsibility than the term suggested in the era of public reliance upon community almshouses and county homes for paupers, whose pathetic fate was summarized in the phrase, "over the hill to the poor house." Through significant developments since the passing of the fabulous 1920s, the public welfare picture has been revolutionized in features and magnitude. For humanitarian and pragmatic reasons, it has acquired the twin supports of public philosophy and professional administration. It expresses the power of the purse of big government, little government, and middle government in a fashion strikingly symbolic of the new "cooperative federalism."

Meaning of the term

Temporary and permanent measures gave centralized momentum to welfare administration in the depression of the 1930s, when millions were unemployed and other millions could not pay debts or taxes. The burden of relief became too much for private or community charities, too much for local units of government, and too much for state governments. The federal government assumed the task in the first term of President Franklin D. Roosevelt, rapidly expanding activities and providing billions of dollars for employment of the jobless on numerous state and local projects. This Emergency Relief Administration became the Works Progress Administration, then the Work Projects Administration. Its various functions included, in addition to the regular farm recovery work, launching a rural rehabilitation program to aid stranded farmers and tenants such as those described by John Steinbeck in *The Grapes of Wrath.* An incidental accomplishment of the WPA was the physical removal of malarial conditions in swampy regions of the South. Inside or outside the WPA there were federal agencies and funds to aid states and municipalities in highway improvement, slum clearance, park development, and other useful work that would offer employment without competing directly with private enterprise. This broad-gauge action stimulated the states and localities to create or authorize agencies and projects of immediate and lasting importance.

Emergency relief

Social Security

The federal Social Security Act of 1935 has become a basic charter of cooperative welfare policy, attested by subsequent expansions by federal legislation and statutory implementation in all the states. It launched four broad programs of action. These are a strictly federal system of old-age and survivors insurance; federal–state systems of unemployment insurance; aid to the states for public assistance to needy persons of specified categories; and aid to the states for maternal and child welfare service. All but the first of these programs require state legislation and cooperation. The first, under federal administration, prevents a certain type of welfare problem from falling upon the states and local jurisdictions. In using federal insurance and welfare funds, state and local agencies must comply with certain standards, including merit requirements for their own personnel.

Unemployment compensation

The unemployment insurance systems of the states are somewhat varied, flexible, and complicated, since they are set up and administered by the states with the support of compulsory payroll taxes levied by federal legislation. The states originally had little alternative but to take "voluntary" steps to use the compulsory levies within their borders. All states have unemployment systems, including Wisconsin which had adopted a plan prior to 1935.

By federal requirement the unemployment insurance plan applies to commerce and industry, exclusive of the railroads, which had already been covered by a separate national system of labor security. In a roundabout process, a payroll tax is paid by each employer or establishment having one or more workers for parts of twenty weeks of the year, and the proceeds are segregated according to states. The maximum levy is 3.2 percent of a worker's annual pay up to $4,200. This includes a flat four-tenths of 1 percent to cover federal grants to the states for administering the program. The remaining 2.8 percent is subject to reduction for a particular taxpayer according to his experience or merit rating as an employer under the state system. This portion of the tax goes into a federal trust account for use by the state concerned in making benefit payments to cover works for temporary periods of unemployment.

State laws vary considerably in details, but essentially they determine the recipients, amounts, and conditions of unemployment compensation. The average benefit per week among the states in 1971 was about $50, and the maximum duration for benefits ranged from twenty-six to thirty-six weeks. A worker earns insurance credits when employed; upon becoming jobless, he files a claim for benefits with a public employment office and also registers with the office for reemployment. The Bureau of Employment Security of the United States Department of Labor administers the federal features of the process with a cooperative eye on state standards and practices. The amount of funds held in the federal treasury for state accounts extends into billions, and the number of workers receiving benefit payments in a year extends into millions.

Welfare assistance and service

Many persons are not protected from poverty or ill fortune by the systems of old-age and unemployment insurance. In recognition of this condition, the federal government aids the states in providing public assistance to four classes of needy persons: the aged, the blind, the permanently and totally disabled, and children without parental support. This help to more than 15 million Americans is administered by state and local welfare offices and financed on a federal–state matching basis. The $10 billion spent in 1971 was three times that spent in 1960 and was for twice the number of welfare recipients than in 1960.

One program inaugurated under the Social Security system affords service rather than financial payments to individuals. It is a matching program under federal requirements and with state or local administration for services in behalf of maternal health, child health, crippled children, and child welfare. The matched funds for these services are handled at the state level partly through health units and partly through welfare agencies. Federal responsibility rests with the Children's Bureau of the Department of Health, Education, and Welfare. Nongovernmental organizations and institutions also cooperate in carrying out relevant phases of the work, such as providing special training and opportunity for physically handicapped children. Red Cross teams move into relief action in case of sudden misfortune or disaster. Welfare policies and administrative practices are advanced by the professional influence of schools of social work and associations of social workers.

Collateral activities

Social welfare for states and local units is also served by funds, activities, and agencies outside the technical scope of public welfare administration. Supervised parks and recreation facilities contribute to the well-being of the masses. Various agencies and jurisdictions of government take up relief tasks in case of a major flood in New England or California. Impoverished veterans of the armed services may avoid local relief rolls through public provisions for their care and benefit. Retirement pensions and job securities for teachers and other public employees contribute to the general welfare. So does public housing for low-income families. Mention should be made of fringe benefits for employees in many collective-bargain contracts with labor union welfare funds mounting to significant proportions since the end of World War II. The proper administration of such funds is a matter of public concern, particularly in the industrial states. Economic and scientific progress ramifies the problems of public welfare and the methods of coping with them.

State and local governments played a key role, and even a controversial one, in the War on Poverty, a program originating in the Economic Opportunity Act of 1964. President Johnson's anti-poverty program was aimed at all ages and all regions, but its primary thrust via the Office of Economic Opportunity was toward the alienated, disadvantaged youth of the nation's cities. The early strategy of the fast-developing program was to cut across all levels of government, to establish new organizational forms—private and public—as well as to utilize existing forms. It was to maintain the spirit of a "crash program" of preparing disadvantaged youth for full participation in modern society by provision of (1) work opportunities, (2) training mechanisms, and (3) educational programs. The development and administration of specific anti-poverty programs called for broadly based community action machinery involving "maximum feasible participation" of the poor.

The War on Poverty

With a speed reminiscent of the early New Deal days in the 1930s, new names and initials for anti-poverty agencies and programs found their way into the vocabulary of officials and the general public. Among these were OEO (Office of Economic Opportunity), VISTA (Volunteers in Service to America, a kind of domestic Peace Corps), CAP (Community Action Program), the Job Corps (seeking to improve the employability of youths sixteen through twenty-one years of age), and Operation Head Start (aimed at helping the disadvantaged preschool child, as well as his parents, to prepare for school experiences). Not all of the programs were oriented to youth, however; some of the community action programs involved elderly poor people, such as a foster grandparent program and staffing community centers in public housing projects for the elderly.

The anti-poverty alphabet

The honeymoon period of the anti-poverty program was brief and by 1967 it was running into rough political waters for a variety of reasons: budget pressures related to the war in Viet Nam added to the normal opposition to welfare spending; "maximum feasible involvement of the poor" in many cases took on the appearance of organizing to "fight city hall," which in turn caused a loss of important political support for congressional appropriations; and the practice of creating private community action agencies in some three-fourths of the cases, rather than governmental agencies, tended in many cases to isolate the program from important coordinating pressures at the local level. In addition to these mitigating factors, weaknesses of the War on Poverty tended to make more headlines in the press than quiet success stories; urban violence in some of the cities that were alleged to have the more successful anti-poverty programs provided ammunition for the militant opponents of the War on Poverty; and inter- and intra-administrative rivalries and competition for control of various aspects of the anti-poverty program weakened it from within.

The politics of fighting poverty

Following President Nixon's landslide re-election in 1972, he served notice in his 1973 budget message to Congress that he favored elimination, contraction, suspension, or transfer of many of the anti-poverty programs.

He called the programs "a hodgepodge of poorly conceived and hastily put together" projects and called for the dismantling of the OEO. The more popular programs were taken over by the older agencies or departments, and the more embattled programs seemed destined to die lingering deaths in the 1970s.

The War on Poverty during its relatively brief and controversial career received more than the usual quota of lumps and bruises for a new governmental program. But it was inaugurated with a more than usual goal—the eventual total victory over poverty, "the most ancient of mankind's enemies." For the interested student of political behavior, intergovernmental relations, and the politics of poverty, the lessons are legion.

1968 Report of the Kerner Commission

In the wake of the urban riots in the summer of 1967, President Johnson appointed an eleven-member Advisory Commission on Civil Disorders, headed by Governor Otto Kerner of Illinois, to investigate and make recommendations. Reporting in March 1968, almost five months ahead of its deadline, the Kerner Commission made sweeping proposals related not only to traditional welfare programs and the War on Poverty, but also to education, housing, employment, and law enforcement. To head off the movement of "our nation . . . toward two societies, one black, one white—separate and unequal," the Commission recommended a massive compassionate effort to eliminate segregation and poverty in the racial ghettoes "created, maintained, and condoned by white society." In addition to calling for two million new jobs and six million new homes for lower income families, it called for drastic overhaul of the welfare system, declaring that the present set-up "is designed to save money instead of people and tragically ends up doing neither." It recommended elimination of residence requirements, elimination of the controversial "man in the house" rule designed to curb illegitimate births among mothers on welfare, increased support for family-planning programs, and an increase of the federal financial share to 90 percent of total welfare costs. The Kerner Commission report was undoubtedly intended to have a kind of shock value directed at white complacency in local, state, and national decision making.[13]

[13] For an in-depth study using social psychology to help explain the political significance of the first Watts riots, *see* David O. Sears and John B. McConahay, *The Politics of Violence: The New Urban Blacks and the Watts Riot* (Boston: Houghton Mifflin, 1973).

SUPPLEMENTARY READINGS

Ashmore, H. S. *The Negro and the Schools.* Chapel Hill: University of North Carolina Press, 1954.

Bell, Winifred. *Aid to Dependent Children.* New York: Columbia University Press, 1965.

Burkhead, Jesse V., with Thomas G. Fox and

John W. Holland. *Input and Output in Large-City High Schools.* Syracuse, N. Y.: Syracuse University Press, 1967.

Carnegie Commission on Higher Education. *Priorities for Action: Final Report of the Carnegie Commission on Higher Education.* New York: McGraw-Hill Book Co., 1973.

———. *Higher Education and the Nation's Health: Policies for Medical and Dental Education.* New York: McGraw-Hill Book Co., 1970.

———. *The Capitol and the Campus: State Responsibility for Postsecondary Education.* New York: McGraw-Hill Book Co., 1971.

Commission on Intergovernmental Relations. *A Study Committee Report on Federal Aid to Public Health.* Washington, D. C.: U. S. Government Printing Office, 1955.

———. *A Study Committee Report on Federal Aid to Welfare.* Washington, D. C.: U. S. Government Printing Office, 1955.

———. *A Study Committee Report on Unemployment Compensation and Employment Service.* Washington, D. C.: U. S. Government Printing Office, 1955.

———. *A Study Committee Report on Federal Responsibility in the Field of Education.* Washington, D. C.: U. S. Government Printing Office, 1955.

Council of State Governments. *State Action in Mental Health.* Chicago, 1960.

Daland, R. T. *Government and Health: The Alabama Experience.* University, Ala.: Bureau of Public Administration, University of Alabama, 1955.

Drake, J. T. *The Aged in American Society.* New York: Ronald Press Co., 1958.

Gardner, John W. "National Goals in Education." In *Goals for Americans,* report of the President's Commission on National Goals. New York: The American Assembly, Columbia University, 1960; reprinted, Prentice-Hall, 1960. Pp. 81–100.

Krist, Michael. *The Politics of Education at the Local, State, and Federal Levels.* Berkeley, Calif.: McCutchan Publishing Co., 1970.

Levin, Henry M., ed. *Community Control of Schools.* Washington, D. C.: Brookings Institution, 1970.

Masters, Nicholas A.; Salisbury, Robert H.; and Eliot, Thomas H. *State Politics and the Public Schools.* New York: Alfred A. Knopf, 1964.

McClure, William P., and Miller, Van. *Government of Public Education for Adequate Policy Making.* Urbana, Ill.: University of Illinois Bureau of Educational Research, 1969.

Means, J. H. *Doctors, People, and Government.* Boston: Little, Brown, and Co., 1953.

National Conference of Social Work. *The Social Welfare Forum, 1955.* New York: Columbia University Press, 1955.

Scotland, E., and Kobler, A. L. *Life and Death of a Mental Hospital.* Seattle: University of Washington Press, 1965.

Steiner, Gilbert Y. *Social Insecurity: The Politics of Welfare.* Chicago: Rand McNally and Co., 1966.

———. *The State of Welfare.* Washington, D. C.: The Brookings Institution, 1971.

TenBroek, Jacobus, ed. *The Law of the Poor.* San Francisco: Chandler Publishing Co., 1966.

White House Conference on Aging. *Aging in the States: A Report of Progress, Concern, Goals.* Washington, D. C.: U. S. Government Printing Office, 1961.

Wyatt, L. R. *Intergovernmental Relations in Public Health.* Minneapolis: University of Minnesota Press, 1951.

Index

A

Abington School District v. *Schempp*, 96, 517
Abrams, Charles, 504
Absentee voting, 152
Adams, Sherman, 304
Adler et al. v. *Board of Education of the City of New York*, 93–94
Administrative organization, 307–318
  problems, 324–328
Admission of new states, 35
Adrian, Charles R., 174, 405, 410, 428
Advisory Commission on Intergovernmental Relations, 46, 333, 336, 339, 345, 346, 348, 350, 352, 374, 429, 453
  creation of, 51–53
  review of work, 52–53
Agger, Robert E., 409
Agriculture, 488–490
  U.S. Department of, 513
Airports, 70, 496
Alabama, 551, 513
  area, 22
  black voting, 144–145
  constitution, 110, 111
  counties, 377
  elected department heads, 295
  federal aid, 44
  governor, 282
  innovation score, 8
  legislative apportionment, 251
  legislative pay, 222
  legislature, 220
  party competition, 169
  population, 22
  urban–rural cleavage, 252
  voter registration, 143–144, 148, 149
  voting qualifications, 148, 149
Alameda County, 437
Alaska
  area, 22
  boroughs, 375
  constitution, 110, 111, 113, 120, 126
  constitutional convention referendum, 121
  earmarked taxes, 350
  federal aid, 44
  governor's reorganization powers, 313
  legislature, 220
  party competition, 169
  population, 22
  short ballot, 294
  voter registration, 148
  voting qualifications, 146, 148
Albuquerque

degree of non-partisanship, 174
Alcoholic beverage control, 347
Alexander, Herbert C., 181
Allen, Tip H., 138
Allentown–Bethlehem–Easton metropolitan area
population, 78
Almond, Gabriel, 186
Altgeld, John P., 33
Altshuler, Alan A., 412
Amendments, constitutional, 119, 129–134
American Assembly, 323
American Bar Association, 371
American Civil Liberties Union, 465
American Farm Bureau Federation, 490
American Judicature Society, 371
American Legion, 188
American Medical Association, 188
Amtrak, 496
Anderson, James, 155
Anderson, John, 226
Anderson, Martin, 504
Anderson, Stanley V., 328
Anderson, Totton, J., 192
Annexation, 429–433
Apodaca v. *Oregon*, 92, 367
Appalachian Regional Development Act, 42
highways, 494
Apportionment, legislative, 248–263
Appropriations, 352–353
Area Redevelopment Act, 42
Arizona
area, 22
constitution, 111
counties, 377
elected department heads, 295
federal aid, 44
governor, 281
innovation score, 8
legislature, 220
loyalty oath, 94
party competition, 169
population, 22
Arkansas, 358
administrative reorganization, 315–316
area, 22
board memberships, 292
budget making, 297
constitution, 111
constitutional convention, 125
counties, 377
desegregation, 98
federal aid, 44
governor's callers, 302–303
gubernatorial accountability, 326
highway commission, 315
innovation score, 8
legislature, 220
loyalty oath, 94
party competition, 169
population, 22
voting qualifications, 148, 149
"Arkies," migration of, 17
Arnall, Ellis, 128, 163, 285
Articles of Confederation, 205
Athens (Tenn.), Battle of, 151
Atlanta (Ga.), 99, 217, 452
Jackson, Maynard, 145
power structure, 407–408
Auditing, 313
Augusta metropolitan area
population, 78
Avery v. *Midland County*, 381
Aycock, Charles B., 164

B

Bachrach, Peter, 409
Bailey, Harry A., Jr., 142
Bain, Chester, 432
Baker, Gordon E., 250, 254
Baker v. *Carr*, 11, 82, 145, 255–263
Ballot forms, 151–154
Balmer, Donald G., 181
Baltimore, 443
legislative apportionment, 249–250
Baltimore metropolitan area
Linear City, part of, 15
Banfield, Edward C., 428
Bank regulation, 481–482

Banovetz, James M., 428
Baratz, Morton S., 409
Barber, James David, 207–208, 208–209, 215, 231, 243
Barnett, Ross, 31, 327
Barnes, Robert Elliott, 54
Barton, Weldon V., 56
Baton Rouge, 445, 446
  city–parish consolidation, 445
Bayes, John R., 390
Beckman, Norman, 46, 72, 226, 439
Beiser, Edward N., 363
Bell, George A., 311
Bell, James R., 310
Bernd, Joseph L., 143, 155
Berry, Donald S., 498
Best, James J., 204
Beth, Loren P., 242, 252
Beyle, Thad L., 288
Bicameralism, 218–219
Bilbo, Theodore G., 163
Billboard legislation, 493
Bill of attainder, 35
Bill of Rights, 91–92
Binghampton metropolitan area, population, 78
Birkby, Robert H., 96
Birmingham, 99
Birth control laws, 96
Black, Gordon S., 159, 174, 276
Black, Hugo, 464
Black legislators, 217
Black militancy, 190
Black politics, 189–190
Black power, 163, 429
Blomme, George W., 498
Blue laws, 85, 95
Blue sky laws, 481
Boards, buffer, 292–293
Bock, Edwin A., 317
Bollens, John C., 15, 386, 390, 434, 506
Bonds
  general obligation, 346–347
  revenue, 346–347
  serial, 346–347
  sinking-fund, 346
Bone, Hugh A., 154, 156, 180
Booth, David A., 134, 449, 504
Boroughs, 375
  rotten, 249
Borrowing, 345–347
Boskoff, Alvin, 154
Bosses, political, 162–163
Boston, 421
  political machines, 162
Boston metropolitan area, 420, 430
  central city decline, 12
  Linear City, part of, 15
  suburban growth, 12
Bosworth, Karl A., 124, 276
Boyd, William J. D., 13, 257
Boynton, Robert Paul, 405
Bradley, Donald S., 408
Bradley, Thomas, 145
Brandeis, Louis D., 32
Braunfeld v. *Brown*, 95
Breathitt, Edward T., 135
Bricker amendment, 105
Brooks, Glenn E., 6, 48, 49, 50, 51, 52
Brown, Pat, 34
Brown v. *Topeka Board of Education*, 30–31, 98, 515
Bryce, James, 157, 183, 392
Buchanan, James M., 350
Buchanan, William, 156, 168, 170, 209–216, 225, 226, 231, 232, 233, 238, 240, 244–247, 520
Buckley, William F., Jr., 32, 147
Budget, 352–354
  reform, 353–354
  state, 297–298
Buffalo, party organization incentives, 159
Bureau of Public Roads, 39–40, 69
Bureau of the Census, U.S., 334, 419, 420, 421, 423
Burger, Warren E., 102–103, 372–373
Burgess, E. W., 19
Burns v. *Richardson*, 257
Burr, Aaron, 319
Business affected with a public interest, 89–90
Busing for racial balance, 516–517
Busing in schools, 100–101

Byrd, Harry, 98, 273

C

Cable television, 478–479
Calhoun, John C., 29, 33, 179
California, 506, 513
  administrative proliferation, 308
  administrative reorganization, 310
  area, 22
  black in-migration, 17
  civil service reform, 320
  constitution, 110, 111, 113, 118
  counties, 377
  double filing, 177
  federal aid, 44
  governor, 283
  innovation score, 8
  interest groups, 194, 195, 197
  judicial appointments, 362
  legislative apportionment, 250
  legislative conflicts, types of, 232–233
  legislative pay, 222
  legislative sanctions, 240
  legislative volume, 234
  legislators, 210, 213, 214, 217, 220, 222, 225
  legislature, 220, 223, 225, 232–233
  party competition, 169
  party influence, 245
  police, 461
  population, 22
  property tax litigation, 340
  tidelands controversy, 30
Callaway, Howard (Bo), 285
Campbell, Alan K., 453, 454
Cardozo, Benjamin, 43
Carnegie Commission on Higher Education, 519, 530
Casper, Jonathan D., 475
Cassella, William N., Jr., 379
CATV, 478–479
Caucus, party, 171–172
Censorship, 93–94
Chaffey, Douglas Camp, 245
Chamber of Commerce, 191, 402
Chambers v. *Florida,* 91
Chandler, A. B. ("Happy"), 276, 283
Charles River Bridge v. *Warren Bridge,* 86
Chattanooga metropolitan area, 78
Chicago, 397, 400
  degree of non-partisanship, 174
  legislative apportionment, 251
  political machines, 162
Chicago metropolitan area, 431
  units of government, 423
Chicago Sanitary District, 440
Chicago Transit Authority, 480
Chief administrative officer (CAO), 313, 400
Chiefs of Police, International Association of, 65
Childs, Richard S., 180, 406
Child welfare, 527
Chisholm v. *Georgia,* 33
Cho, Yong Hyo, 261
Church–state relations, 95–96, 517
Cincinnati, 415
  degree of non-partisanship, 174
Cincinnati metropolitan area
  population, 78
  units of government, 423
Cities, constitutional status of, 59–62
Citizens' Conference on State Legislatures, 263–269
City charters, 392–395
City–county consolidation, 444–452, 522
City–county relations, 383–385, 391, 443–452
City–county separation, 443–444
City government
  administration, 391–406
  airports, 496
  charters, 392–395
  council, 395, 396, 397–398, 399, 400, 402–405
  expenditures, 331–335
  forms of, 395–406
  home rule, 394–395
  leadership, 405
  non-partisanship typology, 174

planning, 412–413
police, 464–469
power structure, 406–410
public works, 500–504
reorganization movement, 313–314
zoning, 412
City–manager plan (*See* Council-manager plan)
City planning, federal assistance, 67–68, 413
Civil defense, 71, 279–281
Civil Rights Acts, 99–100, 143, 148, 515
Civil rights politics, 189
Civil service laws, 293–294
Civil service reform movement, 318–324
Civil War, 20, 29, 206
Civil War amendments, 84–85
Cleaveland, Frederick N., 74
Cleveland, 144, 421, 476
Cleveland, Grover, 33, 163, 272
Clientele politics, 47
Clinton, George, 272
Clinton (Tenn.), 98–99
Closed primary, 175
Cloward, Richard A., 454
COGs (*See* Metropolitan councils of governments)
Colegrove v. *Green*, 254
Cole v. *Richardson*, 94
Collective bargaining in the public service, 323
Colleges (*See* Education)
Collins, LeRoy, 119
Colman, William G., 46
Colonies, original thirteen, 20
Colorado
area, 22
civil service, 320
constitution, 111
counties, 377
federal aid, 44
innovation score, 8
legislature, 220
party competition, 169
population, 22
Columbia (Md.), 413
Columbus (Ga.), city–county consolidation, 445
Columbus (Ga.–Ala.), metropolitan area, population, 78
Combs, William H., 134
Comer, B. B., 476
Commission form, 400–402
Commission on Intergovernmental Relations, 253
Committees, legislative, 239–243
Common Cause, 182, 186, 206
Common law, 84
Communications media, 19
Community affairs, state departments of, 77
Community colleges, 513
Conant, James B., 519
Confederacy, southern, 29, 277
Connally Act, 47
Connecticut, 320, 375
area, 22
birth control legislation, 96
constitution, 11, 120, 124
direct primary, 173
federal aid, 44
innovation score, 8
interest groups, 194
legislative committees, 241
legislature, 220
party competition, 169
population, 22
public defender, 465
public lottery, 343
Tri-State Transportation Compact, 60
Conner v. *Johnson*, 258
Connery, Robert H., 56, 59, 66, 70, 79, 83, 455
Conservation, 504–510
Conservationists, 188
Constable, 463
Constitutional commissions, 127–128
Constitutional conventions, 128
politics, 124–126
Constitutions, state, 107–138, 203–204
commissions, 127–128

common features, 113–116
conventions, 121–127
criticisms of, 116–119
general information, 111–112
length, 110–112
National Municipal League studies, 138
politics, 108–109, 119–120, 124–126
revision, 119–136
tax restrictions, 337–338
Consumerism, 482
Continental Congress, 205
Cooley v. *Board of Wardens of Port of Philadelphia,* 87
Cooperative federalism, 35–48, 525
Cooper, Carole L., 323
Cornwell, Elmer E., Jr., 406
Coroner, 382, 463–464
Corrections
administration, 469–475
employment in, 471
Corruption in government, 199–200 (*See also* Watergate)
Corty, Floyd L., 446
Cotter, Cornelius P., 165
Council–manager plan, 402–405
Council of State Governments, 57, 352
County government, 375–390
board of supervisors, 380–381
chief administrative officer (CAO), 386–387
city–county relations, 384–385
consolidation movement, 384
county–manager plan, 386–387
criticisms, 384
home rule, 387
number by states, 376–377
officers and agencies, 382–384
problems of organization, 440
reorganization movement, 313–314
size by states, 376–377
suburban impact on, 12
County–manager plan, 386–387
County Officials, National Association of, 65
County reapportionment, 381
Court administrator, 372
Court of the union, proposed, 51
Courts
state, 137, 355–373
structure, 471
Coyle v. *Smith,* 35
Craig, James B., Jr., 126
Crain, Robert L., 403, 410
Crane, Wilder W., Jr., 214, 254
Crime, 456–459
Crime Control Act of 1973, 468
Crime control, legislation, 46–47
Criminal justice structure, 470–471
Crump, Ed, 162
Cummins, A. B., 7
Cumulative voting, 179–180
Cunningham, Luvern L., 520
Currigan, Thomas, 65
Cutright, Phillips, 166
Czudnowski, Moshe, 167

D

Dahl, Robert A., 408
Dallas, 431
degree of non-partisanship, 174
Dallas metropolitan area, 424
Danielson, Michael N., 69, 83, 499
Darrah, Earl L., 310
Dartmouth College v. *Woodward,* 86
Dauer, Manning J., 116–117
Davenport–Rock Island–Moline metropolitan area, population, 78
David, Paul T., 156, 183, 258
Davidson County (Tenn.), 466, 447, 449
Davis, Deane C., 119
Daylight saving time, 48
Debt
federal, state, and local, 346
limits, 345
DeGrazia, Alfred, 110
DeGrove, John M., 405
Delaware, 358
area, 22
constitution, 111, 129
counties, 376

desegregation, 98
federal aid, 44
highways, 495
innovation score, 8
legislative apportionment, 251
legislature, 220
party competition, 169
population, 22
Delaware River Basin Compact, 55
Democratic Party, 161, 165, 168–169, 173, 243–245, 278
Denny, Laura L., 181
Denver, 371
Denver metropolitan area, units of government, 423
Derge, David R., 216, 252
DeSapio, Carmine, 164
Desegregation, public schools, 30–31, 514–517 (*See also* Segregation, public schools)
Des Moines, 402
Detroit, 397
Detroit metropolitan area, 124, 431
central city decline, 12
suburban growth, 12
units of government, 423
DeVries, Walter, 200
Dewey, Thomas E., 273, 464
Direct legislation, 269–270
Direct primary, 172–178
Dishman, Robert, 108, 111
District of Columbia, federal aid, 44
Divorce laws, 53–54
Dobriner, W. A., 13
Dodd, Walter F., 117
Dorr rebellion, 33, 140, 284
Dorsett, Lyle W., 162
Double filing, 177
Douglas, Paul, 219
Downing, Rondal G., 362
Driscoll, Alfred E., 118, 128
Drummond, Roscoe, 51
Due process of law, 62, 89–94 (*See also* Fourteenth Amendment)
procedural, 91–92
substantive, 91–93
Duluth–Superior metropolitan area,
population, 78
Duncombe, Herbert Sydney, 379–380, 383, 385, 386, 440, 449
Dunn v. *Blumstein*, 147
Durham, black vote, 145
Dwinell, Lane, 50
Dye, Thomas R., 162, 183, 214, 217, 260, 267, 278, 432

E

East, John Porter, 406
Ecology movement, 189
Economic bigness, 18
Education, 351, 414, 511–520
busing for racial balance, 516–517
community colleges, 513
expenditures, 331–333
federal aid, 43
interstate compact for, 518
and politics, 519–520
state aid, 351
tuition reimbursement, 517
Education, Boards of, 200
Egerton, John, 461
Eisenberg, Ralph, 258
Eisenhower, Dwight, D., 49
Eisinger, Peter K., 13–14
Elazar, Daniel J., 9, 25, 36, 52
Elections, 178–182 (*See also* Voting)
corrupt practice legislation, 181
cumulative voting, 179–180
proportional representation, 180
Eleventh Amendment, 33–34
Elfbrandt v. *Russell et al.*, 94
Eliot, Thomas H., 317, 520
Elliott, William Y., 327–328
Emergency Relief Administration, 525
Employees, state and local, 3–4
Engel v. *Vitale*, 96, 517
English, Arthur, 124–126
English common law, 356–357
Environmental Protection Agency, 507
Epstein, Leon D., 155
Equal protection of the laws, 61, 89, 96–103 (*See also* Fourteenth

Amendment)
Equity, 357–358
Ervien v. *United States*, 35
Eulau, Heinz, 168, 170, 209–216, 225–226, 231, 232, 233, 238, 240, 244–247, 398, 520
Evans v. *Corman*, 147
Evansville metropolitan area, population, 78
Everson v. *Board of Education*, 94
Examining boards, 485
Executive budget, 297–298, 352
Expenditures, state and local, 2–3, 331–335
Ex post facto law, 35

F

Fairbanks, Alaska, 126
Fair, Daryl R., 361
Fair trade laws, 483
Fall River metropolitan area, population, 78
Fantini, Mario, 520
Fargo–Moorhead metropolitan area, population, 78
Farkas, Suzanne, 59, 65, 80
Farley, Edward, 155
Farley, James A., 167–168
Farmers' Union, 490
Faubus, Orval, 31, 98
Federal aid, 41, 343–345
  airports, 70
  beginnings, 39
  block grants, 524
  complexity, 44–47, 74
  constitutionality of, 43–44
  criticisms of, 44–47
  education, 515, 517–518
  "grantsmanship," 524
  growth, 40–41
  highways, 39–40
  hospitals, 523–524
  housing, 65–67
  housing and slum clearance, 501
  open-space preservation, 68
  proportion of state and local revenue (by states), 44–45
  recreation, 68
  sewage treatment, 50
  slum clearance, 66–67
  urban planning, 67–68
  urban renewal, 66–67, 500–504
  urban transportation, 68–69
  vocational education, 50
Federal Bureau of Investigation, 468
Federal–city relationships, 58–82
  airports, 70
  early history, 62–63
  federal limitations, 59–60
  problems, 71–82
  recent programs, 63–71
  water resources, 71
Federal government
  and metropolitan problems, 453
  responsibility for urban problems, 79–82
Federal grants-in-aid (*See* Federal Aid)
Federalism
  composite theory, 37
  constitutional, 8–9
  cooperative, 35–48, 525
  and the courts, 355–356
  defined, 27–28
  and desegregation, 30–31
  interposition, 30–31
  marble cake analogy, 36
  nullification, 30–31
  old and new, 8–9
  in other countries, 27–28
  political, 9, 156
  viewed by aid officials, 37
Federalist, Number 10, 184
Federal Power Commission v. *Hope Natural Gas Co.*, 480
Federal–state cooperation, 35–48
Federal–state relations, police power, 84–105
Federal system (*See* Federalism)
Federated metropolis, 436–438
Feldman, Mark B., 439
Fellman, David, 116, 118
Fenton, John H., 109, 142, 155, 159
Ferguson, LeRoy C., 170, 209–216,

225, 226, 231, 232, 233, 238, 240, 244–247, 520
Ferguson, Miriam ("Ma"), 272, 283–284
Fifteenth Amendment, 139, 176
Fifth Amendment, 35, 369
Fire protection, 414
  expenditures, 332
First Amendment, 185
Fish and game regulation, 505
Fiszman, Joseph R., 520
Fitch, Lyle C., 499
Flinn, Thomas A., 171
Florida
  area, 22
  constitution, 111
  constitutional commissions, 128
  counties, 377
  direct primary, 177
  elected department heads, 295
  federal aid, 44
  inheritance tax, 48, 342
  innovation score, 8
  interest groups, 194
  legislature, 220, 223
  loyalty oath, 94
  party competition, 169
  population, 22
Folsom, James, 272
Forest preserves, 505–506
Fort Smith metropolitan area, 78
Fort Worth, 431
  degree of non-partisanship, 174
Fourteenth Amendment, 29, 35, 88–97, 175, 176, 185, 337
Frankfurter, Felix, 255
Frederickson, H. George, 261
Freedman, Leonard, 510
Freedom
  of press, 92–93
  of religion, 94–96
  of speech, 92–94
Freeman, J., Leiper, 398
Friedman, John, 412
Friedman, Robert S., 252, 495
Fromm, Erich, 19
Frost, Richard T., 56, 163
Full faith and credit, 53–54
Fulton County (Ga.), 452
Functional consolidation, 522

G

Galbraith, John Kenneth, 32
Gallagher v. *Crown Kosher Market,* 95
Galveston, 400, 402
Gantt, Fred, Jr., 288, 303
Gantt, Harvey, 515
Gardner, John, 186, 206
Garfield, James, 320
Gary (Ind.), 144
Gasoline tax, 342
Georgia, 395
  area, 22
  black legislators, 217
  black voting, 143
  constitution, 111, 128
  counties, 376
  county consolidation, 384
  county-unit system, 175
  desegregation, 99
  elected department heads, 295
  federal aid, 44
  governor, 284–285
  governor's power of removal, 295–296
  innovation score, 8
  legislative apportionment, 250
  legislators, 217
  legislature, 220
  lobbying, 248
  party competition, 169
  population, 22
  voter registration, 144, 148
  voting qualifications, 146, 148
Georgia, University of, 99
Gerrymandering, 250
  racial, 145
Gibbons v. *Ogden,* 87
Gideon v. *Wainwright,* 92
Gilbert, Charles E., 168, 380
Ginzburg et al. v. *United States,* 93
Gittell, Marilyn, 520
Glendening, Parris N., 503

Glick, Henry Robert, 374
Gluck, Peter R., 159
Godkin, E. L., 206
Goff, Donald H., 473
Goldman, Ralph M., 156
Goldrich, Daniel, 409
Goldwater, Barry, 32
Gomillion v. *Lightfoot*, 255
Gompers, Samuel, 198
Goodman, Jay S., 406
Goodsell, Charles T., 306
Gould, Jay, 198
Governor
  administrative powers, 291–302
  administrative role, 289–306
  age trends, 273
  appointing power, 291–296
  behavioral perspective, 288
  colonial, 288–290
  congressional candidates, 276
  demands on time, 302–303
  discretionary power, 299
  disputed titles, 284–285
  extra-constitutional powers, 278–279
  financial demagogy, 330
  impeachment, 283–284
  index of formal powers, 301–302
  influence in presidential nominations, 156
  legislative role, 276–281
  ministerial power, 299
  fiscal management power, 297–298
  removal power, 295–296
  presidency, training for, 5–7
  prestige, 272
  recall of, 284
  reorganization power, 285–287, 311
  resignation, 283
  restrictions on power, 292–296
  salary, 274
  and the spoils system, 318–319
  succession, 282–285
  supervisory power, 298
  trends, 285–287
  turn-over, 273–274
  vacancies, 282–285
  veto power, 227, 277–278
Governors' Conference, 49, 286
Gove, Samuel K., 253, 287
Grand jury, 369
Granger cases, 89
Granger movement, 478, 483
Grant, Daniel R., 57, 82, 302, 327, 381, 425, 449, 454
Graves, W. Brooke, 77, 138
Gray v. *Sanders*, 175
Great Society, The, 518
Greenbaum, E. S., 372
Greene, Lee S., 82, 164, 183
Greenstein, Fred I, 164, 270
Greenville (S.C.), 117
Gregg, James E., 186
Griffin v. *School Board of Prince Edward County*, 515
Griswold v. *Connecticut*, 96
Grodzins, Morton, 27, 36, 38, 50
Grovey v. *Townsend*, 85, 176
Growth of government, 2–9
Grumm, John, 437
Grupp, Stanley E., 469, 475
Gulick, Luther, 2, 18, 453

H

Hague, Frank, 128
Hain, Paul L., 276
Hall v. *Beals*, 147
Hamilton, Alexander, 32
Hamilton, Howard D., 257
Hanson, Royce, 413
Hare plan, 180
Harper v. *Virginia State Board of Elections*, 149–150
Harriman, Averell, 294, 305
Harris, Joseph P., 155
Harris, Robert J., 30, 98–99
Hatch Acts, 181
Hauser, Philip M., 11
Havard, William C., Jr., 117, 242, 252, 446
Havens, M. C., 252
Hawaii
  area, 22

constitution, 110, 111, 113
constitutional convention, 125
counties, 377
federal aid, 44
legislature, 220
Ombudsman, 328
party competition, 169
population, 22
short ballot, 294
state planning, 509–510
voter registration, 256–257
Hawkins, Brett W., 449
Hawley, Willis D., 37
Hayes, Donald P., 425
Health Care, 482, 520–524 (*See also* Hospitals)
administrative organization, 522
city–county consolidation, 522
and hospitals, expenditures of, 331–332
Medicaid, 524
Medicare, 524
public v. private, 520–524
Healy, Paul, 196
Heard, Alexander, 181, 206, 214, 218
Heart of Atlanta Motel, Inc. v. *United States,* 104
Hebert, Paul, 504
Heller Plan, 348
Heller, Walter W., 348
Hennessey, Bernard C., 164, 204, 261–262
Hensler, Debora R., 12
Highland Park (Mich.), 516
Highsaw, Robert B., 306
Highways, 491–495
Appalachian system, 494
and billboards, 493
expenditures, 331–333
federal aid for, 492–495
interstate and defense system, 69–70, 493
and the political process, 493–494
rural roads, 69
safety, 494
urban, 69–70
Hill–Burton Act, 523
Hinderaker, Ivan, 174
Hirsch, Werner Z., 354
Hobbs, E. H., 250
Hofferbert, Richard I., 260, 334
Hofstadter, S. H., 372
Holland, Lynwood M., 143
Holloway, Harry, 143
Holmes, Oliver Wendell, 7, 90
Home Building and Loan Association v. *Blaisdell,* 87
Home rule, 394–395
Hoover commissions, 49
Hoover, Herbert, 501
Hospitals, 522–524
administration, 523
expenditures, 332
federal programs, 65–67
legislation, 66–67
Housing and Home Finance Agency, 68
Housing and Urban Development Act, 42–43, 502
Housing and Urban Development, Department of, 67, 68, 75–77, 453
Housing court, 361
Housing legislation (1974), 501–503
Houston, 422, 432
Houston metropolitan area, units of government, 423
Houston, East and West Texas Railway Co. v. *United States,* 88
Hughes, Charles Evans, 87, 90, 173, 310
Humphrey, Hubert, 8
Hunter, Floyd, 407
Huntington–Ashland metropolitan area, population, 78
Hurtado v. *California,* 92
Hyneman, Charles S., 215

I

Idaho
area, 22
constitution, 111

counties, 377
federal aid, 44
innovation score, 8
legislative pay, 222
legislature, 220
party competition, 169
population, 22
sales tax, 340
Illinois, 320
administrative reorganization, 310
area, 22
black in-migration, 17
constitution, 111, 134
counties, 376
constitutional convention, 125
constitutional convention (1970), 110
cumulative voting, 179–180
federal aid, 44
innovation score, 8
Interstate Air Pollution Compact, 55
legislative pay, 222
legislature, 220
party competition, 169
party system, 159
population, 22
Illinois ex rel. McCollum v. *Board of Education*, 94
Impeachment, 228, 283–284
Income tax, state, 342
Indiana, 393
area, 21
constitution, 111
counties, 376
federal aid, 44
governor, 283
innovation score, 8
interest groups, 194
Interstate Air Pollution Compact, 55
legislative apportionment, 251
legislative reapportionment, 259
legislature, 220
multi-member legislative districts, 258
party competition, 169
party system, 159
population, 22
voter participation, 141
Indianapolis, city–county consolidation, 445
Indianapolis metropolitan area, units of government, 423
Indictment, grand jury, 369
Inheritance tax, 342
Initiative, 269–270
Innovation in states, 7–8
Institute for Court Management, 373
Institute of Public Administration, 315–316
Insurance regulation, 481–482
Integration, racial (*See* Segregation, public schools)
Interest groups (*See* Pressure groups)
Intergovernmental Personnel Act of 1970, 320
Interstate commerce, 87–88
segregation in, 104
Interstate Commerce Commission, 478
Interstate compacts, 55–56, 480–481
Interstate relations, 53–57
Intergovernmental relations, cooperative federalism, 35–48
Interposition, 30
Interstate rendition, 54
Iowa
area, 22
constitution, 111, 120
counties, 376
federal aid, 44
governor of, 7
innovation score, 8
interest groups, 194
legislature, 220
Ombudsman, 328
party competition, 169
population, 22
women legislators, 216
Irish, Marian D., 192
Item veto, 277

J

Jackson, Andrew, 28, 318
Jacksonville, 99, 447–451
  city–county consolidation, 445
Jacob, Herbert, 155, 169, 170, 186, 187, 193–196, 206, 217, 259, 275, 318, 364–365, 374, 475, 495
Jassy, Everett L., 439
Jefferson County (Ala.), 387
Jefferson, Thomas, 32, 172, 184, 206, 272, 456
Jehovah's Witnesses, 94–95
Jennings, M. Kent, 183, 407
Jersey City, degree of non-partisanship, 174
Jester, Beauford, 304
Jewell, Malcolm E., 57, 82, 254, 259, 260–261
Johnson, Hiram, 164, 273, 476
Johnson, Lyndon B., 76, 507, 527–528, 529
Johnson, Tom L., 476
Johnson v. *Louisiana,* 92
Joint Federal–State Action Committee, 49–52
  reasons for failure, 51
Jonas, Frank H., 196
Jones, Harold T., 152
Jones, John Hugh, 498
Jones, Victor, 407, 418
Joseph Burstyn, Inc. v. *Wilson,* 93
Judges, 361–366
  compensation, 362–363
  and politics, 363–366
  qualifications, 362
Judicial behavior, state, 363
Judicial councils, 370
Judiciary, 355–373
  common law, 356–357
  equity, 357–358
  hierarchy, 358–361
  judicial councils, 371
  legal aid clinics, 372
  problems of modernization, 370–373
  procedure, 366–370
  small claims courts, 372
Juneau (Alaska), 126
  city–borough consolidation, 445
Jury system, 366–370
Justice of the peace (J. P.), 358–360
Juvenile delinquency, 473–475

K

Kain, J. F., 499
Kallenbach, Joseph E., 274
Kammerer, Gladys, M., 405
Kansas, 320
  area, 22
  constitution, 111
  counties, 376
  desegregation, 97
  federal aid, 44
  innovation score, 8
  interest groups, 194
  legislative pay, 222
  legislature, 220
  party competition, 169
  population, 21
  recall, 284
Kansas City (Mo.)
  degree of non-partisanship, 174
  political machines, 162
  political organization, 162
Kansas City metropolitan area
  population, 78
  units of government, 423
Kaplan, Harold, 410
Kaufman, Herbert, 363–364, 407, 408–409
Keech, William, 145
Keefe, William J., 214, 363
Kelleher, Sean A., 124–126
Kendig, Rodney L., 379, 387
Kennedy, John, 189, 507
Kennedy, Robert, 180
Kent State University, 460
Kentucky, 20
  area, 22
  constitution, 111, 114, 135–136
  counties, 376

desegregation, 98
direct primary, 177
federal aid, 44
governor, 283
innovation score, 8
interest groups, 194
legislature, 220
party competition, 169
population, 22
voting qualifications, 146
Kerner Commission, 529
Kestnbaum Commission, 49, 80, 344
Key, V. O., 155
King, Elizabeth G., 216
King, Martin Luther, 93, 143, 189, 196, 460
Kirk, Claude, 278
Knowles, John H., 524
Kornberg, Allan, 229, 271
Kornhauser, William, 19
Ku Klux Klan, 192

L

Labor
conflicts, 232–233
relations, 487–488
LaFollette, Robert M., 7, 164, 173, 272, 464, 476
La Guardia, Fiorello, 7, 177
"Lakewood Plan," 433–434
Land-grant colleges, 39
Laney, Ben, 292
Lasswell, Harold, 108
Law enforcement, 456–475
assistance, 47
attrition, 458
constable, 463
presidential study, 459
prosecuting attorney, 464
sheriff, 462–463
state police, 460–462
urban police, 465–469
Law Enforcement Assistance Administration, 456, 468
Lawrence–Haverhill metropolitan area, population, 78
Lawyers, 215–216, 485–486
Leach, Richard H., 56, 59, 66, 70, 79, 83, 455
League of Women Voters, 185
Lee, Calvin B. T., 256
Lee, Eugene C., 174
Leeson, Jim, 190
Legislation, state, volume of, 234
Legislators, state
compensation, 222
purposive roles, 211–213
qualifications, 221
reasons for returning, 215
reasons for withdrawal, 215
representational roles, 214
role orientations, 211–213
selection and tenure, 245
women, 216
Legislatures, state
calendars, 236
committees, 239–243
composition, 208–218
conflicts, types of, 233
control of administration, 326–327
criteria for evaluating, 264–265
importance, 205
interstate variations, 231–233
multi-member districts, 257, 258
powers and functions, 226, 228
power structure, 231–233
pressure group activity, 245–248
procedure, 230–248
quorum, 234–235
reapportionment, 10–13, 81–82
restrictions, 207
rules committee, 236
sessions, 222–223
socioeconomic background, 215–216
sources of political interest, 210
speaker of house, 223, 237
structure, 218–226
turnover, 214–215
types, 208–209, 211–213
unicameral, 218–219, 237
unofficial "rules of the game," 238–239

voting, 236–237
working facilities, 225–226
Liberal–conservative conflicts, 233
Licensing, 485
Lieutenant governor, 282–283, 284
Liquor regulations, 484
"Little Hoover" commissions, 304, 310–311
Lincoln, Abraham, 28, 360
Lindsay, John, 7, 34, 61
Lindsey, Ben, 371
Linear City, 15
Lineberry, Robert L., 162
Lipmann, Walter, 202
Lipson, Leslie, 287
List plan, 180
Literacy tests, 148–149
Little Rock (Ark.), 98
school desegregation, 31
Lobbying, 198–200, 245–248
Local government
city, 391–417
county, 375–390
expenditures, 331–335
metropolitan area, 418–455
New England town, 389–390
revenues, 335–352
Local self-government, inherent right doctrine, 61
Lochner v. *New York,* 90
Lockard, W. Duane, 173, 196, 244
Loh, Jules, 65
London metropolitan area, 436–437
Long ballot, 294–295, 308–309
Long, Earl, 282
Long, Huey, 162–163, 189, 272, 365–366, 460
Los Angeles, 422
Thomas Bradley, 145
Los Angeles County, 388
contractual agreements, 433
legislative apportionment, 250
Los Angeles metropolitan area, 432
central city population, 12
Linear City, part of, 15
suburban growth, 12
units of government, 423
Lottery, public, 343
Louisiana, 395, 506
area, 22
black voting, 142, 143, 144
constitution, 111, 129
counties, 377
earmarked taxes, 350
elected department heads, 294
federal aid, 44
governor, 282, 284
innovation score, 8
judicial politics, 364–366
legislative apportionment, 251
legislature, 220
Napoleonic Code, 356
party competition, 169
population, 22
tidelands controversy, 30
voter registration, 144, 148
Louisiana purchase, 29
Louisiana v. *United States,* 149
Louisville, 415
Louisville metropolitan area, population, 78
Loveridge, Ronald O., 406
Low, Seth, 163
Lowden, Frank, 275, 286, 310
Loyalty oaths, 94
Lugar, Richard, 452
Lutrin, Carl E., 270

M

McArthur, Robert E., 381
Macchiarola, Frank J., 61
McGowan v. *Maryland,* 95
McKissick, Floyd, 413
McLaurin v. *Oklahoma State Regents for Higher Education,* 97
McNayr, Irving G., 439
Maddox, Lester, 285
Madison, James, 184
Magat, Richard, 520
Magna Carta, 84
Magrath, C. Peter, 406
Magraw v. *Donovan,* 254
Mahan v. *Howell,* 256

Mahood, H. R., 204
Maine, 20
  area, 22
  constitution, 111
  counties, 377
  federal aid, 44
  innovation score, 8
  interest groups, 194, 196
  legislative committees, 241
  legislature, 220
  party competition, 169
  population, 22
Maleck, Edward S., 204
Malloy v. *Hogan*, 92
Mapp v. *Ohio*, 92
Marcy, Senator William, 318
Margolis, Larry, 263
Marriage laws, 53–54
Marshall, John, 86
Martial law, 460
Martin, Philip L., 389
Martin, Roscoe C., 62, 80–81, 83, 109, 443, 449
Maryland, 320, 395
  administrative reorganization, 310, 311
  area, 22
  constitution, 111
  constitutional convention, 125
  counties, 376
  county-unit system, 175
  desegregation, 98
  federal aid, 44
  innovation score, 8
  legislative apportionment, 250
  legislature, 220
  party competition, 169
  population, 22
  public lottery, 343
Massachusetts, 360, 371
  administrative reorganization, 286, 310
  area, 22
  constitution, 111, 120, 129
  consumer protection division, 483
  counties, 376
  federal aid, 45
  housing court, 361
  innovation score, 8
  judiciary, 362
  legislative apportionment, 250
  legislative committees, 241
  legislature, 220, 241
  lobbying, 248
  party competition, 169
  population, 22
  public lottery, 343
Massachusetts Metropolitan District Commission, 440
Mass culture, 19–20
Masters, Nicholas A., 520
Matthews, Donald R., 142
Maverick (politician), 245
Mayflower Compact, 107
Mayor, 397–400
Mayor–council plan, 397–400
Mayors, U.S. Conference of, 65
Medicaid, 524
Medical examiner, 382, 464
Medical profession, 486
Medicare, 486, 524
Megalopolis, 15
Memphis metropolitan area, population, 78
Mencken, H. L., 11, 249
Mendelsohn, Ethel, 488
Meredith, James, 31, 327
Merit system, 387 (*See also* Personnel administration)
Merriam, Charles E., 418
Metropolitan area government
  city–county consolidation, 444–452
  federation, 436–439
  functional consolidation, 452
  Jacksonville consolidation, 447–451
  London federation, 436–437
  Miami plan, 438–439
  Nashville consolidation, 446–447, 449
  proposed remedies, 429–452
  special districts, 440–443
  Toronto federation, 437–438
Metropolitan areas
  interstate, 77, 78

number, 15
planning assistance, 68
population, 15
school organization, 514
Metropolitan councils of governments, 434–436
Metropolitan districts, 14, 421
Metropolitanism, 14–17, 418–425
Metropolitics, 17, 418–455
Meyer, J. R., 499
Meyerson, Martin, 428
Miami
Cuban in-migration, 17–18
metropolitan area, partial federation, 438
Michigan, 395
area, 22
black in-migration, 17
black officials, 145
constitution, 109, 111, 124
constitutional convention, 187–188
counties, 376
federal aid, 45
innovation score, 8
interest groups, 187–188, 194, 196–197
legislature, 220
party competition, 169
party system, 159
population, 22
public lottery, 343
Migratory bird legislation, 104–105
Milbrath, Lester W., 141, 183, 199
Militia, 28
Miller v. *California,* 93, 484
Miller, William D., 162
Mill, John Stuart, 180, 233
Mills, C. Wright, 407
Mills v. *State of Alabama,* 93
Mills, Wilbur, 349
Minersville School District v. *Gobitis,* 94
Minneapolis, legislative apportionment, 255
Minneapolis–St. Paul metropolitan area, 431
metropolitan council, 436
units of government, 423, 442
Minnesota
area, 22
constitution, 111, 133
counties, 377
federal aid, 45
innovation score, 8
legislative apportionment, 254–255
legislature, 220
party competition, 169
party system, 159, 161
population, 22
third parties, 159
Minor v. *Happersett,* 33
Miranda v. *State of Arizona,* 92
Mississippi, 358
area, 22
black officials, 145, 217
constitution, 111, 133
counties, 376
federal aid, 45
innovation score, 8
legislature, 220, 241
non-voting, 141–142, 144
party competition, 169
population, 22
single-member legislative districts, 258
voting qualifications, 144, 148, 149
Mississippi, University of, desegregation, 31
Missouri
area, 22
constitution, 112, 124, 133, 296
counties, 376
desegregation, 98
federal aid, 45
innovation score, 8
judicial appointments, 362
legislature, 220
party competition, 169
population, 22
Missouri ex rel. Gaines v. *Canada,* 97
Missouri, University of, 97
Missouri v. *Holland,* 105
Mitau, G. Theodore, 155
Mitchel, John Purroy, 163

Model Cities Program, 67
Model state constitution, 114–116
Montana
area, 22
constitution, 112
counties, 377
federal aid, 45
innovation score, 8
interest groups, 194, 196
legislature, 220
party competition, 169
population, 22
Montgomery, "freedom rides," 31
Moore, Dan K., 277–278
Moore v. *Dempsey*, 91
Morals, regulation of, 484
Morehouse, Sarah McCally, 171, 278, 279
Morey, Roy D., 281
Morgan v. *Virginia*, 88
Morrill Act, 489
Morse, Wayne, 32
Moscow, Warren, 244
Mosher, Frederick C., 338
Moynihan, Daniel P., 14, 294, 319
Mulrooney, Keith F., 406
Mumford, Lewis, 492
Munger, Frank J., 267
Municipal corporation (*See* City government)
Municipal home rule, 394–395
Municipalized county, 439–440
Municipal Manpower Commission, 63
Munn v. *Illinois*, 89, 478
Murphy, Thomas P., 390
Murphy, Walter F., 374
Murray, Richard, 155
Muskie, Edmund, 76

N

Nader, Ralph, 196, 482, 483
Nader's Raiders, 483
Nashville, city–county consolidation, 445
National Association of Counties, 386, 387
National Association of Manufacturers, 3
National Association of Utility Commissions, 479
National Center for State Courts, 373
National Crime Information Center, 468
National Guard, 33, 460
National League of Cities, 65
Natural resources, 504–510
National Rifle Association, 186
Near v. *Minnesota*, 92
Nebraska
area, 22
constitution, 112
counties, 377
federal aid, 45
innovation score, 8
interest groups, 194
Ombudsmen, 328
party competition, 169
population, 22
Netzer, Dick, 339
Nevada
area, 22
constitution, 112
counties, 377
federal aid, 45
innovation score, 8
party competition, 169
population, 22
New County USA Center, 386
New Deal, 189
New Hampshire
area, 23
constitution, 112
counties, 377
federal aid, 45
innovation score, 8
party competition, 169
population, 23
public lottery, 343
New Jersey
area, 23

constitution, 112
counties, 376
federal aid, 45
innovation score, 8
legislators, 210, 213, 214, 217, 220, 225
party competition, 169
population, 23
public lottery, 343
Tri-State Transportation Compact, 55
New Mexico
area, 23
constitution, 112, 125
counties, 377
federal aid, 45
innovation score, 8
party competition, 169
population, 23
New Rochelle (N.Y.), 516
New towns, 412–414
New York Authority, Port of, 55, 56, 441, 480
New York City, 321, 415, 437, 441, 504, 509, 521
budgeting, 352
Communist councilmen, 180
judicial politics, 363–364
mass transit, 495
mayor, 7
party system, 161
police, 465, 467
political machines, 162
power structure, 408–409
proportional representation, 180
Puerto Rican in-migration, 17
New York metropolitan area, 12, 418, 434, 437
federal expenditures in, 59
Linear City, part of, 15
population, 78
units of government, 423
New York state, 360, 395, 506, 513
administrative reorganization, 286, 310
area, 23
black in-migration, 17
black officials, 145
civil service reform, 320
constitution, 112, 113, 116, 118
constitutional convention, 125
counties, 377
education, 513
federal aid, 45
innovation score, 8
interest groups, 194
Labor Relations Board, 488
legislature, 220, 222, 234, 279–281
party competition, 169
population, 23
public lottery, 343
Tri-State Transportation Compact, 55
voting qualifications, 149
New York Times Company v. *Sullivan*, 93
Nimmo, Dan, 155, 197
Nineteenth Amendment, 33, 139–140
Nixon, H. C., 384
Nixon, Richard M., 77, 349, 528–529
Nixon v. *Conden*, 176
No-fault insurance, 483–484
Nominating process, 171–178
Non-partisan primary, 173–174
Non-voting, 140–146
Norris, George W., 218
Norris v. *Alabama*, 91
North Carolina, 513
area, 23
black voting, 176
constitution, 112
counties, 376
desegregation, 98
federal aid, 45
highways, 494
innovation score, 8
legislature, 220, 234, 241
party competition, 169
population, 23
voter registration, 148
North Dakota
area, 23

constitution, 112, 129
counties, 377
elected department heads, 295
federal aid, 45
governor, 284
innovation score, 8
legislature, 220, 222, 235
party competition, 169
population, 23
recall, 284
Nullification, 29, 30

O

Obligation of contracts, 61, 86–87
Obscenity regulation, 93, 484
O'Connor, Edwin, 158
O'Daniel, W. Lee ("Pappy"), 304
Oden, William E., 155, 197
Ogden, Daniel M., Jr., 156
Ohio, 320, 371, 393
area, 23
constitution, 112
counties, 376
federal aid, 45
innovation score, 8
interest groups, 194
legislators, 210, 213, 214, 217, 220, 222, 225, 232, 233, 240
party system, 159, 169, 245
population, 23
Ohlin, Floyd E., 473, 475
Oil
regulation, 506
tidelands, 30
"Okies," migration of, 17
Oklahoma, 20
area, 23
constitution, 110, 111, 113
counties, 377
desegregation, 97
federal aid, 45
impeachment, 283–284
innovation score, 8
legislature, 220
party competition, 169
population, 23
Oklahoma City, annexation, 431
Oklahoma, University of, 97
Older Americans Act, 47
Omaha, 415
Omaha metropolitan area
population, 78
units of government, 423
Ombudsman, 327–328
Open primary, 176–177
Open-space preservation, 68
Operation Head Start, 42, 528
Oregon
area, 23
constitution, 112, 129, 136
counties, 377
federal aid, 45
impeachment, 228
innovation score, 8
legislature, 220
Ombudsman, 328
party competition, 161, 169
People's Power League, 309
population, 23
recall, 284
Oregon v. *Mitchell,* 146
Orfield, Gary, 515
Orwell, George, 25
Ostrom, Vincent, 428, 520
Outdoor Recreation Resources Review Commission, 507
Owen, Wilford, 499
Owsley, Frank L., 29

P

Pacific States Tel. and Tel. Co. v. *Oregon,* 33
Palko v. *Connecticut,* 92
Palumbo, Dennis J., 35
Pardons, 275
Parent–Teacher Association (PTA), 200, 513
Parishes, 375
Parkersburg–Marietta metropolitan area, population, 78
Parks and recreation, 506–507
expenditures, 332

Parochial school aid, 517
Parties, political
caucus, 171–172
clubs, 164
competition, 168–171, 278
conflicts, 232–233
convention, 172
legislative role, 243–245
organization, 164–166
primary, 172–178
state systems, 159, 161
traditional image of, 157–158
Patterson, John, 93
Patton, H. Milton, 510
Payne, Thomas, 196
Peel, Sir Robert, 466
Pennsylvania, 460, 506
administrative reorganization, 310
area, 23
constitution, 112
counties, 376
federal aid, 45
innovation score, 8
interest groups, 194
legislature, 217, 220, 222
party competition, 169
population, 23
public lottery, 343
Penrose, Boies, 163
Peoria metropolitan area, units of government, 423
Personnel administration, 318–324
certification, 321–322
discipline, 322–323
examination, 321–322
position classification, 322
problems, 324–328
recruitment, 321–322
retirement, 324
Petit jury, 367–368
Petroleum regulation, 506
Phenix City (Ala.), 460
Philadelphia, 395, 421, 445
political machines, 162
Philadelphia metropolitan area
Linear City, part of, 15
population, 78
units of government, 423
Phoenix (Ariz.), 432
Pinchot, Gifford, 273
Pittsburgh, 397
Pittsburgh metropolitan area, 420, 431, 437
central city decline, 12
suburban growth, 12
units of government, 423
Piven, Frances Fox, 454
Planning, city, 412–413, 509
Planning–Programming–Budgeting, 353
Planning, state, 509–510
Plessy v. *Ferguson*, 97
Plunkett, George Washington, 157
Pocket veto, 277
Poland, Orville F., 338
Police power, 84–105
national "quasi-police" power, 103–105
Police protection, 332, 460–462
Policy innovations, 269
Policy outputs, 7, 171, 267, 333–334
Politics
of constitutions, 108–109, 119–120, 124–126
of education, 519–520
of highways, 493–494
of judges, 363–366
of poverty, 528–529
of reapportionment, 253–255
Politics, state, new interest in, 155–156
Poll tax, 140, 149–150
Pollution, politics of, 507–510
Polsby, Nelson W., 410
Pomper, Gerald, 174
Population
racial characteristics, 17–19
rural, decline of, 10–12
urban, growth, 10–12
Portland (Ore.) metropolitan area
population, 78
units of government, 423
Port of New York Authority (*See* New York Authority, Port of)

Pound, Roscoe, 370–371
Poverty (*See* War on Poverty)
  politics of, 528–529
Powell v. *Alabama,* 91
PPB (*See* Planning–Programming–Budgeting)
Prayer in schools, 517
Precinct, 150, 383–384
Prescott, Frank W., 277
President's Commission on National Goals, 63–64
President's Committee on Administrative Management, 310
Press, the, 189, 201
Press, Charles, 250
Pressure groups, 184–204, 245–248, 316–317
  Catholic, 109
  comparative patterns, 193–198
  ethnic, 109
  farm, 109
  labor union, 109
  methods, 198–204
  Protestant, 109
  sources of strength, 190–193
  taxpayers, 108
  types, 185–190
  veterans, 108–109
Presthus, Robert V., 410
Prewitt, Kenneth, 167, 183
Price, Reginald C., 509
Prison administration, 469–475
Propaganda, 200–203
Property tax, 338–340
Proportional representation, 180
Prosecuting attorney, 464–465
Prothoro, James W., 142, 192
Providence–Pawtucket metropolitan area, population, 78
Public defender, 465
Public health (*See* Health)
Public housing, 501–504
Public opinion, 184–204
Public Personnel Association, 320
Public service unions, 323
Public utilities, 414
Public utility regulation, 477–481
Public welfare, 331–333, 525–529
Public works, 500–504
Public Works Administration, 62–63
Puerto Ricans, migration of, 17, 149
Puerto Rico
  constitution, 112
  party competition, 169

R

Rabinovitz, Francine F., 12, 412
Racial balance in schools, 100–101
Racial segregation, 88, 514–517 (*See also* Segregation, public school)
Railways, 495–496
Ranchino, Jim, 156
Randolph, Edmund, 272
Ranney, Austin, 168, 169, 170, 275
Ransone, Coleman B., 138, 279, 304, 306
Reapportionment, 81–82, 248–263, 279–281, 453
  effects of, 261
  politics of, 253–255
Recall, 284
Recreation, metropolitan needs, 68
Reed, T. H., 453
Reeves, Mavis Mann, 503
Referendum, 269–270, 445
Reformers, political, 163–164
Regional city, 415–416
Regional conflicts, 232–233
Regionalism, 42
Regional poverty, 42
Registration, of black voters, 144–145
Regulation
  of business, 477–481
  of labor, 487–488
  of trades and professions, 485–487
Rehfuss, John, 166
Reorganization, administrative, 286–287, 308–318
Republican form of government, 32
Republican Party, 161, 169, 173, 177, 210, 243–245, 278
  southern strength, 278
Reserved powers, 32–33

Reston (Va.), 413
Revenues, 335–352
  ear-marking, 350
  public lottery, 343
  state and local, 44–45
Revenue sharing, 349
Reynolds v. *Sims*, 11, 82, 255–256
Rhode Island, 375, 395
  area, 23
  constitution, 112, 120
  Dorr rebellion, 33, 140, 284
  federal aid, 45
  governor, 284
  innovation score, 8
  interest groups, 219
  judiciary, 362
  legislature, 220, 222
  party competition, 169
  population, 23
  public defender, 465
Rich, Bennett, M., 283, 314
Ridley, Clarence, 405
Riesman, David, 19
Riker, William H., 26
Riordin, William L., 157
"Ripper bill," 296
Rivlin, Alice M., 518
Roadbuilders, 200
Roberts, George C., 259
Roberts, Owen J., 92
Robinson, James A., 141
Rockefeller Foundation, 523
Rockefeller, Nelson, 61, 279–281
Rockefeller, Winthrop, 278
Rogers, Paul, 479
Rodriguez case, 340
Roman law, 357
Romney, George, 109, 503, 504
Roosevelt, Franklin D., 189, 272, 501, 505, 525
Roosevelt, Theodore, 30, 48, 157–158, 173, 285, 467, 505
Roos, Leslie L., Jr., 196
Root, Elihu, 157–158
Rose, Albert, 438
Rosenberg, B., 19
Rosenberg, Beatrice, 488
Rosenthal, Donald B., 402, 410
Rossi, Peter H., 218, 408, 410
Roth case, 517
Roth v. *United States*, 93
Rouse, James, 413
Ruef, "Abe," 163

S

Sacks, Seymour, 454
Safe Streets Act, 462, 468
Safety regulation, 482
St. Louis, 421, 423
St. Louis Bi-state Development Agency, 441
St. Louis metropolitan area, 420, 441
  central city decline, 12
  population, 78
  suburban growth, 12
  units of government, 423
Sales tax, 340–342
Salisbury, Robert H., 174, 204, 409, 520
San Antonio, 431
San Antonio Ind. School District v. *Rodriguez*, 340
SANGAB, 434
San Diego metropolitan area, Linear City, part of, 15
San Francisco, 443
San Francisco–Oakland metropolitan area, 420, 440
  Linear City, part of, 15
  units of government, 423
Sanitation, expenditures, 332
Santa Clara County v. *Southern Pacific Railroad Company*, 90
Sarasohn, Stephen B., 156
Sarasohn, Vera H., 156
Sawyer, Robert Lee, Jr., 156, 157
Sayre, Wallace S., 363–364, 408–409
Scammon, Richard M., 141
Scheiber, Harry N., 36
Schick, Allen, 353
Schlesinger, Joseph A., 318
Schmandt, Henry J., 15, 434
Schmidhauser, John R., 168

Schneider v. *State (Town of Irvington)*, 92
School
  consolidation, 514
  desegregation, 514–517
Schools and politics, 519–520
Schools, busing for racial balance, 100–101
Schubert, Glendon, 250
Schultze, William A., 417
Screws v. *United States,* 91
Seattle metropolitan area, units of government, 423
Secession, state, 29
Segregation, public school, 97–102
Senate confirmation, 292
Serino, Gustave, 439
Serrano v. *Priest,* 340
Settle, Allen K., 270
Seventeenth Amendment, 140, 227
Shade, William L., 267
Shaffer, William R., 267
Sharkansky, Ira, 162, 297, 329, 333, 334
Sheriff, 495, 462–463
Shivers, Allan, 98, 304–305
Short ballot, 153–154, 286, 294–295
Shuldiner, Paul W., 498
Siffin, William J., 224
Sindler, Allan P., 156
Sing Sing Prison, 473
Sioux City metropolitan area, population, 78
Slaughterhouse Cases, 89
Slochower v. *Board of Higher Education of City of N. Y., 94*
Slum clearance, 67, 500–504
Smallwood, Frank, 437
Smerk, George M., 499
Smith, Adam, 347
Smith, Alfred E., 202, 273, 304
Smith–Lever Act, 39
Smith, Terry B., 276
Smith v. *Allwright,* 85, 176
Smith v. *Holm,* 254
Smyth v. *Ames,* 480
Social changes, impact on government, 19
Social security, 40–41
Social Security Act, 526
Sofen, Edward, 439
Solomon, Samuel R., 273
Sorauf, Frank J., 156, 161, 183
Soul City (N. C.), 413
South Carolina, 515
  area, 23
  constitution, 112, 133
  counties, 376
  desegregation, 97
  federal aid, 45
  governor, 284
  innovation score, 8
  legislature, 220, 234
  party competition, 169
  party organization, 165
  periodic registration, 150
  population, 23
  voting qualifications, 149, 150
  voter registration, 144, 150
South Carolina v. *Katzenbach,* 144
South Dakota
  area, 23
  constitution, 112, 117
  counties, 377
  federal aid, 45
  innovation score, 8
  interest groups, 194
  legislature, 220, 235
  party competition, 169
  population, 23
Southern Growth Policies Board, 55
Southern Manifesto, 31
Southern Regional Education Compact, 56
Speaker of the House, 237
Special districts, 72–73
Spicer, George W., 385
Spoils system, 318–319
Sprengel, Donald P., 183
Springfield–Chicopee–Holyoke metropolitan area, 78
Staebler, Neil, 159

Standard metropolitan statistical area
definition, 14–15
number, 15
Standing, William H., 141
Stanley, David T., 321, 323
State–city relations, state supremacy, 60–61
State geography, 22–25
State government
conservation, 505–510
courts, 355–373 (*See also* Judiciary)
education, 511–520
expenditures, 331–335
health, 520–524
highways, 493–494
hospitals, 522–524
judges, 361–364
penitentiaries, 472–473
planning, 509–510
police, 460–462
regulation of business, 477–481
responsibility for urban problems, 79–82
revenues, 335–352
welfare, 525–529
State histories, 20–22
State–local relations, financial, 350–352
State policy outputs, 333–334
States (*See also* Federalism)
equal footing, 35
and foreign relations, 34–35
guarantees to, 32–33
prohibitions on, 34
suits against, 33–34
States' rights
debates over, 28–32
and desegregation, 30–31
"disunion amendments," 51
and reapportionment, 255
and tidelands oil, 30
Staunton (Va.), 402
Stearns v. *Minnesota,* 35
Steffens, Lincoln, 163, 392
Steiner, Gilbert Y., 253
Stein, Maurice R., 19
Stelzer, Leigh, 205
Steubenville–Weirton metropolitan area, 78
Stream pollution, 71
Strikes, public employee, 323
Sturm, Albert Lee, 109, 126, 138, 187
Suburbanism, 11–13
causes, 11, 422
growth of, 11
and legislative apportionment, 251–252
political impact of, 12–14
Sugg, R. S., 56
Sumter (S. C.), 402
Sunday closing laws, 95, 484
Sundquist, James L., 183
Swann case, 100–101
Swanson, Bert E., 409
Swanson, Wayne R., 124–126
Sweatt v. *Painter,* 97

T

Taebel, Delbert A., 406
Taft Commission on Economy and Efficiency, 310
Taft, Robert A., 32
Taft, Seth, 144
Talmadge, Eugene, 163, 164, 175, 284–285, 296
Talmadge, Herman, 284–285
Tammany Hall, 162–164, 318
Taney, Roger B., 86, 89
Tannenhaus, Joseph, 374
Taxes (*See also* Revenues)
ear-marking, 350
gasoline, 40
inheritance, 48
Tax immunity, 61
Telford, Ira Ralph, 177
Temple, David G., 445–446
Tennessee, 20, 358, 395
administrative reorganization, 310
annexation procedure, 431
area, 23
black voting, 176

- constitution, 112, 114, 120, 134
- counties, 376
- county consolidation, 384
- desegregation, 98
- federal aid, 45
- innovation score, 8
- legislative apportionment, 251
- legislative conflicts, types of, 232–233
- legislators, 210, 213, 214, 217, 220, 225
- legislature, 220, 226, 232–233
- party competition, 169
- party influence, 245
- population, 23
- residence requirement, 147

Tennessee Valley Authority, 48, 490
Tenth Amendment, 32, 61, 355
Terminiello v. *City of Chicago,* 92
Texarkana metropolitan area, population, 78
Texas, 506, 513
- annexation procedure, 431
- area, 23
- black voting, 142–143
- constitution, 110, 112, 117
- counties, 377
- desegregation, 97
- earmarked taxes, 350
- elected department heads, 294
- federal aid, 45
- impeachment, 283
- income, 342
- innovation score, 8
- legislative committees, 241
- party competition, 169
- political system, 197–198
- population, 23
- Rangers, 460
- tidelands controversy, 30
- voting qualifications, 149

Texas and Pacific Railway Co. v. *United States,* 478
Texas, republic of, 20
Texas, University of, 97
Texas v. *White,* 29
Thomas, Norman C., 252
Thompson, "Big Bill," 163
Thompson, M. E., 284–285
Thornton, Robert, 147
Thursby, Vincent T., 56, 57
Tidelands oil, 506
Tiebout, Charles, 428
Times Film Corp. v. *Chicago,* 93
Tobacco tax, 342
Tocqueville, Alexis de, 24–25, 161, 184, 290
Toledo, 415
Toledo metropolitan area, 78
Torcaso v. *Watkins,* 96
Toronto
- metro evaluation, 438
- metropolitan area, federation, 437–438

Township, 383–384
Transportation
- Department of, 69, 498
- mass, 68–69, 480
- urban assistance, 68–70

Treaty power, 104–105
Tressolini, Rocco J., 56
Trial by jury, 367–368
Trial safeguards, 91–92
Truman, Harry, 378, 381
Tuskeegee, black vote, 145
Tuskeegee decision, 145, 258
Twenty-fourth Amendment, 140, 149–150
Twenty-sixth Amendment, 146, 147
Twenty-third Amendment, 147
Twin Cities Area Metropolitan Council, 436
Twining v. *New Jersey,* 92
Two Guys v. *McGinley,* 95

U

Unemployment insurance, 40, 526–527
Unicameralism, 218–219, 237
Uniform State Laws, National Conference of Commissioners on, 56–57
UNIGOV, 449, 452
Unions in the public service, 323

United States
area, 22
population, 22
U. S. Bureau of the Census, 5, 45, 334, 376–377, 380, 423
U. S. Public Health Service, 521
United States v. *Barnett,* 327
United States v. *Classic,* 176
United States v. *McCullagh,* 104
United States v. *Shauver,* 104
United States v. *Southeastern Underwriters Association et al.,* 481
United States v. *Sutherland,* 91
Urban county, 379, 439–440
Urban crisis, 13–14
Urbanism, 10–12, 391–392
Jeffersonian view, 391
and town meetings, 389–390
Urbanized area, definition, 14–15
Urban renewal, 67, 500–504
Urban–rural conflicts, 233
Urbiculture, 10–12, 75
Utah
area, 23
constitution, 112
counties, 377
federal aid, 45
innovation score, 8
legislature, 221
party competition, 169
population, 23
Utter, Kathryn L., 390

V

Van Dalen, Hendrik, 193, 195, 196, 199
Vanlandingham, Kenneth, 394
Vanderbilt, Arthur T., 371–372
Vandiver, Ernest, 99
Vardaman, J. K., 164
Verba, Sidney, 186
Vermont, 20
administrative reorganization, 310
area, 23
constitution, 110, 112
counties, 376
federal aid, 45
innovation score, 8
judiciary, 362
legislature, 221
party competition, 161, 169
population, 23
voter registration, 150
Vines, Kenneth N., 142, 155, 169, 170, 186, 187, 193, 194, 195, 196, 217, 275, 318, 364–365, 495
Virginia, 20, 340
administrative reorganization, 286
area, 23
black voting, 176
city–county separation, 443–444
constitution, 112
counties, 376, 385
desegregation, 97
direct primary, 177
federal aid, 45
highways, 495
innovation score, 8
interest groups, 194
legislature, 221
party competition, 169
population, 23
voter registration, 144
voting qualifications, 149
Washington suburban growth, 12
VISTA, 42, 528
Vose, Clement E., 200
Voter efficacy, 141
Voting, 140–154
absentee, 152
Australian ballot, 151
black, 139, 140, 142–145
machines, 151–152
problems, 151–154
qualifications, 146–151
registration, 150–151
residence for students, 147
residence requirements, 146–147
suspension of literacy tests, 149
Voting Rights Acts, 140, 147, 148, 149, 152

W

Wabash, St. L. and P. Ry. Co. v. *Illinois,* 88
Wahlke, John C., 170, 209–216, 225–226, 231, 232, 233, 238, 240, 244–247, 398, 520
Waite, Morrison R., 89
Waldman, Sidney, R., 159
Walker, Harvey, 327
Walker, Jack L., 7–8, 267, 269, 410
Walker v. *Sauvinet,* 92
Wallace, George, 31, 274, 327
Wallace, Lurleen, 274
Walter, Benjamin, 12
War Between the States (*See* Civil War)
War on Poverty, 41–42, 73, 527–528
Warren, Earl, 51, 98, 177, 283
Warren, Robert Penn, 3, 163, 202
Washington
  area, 23
  constitution, 112
  counties, 377
  federal aid, 45
  innovation score, 8
  legislature, 221
  loyalty oath, 94
  party competition, 169
  population, 23
Washington, D. C., metropolitan area
  central city decline, 12
  desegregation, 98
  Linear City, part of, 15
  population, 78
  suburban growth, 12
  voting rights, 147
Washington, George, 201
Watergate, 182
Water Quality Act, 507
Waterways, 495–496
Watson, Richard A., 362
Wayne County (Mich.), 380
Weaver, Robert, 76
Weaver, Warren, Jr., 279–280
Webber, Ronald E., 267
Webster, Daniel, 28, 32, 86
Welfare, 525–529
  old age assistance, 526, 527
  old age insurance, 526, 527
Wellington, Harry H., 323
Wendell, Mitchell, 56
Werner, Emily E., 216
West Coast Hotel Company v. *Parrish,* 90
West Virginia, 20, 340, 519
  area, 23
  constitution, 112
  counties, 376
  desegregation, 98
  federal aid, 45
  highways, 495
  innovation score, 8
  legislature, 221
  party competition, 169
  population, 23
  restoration of voting rights, 148
West Virginia State Board of Education v. *Barnette,* 94
Wheare, K. C., 28
Wheeler, Burton K., 196
Wheeler v. *Board of Trustees,* 128
Wheeling metropolitan area, population, 78
Whitcomb v. *Chavis,* 258
White, David M., 19
White, John P., 252
White, Theodore H., 519
White primary, 176
White supremacy, 179
Wichita, degree of non-partisanship, 174
Willbern, York, 83, 454
Williams, G. Mennen, 272
Williams, J. Oliver, 288
Williams, Oliver P., 410
Willis, George L., 177
Wilmington metropolitan area, population, 78
Wilson, James Q., 14, 174, 192, 294, 319
Wilson, Woodrow, 203, 272, 290
Winter, Ralph K., 323
Wirt, Frederick M., 12

Wisconsin, 320, 526
  area, 23
  constitution, 112
  counties, 377
  direct primary, 173
  federal aid, 45
  governor of, 7
  innovation score, 8
  legislative apportionment, 250
  Legislative Reference Bureau, 224
  legislators, 217
  legislature, 221, 241
  lobbying, 248
  party competition, 169
  party system, 159
  population, 23
Wisconsin v. *Yoder*, 94
Wohl, Martin, 499
Wolfinger, Raymond E., 270
Wolf, Reinhold P., 439
Women, state legislators, 216
Women's liberation, 189
Women's rights, 488
Wood, Robert C., 12, 14, 76, 418
Wooley, Edward A., 372
Work Projects Administration, 525
Works Progress Administration, 62–63, 525
World War II, federal–city relationships, 63
Wright, Deil S., 37, 52, 299, 300, 314, 318, 354, 405
Wylie Amendment, 96
Wyoming
  area, 23
  constitution, 112
  counties, 377
  federal aid, 45
  innovation score, 8
  legislature, 221
  party competition, 169
  population, 23

Y

Yates, Douglas, 455
Yates, W. Ross, 147
Young, Roland, 216

Z

Zagoria, Sam, 329
Zald, Mayer N., 408
Zeigler, Harmon, 154, 186, 187, 193–196
Zeller, Belle, 180, 214, 216, 241
Zimmerman, Frederick L., 56
Zorach v. *Clauson*, 94